STORY LINES

STORY LINES

Chapters on Thought, Word, and Deed

• •

For Gabriel Fackre

Edited by

SKYE FACKRE GIBSON

WILLIAM B. EERDMANS PUBLISHING COMPANY
GRAND RAPIDS, MICHIGAN / CAMBRIDGE, U.K.

Wm. B. Eerdmans Publishing Co.
255 Jefferson Ave. S.E., Grand Rapids, Michigan 49503 /
P.O. Box 163, Cambridge CB3 9PU U.K.

Printed in the United States of America

07 06 05 04 03 02   7 6 5 4 3 2 1

Library of Congress Cataloging-in-Publication Data

Story lines: chapters on thought, word, and deed:
for Gabriel Fackre / edited by Skye Fackre Gibson.
p.   cm.
Includes bibliographical references and index.
ISBN 0-8028-6082-6 (alk. paper)
1. Theology. I. Fackre, Gabriel J. II. Gibson, Skye Fackre.

BR50.S765 2002
230 — dc21

2002074323

www.eerdmans.com

Contents

Contents

Part II: The Mission of the Story Today

Contents

Part III: The Ministry of the Story Today

Contents

Publisher's Note

I first met Gabe 40? 50? years ago at a church conference in suburban Chicago. At the time the attraction for me was Bill Stringfellow, the fiery young lawyer who radicalized the practice of the gospel (already radical) in the streets of Harlem. Bill was the lay fireball advertised. But then there was Gabe, different in style and more the professional theologian, yet giving nothing away to Stringfellow in prophetic utterance. I was to have the privilege of publishing them both.

Gabe was a trained theologian calling for the word of the gospel to take root in deeds that redeem daily life. Word inscribed in deed became a watchword for Gabe, characterizing his career. It was the "call and response" of his narrative theology, the locus to which doctrinal loci always returned.

Thus his off-hours editorship of a Lancaster, Pennsylvania, citizen's newspaper dedicated to the rights of ordinary workers and people on and below the margins; his protest in the political realm against an overbearing Religious Right and limned in his book *The Religious Right and the Christian Faith;* his ecumenical advocacy of a posture among the churches of mutual "affirmations and admonitions," another healing phrase one identifies with Gabe; his marriage to Dot, if labeled "a marriage made in heaven," its seamless garment stitched in time in one size as befits the Divine Story Book's call of "one flesh," is a testament to the wholeness and integrity of Gabe and Dot's true love on an all-too-famously tested terrain. Lest one think him more practitioner than scholar, there is Gabe's multivolume systematic theology, *The Christian Story,* still in progress, a contemporary systematics of the traditional Christian loci elucidating the divine-human encounter, the Christian story forever alive in Jesus Christ; and not to overlook the Fackre annual newsletter, a diagnosis of the body ecclesia, of what affects and infects it, of what's *au courant* and what's needed for retrieval and renewal: the broad lines of what's happening. A good read for those with an ear to the ground listening to the conflicting voices.

As theologian resident in church and academy, in life on the margins, and in the 'hood, Gabe's life and work permeate all reaches of human experience with the gospel. Thanks, then, Bill Stringfellow.

BILL EERDMANS

Editor's Note

The idea for this *festschrift* was born in a Volvo, hurtling down a Swiss autoroute on the way to Zermatt — a trip to show my father and mother the Matterhorn. We were headed to the mountain of lore, a storied peak and a finger of God, raised like so many fingers and fists of rock in the raw spring Alps. Calvin's landscape flew by the car window, old vistas now bracketed by guardrails and electrical pylons, but still testamentary and enduring, still witness to history and truth, transcendental and mundane. The setting for that Protestant theology was storybook.

As we rounded the end of Lake Geneva, Dad was talking about a *festschrift* to which he then was contributing, reflecting on themes he had discussed, reminding me again how lucid and interesting my father is — a born teacher, a born thinker, a born storyteller. Time for a *festschrift* for Dad, I thought. And so here is a book for him, on Story.

I introduce the book this way because its intention was to be a birthday present from a daughter, and not simply an academic paean. Raised by my parents as a Christian, professionalized as a lawyer, and in my present calling as a mother, I have stayed within range of what I was taught by them as a child: that there is a Story greater than ours alone. My father has spent nearly his whole life telling that Story — from the time he was sixteen and first knew he wanted to be a minister, to this very time as he writes his books and articles, treks to speeches, and discovers that technology can be turned to evangelizing (www.gabrielfackre.com). I wanted the world to know something of what Dad has done. As a present, the book is to honor his belief that one needs to get the Story straight, and to get the Story out.

As it turned out, Dad's own story made this a radically unusual *festschrift*. His history is a bridge between traditions and points of view, and, as such, the likes of Carl Henry and Donald Bloesch and Jürgen Moltmann and Martin Marty all share the pages. The book comprises three sections: Meaning, Mission, and Ministry, and each author sheds his or her prismatic light in one of those categories. Each category represents a part of Dad's theological history. Meaning, or content or systematics, is about narrative theology and basic gospel. There you'll find Martin Marty with a riff on the Story, Donald Bloesch on straight gospel, Avery Dulles and George Lindbeck responding to Dad in the Lutheran-Catholic dialogue about the Joint Declaration on Justification, Elmer Colyer's scholarly treatise on narrative theology, Carl Henry reviewing Dad's work, Mark Heim moving from myth to sacrifice and paradox, Kathryn Greene-McCreight on Mary, Jens Jenson on theological history and objectivity, Roger Shinn talking about the Story in the constellation of stories, Leander Keck telling the good news from Romans, and Paul Westermeyer with his grace note on music.

Mission is about outreach, new frontiers, updating, and social justice. Here you have Jürgen Moltmann on the new millennium, Carl Braaten eloquent about evangelism and mission, Max Stackhouse in conversation about God and globalization, Fred Trost on full communion, George Hunsinger on social witness, Diane Kessler on the United Church of Christ and ecumenism, Jeffrey Gros on the ecumenical vocation of the United Church of Christ, Paul Crow on the history of Faith and Order, Alan Sell's historical overview from the English Reformed heritage on how Reformed preachers have been telling the Story, and Kenneth Mulholland's (Dad's first seminary student) personal overview of Dad's theology and history.

Ministry is about the pastors with whom Dad worked in his Tabletalk group for thirty years and others in center movements, all grounded in Scripture, introduced with sermons by two leading biblical scholars, Elizabeth and Paul Achtemeier, with Rick Floyd and Dick Olmsted taking us from Palm Sunday to Easter, Herb Davis (Dad's old buddy from the "barricades" in the civil rights movement) on the Prodigal Son, Roberta Heath reminding us to trumpet the Story, Lelly Smith on the deep waters flowing around one boy's baptism, Joe Bassett on some core Congregational history, and fittingly closed with Leander Harding's message on ministry and his final words, "Make it so."

The contributors themselves fall roughly into two groups: teaching theologians and pastoral theologians, a distinction Dad taught me to make and one which says a lot about where, how, and whom he believes theology fits. The academy and the ministry entwine. And he himself is a pastor and a professor, a *Doktorvater* to some, a loving father and grand-father, an infinitely devoted husband, a committed Christian, and one of God's children, as the Story tells us we all are. And behind it and through it, as Dad wants me to say and as I know to be true with my whole heart, there is no Gabe without Dorothy, my mother, and his wife of fifty-seven years.

Many happy returns.

Sic Transit Gloria Fackre
Gabe and Dot *in transitu* with mopeds,
at once affirming and admonishing themselves,
cantus firmus, on the importance of *ut unum sint*

PART I

THE MEANING
OF THE STORY TODAY

Story and History:
The Christian Context

Martin E. Marty

There is a story behind this essay on story. One should have no difficulty defending such a sentence in respect to any essay. While not wanting to sound imperialistic or triumphalist about the place and power of story, I do find it easy to make the claim that no essay appears without story behind it. This is as true of writing by Immanuel Kant or Ludwig Wittgenstein as it is of reportage by a war correspondent on the scene, or a paper assigned to and extracted from a college junior. It certainly has to do with everything about religion, everything about Christianity.

Thus, stories about writing usually have to do with solicitations by editors and responses by authors; with tales of Kant taking his walk in Königsberg before retiring to a study to write; with accounts of letters about overdue assignments from editors; with narratives about the burning of the midnight oil; with reminiscences of an idealist philosopher being asked to kick a stone to get in touch with reality; with a prophet announcing that he was asked to write a vision after experiencing a revelation from God.

A sentence with so many semi-colons and "with's" may not be elegant, but its crowded and provocative character suggests the myriad ways story connects with abstract as well as concrete, narrative-based essays. Tell me that the writing you have did not have human origin, as the writer of the Pentateuch tells us about Moses descending to the people as they danced around their Golden Calf, writing carved into stone by Yahweh and none other, and you still will not have divorced writing from a story context. To make full sense of it we would have to talk about Pentateuch and stone-carved tables and more, something we are not prepared to do here. Because "that's another story."

3

The story behind an essay like this has to do with *festschriften* and with this particular collection honoring one person; with that one person, in this case Gabriel Fackre; with my relations with the honoree; with a request and a rationale for the assignment. While "Gabe" and I have not often been in each other's presence, we do have somewhat similar academic pedigrees. We have found ourselves positioned similarly in the spectrum of American religious commitments. We are both ecumenical in outlook. We have both served at a crossroads where neither of us has been willing to surrender "academy" or "research" on one hand or "church" and "ministry" on the other. We both have newsletters; mine is fortnightly and his have been annual, but he has packed so much into his that the yearlong wait has always been worthwhile.

Further, I think that both of us have sensed a similar aspect in our ecumenical postures. Celebrating new relations during "our" half century with Orthodoxy, Roman Catholicism, and the variety of churches that make up mainstream Protestantism has been, strange to say, not all that difficult. But during the past third of the century we have seen the rise to new prominence and vitality of the cluster of evangelicalisms and Pentecostalisms and conservative Protestantisms that sociologists tab in a genus they call "Evangelical." It makes up one fourth of the religious graphic "pie" among Americans polled about their preference.

Such Evangelicalism often defined itself around a Fundamentalism-Modernism polarity, dated ca. 1925, that never did do justice to latter-day "mainstreamism" and evangelicalism. But it was so dramatic and efficient that it served many evangelicals well when they drew boundaries to keep themselves together, or "in," and others "out." On those terms, Fackre and I had to be "out." True, I had begun my ministry and teaching in the Lutheran Church–Missouri Synod, which ought to have led them to classify me as kin to fundamentalists. But my commitments to ecumenism as evidenced by my writing for *The Christian Century* as early as 1956 led me to be "typed" with liberals. And Professor Fackre's denominational home led them to position him as hopelessly mainstream-liberal/modernist.

Neither of us was ever content to be thus typed. Please don't misinterpret, dear Fackre-fan reader or Fackre-foe (are there such?), kibitzer or eavesdropper. Both of our commitments to catholic versions of ecumenism are so rich and so deep that we are not likely to be described as unmoored or adrift. We have anchors and home ports. The Evangelical Lutheran Church in America ("ELCA") and its antecedents, my "home" for thirty years, itself is not easily located on the inherited fundamentalist/

modernist polarity spectrum. Often introduced at evangelical gatherings as "this year's non-evangelical guest presenter," I had to remind conferees that I was the only person in the room who belonged to a church body that had the name "Evangelical" in it. (Sometimes Evangelical Free Church members were present and rose to question that claim for monopoly, but again, "that's another story.") And on grounds connecting us with the New Testament, early Christian, Reformation-era, and nineteenth-century Anglo-Continental Protestant grounds and all definitions inherited from such eras, the ELCA and I are certainly evangelical.

Still, one must make some commitments to be seen as anomalous or boundary crossing. And both Fackre and I have tried to stand at the crossing or on the bridge, to do justice in our reporting of things going on in the cluster sociologists call Evangelical, and to represent "the mainstream" openly among evangelicals. While many of our colleagues disdained anything on the burgeoning right as "uppity," sub-academic, or non-respectable, we have tried to pay respect to the kind of Christian witness and theological aspiration that represents amazing achievement in Christ's cause on the global scale during the past half century and holds great promise for the next.

Fackre has contended and, I believe, shown that many of the features he and I and all would call "liberal" in an open-Christian world can both speak to and learn from features of "evangelical" Christianity, and has encouraged dialogue among once hostile and still suspicious or at least wary parties. Neither of us would say that there are no issues separating the camps; neither of us would be ready to see one collapse into the other and let that other do the defining. But both of us have self-consciously stayed at the dialogical crossover spot and hope to put more energy into action based on that stance in the future.

This is his *Festschrift* and not mine, so it may seem ungracious or arrogant to have inserted myself so frequently into this informal account of where I see him. But the device with which I opened this essay is designed as a tribute to him as someone who has witnessed to me and taught me, and no doubt some of that "criss-crossing" or "crossing-over" or "crossroading" to which I referred has occurred in my own life and career, and in that of so many of his students and readers through the years, that I wanted thus to pay my respects and some of my debts and, I hope, represent others like me.

I have saved until now the intellectual feature of his influence that stands out most of all and is intended to be the theme of this *Festschrift*. That is, his commitment in Christian theology through "story." Would I comment on the subject of story in a contribution to this honoring volume? I would.

That a systematic theologian such as Fackre would be committed to "story" was a somewhat exceptional element in the years of his early career. Systematic theology is supposed to be abstract, in certain ways propositional, thetical, distant, lofty, difficult. The best of such, of course, includes other kinds of discourse, but in the present story I have to use a broad brush to paint the outlines. Fackre has paid his dues and has the credentials to confine himself to life within the boundaries suggested by those six adjectives that made their appearance two sentences ago. But he chose not thus to be narrowed. He devoted himself to story.

Now, between the early years of his career and the present there have been changes in the camps of the systematicians, some of which he helped effect and others which were effected by others that made his life work look more congenial to more people. He has seen and analyzed many theologies: of hope, politics, new, death-of-God, secular, women's, ethnic-based, global, liberation, and others that have come and sometimes gone. And among all of them he has been especially hospitable to what has come to be called "narrative" theology, or narratological theology among those who devour and emit jargon, or "story" theology among those who like to be understood.

Theology rooted in and related to story, of course, and especially at first, sounded like something very obvious to many in the Christian fold. Just as one man was surprised to be informed that he was talking in "prose," so it must have seemed, and in fact it did seem, strange to many Christians that systematic theologians were discovering, celebrating, and systematizing story. What have Christians had to talk about that was not story-based, from Genesis to Revelation, from Big Bang to the present moment? True, they have numbered in their systematic mix philosophers of religion whose style and substance seem remote from story. They relate idea to idea, which is a perfectly legitimate thing to do. But the moment they make their leap from abstract God-ness to any reference, *any* reference, beginning with the name Christ-ian, they are hooking into stories about Christ, anointing, Messiah, and the issue of why any philosopher would bother calling her proofs and propositions by a proper noun that refers to a figure in history, a rabbi on the east end of the Mediterranean twenty centuries ago.

Let the systematicians, then, fuss and argue about narrative theology, thought some, including many preachers. We will cheer them on because they have come lately to discover what we always knew; to put new names on it; to give it new prominence. And the preachers at their best profited from the systematicians, and at their worst thought that the legitimation of narrative theology was a license for them to issue homilies that were nothing but autobiographical. For them, "story" = "biography" = "autobiography" and produced boring, trivial accounts interrupted by occasional dazzling self-reference by some pastors who were particularly attentive, perceptive, articulate, and able to relate their own or other people's stories to the lives of their hearers, their congregants, or their prospects for evangelization. The most conscientious and alert among them also were concerned to deepen their understanding of narrative, of story. And those who followed through on their concern were often aided by Gabriel Fackre more than by most other systematicians.

It is good for the profession that such as he have come along. At this millennial turn we are learning that, both globally and locally, Christian pastors and people are turning less for theological comment to systematic theologians who write on what some derisively and not quite accurately call "Greco-Germanic" models, than to story writers and tellers. One publisher has told the theological communities that the market for books devoted to "serious" theology is limited to about 12,000 people in North America. Evangelicals talk a good line about devotion to theological truth and have produced a number of articulate systematic theologians. But a visit to an evangelical bookstore will quickly convince that seeker that that line often represents good intentions or bad lip service. Much of the ware at such stores is now of the gewgaw, knickknack, bumper-sticker, T-shirt sort, and the books are self-help, inspirational, "spiritual," in genre, while books on the Trinity or Incarnation languish.

The place where high- and mid- and lower-brow meet among those who seek interpretations of revelation, scripture, philosophy, and life is on the shelves of novelists, sometimes of poets, of storytelling essayists: Kathleen Norris, Frederick Buechner, Barbara Brown Taylor, Eugene Peterson, Walter Brueggemann, Walter Wangerin, Nancy Mairs, Madeleine L'Engle, and a cast of dozens tell stories, interpret theology, and reach many who have been turned off by abstract theology, creative and helpful and necessary though it be. But to put such writers and writing in context is the task of a few systematicians, Fackre among them.

So much for the survival and revival of story in narrative or story theology. One would not have suspected any need for concern for the survival or revival of story among historians, whose vocation and profession, whose expertise and curiosities, presumably would be located in story. Yet here a generation is busy beginning to recover story. Let me devote some attention now to my species in the theological community alongside the Fackrean systematicians: the historians of Christianity, a.k.a. church historians. What about story there?

Hard as it may be for non-historians to picture, and taken-for-granted as it will be among historians, "story" has had a bad reputation for some years among elite and avant-garde academic historians. Non-historians would be bemused at such a turn. History never seems to have had it so good among literate nonprofessionals. There are history book clubs, all of them devoted to books that tend to be pure story. For the two percent of the public that watches public television or higher-brow cable TV, there are frequent, well-turned series devoted to history in the form of story. In more weeks than not on the cover or third or fifth page of reviews such as the *New York Times Book Review* or the *New York Review of Books,* a historical work that concentrates on telling a tale or narrating a life will be the main feature.

One has to turn to the professional journals of historians to see that story has been in eclipse. Just as teachers of literature began to write essays on critical theory instead of John Milton or Shusaku Endo, and just as philosophers discussed methodological questions while avoiding the metaphysical, so many of the more prestigious historians put more energy into the theories of Foucault or Derrida or Lacan than they do to telling the story of French peasants in the feudal era or during the Reformation.

As well they might. Historians not only tell stories. They have to think about what they are doing. They may eschew philosophy — Jacob Burckhardt called it a "centaur" among historians — but they drag philosophies of life and philosophies with them. There may well be no "pure story." We have to think about why we chose the narrative we did; why we bring implicit or explicit value judgments to the stories; what are their frameworks and contexts. All that is, somehow, philosophy. So is reasoning and searching for clarity when dealing with tenses past and present and future.

Nor does one profitably remain ignorant of that which makes up the *Zeitgeist,* the fashions and fads and passing scene. The theorists of our time have taught much about bias, for example on the male-female, masculine-feminine, gay-straight, rich-poor, black-white, abused-victimizer fronts. Most of the time they do that depending upon story more than telling stories. They deal with the past synchronically rather than diachronically, taking cross-cuttings of history and not development as their subject matter. But story-minded historians, who have read all the theorists-of-the-moment, tend to absorb, to "internalize" the theories and then go back to the tracings that events of the past leave, and construct — yes, construct; thanks, philosophers of history for pointing that out — their narratives.

Just as there is value in theoretical and critical non-story history, we could put in one more moderating word: those journals of the professional association include hundreds of reviews of books each year, many of them devoted to story. The scene was never all bleak or all black in the sight of those of us who make much of story. But story was in eclipse.

So it was that an influential and honored historian, Lawrence Stone of Princeton, made news in an essay first published in 1979 on "The Revival of Narrative: Reflections on a New Old History" (most recently published in *The Past and the Present* [London: Routledge and Kegan Paul, 1981]). I commend it to anyone who would like to trace the eclipse and the reappearance. There are more militant versions of defense of story among neoconservatives, most notably Gertrude Himmelfarb, who has waged war not only on anti-story theorists, but also on "social historians" who get close to daily life of ordinary people but rebel against political history, because it tends to imply meta-narrative, about which a bit more a bit later. Or there are moderate surveys in the hands of figures like Jacques Barzun, who defends *Clio* among the muses for her stories. But Stone kept company with many who had deserted the narrative scene and, in effect, cried, "Enough!" and helped lead some back.

I wanted to be a writer before I knew I wanted to be a historian. In the years when I was almost accidentally being located among historians in graduate schools, I was reading José Ortega y Gasset in new English translations. It was compelling to read him say, for instance, that humans do not have an essence; they have a drama. A story.

Later I came to read Michael Oakeshott, who as early as 1933 spun out theories about experience and its modes. Modes, for him, are arrests in experience; each has its own kind of subject matter and demands its own irreplaceable language. Thus, science is a mode dealing with measurement. Poetry with imagination. Religion's differentia are seen *sub specie voluntatis* or *moris,* the will and the moral framework, and it is always directed to altering the world within. For history, the differentia is the past and all is seen *sub specie praetaritorum.* That is, the historian as historian has nothing to say until something has happened, until something belongs to the past.

What does the historian have to say, granted all that? Another work that was influential, at least on me, in the 1950s was by the Dutch historian G. J. Renier: *History, Its Purpose and Method* (Boston: Beacon, 1950).

9

Renier cut through the philosophy and asked what had history to deal with. One chapter dealt with history as story; another, history as nothing but story. He would have agreed that there are philosophical questions behind the choice of story and emphasis in it, but it was story.

No sooner was the ink dry on books like his when reaction came in. This is not the place to diagnose all the reasons for the rejection. Some were ideological, also in the religious world: neo-Marxist, Foucaultian, Lacanian, or whatever — critics saw stories to be the product of dominant and oppressive sorts. Winners get to tell stories. Ironically for them, it was at just that moment that we began to hear for the first time, or afresh, assuming we were not part of the communities that produced them, stories from racially and ethnically demeaned peoples; women; the abused and the victimized; the poor. How did any of them seek liberation? Through ideology and philosophy? Academics among them might have, but most did so by telling their story.

Others rebelled against story out of boredom with stories already told and, they would say, over-told. There did not seem to be more to mine about medieval times, the biblical world, Chinese dynasties. It was time to give historians, including religious historians, new themes and tasks. Again, ironically, as these claims were being made, archivists and researchers were turning up unprecedented numbers of documents and traces revealing elements in the past that had been quite literally left alone. There were new stories, and they needed telling.

A third factor might be a kind of faddism. I do not want to elaborate so much on this as to let me fall into the neoconservative camp, which repudiates all theories and argots outside its own. But it seems evident that many in the academy, after having drawn what was valuable out of theorists — more of them French than not — stayed around and dealt only with theory, at the expense of story. The frame of history writing overwhelmed the slight images it framed.

What to do about the theories? Some years ago I conversed with a philosopher about what was integrally human. Every four or five years a new reductionist theory would come along. That year it was AI, artificial intelligence modeling. That meant that the human brain was nothing but a high-speed computer. A few years before there had been neo-behaviorism and before that sociobiology, which followed behaviorism, and on and on. We agreed that we both learned from some of these models; that we could not truly refute them. But we also noted that we, before age sixty, had already outlived eight all-purpose final reductions that explained how humans were "nothing but" this or that.

Eventually they moved on, passively finding a home in the storehouse whence historians soon produce fresh stories. One need not go as far as Renier did with his theme "Nothing but a Story," to see that the concentration on story was a kind of guard against fanaticism of ideology. Many of the critical ideologies will remain in the canon, and can inform the tellers of stories. But in the end, wherever humans look for precedent, ancestry, past causes and explanations, or just delight in a tale, narrative will come back, to be welcomed by those who, like Professor Fackre, never left home.

A word about some Christian implications. Historical theologians and historians need not turn hyperbolic and make too strenuous claims, nor need lovers of story among them try to monopolize. Their discipline is modest, very modest. It can bring perspective, but not shape prediction. It needs sibling disciplines up and down the hall. Its practitioners may get more involved with story than many or most in other disciplines, but that larger involvement will not have meant that they have solved basic problems of human existence and Christian theology. But without them, their pack-rat mode of life, their rummaging through souvenirs and attics, the systematicians, ethicists, comparativists, and, of course, scriptural scholars, would have little to talk about.

In the nineteenth century, some historical theorists claimed that you study history to change history; that you overcome history with history, bad stories with other stories, stories that have a stranglehold with those that can liberate.

Martin Buber liked to say that God created the world because he loved stories. In the end, there is an intrinsic character and value to stories and story telling. They justify themselves. Having told them and responded to them, historians can then see that through stories we can seek the kingdom of God and God's righteousness. And all kinds of other things shall be added unto them.

No ideologue would have invented stories as unsettling and misfit as those about Jacob or David or, of course, Jesus. But they found in the very idiosyncratic particularism of stories a saving power they did not get or transmit through ideology or abstraction. They never run out of material for stories, and will always be providing systematic theology thereby with new raw material. Because Gabriel Fackre both narrates and systematizes, he belongs enviably to two worlds. And since there are so many stories still to be told, we shall have to, and we shall, wish him *ad multos annos.*

Reclaiming the Gospel

Donald Bloesch

I am not ashamed of the gospel: it is the power of God for salvation to everyone who has faith, to the Jew first and also to the Greek.

ROMANS 1:16, RSV

It is a pleasure for me to participate in this festschrift in honor of my friend and colleague in academia, Gabriel Fackre. We have much in common in our critique of a dead orthodoxy and our search for a more dynamic understanding of the gospel and of faith. Both of us are firmly committed to the cause of Christian unity, including Evangelical-Catholic unity. We also are working assiduously for spiritual and theological renewal in our own denomination, the United Church of Christ, which has a splendid theological heritage but a sorry record in remaining true to this heritage. We are both actively involved in renewal fellowships that seek to turn our denomination in an evangelical and biblical direction. I believe that Gabe will empathize with my ruminations concerning the gospel in this brief essay. He will not necessarily endorse all of my theological conclusions, but he will stand with me in upholding a centrist or reformist evangelicalism.

One of the remarkable phenomena in today's Christian world is the growing interest in redefining the gospel. This is due partly to the dawning realization, in both ecumenical and evangelical circles, that the gospel constitutes the bedrock of Christian faith and that there can be no Christian unity apart from a common understanding of the gospel. One might expect that a consensus on this matter would not be difficult to find, but in reality churches and theologians are deeply divided on what the gospel meant originally and also what it means today. In orthodoxy, the gospel is defined primarily as doctrine or teaching. In narrative theology, the gospel is understood basically as story. In the mystical heritage of the church, the gospel is envisioned as the gift of interior illumination, often called the inner word or the inner light; here the focus is on being united with Christ in his death and resurrection. In the circles of existentialism, the gospel is a call to decision to live in freedom (Bultmann). In the neoorthodoxy of Karl Barth, the gospel is the transcendent Word of God that encounters us primarily through the preaching and reading of Holy Scripture. I am closer to Barth than to the other alternatives mentioned above, but in fidelity to Scripture I wish to incorporate mystical and existential themes in a reaffirmation of the gospel.

In reclaiming the gospel, we must sedulously avoid several pitfalls. One of these is confounding the gospel with law, promise with command. This is the error of moralism or legalism, and it has been rampant in the church from the first century onward. It was vigorously combated by the Protestant Reformers in the sixteenth century. A second danger is reducing the gospel to a religious experience. This is the error of spiritualism or experientialism, discernible in Friedrich Schleiermacher, among many others. Then there is the danger of identifying the gospel with kerygma — the apostolic preaching. The gospel certainly includes kerygma, but it contains dimensions deeper than kerygma. It comprises not only the story of salvation but also the "power . . . unto salvation" (Rom. 1:16 KJV). A fourth danger is confounding the gospel with the doctrine of justification. This is the temptation of orthodoxy. The gospel includes the doctrine of justifying grace, but it also encompasses interior cleansing by the Holy Spirit — the lifelong process of sanctification. When justification is separated from sanctification, it becomes exclusively forensic and extrinsic. When it is confounded with sanctification, we then lose sight of the truth that justification is essentially an imputation of righteousness to be received only by faith. Justification and sanctification are not separate blessings (as in much evangelical revivalism), but a twofold blessing (Calvin).

I propose that we understand the gospel as the transforming message of redemption procured through the cross and resurrection of Christ, and sealed within us by the Holy Spirit. It is both a norm that judges and a vision that saves. It has both a historical and an ontological dimension. It is narrational and also existential. It is the power of the new being in Jesus Christ, as well as the ongoing interpretation of this transforming power, an interpretation that is anchored firmly in the apostolic witness. The gospel is not the systematizing of theological concepts, but it is the basis for all valid theologizing.

The gospel is not the law, but it must always be united with law. We are called to go into the world proclaiming the good news of redemption, but our vocation is also to make disciples of all the nations (Matt. 28:19). This involves teaching the precepts of religion, including the commandments that guide us in holy living. The gospel is not the antithesis of the law but the divine criterion that enables us both to understand the law and obey the law. If we maintain the inseparable relation of law and gospel, then we may conclude that one can *live* the gospel as well as *believe* the gospel.

The right understanding of the gospel is best found in the context of a theology of Word and Spirit. *Logos* and *praxis* must not be sundered, but united. The gospel is both the power of personal regeneration and the truth of historical redemption. It is not merely the *doctrine* of justification but the *act* of justification — in past history and in present experience. It is not just an experience, but an experience that points beyond itself to divine revelation in sacred history.

As Christians, we can know the gospel through the power of the Spirit; yet our oral and written renditions of the gospel must not be identified with the gospel itself. The gospel in one sense can be spoken only by God, but we can present a true witness to the gospel as the Spirit makes the Scriptures come alive for us. Our witness must not be mistaken for the gospel itself, but when the Spirit acts both within Scripture and upon our hearts then we can know — not fully or exhaustively, but truly and adequately. We must strive to avoid the twin perils of gnosticism and agnosticism. Now we must walk by faith, not by sight. Apart from the illumining work of the Spirit the gospel remains kerygma. But with the bestowal of the Spirit, the gospel becomes in fact the revivifying Word of the living God. So we must hope that in our broken witness to what God has done for us in Christ, our words might be used by the Spirit to bring others into inner communion with the passion and victory of the Lord Jesus Christ.

This brings us to the thesis that the gospel cannot be adequately understood apart from the Bible. The Bible is the objective norm by which we gain an understanding of the gospel in its narrational and historical settings. In its paradoxical unity with the Spirit, the Bible can even be regarded as an infallible norm. In this context it becomes transparent to the gospel, the norm that rules all other norms. What we say today concerning the gospel must stand in direct continuity with what the prophets and apostles said in their testimony to God's saving acts culminating in Jesus Christ. We are not preaching the gospel unless we preach from the Bible. The loss of the gospel in our churches is due partly to the crisis in preaching.

Our challenge today as theologians of the church is to recover a sacramental understanding of the gospel. The transcendent reality is Jesus Christ, the living Word of God. The historical sign is the biblical and apostolic witness to Jesus Christ. We gain access to the transcendent reality only through the historical or visible sign. We come to know the gospel by faith in Jesus Christ as our minds are opened by the Holy Spirit. Finally, we must resist the temptation to make personal salvation contingent on correct understanding. This is an error often committed by those who wish to stand firmly in orthodoxy. In my opinion, one may have a deficient understanding of the gospel and still be a real Christian. One may even veer toward heterodoxy in the formulation of faith and still be in contact with the salvific reality of the living Christ. So long as we respond to the embrace of the risen Christ in faith and repentance, we are in the family of God, even if we have not thought through the significance and implications of this transformative reality in our lives. Moreover, it is possible to have a correct understanding of the gospel yet nevertheless fall short of being in a right relationship with Christ. This anomaly exists when we profess faith in Jesus Christ, but fail to live in obedience to the imperatives contained in the gospel.

In summary, the gospel is more than story; it is wider and deeper than doctrine. It is the reality of the living God revealed in Jesus Christ; a reality that bursts into our lives when we are confronted by the message of Jesus Christ and him crucified. To proclaim the gospel rightly is to be caught up in the power of the gospel. To teach the truth of justification rightly is to lead others to the One who alone justifies and sanctifies through the power of his Spirit.

Our mandate today, as in days past, is not to impart religious insights or communicate God-consciousness, but to introduce lost sinners to Jesus Christ by sharing the good news of God's saving deeds in the sacred history mirrored in the Bible. May we put on the whole armor of God and trust in the power of the gospel itself to heal those who are spiritually and morally crippled, and to empower those who are intimidated and incapacitated by the forces of darkness. May we be light and salt to those around us by the proclamation of the Word, and the demonstration of a Christian life.

Justification: The Growing Consensus

Avery Cardinal Dulles, S.J.

It is a pleasure to submit a contribution, necessarily all too brief, to celebrate the work of Professor Gabriel Fackre, who has been for many years a friend and a consultant on important matters. I am particularly indebted to him for his assistance to me in Boston in the winter of 1981-1982, when I was writing my Models of Revelation. He gave me invaluable help, especially in identifying the views of American Protestant Evangelicals.

In the past few years, Professor Fackre has several times called attention to the wider ecumenical import of the Lutheran-Catholic Joint Declaration on the Doctrine of Justification ("JD"), signed in Augsburg, Germany, on October 31, 1999.[1] On April 20, 2001, he presented a paper on "The Ecumenical Import of the Joint Declaration on the Doctrine of Justification" to the annual meeting of the American Theological Society. As my contribution to this volume, I shall here reproduce in substance the response that I delivered to that paper.

Professor Fackre's paper, being remarkably comprehensive, clear, and well-structured, could serve as a model for ecumenical discourse in this and many other areas. Especially helpful is his attention to method. He attends first to common affirmations and then follows up with differences, which he treats under the rubric of mutual admonitions. After reviewing the convergences and divergences between Lutherans and Catholics noted in the Joint Declaration, he goes on to consider what consensus could be achieved and what admonitions might be appropriate if Re-

1. "Joint Declaration on the Doctrine of Justification," *Origins* 28 (July 16, 1998): 120-27.

formed Christians were brought into the discussion of justification with Lutherans and Catholics.[2]

Fackre's analysis draws heavily on his distinction between what he calls justification "writ large" and justification "writ small." By the former, he seems to mean what has more commonly been treated under the rubric of redemption. Classical theology took justification to mean the application of the fruits of redemption to people of various times and places. I state this not as a point of disagreement with Dr. Fackre, but simply to facilitate communication. Whichever terminology one employs, it should be clear that justification follows from redemption, a doctrine on which there was relatively little disagreement among Lutherans, Calvinists, and Catholics in the sixteenth century, since they were unanimous in confessing that Jesus Christ had atoned for the sins of the whole world and had sent the Holy Spirit to complete his saving mission.

It is puzzling how Lutherans and Catholics, after anathematizing each other's positions on justification for four hundred and fifty years, could declare in 1999 that their differences on that subject are no longer church dividing — and all this with the claim that neither party has changed its position. To explain this, Fackre suggests that the Joint Declaration was able to achieve its unprecedented agreements by contextualizing the theology of justification within the broader framework of the doctrine of redemption (or justification "writ large"). While this explanation undoubtedly contains a measure of truth, I personally doubt that it is the adequate explanation, since the sixteenth-century theologians were quite aware, I believe, of the trinitarian and christological underpinnings of the doctrine of justification. The early councils had settled the essential doctrines concerning the Trinity and the Incarnation to the satisfaction of all mainline Christians.

A further ingredient in the recent rapprochement is the influence of the Finnish school of Lutheran theologians, who have emphasized that justification by faith alone need not be understood in merely forensic terms, as something extrinsic to the believer.[3] In a number of important

2. For an initial exploration by a Catholic dealing primarily with Calvin, see William M. Thompson, "The Saints, Justification, and Sanctification: An Ecumenical Thought Experiment," *Pro Ecclesia* 4 (1995): 16-36.

3. See Tuomo Mannermaa, "Theosis as a Subject of Finnish Luther Research," *Pro Ecclesia* 4 (1995): 37-48; also David S. Yeago, "Martin Luther on Grace, Law, and Moral Life: Prolegomena to an Ecumenical Discussion of *Veritatis Splendor*," *The Thomist* 62 (1998): 163-91. In his article "The Nature of Justifying Grace: A Lacuna in the *Joint Declaration*," published in *The Thomist* 65 (2001): 93-120, Christopher J. Malloy maintains that

texts Luther himself asserted that the Christ who is grasped in faith dwells in us and divinizes us by virtue of faith itself. Thus, the Joint Declaration was able to state that according to the Lutheran understanding, "justification and renewal are joined in Christ, who is present in faith" (JD 26). Lutherans who accept this interpretation of their own tradition tend to agree with Catholics that transforming grace and the divine inhabitation are essential to the process of justification itself.

In an article for *First Things* published in December 1999, I called attention to some passages in the Joint Declaration in which the authors seem simply to have juxtaposed Lutheran language of imputation and Catholic language of impartation, without indicating how the gulf can be bridged.[4] The text allows Lutherans to hold that justification does not eradicate sin in the justified while Catholics continue to assert that it does. How, I asked, can these contrary positions be harmonized?

My suggestion was that theologians have gained a greater awareness of the inability of all human conceptuality and language to capture the mystery of justification. With this realization, we can see the value of different affirmations that seem on the surface to be incompatible, somewhat as wave-theories and particle-theories might help us to account for different aspects of the phenomenon of light. This, I think, is what the signers of the Joint Declaration were implicitly saying when they allowed the languages of both traditions to stand. But the Joint Declaration did not fully accomplish the theological reconciliation. It did not show to the satisfaction of critical readers that the contradictions are merely apparent or unimportant. The Official Catholic Response of June 25, 1998[5] and the Official Common Statement of June 11, 1999,[6] both called for further studies on the part of theologians to clarify the remaining divergences.

Following a proposal made in each of the two official commentaries just mentioned, I suggested in my *First Things* article that the traditional formulations of the two parties might profitably be enriched by deeper biblical research. The decrees of Trent, while not stating anything false, suffer from certain limitations due to the Scholastic atmosphere in which they were concocted. Trent was within its rights in defining justification,

---

even the Finnish interpretation of Luther does not succeed in bridging the gap between the Lutheran and Catholic positions on sin in the justified (98).

4. Avery Dulles, "The Two Languages of Salvation: The Lutheran-Catholic Joint Declaration," *First Things* 98 (December 1999): 25-30.

5. "Official Catholic Response to the Joint Declaration," *Origins* 28 (July 16, 1998): 130-32.

6. "Official Common Statement," *Origins* 29 (June 24, 1999): 85-88.

as it did, in terms of the effect on the persons justified, and hence as equivalent to rebirth and sanctification. But in so doing they missed the Pauline insight that justification may also be viewed from God's side, as it were, as a forensic decree in which the Father pronounces sinners righteous in view of the merits of Jesus Christ. This forensic act logically precedes the transformation of the justified person through grace and the inhabitation of the Holy Spirit. In acknowledging this, as I think they can, Catholics may be able to find legitimate meaning in certain traditionally Protestant categories such as imputed righteousness.[7] Protestants, for their part, may find greater legitimacy in the Catholic formulations if they will take a broader view of the biblical data, not confining themselves to a few favorite texts from Paul.

If the gap between the Lutheran confessional books and the Council of Trent can be bridged by some such procedure as this, I am optimistic that the conflicts of Catholics with Orthodox, with Anglicans, and with Methodists on the issue of justification can likewise be transcended. As for Reformed Christians, it seems rather difficult for Catholics to achieve agreement with those who belong to nonsacramental churches, like the Southern Baptists, but relatively easy to find common ground with those who, like Gabriel Fackre, adhere to a sacramental vision of Christianity. Their position, inherited from Calvin, is in some ways intermediate between Lutheranism and Catholicism. While admonishing Lutherans in much the same way as Catholics do, they admonish Catholics somewhat as Lutherans do. To put this more concretely, I would say that Reformed Christians, like Catholics, insist on mystical union with Christ, internal holiness, and good works. But, like Lutherans, the Reformed insist on God's utterly free election of those who are to be justified and on faith alone as the instrument by which divine forgiveness is received.

In his anxiety to find material for mutual admonition between Catholic and Reformed Christians on the subject of justification, Fackre, in my opinion, mentions points on which I would think that the two parties already agree. He would like Reformed to admonish Catholics to accept the following four doctrines, all of which Catholics themselves profess:

1. Faith is absolutely necessary for justification. This has been repeatedly taught not only by Trent, but also by popes and councils down through the ages. To the best of my knowledge, no reputable Catholic

---

7. See Avery Dulles, "Justification in Contemporary Catholic Theology," in *Justification by Faith: Lutherans and Catholics in Dialogue VII* (Minneapolis: Augsburg, 1985), 256-77, esp. 257-58.

theologian has ever taught that baptism justifies without faith. The approved opinion is that if the candidate for baptism as yet lacks the gift of faith, that gift is infused by baptism itself. The gift or virtue of faith subsequently expresses itself, and must express itself, by acts of faith. While Reformed Christians and Catholics agree on the necessity of faith, they might have a problem agreeing on the doctrine of baptismal regeneration — a point that Fackre surprisingly neglects to mention.

2. The justification of the sinner is never merited. Catholics teach this as firmly as Protestants do, while adding that justification may be more easily received by those who, by God's grace, are more favorably disposed to accept it. Without God's freely bestowed mercy, no sinner could ever attain righteousness.

3. The offer and bestowal of grace are not restricted to members of the institutional church. According to a thesis that has become common Catholic teaching, all men and women receive sufficient grace to attain eternal salvation. Vatican II leaves no doubt about what Catholics hold on this question.

4. Among the good works required of the justified, one would have to list not only those of a personal and private character, but also those affecting society in its public aspects. The Catholic Church, convinced of this thesis, has produced an immense body of social teaching.

Toward the end of his paper, Dr. Fackre lists some Catholic admonitions to the Reformed. Since he as a Reformed Christian formulates them, we may presume, I think, that the admonitions do not point to deficiencies that are universal among Reformed Christians. Let me comment very briefly on three of these admonitions:

1. Some Reformed theologians have no doubt tended to emphasize predestination and election at the expense of human freedom and cooperation. Theologians like Fackre, as a Reformed Christian, and myself, as a Catholic, are alike faced with the problem of affirming both divine election and human cooperation. Although we cannot fully explain how the two interlock, we can, I suppose, agree that God's grace neither eliminates nor diminishes human freedom.

2. While the church exists most perfectly in believers who are morally and spiritually pure — that is to say, in the saints — its membership is not restricted to the righteous or the elect. In its earthly pilgrimage, it contains sinners also. Perhaps some Reformed Christians have tended to restrict the church to the number of the elect, as Wycliffe did, but today I suppose that most would agree that the church on earth is a *corpus permixtum* containing bad fish, as well as good.

3. For an adequate grasp of the doctrine of justification, or for that matter of any doctrines whatsoever, we must attend to the historic teaching of the church and stand within the great tradition, all the while not allowing ourselves to be confined to past expressions of the faith. If Reformed Christians tend to be more creative and less traditional, as Dr. Fackre suggests, this may bring home the point he so persuasively argues, that groups having different charisms should learn to appreciate one another's gifts for the sake of mutual enrichment.

Gabriel Fackre himself cannot be accused of neglecting the tradition, but he is creative in his ecumenical methodology. I gladly confess that my own thinking has been stimulated and advanced by the paper on which I am commenting. I expect that in coming years, Fackre will be among the foremost artisans in carrying through the ecumenical project that he has so auspiciously launched.

Response to Gabriel Fackre
on the Joint Declaration on the
Doctrine of Justification

George Lindbeck

In responding to Gabriel Fackre's analysis from a Reformed perspective of the Lutheran-Roman Catholic Joint Declaration on the Doctrine of Justification ("Joint Declaration"), I have chosen, with some encouragement from him, not to enter into the details of the argument, but rather to discuss the worthiness of the kind of theological ecumenism represented by his paper and by the Joint Declaration itself. These have succeeded in closing the conceptual gap between the contending parties more completely than I and my colleagues ever managed to do during the decades, beginning with Vatican II, when I was officially part of the dialogue. I have no substantial suggestions as to how to improve on their bridge building at the present time.

Yet successes of this kind (or, for that matter, failures) arouse little interest. As is often said, theological ecumenism is in the doldrums and with it, so I would argue, theology for the church in general. It is in view of this larger enterprise that I shall comment on the growing agreement on justification that Professor Fackre has admirably analyzed on this and other occasions.

Theology for the church or churches (understood as organized communities of faith) can be distinguished from, for example, theology for the academy and theology for the world. Each of these theological activities has its own area of responsibility.

Response given at the American Theological Society, Princeton, New Jersey, April 4, 2001.

Theology for the church is concerned with constructing and nurturing Christian community by scriptural, historical, systematic, or pastoral studies. Theology for the academy engages in the communally "neutral" study of a range of phenomena, in which Christianity along with other communal faith traditions becomes a subdivision of religious studies. Theology for the world, in turn, centers on social and environmental concerns; on what the World Council of Churches calls JPIC (Justice, Peace, and the Integrity of Creation). Each of these domains can profit from the others, and yet much of the work done in one might be unintelligible, uninteresting, or irrelevant to the others.

Neither the Joint Declaration nor Professor Fackre's paper, for example, are academically interesting in that they are not directed at an audience that includes unbelievers as well as believers. (Which does not mean that they may not also be read with interest for academic or JPIC purposes by unbelievers as well as believers.) Both the Declaration and Fackre assume, rather than explain or defend, the importance of visible church unity and of a whole range of distinctively Christian beliefs. Then, without saying why others should care, they investigate the possible compatibility or perhaps even complementarity of historically divisive formulations of a doctrine — that of justification, which might once have been at the living center of Reformation and Roman communions of faith — but now seems marginal.

The very word "justification" is unfamiliar to ordinary Catholics, and its meaning has become obscure to most heirs of the Reformation, including Lutherans, yet both the Joint Declaration and Fackre confine themselves for the most part to old and now largely unintelligible language and concepts. They have to do so or they would not be able to make any progress in their tasks of examining the compatibility and complementarity of the formulations they study. Yet, once again, what difference does this make to anyone outside a small band of specialists? Is it of any real importance to the communities of faith, not to mention the academy or the world at large?

The answer to this question depends, not simply on whether one thinks theology for the church is important, but on how ecumenical discourse operates or is supposed to operate. The ecumenical standard for this discourse as it developed in Faith and Order and in the major bilaterals, was rooted in the historic Christian mainstream. There is (or, at least, was) something like a consensus that theology for the churches should be guided by Scripture and tradition interpreted in the light of the confession of trinitarian faith by the community as a whole (that is, by the *sensus fidelium* in interaction with both those doing theology for the church and those exercising ecclesiastical oversight). The relation between these various elements and the weight given to each vary enormously from church to church, but the characterization I have given nevertheless covers all the bodies in the organized ecumenical movement from the ancient churches of the East and West to contemporary Pentecostals. Though thin, the methodological consensus sufficed to produce so substantive an agreement as the Lima text, "Baptism, Eucharist, and Ministry" ("BEM"), in 1982.

In the last two decades, however, the practice of, even if not the formal commitment to, this methodological standard has greatly weakened within the multilateral (chiefly World Council) part of the ecumenical movement. It seems unlikely in the foreseeable future that multilateral dialogues will again achieve anything comparable to BEM. Progress in theological ecumenism has shifted to the bilateral dialogues, especially those carried on by the Roman Catholic Church with the Christian world communions that stem from the Reformation — Lutheran, Reformed, and Anglican. But here also there is a weakening of the ecumenically standard methodological commitments to, as I put it earlier, Scripture and tradition interpreted in a trinitarian context by theologically and ecclesiastically concerned communities of faith.

This standard mode of ecumenical theology has lasted long enough to make possible the Joint Declaration, but whether it will persist in any comparably effective way is widely doubted. The Declaration may prove to be the climax of what is currently possible in bilateral ecumenism, just as BEM is of the multilateral variety, but its status as an enduring achievement is more solid. It has been officially received by the leaders of the traditions that sponsored the process that produced it, and thus its revocation of the condemnations that were initially central to the break-up of the religious unity of the West now has the status of shared doctrine. Perhaps the Anglican-Roman Catholic *Gift of Authority* (1999) is potentially more important in that it envisages visible unity between Rome and a major Reformation body, but it is still under discussion and is not an authoritative statement of either Anglicans or Roman Catholics. The Joint Declaration stands alone in this respect.

This uniqueness, however, establishes the importance of the Joint Declaration only if the kind of theology that produced it has a future, and it is precisely this that is doubtful. In mainstream Protestantism and in much of Roman Catholicism, ecumenically-oriented traditions of theological inquiry informing and nurturing enduring communities of faith are weakening. The communities that they aim to serve provide them

24

with less and less support, and instead depend on theologies for the world and for the academy to do their work. Where this happens, it is easy to dismiss the Joint Declaration with the "oft-repeated words" that Gabriel Fackre cites from Horst Symanowski: Luther asked, "How can I find a gracious God?" while we lie awake wondering "How can we find a gracious neighbor?" From such a progressive Western perspective, the effort expended on the doctrine of justification is misspent.

On the other hand, it is possible to argue on non-theological as well as theological grounds that ecumenically-oriented theology for the church is indispensable: without it, communities of faith dissolve if not in the short, then in the long run. The groups that practice the ecumenical standard might shrink in size, but they will be the ones which survive, and in the histories they write at some future date, the Joint Declaration (or, more precisely, the development of which it was a part) may figure as of world historical importance.

This potentially world-historical development is a mass phenomenon, which I was reminded of a year ago when I was called upon to respond to an address on the Joint Declaration by Cardinal Cassidy before his retirement as head of the Pontifical Council on Christian Unity. He quoted from a sermon delivered the previous year before the Pope and the Roman Curia. "I often sorrowfully ask myself," the preacher had said, "why it is that, in many parts of the world, thousands of the faithful are drawn away from the Catholic Church so as to hear elsewhere the strong and liberating message that 'those who are in Christ are not condemned' (Rom. 8:1). Why not let this ring out loud and clear in our proclamation to the people of God?" In short, so this homilist was saying, the doctrine of justification belongs also in the Roman Catholic Church where it has been wrongfully neglected. That is why, he suggests, there has been a hemorrhaging of membership to the sects in many places; it is urgently necessary to recover the message that there is no condemnation for those united with Christ Jesus in faith. (Much the same sermon, it should be added, needs to be heard in mainline Protestantism.)

The way I've put this matter is unfair. I have made it sound as if institutional self-interest were the main Roman Catholic incentive for proclaiming that union with Christ delivers from condemnation, but better motives are also at work. One modern-sounding, yet thoroughly biblical, reason is the preferential option for the poor. They constitute the bulk of the "thousands of the faithful [that] are drawn away," which the preacher mentioned. The poor are the ones most likely to recognize their need for this message and to respond to it.

Unlike the rich in a society such as ours (where even the middle-class majority is immensely richer than most of humankind), poor Christians have not been brainwashed into thinking there is no such thing as condemnation, or no such thing as the wrath of God. They do not imagine, as our American culture teaches us to do, that what used to be called sin is an unfortunate (perhaps even disastrous) and yet wholly non-culpable failure to actualize our inner potential. As in the sixteenth century, so in the twenty-first — it is the poor in body as in spirit (for the two are usually, though not always, conjoined) whose consciences most frequently cry out for consolation and who are most open to death-defying faith in Christ. The kingdom of heaven is theirs, as the first of the beatitudes affirms (Matt. 5:3).

What I have just said was not in Cardinal Cassidy's speech, but he said he approved of it. Thus, if I understood him rightly, it is not institutional self-interest (although, in our wicked world, that also operates), but a thoroughly catholic emphasis on God's preferential option for the poor that prompts renewal within the Roman Curia itself of the Reformers' chief concern.

Whether any comparably powerful concern is at work among mainline Protestants is doubtful. They often seem to regard the Joint Declaration as an act of ecumenical courtesy, in which Protestants officially welcome what they think of as an admission by the Roman Catholics that the Reformers were basically right about a doctrine that was once central, but is now marginal. As for the minority of Lutherans who take justification seriously as the article by which the church stands or falls, they are divided into what might be called "catholic" and "protestant" camps. The first favors and the second opposes the Joint Declaration not so much because of differences over justification itself, as over its ecclesiological implications. In short, the mainline heirs of the Reformation tend to be spiritually indifferent and theologically complacent about the doctrine; they have forgotten its importance, on the one hand, and think they know it boringly well, on the other.

Knowing it boringly well, however, is an illusion: there is much unknown territory that remains to be explored. What the Germans call *Wirkungsgeschichte* in particular has been neglected. Justification is a dangerous doctrine, especially when divided, as it has been, between the confessions. The neglect of it by Catholics and the misunderstandings of it by Protestants have been disastrous, as history abundantly displays. Neither the Joint Declaration and the studies leading up to it, nor Gabriel Fackre's contribution has had the time and space to tell this sorry story, but this badly needs to be explored.

Moreover, the exploration needs to be done jointly. Some of the most acute (though very different) pastoral problems experienced by Roman Catholics and Protestants in our day originated in the sixteenth-century schism over justification, and have worsened ever since. Because of their polemical origins, both the Tridentine and the Reformation formulations were from the very beginning one-sided, although not, as the Joint Declaration implies, untruthful. One-sidedness, however, led to disaster.

Roman Catholics, in effect, surrendered the doctrine to the Protestants. Sometimes it was primarily the word "justification" that was omitted (as from the sixteenth-century Roman Catechism that was composed to transmit Tridentine teachings, which had used the term freely), but the substance of the doctrine (the *sola gratia,* for example) was also slighted. Protestants, in turn, butchered the Reformation teaching in their various and often contradictory popular versions, by short-changing the trinitarian and other catholic elements that gave the doctrine its original coherence and power. Roman Catholics and Protestants have been linked together polemically in these developments as inseparably as Siamese twins, and yet they have imagined themselves independent of each other, unaware of the degree to which they have both been shaped by their mutual antagonism. What was affirmed in one tradition was assumed to be false by the other, with the result that there was reciprocal impoverishment.

These illusions are now beginning to be shattered, but there is still far to go. If I may conclude on a pious-sounding note, the Joint Declaration and Gabriel Fackre's reflections will not have their proper *Wirkungsgeschichte* until Roman Catholics and Protestants learn to weep together over the harm they have mutually inflicted by their divisions over justification. Joint repentance is the precondition for learning to work together to repair the damage. It is only by the closest ecumenical collaboration that the catholic and evangelical dimensions of justification in union with Christ through faith by grace will be rejoined for the church as a whole.

Toward the Trinity: Reading the Christian Story with a Holistic Hermeneutic

Elmer M. Colyer

I first met Gabriel Fackre at a theology conference in Wheaton, Illinois, in the mid-1980s. I remember the occasion vividly. Donald Bloesch, my friend and former mentor, introduced me to Dr. Fackre. I was immediately impressed by the polished, gracious, and thoughtful demeanor of the man. He came across as an extremely wise and winsome theologian, Christian, and person. I remember thinking that I would like to get to know Gabe and that he would be a great person to work under in a Ph.D. program. It is no coincidence that I ended up in the Joint Doctoral Program of Boston College and Andover Newton Theological School, a decision I never regretted. Fackre was an outstanding mentor/*Doktorvater*.

The kind of narrative theology Fackre advocates is the most appealing form of this crucial movement to date.[1] That he places greater emphasis on the doctrine of the Trinity in Christian faith and theology than do many narrative theologies, is one of the most promising elements of Fackre's narrative interpretation of Christian doctrine. This brings us to the subject of this essay and my thesis that the Christian Story rendered by the biblical narrative has a trinitarian substructure or deep structure, which can be discerned when that narrative is read with a holistic hermeneutic. (In a brief essay like this, one can do little more than assert one's thesis and leave detailed development and documentation of it for another essay.)

---

1. See Gabriel Fackre, *The Christian Story*, vol. 1, *A Narrative Interpretation of Christian Doctrine*, 3d ed. (Grand Rapids: Eerdmans, 1996), and vol. 2, *Authority: Scripture in the Church for the World* (Grand Rapids: Eerdmans, 1987).

Narrative Theology's Hermeneutical Holism

One of the most significant contributions of the narrative movement is its passionate return to hermeneutical holism. I think it can be demonstrated that the doctrine of the Trinity has not fared well in times in church history dominated by analytic, deductive, and other procedures in biblical interpretation that carve up the Bible and focus on the various parts of the biblical text without seeing them in relation to the whole biblical narrative. It is striking how seldom historical-critical biblical studies have ever led to a robust doctrine of the Trinity.

Hans Frei was certainly not the first to complain that Enlightenment/post-Enlightenment procedures for examining the biblical text proved to be destructive to the holistic integrity of the biblical narrative. Yet his work, *The Eclipse of the Biblical Narrative,* with its painstaking scholarship, demonstrated in an unprecedented and undeniable manner this eclipse of narrative and its holistic way of reading the Bible.[2]

According to Frei, the Bible (and books within it, a Gospel for example) is best read as a whole, somewhat akin to a nineteenth-century realistic novel. The identities of the characters (God and human beings) and the "world" they inhabit emerge only out of their interactions throughout the entire course of "story" narrated in the biblical text. Procedures that focus only or primarily on the constitutive parts of the Bible (or of individual books) eclipse the very fabric, the interconnections and intrinsic structures, of the entire narrative, which renders intelligible the "Christian Story." The Trinity, in particular, is far more deeply, pervasively, and intrinsically embedded in the overall texture of the biblical narrative, than simply present in a few triadic formulae here and there in the New Testament. It is no coincidence that the doctrine of the Trinity suffers in those hermeneutical/theological perspectives which approach the Bible piecemeal. It is little wonder that when the Bible's constitutive parts are interpreted in isolation, the Bible then is regularly transposed into a new idiom in order for it to be intelligible and meaningful to modern readers. (The Bible has to be reinterpreted in light of extrinsic frameworks and warrants brought to the text by the modern interpreter, as Frei astutely points out.)

This problematic kind of analytic, deductive, abstract procedure, which begins by isolating data or phenomena and then developing theoretical elements like concepts or doctrines in light of them, can be found in

---

2. Hans W. Frei, *The Eclipse of Biblical Narrative: A Study in Eighteenth and Nineteenth Century Hermeneutics* (Philadelphia: Fortress Press, 1975).

other disciplines of the modern period like natural science.[3] Similar methods created corollary problems in natural science to those Frei documents in biblical studies. For example, Newton did not (and could not) develop theoretical elements (absolute time and space for instance) by isolating data and deducing or abstracting his theories from them, a point which Hume demonstrated with devastating consequences (as Kant so clearly perceived in his awakening from "dogmatic slumber"). Yet, the deepest problem with this analytic/deductive isolation of "empirical data," is that it breaks up the natural coinherence (form in being) of things (the electromagnetic field or space-time continuum, for example) into individual particles externally related to each other. Procedures of this kind efface the very intrinsic interconnections that define and constitute what an electromagnetic field actually is. Thus natural science has also had to move toward a more holistic and integrative way of investigation.[4]

A common example of a complex integrated entity, which requires holistic and integrative apprehension, is the popular book of *Magic Eye* pictures. At first, a Magic Eye picture looks like a chaotic mass of tiny detailed figures. The creators of it, however, tell us that there is a three-dimensional image embedded in the matrix of intrinsic interrelations of those tiny detailed figures. If we follow their directions, hold the picture close to our faces and slowly move the picture away without focusing on the detail, suddenly the astonishing 3-D image leaps into view. The human mind is able to integrate the subsidiary clues, the intrinsic interrelations between the tiny figures, which render the 3-D image apprehensible. However, if we break up the Magic Eye picture and merely analyze the detailed figures separately, we efface the very fabric of interrelations in the detail that enable us to integrate those subsidiary clues and perceive the 3-D image.

In a similar manner, other holistic, interconnected entities (like electromagnetic fields or the Trinity embedded in the Christian Story) are not amenable to any method or procedure that shifts the focus (unconsciously or by intent) merely or primarily to examining the constitutive elements. In the end, these procedures efface the very intrinsic interrelations that have to be *integrated holistically* in order to grasp the natural

---

3. See Elmer M. Colyer, *How to Read T. F. Torrance: Understanding His Trinitarian and Scientific Theology* (Downers Grove, IL: InterVarsity Press, 2001), pp. 325-59, for a discussion of the problems with analytic, deductive, etc. procedures, their destructive isolation of data, and the need for holistic epistemologies.

4. See Colyer, *How to Read T. F. Torrance,* pp. 331-44.

cohesion (form in being) of the electromagnetic field or the Bible. Interconnected entities require a complex and holistic cognitive *indwelling* of these intrinsic interrelations in order for us to assimilate mentally their integration.[5] Presuppositions or methods that rule out a holistic and integrative approach to the Bible are therefore suspect. Narrative theology is right in its questioning of all forms of hermeneutics that eclipse the holism of the biblical narrative, and right in its call for a more comprehensive and integrative interpretive procedure.

Of course, this does not mean that historical-critical biblical studies have no value and should be discarded. Rather, not unlike the way Einsteinian physics has qualified the Newtonian perspective, a more holistic and integrative hermeneutical approach to the Bible still values and learns from the historical-critical approach and its findings, but acknowledges that they are of only limited applicability at rather rudimentary interpretive levels. In a similar way, one can learn a lot by examining the details of a Magic Eye picture piecemeal, but this cannot take one all that far towards integrating the intrinsic interrelations of the detail in the holistic manner required if one is to apprehend the 3-D image embedded in the picture.

Thus, a holistic hermeneutic calls for a more comprehensive kind of

5. The notion of indwelling comes from T. F. Torrance and Michael Polanyi and refers to the significantly informal, holistic, integrative, and heuristic process by which the human mind assimilates the intrinsic interrelations embodied in complex entities (an electromagnetic field or the biblical narrative). A structural kinship develops out of this informal process between our knowing and what we seek to know. This kinship is not an a priori (independent of experience) or innate conceptual counterpart or cognitive structure (as in Kant). There is not inherent isomorphism between the human mind/thought and that which it seeks to know. Neither is it a cognitive counterpart deduced or abstracted on the basis of isolated data or phenomena. Only as the mind gradually and informally assimilates the intrinsic interconnections constitutive of the entity under investigation in a holistic and integrative manner does this kinship arise, a kinship that is thus neither impossible nor automatic. Thus the cognitive kinship between the mind and the complex entity is neither inherent in the mind, nor a necessary inference deduced or abstracted from the isolated data, nor simply imposed by constructive mental activity, but rather contingent upon the holistic, dynamic, integrative indwelling process of interaction between the mind and the intrinsic interrelations constitutive of the complex entity. It is the fusion of form in being which requires this kind of holistic, integrative form of knowing beyond analyzing distinct particulars and deducing knowledge from them. Genuine knowledge is neither inevitable nor impossible, but requires the generation and discovery of suitable forms of thought and speech both for the apprehension and the articulation of intelligibility. See Colyer, *How to Read T. F. Torrance,* pp. 334-44.

reading (maybe even a different kind of reader) of the Bible. It entails an indwelling and assimilation of the whole biblical text so as to integrate the various elements and events of the Christian Story in their interrelations. As the biblical drama unfolds, previous events are interpreted ever again and anew as later events and their sequences cast new light on those that happened earlier. The Exodus and the Passover Lamb are repeatedly reappropriated and their significance deepened and transformed throughout the trajectory of the biblical narrative, finding their deepest meaning in Jesus Christ himself.[6]

Thus, seeing the trajectory of the entire biblical narrative is a prerequisite to its proper interpretation. One cannot understand Jesus Christ as the Son of God or as the Lamb of God who takes away the sin of the world apart from the Old Testament narrative matrix, just as the New Testament depiction of Jesus Christ leads to a new reading and transposition of all that has happened in the narrative of the Old Testament. Only at the end of the narrative (but in the light of the entire narrative) does the "Christian Story" come fully into view.[7]

This kind of integrative, holistic hermeneutic becomes even more complex and necessary in relation to the trinitarian deep structure or substructure of the Christian Story because the interpreter has to integrate constitutive, interconnected elements at multiple levels: the level of the biblical text itself, the level of the Christian Story depicted by the overall biblical narrative, and the level of the interrelations between the trinitarian Persons and their activities embedded throughout the Christian Story.[8] It is little wonder that it took the early church several hundred years to work out the details of the doctrine of the Trinity. We are dealing

6. We cannot abstract Jesus Christ out of the matrix of his interrelations to the Old Testament and Israel, nor disregard the way in which the overall Gospel narratives depict the identity of Jesus, nor merely examine elements of a Gospel apart from the theological matrix of the entire Gospel, nor only examine various New Testament books independent of one another or the entire Bible.

7. We are faced here with the age-old issue of the hermeneutical circle in the relationship between the parts and the whole. They have to be understood together, in light of one another, or more precisely each has to be understood with simultaneous, subsidiary attention to the other.

8. If God is a real Actor, not just a literary convention, then we cannot avoid the extra-textual reference of the biblical narrative, and with it the need to distinguish between several coordinated levels within our interpretation of that narrative. This does not require a return to the simplistic and problematic way of approaching the question found in the Enlightenment hermeneutics that eclipsed the biblical narrative, nor does it necessitate a form of foundationalism. We will return to this point below.

with a highly complex, multilevel, integrative, and holistic (and I would argue participatory) hermeneutic, which alone is adequate to assimilate the trinitarian deep structure of the Christian Story with the fabric of the overall biblical narrative.

I do not believe that the ecumenical creeds (which affirm that the doctrine of the Trinity is indispensable to a genuine reading of the Christian Story) arose by any primarily analytical, deductive, or logical process, but rather out of the church's holistic and integrative indwelling of the biblical witness within the matrix of the ongoing worship, life, and missionary activity of the Christian community. The Trinity, the Christian doctrine of God, arises out of a holistic, integrative indwelling of the entire biblical narrative. The articulation of the identity of the Chief Actor in the biblical drama takes a trinitarian form for the intrinsic interrelations of the Christian Story are trinitarian in structure and render the comprehensive biblical narrative intelligible in a way that the alternatives do not.[9]

---

9. The trinitarian substructure of the Christian Story, however, is far more complex than a simple three-act drama correlated with the three Persons of the Triune God. There is much greater coinherence in the interrelations between the missions of the trinitarian Persons. See, for example, the way Luke-Acts views the interpenetrations of the missions of Jesus Christ and the Holy Spirit. Jesus is born of Mary by the Spirit, receives the Spirit at his baptism into the humanity Christ assumed from us in the incarnation, and Christ lives out his life and does his ministry in the Spirit. When the Spirit comes at Pentecost, Jesus Christ himself comes again to his disciples, and continues in Acts what Jesus began to do and teach in Luke. So closely linked are the Christ and the Spirit that the narrative even refers to the Holy Spirit as the Spirit of Jesus (Acts 16:7). The missions of the second and third Persons of the Trinity completely interpenetrate one another. Jesus Christ and the Holy Spirit mutually mediate one another through their respective activities and this is at the very heart of the Gospel. It is the way in which humanity is restored to union and communion with the Triune God. See Colyer, *How To Read T. F. Torrance*, pp. 221-33. Thus, I agree with Thomas F. Torrance's contention that it is better to speak of the perichoretic coactivity of the Trinity in which the trinitarian Persons mutually indwell, coinhere and inexist not simply in their *being* but also *in all of their activity*. In this way the distinctive incommunicable properties of the Persons and their activities unite them in a dynamic oneness of activity without in any way detracting from their differences. This, I believe, is much closer to the complex interrelations between the Persons and their activities depicted in the overall biblical narrative (as in Luke-Acts) than is the so-called *law or principle of appropriations,* which allows certain activities of the whole Trinity to be "appropriated" or assigned to one of the Persons — appropriations which lead to viewing the Christian Story as a three-act drama, with each act assigned to a particular one of the trinitarian Persons. See Colyer, *How to Read T. F. Torrance,* pp. 317-21.

Elmer M. Colyer

Why Segments of the Narrative Movement Have Not Been Fully Trinitarian

Now if narrative theology employs a more holistic and integrative hermeneutical approach to the Bible, and if the doctrine of the Trinity arises out of a holistic approach to the Christian Story, why has the narrative movement often not been more comprehensively and forthrightly trinitarian? This is a complex question with many philosophical and historical facets. Overall, the narrative movement has tended to emphasize the *textuality* or *cultural-linguistic* character of the Bible over the question of the precise relation of the Bible to history. This is a crucial corrective to the focus of eighteenth- and nineteenth-century biblical hermeneutics on confirming or disconfirming the Bible's correspondence to external historical or metaphysical referents.[10]

Nevertheless, underlying much of the narrative emphasis on the textuality or cultural-linguistic character of the Bible is a philosophical and historical background in the foundationalist/anti-foundationalist epistemological debate and/or the overall philosophical and cultural movement away from modernity toward postmodern perspectives. (Not all advocates of narrative theology are postmoderns. Fackre is an example *par excellence*.) There is a kind of neo-Kantian stricture against knowing extra-textual realities (the infamous *Ding an sich*) among some in the narrative camp. This is partly due to the long and convincing attack upon all forms of epistemological foundationism (epistemologies which attempt to render the conditions for indubitable knowledge entirely explicit). But it is also rooted in the narrative movement's astute observation that the Bible is "history-like," rather than simple history, and that the biblical narrative is able to depict a followable world of faith with its imperialist claim to be the "real world," even if the events recorded in Scripture did not actually unfold as depicted. (Maybe some did not happen at all — for example, even if Jesus Christ did not actually walk on the water, the narra-

---

10. The emphasis on the Bible's textuality is one of the reasons why many evangelicals have been attracted to the narrative movement; it provides evangelicals with a way to hold on to their long-standing emphasis on the textuality of the Bible while shedding some of the narrow and rigid characteristics of the *propositional* perspective on the character of the biblical witness. Revelation cannot be resolved into propositions, for this abstracts revelation from the being and activity of the trinitarian God and reduces revelation to the communication of information, rather than the complex polyvalent *Self*-communication of God that revelation is, a Self-communication that is always revelatory and redemptive (two sides of a single reality).

tive in Matthew 14:22-36 accurately depicts Christ's identity as Lord of space and time.) We do not have to establish exactly what "happened" in *Historie* in order for the narrative depiction of *Geschichte* to be intelligible and credible. The narrative movement is right on this point.

Yet this disengaging of the biblical narrative and history, when carried to an extreme because of these kinds of philosophical convictions, unnecessarily confuses and obscures the Bible's extra-textual reference to the history of the Jesus story or metaphysical reference to God. An example of this is George Lindbeck, who rightly emphasizes intrasystemic truth, the power of narrative, and the proformative use of language in the Bible and the church, which shape members of the Christian community in specific ways for living as disciples within the followable (and "real") world of the Bible.[11] Lindbeck is surely correct that this kind of use of the Bible is a necessary condition (the total relevant context which includes a form of life) for ontological truth claims. But Lindbeck never fully clarifies how ontological truth comes about.[12] In addition, his "rule-theory" concerning the nature of doctrine, in which doctrines are second-order rules governing first-order discourse, raises all kinds of questions and problems for extra-cultural/linguistic reference of the Bible.

This problem of extra-textual reference is particularly distressing in relation to the subject of this essay, the doctrine of the Trinity, for Lindbeck argues that this doctrine is "not a first-order proposition with ontological reference, but . . . a second-order rule of speech."[13] Now

---

11. See George Lindbeck, *The Nature of Doctrine: Religion and Theology in a Postliberal Age* (Philadelphia: Westminster Press, 1984).

12. See Bruce Marshall's astute analysis of Lindbeck's position on truth in "Aquinas as Postliberal Theologian," in *The Thomist* (July 1989): 353-57. Also see Lindbeck's response in ibid., pp. 403-6, in which he never fully answers Marshall's most pressing questions.

13. Lindbeck, *Nature of Doctrine,* p. 94. Lindbeck maintains that Athanasius' famous dictum, "whatever is said of the Father is said of the Son, except that the Son is not the Father," is a historical precedent of his rule-theory of doctrine. Thus he triumphantly asserts, "Thus the theologian most responsible for the final triumph of Nicaea thought of it, not as a first-order proposition with ontological reference, but as a second-order rule of speech." However, Lindbeck draws this quote from Bernard Lonergan's book, *Method in Theology* (New York: Herder and Herder, 1972), seemingly without checking the context of Athanasius' dictum, a context that Lonergan does not note. Athanasius' whole statement reads as follows: "And so, since they are one, and the Godhead itself one, the same things are said of the Son, which are said of the Father, except his being said to be the Father." See Athanasius, *Contra Arianos,* III:4. This translation comes from Thomas F. Torrance, *Theology in Reconciliation* (Grand Rapids: Wm. B. Eerdmans Publishing Co., 1975), p. 225. When read in context, Athanasius' famous dictum un-

Lindbeck unequivocally affirms the ontological Trinity, but do not his philosophical commitments undermine his own affirmation and also the significance and place of the Trinity in the fabric of the biblical narrative, in the Christian Story, and in theology?

Ronald Thiemann, with his antifoundationalist sensibility, carries these kinds of philosophical convictions to an even further extreme and wants to dispense with the category of revelation completely.[14] In its place, Thiemann views the Bible (the New Testament Gospels, for example) as providing a "narrated promise" that Jesus Christ is risen and is Savior and Lord. It is a promise embraced only in hope, awaiting an "eschatological justification," rather than a firm and certain knowledge. Why an individual comes to believe and embrace this promise as worthy of risking one's life is rooted in a "person-specific act" of faith "with reasons and causes related to that person's individual history" (Feuerbach would have fun with this!), and the explanation of these reasons and causes "lies beyond theology's descriptive competence."[15]

Yet is the biblical narrative simply of human cultural-linguistic construction (no revelation involved)? Or does it not ultimately arise out of God's *oikonomia*, God's patterned interaction with our world?[16] Thiemann's new narrative form of the Kantian destruction of knowledge to make room for faith is extremely problematic and symptomatic of those thinkers beguiled by the antinomies latent in the limited categories (like

---

derscores the ontological grounding and priority of his dictum, rendering it not simply a second-order rule governing first-order discourse, but a dictum with ontological reference specifying something about the interrelational character of the Trinity.

14. Ronald Thiemann, *Revelation and Theology: The Gospel as Narrated Promise* (Notre Dame, IN: University of Notre Dame Press, 1985). I believe that Thiemann also wants to affirm the Trinity, but the question is whether his position and philosophical commitments undermine this intent.

15. Thiemann, *Revelation and Theology*, pp. 94 and 147-48.

16. The Greek patristic concept, *oikonomia*, refers to the distinctive trinitarian pattern of God's revelatory/saving activity in Israel and in Jesus Christ and the NT Church, a pattern imprinted on the events proclaimed in the biblical narrative, out of which the Bible arose. The Bible is not purely of human construction, even though there is no apprehension of God's activity without a human cultural-linguistic framework. This is part of the reason why revelation and its apprehension, assimilation, and articulation by human beings are progressive, and include election (God has to begin somewhere) and a distinctive narrative quality (the progressive character involves a pattern). Since there is no inherent isomorphism between the human mind/language and extra-mental entities, a real apprehension of God involves the progressive generation of the appropriate cultural-linguistic structures (language and a form of life) and entails divine *and* human agency.

that age-old dichotomy between necessity and chance, which is the source of a lot of mischief in the history of theology) of the foundationalist/antifoundationalist debate.[17] It is difficult to see how a robust doctrine of the Trinity or trinitarian theology could ever grow out of this kind of epistemological/hermeneutical soil.

Toward a Narrative Interpretation of the Trinity

There is no reason why the narrative movement must embrace these kinds of philosophical commitments, and a narrative theology freed from them could and would develop quite naturally in a more robust trinitarian direction. I view Gabe Fackre's form of narrative theology as just such an attempt to forge this kind of alternative. Fackre rightly sees narrative as related first and foremost to the theological content, rather than simply literary form, of the Bible. He thoroughly baptizes the literary concept of narrative and identifies it with "the pattern of God's decisive actions among us."[18]

Thus, Fackre refuses to jettison the concept of revelation and the interactionist God-world relation it implies. Fackre's God is Alive and Personal and is a *real* Agent in human affairs. Unlike many narrative thinkers, Fackre rejects the postmodern suspicion (often Kantian dualism in the name of epistemic caution) of meta-narratives and ontology. He rightly sees the value of postmodern epistemic humility, while noting the impossibility of avoiding meta-narratives and ontology.[19] For Fackre, narrative is not a species of a philosophical genus, but is ultimately rooted in the fact that "The being and doing of God are knowable — under the conditions of finitude and sin . . . in particular turns in the revelatory story."[20]

17. See Colyer, *How to Read T. F. Torrance*, pp. 323-60, esp. 342-44. It may be no coincidence that Thiemann and Lindbeck are both Lutheran. Kant, too, was of Lutheran background, with Lutheran Pietist parents who enrolled him in the *Collegium Fridericianum* (a Pietist school) for eight years (1732-40). Behind it all is Luther's *Deus Absconditus* and darkness of faith.

18. See Gabriel Fackre, *The Doctrine of Revelation: A Narrative Interpretation* (Grand Rapids: Wm. B. Eerdmans Pub. Co., 1997), p. 5. As far as I can tell, Fackre here intends something very close to the Greek patristic concept of *oikonomia*, which is neither simple history, nor purely a literary form, but rather the intelligible pattern of God's interaction with humanity in Israel and in Jesus Christ within the world of space and time.

19. Even the term "postmodernity" entails a judgment that history has entered a new stage and that postmodernity represents a "Big Picture" or "totalizing schema," despite various demurrers. See Fackre, *Doctrine of Revelation*, pp. 2-7 & 20-21.

20. Christian faith can make a "plausible" case for its knowledge of God, even if

This helps account for his greater emphasis on the place of the doctrine of the Trinity in Christian faith and theology.

When Fackre indwells the biblical narrative and discerns the Christian Story, he perceives a particular pattern in the course of events, an "unfolding drama of divine deeds" within "the many and varied instantiations of the literary form in which they are described" within the Bible.[21] The identity of the Christian God emerges out of the particular pattern of divine activity in the Christian Story that we come to know in and through the biblical text.[22]

So far Fackre has not fully developed his narrative construal of the doctrine of the Trinity, which I judge to be exceedingly rich with promise. What narrative theology needs is the kind of carefully developed doctrine of the Trinity toward which Fackre seems to be moving. He reads the Christian Story through the overall biblical narrative with the kind of holistic hermeneutic required to discern and develop a doctrine of the Trinity and a fully trinitarian narrative theology. I look forward to Fackre's full treatment of that doctrine in a later volume of his magnum opus, *The Christian Story*.[23]

---

this is not some new form of foundationalism, which renders the conditions for this knowledge entirely explicit. Fackre, *Doctrine of Revelation*, p. 9. Fackre rejects both epistemological dualism (with its subject/object bifurcation) and cosmological dualism (which prohibits any kind of divine Agency in human affairs within the world of space and time).

21. Fackre, *Doctrine of Revelation*, p. 5.

22. Fackre's point here is absolutely crucial pastorally, as well as theologically. His careful linking of divine *ousia* (being) and *parousia* (revelatory/salvific activity) underscores the fact that God is not ultimately different in God's own being, God's intra-trinitarian life, than God is in God's revealing and reconciling activity through Jesus Christ in the Holy Spirit. There is no dark and inscrutable deity *(deus absconditus)* whom we cannot but fear behind the God that we know, face to face in Jesus Christ in the Christian Story, as rendered by the overall biblical narrative. It is also important to note that the doctrine of the Trinity, arising out of the trinitarian deep structure of the Christian Story in the overall biblical narrative, provides a more properly basic understanding of God than does a description of the attributes of God developed abstractly or by merely amassing various isolated biblical references to particular attributes without reference to the Persons and the narrative approach to their identities. The attributes of God must always be defined in terms of the trinitarian Persons and their activities, which are what they are in their perichoretic intercommunion and coactivity.

23. For another alternative account of this kind of holistic approach to theology and the doctrine of the Trinity, see Thomas F. Torrance, *The Christian Doctrine of God: One Being Three Persons* (Edinburgh: T & T Clark, 1996), especially chapters 2-4. Also see Colyer, *How To Read T. F. Torrance*, pp. 285-321.

An Evangelical-Ecumenical Dialogue

Carl F. H. Henry

When Gabriel Fackre's retirement was marked by Andover Newton Theological School in April 1996, his colleagues identified his major theological interests as the United Church of Christ (in which he worked for renewal), theological education, ecumenism, and the church and the world. Especially noted was his involvement in the Lutheran-Reformed dialogue and ongoing conversation with evangelical Christians, as much in person as in print.

The evangelical dialogue might have been mentioned last, but it was not the least among his interests. In later years, "Gabe" counted among the things worth caring about on the theological frontier the evangelical-ecumenical conversation, which he sought not only to encourage but also to advance. His special lectures provided opportunity to probe for ecumenical-evangelical points of contact and of shared theological interests.

In the book, *Restoring the Center*,[1] Fackre gathers essays that may hopefully contribute to evangelical-ecumenical alliance embracing both elements, with its reaffirmation of the centrality of Christ, and bearing bold witness "to Christ the Center in these decentered times." Fackre's autobiographical notes in this book are anything but bland, being laced with involvement in many formative movements over four decades. It is debatable whether Fackre is best characterized as an evangelical theologian with ecumenical sympathies, or an ecumenical theologian with deepening evangelical commitments.

Terms like "perspective" and "faith" — and no less so "ecumenical"

---

1. Gabriel Fackre, *Restoring the Center* (Downers Grove, IL: InterVarsity Press, 1998).

39

and "evangelical" — can provide a linguistic center whereby these conceptualities reflect tensions in contemporary theology, and serve also as an effort to rise above overlooked alternatives and, if possible, also probe differences that explore a deeper investigation of neglected options. Not by mere happenstance does Fackre, at the climax of a long and fruitful life in pursuit of theological synthesis, find in these terms the title of his 1993 survey and overview of his contemplations on the shifting dogmatic scene in America, *Ecumenical Faith in Evangelical Perspective.*[2] More than any other contender, Fackre aims to hold fast to an ecumenical inheritance of conciliar Christianity. At the same time, he plumbs statements of evangelical theology that a full-orbed doctrinal view must retain if it is not to lose cerebral power and spiritual dynamic, readily surrendered by contemporary religious options that value rational consistency less than the pursuit of feeling.

In *Restoring the Center,* Fackre comments on the recent growing favor among some evangelicals for a pliable view of God, one embracing notions of divine mutability. At the end of the first Christian century, an "open" view of God emerged among mediating evangelicals, mainly in respect to discussion of the eternal punishment of the lost. In our time, the controversy has widened, penetrating some evangelical colleges and seminaries, religious publishing houses, theological societies, and radio and television programs. Fackre offers an overview of the controversy involving "an evangelical mega-shift." His survey is comprehensive enough to approach a brief history of recent theology. Fackre seeks to preserve elements from so-called mainline theology and at the same time honor aspects of evangelical piety, thus combining evangelical devoutness, social engagement, and political concern. Although the correlation is at times more verbal than intellectual, it reflects Fackre's desire to maintain continuity with the biblical heritage.

Story and Evangelical Theology

It is no surprise that the Christian message might in part be cast in the form of narrative or story. Christian hymnody preserves and advances this understanding through familiar hymns such as "I Love to Tell the Story." Concentration on pietism leaves to others a ruling on its social dimen-

---

2. Gabriel Fackre, *Ecumenical Faith in Evangelical Perspective* (Grand Rapids: Eerdmans, 1993).

sions. Yet narrative theology can also concentrate on political, social, and economic agendas.

In *Ecumenical Faith in Evangelical Perspective*, Fackre engages the Yale version of interpreting the Story in which "the biblical narrative creates a world of its own, one not knowable by or translatable into the culture's regnant assumptions, with the identity of its chief character, the God incarnate in Jesus Christ, rendered only as the story unfolds."[3] He understands that substitution of the "history-like" for history faces the reader with the question of which distinctions preserve and which surrender the biblical essentials. The evangelical entry point is experience embedded in the church and in the classical creeds — even in claims to truth.[4] Fackre has no doubt that "the Christian Story" is a news story, and at the same time is inspired canonical writing. If anything, that conviction was presented in ever-deepening force through his years as professor of theology at Andover Newton Theological School and in the seventeen books that have followed, including a multi-volume systematics, *The Christian Story*,[5] in which he emerges as "evangelical-ecumenical." The blending may not be as easy a task as, at times, implied. One may assume hurriedly that rational consistency accommodates such coordination, yet their coordination may be traced to unwitting retentions from canonical literature, or ready accommodation to congenial elements of the tradition.

Fackre commends himself to evangelical believers when he insists on the verbal witness of Scripture. He disputes a high regard for the sociology of knowledge, one that relativizes the finality of the Bible in a way that subjectivizes ultimate truth, while he correlates Scripture with the text as "story." The Scripture "story" is indispensable for a proper understanding of the text. The identification of Scripture as story, however, has its problems. It leaves open the function of a transcendental revelation, and leaves indeterminate also the perspectival nature of the story. Is my rendition of biblical narrative so distinctive that other narrative accounts may not be logically derived from it? Does exegesis of the sacred story lay claim to universal truth? Does it preserve the propositional nature of the story and, if so, what claim can be made to the normative role of the scriptural account?

3. Fackre, *Ecumenical Faith*, p. 141.

4. Fackre, *Ecumenical Faith*, p. 209.

5. Gabriel Fackre, *The Christian Story*, vols. 1 and 2 (Grand Rapids: Eerdmans, 1978, 1987).

Carl F. H. Henry

Revelation and Scripture

Fackre senses what many contemporary theologians ignore: that to discuss genuinely Christian theology, one cannot ignore a vital view of revelation and inspiration, and that neither a flimsy view of revelation, nor a view of revelation that lacks conceptual significance can long be powerful. He understands evangelical Christianity to be inscribed or Bible-based, not beholden to secular society and human-centered principles, but committed to an orderly biblical faith, grounded in biblical inerrancy, with a doctrinal stress on divine sovereignty juxtaposed with human depravity and devoted to an aggressive evangelism.

Fackre emphasizes that sin has met its match in Jesus Christ. All claims to ultimate truth must bow before Him. Hence one speaks of contributions by both liberal theology and evangelical theology, and that of C. S. Lewis (regard for whom among evangelicals has reached almost icon status). On the one hand, he cautions evangelicals to guard against disregard of divine sovereignty. On the other, Fackre has a keen eye for a radical perspectival emphasis that introduces its own agenda into the conversation as a serious contender — in which case it disavows a claim to universal truth and allows contexts to control text. What God says in and through Scripture is decisive.

Fackre's comments are, at times, both incisive and penetrating. He emphasizes that the Spirit works internally: the Bible's "authority is grounded in the Holy Spirit's special message to the prophetic-apostolic witnesses." He emphasizes "the epistemological privilege of the Word incarnate, inspired or illumined,"[6] but does not stop there.

Fackre, as a self-defined "evangelical-ecumenical," seeks from this convergence to probe mutual and overlapping interests. He contends that evangelical hermeneutics is "fiercely" pluralistic and that evangelicals should be invited into an ecumenical conversation that is currently restrictive.

Although Fackre seeks to maintain a bridge that arches away from the modernism of the twentieth century to evangelical emphases, he has no sympathy for a so-called "fundamentalist epistemology" that involves a case for inerrant Scripture. He sees inerrancy as standing at the center of the evangelical battle for the Bible, venturing to explore evangelical hermeneutics under the themes of oracularity, catholicity, inerrancy, and infallibility. Avowed fundamentalists affirm oracularity (dictation). By con-

6. Fackre, *Ecumenical Faith*, p. 216.

42

trast, "inerrantists" allow for the Holy Spirit's initiative in inspiration. Fackre cites three views of inerrancy: conservative, moderate, and liberal.

So unrelenting is Fackre's disdain for scriptural inerrancy, that he runs the gamut from ultra-inerrancy, transmissive inerrancy, trajectory inerrancy, intentional inerrancy, to infallibility (unitive, essentialist, and christocentric). He opposes these in the name of modern positions on the authority of Scripture, as if authority can be promoted by a neglect of inerrancy. Inspiration is the functional presupposition of an evangelical view, and Fackre formulates it in a variety of ways.

A new ecumenism, as he sees it, will escape the multiplicity of modernism. But it is, in fact, precisely the failure to follow through with a consistent epistemology that bulwarks ready assertion of an evangelical world-and-life view. To emphasize, as Fackre does, the divine inspiration of Scripture, while at the same time disparaging the emphasis on its inerrancy or infallibility, creates its own set of problems.

Moral Mandates in the Political Arena

Theology is ideally not done in a vacuum; it is engaged with living ideas and ideals. Participants in its dialogue may seem at times like invaders from the outside. Gabriel Fackre's concern with it embraces debates over theism and/or morality. Two small works concern the effort of almost two hundred college and seminary teachers to call President Clinton to account on ethical and theological matters.

Besides *The Day After,* Fackre produced *Judgment Day at the White House* with eleven co-signers and some essays by critics as well.[7] He challenges in these works a religious forgiveness that relieves one of further obligation. Further, the violation of moral standards is not compensated for by faithful adherence to a political agenda. With the skill of a veteran reporter, Fackre gives a blow-by-blow account of the raging controversy in consequence of the Clinton misbehavior in the political arena and of moral judgment and misjudgment by clergy. He repudiates the notion that national leaders are entitled to live by lower moral standards.

Fackre warns not only of political misuse of religion and of religious symbols. He fears that the religious community is in danger, and that it is

---

7. Gabriel Fackre, ed., *Judgment Day at the White House* (Grand Rapids: Eerdmans, 1999); *The Day After: A Retrospective on Religious Dissent in the Presidential Crisis* (Grand Rapids: Eerdmans, 2000).

being called upon for religious accreditation of political activities. He challenges the notion that forgiveness cancels further obligation, so that all wrongs are believed to be relieved by the errant. He deplores the disregard of the impact of one's example on the student world and on children generally.

The debate over the Clinton episode is carried on by professing Christians in terms of Christian principles. For all that, it affirms linkage between Christian and non-Christian participants in respect to ethical and political matters. Those involved wrestle with almost unending concerns: religious manipulation for political ends, overlapping personal and public morality, the propriety of a national prayer breakfast, the respective roles of mainline Protestants and the so-called religious right, and so on. This religion-and-morality debate in American life has fewer instructive participants elsewhere than those engaged in dialogue and disputation mirrored by these issues. We are grateful to Gabriel Fackre for his leadership in these matters.

The Visible Victim:
Christ's Death to End Sacrifice

S. Mark Heim

Gabriel Fackre's theology has always been what he calls "pastoral system-atics": reflection in the service of the church's life and the preacher's task. Those of us fortunate enough to have been his students learned early that the narrative truth of the gospel is an essential dimension of Christian faith.

That insight directs us with special urgency to questions that dog preachers and parishioners today as they pursue their annual Lenten jour-neys, and face a central paradox of the Christian story. Jesus' death saves the world, and it ought not to happen. It fulfills prophecy, but it is the work of sinners. It is a good bad thing. The attempt to give the crucifixion a *general* moral (die to self, be faithful to the end) runs the risk of simply baptizing all bad things, as if with the right approach they, too, can be good things. Given the many criticisms raised against atonement theol-ogy, is there good reason that Scripture puts this specific event at the heart of the redemptive plot?

Let's think about the problem the other way around. What would Christianity need to be to avoid charges of exalting suffering and abuse? What if, in place of the passion narratives of the Gospels, Christians had instead the following text:

> Christ — the living wisdom of God — came down to earth. He visited a
> great city in the form of a stranger, a swarthy carpenter with a with-

This article is adapted with permission from the *Christian Century*, where it first ap-peared.

ered leg, in order to call back those who had fallen into ignorance. He taught many things to those who had the inner ears to hear. But those who saw only his outward form, did not understand the grace he brought. He did many miracles and the people worshipped him for this reason and made him their king. But still their ignorance was not dispelled, and each house in the city was set against another, and great fires burned there day and night. So Christ prepared his final miracle. One day he called to him Mary, his mother and his dearest disciple. He went into the temple and ate the bread in the holy of holies, which no person is to touch. They lay together there near the altar throughout the night. While they lay there the earth shook, and many in the city were stricken with a deadly disease and the people were afraid. He sent Mary away, telling her she must return without fail at the first hour and that whatever she found at that time must be cast outside the gates. In the morning, when the people came to the temple, seeking to know what evil had been done to bring these troubles upon them, they found nothing but the smallest mustard seed lying near the altar. He had taken the form of a mustard seed, carrying the entirety of divinity within him. All the people were greatly distressed at this. Priests and soldiers, foreigners and natives, members of every tribe, all were seized with awe in a kind of trance. Heeding Mary, with one spirit they rushed together to form a procession and carried the seed to a stony hill where they threw it in a great hole that opened there. And each person, without exception, threw in stones to cover it. Miraculously, the seed immediately grew up into a great tree, and Christ himself was in the fruit of that tree, and everyone who ate of this fruit discovered God within themselves and the joy of eternal life. The people returned to the city rejoicing, and health and peace ruled in those walls.

This is a rich, symbolic story, full of allegorical possibilities. There is no offensive violence, no punishment or glorified suffering. It would not pose embarrassing charges of victimization in our Scriptures. We would have the added bonus that the spiritual value of this story is plainly not encumbered with worries about what actually happened. Its spiritual value is no less if we regard it as entirely imaginary rather than historical.

Suppose we added just one additional clarification, namely that this text in fact refers to the event of Jesus' execution, which actually took place as it is described in the Gospels? The drawback to the text, in other words, is that it is a lie about a lynching. If we would be happy to substitute this text for the Gospels, knowing that Jesus' death is perhaps the one thing about which we are historically most certain, it says something interesting about us. We would like to avert our eyes from victims.

René Girard has attracted a great deal of attention by arguing that this is not just a thought experiment but a key to understanding one dimension of Christ's saving work.[1] The cross can be understood only in light of another — indeed the prototypical — "good bad thing" in human culture: scapegoating sacrifice. He maintains that central human myths are in fact transcriptions of a consistent kind of violence, which he calls the "founding murder." Such murder literally stands at the beginning and in the middle of human society. It makes human community possible.

In brief, the story is this. Particularly in its infancy, social life is a fragile shoot, fatally subject to plagues of rivalry and vengeance. Escalating cycles of retaliation are the original social disease. Without finding a way to treat it, human society can hardly begin. The means to break this vicious cycle appear as if miraculously. At some point when feud threatens to dissolve a community, spontaneous and irrational mob violence erupts against some distinctive person or minority in the group. They are accused of the worst crimes the group can imagine, crimes that by their very enormity might have caused the terrible plight the community now experiences. They are lynched.

The sad good in this bad thing is that it actually works. In the train of the murder, communities find that this sudden war of all against one has delivered them from the war of each against all. The sacrifice of one person as a scapegoat discharges the pending acts of retribution. It "clears the air." This benefit seems a startling, even magical result from a simple execution. The sudden peace confirms the desperate charges that the victim had been behind the crisis to begin with. If the scapegoat's death is the solution, the scapegoat must have been the cause. The death has such reconciling effect, that it seems the victim must possess supernatural power. So the victim becomes a god, memorialized in myth.

Rituals of sacrifice originated in this way, tools to fend off social crisis. And in varied forms they are with us still. The prescription is that divisions in the community must be reduced to but one division, the division of all against one common victim or one minority group. Prime candidates are the marginal and the weak, or those isolated by their very prominence. Typically, they will be charged with violating the community's most extreme taboos. The process does not just accept innocent victims, it

1. See René Girard, *I See Satan Falling like Lightning* (Maryknoll: Orbis, 2001); and James G. Williams, ed., *The Girard Reader* (New York: Crossroad, 1996).

prefers them — "outsiders" not closely linked to established groups in the society. This, in a nutshell, is Girard's account of the origin of religion. It is identical with the beginning of culture itself, for without some such mechanism to head off "tit for tat" violence human society could not get off the ground. It is the founding good bad thing, reconciliation in the blood of the innocent.

No one thought out this process, and its effectiveness depends on a certain blindness to its workings. Myth reflects the scapegoat event, but does not describe it. It is the product of a collective killing that all the actors found completely justified, entirely necessary, and powerfully beneficent. It is the memory of a clean conscience that never registered the presence of a victim at all. The unbroken continuity of consciousness between producers and consumers of the myth from generation to generation is precisely the invisibility of the victim as a victim.

So our text is an example of what Jesus' death would look like if it were a true myth in Girard's sense. If we suspect there is an execution behind this story, we can see many tell-tale signs: typical marks of the victim (a physical deformity, a foreigner), indications of social conflict ("fire" sweeping the city), traces of the accusations (incest, profaning holy things), the unanimity of the mob violence (stoning and burying the "seed"), the positive benefits of the death. We can easily see how a ritual would evolve from this story — perhaps the annual offering of a sacrificial victim at the foot of the sacred tree. Above all, of course, what is "mythical" is that the killing has disappeared completely, and no issues of persecution, guilt, or violence are present in the text at all.

Scapegoating is one of the deepest structures of human sin, built into our religion and our politics. It is demonic because it is endlessly flexible in its choice of victims and because it can truly deliver the good that it advertises. Satan *can* cast out Satan, and is the more powerful for it. It is most virulent where it is most invisible. Victims are *called* criminals, gods, or both. So long as we are in the grip of sin, we do not see our victims as scapegoats. Texts that hide scapegoating foster it. Texts that show it for what it is undermine it.

Jesus' willingness to face death, specifically death on a cross, suddenly looks anything but arbitrary, and much more like the "wisdom of God" that the New Testament so surprisingly discovers there. God is willing to die for us, to bear our sin in this particular way because we desperately need deliverance from this particular sin. God breaks the grip of scapegoating by stepping into the place of a victim who cannot be hidden or mythologized. God acts not to affirm the suffering of the innocent victim as the price of peace, but to reverse it. God is not just feeding a bigger and better victim into this machinery to get a bigger payoff. Jesus' open proclamation of forgiveness (without sacrifice) before his death and the fact of his resurrection after it, reveal and reject the victimage mechanism.

C. S. Lewis, who knew the mythical heritage of the world better than most, saw this clearly. In his Christian allegory, *The Chronicles of Narnia,* the Christ-lion Aslan accepts being killed in order that the evil powers release those they hold hostage. This exchange is proposed in the story by the evil powers as a sacrificial process known to all from the earliest times — a law that an innocent one may die on behalf of others and so free them. It is called "Deep Magic from the Dawn of Time." The evil powers love this arrangement and, incidentally, have no intention of keeping their side of the bargain after Aslan is dead. The resurrection comes into this story as an unexpected development, from what Aslan calls "Deeper Magic from before the Dawn of Time," something about which the evil powers knew nothing. And when Aslan rises, the ancient stone altar on which the sacrifice was offered cracks and crumbles in pieces, never to be used again. The gospel is not ultimately about exchange of victims, but about ending the bloodshed.

Some deplore the Bible's brutal representations of violence, its fixation on persecution and murder, and complain that biblical tradition lacks the beauty and imaginative sophistication of great myth. The story of Jesus' death is a cut-rate version of the sacrifice of the corn king, flattened into something that belongs on a police blotter and not in high spiritual culture. To Girard, this puts things just backwards. Major myths are rooted in sacrificial violence, prescribe it and shield us from awareness of our complicity in it. That is why they do not show it directly. The Bible makes violence visible, and therefore makes its victims uncomfortably visible too. The sensitivity to victims now so often turned against the Bible is itself rooted there. We would not accuse the Gospels of encouraging victimization if we had not already been converted by them. We would not look for scapegoated victims in every corner if the magnifying glass of the cross had not become second nature for us.

The workings of mythical sacrifice require that in human society generally "they know not what they do." But in the Gospels, the process is laid out in stark clarity. Jesus says these very words from the cross. Girard recounts the shock of recognition he experienced in coming to the New Testament after his work on violence and the sacred in anthropology and the history of religion. He found there all the classic elements his sacrificial theory had come to expect in myths: the crowd coalescing against an individual, the charges of the greatest crimes and impurities. But he was startled to recognize that the reality of what was happening was explicit, not hidden. It was the same mythic story. The difference was this time it was told from the point of view of the victim, who is unmistakably visible as unjustly accused and wrongly killed. The scapegoating process is stripped of its sacred mystery and the collective persecution and abandonment are painfully illustrated, so that no one, including the disciples, the proto-Christians, can honestly say afterwards that they resisted the sacrificial tide.

The resurrection makes Jesus' death a failed sacrifice, but of a new kind. When mythical sacrifice succeeds, peace descends, true memory is erased, and the way is smoothed for the next scapegoat. If it fails (because the community is not unanimous or the victim is not sufficiently demonized), it becomes just another killing, simply stoking the proliferation of violence, and the search intensifies for more and better victims. But in this case, neither does everyone unanimously close ranks over Jesus' grave (as Jesus' executioners hope) nor is there a spree of violent revenge on behalf of the crucified leader. Instead, an odd new counter-community arises, dedicated both to the innocent victim, whom God has vindicated by resurrection, and to a new life through him that requires no further such sacrifice.

The revelatory quality of the New Testament is thoroughly continuous with Hebrew Scripture, where an awareness and rejection of the sacrificial mechanism are already set forth. The averted sacrifice of Isaac; the prophets' condemnation of scapegoating the widow, the weak, or the foreigner; the story of Job; the Psalms' obsession with the innocent victim of collective violence; the passion narratives' transparent account of Jesus' death; the confessions of a new community that grew up in solidarity around the risen crucified victim: all these follow a constant thread. They reveal the "victimage" mechanisms at the joint root of religion and society and reject them. Jesus is the victim who will not stay sacrificed, whose memory is not erased and who forces us to confront this reality.

This is why anti-Semitism is the infallible test for a healthy atonement theory. One of the crucial things that makes the church a new community is its constitution in solidarity not *against* some sacrificial victim, but by identification with the crucified one. Christians have always been as liable as any others to scapegoating, but the gospel did force them to invent a new kind of sin. Because the dynamic of Jesus' passion made it impossible to be unconscious of scapegoats or to mystify them in myths, Christian persecutors put them in plain sight. Jews were scapegoated with the claim that they were the ones who had scapegoated Jesus. The new sin was to victimize people by accusing them of being victimizers, to make the revelation against sacrifice a new rationale for sacrifice. The moment we point a finger at some "they" as Jesus' killers, we have enacted the sin that the very particularity of the cross meant to overcome. Christians bear a special culpability for this prompt perversion, with less right to claim that we knew not what we did: Our sacrificial violence toward Jews proclaimed the very sin it practiced.

We began by noting the tension seeded through the passion story: the cross saves and it ought not to happen. The tension is there not because the Gospel writers can't get their story straight, but because this tension is the heart of the story itself. The language of sacrifice and blood (with all its dangers) is there to tell the truth. To purge these terms reflects a naïve confidence that we are in greater danger of being corrupted by the language, than of falling prey to the sin it describes. The good/bad tension is there first because of the frank description of sacrificial, scapegoating violence from the foundation of the world. That violence does save us from more violence. And its victims ought not to be sacrificed. God's decision to walk this path makes that fully plain as never before.

Therefore, it is important that Christ's cross is exactly like countless others. Becoming subject to this sin, God takes this tension to a different level. The peace that depends on sacrifice (the "reconciliation" Herod and Pilate aim for in Christ's death), now also registers as something that ought not to happen. The good part of the old good bad thing, sacrifice, now is seen as part of what is bad in the crucifixion. What is needed is a completely new basis for peace. It is hardly accidental that "Peace" is usually the first word of the risen Christ in his appearances. It is an apt greeting in two ways. If a sacrificial victim were to return with power to those who had persecuted or abandoned him, peace is the opposite of what they would expect. And peace not based on new victims, "not as the world gives," is what is now offered. So in the gospel tension it is the entire sacrificial violence complex that becomes the bad thing, and it is God's willingness to suffer its worst in order to deliver us from it that is the good thing.

He is wounded for our transgressions. We can hardly deny that Jesus bears our sin of scapegoating, precisely because of its collective and ubiquitous character. Christ died for us. He did so first in the mythic, sacrificial sense that all scapegoated victims do. That we know this is already a sign that he died for us in a second sense, to save us from that very sin. Jesus dies in our place, because it is literally true that any one of us, in the right circumstances, can be the scapegoat. Is Christ's death unique? It is unique because it is the one of these deaths that have been happening since the foundation of the world, which irreversibly shows us the sin in which we are everywhere enmeshed and offers us a different way.

It is true that there is a transaction of sorts at the cross. God accepts to be "handed over" to our sacrificial process, to bear our original sin and to pay the price that no human can pay. Any human being can be plausibly scapegoated (we are all sinners) and no human can prevail when the collective community turns against her. Nor is it sufficient simply to instruct us about our situation, for we are all too fully enclosed in the scapegoating process to be able to break the spell. It is an extraordinary step even to arrive at the awareness of our own susceptibility expressed by the disciples at the Last Supper, when they piteously ask Jesus, "Is it I, Lord?" Only one whose innocence truly can be vindicated and whose power could have offered escape can, by suffering this sacrifice, reverse it. Here the emphasis on a high Christology is essential. The work of the cross is the work of a transcendent God breaking into a cycle we could not change alone. If we limit Jesus' work to that of a human exemplar, the crucifixion becomes more of a prescription for suffering than if we grasp it as the work of the incarnate one, once for all. It is a saving act of God, a victory over the powers of this world, a defeat of death.

When Christians gather at communion, we hear this story clearly in the unequivocal reminder of Christ's bloody death. When we hear "Do *this* in remembrance of me . . . ," we should hear the implied contrast that comes with emphasis on *this*. Unlike the mythic victims who became sacred models for future sacrifices, Christ is not to be remembered with scapegoating, by taking or being new victims. "This" is a humble meal and prayer, not a new cross. Christ has offered his very real body and blood, so that at the Last Supper he can set a new pattern and say of bread, "this is my body," and of wine, "this is my blood." Following that example, Christians believe this meal of the new community is able to accomplish the peace that sacrificial violence could, and more. In it, we recall a real sacrifice and celebrate a substitutionary atonement. Here on this table, bread and wine are to be continually substituted for victims, substituted for any, and all, of us.

Mother of God:
How Mary Tells the Story

Kathryn Greene-McCreight

There is no rose of such virtue
As is the rose that bare Jesu:
Alleluia.

For in this rose contained was
Heaven and earth in little space:
Res Miranda.

MEDIEVAL, AUTHOR UNKNOWN

In Rome stands the first and largest church of Western Christianity dedicated to Mary, Santa Maria Maggiore. It was founded circa A.D. 350 by Pope Liberius, and financed by a wealthy Roman patrician and his wife who were childless and who had decided to leave their fortune to the Blessed Virgin. She had appeared to them in a dream, telling them to build a church in her honor. There is a legend that a miraculous snowfall outlined the plan of the church in 358, indicating where the church should be built. The legend is commemorated every year on August 5th, when white rose petals are dropped from the dome during the festal Mass. Pope Sixtus III had the church restored in the fifth century to commemorate the declaration of Mary's Divine Motherhood by the Council of Ephesus in 431, and in the nave from this renovation, we can assume, date some of the most spectacular early mosaics of Western Christian art portraying scenes from the Old Testament.

Two particularly significant relics are here at Sta. Maria Maggiore.

One is the remains of St. Jerome, fourth-century Doctor of the Church, colleague of St. Augustine, with whom he carried out a vigorous correspondence, and translator of the Bible into Latin. Jerome was one of the only church fathers of his day to know Hebrew well enough (he admitted his knowledge was second only to that of Paula, his colleague) to translate the Bible from the original Hebrew texts of the Old Testament. He lived out his later life in Bethlehem, translating in a cell near the cave where Jesus was said to have been born and which was venerated as a holy place. Also in Sta. Maria Maggiore in Rome is another Bethlehem relic: a piece from the Holy Manger from that cave near St. Jerome's cell. The crypt which houses the relic of the Manger is arranged as a reproduction of the cave in Bethlehem, so that anyone who has made pilgrimage to Bethlehem will not be left unawares upon visiting Sta. Maria Maggiore in Rome. Sta. Maria Maggiore: Holy Mary, Mother of God, Bethlehem, the birth of God-with-us, Jerome's study of the Word in the Old Testament, scenes from the Old Testament flanking the nave, the crèche kept here inviting us to have our hearts be crèches ever anew, just as Mary "kept these things, pondering them in her heart." The effect of being in this place is to be flooded with the Christian story, to use Gabe Fackre's fond term.

The mosaics of the nave of Sta. Maria Maggiore themselves tell a story, and a surprising one in a certain sense. If the mosaics are indeed from 432-440, from the pontificate of Sixtus III, this would make them the oldest surviving Christian mosaics in a church in Rome. There are some twenty-five panels remaining from the original forty-two, some having been lost, and some restored at different points in the history of the church. The remarkable thing about the mosaics from a theological point of view, when one considers them in the context of a church in honor of Mary, is that these mosaics all are scenes from the Old Testament. Why would a church dedicated to the Mother of God, the apse mosaic of which depicts Mary being crowned Queen of Heaven by Christ and her Dormition just below, why would these nave mosaics give such prominence to Old Testament stories?[1]

1. Although the apse mosaic is a thirteenth-century work, it is now generally considered to have been a copy of the antique classical mosaic originally constructed in the apse in the fifth century in the time of Sixtus III, contemporary with the nave mosaics. Walter Oakeshott, *The Mosaics of Rome: From the Third to the Fourteenth Centuries* (Greenwich: New York Graphic Society, 1967), p. 73. Therefore, one cannot simply argue that there has been a "time lag" or a theological blip on the great computer screen that planned Sta. Maria Maggiore. Neither can one use the argument that the nave mosaics may have been made for another church to account for the disjunction; this argument has been disproven (ibid., p. 73).

The key is the content of the scenes of the Old Testament. They are not just any scenes taken at random, but are understood to be among those stories that weave the greater narrative of redemption. They are typologies that point to Christ, and which ultimately tell the story of *sola gratia,* grace alone.

The mosaics take us from Abraham, notably Abraham and the priestly figure Melchizedek, whom the writer of Hebrews links with Christ (Heb. 6:20), through the sons of the promise, the giving of the law, the conquest of the land, even the apparent conquest of the very sun itself, to the conquest of the known Gentile kings of the earth. Noteworthy also is the fact that the scenes end with Joshua, whose very name means "who saves" and in the Greek Bible is the same name as Jesus. Joshua is understood to be a type of Christ throughout the history of Christian art and iconography, and, more broadly, theology. And even while we do not move beyond Joshua in the narrative of redemption, we can nevertheless call this broad plan which these mosaics of Sta. Maria Maggiore present for us a sort of family tree of Jesus, or maybe more appropriately a typological tree. And the fit between typology and history is profound: Mary grounds Jesus' humanity and history, without which this typological foreshadowing would have no fulfilling. Yet, just as grounding his humanity, she is the mother also of his divinity. Just as she is the Mother of the Son of Man, so she is the Mother of God, for Jesus is confessed to be "truly human and truly divine," indivisibly so.

Let us move from the mosaics of Sta. Maria Maggiore to the pages of the New Testament, where Mary herself comes alive. Briefly, the texts in which Mary appears are Matthew 1-2; 12:46-50; 13:55; Mark 3:31-35; 6:3; Luke 1-2; 8:19-21; 11:27-28; John 2:1-12; 6:42; 19:25-27; Acts 1:14; and Galatians 4:4. These can be grouped into five, broad thematic categories. The first category is the infancy narratives, Matthew 1-2 and Luke 1-2, where Mary appears as mother and wife. Secondly comes Jesus' relativizing of the ties of motherhood and family, as in Mark 3:31-35: "Whoever does the will of God is my brother, and sister, and mother" (cf. also Matthew 12:46-50; Luke 8:19-21; 11:27-28, the last where Jesus responds to "blessed is the womb that bore you . . ." with "blessed rather are those who hear and keep the word of God"). The third category is Mary's presence at distinct moments of revelation, such as her presence at Jesus' first sign (John 2:1-12) and at his last breath (John 19:25-27), where Mary stands by. The fourth category presents Mary as believer among the believers, praying with the disciples after the resurrection (Acts 1:14), and Mary as first disciple, as she "kept these things in her heart" (Luke 2:19; 2:51), believing even where she could not see. Fifth, Mary appears as theological datum for Paul (Gal. 4:4, "born of a woman, born under the law"), where Mary grounds Jesus' humanity and our election. Surely for our understanding of Mary in the Protestant wings of Christendom, the texts that bear Mary in the New Testament will be of greatest importance and bear greatest authority for our embrace of her. Mary thus tells the story of Jesus as his mother, as his disciple, as witness of his crucifixion, as grounding his humanity, as witness to his resurrection appearances.

What then does the church say about Mary? The Roman Catholic Church layers upon the biblical witness four official dogmas about Mary. The first is Mary as the Bearer of God, or *theotokos*. This was first formulated at the Council of Ephesus in 431. More will be said of this later, because of its importance in telling the story of Jesus' divinity and, paradoxically, his humanity as well. The second dogma is the Perpetual Virginity of Mary, accepted by the Lateran Council in 649, which declares that Mary was a virgin before, during, and after Jesus' birth. The third dogma is the Immaculate Conception, which was promulgated by Pope Pius IX in 1854. This is often misunderstood to refer to Jesus' conception, but rather refers to Mary's sinless conception. The fourth dogma, that of the Bodily Assumption, was promulgated by Pope Pius XII in 1950. It declares that Mary was taken up into heaven and that Mary's body is not under the laws of nature of decay and corruption. In addition, there is a body of "pious beliefs" that are known as the Marian Theses, which are not dogmas binding on the faithful, but beliefs which are acknowledged by the Magisterium. These are: (1) Mary as Co-Redemptorix with Christ; (2) Mary as Mediatrix; (3) Mary as the Dispensatrix of All Graces; (4) Mary as the Queen of Heaven; and (5) Mary as the Prototype of the Church.

But what does this mean for Protestants, those for whom and among whom Gabe worked so faithfully? To consider Protestantism alone today, one would think that Mary is nonexistent liturgically, devotionally, and theologically. Insisting that Mary not eclipse Christ, Protestant churches have ended up with the almost complete suppression of Mary. However, we must hold on to Mary not just as any character in the story of Jesus, but as the very Mother of God, while eschewing any devotion to Mary herself.

The twentieth-century Swiss theologian Karl Barth discusses Mary in much this sense in his section on "The Mystery of Revelation" in *Church Dogmatics*.[2] Why would this discussion of Mary come under the "Mystery

2. Karl Barth, *Church Dogmatics*, ed. G. W. Bromiley and T. F. Torrance (Edinburgh: T & T Clark, 1975), I.2, *The Doctrine of the Word of God*. The section "The Mystery of Revelation" comes under the heading "The Incarnation of the Word."

of Revelation"? Because, fundamentally, any statement about Mary is a statement about her "fruit," Jesus, to use a term from the Hail Mary. That is, for Barth, any statement about Mary must be a christological statement. To this extent, the church must, even while disavowing Mariology, hold to the confession of Mary as the "Mother of the Lord," *theotokos*. Holding Mary to be *theotokos* is "a test of the proper understanding of the incarnation of the Word."[3] Barth points out that Luther fully agrees that Mary is *theotokos*, or Mother of God, and that Reformed orthodoxy also upholds the *theotokos*. In addition to her being Mother of God, Barth understands Mary's significance within the Christian story to be in the Virgin Birth: in her specifically passive role in the conception of Jesus she is the type of the Christian soul, and the contradiction (anachronistically!) of all Mariology with its Pelagian trappings. Thus, the story of the very gospel of *sola gratia* is told by and through Mary.

While Mary is distinctly important theologically for Barth, she in and of herself is not a theological datum. She is indeed and irreducibly *theotokos*, but is not herself the object of theological statements. Such would be to engage in idolatry. Instead, every statement about Mary should be a christological statement, and this is true even of the biblical stories about Mary, even the scene between Mary and the angel Gabriel in Luke I. Like John the Baptist, Mary points ever away from herself to Jesus: Both figures, in fact, says Barth, are the "climax of the Old Testament penetrating into the New, and the first among humanity to receive Jesus. 'Behold I am the handmaid of the Lord; let it be to me according to your word' (Luke 1:38)."[4] Here Barth would approve of the nave mosaics in Sta. Maria Maggiore, with their Old Testament scenes, honoring Mary. Mary is the first to receive the miracle of revelation, and the first to take up the call to discipleship: "Behold, I am the handmaid of the Lord. . . ." Mary thus represents the disciples in her receptivity to the divine Word.

Barth, therefore, agrees with Luther insofar as he understood the greatness of Mary to consist in the fact that all interest is directed away from her to the Lord. She is the handmaid, not the demi-goddess. Barth points out that this was a common feature of early interpretation of Mary. Ambrose made it clear in his dictum: "Mary was the temple of God, not the God of the Temple."[5] The dogmatization of the *theotokos* at Ephesus (431) and confirmation by Chalcedon (451), says Barth, must be upheld. These

---

3. Barth, *Church Dogmatics*, I.2, p. 138.
4. Barth, *Church Dogmatics*, I.2, p. 139.
5. Ambrose, *De Spiritu*, III.11, 80; Barth, *Church Dogmatics*, I.2, p. 140.

councils take an expressly christological interest in Mary. The entire scene between Gabriel and Mary points away from Mary to Christ. But Barth rejects all Mariology as "an arbitrary innovation in the face of Scripture and the Early Church" and "a falsification of Christian truth."[6]

Barth basically believes that Mariology amounts to Pelagianism, which formed one of the greatest struggles which Augustine faced in the late fourth and early fifth century, and which arose again as one of the principal problems of the Protestant Reformation. This chief heresy of Roman Catholicism, according to Barth, presumes that in Mary as the head of all creatures, humanity has an openness or receptivity to God simply by dint of being human. This receptivity brings with it in Mary's case her own capacity for redemption, and she becomes "Co-Redemptorix," as one of the Marian theses claims. Barth points out that this means that Mary shares in the work of Christ, thereby engaging the human creature also as co-redeemer, which, says Barth, is a "relative rival with Christ."[7] Here then is Barth's objection to Mariology: that the statements which see Mary as doing anything other than pointing away from herself and toward Christ fall into the Pelagian mode, which sets the creature on par with Christ as co-redeemer. This inner link, which is created between Mary and Christ in the work of redemption, is then passed on to the church: "Like Mary . . . the Church also possesses a relatively independent place and function in the redemptive process. It, too, vies with Christ . . . not only is it born of Christ but, particularly in the eucharistic center of its life, Christ is also born of it. Not only does it need Christ, but in all seriousness Christ also needs it. . . . The Church in which Mary is venerated is bound to regard itself as it has done in the Vatican decree" (of papal infallibility, 1870, which, Barth notes, together with the dogma of the Immaculate Conception [1854], was promulgated under Pius IX).[8]

Having given his biting caution of Mariology,[9] Barth points out that in the clauses of the creed, "born of the Virgin Mary" and "suffered under

6. Barth, *Church Dogmatics,* I.2, p. 143.
7. Barth, *Church Dogmatics,* I.2, p. 145.
8. Barth, *Church Dogmatics,* I.2, p. 146.
9. One wonders what Barth's argument would have looked like if by this point he had known of John XXIII's statement that "the Madonna is not pleased when she is venerated above her Son." Of John XXIII we do have record of Barth having said, "It seems to me remarkable that this old Angelo Roncalli has in fact shown the papacy to be so rich. After a man like that one cannot continue to argue as insistently against this institution as one could in the past. He was a good man." Eberhard Busch, *Karl Barth: His Life from Letters and Autobiographical Texts* (Philadelphia: Fortress Press, 1976), p. 467.

Pontius Pilate," the only historical people mentioned in the creed other than Jesus himself, both serve to underscore Jesus' humanity. They both (the Virgin Birth and the empty tomb) belong together, as a "single sign," which marks off this life from its beginning to its end from all others. In the Virgin Birth, the initiative is solely with God. There is no explanation of how, or even why, but simply the "that," and all from God's side. "The Virgin Birth denotes particularly the mystery of revelation. It denotes the fact that God stands at the start where real revelation takes place — God and not the arbitrary cleverness, capability or piety of man."[10] The empty tomb itself denotes the "revelation of the mystery . . . [that God] has no need of human power and is free from all human caprice."[11] In the Virgin Birth, man is "the object of sovereign divine action. . . . God Himself and God alone is Master and Lord." The Virgin Birth is "an event in this world of ours, yet such that it is not grounded upon the continuity of events in this world nor is it to be understood in terms of it."[12] And here is where Barth shows how the Virgin Birth as biblical doctrine functions exactly the opposite of how the dogma functions in Roman Catholicism: it shows that there is no capacity in human nature to become "the human nature of Jesus Christ," that is, the place of revelation. "The virginity of Mary in the birth of the Lord is the denial, not of man in the presence of God, but of any power, attribute or capacity in him for God."[13]

This theme of the willing and achieving of the self-declaredly sovereign creature, a "point of contact" between the human creature and the divine, is of course one of Barth's greatest bêtes noires. That it should find place in the discussion of the Virgin Birth is no surprise. Barth states that the capacity of the creature for God is simply not a possibility. It is not that Jesus is conceived of the Virgin Mary because women are naturally less in need of conversion than are men (so Schleiermacher),[14] nor because Mary herself was free from sin (so the dogma of the Immaculate Conception). Rather, she was a fallen creature like all others, and her virginity does not exclude her from the taint of original sin. If this were not the case, a way to Mariology would be opened. But as it is, "human nature . . . is made worthy to be a partaker of the divine nature by grace and by a miracle of grace."[15] The *natus ex virgine* means, then, "the inconceivable

10. Barth, *Church Dogmatics,* I.2, p. 182.
11. Barth, *Church Dogmatics,* I.2, p. 183.
12. Barth, *Church Dogmatics,* I.2, pp. 186, 187.
13. Barth, *Church Dogmatics,* I.2, p. 188.
14. Barth, *Church Dogmatics,* I.2, p. 195.
15. Barth, *Church Dogmatics,* I.2, p. 196.

act of creative omnipotence in which He imparts to human nature a capacity, a power for Himself, which it does not possess of itself and which it could not devise for itself."[16] The Virgin Birth is thus an instance of the Reformation concept of *sola gratia,* grace alone.

This makes it clear that it is not Mary herself that is "theologically dangerous." In declaring her Motherhood Divine at the Council of Ephesus in 431, the church did not mean that Mary herself was divine, but that because the son whom she birthed was fully human and fully divine, it was appropriate to call her Mother of God. As we saw earlier with the profound impact of the mosaics at the basilica of Sta. Maria Maggiore, the Old Testament types tell the story of the humanity of Jesus, of the "family tree" of the people of Israel, and why this would be appropriate to include in a church in honor of Mary, who grounds Jesus' humanity. They also reflect Mary's humanity, who is, as Barth says, the last of the Old Testament figures and the beginning of the New. In the apse mosaic we begin to see elements of divinity: Christ and Mary sit enthroned in a roundel, in a blue ground representing the firmament; the sun and moon are below the footstool of Christ as he crowns Mary Queen of Heaven. Even here, at the moment of her coronation, she does not participate, but Christ alone bestows it upon her. Here we see, even in this portrayal of Mary as crowned Queen of Heaven, elements of what Barth saw in the Virgin Birth: an instance of grace alone. One can imagine Barth turning in his grave at this point, since Mary's coronation is not a dogma bearing upon Evangelical Christians, being as it is "repugnant" to Holy Scripture, but nevertheless the observation stands: Mary herself is not necessarily "theologically dangerous" when she tells the story of Jesus' humanity and divinity, the gospel of *sola gratia.*

Now, back to the twenty-first *(mirabile dictu!)* century. The United Church of Christ "claims as its own the faith of the historic Church expressed in the ancient creeds" (*Preamble to the Constitution,* United Church of Christ). Gabriel Fackre has worked tirelessly for the United Church of Christ as its faithful servant, both internally as pastor and teacher and externally as an ecumenical leader, and he has taught us all so much about what it means to confess Christ. To put a new spin on a christological question, as Gabe has asked so many christological questions of his denomination in his time, how does the United Church of Christ embrace or reject Mary? This is an important question, not only for the UCC's relation with Catholics, but also with Lutherans and Episcopalians, and

---

16. Barth, *Church Dogmatics,* I.2, p. 201.

other bodies as well because, as has been shown, one's view of Mary is really a question of one's view of Jesus. Mary is by far the single most important human figure in the life of Christ, and the fact that that person is a woman should not be wasted on us, especially in this day when the needs of feminist theology mount. Claiming as it does "the faith of the historic Church expressed in the ancient creeds," the UCC has great resources for hearing how Mary tells the story of the gospel of *sola gratia* for today.

The Christological Objectivity of History

Robert W. Jenson

On some recent occasions I have floated my more culturally incorrect ideas in friends' *festschriften,* in essays written more or less off the top of my speculative head and with very little scholarly apparatus. I propose here to do it again.

I

The possibility of an "objective" historical account, of a narrative describing *wie es eigentlich gewesen ist,* has of late been much doubted; derision of "Enlightenment dreams of objectivity" is very much the mode. At a recent meeting of scholars from various theological disciplines, a historian of Christian origins somewhat ruefully described himself as "neo-modernist," meaning that though he supposed he had to give up hope of achieving *the* truth about the past, and surrender much of historians' erstwhile domain to the free play of interpretation, he still thought there must be something or other back there and that a few bits of universally reliable knowledge could be assembled about it.

He did not have much argument for his insistence, except the — of course quite possibly dispositive — feeling that it *must* be so: "Otherwise, we are silenced!" The rest of us shared both the feeling and the lack of further warrant. The present essay is a very preliminary and incautious attempt to make up that lack, with a *theological* theory of historical objectivity — readers will at least agree that I have not chosen to honor Gabe Fackre by writing on a light subject.

"Objective" knowledge must, one supposes, be knowledge of an "object," presumably by a subject. Historians are indeed interpreters, storytellers — that is, they are subjects, and so they are not mere intelligences, that is, makers of lists[1] or analysts of causal factors.[2] They cannot be replaced by computers. But if our interpreting is not to be endlessly deferring fantasy, it must from time to time bump up against the *interpretandum* in such fashion as thereby to be corrected, must encounter something that is what it is regardless of our construals,[3] and is available to us in that character. And therein lies the difficulty. For how is the past thus our object?

Historians do of course deal with objects of a certain kind, "traces" of the stories they seek to re-create: texts and artifacts. Traditional accounts of historical method have regarded these as the objective controls on historical imagination, as *evidences* of the past. And surely that is right, so far as it goes. Texts and artifacts are clues from which we can rightly conclude to something. The question is, "To what?"

It is historical actors and the events they perpetrate, *persons* and their mutual involvements, which historians want to know — or did before so many gave up. But the past persons themselves would seem to be unavailable merely on account of their pastness; we seem indeed to be wholly dependent on the texts and artifacts. And the relation between these and defunct historical *personae* has become unclear in the culture — certainly some act of writing left the traces we call *The Gallic Wars,* but did exactly *Caesar* or *Rome* therein trace themselves? It is precisely this undecidability that is exploited by postmodernist critiques.

To be sure, neither are a host of subatomic and cosmological entities available for direct inspection, and both modern skeptics and postmodern ideologists have exploited this to carry their demolition of objectivity also into the "natural" sciences. Whereupon some historians have turned the argument around, and responded that if the sciences and history are thus equally subject to postmodernist critique, then history must be as objective as the sciences, whose objectivity no one doubts in their heart of hearts.

But the extension of postmodernist critique to the sciences is decidedly counterintuitive, for at least *some* entities posited in the natural and social sciences — e.g., amoebae and governments and molecules and per-

---

1. Works coming from the *Annales* school are often fascinating, but precisely insofar as they violate their announced method.

2. Those in history departments who could just as well be, are some part of the problem.

3. Our discourse must "have a body."

sons named Robert and glaciers and occasionally atoms — seem quite straightforwardly to be our present objects, and even tracks in cloud chambers have an air of immediate presence not attaching to a text or inscription. It does seem difficult to ask Karl Barth whether I have read him right, or the occupant of a sarcophagus bearing a cross what he *really* thought about God, but those possessed of the technique can put a shower of nuclear debris "to the question," looking to exclude deceptive appearances. So natural scientists with one accord regard postmodernist "critique" as bunk, and nineteenth- and early-twentieth-century positivists as irrelevant, whereas history departments have surrendered *en masse.*

The difficulty is not only now discovered. The Enlightenment began to lose its bravado almost immediately upon its establishment, and from Schleiermacher on theories of historical knowledge were developed that based the reliability of historical knowledge not on the availability of the object of knowledge but in one way or another on a relationship between the knowers. Unfortunately to the present point, the supposition that universally reliable knowledge comes to pass in this fashion depends on the (at least subliminal) posit of a universal community, and despair of such community is exactly what drives late modern and postmodern suspicion in the first place. Thus by this move we in fact come full circle; and it indeed appears that idealist and existentialist solutions to the problem of historical knowledge have fed directly into our current lack of one.[4]

In fact, the problem was felt long before any variations on "modern." Antiquity's greatest work of self-reflective history-writing, Augustine's *Confessions,* is haunted by the question, "Where then is the past, that I should be able to describe it?" That it cannot be an object "back there" was as clear to Augustine as to any postmodernist: the past is precisely what *is not* any more. Augustine's first and, to him, obvious step was to say that the past is "in memory." But then, what sort of space is *that?* Augustine's eventual solution is that the remembered past is accommodated by a "distention" of the soul, which itself abides in the present tense, so that what it encompasses is always available. I have elsewhere criticized and adapted his proposal,[5] but will here take it simply as a wonderful hint. And Augustine did something else: he uttered the whole of his *Confessions* as a prayer. That, I will argue, is the main part of a solution.

---

4. I have just recently been helped to clarity on this point by an unpublished manuscript of Carver Yu, on Dilthey and Mannheim.

5. For this, and much more also on the present proposal, I must refer to my *Systematic Theology,* vol. 2 (New York: Oxford University Press, 1997), pp. 20-35.

II

Generally reliable, "objective," knowledge must confront objects. So far, so good. But there are lifeless objects and there are lively objects, even person-type objects. Augustine's evocation of soul, of the personal aliveness of some objects, leads to my first suggestion.

Our difficulties with objective historical knowledge result, I suggest, from modernity's *mechanism,* which persists in "the humanities" even as it is driven out from the sciences. We subliminally think of temporal succession as a mechanism, even when we talk of plots and battles and great leaders; and then we think of the past as a *stilled* mechanism, and so as an assemblage of objects that are *only* objects. *Such* objects must of course be out of our grasp; if they were persons they are now dead persons, and are indeed back there where we are not. On these terms, only the specious present can be available.

But what if past persons had not been turned into *mere* objects? But were also subjects? Christians, after all, would seem bound to regard them so. According to Jesus, God can be identified as "the God of Abraham, Isaac, and Jacob," and is metaphysically "the God of the living and not of the dead." Therefore Abraham, Isaac, and Jacob, if Jesus is right, must be alive and not merely lifeless objects in the past, and their liveliness is a corollary of the specific identity of the true God. Here we must plumb a depth.

God's history with his people is, according to the doctrine by which the church identifies God, the doctrine of Trinity, not only our history but first and foremost *his:* the tale told by Scripture from creation to fulfillment is the deep truth about God, and the *personae* of this drama are who God is. Therefore as Father, Son, and Spirit in the lively relations of begetting and being begotten, enlivening and being enlivened, liberating and being liberated, God is himself from all temporal directions and in every aspect the other whom we encounter when we face plotted temporal succession, when we turn to what we know as history. Having said that, we must of course immediately note that he is of course not identical with our history, for when *he* turns to his history with us, we are his other precisely in our condition as creatures he has called into being.[6]

Thus, the reality of history is not that of a set of mere objects, but is sustained and enveloped in God's *life*. That God "creates,"[7] rather than

---

6. It is this point, by the way, which seems overlooked by critiques of recent trinitarianism who worry about too close an identification of God's history with ours.

7. The verb has a clear technical and restricted use in Scripture.

makes or emits, means that what he posits as other than himself is not a some*thing* but a history. To create is to make history as history is made, by the lively word. Thus all that is, is *summoned* into being at every moment and in every aspect by the triune God's lively address. Considering specifically the past, Abraham and Isaac and Jacob — and Caesar and Socrates — are indeed located in a memory, in the "distention" of a consciousness. But this is *God's* consciousness. And those who are located in God's memory cannot be a set of mere objects,[8] for God is not only alive, he is life. He holds them in his memory precisely by *addressing* them and so maintaining them as living subjects. *The Gallic Wars* can be the trace of Caesar, and not just of an unidentifiable act of writing, because as we attend to them God is present to our intention, and because in God's presence to our attention Caesar is summoned, and is himself present to claim his traces.

The historian's earlier assumed method is not thereby changed. He or she is still dependent on traces, on texts and artifacts. In my understanding, all history-knowing begins as aetiology, as wonder provoked by the way things now are. It begins indeed as free imagination of a past — whose very status as *past* is thus, of course, ambiguous. If aetiology becomes history, it is because it comes to be checked and steered by inference from traces, which is the point postmodern suspicion attacks. The warrant against this suspicion is the doctrine of Trinity.

Or rather, not quite the *doctrine*, but the fact. Our claim to be in living contact with the past when we reason from its traces, is warranted if and only if the life of God is itself available to us as what he is, with or without our construals. Now as the patristic formula has it, all God's works originate from the Father, are perfected in the Spirit, and have their objectivity as the Son, who is the one in whom the Father contemplates his own works and in whom the liberating, fulfilling Spirit encounters his own "check," the determining content of the freedom he is. It is, therefore, insofar as we know the Son that we know the past. And the Son is our object, and a subject who has us as his objects, as we participate in the life of his church, centrally to this point, in the Eucharist. It is when we are assured, "This is the body of Christ," that we are assured, "The past is not dead." The anchoring object of historical knowledge is the body of Christ.

---

8. The wonderful "Knechtschaft und Herrschaft" passage of Hegel's *Phenomenologie des Geistes* is relevant here as in so many contexts. For you and I to address each other, each must take the other for his object. But if I do not just so allow you to be a subject, or you allow me, our discourse is instantly a struggle for hegemony.

III

History telling is interpreting a past which somehow is just there for us. If the foregoing is in the vicinity of the truth, we can do this because, and only because, in every attention to reality we encounter the living God, in whom the past is alive because he addresses it. Which is to say that when we attend to the past we are spoken to, and that our interpreting is a response. Response in this situation has a name, *prayer.* Moreover, if the foregoing is in the vicinity of truth, we can be objective in prayer because Christ is in our community.

It is the truly contrarian final proposal of this essay: The founding act by which to pursue historical objectivity is that we pray for it. We should address our tale of past persons and their doings first to God and only then to each other. Augustine's "Dear Lord, let me rightly say what happened" at the beginning of a history may doubtless often remain implicit, but a historiographical culture that does not assume it must be in permanent epistemic crisis.

In this matter as in so much, Western modernity has been parasitic on the faith from which it claimed to emancipate. Obviously, such a relation must eventually run out its time. The time has come, and therefore the community of historians has lost its nerve. Since it no longer knows *why* the past can be its object, it cannot confidently claim *that* it is. Within the Christian church, we need not be so defeatist.

IV

Can then history not be done outside the church? It is indeed noteworthy that history telling, as against chronicling or myth making, is not an enterprise generally undertaken, and seems to appear where the gospel comes. But we need not be quite so imperialist as that may sound — though in general we should not be much frightened by accusations of this offense. We can adapt a principle from Karl Barth.

Since God creates by speaking, so that no one is unaddressed by him, and because his speech is coherent, we should not be surprised to find the possessions of the church popping up here or there outside the church. When and where this happens can be determined only by observation from case to case. So if folk succeed in telling history in ancient Greece or China or wherever, without any of the warrants just described, blessings on them.

Many Stories and "The Story"

Roger L. Shinn

Christian faith is rooted in stories. Its Scripture is a long book of stories — much more than that, but surely no less than that. Even in as secularized a culture as ours, those stories are part of the common heritage of society. Parents still name their children after the characters of the Bible. Our cultural memory includes the stories of Adam and Eve, of Noah and his family, of Abraham and Sarah, of Isaac and Rebekah, of Jacob and Rachel. Of Moses and Aaron and Miriam. Of Joshua and Deborah and Gideon. Of Ruth and Naomi and Hannah. Of Samson and Saul and David and Solomon. Of Elijah and Ahab and Jezebel. Of Amos, Hosea, Isaiah, Jeremiah, Ezekiel, and Daniel. Of Job. Of Mary and Joseph and Jesus. Of Herod and Peter and Judas and Pontius Pilate. Of Mary Magdalene and the other women who were the first witnesses to the resurrection. Of Paul, Silas, Timothy, and Onesimus. Of many, many others. Some of these we remember as "saints who from their labors rest." Some were notorious villains. Some, like "a man from Cyrene named Simon," were virtual nonentities who, by the quirks of biblical history, got thrown into sudden prominence. All had their stories.

We today know of those stories because they are encompassed by a greater story, which for Christians is "The Story." It is often called, usually too glibly, the greatest story ever told. In principle, no greater story *can* be told. For it begins with the "genesis" of all things, with God's creation of the heavens and the earth. It ends with the apocalypse, the Book of Revelation, which tells of the final judgment and the "new heaven and new earth," breaking into history and introducing the ultimate reign of God. In between is the human story, beginning as the story of all nature and

68

humanity, then focused on the specific people of a covenant with God, then expanded to include again all being.

The Bible includes extensive, sometimes detailed ethical teaching, the law and the prophets, the Sermon on the Mount, the exhortations of the Apostle Paul. It includes Psalms and liturgies. It includes doctrinal essays. It includes agonizing struggles with the problems of suffering and "the mystery of iniquity." But many of these emerge from the innumerable stories of Scripture and address specific occasions. All are embedded in the Story — the story of first and last things, of humankind, of Israel, of the coming of Christ, and the first years of the church. Within the Story are many types of stories. In modern terms, these are differing genres of literature, although that language would not have occurred to any biblical writer. Some of these types deserve special mention.

One of these is empirical, factual history with its references to time and place. Events occur before or after the Abrahamic covenant, the Exodus, the year that King Uzziah died, the exile, and Christ. They take place in geographic locations. They can be located in relation to the Lake of Galilee, the Jordan River, and the Dead Sea. People with historic memories still visit Bethlehem, Nazareth, and Jerusalem, the Areopagus of Athens. "From Dan to Beersheba" is a distance that is recognizable on a map and measurable in miles or kilometers. The road to Damascus was an actual road, as real as any road in history, though loaded with meanings unique to that road. Tourists can retrace the journeys of the Apostles as they spread the gospel. Modern archeological discoveries help us to locate some of the historical events of the Story. The concern of the Bible is not only with eternal truths; it is with specific happenings in history. Publications of the Bible, unlike most writings in theology, commonly include maps.

Others of the stories are legends, associated with historical characters. Presumably Samson and Goliath were actual individuals, but there is no way of knowing by historical methods which details of their stories are precisely accurate. Some of their adventures have remarkable similarities to those of other "strong men" in many cultures. David was undoubtedly a specific individual of tremendous importance, but not all the stories about him are verifiable by the normal methods of historiography. Like George Washington and Abraham Lincoln, he has become the center of both factual and imagined stories. The only history we can know is remembered history, and memory is fused with imagination.

Still other stories are parables, telling of events that are true to human experience but that are told to make a point. We need not know or care whether the Good Samaritan and the Prodigal Son were actual individuals. They tell us something true about ourselves and our neighbors. As the Gospel of Matthew (13:3) tells us, Jesus "told them many things in parables."

Then there are — extremely important — myths. In contemporary language, myth may be a term to dismiss a story as illusory. Or it may signify a story of utmost importance, a story that is nonsense if taken as science but that grasps for meaning that cannot be stated literally. To take a very rough analogy, any flat map of the globe misrepresents geography even as it communicates important understanding of the real sphere. Finite minds are capable of genuine insights into infinity, even though they cannot construe it adequately. As Paul Tillich has said, "there is no way of speaking about God except in mythological terms," and "complete demythologization is not possible when speaking about the divine."[1] The two stories of the Creation (Genesis 1:1–2:3 and Genesis 2:4–25) are not scientific accounts of the origin of our universe. For many centuries believers have recognized that they cannot, in their details and their chronologies, be reconciled with each other or with our understanding of cosmic history. But they are irreplaceable accounts of the relation of God to his creation. As Paul Ricoeur puts it, we do not displace such myths with a scientific history; we "reinvent" them.[2]

There are other types of biblical literature. There are doxologies, songs of praise, but even the Psalms are remarkable for their historic specificity. There are occasional fables (Balaam and his donkey). There are confrontations and conversations; think of Elijah and Ahab, of Job and his "comforters," of Jesus and his disciples and his enemies. There are touches of allegory, but very few, because the biblical characters are individuals, not representatives of abstract qualities. There are dreams, recognized as dreams, yet always related to actual events. All these are comprehended within the Story.

Readers of the Bible discern both its unity and its variety. My primary teacher of Old Testament, Julius Bewer, wrote: "The Old Testament is not a single book but a little library of thirty-nine books as we ordinarily count them." In a later generation, a colleague, James Smart, influenced by Karl Barth, wrote: "The authority of the Scriptures is that there

---

1. Paul Tillich, *Systematic Theology*, I, p. 223 (Chicago: University of Chicago Press, 1951); II, p. 29 (1957).

2. Paul Ricoeur, "Myth: Myth and History," *The Encyclopedia of Religion* (New York: Macmillan, 1987), X, p. 281.

sounds forth from them a single Voice, completely consistent in its demands and its promises, manifesting from beginning to end one purpose and one will, and evidencing itself to the mind and heart and conscience of man as the voice of God." Each of these statements needs correction by the other.[3]

In general, this literature of Scripture expresses no neutral or objective or uncommitted stance. In Davie Napier's vivid phrase, it is written "from faith to faith."[4] Even that profound generalization needs qualification. Skepticism and heresy appear from time to time, keeping a door open to outsiders. Many of us have occasions to be grateful for Job and Ecclesiastes. Much of the language of the Bible is clearly not literal. We read of the "corners" of the earth. God is pictured with wings and feathers, with a mighty hand and an outstretched arm. Often he is called a rock or a fortress. He breathes, sometimes through his mouth, sometimes through his nostrils. His weapons include the spear, javelin, sword, bow and fiery arrows. He is a father who resembles a mother comforting her child. He gasps, pants, and cries out like a woman in labor. Jesus describes himself as a door and a vine, as the bread of life, as a shepherd. He is called both the lamb of God and the lion of the tribe of Judah. The Christian tradition through the centuries remembers these metaphors and adds new ones, like "The Hound of Heaven." Christians argue, sometimes bitterly, over which biblical expressions are to be taken literally and which figuratively. Between American fundamentalists and Rudolf Bultmann, for example, there is a vast distance. Yet all understand the Bible sometimes literally and sometimes symbolically. All remember and retell the Story.

It is the Story, above all else, that is commemorated in Christian tradition and communicated from generation to generation. In centuries when most Christians could not read the Bible, they learned the story from stained glass windows, statues, paintings, sometimes icons. The church calendar celebrated high points in the Story — Advent, Christmas, Passover and Good Friday, Easter, and Pentecost. Plainsong, chants, and hymns recalled the Story. Think of some of the hymns familiar to past generations, some naive and sentimental, some profound: "I love to tell the story"; "Tell me the old, old story"; "Tell me the stories of Jesus";

---

3. Julius A. Bewer, *The Literature of the Old Testament*, rev. ed. (New York: Columbia University Press, 1933), "Introduction." James D. Smart, *What a Man Can Believe* (Philadelphia: Westminster Press, 1943), p. 77.

4. B. Davie Napier, *From Faith to Faith* (New York: Harper, 1955).

"We've a story to tell to the nations." Think of many Christmas carols. Think of hymns of the passion: "In the cross of Christ I glory"; "On a hill far away stood an old rugged cross." Think of the eloquent African-American spiritual that begins with a memory of Jeremiah: "There is a balm in Gilead, to make the wounded whole," then concludes with the lines: "If you cannot preach like Peter,/if you cannot pray like Paul,/you can tell the love of Jesus,/who died to save us all." If that seems unsophisticated, notice how closely it resembles Reinhold Niebuhr's frequent description of the core of the gospel: the character of Jesus and the drama of redemption.

The Story persists. It encourages great freedom of exploration. Through the centuries it has sought alliances with a variety of philosophies: Stoicism, Neo-Platonism, Aristotelianism, medieval realism and nominalism, Kantianism, pragmatism, process philosophy, existentialism, and more. These come and go; the Story continues. Alfred North Whitehead wrote: "Buddhism is the most colossal example in history of applied metaphysics." Christianity, by contrast, "is a religion seeking a metaphysic."[5] If so, what is the continuity of Christianity that gives rise to all the seeking? What but the Story?

The Story has sometimes been submerged in the desire of Christians to build theological systems. Could it be that the term, so common in theological education, "systematic theology," is a mistake? It could not be totally a mistake. The Story is theological from beginning to end. Even the Gospel of Mark, generally regarded as the earliest of the Gospels and certainly the shortest and the least systematic, is inescapably theological. Look at the first verse: "The beginning of the good news of Jesus Christ, the Son of God." That sets the tone for the whole Gospel. It cries out for elaboration. In what way was Jesus "good news," when he represented bad news to so many people? What does it mean to call Jesus "Christ" and "the Son of God"? Christians rightly want to explore the meanings of those terms, to distinguish them from alternative beliefs, to guard them against misinterpretation. That led to the great doctrinal controversies of centuries, including our own time. Yet too often it led to definitions of Christianity that would have been utterly incomprehensible to the Man of Nazareth. It led to hostilities utterly contrary to his spirit.

In the last generation or two we have seen a recovery of the Story as

5. Alfred North Whitehead, *Religion in the Making* (New York: Macmillan, 1926), p. 50.

the primary source of Christian theology.[6] Biblical scholars have identified the oldest confessional statements in Scripture and have shown that these take the form of narrative. Gerhard von Rad identifies one of these, perhaps the oldest, as part of a liturgy older than the book of Deuteronomy, in which it is imbedded:

> A wandering Aramean was my ancestor; he went down into Egypt and lived there, as an alien few in number, and there he became a great nation, mighty and populous. When the Egyptians treated us harshly and afflicted us, by imposing hard labor on us, we cried to the Lord, the God of our ancestors; the Lord heard our voice and saw our affliction, our toil, and our oppression. The Lord brought us out of Egypt with a mighty hand and an outstretched arm, with a terrifying display of power, and with signs and wonders; and he brought us into this place and gave us this land, a land flowing with milk and honey. So now I bring the first of the fruit of the ground that you, O Lord, have given me.[7]

A contemporary version of this confession might be less confident in the identification of "us" and our enemies, more restrained in its certainty of God's direct causality in nature and history. But notice three enduring elements of this early version of the Story. (1) It is a narrative of action, with verbs prominent in the telling. (2) It identifies the present generation with ancestral generations: the Lord "brought *us* out of Egypt" and into this place. (3) The narrative is recited in faith and calls for a response of grateful action.

Similarly, New Testament scholars have identified some passages as the content of the earliest Christian declarations. These are often called the *kerygma*, literally the cry of a herald, the root proclamation of the faith. As H. Richard Niebuhr put it, "The preaching of the early Christian church . . . was primarily a simple recital of the great events connected with the historical appearance of Jesus Christ and a confession of what had happened to the community of disciples."[8] Again, the emphasis is on events, on action, on narrative. The theologies most true to the *kerygma*

---

6. This and the next two paragraphs echo my book, *Confessing Our Faith: An Interpretation of the Statement of Faith of the United Church of Christ* (Cleveland: United Church Press, 1990), pp. 15-17. The Statement of Faith, endorsed by the General Synod of 1959, is an attempt to interpret the biblical *kerygma* in "words of our time."

7. Deut. 26:5-10; see comparable declarations in Deut. 6:21-25 and Joshua 24:17-18.

8. H. Richard Niebuhr, *The Meaning of Revelation* (New York: Macmillan), p. 43.

are those that never forget the Story. A notable example is Gabriel Fackre's book, *The Christian Story: A Narrative Interpretation of Basic Christian Doctrine.*[9]

Christians, then, can welcome the preference for stories and the distrust of pretentious systems that lurk in "postmodern" thought and "deconstructionism." But these movements, often infatuated with individual stories, may scorn the Story. It is currently fashionable to recognize the many pluralisms — religious, cultural, esthetic, and even scientific — in the world of today. This recognition is accurate and can be exhilarating. The Story, to recall a point, encompasses many stories. To stifle the many various stories can be deadening. Søren Kierkegaard, a postmodernist before the invention of the term, was not entirely wrong in insisting that "truth is subjectivity." But a chaos of subjectivities can lead to a normlessness, an anomie as burdensome as any confining authority.

Applications for entrance into theological schools are, in our time, far more autobiographical than those a generation ago. The same is true of papers submitted by candidates for ordination. My students often appeal to their highly personal stories as authoritative for them. On occasions I reply, I hope not too professorially, "Hitler, too, had a story. So did Stalin. So does every tyrant and fool. How do you validate *your* story?"

A question for our time is: What stories have a claim on us? Can we respond to the Story, recognizing that it tells us as well as those we dislike of our incompleteness, our sin, our need for healing, our opportunities for rebirth and fresh ventures? A challenge to Christian theology today is to tell and re-tell the Story without pretension, without disdain for other stories, with respect for the varieties of human experience.

---

9. Gabriel Fackre, *The Christian Story: A Narrative Interpretation of Basic Christian Doctrine,* rev. ed. (Grand Rapids: Eerdmans, 1984; first edition, 1978). There are shades of difference between Fackre and me in his advocacy (p. 3) and my questioning of systematic theology. But there is also a kinship. He recognizes that systematic theology is "a frightening phrase!" With Dorothy Fackre he finds it filled with paradoxes, holding together "seemingly contradictory points." The Fackres, pointing to the mysteries of faith, write: "We can *explore* these mysteries, but we can't *explain* them" (Dorothy and Gabriel Fackre, *Christian Basics: A Primer for Pilgrims* [Grand Rapids: Eerdmans, 1991], p. 45). For my part, I agree with his determination to go beyond "both timid *ad hoc* theologizing and too easy acquiescence to the feeling fads of the day" (*The Christian Story,* p. 4). From ecologists I have learned that "everything is connected with everything else," and I want to explore those connections. I am, I suspect, more skeptical and distrustful of systems than is Fackre. I hope for opportunities in continuing conversations to learn more about our kinships and our differences.

A favorite saying within the Story is, "You will know the truth, and the truth will make you free" (John 8:32). It is not our privilege to claim possession of that truth. It is a gift that calls for our response. We can trust that this truth, both hidden and revealed in the Story, has a liberating power for those who respond to it in faith, hope, and love.

Good News for Us Gentiles:
Reading Romans from the Bottom Line

Leander Keck

As an avowed church theologian, Professor Fackre has not forgotten that the discipline of theology is to serve the church's proclamation of the gospel. Moreover, he has insisted that the Jesus story is the core of the Great Story of God's justice-creating redemption — a story that arcs from creation to consummation, from Genesis to Revelation. It is appropriate, then, for a volume honoring Professor Fackre to include an essay that examines, albeit briefly, what Paul's Letter to the Romans says about the gospel, for it is actually the earliest written theology of the gospel for us Gentiles. Romans neither summarizes what Paul preached to Gentiles nor presents a full-orbed exposition of the theology that undergirds what he preached, for its readers were already Christians, most of whom were Gentiles, as Rom. 1:5, 14 clearly indicates. Since Rom. 15:22-29 alerts them to Paul's plan for a mission to Gentiles in Spain, it is not surprising that what the letter says about the gospel has special pertinence for non-Jews. Moreover, Paul presents himself as a Jewish (9:1-5) apostle to Gentiles (11:13; 15:16). At the same time, the letter's discussion of the law, like its extensive reliance on Scripture (apart from chs. 5–8), reflects his concern to clarify matters of special importance for Christian Jews. Instead of regarding these "Jewish" features as evidence that Paul is engaged in a critique of Judaism, one should view them as expressions of his conviction that Christian Gentiles can understand properly neither the content nor the significance of their faith without seeing that God has anchored it in the story of God's dealings with Israel. Paul's letter remains important in that it tells us Jesus is good news *for us* precisely because the good news pertains "to the Jew first" (1:16) and last (11:25-26).

Since for centuries the vast majority of Christians have been Gentiles, we do not fully grasp the import of Paul's argument so long as we regard what Paul said about Gentiles as pertaining only to "them" — to the "pagans" of the Greco-Roman world. Two millennia of predominantly Gentile Christianity have not erased the theological significance of Paul's understanding of good news for us non-Jews. Unless this is made clear, why should we non-Jews care that Jesus is the Christ, the Messiah expected by Jews? Indeed, given the rapid growth of Christianity in Africa and Asia, the issue is even more pertinent today than in Paul's time.

Paul's understanding of Jesus Christ as good news also for Gentiles, especially as expressed in Romans, is inseparable from two convictions, the one pertaining to his overall view of Jews and Gentiles, the other centered in his construal of the Jesus-event as *the* eschatological act of God. This essay must therefore attend to both before turning to the bottom line of his argument in Rom. 15:7-13, where they come together.

Paul's View of Jews and Gentiles

Our common ways of thinking about the peoples of the world differ markedly from Paul's. He grouped them neither according to skin color nor according to stages in economic/technological "development." Nor did he contrast Jews with various ethnic groups, such as Arabs, Celts, Gauls, or Germans. When he says he has an obligation to "Greeks and barbarians" (1:14), he simply uses this conventional distinction to refer to all Gentiles. For him, it was self-evident that all non-Jews are Gentiles, whatever their skin color, technological advancement, cultural heritage, or geographic homeland. Nor do his letters take the slightest interest in distinguishing the various kinds of Gentile religions found in the Greco-Roman cities, whether to understand them in their own terms or to find in the more "advanced" ones some basis for "inter-religious dialogue." In his perspective, there were Jews and "pagans" — though he neither used nor knew this term.

To be sure, most peoples have distinguished themselves from all "others" as a way of asserting, valuing, and preserving group identity — especially if the group sees itself threatened, whether by absorption or by its opposite, persecution. In the Greco-Roman world, faithful Jews had to contend with both, partly because they insisted that the God they worshiped was the one God, not a Jewish brand of a generic deity worshiped also by others who had their own names for the One. As Paul sees it, whatever gods the Gentiles worship, they do not know *God* (Gal. 4:8); what they know are but "idols," no matter how "meaningful" the devotee may have found their sundry rituals, sacrifices, processions, prayers, sacred days, and dietary customs. From Paul's angle, the devotees are "enslaved to beings that by nature are not gods" (Gal. 4:8). We are not surprised, then, that he reminded the new Christians in Thessalonika that they "turned to God from idols, to serve a living and true God" (1 Thess. 1:9). We may assume that this "turning" included abandoning their moral habits (in Paul's eyes, the degradation to which God had given them up because they refused to honor God as God, as he asserted in Rom. 1:18-32). In Rom. 6:17, 20, he reminds the Christian Gentiles in Rome that they had been "slaves of sin." Paul did not become an apostle to Gentiles because he thought they deserved to hear the gospel but because they needed to. At the same time, he did not hesitate to appropriate the language, values, and theological thought of the "pagan" world, especially those of the popular moralists,[1] when he deemed them valid enough to "capture" for Christ (2 Cor. 10:5).

We may also assume that Paul, like many Jews of the day, also believed that someday the gulf between Jews and Gentiles would be overcome, for the prophets had foreseen that the God of Israel would be acknowledged by the nations as the one true God. There was, however, no standard view about when or how this would occur.[2] In the meantime, some individual Gentiles could, and did, do so by conversion, while others — the so-called "God-fearers" — accepted Jewish beliefs while declining the mark of conversion, circumcision. Even if much daily Jewish life was "Hellenized" (not only in the diaspora), the difference between God's chosen and all the unchosen remained basic to Paul's thinking, for it was a conviction, not an idea.[3]

---

1. This aspect of Paul's work has been well-documented by Abraham J. Malherbe. See, e.g., his *Paul and the Thessalonians: A Philosophical Tradition of Pastoral Care* (Philadelphia: Fortress Press, 1987), and *Paul and the Philosophers* (Minneapolis: Fortress Press, 1989), as well as his recent commentary, *The Letters to the Thessalonians*, Anchor Bible (New York: Doubleday, 2000).

2. For a concise survey of views, see Terence L. Donaldson, *Paul and the Gentiles: Remapping the Apostle's Convictional World* (Minneapolis: Fortress Press, 1997), ch. 3.

3. For the distinction between a conviction and an idea, see Daniel Patte, *Paul's Faith and the Power of the Gospel: A Structural Introduction to the Pauline Letters* (Philadelphia: Fortress Press, 1983). For Patte, "a conviction is a self-evident truth"; moreover, whereas "we have power over ideas" (because we modify and manipulate them), "convictions have direct power over us" (pp. 11-12). Donaldson uses Patte's distinction to argue that while

Paul's awareness that being a Jew in a sea of Gentiles made him "different" was not obliterated when he came to faith in Jesus as the Christ; indeed, it was an essential ingredient of his sense of vocation of being Christ's emissary to Gentiles.[4] This is implied in his adaptability to become "as a Jew in order to win Jews," and then to become "as one outside the law" (to live as a Gentile) in order to win Gentiles to the faith (1 Cor. 9:20-21). True, for those "baptized into Christ . . . there is no longer Jew or Greek," just as there is "no longer slave or free . . . male and female" (Gal. 3:27-28), but Paul's point is that these distinctions no longer define one's identity "in Christ" even though they remain; that they did remain is shown by his counsels in 1 Corinthians 7. "In Christ" the new relationship between Jew and Gentile is a given; it does not need to be negotiated. It does, however, need to be actualized. For Paul, that included his freedom to be adaptable precisely because in Christ the relation between Jew and Gentile was radically transformed, not terminated (Gal. 5:6).

For Paul, the Christ "into" whom believers are baptized is the crucified Jesus whom God resurrected. At the outset of Romans, Paul reminds his Christian Gentile audience that the good news, "which God had promised beforehand through his prophets in the holy scriptures," is about God's Son, "who was descended from David according to the flesh, and was declared to be the Son of God with power . . . by resurrection from the dead" (1:2-4). One can understand why word of this would be good news for those Jews who read the prophets and who expected a Davidic deliverer, but why would it be good news for Gentiles? Understanding Paul's answer to this question requires grasping his view of the Jesus event. This entails more than understanding Paul's ideas; it includes sensing imaginatively their power when one is so utterly convinced that they are true, that they are not negotiable. In short, Paul's understanding of the Jesus-event is his transforming conviction.

Paul's convictions about Gentiles remained unchanged (they could become full members of Israel on equal terms), his new conviction about Jesus caused a shift in these terms — now faith in Christ, not Torah, was decisive (*Paul and the Gentiles*, pp. 74-78). In chapter 12, he discusses the "reconfiguration of Paul's convictions" in detail. Donaldson holds that Paul had engaged in efforts to convert Gentiles even before his conversion (see, e.g., p. 259).

4. Donaldson rightly asserts that "for Paul to define his apostolic role as having to do with *Gentiles* is to signal not his abandonment of a Jewish perspective, but the degree to which his mission depends on such a perspective for its rationale" (*Paul and the Gentiles*, p. 252).

The Jesus-Event

Just as Paul thought differently about the peoples of the world from the way we commonly think of them, so his way of thinking about Jesus differed from that of many Christians. One cannot overemphasize the central point: for Paul, Jesus is good news for us Gentiles *not* because of anything Jesus had said or done during his lifetime, but because the event as a whole was the decisive act of God.

Even if Paul had known the entire body of Jesus traditions that later ended up in the four canonical Gospels, he would have discovered that, except for Jesus' positive comment about the Roman officer who asked Jesus to heal his son (Matt. 8:10), Jesus had said not one good word about Gentiles, but rather expressed his disdain for them by using them only as negative examples of what to avoid.[5] Paul would also have seen that there is not much point in telling his Gentile audience that Jesus was a wise, insightful teacher who lived what he taught, healed the sick, criticized pretensions and the misuse of religion (e.g., Mk. 7:9-13), and invited people to follow his way, for such figures were found in the Greco-Roman world already. Had Paul presented Jesus in such terms, he might have found himself comparing Jesus with such figures, arguing that Jesus was wiser, more insightful, more consistent, more penetrating in his critiques, and his hearers might have heard him commending an unusual Cynic-like Jew who was "done in" by the established authorities. But even if some hearers would have welcomed the news of such a figure, that information would not have been the good news as Paul understood it.

What made the Jesus who died on a despicable cross good news was the framework, the context — or as Professor Fackre would say, the Great Story — in which Paul saw the Jesus event as a whole; namely, Jewish apocalyptic thought, for this enabled him to understand the meaning of Jesus' resurrection. While a Pharisee, Paul had believed there would be resurrection (Acts 23:6-8) long before he came to believe that it had occurred in the case of the crucified Jesus, and *only* in his case. For Paul the Pharisee as for Paul the Christian, resurrection was not confused with mere resuscitation (which is devoid of theological significance anyway), but was part of the expected future scenario that signaled the end of This Age and the irruption of the Age to Come into the present. This transition, moreover, was

---

5. For a somewhat fuller discussion of Jesus' attitude toward Gentiles, see my *Who Is Jesus? History in Perfect Tense* (Columbia: University of South Carolina Press, 2000), pp. 55-58; a paperback edition was published by Fortress Press in 2001.

to inaugurate much more than a new phase of Jewish history; it entailed the eschatological (and hence definitive) transformation of the present state of affairs. Paul's word for the result was "new creation" (Gal. 6:15), marked by reconciliation between Creator and creation (2 Cor. 5:17-18). If God indeed resurrected Jesus from the realm of the dead, then the whole Jesus-event is God's act, and if that resurrection announced the New Age, then Jesus is indeed good news for the whole human world, for Gentiles no less than for Jews, because by definition "new creation" means a fresh start, inaugurating the time when everything is made right.

Paul's impassioned letter to the Galatians shows that not everyone saw the new situation as he did. In this letter, Paul strives to thwart the influence of opponents, whom Martyn calls "Teachers" instead of the pejorative "Judaizers";[6] they also insisted that now the Gentiles could cease to be "outsiders" and become members of the people of God. At issue between the Teachers and Paul was what was required for this inclusion. For Paul, it was solely by believing the good news of God's act in Christ, followed by baptism "into Christ," Abraham's "seed" (offspring).[7] For the Teachers, however, this first step must be followed by the second: baptized male Christian Gentiles must also be circumcised and so *become* Jews, thereby completing their justification (being made right with God) by faith. Paul, however, insisted that the Teachers' way was not good news for Gentiles at all, for the Teachers did not see that Jesus' resurrection brings new creation. Although Paul does not actually say so, he apparently realized that even in the Old Age Gentiles could become Jews by conversion. If even after faith and baptism they must still become Jews in order to be included in God's people, then the Jesus-event was irrelevant; indeed, "if justification were through the law [which requires circumcision for Jews], then Christ died for nothing" (Gal. 2:21).

Since Paul had already fought this battle when he produced Romans, he does not repeat what he had argued in Galatians but assumes, and modifies, it. Now, freed from the need to *dissuade* readers from the

---

6. J. Louis Martyn, *Galatians,* Anchor Bible (New York: Doubleday, 1997), pp. 117-26. In Martyn's reconstruction of the "Teachers'" mission and message, they are much more than the catalysts that prompted Paul to write Galatians; rather, throughout the letter, Paul's teaching counters theirs, point by point.

7. A good part of Paul's complex argument in Galatians 3 turns on his observation that in Gen. 12:7, God's promise refers to Abraham's "seed," which, being singular rather than plural, Paul takes as referring to Christ (3:16). Accordingly, those who are baptized "into" Christ "belong to Christ" and so are already Abraham's seed, members of Abraham's family, without becoming Jews by circumcision.

theology of the Teachers, he seeks to *persuade* the Christian Gentiles in Rome that the Jesus event is such good news for Gentiles that they will both stand by him in prayer as he goes to Jerusalem and later support his mission to Gentiles in Spain after his arrival in Rome (15:22-32). This effort to persuade reaches its bottom line in Rom. 15:7-13. To understand this passage, therefore, one must be alert to its allusions to what Paul had said before.

Romans 15:7-13[8]

From 14:1 through 15:6, Paul addresses a conflict in the Roman house churches in which "the weak" (often thought to be Christian Jews) and "the strong" (commonly regarded as Christian Gentiles) were hectoring each other over the observance of diets and (unspecified) special days, summing up his admonitions in 15:1-6. At first glance, verse 7 ("Welcome one another, therefore, just as Christ has welcomed you, for the glory of God") appears to resume his counsel, but it actually serves to link verses 1-6 with the somewhat similar verses 8-13. Since Jesus had not been to Rome, Paul implies that Christ arrived there when the gospel arrived. Thus, Christ is not just the subject matter of the gospel; the risen Christ is also the subject who acts when the gospel is preached and believed (as also 15:18 implies). Christ welcomed the Romans; they did not welcome him, however happy they might have been to receive the gospel. The little word "for" at the beginning of verse 8 signals that what follows provides the warrant for the exhortation in verse 7. And that warrant (verses 8-12) states the outcome of the Jesus event for Jews and Gentiles, and for the relation between them, and so is the bottom line of the whole letter's argument.

NRSV (like most modern translations) renders verses 8-9 in a way that makes Paul's syntax clearer than his Greek:

> For I tell you that Christ has become the servant of the circumcised on behalf of the truth of God in order that he might confirm the promises given to the patriarchs, (9) and in order that the Gentiles might glorify God for his mercy.

---

8. The discussion of this passage draws on, modifies, and goes beyond my more detailed treatment of it in "Christology, Soteriology, and the Praise of God (Romans 15:7-13)" in *The Conversation Continues: Studies in Paul and John in Honor of J. Louis Martyn,* ed. R. T. Fortna and B. R. Gaventa (Nashville: Abingdon Press, 1990), pp. 85-97.

However, Wagner's alternative translation has much to commend it:[9]

> ... the Christ has become a servant of the circumcision on behalf of the truthfulness of God, in order to confirm the promises made to the patriarchs, (9) and [a servant] with respect to the Gentiles on behalf of the mercy [of God] in order to glorify God.

This translation exhibits more accurately the rhetorical balance of the sentence; above all, it makes Christ (not the Gentiles) the one who glorifies God — a shift that leads more smoothly into the rest of verse 9, where Paul takes the quotation from Ps. 18:49 as the words of Christ. As a result, the whole of verses 8-12 constitutes a coherent christological warrant for the exhortation in verse 7. While the whole passage concerns the significance of Christ for the relation of Jews and Gentiles, the focus is on the Gentiles.

However, in this highly compressed sentence, Paul first insists that the aim of the Christ event is the confirmation of the promises given to the patriarchs — an allusion to "the promises" that belong to Israel in 9:4 and to the discussion of Abraham as "promise" in chapter 4, and especially to the gospel "promised beforehand ... in the holy scriptures" (1:2). By using the perfect tense (rendered "has become") instead of the aorist ("became"), Paul implies that Christ was and now continues to serve as the witness to God's truthfulness — an allusion to the axiomatic truthfulness/faithfulness of God in 3:1-8, as well as to its equivalent, God's righteousness, or rectifying rectitude (righteousness that makes right) apart from the law, yet "attested by the law and the prophets" (3:21, 26). Christ is the servant *of* the Jews (not *to* them, as in RSV), partly because according to 9:5, he comes "from them, according to the flesh," while being the Son whom God "sent ... in the likeness of sinful flesh" (8:3), but mostly because he facilitates the achievement of Israel's role with regard to the nations (Gentiles). In short, with this dense assertion Paul certifies (as "I tell you" implies) that "God has not rejected his people" (11:1), and that to the contrary, "the gifts and the calling of God are irrevocable" (11:29). For Paul, the actualization in Christ of God's promise to Abraham is essential also for Gentile believers, for he may have sensed that if they ignore this point, they would end up where Marcion ended up in the next century. And Paul's premonition was right.

According to NRSV's rendering of verse 9, Christ's becoming "a ser-

9. J. Ross Wagner, "Christ, Servant of Jew and Gentile: A Fresh Approach to Romans 15:8-9," *JBL* 116 (1997): 481-82.

vant of the circumcised" also has a second purpose — "that the Gentiles might glorify God for his mercy." How that purpose is achieved, however, is not obvious. On the other hand, although Wagner's rendering posits an ellipsis (Paul assumed that the reader would understand that Christ has two servant roles, though only one is mentioned), it has the advantage of keeping the focus on Christ and so avoids an awkward change of subject from "Christ" to "the Gentiles" and back again to "Christ" (the speaker of the quotation that follows). Moreover, by taking Paul's *ta de ethnē* as an accusative of respect, Wagner's rendering discloses a subtle but significant difference between Christ's servant roles: he is not a servant *of* the Gentiles but *with respect to* them. While he does not come "from" them (as the Messiah "according to the flesh" comes "from Israel," 9:5), he is nonetheless God's servant for them, on behalf of (i.e., for the sake of actualizing) God's mercy — an allusion to God's gracious action toward the "objects of mercy," who included the assorted Gentiles whom God has called "my people" (9:23-26, where Paul interprets Hos. 1:10;[10] see also 11:30, "you [Gentiles] . . . have now received mercy"). In short, just as Christ served God's purpose for Jews by confirming God's promises, so through the gospel Christ served God's purpose as the means by which God's mercy made Christian Gentiles into part of God's people. Had Christ not confirmed the promises, he could not have served this goal.

To show that this remarkable understanding of Christ's dual servanthood is not merely Paul's fanciful idea, the Apostle goes on to say that it accords with Scripture ("As it is written"), namely, with four quotations drawn from all three parts of the Hebrew Bible: the law (v. 10 is from Deut. 32:43 [Septuagint], the prophets (verse 12 is from Isa. 11:10), and the writings (verse 9 is from Ps. 18:49; v. 11 from Ps. 117:1). All of these quotations concern the Gentiles, though in differing ways.

In the first quotation, Christ speaks to God: "Therefore I will confess you among the Gentiles, and sing praises to your name." Hays notes that these lines are from Psalm 18, which celebrates David's deliverance from enemies, and so infers that Paul would have read it as a "prefiguration of the Messiah's sufferings and glorification," a celebration of "the

---

10. Rom. 9:25-26 claims to cite the words of Hosea. But only verse 26 quotes Hos. 1:10 (2:1 in LXX); verse 25, which has "I will call [them] 'my people,'" is actually Paul's interpretation of Hos. 1:9 (where God says, "You are not my people," a word of judgment on Israel), in light of verse 10. In other words, it appears that Paul applies to Gentiles what in Hosea pertains to God's judgment on Israel and the reversal of that judgment. Donaldson points out that Paul makes the same move also at 10:11, 13, 20 (*Paul and the Gentiles*, p. 101).

eschatological triumph of God,"[11] not as the promise of the preexistent Christ about the purpose of his impending incarnation, as I had proposed.[12] Hays may well be right about how Paul read the whole psalm — *before* he used it here. He is not equally right, however, in saying that the text "must be interpreted not as an isolated prooftext about Gentiles but as an allusion to the narrative of the psalm as a whole" (134), for it is precisely the reference to the Gentiles that makes the psalm useful for the argument here, as is true also for each of the other quotations that follow.

But how does Paul understand the resurrected Christ to be confessing and praising God among Gentiles? Though the Apostle does not explain what he has in mind, one can surmise the import of his quoting just these lines here. Because in verse 7 Christ "received" the Gentile readers for the glory of God, and because verse 9 sees the purpose of Christ's servanthood with respect to the Gentiles as his glorifying God, one may infer that Christ's receiving Gentiles, his glorifying God, and his confessing and praising God among Gentiles interpret one another, and so make essentially the same point: the Christ who receives Gentiles points them to God by his own praise of God, and thereby is "the servant of the circumcised," the one by whom Gentiles now look to Israel's God. The second quotation now follows smoothly, for it summons Gentiles to rejoice with God's people; the third emphatically summons "all you Gentiles" to join in the praise of God.

Behind Paul's use of Deut. 32:43 ("Rejoice, O Gentiles, with his people") in verse 10 lies Rom. 11:13-24, where he pointed out that believing Gentiles are wild olive branches grafted into the orchard olive, Israel. That is, by faith in Christ, we become part of this odd tree ("grafted, contrary to nature," 11:24) in which we are nourished from the same root (11:17), God's inexplicable freedom to choose and to show mercy (9:15), while we remain Gentiles, though now "*with* his people." And behind 11:13-24 stands 9:26, as already noted. And behind 9:26 lies the precedent of Abraham, who gave God glory *before* he became a Jew by circumcision (4:20, 11-12), and so became the prototype of all who are justified/rectified by faith (4:24-25). In short, giving glory to God as Abraham did is a sign that our refusal to "honor God as God" has ceased. When and where that occurs, God has indeed rectified (justified) us, the ungodly (4:5).

---

11. Richard B. Hays, "Christ Prays the Psalms: Paul's Use of an Early Christian Exegetical Tradition," in *The Future of Christology* (L. E. Keck Festschrift), ed. A. J. Malherbe and W. A. Meeks (Minneapolis: Fortress Press, 1993), p. 135.

12. Leander Keck, "Christology, Soteriology, and the Praise of God," p. 93.

Important as the rectification of our relation to God is, one cannot avoid asking whether, even when we join Israel in praising God, this suffices to deal salvifically with the deepest level of our plight. What if our deepest problem is not relational but structural, if it pertains not only to what we do and do not do but primarily to what we have become? Paul's fourth quotation (verse 12) alludes to his response to just such questions.

The fourth quotation alludes not only to Christ's dual role stated in verses 8-9, but also to another aspect of the good news, the decisive significance of Jesus' resurrection:

> The root of Jesse [an allusion to the Messiah] shall come,
> the one who rises to rule the Gentiles.
> In him the Gentiles shall hope.

It is doubtful that Paul sees here either the Messiah's political sovereignty over the nations (Gentiles), as in some Jewish apocalyptic texts, or an allusion to another apocalyptic motif, the Gentiles coming to Jerusalem as in a pilgrimage.[13] Rather, he understands "rises" as a reference to Jesus' resurrection and exaltation. It is the resurrected Jesus Christ in whom the Gentiles hope when they acknowledge his "rule" as Lord, as 10:9-13 already said.

One may doubt whether Paul's preaching to Gentiles in order to win their positive response to the gospel put up front their inclusion in the people of God, for his Gentile listeners might well have heard such a message as an answer to a problem they didn't have. Moreover, given the widespread antipathy toward Jews, it is unlikely that many Gentiles thought that their religious needs would be met by identifying with Jews. Indeed, even as Christians, the Gentiles in Rome appear to have been reluctant to associate closely with Christian Jews, thereby prompting Paul to write Romans 9-11 (especially 11:13-32) and 14:1–15:7 as he did. Nor did Paul think that Gentile immorality, portrayed in 1:26-32, would be transformed into morality if Gentiles adopted the Torah as the norm of an alternative ethos, because for him, living by that alternative norm requires both a positive response (faith/trust) to God's act in Christ, which deals decisively with the *human* condition inherited from the past, in which both Jews and Gentiles are caught, *and* the presence of the Spirit that empowers for the future.

---

13. Donaldson discusses, and rightly rejects, this interpretation. He does so not only of this passage, but also as an explanation of Paul's view of the Gentiles' relation to Israel as a whole (*Paul and the Gentiles,* pp. 186-97).

So it is not surprising that Romans 5-8 addresses the Adamic situation, in which sin and death rule as inescapable tyrannical powers over everyone. In this *human* plight there is no difference between Jew and Gentile ("death spread to all because all have sinned," 5:12).[14] Because neither Abraham (Israel's election) nor Moses (obedience to Torah) can liberate from these tyrants, there is no point in requiring Gentiles to become Jews. According to Paul's gospel, however, this liberation occurs to both Jews and Gentiles when they believe that in Christ's resurrection God broke the power of death, for Christ, "being raised from the dead, will never die again; death no longer has dominion over him" (6:9-10). Those who believe this, and so are baptized into the living Christ, are participatory beneficiaries of this event that defeated death and sin. Moreover, just as Jews and Gentiles share the Adamic condition, so for participants in Christ, the new Adam, "there is no distinction between Jew and Greek; the same Lord is Lord of all and is generous to all who call on him. For 'everyone who calls on the name of the Lord shall be saved'" (10:12-13, paraphrasing Joel 2:32).

In other words, allusion to Christ's resurrection in the fourth quotation in verse 12 points back to chapters 5-8, in which Paul goes most deeply into the human dilemma and its resolution by arguing that Christ's death and resurrection liberates the baptized believers from bondage to sin and death. The Gentiles to whom Paul preached would have heard *this* presentation of Jesus' significance as good news, because it offered redemption from the human plight that they recognized when Paul presented the gospel. Even in penetrating to the *human* dilemma, "Paul sees himself as a Jewish apostle to Gentiles, not simply as the bearer of a universal message to an undifferentiated humanity."[15] Because the Christ whose death and resurrection effected this liberation was the Messiah who confirmed the promise to Abraham, he is indeed the one in whom Gentiles hope, as the fourth quotation says.

When Paul dictates 15:7-13, he counts on the reader to bear in mind what he had said up to this point. Consequently, he envisions the Gentiles' praise of God as their response to what the promise-keeping God of the patriarchs has done for them in Christ's death and resurrection. And since it is truth that distinguishes praise from flattery, in praising of God, Gentiles acknowledge that what Paul has written is true, and that he has good news for all of us.

---

14. This claim accounts more adequately for the human condition than 1:18–3:8 does for the assertion that "all, both Jews and Greeks, are under the power of sin" in 3:9.

15. Donaldson, *Paul and the Gentiles*, p. 159.

87

Concluding Remark

In pondering the current import of what Paul asserted and argued about Jews and Gentiles, as well as the significance of Jesus' resurrection, we, too, can begin at the bottom line. For us, that bottom line is the question that goes to the heart of Christian theology — Is Paul's gospel still good news for us Gentiles? If the answer is not an immediately self-evident *yes,* it is because a convincing *yes* must come to terms with those considerations that can evoke a robust *no.* Paul's Romans is written in such a way, however, that if we Gentiles attend seriously to Paul's bottom line in 15:7-13, we will find ourselves contending with the whole letter. And it is just such an engagement that makes exegesis significant, particularly for a church theologian like Gabriel Fackre — who, fortunately, does not need to be informed about the role of exegesis in Christian theology.

Singing the Story

Paul Westermeyer

"O sing to the Lord a new song," the Psalter calls out to us again and again. It is the Christ hymn, new every morning, that a community living together begins to sing in the early morning, the new song that is sung by the whole community of faith in God on earth and in heaven. We are called to join in the singing of it. It is God who has prepared one great song of praise throughout eternity, and those who enter God's community join in this song. It is the song that "the morning stars sang together and all the children of God shouted for joy" (Job 38:7). It is the victory song of the children of Israel after passing through the Red Sea, the Magnificat of Mary after the Annunciation, the song of Paul and Silas when they praised God in the darkness of prison, the song of the singers on the sea of glass after their deliverance, the "song of Moses, the servant of God, and the song of the Lamb" (Rev. 15:3). It is the new song of the heavenly community.[1]

The new song tells a story of victory, not without pain and sorro*w*.

Or, more broadly, the pain and sorrow of the new song are contextualized by the joyful foretaste suggested by the leading tone *ti*.

Gabriel Fackre, in his *Theology and Culture Newsletter* 40,[2] said that

---

1. Dietrich Bonhoeffer, *Life Together; Prayerbook of the Bible,* ed. Geffrey Kelly, trans. Daniel W. Bloesch and James H. Burtness, vol. 5 of Dietrich Bonhoeffer Works (Minneapolis: Fortress Press, 1996), p. 65.

2. Gabriel Fackre, *Theology and Culture Newsletter* 40 (Advent 2000), p. 4.

"Christians are called to tell their story with its promise of singular truth and life." In arranging this festschrift, Gabe's daughter noted this theme of "telling the story" in her father's work "from parish days to his semi-retirement," and then called on Dietrich Bonhoeffer to "stimulate some thoughts." With that in mind, the above quotation from Bonhoeffer suggested itself. It indicates that with the story goes the song, that the story is embodied in song. To tell the story then is at least in part to sing i*t*.

Although he is neither unaware of it nor interested in denying its importance, I suspect the story in song is not exactly what Fackre has in mind by "telling the story." His work has to do with a careful precision that is its own kind of discourse, its own systematic reflection so needed in the life of the church. The ballad the church sings is likewise *its* own form of discourse. The narrative it voices in song is not so much careful precision as it is ordered but multi-spectral material that lives beneath the systematic reflection. It's the "world-making" of which Walter Brueggemann speaks, the "world of justice, mercy, peace, and compassion . . . created in the imaginative act of liturgy." It's the doxology the "empire tries to silence," the "song that breaks out in newness because Yahweh's power for life will not be contained."[3] The radical newness of freedom inheres in the song given by Yahwe*h*.

Bonhoeffer and Brueggemann point to potent stuff. This is not pious treacle that tries to trade on how we feel. It is not manipulative musical drizzle that summons up a god who fades like the morning mist. This is the Christ hymn of the whole church in heaven and earth that is new every morning whether we feel it or not — the utterances of Miriam and Moses, Mary, Paul and Silas — one great song of praise throughout eternity, whether we know it or not. It began at creation and continues as the song of the Lamb at the heavenly banquet. It "evokes the power of Yahweh [and] the possibility of Israel." "[T]hrough the liturgy" it is about life shaped as "equity, righteousness, and truth," and it "means to 'uncreate' . . . other worlds."[4] It has to do with our very being.

Rarely are Bonhoeffer's and Brueggemann's insights expressed among us. We are more likely to focus on the song in relation to our personal states, not our states in relation to God and the song God gives. Rather, we focus on the song in relation to us as isolated flotsam and jetsam on a sea devoid of meaning and cohesion where equity, righteous-

---

3. Walter Brueggemann, *Israel's Praise: Doxology against Idolatry and Ideology* (Philadelphia: Fortress Press, 1988), pp. 52, 53.

4. Brueggemann, *Israel's Praise*, p. 53.

ness, and truth are meaningless or obliterated. Are there two mutually exclusive views here? Is the song either about us in our isolated bubbles, or is it a delusion? Are Bonhoeffer and Brueggemann proposing a phantom of our imagining that is equally as meaningless, foreign, and misty as the isolated songs of our personal states? Is there anything to sing at all? Are we forever at odds with ourselves and with one another, having no song but a delusion to sing, driven to a perpetual state of war?

In the mercy of God there is another possibility. As the two propositions that head this article suggest, the song of victory is a real song that enters into our pain and sorrow and that is contextualized by the joyful foretaste suggested by the leading tone ti. To see where these lead us, we will begin with the first proposition. We note here, however, that the second one requires getting at the raw material of musical syntax. Ti is a scale degree, one of the pitches from the upward sequence "do, re, mi, fa, sol, la, ti, do." Ti is the "leading tone" of the sequence, the note that leads to the tonic (do) and follows the sixth degree (la).

Even though Bonhoeffer's words, and the songs to which they refer, are fundamentally about victory and joy in what God has done and does, pain and sorrow are not absent from them. The pain of the Egyptians with their clogged chariot wheels driving heavily and trapping them in the sea (Exodus 14) stands for a pain we cannot forget in the sense that we are called to remember and even pray for our enemies. They too have burdens to bear. The Psalms recount other kinds of laments and sorrows. Why, for example, does God forsake even those who know the "story with its promise of singular truth and life" (Psalm 22) and leave them in darkness (Psalm 88)? Or, again, Job speaks for many people with his bitter complaint and groaning at God's absence (Job 23:1-2). There are times in the big story and in all our little stories when we not only mourn in sorrow, but mourn that God is gone and we are lost.

Lest we forget the depth of the societal and systemic abyss we have to contend with, let us recall Mary's *Magnificat*. It, too, is a song of God's victory and of our liberation, but, as Samuel Terrien reminds us, it "predicts in no uncertain terms the eventual end of any civilization that cultivates material pleasure at the expense of an ethic of sharing." The rich industrial states today "devour . . . a third of the [planet's] natural resources. . . . In the imagination of our hearts" we are "lulled by the conceit of [our] technology."[5] Our ingrown conceit also dupes us into amusing ourselves

5. Samuel Terrien, *The Magnificat: Musicians as Biblical Interpreters* (New York: Paulist Press, 1995), p. 52.

to death.[6] But, in Mary's subversively truthful words, "the rich are sent away empty." J. S. Bach knew this and expressed it in his typically astonishing setting of this text. The flutes play parallel thirds up to the last cadence of the piece, but stop on re and fa. The final notes, do and mi, are missing. There is no resolution. "We are left in mid-air. . . . We face the void. Bach [ever the musical exegete] knew the meaning of heaven, but also of hell — nothing."[7] This is what it means to be sent away empty *(inanes),* but fortunately pain, sorrow, lament, nothingness, and emptiness are not the full story — which brings us to the context of joyful foretaste and the leading tone *ti.*

Finality is not our portion in this life. In the words of Hebrews (13:14), set so well by Johannes Brahms, "Denn wir haben hie keinen bleibende Statt" ("Here on earth have we no continuing place"). The best we have is a foretaste of the feast to come. The leading tone (ti) expresses this foretaste. It wants to resolve to the tonic (do). We live on the leading tone, so to speak, just before it resolves, knowing that in God's victory it will resolve and waiting with eager expectation and joyful longing for the resolution. In Susan Cherwien's words, we "remember well the future God has called us to receive."[8] Any cadence where the melody moves from the leading tone to the tonic, from ti to do, will demonstrate this musical trai*t.*

Actually, there is a more telling way to demonstrate it. Staying with Brahms' *German Requiem* for a little longer, consider the fugue at the end of the third chorus where the composer sets Psalm 37:17b, "but the righteous souls are in the hand of God." Just before the fugue the text from Psalm 39:7, "My hope is in Thee," is strung out on an extended dominant (sol),[9] yet another aspect of musical longing that pulls toward the leading tone ti. When the dominant resolves, the fugue sets out resolutely in D major. This is some resolution. Throughout the whole fugue the organ, the double bass, the tuba, the trombone, the contrabassoon, and the timpani all play a low D.[10] This "pedal point," a note that begins and ends as a consonance but runs into dissonance in between, is relentless.

6. See Neil Postman, *Amusing Ourselves to Death: Public Discourse in the Age of Show Business* (New York: Penguin Books, 1985).

7. Terrien, *Magnificat,* p. 54.

8. Susan Palo Cherwien, "Rise, O Church, Like Christ Arisen," in *O Blessed Spring* (Minneapolis: Augsburg Fortress, 1997), p. 109.

9. Johannes Brahms, *Ein Deutsches Requiem,* third movement ("Herr, lehre doch mich"), measures 164-172.

10. Brahms, *Requiem,* third movement, measures 173-208.

Brahms places the low D (do) as an anchor and resting place, a musical way to reflect the text's assurance that the righteous are in the hand of God and that neither grief nor pain will come near them. But the leading tone C sharp in the fugue subject does come near the D. It scrapes very closely and creates considerable dissonance in a longing for resolution that we know will eventually come. Though here but not yet fully here, we "remember the future God has called us to receive" and know the foretaste now will then be feast, banquet, fiesta, lua*u*.

Chasing through this life is not without its pain. The anchor and resting place of God may be secure, but the journey is not all sweetness and light. That may be what Brahms is saying with his music as all sorts of harmonic dissonances push against the tonic (do) pedal point. The most telling of all the dissonances is this: when the leading tone (ti) of the fugue subject scrapes against the tonic (do), it does so on the lengthened first syllable of the words "Gottes Hand." It is precisely in "God's hand" that Brahms fashions this strong dissonance and longing for resolution. What does that mean? We can all make our own suppositions. Here's one. Perhaps the music says that both the victory and the sorrow we experience and sing reside in Go*d*.

Keeping this discussion within Western common practice harmonic bounds has characterized it. That is one way to proceed, but not the only way. There are other ways, Western and non-Western, to exegete texts. There are traditions that may not want to engage in this kind of musical exegesis at all. The way I have gone at the topic does not invalidate the other ways, nor do the other ways invalidate the one I have followed. Telling the story is more multi-valent and luminescent than any single way would suggest. Let us respect the hearty richness of the far*e*.

Remembering that the story is not only sung in large choral works like a Bach *Magnificat* or a Brahms *German Requiem* is another important insight. It is also sung in the hymns and tunes of the faithful, like "O Love, How Deep," where the tune *Deo Gracias* boldly breaks open the text by a strong rhythmic pulse in which the leading tone (ti) is *avoided*. We could start over now and figure out what that might mean. Or we could return to Susan Cherwien's text — "remember well the future God has called us to receive" — and see how Timothy Strand's tune *Surge Ecclesia* sets it. Whatever any of this means or does not mean, it does not require any of the various strata of the song or any of the analytical avenues to sto*p*.

Eventually this topic compels one to conclude what the church always senses but seldom expresses: whatever the musical syntax of our song, however and wherever we sing it, and however we try to understand what it means, if we are faithful we come to recognize that at its center the story it tells is far bigger than our individual stories. To sing the choral literature and hymns of the church is to join the great song of earth and heaven that the body of Christ expresses. Bonhoeffer knew this well and *did* express it. In the quotation which follows, he had in mind "essentially" hymns sung in unison,[11] not choral literature nor even hymns sung in harmony — though he knew a lot about all of that, had a deep appreciation for it, and did not want to be "doctrinaire." We should probably pay more attention to his ideal of unison singing, which has much to commend it, but I would nonetheless want to fold a broader musical syntax of hymns in harmony and choral music into his vision as well. The central affirmation he makes, however, is on target. Bonhoeffer realized the story the church sings each day is always as fresh as, but never evaporates like, the morning de*w*.

> *It is the voice of the church that is heard in singing together. It is not I who sing, but the Church. However, as a member of the Church, I may share in its song. Thus all true singing together must serve to widen our spiritual horizon. It must enable us to recognize our small community as a member of the great Christian church [Christenheit] on earth and must help us willingly and joyfully to take our place in the song of the church with our singing, be it feeble or good.*[12]

11. See Bonhoeffer, *Life Together,* pp. 66-68.
12. Bonhoeffer, *Life Together,* p. 68.

PART II

THE MISSION
OF THE STORY TODAY

Christian Theology for the Future of Humankind

Jürgen Moltmann

The great event of the twentieth century was the end of the "Christian world," the Christian century, the Christian empires and the Christian nations, and the beginning of the rebirth of the church of Christ, an independent and resisting community, a church with a universal mission, a church of the all-embracing Hope in the coming kingdom of God and God's righteousness.

Post-war Christianity

The Christian nations of Europe destroyed themselves in the two world wars. World War I is rightly called "the fundamental catastrophe" of the Christian world. It was, on the other hand, the beginning of the liberation of the colonized peoples in Asia, Africa, and Latin America. The European superpowers were just on the way to divide between themselves China, the last independent nation, in the so-called Boxer Rebellion, when their enmity against each other led to their downfall. With World War I, the political "christianization" of the world ended.

The Christian world then internally disintegrated in the following decades: the unity of "throne and altar," of "church and culture," and of "faith and public morality" was dissolved. The confessionally unified states disappeared. There are no more strictly Catholic or Protestant nations. Only in the Balkans are there still one or two "Orthodox nations" (Serbia, Rumania). Governments were secularized and Catholic, Protestant, and Orthodox people learned to live together in peace. The long "confessional age" was over. Today we live in Europe in multireligious societies and religiously neutral states. This is, in fact, the end of the 1700-year-old "Constantinian age," the Christian empire or the Christian civilization. In every multireligious society, Christians are or will become minorities. But they are a universal minority in the world, two of six billions. What now are the consequences for the Christian church and theology?

For European theology, the locus theologicus, the *Sitz im Leben,* has changed and is still changing dramatically. Our context, our kairos, and our community are no longer determined by what was called the Christian world, "Christendom," or *Cristiandad.* The Christian religion is no longer the civil religion of our society or the political religion of our nation, not even in the United States, the "one nation under God." The Christian churches are now one religious community among others in this multireligious society, or one religious community in an otherwise secular, atheistic society.

Shall Christian theology retreat into the circle of believers and become "Church Dogmatics," or shall Christian theology try to present itself in public as "public theology"? Shall the church give up its universal claim of the gospel and become an introverted, self-related religious group? Or is there something beyond these poor alternatives: a church with a universal mission and a missionary theology, rooted in the risen Christ and aiming at Christ's universal coming?

Ecumenical Solidarity

The first step in this direction is ecumenical theology. We have left behind the confessional age and we are entering the ecumenical age of Christianity. It is astonishing: when the Christian world came to an end, the ecumenical movement began. In a multireligious or atheistic society, only whether you are a Christian or not is important. The denominational qualifications of Lutheran, Reformed, Baptist, Catholic, etc. are less and less important. This Christian diversity should not die, because our differences are also our treasures. But they no longer divide us at the Lord's Table and in the Christian community. In a "reconciled diversity" we can learn from each other and make our differences productive. Being Christian is the one necessary thing. In the church struggle in Germany, in painful persecutions in the Archipelagus Gulag in Russia, and in the cultural revolution in China, Christians have learned this lesson: To be or not to be a Christian: that is the question.

A theology learning this lesson can no longer maintain the old confessional traditions as Lutheran Theology, Methodist Theology, Roman-Catholic Theology, Orthodox Theology, or whatever, but must become the one Christian Theology. Up to now, popes were quoting only popes, Catholic theologians only Catholics, Lutherans only Lutherans and so on; each one stayed in his confessional family. With the new ecumenical hermeneutics, we read books from Catholic, Orthodox, Methodist, and Reformed theologians and interpret their truths as fragments of the one Truth of a common Christian Theology. We no longer analyze what divides us, but create what brings us together out of our differences.

Ecumenical solidarity will become more and more important for the Christian minorities in our different countries. Especially in times of oppression and persecution, this worldwide ecumenical solidarity is simply life saving and necessary for resisting Christian churches and communities. Keeping Christian solidarity with oppressed churches in other countries can become stronger than the loyalty to one's own nation, class, race, and sex. I am, first of all, a Christian, and, secondly, a Christian in Germany. Germany is the place where I live, but my life is determined by Christ. This simple insight was the reason why our church changed its name after 1945 from "The German Evangelical Church" to "The Evangelical Church in Germany." We are first of all members of the worldwide community of Christians, and then we seek to do the best for the countries and cities in which we exist.

We are doing theology in our faculties and seminaries not only for our own denomination, but also for ecumenical Christianity; not only for our own regional churches in our countries, but also for the World Christianity. Up to now, in the theological faculties of Germany, the horizon for doing theology was only our own theological tradition. Lectures and seminars dealt with Karl Barth, Schleiermacher, Luther, Calvin, Thomas Aquinas, Augustine, Athanasius, and the apostle Paul. French, British, American, Latin American, African, and Asian theology were not in our eyes. Our faculty members simply didn't know anything about theologies beyond our borders, or put this task in the hands of specialists for Eastern theology, or African, or Asian theology. Those of you who have studied at European theological faculties know about our limitations. Whenever a new universal claim emerges, we call a specialist and give him or her an institute — and go on unchanged as before. We need you to overcome our dilemma. Christian theology in Asia must become better than Christian theology in Europe, so that as many students go from us to you, as from you to us.

99

Church Structural Unity

I think this new millennium will become for us the Millennium of the Holy Spirit. We shall experience in a new way the energies of the Spirit and, more than before, the fellowship of the Holy Spirit. With this statement I do not just praise the Pentecostal movements and the new Charismatic communities; I mean much more. Let me illustrate it with the structures of the church known to us up to now.

The unity of the church was legitimated by the ancient hierarchical church with the monarchy of God the Father. Beginning with Ignatius of Antioch and still working in the Roman Catholic church today is the "monarchical episcopate": One God — one Christ — one bishop — one church. This is a hierarchical pyramid from God the Father down to *Il Papa* in Rome, an authoritarian structure secured by the infallibility of the pope. In this hierarchical church, there was and is a discrepancy between the priests and the laity: the first are called "spirituals" *(Geistliche);* and the second the "people of the church" *(Kirchenvolk).* Up to Vatican II, only the ordained hierarchy was understood as the church. After Vatican II, the "people-of-God-concept" won ground so that priests and lay people together are the "people of God." But there is no "priesthood of all believers" which includes the special priesthood of the ordained. In order to combine hierarchy and community, Roman Catholic theologians speak of a *communio hierarchica,* a hierarchical community.

Protestant churches have since the Reformation introduced another principle of the unity of the church: Christocentrism. Christ the Son of God is the unity of the church, and Christ is the "first-born" of many brothers and sisters (Rom. 8:29). The Christian church is therefore "the community of brothers and sisters, in which Jesus Christ acts presently through word and sacrament in the power of the Holy Spirit," as the Barmen Theological Declaration, Thesis III, of our confessing church in Germany says. The community with Christ makes this church the brotherly and sisterly fellowship. In this community with the incarnate Son of God, we are all priests and kings. A general priesthood of all believers dissolves the discrepancy between priests and the laity. All of them are filled with the Holy Spirit. And there is also a universal theologianship of all believers. Anyone who believes and tries to understand is a theologian. In Christ, the first-born of many brothers and sisters in the unity of the church, we find an egalitarian community. As the Apostle said in Gal. 3:28: "They are all one in Christ Jesus." The Spirit of mutual trust replaces the Spirit of hierarchical obedience. The authoritarian structure is replaced by the covenant of brothers and sisters. This is also the community experience in Catholic-based communities in Latin America.

Today we discover in different churches and countries the charismatic community. Here, everyone is accepted as he or she is, and engaged with his or her gifts and energies. "There are diversities of gifts but the same Spirit" (1 Cor. 12:4). And "the manifestation of the Spirit is given to everyone to profit with all" (12:7). The life-giving Spirit of God is the source of the energies of life and gives everyone his or her own. In the colorful diversity of gifts and tasks the unity is found in the one Spirit, as Paul summarizes:

> There are diversities of gifts, but the same Spirit.
> There are differences of administrations, but the same Lord.
> There are diversities of operations, but the same God,
> who works all in all.
>
> (1 Cor. 12:4-6)

This is to say that the unity of the charismatic community lies in the one and same Spirit. If I understand this correctly, this is a trinitarian foundation of the unity in diversity of gifts, tasks, services, and energies in "the same Spirit, the same Lord, the same God."

The hierarchical church guards the difference between priesthood and laity. In the brotherly/sisterly community, they are all equals. In the charismatic community, they are all experts and taken seriously as experts of their own lives and their own contributions to the community. They are a community of friends, bound together by friendship, i.e., love and respect.

We may say that after the hierarchical church of God the Father, we learned the brotherly church of God the Son, and now we are discovering the charismatic church of God the Spirit. It is in this sense that we may call the next, the third Christian millennium, the "Millennium of the Holy Spirit." We must, however, keep in mind that the church is not united by the monarchy of the Father, nor the brotherhood of the Son, nor the superabundant life of the Holy Spirit alone; but by the trinitarian unity of the Father, the Son, and the Holy Spirit. Remember the high-priestly prayer of Jesus in John 17:21: "That they all may be one, as your Father in me, and I in you, that they also may be one in us." We call the trinitarian unity of the trinitarian persons *Perichoresis:* mutual indwelling and embracing. The unity of the church shall correspond to this perichoretic unity of the triune God and shall furthermore share and dwell in the open space of the Holy Trinity. Wherever love forms the unity of the Christian community, there God lives in us and we live in God (1 John 4:16). This is the mystical dimension of the Christian and charismatic community: Here God dwells among us.

Eschatology

At the beginning of the new millennium, Christians are becoming aware of their own future-oriented eschatological expectation. Some apocalyptics count again the "biblical chronology" with the result that, after "2000 years chaos — 2000 years Torah — 2000 years the Messiah," the course of world history must soon come to an end. They expect catastrophies, as I found on a poster in Jamaica some years ago: "Behold, the Lord cometh! Expect earthquakes, famine, diseases, etc." Apocalyptically this is correct, but is it Christian? In Christian faith we see the future in the light of the resurrected Christ: "The kingdom of heaven is open, hell is closed, life is triumphing, death is overcome. Trust in this great promise of God is the only possibility, mistrust is the excluded possibility."[1]

What we hope for the future always determines how we understand ourselves in the present and what we are doing here and now. If there is positive hope, we invest in the future. If there is no hope anymore, we incur debts. The divine future of the church is the kingdom of God and its righteousness. Therefore, we understand the present church as promise and anticipation of the coming kingdom, and the righteousness of God under the present conditions of history. Historical Christendom has always been a strange mixture of church and the anticipated kingdom in terms of the "thousand-years reign" of Christ, where the saints will rule and judge together with Christ the peoples of the world (Rev. 20). The church was then dissolved into the religion of the Christian world, and the Christian world became the political Body of Christ. When this "impossible dream" is over now, the church can become the church again and will, as such, proclaim the coming kingdom of God to the society in a critical and prophetic way. What corresponds to the righteousness of God will get our support; what contradicts it must be criticized. As a confessing minority in multireligious societies, the church can proclaim God's kingdom much better than as a majority, which must express the ruling opinions of the society, as was the case in Christian nations, especially

1. Karl Barth, *Church Dogmatics* (Edinburgh: T & T Clark, 1975-), II/2, p. 358.

during war. If the church is the bearer of hope for the kingdom of God, the church will exist there, where Jesus proclaimed and executed the kingdom: with the poor, the sick, the downtrodden and heavy-laden, those who in our societies live in the shadow. As the resurrection happened to the crucified One, the kingdom enters into this world from below, turning our value systems upside down: The last will be the first.

Bios and Zōē

For the church as a minority with a universal mission, it is the mission of Christ that combines the particular with the universal without giving up the universal in favor of the particular or the particular in favor of the universal. The Christian mission embraces evangelism and peace making, healing and comforting. This mission is grounded in the *Missio Dei* and directed towards the coming kingdom of God and its righteousness. It is not the globalization of a Christian empire, as we have had it in a long past. It is not the globalization of the given church, as was done in the *plantatio ecclesiae* idea, and which has spread Christian denominationalism around the world. Grounded in the *Missio Dei,* Christian mission participates in the messianic work of Jesus (Matt. 11:5 and 10:7-8: "Heal the sick, raise the dead, cleanse lepers, cast out demons and preach that the kingdom of God is at hand"). Grounded in the *Missio Dei,* Christian mission takes place in the "outpouring of the Holy Spirit on all flesh." God sends the life-giving Spirit before the end of this world as the beginning of his eternal kingdom. The Gospel of John can say very simply: what God has brought into this world through Christ is life: healed, accepted, shared, entirely lived; in short, eternal life (cf. also 1 John 1:1-3 about "the life that has appeared").

This life is not just *bios,* but *zōē,* to use the two Greek words for life. What is "poured out on all flesh" are the life-awakening "energies of the Holy Spirit." Therefore, God's Spirit is called *fons vitae* and *vita vivificans.* These energies of life are the charismata. They are not "super-natural," as some who are fascinated by the miraculous think. They are "the powers of the age to come," as Hebrew 6:5 says: anticipations of the new world of God, life — power from the power of resurrection from death to life. In short: the mission of Jesus and the mission of the Spirit are nothing other than creative movements of life; movements of healing; movements of faith awakening; movements of liberation for justice and peace. Jesus did not bring a new religion into the world in order to enlarge our multireligious societies. What

Jesus brought was new life. The new vitality of love and the rebirth to a living hope in God's coming, whatever may happen to this world.

Millennial Ecology

Christian mission serves life looking toward the End. But what is the "End"? In 1992, the American Baptist Church invited me to a National Evangelism Convocation. Its theme, and then mine as well, was: "All Things New: Invited to God's Future." This is, indeed, the eschatology of the Christian mission. The last word of God is Rev. 21:5: "Behold, I make all things new." God's last word is not the final judgment, but the new creation of "all things." The last judgment is penultimate. It serves to establish the judging and saving righteousness of God for all and everything. There can be new creation only on the foundation of God's universal justice. Just as world history did not begin with the fall of sin, but with the original blessing of the creation, so the end will not be the final judgment, but the eternal bliss of the new creation in glory.

In this sense we say that Christianity is in origin and by its very essence a missionary religion of life. If this is essentially true, Christianity cannot end in a family religion, a tribal religion, a white religion, a male religion. Consequently, Christianity is not dependent on family ties, tribal identity, or on male clubs. With its life-awakening message it reaches out for the faith of each and every human being. Family, tribe, a nation, or whatever forms the reality of the Christian community takes, can be used as vehicles for its mission. In itself Christian mission is reaching out as far as the Coming God: "Behold, I make all things new." Its internal power is this all-embracing Hope.

Christian Mission in an Age of the Globalization of Capitalism

In the time of the "Cold War" and the division of the world into East and West blocs, Christianity was able to maintain its ecumenical community and, by doing this, contribute to peace in the one world. The World Council of Churches in Geneva kept the churches in West and East together. Ecumenical Christianity claimed and promoted justice in the North-South conflict between the rich and the poor nations, and was a strong power for overcoming the racist apartheid regime in South Africa.

But how can Christianity witness to the righteousness of God and God's future in an age of globalized competition and capitalism? Well, first of all we must see that capitalism is in itself a utopian movement, creating ever new needs and greeds. Capitalism knows only growing or shrinking; it can sustain no equilibrium, no peace. The goal of the present world economy is the domination of nature and all natural resources by always bigger and fewer "global players." The driving force is the utopian thought that man can do and have whatever he wants.

The goal of an ecumenical Christianity is, as the name "ecumene" says, the habitability of the earth. So that the earth may be a dwelling place for humankind and all earthly creatures, we must stop the destruction of nature and start with the healing of nature. Only a reconciliation between human culture and the nature of the earth can bring peace, a certain equilibrium, and a "sustainable development." For this we must not only respect human rights, but also the rights of nature, and of our fellow creatures. We must give up the power-dream of modernity and the modern God-complex — that we humans can, by the use of science and technology, become "masters and owners of nature," as René Descartes postulated.[2] Anyone who is part of nature and dependent on nature cannot become the lord of nature, without destroying nature and himself. If we want the earth as home for us, our descendants, and all living beings (Genesis 9), we must accept our finitude, vulnerability, and mortality and become human again, and cease to play proud and unhappy mini-gods on earth.

I believe that after two centuries of economy, we must enter with the next century or millennium into the ecological age, if we want to survive and want life for our future generations. In the ecological age, the earth, until now the silent partner of everything humans are doing in politics, economy, lifestyle, and religion, must be respected more and more. World politics should change into "earth politics," world economy into "earth economy," specialized natural sciences into integrated earth-sciences, all in order to understand our earth-organism better. And, last but not least, what we have called world religions must change into the religions of the one earth. Only a religion that respects and sanctifies the earth can in the future be called a "world" religion. Biblical religions may rediscover the "solemn Sabbat of the Earth" in the Old Testament and the cosmic Christology in the New Testament, in order to serve the healing of life and of the life-giving earth.

2. René Descartes, *On Method*.

Christology and the
Missionary Crisis of the Church

Carl E. Braaten

Dominus Iesus is the title of a document issued in 2000 A.D. by the Vatican Congregation for the Doctrine of the Faith, signed by Cardinal Ratzinger. It is a timely affirmation of the uniqueness of Christ and the universal validity of his gospel. The declaration condemns the views of the multicultural relativists and religious pluralists, who teach that the Christian churches are promoting religious imperialism when they propagate a Christ-centered faith to people of other religions. Many profess to be embarrassed by the missionary movement of recent centuries, which succeeded in bringing the gospel to every continent, country, and culture throughout the world.

Gabriel Fackre and I have for a long time shared a concern, not only for the integrity of the gospel, but for its universal significance. He has applauded the intention of *Dominus Iesus*,[1] and in this brief essay I want to add my wholehearted support. Today, many pastors and theologians are reluctant to affirm the uniqueness and significance of Jesus Christ as Lord and Savior, not only for those who already believe, but also for the billions who do not yet believe. The fundamental theological question is "What do we think of Christ?" So many have retreated to the kind of nineteenth-century liberalism that treats Jesus of Nazareth as an exemplary pious Jew looking forward to the kingdom of God. This is what is going on with the so-called "third quest" of the historical Jesus of the Jesus Seminar. For these scholars, Jesus is not the One the apostles declared him to

---

1. Gabriel Fackre, "*Dominus Iesus*: A Reformed Response," *Pro Ecclesia* 10 (Winter 2001): 13-15.

be, the only begotten Son of God, born of the Father before all time. He is not very God of very God, as the Nicene Creed of the ancient church confesses. Instead, he is depicted as a kind of second Moses, one who perhaps gives us the right kind of ethics, or one who models a cool lifestyle, merely a good example to follow.

Dietrich Bonhoeffer posed the question, pondering the ultimate concerns while sitting in a Nazi prison cell, "Who is Jesus Christ for us today?" Is he only a human being who sets for us a good example, or is he the crucified and risen Messiah who constitutes good news for humanity and the world? The Christian faith has always centered on the person of Jesus of Nazareth, not merely as a pious Jew modeling the good life, but as the living Christ bringing the presence of God into our life and history.

The reason that the issue of Christology is so important in the life and mission of the church, is that Jesus Christ is the sum and substance of the gospel, and the gospel is the only unique gift the church has to offer the world. As Christians, we do not offer a better political ideology, a better economic system, or a more sophisticated philosophy. We do not have better solutions to the problems of overpopulation, environmental pollution, world hunger, global warming, illegal aliens, and so forth, though we must always participate as good citizens in the efforts to find provisional solutions to these problems. We have a gospel to tell to the nations in Jesus' name. And that's it. In Mark's Gospel, people were buzzing about Jesus' true identity: "Who is this one who teaches with authority? Who is this one who forgives sins? Who then is this one, that even the wind and the sea obey him?" If we as latter-day Christians answer this question of the true identity and meaning of Jesus correctly, we will have a sufficient reason to get back into the business of mission. For his mission is just the sap that flows from the tree of faith.

Only the high Christology of the church, the confession of Christ of the ancient fathers and doctors of the church, will keep the world mission of the church on track. This confession is anchored in the Easter witness of the disciples. On account of the resurrection of Jesus, God and Jesus are spoken of in the same breath. Jesus is none less than the true presence of God in our midst — Immanuel — God in the flesh and blood of a human being. Jesus is the Savior because he will save the people of God from their sins, something only God can do. Jesus is the Lord because God has exalted him above all others. In the witness of the Bible and the ancient church, Jesus is depicted not as a son of God, but as the only begotten Son of God; not as a savior, one among many, but as the one and only Savior of the world. Jesus is absolutely unique, one of a kind, in whose name alone there is salvation, before whom every knee will bow and every tongue confess that Jesus is Lord to the glory of God the Father. Take this away and the whole missionary movement goes flat. And how much flatter can it get than it is at the present time in our Western mainline denominations?

It has been my privilege to listen to the personal testimonies of individuals who have converted to the Christian faith from many diverse cultures and religions. I have listened to former Jews and Muslims and Hindus and Buddhists tell their stories of coming to faith in Jesus Christ as their personal Lord and Savior. Some of these came from Asia and Africa to study for advanced theological degrees at the Lutheran School of Theology in Chicago, where I taught for thirty years. Many of these foreign students have paid a high price for their faith. They have been ostracized from their families. They have borne the brunt of the criticism that they have allowed themselves to become pawns of Western colonialism and imperialism. Yet, they are totally committed to Christ and the gospel. They have personally experienced the difference Christ makes in their lives and are bold to witness to the truth. But many have told me that they experienced the shock of their lives when they came to the United States, supposedly a Christian country, only to discover that many American Christians, respected professors among them, teaching at divinity schools and seminaries of the church, whose books they had read and admired, admit they simply do not believe in converting people from one religion to another.

They hear, to their amazement, that many American theologians and church leaders have bought into the pluralistic theory that regards all religions as more or less equal, and holds that the same liberation and salvation can be experienced in all the different religions of the world. So what's the point of the Christian mission? The pluralists say that its sole purpose is to make Buddhists better Buddhists, Hindus better Hindus, and so forth. So these new converts have had to ask themselves, why become a Christian at such high personal cost? If there is equal salvation in being a Buddhist, why choose to be baptized? Their answer is clear. In Christ they have found forgiveness of sins, the hope of eternal life, and the peace that surpasses understanding.

We can do no better than to imitate the first Christians. They could not keep secret the reality of their new life in Christ. The Spirit of Pentecost came upon them like a gale of wind and flames of fire and virtually blew them into a pluralistic world of Jews and Greeks and Romans and Persians, and there they tangled with a myriad of philosophies, mythologies, ideologies, and mysteries. We should again be like the earliest evangelists and missionaries who took their show on the road — yet not their show, but God's drama of salvation. So they preached and witnessed to Jesus as the turning point of the ages, as the fulcrum of history, as the One whose coming had split all time in two, into B.C. and A.D.

Every epoch has found a way to salute and celebrate the absolute significance of Christ's coming in history. In the second century, Jesus was preached as the light of the Gentiles. To the Romans, Jesus was preached as the king of kings, giving people a choice to worship Christ or Caesar. In the third century, Jesus was proclaimed as the universal Logos, who the Greek philosophers taught was the very reason and meaning of the universe. To the Jews and the Greeks and the Romans, the early Christians confessed that their faith was not in a set of laws, ideals, or beliefs, but in a Person. Christianity is not an "ism," like Platonism or Marxism or socialism or capitalism. It is not essentially an abstract system of categories and concepts that can be detached from the person of the founder. In the Christian faith, the person of Jesus is the heart of the matter, the secret that makes the message of salvation work for all who believe in his name — the name that is above every name.

The great tradition is so rich with testimonies to the supreme significance of Jesus. Devotion to Jesus as the Christ of God has inspired the art and architecture of the Byzantine culture in the East, as well as the Gothic and Baroque cultures of the West. Poets and monks and mystics and prophets and reformers: all these have grasped the mystery of Christ in their own ways. What is the special way in which we can grasp the mystery of Christ, the identity and meaning of Jesus, in our own time and history? There can be no doubt about it. The leitmotif of this century is the search for freedom and liberation. All the different kinds of liberation movements bear witness to that. These movements are signs of the tremendous oppression and bondage people have suffered in our time: the world wars, the severe depressions, the Holocaust, the gulags, genocide, ethnic cleansing, massive poverty and hunger, and totalitarian dictatorships. Liberation is the longing of our era.

In Paul's letter to the Galatians, we find the *Magna Carta* of Christian freedom: "For there is no Jew or Greek, there is neither slave nor free, there is neither male nor female; for you are all one in Christ Jesus. . . . For freedom Christ has set us free; stand fast therefore, and do not submit again to the yoke of slavery." Christians look to Jesus as the great source of the freedom for which they long.

But just at this point we need to be extremely careful, lest we try to recruit Jesus to sponsor our own self-chosen definition of freedom and liberation. Does it mean pro-choice? Does it mean choosing our own lifestyle? There are pseudo-liberation movements, which have nothing to do with the freedom that Jesus was sent by his Father on a mission to deliver. While many in our generation are longing for liberation, some insist on defining liberation as license and licentiousness, the right of self-fulfillment and self-gratification.

We must let Jesus define for us the kind of liberation that God had in mind through his life and ministry, his death and resurrection, his ascension and the promise of his return in glory. Jesus said, "My kingdom is not of this world." Real liberation is deliverance from the powers of sin, death, and the devil. Real liberation is what we receive in baptism, forgiveness of sins, life and salvation.

However, the liberation that we receive from God through Christ has far-reaching implications for life in all its daily aspects. It cannot be confined to the private sphere of life or matters of personal piety. Jesus' ministry of the kingdom showed signs of breaking into every dimension of life, healing physical illness, exorcising demons, feeding the hungry, speaking out against corrupt public officials and religious authorities, and caring for the weakest people in his society.

Correspondingly, the church is to be a Christ-like medium of the kingdom of God in this world, bringing its mission to the frontlines of human struggle. In the present context of the church's global mission, the gospel includes promises that point to both personal salvation in the vertical dimension and human liberation on the horizontal plane. The church is unfaithful to the gospel whenever it separates believing in Christ from following Jesus in Samaritan-like service to the world. The promises of the kingdom embodied in Jesus the Christ address individuals in their deepest struggles for meaning and fulfillment, but they also invite the church to be engaged in the widest range of issues in the social, political, and economic realms. A church with a holistic sense of mission will join its efforts at world evangelization with a sense of solidarity in the struggles of people against all systems of domination, oppression, and exploitation.

Faithfulness in mission means taking up the cross of discipleship and following our leader Jesus into suffering, and even martyrdom. Mission that conforms to Christ takes the form of the cross. Luther placed the cross and suffering among the essential marks of the church, unavoidable in being faithful witnesses to the gospel. Mission under the sign of the cross means announcing the good news of God's acceptance of sinners, and, at the same time, public advocacy for the poor and oppressed, for peace and justice in the situations of hostility and brutality.

In Jesus Christ, we witness the total love of God that seeks justice for the poor as well as justification for sinners, neither one at the expense of the other. When the Messiah comes, the signs of the kingdom are that "the blind see, the lame walk, lepers are cleansed, the deaf hear, the dead are raised up, and the poor are hearing good news." That is holistic mission — responding to the needs of the poor who cry out for justice and freedom, and of sinners who long for peace with God and clean hearts.

The world is so large, and the needs are so great, that the list of all that we should do is enormously long, and we run the risk of becoming confused, of losing a sense of proportionality. We are not utopians. We know that the final victory of God over all the powers of sin and evil will come only at the end of time and history. In the best of times, we will still encounter physical death, disease, destruction, and deprivation, and all attempts to find solutions will remain only partial and temporary. Nevertheless, our vision of the Christian mission covers a spectrum of issues and challenges as great as the suffering body of humanity. We are not called to be successful in mission: we are called to be faithful.

But we run a grave danger that when we cast the net of global mission so broadly as to encompass all dimensions of human existence — and I wouldn't for a minute want to ignore any one of them — we still run the risk of being like Martha, "distracted by many things," so that we neglect Mary's concern for the "one thing needful." What is that? Evangelism is that one thing needful: it constitutes the heart of the mission task, the engine that drives the whole enterprise. The heart is not the only organ of the body, but when it stops pumping, the entire body quits moving. Holistic mission does not mean leveling everything down to the same size. Our priority in mission must always be evangelism, pumping living blood into all the other organs and members of the body.

The current concept of mission is undergoing a great inflation; every agency and institution must have a mission statement. The danger is great that evangelism will be buried in an avalanche of church activism. The occupational hazard of *talking about* rather than *being about* the evangelistic task strikes the church at its most vulnerable center. There are many non-Christian people and institutions working on all possible frontiers of mission, except evangelism. Only a believing church can bear witness to Christ. No other agency in the world can do it, no government, business, or the entertainment industry. Only believing Christian people will be martyrs for Christ's sake and the gospel's. Yet progressively, we have decreased our total commitment of resources to that one thing needful, that one thing that only the church can do — the task of evangelizing.

Many seem to take the attitude that the basic evangelistic task has already been accomplished with the establishment of local churches on every continent. The thinking is, we'll take care of our continent, they'll take care of theirs. The responsibility for evangelism is primarily the responsibility of the local churches in their contextual setting. True. But this happens to be the old Protestant scholastic view of missions, before the rise of the modern missionary movement with the Pietists in Halle, Germany.

In 1651, the theological faculty of Wittenberg University issued a judgment that the apostles had already taken the gospel to all the nations. If any particular people failed to respond, they deserve to be forgotten. To hell with them. Others are saying now, well, of course, it is our responsibility as the church to be engaged in proclaiming the gospel to the unevangelized mega-populations of the world, but this is not a good time for Americans and Westerners in general to go abroad as missionaries. We carry too much baggage from our colonialist and imperialist past. But consider the absurd irony in the fact that we have no compunctions at all in exporting our weapons systems, decadent music and entertainment, technology and scientific culture to every corner of the world, but we think that due respect for people of other religions and cultures requires us to refrain from offering the gospel of Jesus Christ to the unevangelized parts of the world. Where does all this fake humility come from? The source is rank unbelief. We believe strongly in the potential benefits of the information superhighway, but we seem to have lost confidence in the power of the Supername of Jesus to save, the name that is above all names.

We cannot accept a pluralistic theory of religions in which the gospel of Christ is relativized to be on a par with all other religions on the face of the earth. The belief in the absolute supremacy of Christ in a world of competing religious claims is not a function of cultural arrogance; it is an immediate implication of the biblical-Christian gospel of Jesus Christ as God and Savior.

In this presentation, I have addressed the question of the identity and meaning of Jesus Christ and the church's call to global mission. We could be easily discouraged by the magnitude of the tasks. There are gloomy predictions that Christianity is rapidly becoming a minority religion, and the other isms will sweep us off the face of the earth: secularism, atheism, another religion like Islam, or what have you. But we have the promise that the Holy Spirit will lead the church into the fullness of truth and that the gates of hell will not prevail against her.

Christ and Other Faiths in the World

Max L. Stackhouse

For many of the years that I taught at Andover Newton Theological School, Gabe Fackre and Mark Heim were among my closest companions in theological reflection. The relative priority of Trinity or Christology and the relationship of Christian thought to social and ethical issues were among the central issues of discussion. Now, both Gabe and Mark have published major books on these topics, and I am working on one as well. And we each have also turned to treat the non-Christian religions in various ways, an area that we discussed together too little. I think particularly of Gabe's *What of Those Who Have Never Heard?* written with Ronald Nash and John Sanders, and Mark's *Salvations* written in critical dialogue with Paul Knitter, John Hick, and Wilfred Cantwell Smith. This is an issue that also concerns me greatly, given my present research, and I use this opportunity of paying tribute to Gabe to renew our trilateral dialogue.

My contribution grows from an involvement in a fascinating research project on *God and Globalization*. Globalization is the dynamic that is shaping the future of us all and forcing us to think in new ways about our relationship to those of other faiths. It is, after all, not only about economics and spreading capitalism, as some seem to think. These are obviously involved, but they are themselves brought about by communications, transportation, international politics, and a host of changes in education, science, technology, law, and medicine. Together, these are laying the material foundations for a new global civilization that will have many cultures, many peoples, and many faiths within it. This whole cluster of processes is deeply influenced by historic Christianity, which stamped the culture, and which generated the present globalizing forces.

This is not at all strange, if you think about it; for it surely did not grow out of the cultures born of Tribalism, Hinduism, Buddhism, Confucianism, Islam, or any other religion.

This is one of the things that has become clear to our research team: the pressures toward globalization have come from several sources — but, at root, also from Christianity itself. This faith is not a stay-at-home-and-say-your-prayers religion; it is a get-out-there-and-convert-the-world religion. It does not say that people are born into an ethnic, national, or cultural identity that has a religious component that belongs only to it. It says, as Paul writes, "we can become what we are not." Not only has Christ's commission to "go, . . . make disciples of all nations," at the end of Matthew's Gospel made this faith a missionizing one from the very beginning, but Paul set the pattern when he traveled to many cities of the ancient world. That is how he got to Athens, where he was preaching Christ in the midst of monuments to other deities. Others later went to Slavic, Germanic, or African peoples, and still others, even later, to India or China. Many were converted, and the faith continues to spread around the world. However, it has not spread rapidly where other faiths are strong and where they have helped to form complex civilizations.

I do not refer only to the fact that only a minority of Jews converted. Christians have, in principle, always had a special relationship to the Jews, too often betrayed in history, but now largely understood by Christians to be a brotherhood and sisterhood as two parts of God's one covenant with the people of God, properly expanded and fundamentally renewed, Christians believe, in Christ. More striking is the fact that, in the East, very few Confucians ever converted, although after its disestablishment by Maoism, it is growing rapidly in the area. Yet, in India, while Hinduism spread throughout the subcontinent over many centuries, less than three percent have become Christian since this new faith was introduced at least fifteen hundred years ago. Buddhism, developed as a faith five centuries before Christ, spread into many parts of South East Asia, and, blending with Confucianism and Tao in China, with Shinto in Japan, and Shamanism in Korea, developed a tradition that was quite resistant to Christianity. And Islam, born as a faith six centuries after Christ, and claiming a revelation that superseded Christ, spread throughout the Mid-East and then from West Africa to southern Russia and east to Indonesia, conquering some areas and peoples that had become Christian. What are we to make of such matters?

Today, all these traditions have spread to America. People from these traditions are in our schools, in our communities, and sometimes in our families. People we know, many in our churches, are attracted to them, or parts of them. Some like Indian Yoga, or Japanese poetry, Sufi meditation, African drums, or Chinese acupuncture — all connected to distinct spiritual traditions. Christians are often also repelled by these traditions, or parts of them. They can't stand tribalist solidarities that breed ethnocentrism and racism at home or abroad, the Hindu caste system, the Islamic treatment of women, Confucian deference to imperial authority. A friend of mine recently visited a Buddhist temple. He liked its beauty and spare simplicity, he said, but he also said that devotees seemed like survivors in lifeboats, trying to drown their thirst by drinking salt water. I must say that I partly sympathize; in my research and lecturing travels related to the globalization project, I must admit that I have been troubled by the corruption, exploitation, and closed-mindedness of cultures produced by these religions. Of course, it is today bad form to criticize other faiths or cultures. The danger of arrogance is ever present to be sure; but so is timidity when truth and justice are at stake. And issues of truth and justice are at least as much at stake in societies stamped by non-Christian religions as in the West, and it is dishonest and unjust not to say so.

Of course, we should be all sensitive to the importance of tolerance. We know the terror of religious wars and conflicts, and we are well aware of the fact that Christians have sometimes been no less imperialistic, crude, and cruel, as have the non-Christian religions. Moreover, we ought not to hate these people, and a Christian-influenced culture ought to make it safe for them and for their forms of worship. We want our children and our laws to accept others and to respect their faiths, even if we do not agree with them. But, as a result, many are unsure how to remain true to our faith in the face of other faiths. How can we have real pluralism and simultaneous claims about what is true for all?

Here, then, is a key question: In a global era, when we increasingly live in proximity to the other religions, how are we to think about the relation of Christ to the other faiths? There are many possibilities. We can gather in our churches and say our prayers, while others gather in their synagogues, temples, or meditation groups to do their thing and let neither our faith nor theirs make any difference in our public lives together. Secularists love this possibility: hide the faith under the bushel of civility, and remove faith issues from claims about truth — leave that to science. Or we can respect the sincerity of their faith, while doubting its truth. After all, we don't really think that Krishna or Buddha is the true Lord, that Master Kung (Confucius) is the true Master, or that Mohammed is the final and truest prophet. But most of us would not want to say this out loud. Again, we hide what we believe. Who would say to non-Christian neighbors with whom we do business, vote, live in our communities, and work in our office, shop, or factory that "there is salvation in no one else (than Jesus Christ)," as we read in the Bible? Isn't it impolite, even arrogant to say to them what we find in another text: "every knee shall bow and every tongue confess that Jesus Christ is Lord"?

Another approach, of course, is that we could recognize that to be human means to be religious, but also recognize that for all sorts of historical and cultural reasons, or by election, or by some combination of these, we ended up in the church and not in one of those other groups. We might even form an appreciation of people's quests for God and ultimate meaning, or even develop a pity for people who say they have no need of religion. Are they not like those who are tone-deaf or color-blind or frigid — incapable of a range of experience that makes life whole? We could also pray forgiveness for those Christians who have damaged the capacity of other people to turn to Christ or to trust the church because of the way it represented Christianity in their experience. Or, we might want to claim, as I would, that the drive to find God and the most compelling articulation of the nature and character of God's truth and justice are best accounted for by Christian theology. However, we have to recognize that it is an argument that has not convinced everyone, and that, if we hold this claim to be true, we would have "to give an account of the faith that is within us."

I do not think that any of these approaches are quite complete, although there are valid insights in each of them. I have become convinced that we also have to think of this problem in a different way. It is not a single, clean, simple, all-or-nothing matter. It has several dimensions, among them a dimension neglected by these approaches and, so far as I have read, also by my closest companions in theological dialogue from Andover Newton days. I want to make some proposals.

In some ways, we stand in basic communion with people of other faiths, and can even say that Christianity is, in certain respects, no different from other great religions. Every one of the great traditions holds that behind the surface of things, there is something more than meets the eye. That is, some things are not clearly empirical but are transcendent; and the great religions all seek to point to this reality that is more real than what we usually call reality — the finite world that we can see, and touch, smell, and manipulate. Moreover, all the world religions see in this reality, even if they dispute its nature, the source and norm of the principles of ethical life — do not dishonor what is noble and true and good, do not lie, or cheat, or steal, or murder, or rape, or torture, or covet what is not yours. This dimension of the great faiths allows people to recognize virtuous persons from other traditions. It also allowed representatives from most of the religions of the world to agree that the Nazi and Stalinist terrors of the last century were against all that is holy and to sign the United Nations Declaration of Human Rights, while understanding these rights in terms of their own faiths. This is also why the Parliament of World Religions could pass a consensus document about a global ethic, and why we can all recognize the authentic morality of a Dalai Lama, a Václav Havel, a Nelson Mandela, a Pope John XXIII, a Martin Luther King, Jr., an Aung San Suu Kyi, a Mother Teresa. As Christians, we can even see in each of these some deep trace of a Christ-like model.

But that is not the only dimension that is at stake. It is also possible to recognize the ways in which great faiths have shaped civilizations that have endured and flourished over centuries, in part by a profound wisdom and a deep inner spiritual architecture that allows grace-full living. Some religions cannot do this, and the archeologists could tell us that the rubble of history is littered by the residues of societies that could not sustain viable civilizations. Of course, sometimes they also leave partial legacies that are taken up by others. It is not at all an accident that the Old Testament includes wisdom material that comes from non-revelatory sources, as we can read today in Job, Ruth, or Proverbs. Nor is it surprising that the early Christians admired the philosophy of the Greeks and the legal theory of the Romans, and borrowed so deeply from them that Western Christian theology and ethics are laden with them. In fact, many modern thinkers have also became attracted to the wisdom and spirituality of the Hindu *Vedas,* the Confucian *I Ching,* the Buddhist *Sermons,* and so on.

In each of these cases, civilizations have been formed and cultural shape has been given to the spheres of common life. Faithfulness in family life, economic sufficiency and sometimes plenty, political order and sometimes justice, and a high respect for learning and beauty have been cultivated by each of these traditions in ways that have endured for thousands of years. Today, our faith is continuing to develop as Christians from non-Western traditions baptize aspects of these traditions of wisdom and spirituality, extending the development of Christian doctrine by enriching it with philosophical and spiritual insights that we did not see before. Moreover, as Christ becomes more widely known, the traditions of others are enlivened, if not converted, in ways we did not anticipate. Traditions of hymnology, liturgy, and theological reflection that modulate culture, and efforts at social amelioration, service, and advocacy that alter social practices and expectation, for example, can be found in Buddhist, Hindu, and Tribal traditions that are obviously borrowed from the Christian heritage. Christ sometimes transforms cultures and religions before persons are converted — or without their conscious conversion.

But, neither our common universal morality, nor our particular wisdoms and spiritualities that shape civilizations tell the whole story. It is true that the moral law is written on the hearts of all, and it is also true that great wisdom and profound spiritualities have formed great cultures. That is something! But it is not everything. At some point, morality, wisdom, and spirituality cannot solve the whole human problem. They can help us resist wrong and evil, and they can help us build grace-full societies, and this is what makes it possible for us to live in peace and mutual respect with neighbors of other faiths. We have too seldom paid attention to these real factors in our preaching and teaching. But there is more: in Christ, we also see grace, a gift of undeserved forgiveness and reconciliation with God that allows us to love more fully. This cannot be gained by even the best morality, the highest wisdom or the most cultivated spirituality. This gift of grace changes our world if we accept it. Indeed, it allows us to renew covenants of right and to enter federations of cooperation with a new spirit, a sanctifying spirit.

It is in this sense that we speak of the "salvation" that is offered only in Christ. This view differs from the recent Roman Catholic teaching in *Dominus Iesus,* which suggests that only in the Catholic Church (not only in "the catholic" church, but the Roman Catholic Church) can we find salvation, and it differs from what Mark Heim argues when he suggests that every religion has its own kind of salvation. He is surely correct in some ways: if the basic human problem is that we do not submit enough to God's moral law, then we should become an orthodox Jew or Muslim, for they have greater clarity about law and submission to it than Christians do. If the basic human problem is that we are too attached to things, then we should become Buddhists, for that will detach us. And so on one could go. But that approach only bumps up the question to another level: which understanding of the basic human problem is the most valid?

Finally, I do not think that it is a matter of one church or many salvations, and the critical questions will take more deliberation than is possible here. Still, it is more likely that we must face a cluster of profound proposals that wrestle with the basic issue of what, ultimately, do we need to be saved from, saved for, and saved by, and no answer is known with absolutely certainty. That is why faith is required, and why faith requires a grace that cannot be gained by "faithing" harder only in our own tradition. I do not know of any other great tradition that sees humanity as having a problem that cannot be solved by the deeper learning of wisdom, the higher attainment of morals, a more intense commitment to solidarity, and a more expansive spirituality. Christians see these things as good and seek to cultivate them with others, learning from them; but we hold also that Christ offers something else. This "else" we call "salvation," a kind of gracious healing and fulfilled transformation that overcomes the disabilities we humans cannot overcome by ourselves — not only our foolishness, our immorality, and our materiality, but our separation from God. Thus, we find an unconditional love that attaches us to duties and responsibilities, to our neighbors, and to the "more than meets the eye" that we cannot otherwise attain.

We can honor and learn from other traditions, but we should be cautious in claiming that all religions are the same or even that all the salvations are equally valid. A multidimensional view allows us to honor others and also to bring something distinct to the table of respect: Christ offers salvation by grace, believers are those who celebrate that fact, and we can invite all those of other faiths who want to share in it to do so too, lovingly. The most pressing question before us today is whether such a faith can give moral and spiritual shape to the global civilization that is emerging around us, renewing wisdom, righteousness, and material culture and inviting others to join in the creation of a new, global, integrative theology — so that our future does not explode into a clash of contrary civilizations, crumble into ruins, or become a hegemonic terror.

What do you think, Gabe (and Mark)?

Who Do We Hear?

Frederick R. Trost

"To be a Christian . . . means to have the courage to preach the true teaching of Christ, and not be afraid. . . ."

MSGR. OSCAR ROMERO, DECEMBER 5, 1977

For many Christians (and other persons of faith) living in the United States, the name of Archbishop Oscar Romero brings immediately to mind a human being of compassion, courage, and faith. The story of his brief career is already part of the ecclesiastical and political lore of the past century. We remember his discipleship as archbishop of San Salvador, his concern for the poor of his archdiocese, his willingness to address the principalities and powers, his simple love of the gospel, his powerful preaching, his pastoral care, and his ability to connect word and deed. He was, as Dietrich Bonhoeffer might observe, one who took joyous delight in the faith of the church, a person who understood the nature of the term "servant of Christ." Oscar Romero was one capable of asking, "Who is Jesus Christ for us today?"

What does a Roman Catholic archbishop, from a tiny country in Latin America, have to do with "full communion," the unity of the body of Christ? I recall traveling about fifteen years ago as part of a human rights delegation into the war-ravaged villages of Chalatenango province in northern El Salvador. We came to a small community that had recently been devastated by gunfire from the sky. Death had come to that community. But the people met us at the entrance to the village with songs. They carried flowers in their hands. They had been assaulted, but not crushed.

They had been assailed, but they had not lost hope. I remember especially a woman who addressed the crowd in the center of the village that day. She turned to us and said: "Msgr. Romero visited us here. He gave us back our voice." When I think of full communion and the unity of the church, I think of the words of the woman of Chalatenango: "We have gotten back our voice."

Throughout the history of the Christian church, there have been those servants of the Word who have encouraged us to hope, to live out the meaning of our baptism despite our weakness, to remember our calling as ministers of reconciliation. There have been those "friends" who have taught us to explore the faith we proclaim, to challenge the "forces of darkness," to sing with the angels, to take steps in obedience to the word made flesh. Msgr. Romero and Dietrich Bonhoeffer are among those friends. But there are also friends closer to home, colleagues in our midst who summon us to faith through their teaching and their acquaintance with our "situation." These friends of ours call us by name. They are familiar with our gifts. They share our weakness. By their example, they help us to "lift up our hearts" and to raise our voices as part of a community of believers.

One of those friends to a large number of pastors and laity in the church is the one we honor in this *festschrift*. He has been to many of us both teacher and companion for as long as we can remember. His dedication to the relationship of word and deed has brought encouragement as we have gone about the tasks of parish ministry. His commitment to the unity of Christ's church, to "full communion" within the holy catholic church, has broken down some of the walls that have long divided the Christian community. Within the United Church of Christ in the USA, he has been a dear friend to those of us who have looked to the "academy" for guidance and help at crucial moments. The brief essay that follows reflects on the meaning of church unity as it is expressed in "full communion" between the United Church of Christ in the USA and the Evangelical Church of the Union in Germany. "Full communion" between our two churches has been among the many interests of Gabriel Fackre over the years, as he has challenged the church to claim the unity that is God's gift to us in Jesus Christ.

"Full communion" between the United Church of Christ (UCC) in the USA and the Evangelical Church of the Union (EKU) in Germany, dates back to synods that took place in both countries in 1980 and 1981. But what is "full communion" really? "Full communion" is many things. It is friendship among people of faith. It is an exchange of viewpoints. It is mutual hopes, mutual longings, and mutual concern for the integrity of the church and for life in the world God loves. It is testimony to the unity of Christ's church. It is singing, it is confession, it is tears. When I think of "full communion" at the beginning of the twenty-first century, I think of it as an effort within the church, modest to be sure, to reclaim its voice. "Give us . . . our voice!"

The church in every generation faces the danger of losing its voice. To say it another way, we are challenged in every generation to lift up our voice. We are summoned on a daily basis to claim our baptism, to affirm our vocation as images of Jesus Christ and as witnesses to the gospel. To do this in the midst of the wounds and crucifixions of God in the world around us, the hunger in a world of plenty, the fear in a world armed to the teeth, and the materialism that suffocates while millions have no place to lay their heads. As one who served as a pastor in a congregation for twenty years, I know many of its joys and I am aware of its weaknesses. I love to hear its voice, that is, a voice that seeks to proclaim in new, fresh, and imaginative ways, in word and in deed, the truth of "God with us." But few of us are aware of how the voice of the congregation, its life and ministry, has a way of becoming uncertain, muffled, afraid, out of touch with God, out of touch with the realities of the world around us. The fact is, the congregation is tempted to lose its way. From the beginning, "full communion" has been an effort to encourage the church and the congregation to think, to imagine, to dream, to hear the song the angels sing, to speak, to serve, to point to truth, to respond to the presence of Jesus Christ, to be shaped by the voices of Scripture, to examine, gratefully yet critically, the faithful testimony of previous generations, and to see in the faces of our wounded neighbors the reality of God. To put it another way, "full communion" calls us to study, to reflect, to think, while insisting that the "knowledge of God is not an escape into the heights of pure ideas. . . ." But rather, "Entry into the need of the present, sharing in its suffering, . . . its activity . . . and its hope." "Full communion" knows that "there is work and struggle at every point" (Karl Barth).

Full communion between the EKU and the UCC is a summons to life. It is a reminder that each congregation (despite the temptation to believe otherwise), is entrusted with a vocation that is not of its own making. It is a vocation that comes to us from beyond ourselves, that is, from the power and patience of the Holy Spirit to work with our fallible faith and in our very fragile lives. "Full communion" knows that all ministers of the word, ordained and non-ordained, are (as one of the teachers of the church put it years ago) "like trumpets, which make no sound if breath be not breathed into them, . . . or like Ezekiel's wheels, which move not unless the spirit move them, . . . or like Elisha's servants, whose presence does no good unless Elisha's spirit be there also" (John Flavel).

"Full communion" believes in the recovery of the teaching ministry of the church. It believes that theological work is essential to the sound of the trumpet, to the movement of the wheels, to the life of the servant church. "Full communion" involves memory. It involves hope. It remembers. It is expectant. "In theological terms, [memory and hope] are of the essence of discipleship. To remember . . . the cross, and to hope . . . is to be set down in the world as an enduring alternative to what the world regularly offers, which the Bible . . . calls death" (John Douglas Hall). "Full communion" cares about this. It cares about articulation. It cares (to use a term of Dietrich Bonhoeffer) about conformation, conformity to Christ. It understands it must be willing to take risks.

There is a story Martin Buber used to tell his rabbinical students about two farmers who went into the fields in springtime. They saw the work ahead. One turned to the other and said: "I'm not going to plant this year, because last year there was a drought and nothing grew." The other farmer agreed, saying, "You're right. I'm not going to plant either, because if God wants the crops to grow, God will take care of it." So neither farmer lifted a finger. Neither farmer did a thing. And when it came time for harvest, there was nothing except the weeds. Buber turned to his students and said: "Faith is like the wise farmers who sow their crops in the face of the possibility the floods will come and carry everything into the sea, in face of the possibility the sun will bake the land and all the crops shall wither, in face of the possibility the wind will blow fiercely and knock the crops down." Then he said, "You cannot live by faith without a willingness to take risks." "Full communion" understands Buber.

I remember early conversations about "full communion" between the UCC and the EKU, following the synods of 1980 and 1981. We expressed the hope at that time that our full communion would involve vital theological dialogue, and that words and thoughts be related to actions and deeds. So we spoke in those days not only of theological reflection, but of joint mission to be undertaken by the UCC, the EKU, and by the church in Africa, in Asia, and in other parts of the world.

This has happened in several of the conferences of the UCC, including Wisconsin, where we (together with the Moers district of the Evangelical Church in the Rhineland) have sent, at the invitation of the Roman Catholic diocese of San Cristobal de Las Casas, working groups of young people into Chiapas, to serve alongside the church there and to reflect on the faith as it is lived daily in the shadow of the cross. "Full communion" has involved laity and clergy in theological reflection, exploring "the hope that is in us," and learning from one another. Congregations, associations, districts, conferences, and regional churches have established partnerships, which have brought the two churches closer together. Issues such as a just peace, disarmament, nuclear weapons, racism, and economic justice have been probed, alongside the liturgy, the meaning of *diakonia,* catechesis, and the authentic place of stewardship in the life of people of faith. I recall how important it was at the inception of "full communion" that the theological faculties at UCC seminaries be encouraged to move to the center of "full communion," to work with the conferences of the UCC on several projects, and to engage in discussion with their counterparts in Germany. This happened most recently when the entire faculty of Eden Theological Seminary in St. Louis journeyed to Halle, where it met with the theological faculty there. To the best of my knowledge, this has never happened before, though in the nineteenth century, individual faculty members from seminaries of the predecessors to the UCC made regular visits to Berlin, Halle, Basel, and other places. In those early years of theological education in the United States, such "full communion" was seen, literally, as a matter of life and death.

But what of the future? As we think about the future of "full communion," it is important to remember what has been, but then to move beyond what has been to what can be. "Full communion" is like a composition of Bach or the music of the Beatles, or a Dixie-land jazz band, with a main theme (faithfulness to the gospel) and many variations, most of which have yet to be conceived. "Full communion" is the capacity to dream, to think, to imagine what the church at its faithful best will look like in the century that is ahead. Hopefully, the Bible will be at the center of its life, and Jesus Christ will be seen not only where all is well in Zion, but in the faces of the bruised, the wounded, the crucified. "Full communion," however conceived, will want to take the form of the deed. But it will take the form of the deed best where it is rooted in prayer for the guidance of the Holy Spirit, and in joyous and sincere theological reflection and dialogue.

This dialogue, in my view, must eventually include voices not presently engaged in our discussions. One of the challenges ahead will be to celebrate "full communion" by paying attention to the margins. To do this, the church will need to look at the question of ecclesiology. What does it mean in the twenty-first century to be a people of faith? What is the relationship between our words and our deeds? How do we give expression to the truth of our many confessions? What is the relationship between the eucharist and the first commandment, between the bread, the cup, and the river of blood and tears that flows in a torrent across the earth? How do we come, as Peter Taylor Forsyth wrote, "to sing the new song of those who stand upon the rock, . . . [filled with] the devotion of those whom grace found, scarcely saved from the jaws of death, (capable of faith that is) a power and a passion . . . among the passions and powers of humanity"? "Full communion" asks if these questions (and others we might name) do not belong to the heart of our "life together." "Full communion" abhors the idea that it may, itself, become just a toy; a plaything, a hobby of those who like to dabble in faith, a kind of ecclesiastical "decoration." It involves wrestling — wrestling with God, wrestling with one another, wrestling with the church, wrestling with the world, wrestling with ideas, wrestling with events, wrestling with absurdities, wrestling with injustice, wrestling with the contradiction of faith present in the little movements, fads, and systems that claim human allegiance, wrestling with the reality that God is mocked by indifference to teaching and to the demands of faith.

"Full communion" is a confession that we cannot handle these things alone; it knows Christians need one another. Christians need the encouragement that comes from traveling the way of a pilgrim together. "Full communion" means hearing "yes" from each other, and also "no" from each other. "Yes" to humble, sacrificial service. "Yes" to costly grace. "Yes" to God's dream of shalom and jubilee. "No" to arrogance. "No" to idolatry. "No" to "politics without principle" (Bryan Sirchio). "Full communion" is not being embarrassed to express our Christian hope.

"Full communion" will have a stubborn streak. It will resist the notion that the appropriate place for the church is where "all is calm, all is bright." It will have little empathy with the church's tendency, at least in North America, to move away from the public square. It will seek to resist the temptation of the church to let its voice be muffled or silenced in an effort to achieve respectability in the world. It will reject the thought that the prophetic tradition and the teaching of Jesus have little relevance in the world. It will begin to sweat if the church becomes content with the role of counselor or chaplain to society.

Article 3 of the famous Barmen declaration states that "The Christian church is the congregation of brothers and sisters in which Jesus Christ acts presently as the Lord in word and sacrament through the Holy Spirit." The church, Barmen declares, is Christ's "property," not ours. It "lives and wants to live solely from his comfort and admonition." "Full communion" asks: what does this mean today? What does it mean, if anything at all, that the church is to testify "with its faith as with its obedience, with its message as with its order"? What does it mean, if anything at all, that we are called "to dry our tears, [to] put out our mourning lamps, [to rejoice] for the sun of Christ is shining" (Wilhelm Loehe)? What does it mean, if anything at all, that "the single, visible sign of God in this world is the cross" (Dietrich Bonhoeffer)?

If we do not teach this, what do we teach in a world bruised and fractured nearly everywhere we look, crushed by the weight of conflict, arrogance, and power? In short, what does it mean, if anything at all, that "the church is only the church as it is present for others" (Dietrich Bonhoeffer)? In what sense, if any, is the experience of transcendence related to Christians being with and for our neighbor, and what importance has this for Christian formation, the liturgy, congregational life, and mission? What might this mean for common mission, common study, and our willingness to embrace those who dwell at a distance from our own experience? What might it mean for the future, were we to open the Scriptures together and listen to the Word proclaimed to us through the power of the Holy Spirit, and to discover to our amazement, that we "are given back our voice"? What could it mean to look into the world together and to see there the tears of God, and Mary racing from the empty tomb with good news of redemption? What does it mean that we, together with our gifted neighbors, so many impoverished materially, yet abounding in spiritual gifts, are kept together by "the confession of the one Lord of the one holy, catholic and apostolic church"? As Archbishop Romero said, "to be a Christian . . . means to have the courage to preach the true teaching of Christ and not be afraid. . . ." "Let not your word, O Lord, become a judgment upon us, that we hear it and do it not, that we know it and love it not, that we believe it and obey it not" (Thomas à Kempis).

"Full communion" asks: "What is our only comfort in life and in death?" (Heidelberg Catechism). It asks: "What does our communion daily require of us"? (Evangelical Catechism). "Full communion" asks: "Who stands firm . . . ?" (Dietrich Bonhoeffer). What is the future of "full communion"? Its future is contained in the answers the churches give to the questions: "Who do we hear?" "Who do we trust?" "Who do we seek to obey?"

Social Witness in Generous Orthodoxy

George Hunsinger

The twentieth century has witnessed a number of initiatives to encourage political responsibility in the church. Each achieved a measure of success before hitting diminishing returns. Religious socialism of the 10s and 20s in Switzerland and Germany, the American social gospel of about the same era, the worker-priest movement in postwar France, Latin American liberation theologies in the 60s and 70s with their base communities, the black theologies of the same decades in the United States and Africa, and the slightly later feminist and womanist theologies in industrialized nations — these and other efforts were progressive campaigns that made a mark, but did not prevail. The recurring pattern of early promise broken by arrest and eventual decline surely had causes that were various and complex. Yet these campaigns all had at least one thing in common. Each in its own way forced the church to choose between progressive politics and traditional faith. Each made it seem as though the two were mutually exclusive. Each, therefore, forged an unwitting alliance with its opposition, which shared the same diagnosis, only from the opposite point of view. Each failed to see that confronted with a forced option, the church will inevitably choose not to abandon traditional faith. Equally tragically, each failed to see that the forced option between progressive politics and traditional faith is false.

The falsity of the option might have been plain from the existence of

---

This essay has been excerpted from George Hunsinger, "Social Witness in Generous Orthodoxy," *The Princeton Seminary Bulletin* 21 (2000): 38-62.

any number of prominent figures. Dorothy Day, William Stringfellow, Fanny Lou Hamer, Oscar Romero, André Trocmé, Marietta Jaeger, Helmut Gollwitzer, Lech Walesa, Kim Dae-jung, Ita Ford, Desmond Tutu, and not least Karl Barth, are among the many twentieth-century Christians known for their progressive politics. They saw no reason to choose between their love for Jesus Christ as confessed by faith and their love for the poor and the oppressed. They had learned from initiatives for political responsibility, while refusing the fatal choice. Traditional faith was for them not a hindrance, but an incentive for progressive political change. It sustained them in struggle through their darkest hours. It was not for them something disreputable to be hidden from those in need. Nor was it something to be rejected because dishonored by injustice and failure in the church. It was, rather, the hard won and priceless deposit of truth that withstood every effort to discredit its relevance.

Christians are called to bear social witness to Christ in two ways: first, through the ordering of their common life; and second, through direct action in the surrounding world. Ecclesial ordering and secular intervention comprise a unity in distinction. They are not alternatives, and may well at times blend together. Nonetheless, they are ranked in a particular way. Priority belongs (in principle) to the ordering of the church's common life. The church does not have a social ethic, so much as it is a social ethic. A church whose common life merely reflects the social disorders of the surrounding world is scarcely in a strong position for social witness through direct action. In such cases — and where is this not the case? — the gospel must progress in spite of the church, and against its failures.

Here, too, there is more grace in God than sin in us. Note that social witness, whose direct action cannot always wait for the proper ordering of the church's common life, must proceed on several fronts at once. Nevertheless, social witness in discipleship to Christ requires the church to be a countercultural community with its own distinctive profile. It must stand over against the larger culture when that culture's values are incompatible with the gospel. No doubt a church that emphasizes distinctiveness at the expense of solidarity falsifies itself by becoming sectarian. A church that loses its distinctiveness, however, through conformity and capitulation, evades its essential vocation of discipleship, especially when it means bearing the cross for being socially dissident. A Christian is an unreliable partisan who knows that peace with God means conflict with the world (even as peace with the world means conflict with God). "You are the salt of the earth; but if the salt has lost its taste, how shall its saltiness be restored?" (Matt. 5:13). "You are the light of the world" (Matt. 5:14). Disciples are not above their teacher (Matt. 10:24). The very idea of "social witness" implies an orientation toward the centrality of God. It means that Christian social action, whether within the community of faith or the larger world, is more than an end in itself.

This action does not simply aim to alleviate social misery in the form of hunger, nakedness, homelessness, terror, illness, humiliation, loneliness, and abuse. Efforts to name and oppose social injustice, no matter how important and necessary, are only one aspect of "social witness." As Aristotle has pointed out, any given action or policy can be an end in itself while also serving as the means to a greater end. As important as bread is to us, we do not live by bread alone. Human flourishing, as we know from the gospel, depends on more than the alleviation of social misery and the satisfaction of earthly needs. The main purpose for which we were created is to glorify and enjoy God forever.

This purpose is acknowledged by social witness in at least two ways. First, Christian social witness is parabolic in intent. It aims, in all its forms, to enact parables of God's compassion for the world. Although not all needs are alike, with some lesser or greater than others, God cares for us as whole persons in all our needs. The highest purpose for which we were created is not always remembered in this context. Being created to live by and for God, we know a need which only God can fulfill. Being creatures fallen into sin, moreover, we also endure a terrible plight, fatal and self-inflicted, from which we are helpless to free ourselves, but can be rescued only by God, without which we would be cut off from God and one another forever. According to the gospel, God has not abandoned us without hope to this plight, for God does not will to be God without us. On the contrary, God has spared no cost to rescue us. The point is this: No human action, not even by the church, can do for us what God has done, or be for us what God indeed is, at the deepest level of human need. Human action can nonetheless, by grace, serve as a witness. It can point away from itself to God. It can enact parables of compassion that proclaim the gospel. In addressing itself wholeheartedly to lesser needs, Christian social witness points at the same time to God as the only remedy for our greatest need.

Christian social witness, in its efforts to alleviate social misery, is thus at once an end in itself, while also serving as the means to a greater end. Secondly, social witness cannot be parabolic in intent without also being analogical in form. It must correspond to the content it would attest. It cannot point to God without corresponding to God. Correspondence to God is the basic criterion of social witness, and it is this criterion that makes faithfulness more important than effectiveness. The validity of Christian social witness cannot be judged by immediate consequences alone. It must rather be judged, primarily, by the quality of its correspondence to God's compassion as revealed and embodied in Jesus Christ. No social witness can be valid which contradicts faithful correspondence, even when that means leaving the consequences to God. Consequences are in any case greatly overrated with respect to their predictability and controllability, just as they are also commonly misjudged when uncompromising faithfulness results in real or apparent failures.

It is no accident that the words witness and martyr are semantically related. The promise of the gospel is that faithful witness, whether successful in worldly terms or not, will always be validated by God. To believe that supposed effectiveness in violation of faithfulness is promised similar validation can only be illusory. No comprehensive policy of social action, regardless of what it is, will ever be without elements of helplessness, tragedy, and trade-off in the face of human misery. It is always a mistake for faithfulness to overpromise what it can deliver in resisting evil or effecting social change, though it may sometimes be surprisingly effective, or even compatible with maximal effectiveness, depending on the case. Social witness qua witness, in any case, cannot allow itself to be determined primarily by the question of effectiveness, but rather by faithful correspondence to the cruciform compassion of God.

A recurring phenomenon in the history of Christian theology has been the displacement of central truths by lesser truths. Usually these displacements are more or less temporary. Nevertheless, they can cause great confusion while they last. Polarizations and animosities typically form between two groups — those in their wisdom who passionately reject one truth that they might recover the centrality of another, and those who do much the same thing only in reverse. In such cases, the solution arises when central truths are allowed to be central and lesser truths are allowed to be lesser. The truth of neither is denied, and room can even be found for allowing the lesser truths, perhaps previously unnoticed or neglected, to assume the urgency of situational precedence. During the last twenty-five years or so, the church has increasingly witnessed the emergence of victim-oriented soteriologies. The plight of victims, variously specified and defined, has been urged by prominent theologians as the central soteriological problem. It can scarcely be denied that the history of the twentieth century has pushed the plight of victims to the fore. Nor can it be denied that the church has too often seemed ill-equipped to bring the plight of victims, especially victims of oppression and social injustice, clearly into focus for itself so that reasonable and faithful remedies might be sought. Victim-oriented soteriologies have undoubtedly made an important contribution to a better understanding of the church's social responsibility.

Polarizations and animosities have developed, however, to the extent that the plight of victims has displaced the soteriological plight of sinners, or even eclipsed it. Victim-oriented soteriologies have unfortunately tended to define the meaning of sin entirely in terms of victimization. Sin ceases to be a universal category. It attaches to perpetrators and to them alone. Since by definition victims qua victims are innocent of being perpetrators, they are to that extent innocent of sin. If sin attaches only to perpetrators, however, victims can be sinners only by somehow becoming perpetrators themselves (a move not unknown in victim-oriented soteriologies). Victim-oriented soteriologies, with their bipolar opposition between victims and perpetrators, display a logic with sectarian tendencies.

How the cross of Christ is understood by these soteriologies is also worth noting. The cross becomes meaningful because it shows the divine solidarity with victims, generally ceasing to find any other relevance, at least positively. (In extreme cases the theology of the cross is trashed as a cause of victimization. But such denunciations, when meant de jure, exceed the bounds even of heterodoxy and so cease to be of constructive interest to the church.) The cross, in any case, is no longer the supreme divine intervention for the forgiveness of sins. It is not surprising that more traditional, sin-oriented soteriologies should react with unfortunate polarization. When that happens, sin as a universal category obscures the plight of oppression's victims, rendering that plight just as invisible or irrelevant as it was before. Atonement without solidarity seems to exhaust the significance of the cross, and forgiveness supposedly occurs without judgment on oppression.

The task of generous orthodoxy in this situation is to dispel polarization by letting central truths be central, and lesser truths be lesser, but in each case letting truth be truth. No reason exists why the cross as atonement for sin should be viewed as logically incompatible with the cross as divine solidarity with the oppressed. Good reasons can be found for connecting them. The great historical ecumenical consensus remains, however, that the central significance of the cross, as attested by Holy Scripture, is the forgiveness of sins. This established consensus pervades every aspect of the church's life, not least including baptism and the Lord's Supper. It has, by this time, withstood all the onslaughts of unbelieving modernity (so that the only question today is not whether the ecumenical consensus will survive, but whether those churches devitalized by modern skepticism will). No ecclesial catechesis can be valid, which fails to affirm the forgiveness of sins as the central truth of the cross.

Lesser truths, however, ought not to be pitted against central truths. Lesser truths, moreover, gain rather than diminish in significance when decentered, for they no longer have a role foisted upon them that they cannot possibly fulfill. Generous orthodoxy attempts to do justice to both central and lesser truths in themselves, as well as to their proper ordering. The oppressed have always understood that the cross brings them consolation and hope by placing God into solidarity with their misery. The African-American spiritual is exactly right when it laments, "Nobody knows the trouble I've seen. Nobody knows but Jesus." The gospel does not obscure that our Lord was "mocked and insulted and spat upon" (Luke 18:32), that he was "despised and rejected" by others (Is. 53:3). Admittedly, the church has not always kept pace with Scripture in recognizing that "The Lord is a stronghold for the oppressed, a stronghold in times of trouble" (Ps. 9:9). It has not always prayed fervently enough with the psalmist: "May he defend the cause of the poor of the people, give deliverance to the needy, and crush the oppressor" (Ps. 72:4), nor has it always acted conscientiously enough on the basis of such prayers. Social witness has a perpetual obligation to solidarity with the oppressed. This obligation, however, is entirely consonant with the truth (which can be displaced only at our peril) on which the entire gospel depends: "For our sake he made him to be sin who knew no sin, so that in him we might become the righteousness of God" (2 Cor. 5:21).

When the universality of sin is recognized as the central soteriological problem, the results can be liberating. All illusions are dispelled: for example, that though others may be needy, I am not, and that I am, therefore, somehow above others if I am in a position to help them in their need. Acknowledging my need, conversely, brings no implication that I am beneath others who may help me. When recognition is accorded to the universality of divine grace, moreover, I am freed from moralistic forms of obligation. For when grounded in the reception of grace, social obligation is not an externally imposed duty, but a response to the needs of others in gratitude to the God who has already responded so graciously to me. My response to others is based on a solidarity in sin and grace. It occurs as an act of witness to the gospel and through participation in the grace of God. "Walk in love, as Christ has loved us and gave himself up for us" (Eph. 5:2).

Our lesser needs are related to our central need by a unity in distinction. Concern for the poor and needy stands in inseparable unity with the forgiveness of sins, without displacing it or becoming a substitute for it. Concern for the poor and the needy has a solid basis in traditional faith, as when linked with the petition for daily bread in the Lord's Prayer. Through the recovery of sound catechesis, concern for the poor, among other things, could become more deeply embedded in the life of the church. A person who fears and blesses the Lord "opens her hand to the poor, and reaches out her hands to the needy" (Prov. 31:20). It will be a great day when congregations not only give money to help the poor, but also create situations in which the poor feel welcome to participate in the life and work of the congregations themselves.

Teaching the Story:
An Ecumenical Trajectory

Diane C. Kessler

I was a religion major in college. That was where I had my first encounter with the subject of theology. It was not a positive experience. The professor there shall remain nameless, although I remember him well. He took this inexperienced product of public high school and asked her to read Alfred North Whitehead with little preparation. I was drowning in a sea of obfuscation. So I arrived at Andover Newton Theological School thoroughly intimidated by the topic.

A lack of familiarity with Christian theology is a serious lacuna in the fundamentals! Lack it I did, however, until Gabriel Fackre led me out of the wilderness. He made the subject of basic Christian doctrine clear, understandable, connected, relevant, and even exciting! I never will forget this gift Gabe has given to me and so many others, through his teaching, through *The Christian Story*, Parts I and II, and through numerous other writings.

This same capacity for clarity of thought and expression is a gift Gabe has given to the ecumenical movement, on behalf of the United Church of Christ ("UCC"). The UCC looks better as a denomination because, in his teaching office, Gabe has represented his church in a variety of ecumenical gatherings. He puts that church's best foot forward in the ecumenical world — always with honesty and integrity, but using classical theological and ecclesiological categories which help others understand the United Church of Christ, and which help members of the UCC understand themselves, as well.

Gabe grasps from whence the United Church of Christ came as a denomination. He lived it. He knows that passionate and persistent ecumenical commitment formed this united church, and is an essential part of UCC identity, emblazoned on its logo. He has shared the frustrations of many who saw how the post-merger quest to stabilize this newly formed church sometimes diminished the ecumenical emphasis. Gabe would put this observation in the context of Christian understandings of human nature and of the nature of the church, and say with the Apostle Paul that we "have this treasure in clay jars" (2 Cor. 4:7).

The purpose of councils of churches should mirror the nature of the church itself. Churches through councils are called to heal the divisions among them for the sake of the world. Gabriel Fackre's personal commitments have mirrored the balance articulated by the conciliar form of the ecumenical movement — seeing that a full-orbed ecumenism embodies matters of faith, order, life, and work. He has not been an ivory tower theologian. He's been willing to mix it up, to get his hands dirty. When Good Friday was a time for a witness for peace on the Boston Common, Gabe and his wife Dorothy were there. When the United Church of Christ has seemed in danger of slackening the tension, focusing too much on matters of life and work and neglecting issues of faith and order, he has zealously sounded the alarm.

Another place where Gabe and other colleagues have encountered human frailty is in ecumenical dialogue. Churches and church leaders often are tempted to indulge in comparative ecumenism: "We do things this way, you do them another." If the purpose of this dialogical exercise is to test assumptions and refine understandings, then it can be a healthy first step in ecumenical dialogue. What often happens, however, is that the dialogue partners compare their best with the other's worst. Although this is patently unfair, it happens all the time. Gabe recognizes the ploy when it surfaces, calls folks on it, and restores the level playing field — all with a gentle smile and unassailable authority.

I have witnessed Gabe on several occasions when this has happened. He was one of the UCC representatives in clarifying conversations with the Evangelical Lutheran Church in America — discussions that resulted in the document *A Common Calling*. This text was a vital step toward the now completed relationship of full communion between the ELCA and the three participating Reformed churches. Throughout this process, he could be found in Craigville, hunched over his computer, lurking on the Internet, articulately countering misperceptions.

Gabe is able to keep folks honest in ecumenical dialogue — to push for a level playing field — because he respects traditions and the texts that embody them. "Go back to the documents," he'll urge. "What have we said in our official texts?" He has said this with such consistency that his maxim is embedded in the conscience of many who have worked with him. In preparation for this essay, I reread the six-page endnote in *A Common Calling,* titled "Reformed Heritage and Lutheran Connections in the Life of the UCC." It is a brilliant exposition, with Fackrean phraseological tracks woven throughout.

The United Church of Christ often is pressed in ecumenical contexts about the relationship between its stated beliefs, its polity, and its praxis. What do its members really think about their faith, and how do they enforce it? Do members of the United Church of Christ care about theology? Do they have a capacity to think in such terms? Gabe has been instrumental in forming structures which help shape new generations of UCC leaders: theological table talk — an early morning series of conversations using key theological texts as the starting point; the Craigville Colloquy — an opportunity for a summer retreat to tackle a variety of timely issues; the confessing Christ movement — a network of people in the UCC who share similar concerns about "getting the story straight" as we "get the story out."

The phrase "testimonies, not tests" is an example of the kind of memorable image Gabe has given currency to help people remember key ideas. The UCC is vulnerable on the challenge of authority. Who speaks for the United Church of Christ? How can we claim with confidence that what is officially said will be heeded? How do congregations hold each other accountable? Gabe has helped members of the UCC and its dialogue partners understand more fully *why* the UCC and its congregations sometimes are vulnerable. If its members take seriously what is said in official documents about the autonomy of conferences, associations, and local churches being understood in the context of "mutual Christian concern and dedication to Jesus Christ, the Head of the Church," they behave with more accountability and responsibility, consistent with official proclamations. Sometimes the independent leanings of clergy and congregations have less to do with an ever-reforming Christian conscience honed in community than they have to do with rampant secular individualism.

At the same time, Gabe has correctly noted that other polities, with firmer structures of authority and accountability, do not insulate their churches from aberrations. There are no guarantees.

These are some of the contributions that Gabriel Fackre has made to the United Church of Christ as this denomination participates in the ecumenical movement. These are things many people will remember. These are gifts for which we give thanks. These are models he has provided to his students and colleagues.

What, then, about the future — the "trajectory," to use a Fackreism? How might these gifts relate to the United Church of Christ's participation in the ecumenical movement in this new millennium?

The United Church of Christ undoubtedly will continue to wrestle with issues of authority, oversight, ministry, accountability, and continuity with the Christian tradition. The UCC would be pressed to deal with these issues by its own internal diversity, but the UCC also will be asked probing questions whenever we relate to the church catholic. The work Gabe has done to define and interpret the official texts of the United Church of Christ will continue to help its members as they see themselves through the lens of other churches — the Christian Church (Disciples of Christ), with whom the United Church of Christ has a partnership; the Lutheran and other Reformed churches (Presbyterian Church, U.S.A.; Reformed Church in America), with whom the UCC is in full communion; the eight other members of the Consultation on Church Union, who became the Church of Christ Uniting in January 2002; partner churches around the world and in councils of churches. Furthermore, Gabe's work in understanding and interpreting Christian evangelicals will help many churches as they struggle to take seriously the Body of Christ in its fullness.

Issues of inclusive language, of how to define and interpret the trinitarian Godhead, of ways this is lived out liturgically through the baptismal formula, of how to teach and proclaim the Protestant spiritual expressions through the hymns we sing — all this ferment will be with the United Church of Christ and with other churches well into this new century. We will do well to follow Gabe's example as we chart our way through these turbulent and murky waters: to know and respect the tradition; to be mindful of the pitfalls made in the past and of ways to avoid them; to appreciate the context in which we now live and work; to understand that our view of the world is colored by our own particular situation and that it may look different to someone living in another part of the world and speaking another tongue; to cautiously, yet bravely, reach toward new expressions of the faith; to do this in Christian community; to maintain a spirit of humility, love, justice, charity, and unity.

Whenever any church participates in ecumenical relationships, whatever their form, we see ourselves as others see us. We dig deeper into our own identity. We take the risk that we will be transformed in this process. Members of the United Church of Christ are not always self-consciously reflective about the nature of the church and its ministry. Others push us to think in these categories. Gabe's careful, systematic work helps us as we move into the future.

Many churches are approaching several ecumenical crossroads in the next few years. The outcome is not clear. We do not know whether the light will turn green, red, or stay a confusing shade of orange. Our faithfulness to the quest may be tested. How will we behave if we encounter disappointments? Will we treat the ecumenical mandate as a casual add-on, to be muted if the path gets muddy, or will we get to the roots of our Christian faith and hang on because this work is fundamental to the gospel of reconciliation?

A colleague who spends an extraordinary amount of time in airport terminals traveling from one meeting to another recently told me about an experience he had someplace in the Southwest. He rushed into the airport chapel on a Sunday morning — a harried, tired Protestant church executive wanting to worship before the next flight. Before the beginning of the service, the Roman Catholic priest said to the congregation, "Wherever you've been, wherever you're going, while you are here, welcome home." And then the gathered community began to worship.

The spirit of those remarks is what we are after in the ecumenical movement. For that, we work and watch and pray. And we give thanks for that cloud of witnesses, Gabriel Fackre among them, who respect the past even as they help chart the future.

Pilgrims toward the Unity of God's People

Brother Jeffrey Gros, FSC

As I cycle on a Saturday morning in Prince George's County, Maryland, the notice before Amistad–St. Paul's United Church of Christ draws me into prayer and reflection with the cloud of witnesses that stand with that and so many other congregations of the United Church of Christ. Indeed, not only the sainted abolitionists and their puritan piety; not only the great minds of American Christianity — Jonathan Edwards, Philip Schaff, the Niebuhr brothers and the like; not only the hundreds of friends and colleagues in the faith; but particular pillars of the present ecumenical witness of the United Church of Christ come to mind, like Gabe Fackre, whose leadership and contribution we celebrate in this volume.

When I was growing up, in Memphis, Tennessee, there were only two United Churches of Christ, one in the white community and the other in the black community. However, I knew that this church must be important, even before reading about the Pilgrim Fathers or the Prussian Union, since it sponsored a local college, the African American Le Moyne-Owen College.

By the time I knew a bit more about Christian history, we were working side by side with our United Church of Christ ("UCC") colleagues, in the 1960s, trying to find a wedge into the racist society of the South. UCC ministers, Catholic bishops and priests, and a variety of other colleagues were standing with Dr. King and before the economic and political establishment of Memphis and the states of Tennessee and Mississippi, to provide a prophetic Christian witness in a fragmented society.

It was in those days, in the first years after the Second Vatican Council, and during the turmoil of concern for civil rights and world peace —

first in Viet Nam, then during the 70s and 80s in Latin America — that we found a common ground for reflecting on the ecumenical imperative for Christians to work together and to think together about the demands of the gospel.

It was also during this era that the Catholic Church was so richly gifted by the presence, at our council, of a small core of ecumenical observers whose influence helped the Catholic bishops formulate new directions for our church.[1]

It was in the celebrations of the Consultation on Church Union liturgies, in Memphis, with the leaders of civil rights struggles, black and white, in the Episcopal Cathedral that we, as Catholics, could begin to imagine how the great sacramental divide of the Reformation might be healed — among the Protestant and Anglican churches, and in due time, with Orthodox, Catholic, and other churches of the Reformation. It was only gradually that it became clear that the United Church of Christ, as a pilgrim people beginning the uniting process among its own members, but stimulating among the rest of us the hunger for full unity, was witnessing to Christ's prayer that we all may be one. This is another moment in the prophetic demand of the gospel.

During this same decade of the 60s, I had the good fortune of deepening my own understanding of the faith, and the testimonies of the United Church of Christ, by studying the confessions of the church under Dr. Elmer Arndt at Eden Seminary. He was able not only to reflect on the sixteenth-century context of the heritage drawn together in the UCC, but also to share the hermeneutical developments that made union possible, and the relationship of these affirmations to what he had observed at the Vatican Council and in the Faith and Order movement, which had been so productive in its 1963 Montreal meeting.[2]

It was also during this period that Alan O. Miller, also of Eden, was so generous as to come into high school classes, in St. Louis, and to our Christian Brothers novitiate nearby, to share the experience of this church

1. Giuseppe Alberigo, Joseph Komonchak, eds., *History of Vatican II,* vols. I-III [two more in preparation] (Maryknoll/Leuven: Orbis/Peeters, 1997-2000). It is instructive to note, in these volumes, the frequency with which the observations of Douglas Horton are cited. One must remember that the Catholic bishops were bound to secrecy about the proceedings, a regulation that could hardly be enforced among the Protestant and Orthodox observers! Cf. Douglas Horton, *Vatican Diary* (Philadelphia: United Church Press, 1966).

2. Gunther Gassmann, ed., *Documentary History of Faith and Order: 1963-1993* (Geneva: World Council of Churches, 1993).

on its pilgrimage toward full visible unity, and his experience at the council. Indeed, the witness of the United Church of Christ stands as a beacon on the path we all walk in remembering the divided churches.[3]

While celebrating, learning, and struggling with UCC colleagues in St. Louis and Memphis, I had no sense of the burdens and challenges ecumenical and prophetic leadership had laid upon this community. It was only in due time that I was to realize that Douglas Horton's hopes for an ecclesiological vision statement were not able to be realized because of the urgencies of the prophetic agenda of the 1960s. The tensions between congregational and synodical dimensions of the church's comprehensiveness remain as continuing tensions and ecumenical enigmas for partner churches into our own time.[4]

Those of us who have an appreciation of the UCC and its history, possibly overromanticized at times, long for the day when there is an articulate ecclesiological statement, which stands among the testimonies of the church, that can be held up as a witness to the deep ecclesial commitment we hear from UCC leadership and colleagues. My early experience of the UCC was of a prophetic, just-peace church, grounded in a comprehensive integration of the Reformation traditions, formed by the best of the American Protestant heritage, critical in scholarship and therefore more deeply committed to biblical and confessional resources than the fundamentalist environment in which I grew up. This was a church receptive to a catholic unity, which included both the sacramental and ministerial heritage of the church through the ages.

In a Baptist and Pentecostal cultural context, it was clear to me that United Church congregationalism was not divorced from the catholicity of the church in its ethical, international, historical, and ecclesial comprehensiveness and accountability. It was only later that I came to understand that the confessional integrity and catholic continuity of the tradition, represented by UCC churches and individuals, were not transparent to all ecumenical partners, and not, in fact, a comfortable self-understanding even for some of the church's own members.

Certainly the conversations generated by the Craigville Colloquy, the Confessing Christ movement, and a variety of other projects to which Gabe Fackre has contributed, assist in witnessing to the commitment of

---

3. Douglas Horton, *Toward an Undivided Church* (New York: Association Press, 1967).

4. Robert S. Paul, *Freedom with Order* (Cleveland: Pilgrim Press, 1987); Louis Gunneman, *United and Uniting: The Meaning of an Ecclesial Journey* (Cleveland: Pilgrim Press, 1987).

the church — in both the universal theological, and the particular UCC senses of that word — to the classical trinitarian and christological faith, and its contemporary and critical witness.

Indeed, those who represented the church in dialogue with the Evangelical Lutheran Church, Gabe Fackre among them, were able to provide this witness. The final success of that ecumenical venture into full communion must be credited more to the personal testimonies of individual spokespersons for the UCC tradition, than to the texts of UCC ecclesial self-understanding. Subsequent work on the nature of the church and on authority has enriched this agreement, and laid a groundwork for deeper mutual understanding and solid bonds of communion.[5]

The United Church of Christ has been characterized as an expression of "liberal" Protestantism. In fact, it emerged in the rich theological days of the neoorthodox movement, with its particular U.S. expression in Christian realism, and salvation history approaches to the biblical narrative. If liberal means using critical tools to ascertain the intent of the Scriptures and the confessional heritage, presuming the compatibility of faith and reason as Pope John Paul does, for example, in *Fides et Ratio,* and discerning how the prophetic ethical demands of the gospel apply in church and world, then there is a liberal impulse at the very center of the gospel of Jesus Christ. He brought a critical perspective to both his interpretation of the Torah and the institutions of Judaism in his day. He engaged in the classical rabbinical discourse, which uses ironic parables and a reason rooted in divine compassion, to unsettle the communities of his time. Finally, he called his followers out of complacency to take up the cross and follow him into the thick of the contradictions of society in the great tradition of the prophets of Israel.

It was much to my surprise, moving out of the fundamentalist environment of the South, to find those who took the name "liberal" were as much into "proof texting" of Scripture and the historic confessions, the instrumental use of religion for institutional and political purposes, and the disparagement of the intellectual challenge of the church and its tradition, as any conservative Christian or integrist in my own church. Much of Gabe's work has been about mending the weaknesses of a theological tradition and a church whose grand birthright can be diminished by taking its faith content less seriously than the great "liberal tradition" would warrant.

5. Gabriel Fackre and Michael Root, *Affirmations and Admonitions: Lutheran Decisions and Dialogue with Reformed, Episcopal, and Roman Catholic Churches* (Grand Rapids: Eerdmans, 1998).

The ecumenical vocation of the UCC has been a marvelous contribution to me in my more mature journey of faith and my professional life as well. When I came to work at the National Council of Churches in 1981, I was introduced to a serious feminist scholarship, which was bringing the best of the critical tradition to biblical, patristic, and historical studies. Central among these voices were members of the UCC delegation. Indeed, I also had the historic experience of being able to help place these scholarly feminist voices in dialogue with Orthodox, Lutheran, Quaker, and evangelical voices who came at the common task of promoting women, building the unity of the church and exploring the truth of the gospel, from other angles.[6]

It was also during this period that I was so generously tutored into the catholicity of the UCC, first in space, with an introduction to the rich variety of communities and traditions that made up its heritage.[7] My studies at Eden had introduced me into catholicity in time — its affirmation of a variety of testimonies from the Reformation and patristic heritage of the church. However, the hidden histories of minority communities within the UCC provide a rich witness to the catholicity of the church. It has only been in the 90s that we have emerging a resource that catalogues, for the leader and scholar, these testimonies with the wider and longer tradition in ways accessible to a wider public.[8]

One of the most rewarding ecumenical developments of the last three decades has been the entry of the Pentecostal, holiness, and evangelical scholars into the ecumenical discussions. The early-twentieth-century schism among Protestants, which we call the fundamentalist-modernist controversy, is one of the greatest burdens on those who seek Christian reconciliation. The United Church of Christ has shown some important leadership through relations with Pentecostal churches in Latin America. However, in the United States bridging these gaps has been more challenging.

Gabe Fackre has given important leadership to us through taking serious evangelical scholarship into account in his work, and providing bridges between two intellectual communities that tend to live in differ-

---

6. "Gender and Language in the Creeds," *Union Seminary Quarterly Review* 40:3 (August 1985).

7. Barbara Brown Zikmund, *Hidden Histories in the United Church of Christ* (New York: United Church Press, 1984).

8. Barbara Brown Zikmund, series editor, *The Living Theological Heritage of the United Church of Christ*, vols. I-IV (Cleveland, Ohio: Pilgrim Press, 1995-99). We are led to hope for nine more volumes in this excellent series!

ent thought worlds.[9] Of course, Gabe's contribution in this dialogue, like his contributions to all of his ecumenical work, has not been without its critical edge.[10]

However, in addition to UCC contributions to the Faith and Order movement and to building theological bridges with the evangelical community, I must testify to the appreciation that I have, as a Roman Catholic committed to the unity of the church, to the openness of the UCC and Gabe Fackre to our common pilgrimage toward Catholic-Protestant full communion. This is, of course, a slower process than can be expected among the Reformation churches, whether in the Lutheran-Reformed full communion, or among the eight member churches of the Consultation on Church Union. However, healing the Reformation division must be among our priorities as biblical Christians.

The recent discussions of Pope John Paul's invitation to reform the papacy to better serve the ecumenical movement, in his 1995 encyclical *Ut Unum Sint,* is a case in point. The initial response of the General Secretary of the World Alliance of Reformed Churches, of which the UCC is a member, was that there was a lack of interest among the Reformed churches.[11] He did not seem to take account of the fact that the Reformed churches in the United States, Presbyterian, UCC, and Reformed Church in America, had not only been willing to talk about these ideas, but as early as the 1970s had issued reports on polity and authority which did not avoid these sensitive issues.[12] The Catholic Church has very much to learn from the Reformed tradition and the UCC.

As Lutherans and Catholics have moved more closely together with the 1999 *Joint Declaration on Justification by Faith,* Gabe has made the bold suggestion that other Protestant churches can engage in this process, affirming agreement with the Catholic Church on this theme, which was at the headwaters of the Reformation divide.[13] This is a particularly important initiative in light of the full communion between Reformed and Lu-

9. Gabriel Fackre, *Ecumenical Faith in Evangelical Perspective* (Grand Rapids: Eerdmans, 1993).

10. Gabriel Fackre, *The Religious Right and Christian Faith* (Grand Rapids: Eerdmans, 1982).

11. Cf. also Lukas Vischer in *Petrine Ministry and the Unity of the Church,* ed. James F. Puglisi (Collegeville: The Liturgical Press, 1999).

12. Cf. Jeffrey Gros, "Evangelical and Catholic: The Reformed/Roman Catholic Encounter," *The New Mercersburg Review* 14 (Autumn 1993): 18-38; "A Journey of Faith: Reformed and Catholic," *Reformed Review* 52:3 (Spring 1999): 235-53.

13. To be published by Liturgical Press in a volume edited by William G. Rusch.

theran churches, the Catholic-Reformed results in the international dialogues, and the full participation of German Reformed and United churches in the dialogues on the condemnations of the sixteenth century that were among the studies that made this historic moment possible.[14]

It must be said, honestly, that the results of the Reformed-Catholic dialogues, both in the United States and on the global level, have not yet reached the level of both agreement and reception that characterize the Lutheran dialogues. However, the Reformed churches have the reservoir of scholarship and the ecumenical spirit that may, in due time, produce the theological bases for unity and the will to move forward in response to Christ's will for the church.

The Catholic Church has been much slower to move on many issues than has the UCC. It is to be expected that a church so large, so diverse, and so recent in the ecumenical movement, must move with deliberate and measured speed in response to the Holy Spirit's bidding. However, all Catholics can be grateful to the United Church of Christ and to ecumenical scholars like Gabe Fackre for stimulating, prodding, and enabling us to work together as pilgrims on the way to that unity for which Christ prayed.

---

14. Karl Lehmann and Wolfhart Pannenberg, eds., *The Condemnations of the Reformation Era: Do They Still Divide?* (Minneapolis: Fortress Press, 1990).

Telling the Story: Then and Now

Alan P. F. Sell

Had you all the refined science of Plato or Socrates, all the skill in morals that ever was attained by Zeno, Seneca or Epictetus; were you furnished with all the glowing oratory of Cicero, or the thunder of Demosthenes . . . you could have no reasonable hope to convert and save one soul in Great Britain . . . while you lay aside the glorious gospel of Christ, and leave it entirely out of your discourses.[1]

With this paper I am pleased to honor a theologian who has never lost his foothold in the church and who, to a greater extent than many, has sought to locate his theological endeavors in the realities of the pastoral situation. Indeed, he is producing a multi-volume "pastoral systematics," at the heart of which is the good news of God's redeeming love in Christ. This is the story, as evangelical as it is catholic, which Gabriel Fackre has delighted to tell to diverse churches, to industrial workers in Pittsburgh, to students in Lancaster and Andover Newton seminaries, and, through his many writings, to a much wider constituency.

It is no secret that "telling the story" has been a central feature of the Reformed family's life. Truth to tell, the sermon has sometimes been so elevated in importance that other components of the liturgy have been demoted to "mere preliminaries." Again, the Reformed tradition

---

1. Isaac Watts, *An Humble Attempt towards the Revival of Practical Religion among Christians,* in *The Works of the Reverend and Learned Isaac Watts, D.D.,* 6 vols. (London: J. Barfield, 1810), III, p. 15.

has contributed considerably to the literature of homiletics, and that there is still work to be done in this field is exemplified by a remark made to me: "His sermons are just a lot of hot air, but doesn't he do a wonderful 'pause for profile'?" But my concern here is not with the place of the sermon in the liturgy, or with the techniques of preaching. I simply wish to ask, how has the privilege of preaching been viewed in the Reformed family, and what have our forebears in the faith to teach us on the matter? I propose to limit this vast subject by summoning two principal witnesses from the English Reformed heritage: Richard Baxter (1615-1691) and P. T. Forsyth (1848-1921). In the case of each of these a caveat must be entered. Although Baxter is the seventeenth-century's Reformed pastor *par excellence,* we should remember that in a period of ecclesiological fluidity devoid of denominations in our modern sense, he regarded "Presbyterian" as "the odious name" and, in the interests of Christian unity, was not averse to "moderate Episcopacy."[2] In 1681 he declared, "You could not (except a Catholick Christian) have trulier called me than an Episcopal-Presbyterian-Independent."[3] As for Forsyth, I annex this Scot to England only because his five pastorates and his principalship of Hackney College, London, were all on English soil, and because his contribution to English Congregationalism, and through it to the wider church, was of great significance.[4]

I

In the wake of a period of civil and religious unrest, and with toleration under the law denied to Dissenters until two years before his death, Richard Baxter returned time and again in his writings to the solemn responsi-

---

2. See *Reliquiae Baxterianae,* ed. M. Sylvester (1696), I.ii.373, para. 242; I.ii.281, para. 120. See further, Alan P. F. Sell, *Commemorations: Studies in Christian Thought and History* (Calgary: University of Calgary Press, 1993; reprinted, Eugene, OR: Wipf & Stock, 1998), ch. 3.

3. R. Baxter, *Third Defence of the Cause of Peace* (1681), I, p. 110.

4. For the welcome revival of interest in Forsyth's theology see Trevor Hart, ed., *Justice the True and Only Mercy: Essays on the Life and Theology of P. T. Forsyth* (Edinburgh: T&T Clark, 1995); Leslie McCurdy, *Attributes and Atonement: The Holy Love of God in the Theology of P. T. Forsyth* (Carlisle: Paternoster Press, 1999); Richard L. Floyd, *When I Survey the Wondrous Cross: Reflections on the Atonement* (San Jose, CA: Pickwick Publications, 2000); Alan P. F. Sell, ed., *P. T. Forsyth: Theologian for a New Millennium* (London: The United Reformed Church, 2000).

bility and awesome privilege of proclaiming the gospel, the heart of which he construed in these terms: "By sin we have all forfeited our right to heaven; but Eternal love hath given us a Redeemer, who is God and man. . . . To acquaint men with this, is our ministerial office. . . ."[5]

It is no light task to proclaim such a gospel: "All our sermons must be fitted to change men's hearts, from carnal into spiritual, and to kindle in them the love of God,"[6] and "You cannot break men's hearts by jesting with them, or telling them a smooth tale, or patching up a gaudy oration."[7] The problem is that "Multitudes have such dead and hardened hearts, that, when we tell them that they must shortly be in heaven or hell, as they are here prepared, we speak almost as to blocks, or men asleep: they feel not what we say, as if they did not hear us."[8] Hence the urgency of preaching — an urgency which emerges in the often-ailing Baxter's oft-repeated words,

> I Preach'd as never sure to Preach again
> And as a dying man to dying men.[9]

Baxter was concerned, however, not only with the content of the message, but with the condition of the preacher: "When your minds are in a heavenly, holy frame, your people are likely to partake of the fruits of it. . . . If we let our love go down, we are not likely to raise up theirs."[10]

One further point of importance should be noted: for Baxter, preaching was grounded upon, and presupposed, consistent catechetical instruction. He exhorted church members to "Learn first your catechisms at home, and the great essential points of religion, contained in the creed, the Lord's prayer, and the ten commandments. . . . You can scarce bestow too much care and pains in learning these great essential points."[11] He did not, however, stop at exhortation. He summoned those of his people who lived in the town of Kidderminster to his home, or to that of his assistant, and he dispatched his colleague to the homes of those who lived further

---

5. R. Baxter, *Reasons for Ministers Using the Greatest Plainness and Seriousness Possible,* in *Works,* XV, p. 535.

6. R. Baxter, *Knowledge and Love Compared,* in *Works,* XV, p. 229.

7. R. Baxter, *Gildas Salvianus: The Reformed Pastor,* in *Works,* XIV, p. 225.

8. R. Baxter, *Reasons for Ministers Using Plainness with Their People,* in *Works,* XV, p. 537.

9. From Baxter's *Poetical Fragments* (1681); cf. *Reliquiae Baxterianae,* I.i, paras. 137, 32; I.i, para. 114.

10. R. Baxter, *Gildas Salvianus: The Reformed Pastor,* in *Works,* XIV, p. 223.

11. R. Baxter, *Christian Directory,* in *Works,* IV, p. 253.

afield — and all of this with pastoral and catechetical intent: "I set two Days a Week apart for this Employment: my (faithful unwearied) Assistant and my self, took fourteen Families every Week . . . bestowing about an Hour (and the Labour of a Sermon) with every Family."[12]

II

Between the death of Baxter and the working life of Forsyth there intervened a number of significant intellectual and ecclesiastical movements. There was the Enlightenment, which, insofar as it encouraged the individual's quest of conscientious and reasonable religion over against untoward authorities whether biblicist or ecclesiastical, and fostered the moral critique of a scholastic theology (which in some hands had perpetrated the blasphemous view that the Father had to be cajoled into being gracious by the death of his Son [a false "gospel" which may still be heard in some quarters to this day]), by no means merits the blanket denunciations which have been pronounced against it of late by some prolific but insufficiently discriminating theologians. This is not at all to deny that from the Enlightenment there also flowed an individual*ism*, which adversely affected church and society alike. Indeed, from one point of view the Evangelical Revival is Enlightenment individualism gone pious. This diagnosis is confirmed with particular clarity in the Congregational branch of the Reformed family. From about 1820 onwards the local covenant was in decline,[13] and with it Church Meeting — that christocratic, credal assembly of the saints, in which Christ's Lordship over the church's life was proclaimed and God's will for its mission was sought, unanimity in Christ being the objective (this was no democratic assembly with one person, one vote, and government by the majority). Baptism was a further casualty. In some quarters it was demoted and even regarded as optional, for the great thing now was a prospective member's experience of conversion.

Concurrently there were the rise of modern biblical criticism and the explosion of evolutionary thought, and these elicited Christian responses on a continuum from the petrified to the incautious.[14] There

12. *Reliquiae Baxterianae*, I.ii, para. 41.

13. For the evidence see Alan P. F. Sell, *Dissenting Thought and the Life of the Churches: Studies in an English Tradition* (Lewiston, NY: The Edwin Mellen Press, 1990), ch. 1.

14. See further, Alan P. F. Sell, *Theology in Turmoil: The Roots, Course and Significance of the Conservative-Liberal Debate in Modern Theology* (1986; Eugene, OR: Wipf & Stock, 1998).

were also the question of Catholic emancipation, perceived as a threat by many Nonconformists, and the growth within the Church of England of an Anglo-Catholicism, which in some cases seemed more Roman than the Romans, and which propelled numerous Nonconformist pamphleteers into anti-sacerdotalist mode. Some of the Congregationalists among these, seeking to beat the devil at his own game, trumpeted their conviction that in view of their acknowledgment of the sole headship of Christ over the church (subtext: not Christ plus the pope or the monarch of the day), *they* were the true high church people.

III

Into this context stepped Forsyth, a Congregational high churchman if ever there was one, and one whose language is of particular interest. He takes the terms of the ecclesiastical "opposition" and rebaptizes them into his own ecclesiology. Thus, he emphasizes the *priestly* role of the minister, and the *sacramental* nature of preaching, even utilizing such words as "host" and "transubstantiation":

> The ministry is a prophetic and sacramental office; it is not secretarial, it is not merely presidential. It is sacramental and not merely functional. It is the outward and visible agent of the inward gospel Grace. It is more sacramental than the elements. It is a living host, produced by a conversion that goes deeper than transubstantiation. It is the trustee of the one sacrament of the Word, the Word of New Creation.[15]

Elsewhere he underlines the point: "In true preaching, as in a true sacrament, more is done than said."[16] As if to encourage the fainthearted, he immediately adds, "And much is well done which is poorly said." In any case, it is the church, as the community of those living the new life, that is the preacher: "The one great preacher in history, I would contend, is the

15. P. T. Forsyth, *The Church and the Sacraments* (1917; London: Independent Press, 1953), pp. 132-133. In the very year in which this book was first published, Constance Mary Coltman became the first woman to be ordained to the Congregational ministry in England. Thereafter masculine personal pronouns were no longer appropriate when referring to those in that ministerial role as a whole.

16. P. T. Forsyth, *Positive Preaching and the Modern Mind* (1907; London: Independent Press, 1964), pp. 53-54.

Church. And the first business of the individual preacher is to enable the Church to preach."[17]

As to the content of preaching, Forsyth, the erstwhile liberal, set his face against the gospel of brotherhood, the gospel of love-gone-sentimental, any gospel in which God's holiness had been extruded from his love. He trounced any doctrine of the atonement which suggested that the Cross was exclusively to do with humanity, its sin and need. On the contrary:

> The Holy Father's first care is holiness. The first charge on a Redeemer is satisfaction to that holiness. The Holy Father is one who does and must atone. As Holy Father he offers a sacrifice rent from his own heart. It is made to him by no third party, but by himself in his Son. . . .[18]

Hence, "The Gospel of Christ is the Gospel of HOLY LOVE and its victory."[19] Conversely, "So long as the chief value of the Cross is its value for man . . . then so long shall we be led away from direct contact with reality at our religious centre. . . ."[20]

Not surprisingly, therefore, Forsyth had no patience with the idea of Christ as the first Christian. On the contrary: "A Christ that differs from the rest of men only in saintly degree and not in redeeming kind is not the Christ of the New Testament nor of a Gospel Church."[21] Fearing that "The homely may have belittled the holy," he was equally concerned to pose a further question: "The dear Christ of the Gospels — has He not obscured the great Christ of Ephesians?"[22] Above all, he could not tolerate the way in which, in some quarters, the gospel was being pared down to suit the modern mentality. While enunciating the prescription, "Reduce the burden of belief we must. The old orthodoxy laid on men's believing power more than it could carry,"[23] and while in no way an enemy of bibli-

---

17. P. T. Forsyth, *Positive Preaching and the Modern Mind*, p. 53; cf. *The Church and the Sacraments*, p. 131.

18. P. T. Forsyth, *God the Holy Father* (London: Independent Press, 1957), p. 4.

19. P. T. Forsyth, *Congregationalism and Reunion* (London: Independent Press, 1952), p. 40.

20. P. T. Forsyth, *Positive Preaching and the Modern Mind*, p. 121.

21. P. T. Forsyth, *The Church, the Gospel and Society* (London: Independent Press, 1962), p. 99.

22. P. T. Forsyth, *The Charter of the Church* (London: Alexander & Shepheard, 1896), p. 47.

23. P. T. Forsyth, *Positive Preaching and the Modern Mind*, p. 84, though see his qualification on p. 97.

cal criticism as such, he nevertheless protested that "too many are occupied in throwing over precious cargo; they are lightening the ship even of its fuel."[24] In face of all reductionism, trivializing, sentimentalizing, he reminded preachers in no uncertain terms that

> The solution of the world . . . is what destroys its guilt. And nothing can destroy guilt but the very holiness that makes guilt. And that destruction is the work of Christ upon His Cross, the Word of Life Eternal in your hands and in your souls.[25]

IV

"Telling the story: then" — but "now"? Perhaps the most prudent course would be to invite readers to ponder Baxter and Forsyth and draw their own conclusions. But since that might also be the cowardly course, I shall venture a few modest observations.

First, I value Forsyth's emphasis upon the fact that just as it is the church (and not the ministry) which celebrates the sacraments, so it is the church which is called to proclaim the gospel. In this connection, it is worth pondering the Greek terms used in Acts 8:4, 5. The church members, persecuted out of their homes following the death of Stephen, "went through the country preaching the word ('telling the good tidings')," whereas Philip, the appointed evangelist, went to Samaria and "began proclaiming (heralding — something official) the Messiah there." Acts 11:19-21 records the expansion of the church in the wake of the testimony of the "ordinary" church members. It is a humbling thing for ministers to reflect upon how much good can be done when they are nowhere in sight![26]

Secondly, I propose that we who are called to preach examine ourselves (wholesomely, not morbidly) in the light of Baxter's remarks concerning our own spiritual condition. It is not a matter of clearing our diaries so that we can accommodate a week at Iona or a fortnight at Taizé, or even a one-day course on spirituality. Hear Baxter once more:

24. P. T. Forsyth, *The Principle of Authority: Its Relation to Certainty, Sanctity and Society* (1913; London: Independent Press, 1952), p. 261.

25. P. T. Forsyth, *Positive Preaching and the Modern Mind*, p. 228.

26. This is, of course, a testimony to God's providence, not an inducement to ministerial laziness.

O brethren, watch, therefore, over your own hearts! . . . Remember, you cannot decline and neglect your duty to your own hurt alone; many will be losers by it as well as you. For your people's sake, therefore, look to your hearts.[27]

For a blunter and more concise word along the same lines, we may invoke a Baptist (albeit he was raised in Congregationalism and converted in a Primitive Methodist service). Said Charles Haddon Spurgeon (1834-1892) to his budding preachers: "We may not be butchers at the block chopping off for hungry ones the meat of which we do not partake."[28]

Thirdly, I suggest that we have much to learn from Baxter's way of supplying the pastoral and catechetical foundations for preaching. As Baxter's Congregational contemporary, John Owen (1616-1683), said, "It is the duty of a shepherd to know the state of his flock; and unless he do so he will never feed them profitably."[29] What then are we to make of such a present-day ministerial designation as, "Minister for preaching and Christian administration"? Incredible as it may seem, such persons exist; can they truly preach? "The pastor's work," said Forsyth, "is not merely to go about among the people with human sympathy and kindly help, [but to carry] Christ to the people individually, sacramentally [there is that word again]. . . . The pastor is only the preacher in retail."[30]

And how is it with the catechetical task in an age in which, in so many Western churches, pastoral visitation and Christian education are vitiated by members' personal and family timetables, and when enormous pressure is put upon the one hour per week which is all some are able to allow for churchly concerns? What are the implications of this for the size of our local churches? I was recently informed that in the Presbyterian Church U.S.A, 50% of the churches have fewer than two hundred members, while 60% of the total membership dwell in churches having more than five hundred members. If we take the relations of preaching-catechizing-pastoring seriously, the latter statistic may be ecclesiologically more problematic than the former.

Fourthly, may not Baxter and Forsyth together recall us to the solemnity and urgency of the preacher's task? This is not the place for one

---

27. R. Baxter, *Gildas Salvianus: The Reformed Pastor,* in *Works,* XIV, p. 224.

28. C. H. Spurgeon, *An All-Round Ministry* (1900; London: The Banner of Truth Trust, 1960), p. 66.

29. *The Works of John Owen,* ed. William Gold (1850-1853; London: The Banner of Truth Trust, 1968), IV, p. 511.

30. P. T. Forsyth, *The Church and the Sacraments,* p. 145.

more diatribe against "feel good" religion; but let us at least heed Forsyth: "There are crowds and crowds of even Christian people who are sympathetic for every human ache . . . who have a heart for every plea of man, but they are entirely heartless for the affliction of the God of a prodigal race with the iniquity of it all laid upon His holy Soul."[31] How dare any preach half a doctrine of atonement — as if the sacrifice of Christ were for humanity alone?

Fifthly, in their different ways, both Baxter and Forsyth understood the distinction that Isaac Watts drew for preachers in these terms:

> Let your hearers know that there is a vast and unspeakable difference betwixt a saint and a sinner, one in Christ, and one out of Christ. . . . [The change is made] by the operations of the word and Spirit of God on the hearts of men, and by their diligent attendance on all the appointed means and methods of converting grace. It is a most real change, and of infinite importance. . . .[32]

It is not too much to say that the entire Congregational polity turns upon this distinction. What are the implications of this for our churches' present bearing in society? Undeniably, churches and Christians can be "different" in obnoxious ways, which are a woeful hindrance to the gospel. But can they not also be so identified with the world around that any distinctiveness is lost, and with it the challenge of the gospel, the rigor and exhilaration of the "godly walk," and the ability to utter a prophetic word?[33]

This uncritical blending may even be revealed in our language. We saw how Forsyth took the terms of others and rebaptized them to his own use. May it not be that we in the West have poached the terms of the corporate world and shown no inclination to rebaptize them (were that even possible)? Can we imagine that Baxter or Forsyth would think of the ministry as a "job," that they would be impressed by talk of "ministerial career patterns" or the "hiring and firing" of pastors; that they would rate the person in a four-point charge lower than one in a "tall steeple church," or think of the latter as having been "promoted"? By their language ye shall know them.[34] Where in all of this has gone the doctrine of vocation? It

---

31. P. T. Forsyth, *Faith, Freedom and the Future* (1912; London: Independent Press, 1955), pp. 282-283.

32. Isaac Watts, *Works*, III, p. 18.

33. See further, Alan P. F. Sell in *P. T. Forsyth: Theologian for a New Millennium*, ch. 9.

34. See further, Alan P. F. Sell, *Aspects of Christian Integrity* (1990; Eugene, OR: Wipf & Stock, 1998), ch. 6.

may be that the introduction of the corporate model is to some extent a function of congregational size, to which reference has already been made. But this simply raises again the questions: Can local churches be too large? May we not have lost more than we have gained in our carving up of ministerial functions into "specialisms" — even granted that an individual minister may not be equally competent in all aspects of the work?

Finally, it must be granted that Baxter and Forsyth cannot do all our work for us. However it may have been in their own preaching, in their writings on preaching they do not have much to say concerning the need to ensure that the major themes of the Christian faith are regularly enunciated from the pulpit. Perhaps they could take it for granted. I have good reason to think that we cannot. Too many worshippers are deprived of the eschatological note; Pentecost can be transmogrified into Animal Sunday; and in itinerant situations, the situation can be even more haphazard. While I should not wish to belong to a church which required the slavish use of a lectionary, it is not too much to ask that preachers at least heed the Christian Year, and treat their hearers to biblical expositions which will acquaint them with the main arteries of that "body of divinity" about which some of our forebears unburdened themselves at such great length.

Baxter, and even Forsyth to a lesser degree, could accept the assumptions of Christendom, whereas we can no longer do so. Thus, Baxter specifies the matters that the minister is obliged to teach to the people, and these matters assume the existence of God, the viability of natural theology, and the pre-critical recourse to biblical evidences.[35] While our sermons should not become disquisitions on apologetics, we should certainly be aware that many faithful church members harbor doubts concerning basic Christian doctrines which they may feel inhibited from articulating, either because they fear that the minister's reply will not rise above banalities or platitudes, or because the godly will pronounce them lacking in faith, or both. In too many cases such people, having looked up and not been fed, drift elsewhere, or worship nowhere.

Again, although they were both staunchly trinitarian, neither Baxter nor Forsyth related this aspect of their faith in detail to their remarks on preaching. They were, like Paul and Augustine before them, occasional writers rather than Barth-like systematicians.[36] For my part, however, I should like to express my opinion that, no matter how varied the cultural,

---

35. See R. Baxter, *Christian Directory,* in *Works,* V, pp. 120-130.

36. See further, Alan P. F. Sell, "P. T. Forsyth as Unsystematic Systematician," in *Justice the True and Only Mercy,* ch. 8.

intellectual, sociopolitical contexts of Christian preaching may be, *the* context of preaching is the gracious work of the triune God who, on the ground of the Son's saving work at the Cross, calls out a people by his Holy Spirit, who shall praise and serve their heavenly Father now and eternally.

It is a happy thought that both streams of the English Reformed tradition[37] — the Presbyterian and the Congregational — were involved in the Westminster Assembly. That Assembly's Larger Catechism contains the question: "How is the word of God to be preached by those that are called thereunto?" The answer is:

> They that are called to labor in the ministry of the word, are to preach sound doctrine, diligently, in season and out of season; plainly, not in the enticing words of man's wisdom, but in demonstration of the Spirit, and of power; faithfully, making known the whole counsel of God; wisely, applying themselves to the necessities and capacities of the hearers; zealously, with fervent love to God and the souls of his people; sincerely, aiming at his glory, and their conversion, edification, and salvation.

More than 350 years on, that answer remains as challenging as it is comprehensive.

---

37. I do not, of course, deny that among the Anglicans and the Baptists there are those who have swallowed gallons of Reformed doctrine in eager gulps. Here I refer to the Reformed family as such, in distinction from the Anglican and the Baptist.

The Formative Role of the American Churches in the Origin and Development of the Faith and Order Movement

Paul A. Crow, Jr.

To share in a Festschrift in honor of Gabriel Fackre allows me to celebrate a dear friend and a great American theologian. The Crow-Fackre friendship was cemented during a common sabbatical year (1967-1968) at Oxford University, where Gabe and I engaged in theological conversations amid sherry hours and stately high table dinners at Mansfield College. In later years, those conversations were transferred to visits at our home in Princeton and their home on Cape Cod. My simple theology was chastened and deepened by his gifts of friendship and gentle tutoring.

Gabe's books have been distinctive landmarks in theology arising from the American experience, and incidentally in my own. To this day, *The Christian Story* series remains a treasured resource on my library shelves as a sign of stability offered by a theologian who wrestles with the gospel in an ever-changing world. His *Ecumenical Faith in Evangelical Perspective* named one of my ecumenical blind spots. While I always believed myself to be an "evangelical catholic," Gabe led me to confess my sin of not taking evangelical Christians seriously enough as partners in the Ecumenical Movement. So, too, this Cape Cod theologian counseled me and countless others in our encounter with radical pluralism. Regardless of the perimeters of the culture, the ultimate truth is still known and confessed in Jesus Christ through Scripture and tradition. In today's theological and missional crisis we are called to be a "church of the Center," whose theological identity is grounded not in chasing the cultural moment, but in the permanence of the gospel expressed in the doctrines of Christology, the Trinity, and soteriology. Gabe Fackre is a premier theologian in America, whose humble yet forceful brilliance has tutored all sorts and conditions of Christians, and drawn the right and the left into dialogue about the eternal gospel.

The Faith and Order Movement, born in the early years of the twentieth century, has been central to the modern Ecumenical Movement.[1] Its fundamental purpose, articulated in its present constitution, is "to proclaim the oneness of the Church of Jesus Christ and to call the churches to the goal of visible unity in one faith and one eucharistic fellowship, expressed in worship and in common life in Christ, in order that the world may believe."[2] This vision and its expression in a movement of the churches are inspired by the biblical vision of the one people of God, and the Church's calling to be a reconciling and healing presence in a divided world.

What is rarely known or written, even by ecumenical historians, is the formative role that the churches in the United States played in the founding and development of the Faith and Order Movement. The movement actually originated from a fascinating trilateral initiative — in the same week in 1910 — of the Protestant Episcopal Church, the Disciples of Christ, and the Congregational Church in the U.S. This fact is evidence of the diversity of traditions which shared the same vision.

Charles Henry Brent, a missionary bishop of the Protestant Episcopal Church (USA) in the Philippine Islands, was a delegate to the historic World Missionary Conference in Edinburgh, Scotland in August 1910. For the sake of a wider participation of churches and missionary societies, Edinburgh deliberately excluded faith and order issues from the agenda. Bishop Brent's passion for Christian unity, however, led him and others at Edinburgh to envision another world conference that would address the

---

1. For introductions to Faith and Order's history covered in this essay, see Herbert Newell Bate, "Faith and Order, 1910-1927," in *Faith and Order: Proceedings of the World Conference, Lausanne, August 3-21, 1927* (New York: George H. Doran, 1927), pp. vii-xv; Tissington Tatlow, "The World Conference on Faith and Order," in *A History of the Ecumenical Movement, 1517-1948*, ed. Ruth Rouse and Stephen Charles Neill (Philadelphia: The Westminster Press, 1954), pp. 405-441; David P. Gaines, *The World Council of Churches: A Study of Its Background and History* (Peterborough, NH: Richard R. Noone, 1966), pp. 139-145. All of these authors eclipse the formative roles of the Disciples of Christ and the Congregational Church in the U.S. in the origins of Faith and Order.

2. "By-laws of the Faith and Order Movement," in *On the Way to Fuller Koinonia; Official Report of the Fifth World Conference on Faith and Order, 1993*, ed. Thomas F. Best and Gunther Gassmann, Faith and Order Paper No. 166 (Geneva: WCC Publications, 1994), p. 309.

theological divisions that had shattered the fellowship of all Christian churches. Faith and order issues might be postponed, but they cannot be avoided forever.[3] Thus, when the General Convention of the Protestant Episcopal Church gathered at Cincinnati, Ohio in October 1910, a resolution — under Brent's inspiration — was passed by the House of Deputies and the House of Bishops, stating:

> That a Joint Commission [of clergy, laity and bishops] be appointed to bring about a Conference for the consideration of questions touching Faith and Order, and that all Christian Communions throughout the world which confess Our Lord Jesus Christ as God and Savior be asked to unite with us in arranging for conducting such a conference.[4]

The commission was duly appointed with Bishop Charles P. Anderson of Chicago as president; Robert Hallowell Gardiner, a lay person and Boston lawyer, as secretary; and George Zabriskie, a Wall Street lawyer, as treasurer. After the General Convention, Bishop Brent returned to his ministry in the Philippines, although his leadership remained constant through correspondence and visits to the United States. John Pierpoint Morgan, a wealthy financier and lay person, generously contributed $100,000 toward the expenses of planning and convening the world conference.

By providence or coincidence, the International Convention of the Disciples of Christ gathered at Topeka, Kansas during the same week in October 1910. Peter Ainslie, pastor of the large and influential Christian Temple (Disciples of Christ) in Baltimore, Maryland, was that year the president.[5] His presidential travels throughout the United States the previous year alarmed Ainslie about the sectarian spirit among American Protestantism, and particularly the loss among the Disciples of the vision of a united church, which they had inherited from their nineteenth-century founders, Thomas and Alexander Campbell and Barton Warren Stone, and which was uniquely the reason for the Disciples' existence.

3. See Alexander C. Zabriskie, *Bishop Brent: Crusader for Christian Unity* (Philadelphia: The Westminster Press, 1948); and Eugene C. Bianchi, "The Ecumenical Thought of Bishop Charles Henry Brent," *Church History* 33 (December 1964).

4. An official Statement by the Joint Commission of the Protestant Episcopal Church in the United States of America. Faith and Order Pamphlet No. 14, pp. 15-16.

5. See Finis S. Idleman, *Peter Ainslie: Ambassador of Good Will* (Chicago: Willett, Clark and Co., 1941); Charles Clayton Morrison, "Peter Ainslie — A Catholic Protestant," *Christendom* 1 (Autumn 1935): pp. 44-65; Paul A. Crow, Jr., "Peter Ainslie," in *The Encyclopedia of the Stone-Campbell Movement* (Nashville: Disciples of Christ Historical Society, 2001).

Ainslie's address to the assembly, a classic in ecumenical literature, called upon the Disciples to reclaim their original commitment to Christian unity and catholicity by taking immediate actions that would lead to a united church.[6]

In response to Ainslie's prophetic call, the convention took two far-reaching actions on October 18, one day prior to the Episcopal action. First, the Disciples called for "a world conference on Christian Unity." (Immediately after this decision, Peter Ainslie sent a telegram to the Episcopal General Convention announcing the Disciples' action and pledging their commitment to participate in the preparations for a World Conference on Faith and Order.) Second, at Topeka, the Disciples of Christ established a Council on Christian Union (later changed to the Association for the Promotion of Christian Unity and still later to the Council on Christian Unity). Its mandate was "to promote Christian union at home and throughout the world until the various Christian bodies are knit together in one organic life." Its functions were to create and distribute literature "bearing on Christian union," to arrange for conferences with other communions, and to make plans for a World Conference on Faith and Order.

In this action, the Disciples became the first American church to establish a permanent national church agency with such a representative mandate. Peter Ainslie was elected the first president. Henry C. Armstrong, Ainslie's associate in Baltimore, was elected secretary. Frederick W. Burnham, president of the Disciples' American Christian Missionary Society, was made the secretary of the Disciples Commission for the World Conference. In 1911, the Council on Christian Union was founded and Ainslie began to edit *The Christian Union Quarterly* (1911-1934), a popular international journal that became the unofficial carrier of articles and reports interpreting the Faith and Order Movement and church union negotiations in different parts of the world.[7] Ainslie also convened numer-

---

6. Peter Ainslie, "Our Fellowship and the Task," *Christian Union Library*, No. 4 (April 1912), pp. 15-27. For Ainslie's account of the Disciples of Christ's involvement in the origins of Faith and Order, see his autobiography, *Working with God* (St. Louis: Christian Board of Publication, 1917), pp. 297-330.

7. The original name of *Christian Union Library* was changed in 1913 to *The Christian Union Quarterly*. Upon Ainslie's death in 1934, *The Christian Union Quarterly* was broadened in scope and renamed *Christendom* by its new editor Charles Clayton Morrison, editor of *The Christian Century* and Disciples ecumenist. When the World Council of Churches ("WCC") was in process of formation, Dr. Morrison stopped publication of *Christendom* and urged the WCC to publish a major ecumenical journal. There is distinct continuity

ous conferences across the United States, interpreting the hopes and prospects of the nascent movement. Although ecumenical historians have ignored or scarcely noticed him, Peter Ainslie, a close friend of Bishop Brent, was a central voice in the creation of Faith and Order.[8]

The third churchly action which led to the formation of the Faith and Order Movement came, also in October 1910, by the decision of the National Council of the Congregational Churches in the United States, meeting in Boston. Certain Congregational leaders had been inspired by the encyclical on Christian unity issued by the 1908 Lambeth Conference of Anglican bishops. The Congregational assembly, also on October 18, unanimously passed a resolution stating their willingness to participate in any overture toward unity from Anglicans that "desires not compromise but comprehension, not uniformity but unity." The prime movers in this action were Newman Smyth, minister of the Center Congregational Church in New Haven, Connecticut and a friend of Peter Ainslie; Raymond Calkins, Congregational minister in Portland, Maine; and Nehemiah Boynton, pastor in Brooklyn, New York and moderator of the church. A committee was then appointed to consider any overtures that might come, and — like the Disciples — sent a telegram to the Episcopal General Convention expressing the willingness of the Congregational Church to join in the preparations for a World Conference on Faith and Order.[9] Obviously, the winds from Cincinnati and Topeka had reached Boston.

In later years, Peter Ainslie interpreted these actions as "each body

---

from Ainslie's *Christian Union Quarterly* through *Christendom* to *The Ecumenical Review*, the official organ of the WCC.

8. When John R. Mott addressed the First Assembly of the WCC at Amsterdam in 1948, he lauded "the twelve apostles of the modern Ecumenical Movement." One of his twelve was Peter Ainslie. In his Hoover lectures in 1948, ecumenical theologian Walter Marshall Horton wrote of Ainslie: "If Bishop Brent (who first conceived the idea of Faith and Order, launched the movement, and eventually presided at Lausanne) is justly numbered among the ecumenical pioneers and patriarchs, along with Mott of Edinburgh and Soderblom of Stockholm, *Ainslie is his twin*, who should always be remembered with him." See his *Toward a Reborn Church: A Review and Forecast of the Ecumenical Movement* (New York: Harper and Brothers, 1949), p. 8. Also, the judgment of Alexander Zabriskie's biography of Brent throws a similar accolade: "If this biography were a history of Faith and Order, there would have to be a full discussion of the part played by leading clergymen and laymen of other churches, like John R. Mott, William Adams Brown, Peter Ainslie, John D. Rockefeller, and many others." See *Bishop Brent*, p. 150.

9. See Report of the Committee on Church Unity of the National Council of the Congregational Churches, Faith and Order Paper No. 25 (1913), pp. 5-16.

acting independently and without any knowledge of what the others were doing, indicating that the Spirit of Christ was moving the hearts of Christians in various Communions at the same time."[10] J. Robert Nelson, Faith and Order historian and former staff member, once mused: "Three initiatives, virtually simultaneous, and yet unknown to one another at the time! Was it coincidence? Personal agreement? Providence?"[11] To any modern ecumenical skeptic, the beginning of Faith and Order among American churches was a matter of good friends and visionaries, led by the Holy Spirit, acting in concert.

Once the movement was proclaimed, an Episcopal layman and lawyer in Boston became its primary catalyst. Robert H. Gardiner, at the age of fifty-five, undertook what he called "a late vocation to unity" and assumed the voluntary office of secretary of the Episcopal commission with fervor and grace. From the perspective of history, it would be impossible to overestimate his spiritual and administrative leadership within the Faith and Order Movement from 1910 until his death in 1924. He was a quiet person of sound judgment and a deep spirituality. His openness to all Christian traditions and diplomatic gifts calmed many an ecclesiastical hesitancy and attracted very diverse churches to commit themselves to the new movement.[12] Gardiner's phenomenal correspondence is unique in the annals of church history. In the first three years (1910-1913), 600,000 letters and pamphlets were mailed to leaders of most churches in the world — Protestant, Orthodox, Old Catholic, and Roman Catholic. In the same period, Gardiner wrote an astonishing 30,000 letters to all sorts of correspondents. In a creative stroke, Gardiner began in late 1910 to print and widely distribute throughout the world a series of Faith and Order pamphlets, which shared the vision and reports of theological studies and conferences of the movement. All of this administration and diplomacy was accomplished by one man, assisted by secretaries, labor-

---

10. Peter Ainslie, *Towards Christian Unity* (Baltimore: Association for the Promotion of Christian Unity, 1918), p. 45.

11. J. Robert Nelson, "Faith and Order: Five Decades and a Forward View," *Mid-Stream: An Ecumenical Journal* 16 (October 1977): 264.

12. See the commemoration of Gardiner in *Faith and Order: Proceedings of the World Conference, Lausanne, August 3-21, 1927*, ed. H. N. Bate (New York: George H. Doran Company, 1927), pp. 12-13. See Brent's tribute to Gardiner in *The Christian Union Quarterly* 14 (October 1924): 193-195; also Ralph Ruhtenberg, "Robert H. Gardiner: Laie und Organisator der Bewegung für Glauben und Kirchenvegussung," in *Ökumenische Profile: Brückenbauer der Einen Kirche,* ed. Günter Gloede, lst volume (Stuttgart: Evangelische Missionsverlag, 1961), pp. 190-200.

ing in an office in the small village of Gardiner, Maine, his ancestral home.

After these initiatory actions, the Episcopal Commission assumed the primary roles of leadership and decision making. Their first action was to invite churches from different parts of the world, "which confess Our Lord Jesus Christ as God and Savior," to commit themselves to the movement and appoint commissions or committees to prepare their churches for the World Conference. In the first year (1911), eighteen commissions were appointed; seventeen in the U.S. and one in Canada. By 1913, thirty commissions and, by 1920, seventy commissions in forty countries were engaged in preparations for the Lausanne Conference. After the Episcopal, Disciples, and Congregationalist, other commissions included Presbyterian (Southern and Northern) and Reformed; the American section of the Alliance for Reformed Churches Holding the Presbyterian System; the Methodist Episcopal Church (North and South); the Southern Baptist Convention; the Northern Baptist and the Free Baptist churches; the Moravian Church; and the Evangelical Lutheran Church. A tangential Canadian presence was insured when the Episcopal Commission invited the Church of England in Canada — but not the Presbyterians, Congregationalists, Methodists and Disciples — to participate.

Great care was given in these early years to exegeting the purpose and character of the embryonic movement. In April 1911, a special Committee on Plan and Scope (later renamed the Executive Committee) met and produced a preliminary statement of the Faith and Order Movement's ultimate aim and purpose, as well as the next steps to be pursued. Envisioned was a world conference that would involve the full participation of representatives of the whole Christian world — Catholic, Protestant, and Orthodox. The method would involve study and dialogue "without the power to legislate or to adopt resolutions." As was agreed, "The Conference is for the definite purpose of considering those things in which we differ, in the hope that a better understanding of divergent views of Faith and Order will result in a deepened desire for reunion and in official action on the part of the separated Communions themselves."[13] It is important to observe that this early plan of action placed prayer for Christian unity at the center of the movement. Expressive of this commitment was an early Faith and Order pamphlet titled *A Manual of Prayers for Unity* (No. 29), which con-

---

13. Report of the Committee on Plan and Scope, Faith and Order Pamphlet No. 3 (1911), p. 4.

tained litanies, private and public prayers, and a service of intercession for unity offered as a resource for the churches.[14]

In order to gain the confidence and eventual participation of the churches outside the United States, it was decided to send several deputations to meet church leaders personally in other parts of the world. Three were envisioned: to the Church of England and to Anglicans in Scotland, Wales, and Ireland; to Nonconformist churches in Great Britain and Ireland; to Protestant and Orthodox churches in Europe and the Near East; and to the Vatican.

In June 1912, the Episcopal Commission sent a deputation to their sister Anglican churches in Great Britain and Ireland, "especially the mother Church of England," with the intent of securing their participation in the preparations for the World Conference. Included in the delegation were Bishop Charles P. Anderson of Chicago, Bishop Boyd Vincent of Southern Ohio, Bishop A. C. A. Hall of Vermont, and Dr. William T. Manning. A private conference, chaired by the Archbishops of Canterbury (Randall Davidson) and York (Cosmos Lang), was held in Lambeth Palace in London. The result was the appointment of a Church of England committee to monitor the progress towards the World Conference, organize support and participation throughout England, and encourage prayers for the process among the parishes and dioceses. Hope was expressed for the participation of other English denominations, although it was admitted that such was more likely to come from the encouragement of their "co-religionists in America." In his concluding statement to the delegation, Archbishop Davidson urged that it would be "helpful to the satisfactory working of the whole plan [for a World Conference] that its American origin should be borne in mind, as also the possibility or probability that the ultimate Conference, when held, would be on American soil."[15]

In January of the next year (1913), a second delegation was sent by the Episcopal Commission to confer with the Nonconformist churches in Great Britain.[16] The prospects were a little more tender, because none of these churches had yet taken action to participate in the Faith and Order conferences. This slowness to engage in the movement was veiled in a suspicion that reflected the deep wounds in the ecclesiastical history of Great

14. A Manual of Prayers for Unity, Faith and Order Pamphlet No. 29 (1915).

15. The report of this delegation appeared in the Report of the Joint Commission of the General Convention of the Protestant Episcopal Church, Faith and Order Pamphlet No. 23, 1913. See p. 10.

16. See Report of the Second Deputation to Great Britain, Faith and Order Pamphlet No. 27 (1914), pp. 4-10.

Britain. An observation of American church historian Winfred E. Garrison gets at the issue: "So much did the incipient Faith and Order movement take on the appearance of an Anglican project that the British Nonconformists had some difficulty in seeing that there was a place in it for them."[17] The members of this deputation included Peter Ainslie (Disciples of Christ), Newman Smyth (Congregationalist), and William H. Roberts (Stated Clerk of the General Assembly of the Presbyterian Church in the U.S.A.), all key leaders in the movement from its beginning.

As would be expected, this triad of mainline Protestant leaders met with a variety of churches. Thirty-one conferences took place with officials of all the leading communions, including the Archbishops' Committee, the Presbyterian Church of England, the Congregational Union, Wesleyan and United Methodists, Primitive Methodists, the Welsh Calvinist Methodists, the Churches of Christ (Disciples of Christ), Baptists, and the Society of Friends. Conferences were held with representatives of the Free Church Council, as well as joint Anglican and Free Church groups at Oxford and Cambridge. In Scotland, large gatherings brought together representatives of the Church of Scotland, the United Free Church, the Congregational Church of Scotland, the Presbyterian Church of Ireland, and others. In all instances, promises were made to form Faith and Order committees leading to support for the World Conference. Upon their return, Smyth, Roberts, and Ainslie reported to the Advisory Committee (March 12, 1914) telling publicly of the exceptionally positive responses to Faith and Order among the Nonconformists in Great Britain. Yet, confidentially, they described a sense of ecumenical pathos they found among these churches, "a feeling of the utter hopelessness of any inter-relationship, outside the personal ones, with the Established Church."[18] Yet also, they confessed, the brokenness of the church in Britain validated the necessity of a movement for unity that might bring new ecumenical perspectives.

In the meantime, a series of preparatory conferences in the United States began to chart the route toward the World Conference. The first

17. Winfred E. Garrison, *Christian Unity and the Disciples of Christ* (St. Louis: The Bethany Press, 1955), p. 185.

18. See this discussion in Faith and Order Pamphlet No. 27, pp. 11-25. The historic alienation between Nonconformists and Anglicans had the year before (1913) been exacerbated by the Kikuya (East Africa) controversy. The Anglican bishop of Zanzibar made a "tempestuous denunciation" of a eucharistic service presided over by the Anglican bishop of Mombasa and shared by Anglicans, British Methodists, and Church of Scotland ministers and members. See Roger Lloyd, *The Church of England, 1900-1965* (London: SCM Press, 1966), pp. 424-428.

occasion when appointed representatives of other churches met with the Episcopal commission was on May 8, 1913, at the Astor Hotel in New York City. William T. Manning, rector of Trinity Episcopal Church in New York and later Bishop of New York, was chosen chairperson and Robert H. Gardiner, secretary. The spirit of this gathering was optimistic, although the minutes recorded "a deep realization of the difficulties with which this undertaking is confronted."

It was in this meeting that these early architects of Faith and Order came to a common mind about the character and nature of a World Conference, saying:

1. That the true ideal of the World Conference is of a great meeting participated in by men [sic] of all Christian churches within the scope of the call, at which there shall be consideration not only of points of difference and agreement between Christians, but of the values of the various approximations to belief characteristic of the several churches.

2. That while organic unity is the ideal which all Christians should have in their thoughts and prayers, yet the business of the Commissions is not to force any particular scheme of unity, but to promote the holding of such a Conference as is above described.

3. That in order that the World Conference may have a maximum value, the questions there to be considered shall be formulated in advance by committees of competent men [sic] representative of various schools of thought, these committees to be appointed at as early a date as is consistent with assurance that their truly representative character cannot be successfully challenged.[19]

Significant at this meeting was the presence of the Very Rev. Alexander A. Hotovitzky, dean of the Russian Orthodox Cathedral in New York and the first Orthodox to appear at these meetings. In the spirit of candor he proposed that the first step toward the realization of Faith and Order purposes might be "to embrace your Protestant churches all together. . . . If you cannot do that, how can you expect to reconcile such differences as exist with the Eastern Orthodox Church or the Roman Catholic Church?"[20] Yet, Dean Hotovitzky expressed his conviction that his Russian Orthodox Church would participate in the World Conference.

19. A First Preliminary Conference, Faith and Order Pamphlet No. 24 (1913), p. 46.
20. Ibid., p. 48.

Six months later (November 19, 1913), an Advisory Committee — composed of the Episcopal commission and one representative from each church committed to the World Conference — began to meet and oversee the work of Faith and Order. This move represented an official sharing of leadership indicative of a truly ecumenical spirit. It symbolized the eventual shift from Faith and Order being perceived as "the Episcopal movement," to a movement in which leadership with other churches was truly collegial. This multichurch Advisory Committee met at least annually from 1913 to 1919, until the pivotal preparatory meeting at Geneva in 1920.

In August 1914, the First World War broke upon an unprepared world. Obviously all international contacts and meetings had to be postponed for an indefinite future. Providentially, however, the churches in the United States decided to continue their preparations for the World Conference until such time as relationships with their partner churches in Europe and other parts of the world could be resumed. Sadly, these war years and their aftermath created new enmities and suspicion among nations and churches. In terms of ecumenism, however, both the sense of division and the search for reconciliation were intensified.

In order to press forward during the war, a North American Preparatory Conference was convened at Garden City, Long Island, New York, January 4-6, 1916. Invited were members of all the Faith and Order commissions in the United States and the Church of England in Canada. Sixty-three men attended, representing fifteen churches. For the first time, the moderators of this meeting represented diverse traditions: Episcopal, Presbyterian and Reformed, Methodist, Baptist, Disciples of Christ, Congregational, and Lutheran. The focus of the agenda was upon the next steps to be taken toward the World Conference.

The substance of the Garden City Conference was expressed in a document titled "Direction and Spiritual Basis of the World Conference." The Declaration, drafted by Newman Smyth, placed the search for visible unity among the churches in the context of war and social instability: "The catastrophe which has fallen upon modern civilization may be hastening the time for a united church to come forth as one power and with one obedience to make the rule of Christianity the law of the nations. . . . To do our part we must study seriously, as we never have done before, the things that make for peace." Further, the document identified the theological basis of the World Conference as "the faith of the whole Church, as created by Christ, resting on the Incarnation and continued from age to age by His indwelling Life until He comes." The proposed method must accentuate the universal. "It is for each communion to think and act in terms of the whole. In and through our relation to the whole Church may we rightly and finally determine our relations to one another." Above all, it is critical to understand that the call for a World Conference is "the call of Christ's love for a whole Church to carry salvation to the whole world."[21] This language made clear the essence of the Faith and Order Movement.

The Garden City Conference identified five "larger questions," which they proposed as the theological substance agenda of the World Conference:

1. The church, its nature and functions
2. The catholic creeds, as the safeguards of the faith of the church
3. Grace and the sacraments in general
4. The ministry, its nature and functions
5. Practical questions connected with the missionary and administrative functions[22]

This list of themes, with several additions, became the working agenda for the World Conference when it convened at Lausanne, Switzerland in 1927.

At the end of this meeting, a North American Preparation Committee was appointed to continue the groundwork for the conference, anticipated to be convened after the end of the war. Its identified tasks were: to gather a committee of theologians, canonists, and other persons to flesh out the five issues; to secure from all the participating denominational commissions a formulation of the perspectives of their communion on these issues; and to compile a bibliography of books and documents which expound their communion's teachings. Also, each church was requested to prepare a statement identifying their theological perspectives on the five issues and especially making clear where their tradition agrees and where it disagrees with other communions. The intent of these denominational statements was to bring "clarity and charity and be respectful of diversity." It is important to observe that at this early juncture in the history of Faith and Order, the method of what later was called "comparative ecclesiology" came into play.

21. "Declaration and Spiritual Basis of the World Conference," in Faith and Order Pamphlet No. 30 (1916), pp. 3-5.
22. See typescript of the *Proceedings of the North American Conference in Preparation for the World Conference on Faith and Order, Garden City, Long Island, New York, January 4-6, 1916,* p. 236. Faith and Order Archives of the World Council of Churches, Geneva.

Upon the signing of the armistice in 1918, the Episcopal Commission resumed plans to send a deputation to continental Europe and the Near East.[23] Those appointed were Bishops Charles P. Anderson (Chicago), Boyd Vincent (Southern Ohio), R. H. Weller (Fond du Lac), E. L. Parsons (later bishop of San Francisco), and Dr. B. T. Rogers. In March 1919, the first leg of their journey to Greece was complicated by postwar delays that required them to travel via a French war cruiser, an American submarine, and military cars of several nations before reaching Athens. Once there they met with the Metropolitan and Holy Synod of the Church of Greece, who enthusiastically agreed to appoint representatives to the World Conference. In Constantinople, the spiritual center of the Eastern Orthodox Church, Ecumenical Patriarch Dorotheos welcomed them with open arms and the Holy Synod expressed its readiness to send competent delegates to the conference. A visit was also made to the Orthodox Theological College on the sacred island of Halki for conversations with President Germanos Strenopoulos, later to become Archbishop of Thyateira and a president of the World Council of Churches.

While at Halki, serious conversations took place with Metropolitan Platon, Russian Orthodox Metropolitan of Odessa, who was in exile from the Marxist regime. He reported with a sense of pathos: "The Church of Russia is now sick in body, mind and spirit, but when she gets well again she will doubtless be represented at the Conference." With deliberate and extensive focus on the hoped-for presence of the Orthodox Church in Faith and Order, the delegation made visits to Smyrna, Sofia, Bucharest, Belgrade, Alexandria, Cairo, Jerusalem, and Damascus. In all these places it was agreed to send representatives to the World Conference, believing, as Metropolitan Dimitrije of Belgrade said, it "would be of great advantage for the most effective teaching of the Gospel of our Lord to all mankind." Later in London the delegation met with the Orthodox Archbishop of Cyprus, who pledged the unanimous support of his synod.

The delegation's European itinerary took them to France, Norway, and Sweden. In Paris, they met with Professor Wilfred Monod, President of the Reformed Churches of France, and other French Protestant leaders. In Norway, the bishops of Bergen and Christiania became advocates of the cause. In Sweden, a major conference of Lutheran theologians was convened by Nathan Soderblom, the Archbishop of Uppsala, the inspirational leader of the Life and Work Movement, and a pivotal voice at the

23. Report of the Deputation to Europe and the East, Faith and Order Pamphlet No. 32 (1919).

Lausanne Conference in 1927. Problems of travel and communication precluded intended visits to Finland, Denmark, and Holland, although formal invitations were later sent by mail. The delegation discovered that Germany was "inaccessible on account of internal conditions." The brokenness created by the war remained to be healed among Christians, and confidence in the World Conference needed to be regained. Many German Christians believed Faith and Order was "a veiled Anglican imperialistic plot," which obviously was "a misgiving shared, to some extent in certain other Continental nations."[24] For the moment, the German churches refused all invitations to share in the World Conference.

A dramatic event in our story happened when the delegation traveled to the Vatican to interpret the conference, and to invite the official participation of the Roman Catholic Church. The idea for such a visit came from Gardiner's earlier correspondence with Cardinal Gasparri, the Secretary of State during the pontificate of Benedict XV. Archbishop Cerretti, the Secretary of Extraordinary Affairs, arranged for this diplomatic visit, which Fr. Thomas F. Stransky, Catholic ecumenist extraordinaire, calls "the first face-to-face contact between a post-Reformation pope and the bishops of another church."[25] In advance of their audience, the delegation conveyed to the Pope a formal invitation — in Latin — to the World Conference and a statement — in English — about the nature and issues of Faith and Order. At the audience, they were graciously received by Cardinal Gasparri and Benedict XV, who listened with utmost graciousness to their appeal. As the delegation left the audience, they were handed a statement:

> The Holy Father, after having thanked them for their visit stated that as the successor of St. Peter and Vicar of Christ he had no greater desire than that there should be one fold and one shepherd. His Holiness added that the teaching and practice of the Roman Catholic Church, regarding the unity of the visible Church of Christ was well known to everybody and therefore it would not be possible for the Catholic Church to take part in such a Congress as the one proposed. His Holiness, however, by no means wishes to disapprove of the Congress in question for those who are not in union with the Chair of Peter; on the contrary He earnestly desires and prays that, if the Congress is practicable, those who take part in it may, by the grace of God,

---

24. David P. Gaines, *The World Council of Churches: A Study of Its Background and History*, p. 143.

25. Thomas F. Stransky, CSP, "A Basis Beyond the Basis: Roman Catholic/World Council of Churches Collaboration," *The Ecumenical Review* 37 (April 1985): 214.

see the light and become reunited to the visible Head of the Church, by whom they will be received with open arms.[26]

In their later report to the U.S. Advisory Commission, the bishops pointed to the contrast between the Pope's demeanor while in their presence and the nature of his reply. His personal disposition was "irresistibly benevolent," while his official response was "irresistibly rigid." The ceremonial cordiality did not mask the force of the Pope's negative answer and the call for these Christians to leave their tradition and "return" in penitence to the true church. On the other side, the delegation's frustration and disappointment was undoubtedly heightened by the unrealistic optimism that these Americans brought to that historic moment. They learned, as all those who labor for the unity of Christ's church, that the road to reconciliation and visible unity is often painful and strewn with opposition.

After a first decade of essentially American leadership at the helm of Faith and Order, the kairos dictated that the movement should become truly international. To this end a preparatory conference — first thought to be held in the United States — was wisely convened in Geneva, Switzerland in August 1920, under the theme "A Pilgrimage Toward Unity."[27] With this action, the total responsibility for Faith and Order was passed from the Protestant Episcopal Church and the other churches in the United States to an international Christian community, Protestant and Orthodox. One hundred and thirty-seven church leaders from seventy "autonomous Churches" from forty countries met at the stately Athénée in Geneva. The presence of eighteen Orthodox hierarchs and theologians was prompted by the Ecumenical Patriarch of Constantinople, whose ecumenical vision was proclaimed the same year in the historic encyclical "Unto the Churches of Christ Everywhere."[28] Several representatives of the churches in Germany attended. Ironically, the officers elected were three trusted American Episcopalians: Charles H. Brent, chairperson; Robert H. Gardiner, secretary; and George Zabriskie, treasurer. The most important decision by the Geneva conference was the appointment of a fifty-one person Continuation Committee, which became the center of authority and planning. Two working committees were appointed from

26. Report of the Deputation to Europe and the East, p. 12.

27. See Report of the Preliminary Meeting at Geneva, Switzerland, August 12-20, 1920. Faith and Order Pamphlet No. 33 (1920).

28. See *Orthodox Visions of Ecumenism*, ed. by Gennadios Limouris (Geneva: World Council of Churches, 1994), pp. 9-11.

the Continuation Committee: a Business Committee, eight of whose ten members were Americans; and a Subjects Committee authorized to refine the theological subjects to be addressed at the World Conference, and to encourage study among the churches of the Conference's subjects. The main theological discourse at Geneva was "The Meaning of the Church and What We Mean by Unity," or, as alternately described, "The Church and the Nature of the Reunited Church." A foretelling dialogue was begun with papers by James Vernon Bartlet, a Congregational church historian at Mansfield College at Oxford University, and Anglican Bishop Charles Gore, a staunch Anglo-Catholic, regarded by many as the greatest theologian of his generation in the Church of England.[29] In an action relatively unnoticed by the press, a resolution called upon the churches of the world to begin to celebrate a special Week of Prayer for Christian Unity, ending with Whitsunday (Pentecost). From its origins and throughout its history, Faith and Order has intertwined the call to unity and the call to prayer.

So the vision, leadership, and resources of the churches in the United States gave first life to the Faith and Order Movement. As the second decade of its history unfolded and the First World Conference on Faith and Order was on the horizon, to be convened in 1927, the legacy of the leadership of the American churches was a firm reality. In God's irony, the nation where the churches are the most fragmented is where God, through Christ in the Holy Spirit, raised up a theological movement for the visible unity of the one Church of Christ. And this leadership and legacy came from the passion and astute gifts of a relatively small number of Christian pastors, laypersons, and teachers of the faith, who worked heroically with meager finances and big dreams. These Americans laid the foundations of Faith and Order, and literally gave their lives for the unity of Christ's Church.

---

29. See Faith and Order Paper No. 33, pp. 38-43 (for Gore's paper) and pp. 44-48 (for Bartlet's paper).

The Enduring Impact of
Gabriel Fackre's Life and Teaching

Kenneth B. Mulholland

It is an awesome task to review not just a book, but a life — the life of a prominent theological professor, author, and churchman, especially if forty years ago you happened to be that teacher's first student!

Gabriel Fackre is a blend of many ingredients. His writings display the multiple concerns and emphases that have marked his theological pilgrimage through the years: his passion for communicating the faith in a relevant manner; his concern for the alienated industrial worker, which marked both his doctoral struggles with Marx and Kierkegaard and his urban ministerial experience; his immersion in historical theology, which informed the critique of his denomination's attraction to theological fads; his unquestioned and longstanding commitment to the local parish; his fascination with Christology, bibliology, and ecclesiology; his ability to maintain an evangelical focus while interacting with the social issues of his time; and his love of family reflected not only in his partnership with Dorothy, but his commitment to the welfare both of his parents and his children.

The faculty of Lancaster Theological Seminary was small when Fackre began his teaching career there in the summer of 1961. Professors taught a broad range of courses related to their discipline field and personal interests. The papers I remember writing for him reflect the immense scope of his competency: "Grace, Faith, and Baptism" for an interseminary seminar, "The Theology of Justin Martyr" for a course on historical theology, "The Life and Thought of Bishop Fulton J. Sheen" for a course on Roman Catholicism, "The Radical Monotheism of H. Richard Niebuhr" for a course on social ethics, a review article on Vance Packard's works for a course on American culture, and later, "The Pentecostal Movement" for an S.T.M. course on church renewal.

Fackre's large office, located in the basement of the building which housed classrooms, administrative offices, and the chapel, was perpetually cluttered with bulging files jammed with notes and clippings as well as projects in process spread on every available surface. Nevertheless, there we enjoyed stimulating interaction. We dialogued over coffee in the refectory following morning chapel services. We argued in the hallway outside the door of the room where he had just concluded class. We debated publicly the legitimacy of infant baptism. Even a supper invitation to his home — all contributed to his impact as a teacher and mentor. And he modeled what he taught by his involvement in the local community.

His educational impact upon me did not conclude when I marched across the platform to receive first a B.D. in 1962 and later an S.T.M. in 1971. It continued through the affirmative responses to occasional invitations I extended to him to minister in the three-point rural charge I served and then by the newsletters that periodically arrived in my mailbox. He continued to broaden my horizons and sharpen my insights through the perusal and at times serious study of his multiple writings. Correspondence through the years has nourished the relationship. Also, an encounter with him and Dot at a weekend conference in Wheaton, Illinois, provided an opportunity for extensive conversation and personal updating. Just as Paul never abandoned the churches he founded, so Fackre never abandoned the students he taught.

I have selected five themes derived from Fackre's life and thought, which continue to exert influence upon my ministry.[1]

I. Personal Savior and Public Lord

In the evangelical circles in which much of my ministry takes place, great emphasis is rightly placed upon the importance of a personal relationship with Jesus Christ. Unfortunately, the Lordship of Christ is sometimes viewed as merely an option for those who want to take a second step be-

---

1. My own career in ministry has been marked by five years of pastoral experience in rural Pennsylvania, fifteen years of missionary experience in Central America, and twenty years as a missions professor, the last thirteen of which I have also served as dean of Columbia Biblical Seminary and School of Missions of Columbia International University, Columbia, SC, a trans-denominational university divinity school in the evangelical tradition which each fall enrolls a total of about 750 resident and extension students.

yond their initial commitment to Christ as Savior. However, Christ cannot be divided. He is both Savior and Lord. As Fackre clearly pointed out in *The Pastor and the World,* Savior may be a personal term, but Lord is a public term. This theme runs through much of his work, even on the backs of the denominational church bulletins to which he contributed. For instance, "Lord of the Streets" was the title of an interpretive paragraph for a Palm Sunday bulletin.

Although the focus of the gospel is personal, it has a social dimension that can be ignored only at the risk of distorting the faith. This emphasis helped me to lead the rural Pennsylvania Dutch congregations that I served, to embrace openly on biblical grounds the civil rights movement. It guided me to support the legitimate call for social justice in Latin America as mediated by the Latin American Theological Fraternity, of which I have been a longtime member, while at the same time resisting the reductionist tendencies which characterized Latin American liberation theologies. Years later, I made August Hermann Francke's fourfold basis for ministry my own: "A life changed, a church revived, a nation reformed, a world evangelized."

II. The Mystical Body of Christ and St. John's by the Gas Station

Another of Fackre's contributions was to help me embrace with equal ardor both the universal body of Christ and the local congregation. Above all, Fackre was and is a churchman. There was no place in Fackre's thought for the kind of docetic ecclesiology that cultivates individualistic piety at the expense of commitment to the community of believers. After all, how can you love the Lord and at the same time despise His people? His emphasis on historical theology and his immersion in the Mercersburg theology while at Lancaster encouraged me to appreciate the universal church as Christ's Body extended through the centuries, and yet understand the soft underbelly of the church in its local expression. This emphasis kept me from falling into despair in the face of shortcomings and even failure on the part of the local church to reach its full potential. On the other hand, it gave me hope as I came to view the church as an arena in which genuine healing and authentic transformation can take place, a truly therapeutic community, a pilot project of God's Kingdom where Christ's reign, though partial, is real and substantial.

Congregational renewal was high on Fackre's agenda. As he sought to enable us to move the congregations we served from tradition to mission, he encouraged experimentation, pointed us to effective models, and sought to help us engage the culture. Furthermore, through both his pulpit and his pen (later on, thankfully, his typewriter and computer; his handwriting was only semi-legible), he kept his former students abreast of resources that would enable them to lead their churches in full-orbed renewal. The experiences growing out of his ministry in the Pittsburgh area and his relationship with Dr. Wally Fisher, longtime pastor of Trinity Lutheran Church in downtown Lancaster, enriched his own teaching with practical examples that were both pastoral and theological.

Fackre's ecclesiology was missional as well. His early work as a mission pastor in a steel mill town and a mushrooming suburb, infused in him the significance of communicating the gospel across barriers of class. He learned early on, both from his doctoral studies and his work in an urban industrial setting, that effective ministry among blue-collar workers called for variables distinct from effective ministry among the burgeoning suburbanites of the time. Although his Lebanese heritage made Fackre aware of cross-cultural issues and sensitized him to the global dimensions of ethical issues, his missiological instincts were never developed to their fullest potential. Nevertheless, amid the tumultuous sixties and early seventies, when conciliar missiologists and theologians were asking the right questions about the nature and mission of the church, but consistently coming up with wrong, and often disastrous answers, Fackre's ecclesiology, although occasionally sounding an unclear or uncertain note, emerged theologically sound and missiologically intact. Currently, I am a member of a task force of the Missions Commission of the World Evangelical Fellowship led by a Norwegian Lutheran, charged with developing a missional ecclesiology for the twenty-first century. Once again, I look forward to drawing again upon the insights gained from Fackre's thinking about the church.

III. Evangelical and Ecumenical

Just as Fackre affirmed the church both in its universal and local expressions, so the breadth of his ecclesiology found expression in a stance that was both evangelical and ecumenical. In his books *Restoring the Center* and *Ecumenical Faith in Evangelical Perspective,* as well as elsewhere, his call for "Evangelical Catholicity" sought to overcome the polarization separating the two constituencies through the recovery of a christocentric emphasis. In company with an early colleague, Dr. Bela Vassady, he delighted in recognizing the church as simultaneously Catholic, Reformed, and Evangelical.

Ordained by the American Baptist Convention in the waning days of the fundamentalist-modernist struggle as they played out in the tension between Northern Baptist Theological Seminary and the University of Chicago, Fackre never lost his evangelical roots, even though for a period of time in the late sixties, they seemed to go underground. Though he rejected the separatism of fundamentalism, was keenly critical of the rationalism to which evangelical theology was prone, and rebuked the so-called Religious Right for the ecclesiastical legitimation of essentially secular premises and the cultural captivity of their basic theological assumptions, his writings reflect a wholesome appreciation and accurate understanding of evangelical thought and heritage. Especially notable is his treatment of Carl F. H. Henry.

At the same time, Fackre was committed to the unity of the body of Christ. While not enamored with unity for the sake of unity, he was passionate about unity for the sake of mission. Essentially an evangelical theologian with strong ecumenical commitments, he involved himself deeply in ecumenical affairs, whether in the form of a community action project or inter-confessional theological dialogue. In his writings, he draws heavily on such ecumenical theologians as Newbigin, Niles, Minear, Visser 't Hooft, and Kraemer, and demonstrates a keen awareness of theological developments both in Orthodox and Roman Catholic circles.

The insights derived from his course on Roman Catholicism helped me understand the new currents that emerged from Vatican II against the backdrop of the traditional, neo-medieval Catholicism, which I encountered in Latin America at the beginning of my missionary career. Also, these insights enabled me to relate constructively and with credibility among renewal elements within the Roman Catholic Church, without compromising either the Reformation tenets or the evangelistic focus which characterized my ministry.

IV. Christianity: Classical and Contemporary

Gabe Fackre has been both true to the faith and in tune with the times. He urged us as students to be both faithful to the faith once revealed to the saints and relevant to the culture in which we lived. Doctrine did not have to be dull. Whether delivered in a seminary chapel or in a wide assortment of local congregations, his own sermons, invariably scriptural, but laced with contemporary illustrations, demonstrated this dual commitment. Furthermore, he taught us to break the stained glass barrier and meet people where they live and work. His example encouraged me on occasion to conduct Bible study in factory lunch rooms, and also to include the local taverns in my visitation rounds; to initiate a released time religious education program in our community while establishing a broad-based prison ministry in the county jail. The same dual commitment inspired me to launch with John Lindner and Carl Knoch the Evangelical Fellowship of the United Church of Christ (an early forerunner of both the Biblical Witness Fellowship and the Confessing Christ movement), while heading up the United Way in our Pennsylvania township; and, finally, to defend the historic Christian position with regard to sexual ethics, while at the same time supporting the civil rights movement.

Fackre emphasized not only getting the gospel out, but getting it straight. The classical emphasis comes through strongly in *The Christian Story* and the subsequent tomes on systematic theology. Fackre was uncompromising when it came to the attempts to dilute the unique nature of Christian faith. Often, he spoke of the "scandal of particularity." God chose Israel out of all the then-existing nations of the world to be His people and later became incarnate not in humanity in general, but in the person of a first-century Jew. Always, but particularly in *The Rainbow Sign,* he insisted upon the inseparability of authentic eschatology and ethical action. Later, he defended the trinitarian nature of baptism against the use of quasi-Unitarian baptismal formulas promulgated in some sectors, and questioned the retreat from classical Christian terminology evidenced in the New Century Hymnal and the Revised Statement of Faith of his denomination. While committed to cultural relevance, he opposed cultural relativism and was determined not to sacrifice the full-orbed nature of classical faith upon the altar of reductionist cultural fads. Recently, I served on the drafting committee of the "Millennial Manifesto: Covenanting Together for the 21st Century," the legacy document of the AD 2000 and Beyond Movement. While working through the section on Theological Foundations, I was reminded again of lessons learned at Fackre's feet.

Fackre's periodic newsletters provided the reader with overwhelming annotated bibliographies encompassing an incredibly broad range of works, with special emphasis on theology and culture. He was among the first to detect the resurgence of systematic theologies among evangelical writers at a time when many thought that the writing of full systematic theologies had ended with the demise of neoorthodoxy. However, the really impressive nature of his bibliographical work was the breadth of his awareness of emerging cultural trends and the social issues occasioned by those trends. Historic Christian thought engaged with current issues and expressed in fresh ways has characterized Fackre's theological reflection and placed him in the vanguard of classical Christian theologians.

V. Word in Deed

Preaching grace and doing justice are not polar opposites in the thought of Gabe Fackre. Like husband and wife, no person was to put asunder what God had joined together. During the heady and polarizing days of the sixties and the early seventies, Fackre sought to mediate between the activists and pietists who sought to mutually exclude the other. He recognized that deed authenticates word and word explains deed. Both are essential to the effective communication of the gospel message. At the same time, he insisted upon the importance of a call to decision and underscored the essential rightness of properly understood church growth as a legitimate expectation of mission.

Nearly twenty years ago, I wrote that the relationship between evangelism and social responsibility would be one of the six most significant issues facing the church during the decade of the eighties and nineties. That issue remains with us. Although I hold to the position expressed at the Lausanne Congress on World Evangelization, namely that in the ministry of sacrificial service, evangelism is primary, and though I continue to advocate the priority of evangelism, I am both in agreement with and in debt to Gabe Fackre for holding word and deed in dynamic tension one with the other.

The commitment to the prioritization of evangelism does not diminish my concern for the issues which confront all voyagers on the good ship Earth: oppression, be it economic, religious, political or ethnic in nature; conservation of natural resources; poverty; child abuse; and violation of human rights. These issues cannot be evaded. They must be addressed from a perspective that is at the same time biblically informed and scientifically responsible. Pronouncement must be followed by action. Compassion must be balanced by justice and justice must be tempered by mercy. Fackre's forays into the ethical area have met these criteria. They have been as timely as his perspective on Bill Clinton's escapades, sensitive to the multiple ways in which power can be used and abused, aware of the temptations to elevate cultural biases to theological principles, cognizant that religion can serve as the agent of accommodation as well as the vehicle of transformation. Above all, they have been refreshingly transparent and humble. I recall a conversation with Fackre during the early days of the Viet Nam War when he referred to himself as a liberal with regard to race relations, a conservative with regard to sexual ethics, and just plain confused about Viet Nam. A man of action as well as thought, Fackre has involved himself personally in many of the arenas about which he has written.

Five themes. I could mention more. Gabe Fackre has been the epitome of balance. He has sought to live in the center of biblical tension while avoiding the easier path of going to a consistent extreme. Do I differ with him at any point? Yes. Among other things, I would like to see him embrace more fully the Chicago Statement of the International Conference on Biblical Inerrancy. I would like to see him assume an eschatological stance more congruent with his emphasis on the uniqueness of Christ. I would like to see him interact more extensively with the vision of a church for every segment of the human mosaic in order that the gospel be made accessible to every person. However, he would be glad to know that, although I remain concerned about the corruptibility of its practice in nominal Christian circles, I now share his views on infant baptism!

I am grateful for him and wish him the very best on the occasion of his seventy-fifth birthday. He was and continues to be one of my finest teachers; a faithful correspondent through the years; a great influence for good on my own ministry; a man of integrity; a model; a mentor; a friend; a brother in Christ.

PART III

THE MINISTRY
OF THE STORY TODAY

What's It All About?
Telling the Story by Means of a Sermon

Elizabeth Achtemeier

Scripture Lessons: Genesis 12:1-9
Matthew 9:9-13, 18-26

Do you ever wonder what our lives are all about? Sometimes, if you just sit back and contemplate the passing of the years and think in terms of family histories, human life can seem rather pointless. After all, we pour our hearts and labors and countless hours into raising our kids, and then they grow up and raise their children, and those children raise theirs, and those in turn raise theirs. And on and on it goes, one generation after another, in a seemingly endless circle of life that goes nowhere. What's the point of it all? And more importantly, what does it all have to do with God? Is he involved in any way in this endless tale of birth, life, and death that we experience, or is it indeed a meaningless story? What's it all about?

Surprisingly enough, our Scripture lesson from Genesis can give us at least part of the answer. In that Scripture passage, God breaks into human activities in about 1750 B.C., and he calls one man named Abraham out of his home in Mesopotamia in the Middle East. "Abraham," the Lord says, "Pack up all of your belongings, and take your wife Sarah and your nephew Lot. Say goodbye to the rest of your relatives and leave your home and country behind you, and journey to the land that I am going to show you."

So, says Genesis, Abraham went, as the Lord had commanded him. Now Abraham didn't have the foggiest notion where he was going, and I'm sure Sarah and Lot were pretty upset about that. But Abraham obeyed the command of the Lord because the Lord gave him a promise. "Abraham," God declared, "I'm going to make you a great nation by giving you lots of descendants, and through them and you, I'm going to bring my blessing on all of the people in the world." So Abraham went.

The key to the whole story, in fact the key to the meaning of our lives and to what God is doing right here and now, is in that word "blessing." To be blessed by God, according to the Bible, is to be given fullness of life — joy, peace, love, righteousness, well-being, vitality, life abundant in all its facets. God, through Abraham and his descendants, wants to give abundant life to all of the people on this earth.

Heaven knows we need that blessing, that abundant life, don't we? The first eleven chapters of Genesis tell us that human beings were intended to have that kind of life in the beginning, because those chapters are written to be the story of all people and of you and me. "God saw everything he had made," reads Genesis 1, "and behold! It was very good." God created this world of ours very good. And the second chapter of Genesis spells out that goodness. It says that the Lord God created each one of us, very carefully, to be unique individuals. And then he surrounded us with all sorts of good gifts. He gave us the beauty of the natural world, and food, and creative work to do. He gave us loving relationships with our spouses and families, and above all, with him personally, because that was the way he wanted to be with us — in constant fellowship and love, caring for us, guiding us, showering us with every good thing forever.

But somewhere along the line we messed up that paradise, didn't we? And we turned God's good world into a cursed place that he never intended. Do you remember the story of Eve and Adam in Genesis 3? It's really the story of all of us, because what did they want? Well, they wanted to run their own lives, just as we do. "Come," the serpent told them, "you can be like God, knowing good and evil." You can make up your own rules, you see. You can decide what's right and wrong. You don't need God to tell you what to do. You can be your own god, and therefore you can map out your own plans for the future, and do whatever you desire. Never mind the commandments of God — you shall not kill; you shall not commit adultery; you shall not steal; you shall not covet; you shall have no other god besides me. No. Take charge of your life. Be your own god.

And that has had dreadful consequences in our world, as the following stories in Genesis tell us. Remember the story of Cain and Abel in Genesis 4, where Cain becomes so jealous of his brother that he kills him? And when God confronts him with what he has done, Cain sneers, "Am I my brother's keeper?" We feel that way a lot of times, don't we? Why should we care about our neighbor whom we don't like very well? Why should we be concerned with the people on welfare and the homeless bums and all of those dregs of society? Why bother with those people abroad who are hungry or ignorant or warring? Let them die, or let them kill one another. We're not our brothers' keepers.

And then there's the story in Genesis 11 of the Tower of Babel, which pictures us so well. "Come," they say to one another, "let's make a name for ourselves." And we're all after that, one way or another, aren't we? — to have a good name, to be respected, noted, with a good image in our town or in our church or in our social circle. But we also want to be secure, just as did the people at Babel, creating for ourselves our own safety and protection from the anxieties and sufferings of daily life, trying vainly to ward off want with our money, or counting on insurance to protect us from future harm, and finally trying desperately to deny that we will die by looking young and staying fit. Thus we rely not on God's security, but on whatever we can fashion for ourselves. And so, says the story, we become turned in on ourselves, and somehow we can't understand one another, and we can't get along with one another — and strife and hatred and misery fill the world, with husband against wife, brother against brother, nation against nation, and all of us under that sentence of death that our sin has brought upon us: "Dust you are, and to dust you shall return."

Yes, we do need God to turn all that into blessing, because our attempts to live without God most of the time have corrupted every good gift he has given us. We continually trash the beauties of nature that God lavishes upon us. We have the food he gives us, but we let millions of people go to bed hungry every night. We take the good gift of work and turn it into drudgery for some people, or we consider it just a way to earn a buck. And as for our relationships, well, one out of two marriages ends in divorce, sometimes we won't even speak to our relatives, and often we turn the raising of our kids over to the television set. God's good world is no longer the way it was meant to be, because we have tried often to live without God. And instead of the blessings he would pour out upon us, we often find ourselves accursed.

But you see, God won't leave it at that. God wants us to have abundant life. Out of his love and mercy for every single person and family in the world, God starts a history in which he intends finally to save us all. God calls one man named Abraham out of Mesopotamia, and he promises Abraham that through him and his descendants he will bring blessing on all the families of the earth. That's what the Bible is all about, friends, and that's what is happening in your life and mine, right now. God is working in our world to bring abundant life once more to us all.

How does he do that? First of all, he tries to do it through his people Israel, through all of those descendants of Father Abraham. But Israel in the Old Testament is like we are, always trying to run her own life and to shape the future without God. And so to fulfill his promise to Abraham, God finally centers down on one descendant of the patriarch, on Jesus of Nazareth, the Son of God, born of the virgin Mary in Bethlehem, anointed with the Holy Spirit, and appointed to bring God's abundant life to us all.

We find Jesus in our New Testament lesson giving that life. He's surrounded by a crowd of people, but one desperate woman pushes through the crowd just to try to touch his robe. She's been passing blood for twelve years, and Mark's version of the story says she's been to all sorts of doctors, spending every cent she has and going through all sorts of treatments. But no one has made her well, no one except Jesus — Jesus, who she believes can heal her, and who in that moment gives her back her life, just as he gives life to the dead daughter of the synagogue ruler who everyone else thinks is gone forever. God wants us to have life. He wants to bring blessing upon us, as he promised to Abraham. And Jesus Christ is the fulfillment of that promise and the Source of blessing and life.

But, Jesus says in our Gospel reading, "I came not to call the righteous, but sinners." And that means that to have the abundant life God would give us through Christ we must acknowledge the fact that we need him. We must confess that only through Christ can we be what we were meant to be, persons over whom God would pronounce those words, "Behold! They are very good."

That goes against all of our American inclinations, of course. After all, we look up to the self-made man. We admire the competent woman, and we honor those who can perform — those who lead and shape affairs and really have it made. Should such persons suddenly become dependent on God?

Or take all of us pious people, who support the church and do kind deeds, and who anyone would say are Christians. Should we say we are dependent on Christ to be counted good?

I don't know about you, but I do know that apart from the death and resurrection of Jesus Christ, I am not good in the eyes of God. I'm much too selfish, much too wrapped up in my own affairs, much too concerned about my own skin. And unless when God looks at me, he sees the unfailing faith and goodness of Christ instead, I have no way that I can inherit his abundant and eternal life.

As for running our own affairs without God in Christ, have we done so well on our own? Have we solved the problems of hunger and poverty, of warfare and suffering? Is even the life we carry on in our homes entirely the way it is supposed to be? Do we know for sure the right way to bring up our kids? And what about when we die? Can you and I give ourselves eternal life beyond the blackness of the grave? Or do we need a God who constantly guides us, strengthens us, and forgives us? Who loves us more than we love ourselves, and who does not want us to die forever? And who therefore gives his own Son to ensure that we will have eternal life?

Through you and your descendants, God promised Abraham, I will bring my blessing on all the families of the earth. And through the centuries God made the fulfillment of that promise possible by sending his only Son. That's what human life is about, good Christians. That's what God is doing — working to bring all persons into his abundant life through Jesus Christ our Lord, working to pour out his promised blessing on you and on me. In faith — by faith in Christ — we can receive that blessing and enter into life.

Amen.

Give Us a King

Paul J. Achtemeier

Scripture Lessons: OT Lesson: 1 Sam. 8:1-22
Epistle: 2 Cor. 4:13-5:1
Gospel: Mark 3:20-35

Grace to you and peace from God our Father and the Lord Jesus Christ, Amen.

Whatever else one may say about the story of God's dealings with his human creatures, one must admit that the plot line is not always immediately clear. That is demonstrated every now and again when a passage comes along in the Bible that baffles the reader and preacher alike. I suppose we should not be surprised if the Word of God seems confusing every now and then. It is, after all, the Word of God, and whatever else we are, we are not God, even though at times we seem to want to think we are.

Such a passage is the account in 1 Samuel, the story of Israel's request for a king. To see why it is a problem, we must look at it carefully, and to look at it carefully, we have to go all the way back to Israel's beginning as a people.

The act that had made them a people, that had created a nation out of a band of slaves in Egypt, was the exodus from that land. It is a familiar story — the plagues God brought on Egypt, Pharaoh's unwillingness to let

It is a pleasure to take part in this tribute to my colleague and friend, Gabriel Fackre, as a token of my esteem for all that his friendship has meant to me, both personally and professionally.

Israel go, the slaying of the firstborn and the escape in the night, the parting of the sea and the escape into the wilderness. It was those mighty acts of God that had created Israel a people.

But more than that, it had created Israel a special people. They were God's own people, created by his mighty power. God had sealed that creation of a people with the covenant: "I will be your God, and you shall be my people," God had told them.

Now this covenant was an act of sheer grace, an act of undeserved love by God. It had nothing to do with any virtue on Israel's part. Moses said as much when he told Israel how God's choice was made:

> It was not because you were more in number than any other people that the Lord set his love upon you and chose you, for you were the fewest of all peoples, but it was because the Lord loves you, and is keeping the oath which he swore to your fathers, that the Lord has brought you out with a mighty hand, and redeemed you from the house of bondage, from the land of Pharaoh, king of Egypt. (Deut. 7:7-8, RSV)

So Israel was a special people, with a special covenant with God, and a mighty deliverance from Egypt, and God's law given on Mount Sinai, and finally their occupation of the promised land — all pointed to that special relationship with God.

The problem was, the Israelites had difficulty wrapping their mind around the fact that they were to be a special people, unlike any other people in the world. And because they had difficulty understanding that, they kept getting into trouble. It started in the desert with the golden calf — after all, everybody else had idols to worship — and continued right on into the promised land. Israel kept getting into trouble, and God kept bailing them out.

That story is told in the book of Judges: When they went astray, when they were tormented by their neighbors, they would call on God to help, and God would raise up a leader, a judge, who helped them get out of trouble — warriors, for example, like Gideon and Samson. That happened over and over again.

One of those judges was Samuel, and with him we finally get to our troubling passage. In this passage in 1 Samuel, we have a description of the way that process of God raising up judges to save Israel was beginning to break down. Samuel was old, we hear, so he set up his sons to help him run the country. But such a hereditary arrangement had a fatal flaw: Samuel's sons were corrupt; they began to take bribes and pervert justice. But if the very people who are to show God's justice are corrupt, then the system has really ceased to function. What was Israel to do? Well, the elders of Israel had a solution, and it was a solution they borrowed from their neighbors who lived in the surrounding lands.

The solution: Give Israel a king. After all, Israel's neighbors who had kings found that it worked nicely, or at least so it seemed to the elders. The king led the people into battle and protected them from raids by their enemies. In other words, the elders said in effect, we do not want to be a special people any more. We want to be like every other people, and have a king to rule over us. What good is being a special people if all it brings is trouble? Who needs that? Why not be like every other people, and have a king to protect us?

So, they come to Samuel and say: find us a king! Now this troubles Samuel, and rightly so. The request for a king is a direct rebuke against him, whom God himself had chosen to be judge, back when Samuel was a member of Eli's household. So, good judge that he is, Samuel takes it to the Lord in prayer. There Samuel hears words of comfort, but they are ominous words for all that. They have not rejected you, God tells Samuel, they have rejected me. I am the one who has been king over this covenant people, and now they want another king.

In other words, the request for a king is simply an act of rebellion against the God who chose them and delivered them from slavery in Egypt. But such rebellion is nothing new — God concedes that such rejection and rebellion have characterized Israel from day one. Ever since Egypt, they have wanted someone else to be their God. They are simply acting in character.

Israel is here sort of like the child who wants to do something, and, when told no, argues that all the other kids can do it, so why can't I? A familiar argument in most families. Why can't I be like everyone else, and do what everyone else is doing? That is Israel's argument here: Other people have kings, and so Israel wants one for herself as well.

But there are other problems with Israel's desire to have a king. Ancient near-eastern kings had a way of becoming despots, who ran the state for their personal benefit, and not for the good of the people. God points that out to Samuel, who is to report it to the people.

But for all that, the central problem here is the rejection of God as king. With their request, the elders want to throw over the covenant agreement that constituted Israel as a special people. They want to throw over the freeing results of the exodus that released them from slavery in Egypt.

Their new king will take away the liberties gained in the exodus. Israel will now once again have someone over them who will take away their sons for the army and their daughters to work in the court. The king will take away their fields and vineyards to give to his cronies, their property and their hard-earned money, so that the king can live a life of ease.

That will be the result of their rebellion, of their rejection of God as their king, and their desire to have the kind of king everyone else has.

Now, faced with such rebellion, it seems clear God has only one choice. God must tell Samuel to tell those elders to shape up, that they must respect the covenant their ancestors made with God. They have God as their king, and that is all there is to it. Like the wise parent, God will surely tell them that their lives are not to be determined by what other people do. They are after all a special people, and for that reason they cannot have a king and be like all the other nations.

But that is not what God does, and it is here that the passage becomes confusing. Having warned Israel of what to expect, God does not tell Samuel "no king." What he tells Samuel is: "Give them their king!"

Now why does God do that? Why in the world does God give in to their rebellion? Has God given up on the idea of chosen people? What does God have in mind with this granting their request to have a king?

Well, perhaps God has a particular king in mind. Maybe a king like David. David, after all, was the king who led the chosen people in triumph over their enemies, who stretched Israel's borders to their furthest extent, who had God's favor in his battles with Israel's enemies.

Yet David is not without his faults. David, too, will prove to be something less than an ideal king. There is his sordid business with Bathsheba, and, as punishment, the death of their child. Then, when David became too much of a tyrant, there was the rebellion against him led by his own son.

Is that really the kind of king God has in mind when he tells Samuel, "Give them their king"? Or perhaps God has another king, a different kind of king altogether, in mind. That would not be surprising. The Old Testament contains a whole host of passages where God's word, God's promise, points beyond itself, indeed beyond Israel as chosen people, to find its fulfillment.

But if God does have another king in mind, who would it be? Well now, for Christians, that is not a hard question to answer at all. That king must be Jesus Christ.

Yet if that is the case, what a very different kind of king he will be, as our Gospel lesson points out. Would this really be the kind of king God intended? First of all, if Jesus is king, he is a king who can be completely misunderstood even by those closest to him. Jesus returned home, Mark tells us, and the usual crowds surrounded him. But those closest to him — the Greek phrase means both friends and family — come to the conclusion that Jesus has lost it. They conclude he is "beside himself," that is, he is not in complete control of his actions.

Now it is not hard to understand how they could come to such a conclusion. Jesus, as a grown man, suddenly left his home and his native village, called some men to follow him, and went around announcing that God's Kingdom was about to appear. It seemed even the demons listened to him — but more on that in a moment. Now we all know the kind of reaction generated in our time when someone goes around announcing "The end is near." Universal respect is not what is usually accorded such a person. He is more likely to be the subject of a cartoon, with long robe and beard and a sign on his shoulder.

Yet here is Jesus, announcing just that. Any wonder his family and friends wonder what has gotten into him? And we can wonder, too. What kind of a king would do such things?

Secondly, Jesus can be, and regularly is, completely misunderstood by the religious and civil authorities. Actually, in Jesus' world, religious and civil authorities are the same people. Sometimes we lose sight of that. So among the Jews of Jesus' time, those who had religious authority were precisely those who also wielded civil authority. And it is just those people who completely misunderstand Jesus and where he is coming from.

Jesus casts out demons? Then, they conclude, it must be because he is in cahoots with the leader of the demons, namely Satan, and that is why the demons obey him. Jesus points out how silly this is. Why would Satan suddenly be undermining his own power by removing his demons from their tasks of controlling people? If Satan is acting like that, Jesus says, then his reign has come to an end.

Ironic, Jesus points out, that Jesus' own actions, whether with Satan or against him, point to the end of Satan's power, the point Jesus has been making all along. But I am not with Satan, Jesus says, I am against him. I am like one who has overpowered another, tied him up, and is plundering his possessions. In fact, says Jesus, to say I am working with Satan is the ultimate sin — it is to confuse God with Satan. So badly have the authorities misunderstood Jesus.

Thirdly, our Gospel passage reports that Jesus is visited by his immediate family. They have obviously come to get poor, confused Jesus and take him back to the safety of his own home. Yet with his family standing outside, Jesus completely turns on its head the notion of who his family really is. Not blood relatives, Jesus says, but those who hear and do what I say — those are members of my immediate family. So much for any dynasty to follow Jesus as king. Not his blood relatives, but those who follow what he says — they are his true family.

Now what kind of a king is it who is thought to be crazy by those closest to him, is totally misunderstood by the authorities, and who radically alters the notion of who belongs to his true family? Well, for starters, he is a king utterly unlike the kings described by Samuel, kings who exploit others for their own benefit. Jesus does not exploit others for his personal gain. He does just the opposite — he exploits himself for the good of others.

Mark remembers another saying of Jesus about himself: The son of man came not to be served, but to serve, and to give his life as a ransom for many. If Jesus is God's king, then he is not a king who sacrifices others for himself. He is a king who does just the opposite: he sacrifices himself for others.

Again, Jesus does not call people to follow him into battles, to add to his own glory by way of military victory. Kings of the world do that, but Jesus does not. Put away your sword, he tells Peter who tried to defend him against those sent to arrest him.

That is not the kind of king Jesus is. In that situation, Jesus shows himself to be a king willing to give up his own life on the cross precisely for those who misunderstood and vilified him. While we were God's enemies, Paul tells the Romans, God sent his son Jesus to die for us. Jesus' glory lies not in battle where others are killed, but in his own death on a cross.

Finally, Jesus is not the kind of king for whom his followers build a magnificent tomb, to remind later generations of his years of royal glory. Jesus does not leave behind a magnificent tomb, he leaves behind an empty tomb — empty, to remind all future generations of his living glory and his eternal kingship.

That is the kind of king God chose for his chosen people, the kind of king God has chosen for us. That is the kind of king God had in mind when he so unexpectedly gave in to the request of the rebellious elders of Israel, so long ago. Strange how God used their rebellion to set forth his own purposes — to set over them, and over all people, a divine king, who would rule in love and mercy and peace. Who can defeat a God like that, a God who uses even our sin to achieve his righteousness and salvation?

That is the God who is revealed in these strange passages that make up the story in the Bible of the way God deals with his human creatures. It is a story of the God who will save us in spite of ourselves.

Surely such a God is One we can trust, One who will bring our story to the conclusion he desires, a conclusion full of love and mercy and peace. In the name of the Father and of the Son and of the Holy Spirit. Amen!

They'll Know Him in His Cross:
A Sermon for Palm/Passion Sunday

Richard L. Floyd

When Jesus entered Jerusalem on that first Palm Sunday, many looked to
him to overthrow the Roman oppressor. His entry, not on a charger but
on a donkey, was a living parable that here was a different kind of power.
And those who shouted "Hosanna!" on Sunday, were quick to shout
"Crucify him!" on Good Friday, when he didn't show the kind of power
that the world understands all too well.

Christ's cross confronts us still as the place where divine power and
human sin collide. He took our sin to that cross, and it died there along
with him. It is no accident that the cross is the symbol of our faith. Paul
tells the Philippians:

> Let the same mind be in you that was in Christ Jesus,
> who, though he was in the form of God,
> did not regard equality with God
> as something to be exploited,
> but emptied himself,
> taking the form of a slave,
> being born in human likeness.
> And being found in human form,
> he humbled himself
> and became obedient to the point of death —
> even death on a cross.
> Therefore God also highly exalted him
> and gave him the name
> that is above every name,

so that at the name of Jesus
every knee should bend,
in heaven and on earth and under the earth,
and every tongue should confess
that Jesus Christ is Lord,
to the glory of God the Father.

(Philippians 2:5-11, NRSV)

Let us be very clear what is claimed here: that it is the fact of Jesus' death as a slave that makes him Lord, his death as a nobody that makes him exalted at the right hand of God. And if God, the Father Almighty, who created the heavens and the earth, and Jesus, the man of Nazareth, share a divine identity, what does the cross tell us of the identity of God?

It tells us first of all that what the world values is not what God values. The Roman Empire that crucified Jesus was constructed on power, violence, and might, all delivered with ruthless efficiency, and the cross was the supreme instrument of Roman values. The cross was a slave's death, designed to dispose of the nobodies of the world and put fear into the hearts of other nobodies, so they wouldn't challenge Rome's power.

But the crucifixion puts God squarely on the side of the nobodies. The cross condemns the brutal social arrangements then and now that trample the poor, which put the concerns of the powerful ahead of the nobodies of the world. The cross condemns every injustice that treats people as expendable; every cynical deal that seeks gain at the expense of others.

The cross says God has different values, seeks a different way, a way of servanthood and humility, a way that seeks the good of others, a way that rejects violence and injustice, a way in which everybody is somebody. In God's values, there aren't any nobodies, for God's own son was once regarded as a nobody and died a nobody's death, forgiving those who killed him even as he cried out in utter forsakenness.

This is the Christian God, the crucified God, who turns the world's values upside down. If you want to know about this God, take a good look at Jesus. Notice how he befriends the poor, touches lepers, eats with sinners. There weren't any nobodies in Jesus' book. Only sinners to be saved, broken people to be made whole, dying people to be given new life, sorrowful people to be made glad, remorseful people to be forgiven.

Look to Jesus: that is where the Christian finds identity and purpose, from Jesus Christ and him crucified. And not just for our personal spiritual life, but for the whole world. For his cross redeems our sins, but also our politics, our marriages and families, our business practices, our churches, and everything else about our world. George MacLeod, the founder of the Iona Community, once wrote:

> I simply argue that the cross be raised again at the center of the marketplace as well as on the steeple of the church. I am recovering the claim that Jesus was not crucified in a cathedral between two candles, but on a cross between two thieves; on the town garbage heap; at a crossroads so cosmopolitan that they had to write his title in Hebrew and in Latin and in Greek . . . at the kind of place where cynics talk smut and thieves curse, and soldiers gamble. Because that is where he died. And that is what he died about.

People have asked me why my theology is so centered on the cross of Jesus. Why should somebody as generally cheerful as I am want to focus on such a gloomy subject? The story of my coming to the cross is a story of coming to know God in a whole new way. Although I was raised in the church as a child, I decided to be a Christian as an adult, because the cross of Christ rang true for me, as an answer equal to the world's harsh truths. My mother died when I was eighteen, and my sunny childhood faith was tested and found wanting. We live in a world where people we love can get sick and die, where injustice is often done, where bad things happen to good people as well as bad, but in my young life I had never known this and I had a lot of trouble accepting it. At this vulnerable time in my life, the time when I was leaving home, my world was turned upside down, and I found myself in a darkness I had never known.

Some of you, probably most of you, have known such darkness, because the world brings it to us in time. There is, in such times, no light, no hope, no word of comfort. Nicholas Wolterstorff, who teaches theology at Yale, writes about such a time, when his son died suddenly at the age of twenty-five. Wolterstorff wrote this about his time of darkness:

> I am at an impasse, and you, O God, have brought me here. From my earliest days I heard of you. From my earliest days I believed in you. I shared in the life of your people: in their prayers, in their work, in their songs, in their listening for your speech and in their watching for your presence. For me your yoke was easy. On me your presence smiled. Noon has darkened. As fast as she could say, "He's dead," the light dimmed. And where are you in the darkness? I learned to spy you in the light. Here in this darkness I cannot find you. If I had never looked for you, or looked but never found, I would not feel this pain

197

of your absence. Or is it not your absence but your elusive troubling presence?

Will my eyes adjust to this darkness? Will I find you in the dark — not in the streaks of light which remain, but in the darkness? Has anyone ever found you there? Did they love what they saw? Did they see love? And are there songs for singing when the light has gone dim? The songs I learned were all of praise and thanksgiving and repentance. Or in the dark, is it best to wait in silence?[1]

Wolterstorff asks whether anyone has ever found God in the darkness. I did. It took time, and not a little waiting in silence. But as I look back at it, I would say that it wasn't I that found God, so much as God who found me. Found me in the darkness! And the God who found me was not a stranger to darkness. Here was a God who knew what I knew, who experienced what I had experienced. Who knew sorrow and was acquainted with grief.

And in this solidarity of suffering, I recognized something I had never expected to know in the dark. I knew I was loved, loved by the crucified God, the God who, by some mystery, fully and passionately entered into human life to redeem and transfigure it. And not human life at its best, but human life at its very worst, at a state execution, where a man was beaten half to death and nailed to a tree to die a slow, humiliating, and painful death. "It was now about noon," Luke writes of the crucifixion, "and darkness came over the land."

In my time of darkness, I finally realized that I didn't have the resources to fix the world, much less my own life. I couldn't even heal the deep grief and loss I felt. But I knew, believed, trusted, the presence of God in all my troubles and trials. Knew and believed in God's power to transform, renew, heal, and restore the broken suffering world.

And thirty years later, I still believe it. And when I look at the world today, in Africa, the Middle East, the Balkans, or even on North Street in Pittsfield, I see a world that cannot save itself and needs the redemptive power of God, which is demonstrated in the cross.

And I try never to forget what I know, that the Risen Christ of Easter is the crucified Jesus of Good Friday. The Risen Christ of Easter still bears the marks of the nails that killed him. Because when I am happy and healthy and well-fed, I want a God without a cross, a God who will prop up my life and maintain the things I want, and not cause me too much

---

1. Nicholas Wolterstorff, *Lament for a Son* (Grand Rapids: Eerdmans, 1987), p. 69.

trouble, a nice God who dwells in sunlight and doesn't trouble my conscience or demand too much of me. No elusive troubling presence, thank you, just God in his place.

And God's place, it is sad to say, is often the church, for even the church tries to domesticate God. Even the church tries to sell God like so much snake oil as a nostrum for being healthy and happy, but, if the truth be told, faith should come with a warning label. Maybe that is what the cross is, a warning label! Because those who look to Jesus Christ and his cross for their identity will find that they will invariably share his passion for this world, and his vocation to be the love of God for a fallen world, and like him go out to embody God whatever the cost. "Take up your cross," he says, "and follow me!"

That doesn't make life easy, but it makes it interesting, and in the end deeply satisfying in a way that others cannot know. For by some strange gospel equation, only the empty know what it is like to be filled, only the humble know what it is to be exalted, only those who have wept can know what real joy is, and only those who in some very real way have lost their lives will find the true life that comes from God. The Christian might start out as a consumer of religion, but will soon be called to be a servant, "just as the Son of Man came not to be served but to serve, and to give up his life as a ransom for many."

Jesus gave up the form of God to take the form of a slave, even unto a slave's death on a cross. But now the slave is master, whom we call Lord! Now the humbled one is the exalted One who sits at the right hand of God the Father! Now by his cross we, nobodies in the eyes of the world, and too often in our own eyes as well, are raised up to new life in him and with him.

And someday, in the fullness of time, in God's good hour, the whole world will see and know Jesus as he is, no longer in darkness but in unspeakable light! They'll no longer view him as an executed slave, a loser and a nobody, dead on a cross, but as the Lord of time and eternity; the Lord before whom every knee should bend, and every tongue confess that he is Lord. And when they do, they'll see that the risen Christ is still the crucified Christ, that the glorified Lord still bears the visible wounds on his hands and feet and side. Because the only way to really know Jesus, is to know him in his cross!

> He died upon the lonely tree,
> forsaken by his God.
> And yet his death means all to me
> and saves me by his blood.

The world will never know his worth,
the wise will never see;
but those forsaken, broken, bowed,
will recognize that tree.

And know that there God's love does reign
and conquers sin and death;
thwarts hate and evil, comforts pain,
gives hope while there is breath.

The nations grasp at wealth and power
while wars like tempests toss,
but finally in God's good hour,
they'll know him in his cross.

Then wars will cease and weapons fall,
and fear will melt away.
For Christ will be their all in all,
from day to endless day.

Death, Thou Shalt Die:
An Easter Sermon

Richard H. Olmsted

Scripture Lessons: 1 Cor. 15:51-58
John 11:17-27

> Death is swallowed up in victory.
> O death, where is thy sting?
> O grave, where is thy victory? . . .
> Thanks be to God who gives us the victory
> through our Lord Jesus Christ!

With these ringing words, Paul proclaims the message of Easter, the triumph of life over death. Christ is risen! Having taken on sin, death, and the evil one upon his cross, Jesus is now made manifest as the victorious Lord of life. He wins! Death loses! Because of him, death will always lose. With a poetic power to match St. Paul's, John Donne said it for the ages:

> Death be not proud, though some have called thee
> Mighty and dreadful, for thou art not so.
> For, those whom thou thinkst thou dost overthrow,
> Die not. Poor death, nor yet canst thou kill me. . . .
> One short sleep past, we wake eternally.
> And death shall be no more; death, thou shalt die.

Nothing less than this is the meaning and message of Easter. This is the great good news, the unqualified "Yes" which God speaks to each of us this day.

But is it true? How can we be certain of it? And what difference does it make to our lives here and now, to the way we do our living and our dying?

We still have to face death. Unless (as Paul speculates in our lesson) the Lord should come again before it happens to us, we will certainly die. Death continues to be a threat at all times to all life in this world. As an old German proverb puts it: As soon as a person is born, he or she is old enough to die. This is the truth, and what difference can Easter make to this truth? That is the question I would like to think about briefly with you, this Easter day.

Christian ethicist, Stanley Hauerwas, often begins a speaking engagement by asking his audience how they would like to die. He reports that he always gets the same answers to that question. Without fail, people say: "painlessly," "quickly," "in my sleep," "without causing great trouble to those close to me." Such desires seem eminently sensible. They express what any of us would want if we thought about it. We want to die without knowing what is happening to us, without causing great pain to ourselves and others.

But Hauerwas, after getting these answers, catches his audiences up short by reminding them that in other places and at other times such wants in relation to death would have been considered irrational, if not immoral. To have death take one unawares, without any opportunity for spiritual preparation, was regarded as the height of misfortune.

The Great Litany of the old Book of Common Prayer includes the petition: "From all oppression, conspiracy, and rebellion; from violence, battle and murder; from dying suddenly and unprepared, Good Lord, deliver us." One of the slaves of Philip of Macedon had a standing order. Every morning he was to enter the quarters of the king and shout, "Philip, remember that you must die."

It seems to me that this *memento mori,* this reminder of death, is expressive of a deeper attitude toward the conditions of our existence than any the modern world encourages us to take. I also think it is more conducive to recognizing and appropriating the meaning and message of Easter.

One of the things that robs the message of the resurrection of its power, is to think of it simply as something that might have happened a long time ago to Jesus and that might happen some time in the distant future to us. French theologian Louis Bouyer speaks of those "who believe in the light, but as they would believe in the existence of a world never to be seen by them, or which they expect to visit at some date so distant that it seems unreal."

It was along these lines that Martha was thinking as she talked to Jesus outside her brother's tomb. "Oh, I know," she said, "that he will rise again in the resurrection of the last day." But Jesus contradicted that kind of distancing of the power of new life in him. "Martha," he said, "I am the resurrection and the life; he who believes in me, though he die, yet shall he live, and whoever lives and believes in me shall never die." Here the Lord of life is speaking the words of eternal life, and offering them as a gift to us right here in the midst of life. It is hard, however, for us really to hear those words, to fit them into our lives. For our culture gives us very little help in facing up to the issues of life and death. Rather, it encourages us to screen out that kind of talk and reflection.

One of my favorite stories about not hearing what we don't care to attend to has to do with Franklin Roosevelt, who sometimes wearied of the long receiving lines on occasions of state at the White House. He complained that no one paid any attention to what was said. One day, during a reception, he decided to try an experiment. To each person who passed down the line and shook his hand, he murmured, "I murdered my grandmother this morning." The guests responded with phrases like, "Marvelous," "Keep up the good work!" "God bless you, Mr. President." It was not until near the end of the line, while greeting the ambassador from Bolivia, that his words were actually heard. With stunning diplomatic aplomb and a twinkle in his eye, the ambassador leaned over and whispered, "I'm sure she had it coming."

As far as death is concerned, we all have it coming. But what clues does the modern world have to offer us on how to die well, on what it might mean to make a good death? In the Middle Ages, there was a whole tradition of reflection on the art of dying. I think we badly need to begin to piece together a similar tradition for our day. Let me suggest one item I would include in such a tradition.

It is a scene from Dostoevsky's novel, *The Brothers Karamazov*. There are two characters in the scene: a wise and holy man, Father Zossima, who is ill and drawing near to the end of his life, and Madame Khohlakov, a widow in her thirties, who is described as a wealthy society lady. She is a self-preoccupied, but honest person. She has come to see Father Zossima at the monastery where he is the presiding elder. She is seeking relief from her spiritual suffering; more precisely, from her fear of death. This is how she describes her torment to him:

> The thought of the grace distracts me to anguish and horror. You see, I shut my eyes and ask myself: If others have faith, where did it come

from? There are those who say it all comes from terror at the menacing phenomena of nature, and that none of it is real. And I say to myself, "What if I've been believing all my life, and when I come to die, there's nothing but the flowers on my grave?" It's awful! How can I get back my faith? The truth is I only believed when I was a little girl, mechanically, without thinking or anything. But, dear God, how can I believe now? How, how is one to prove it?

Father Zossima gently responds that there is no way to prove it, but that she can become convinced of it. He tells her how in these simple words of advice:

Strive to love your neighbor actively and tirelessly. As you advance in love, you will grow surer of the reality of God and of the immortality of your soul. Insofar as you attain to self-forgetfulness in the love of your neighbor, you will believe without doubt, and no doubt can possibly enter your soul. This has been tried. This is certain.

As that wonderful passage suggests, the art of dying is, at the same time, the art of living. Our lives can become a series of little good deaths as we forget about self in our reaching out to those in need, a continuing process of dying to self, so that we come more and more to live in the joy of God and for the sake of others.

And those little good deaths will prepare us for the final moment of our lives in this world. Let me conclude with a reassuring hint about that final moment. It comes from the pen of the great Roman Catholic priest and author, Henri Nouwen.

Nouwen died in September of 1996. But several years earlier, he had a close brush with death. He was struck by an automobile while walking along the side of a road. Because of serious internal bleeding, for several days it was uncertain whether he would live or die. He wrote about what he learned from this experience in a little book called *Beyond the Mirror*. It is my favorite of his books. It has many fine insights, but let me share with you what he has to say about the critical time when he was close to death.

Nouwen describes himself as being normally a tense, nervous, and anxious person. But, to his surprise, he did not react with panic when he felt the nearness of death. Rather, something happened that brought him great peace. He writes:

What I experienced then was pure and unconditional love. Better still, what I experienced was an intensely personal presence, a gentle, non-judgmental presence that pushed all my fears aside. . . . He was there, the Lord of my life, saying, "Come, don't be afraid. I love you."

That, I believe, is in the future of all of us. But we don't have to wait till the end or have a near-death experience to know that it is true. We can live self-forgetfully in the power of the resurrection right here and now. This is what Jesus promised Martha outside her brother's tomb. And it is what he proclaims to us this Easter day.

If we don't screen him out, he can and will do that. He will say to us: "Come, follow me. Don't be afraid. I love you." He can indeed say this to us both now and in the moment of our dying because he is risen. The grave could not hold him. Death is swallowed up in victory. Glory be to God! Amen.

That's the Gospel

Herbert Davis

Scripture Lessons: Romans 5:6-11
                     Luke 15:11-32

Grace to you and peace, from God our Father and the Lord Jesus Christ.

Hear again these words from the Epistle: "But God proves his love for us in that while we were still sinners, Christ died for us" (Rom. 5:8).

The words of St. Paul in the Epistle to the Romans, "while we were yet sinners, Christ died for us," are a summary of the parable about the son who took his inheritance and left home. I suspect you know this parable of the two sons; one leaves and the other stays at home. I suspect the story is more about God than us. I don't think I'll have anything new to say about the story and that's part of the difficulty. We know it so well. On the other hand, I think it is hard for us to identify with the folks in the story. In our culture, no one would ask for his or her inheritance, and children are expected to leave home. Our problem is, or at least mine was, with the kids that left home and returned. I was always excited about them coming home, only to discover their plans were not the same as mine. We believe that to grow up, children need to leave home, to become their own person. We assume that separation is a normal process. We expect the cutting of the apron strings will come in those dreaded teenage years. I had a friend who was terribly depressed because his daughter likes

Sermon preached at East Falmouth, June 24, 2000; Cotuit, Massachusetts, September 24, 2000.

him. He felt he did something wrong. He was ready for the alienation of growing up. He was surprised by love.

But in this Bible story, where children and parent were expected to be together, the young son says to his father one morning, "Dad, how about giving me my inheritance and letting me go?" And the father gave him the inheritance and let him go. That must have been part of the rules of that day. If the son wants to go, you give him the inheritance and let him go. The son can't leave home fast enough. The father embarrasses him. He sees the father as limiting his potential, curtailing his pleasure. There is no love lost between the father and son. There are ways of leaving home, which embrace love and honor the parent. Ways that declare one's love for the parent.

As a young pastor, I served a congregation with a large number of members who came from the Caribbean. I was having a very difficult time with marriage services. The bride would never get to the church on time. Often, she arrived forty-five minutes late. The organist had played her prelude. I had paced the floor. Finally, the bride would arrive as though nothing had happened, ready for the liturgy to begin. At marriage counseling, I would threaten the bridal party with time limits. I would insist they sign a covenant that they would get to the church on time. Nothing made any difference. The bride was always late, at least thirty minutes late. Finally I went to an elder and asked, "Why is the bride always late?" The elder explained, "In our land, time is not as important as it is in America. So thirty minutes waiting is not a great inconvenience. We have a ritual to honor the parents and to express one's love as the bride leaves for the wedding. She kisses her parents and moves to the door. She cries, turns to leave and then runs back, embraces her mother and says she can't go. Her mother insists. The bride opens the door, bursts into tears and again returns to hug her parents. This process may be carried on for thirty minutes, so that the parents know how deeply the bride loves her family and how hard it is to leave. To leave in a hurry would be an embarrassment to the family. Please don't be embarrassed or upset if a bride loves her family so much that she never gets to the church on time." You might say this is to leave home with love.

However, I think the clue to what is going on in the parable comes a little later in the story when the son has wasted his inheritance on wild living, irresponsible behavior, smoking and drinking and never going to the office. He ends up as far from home as a Jew could go — feeding pigs and eating what fell from the pigs' table. And he says to himself, "I would be better off as a servant in my father's house, than here feeding the pigs."

Did you hear any love, any longing to be with the father? Is it possible the only relationship between the son and the father was economics? Is the father simply a meal ticket? Is the father a problem solver? Is it possible that the son does not know how much the father loves him?

Coming home is never easy. The younger son had to pay a price for squandering his father's inheritance, because it reflected not only on his family, but also on his community. He had destroyed part of the community's potential in his reckless living. There was a tradition that a son returning to his family, after squandering his resources, was met by a group of elders who beat him as he ran through the village to his father's home. The son must pay the price for his sin. It is possible that the hearers of this parable understood this old tradition when the text claims, "But while he was still a long way off, his father saw him and was filled with compassion for him. He ran to his son, threw his arms around him and kissed him." In our parable, we find it is not the irresponsible son who runs the gauntlet, it is the father. The father runs to meet the son; the father takes the blows for the son; the father takes on sin for the son. The father is filled with compassion. The father loves the son and welcomes the son home with a wild, joyful party.

Does the runaway son now know he is loved? The text doesn't make that clear. We can only hope he does, but we are not told if he changes his relationship from a hired servant to a beloved son. If we come home as servants and not as children, we do not know the Father.

But staying at home does not mean we know the father's love either. Many folks in America have never left the church, have never been disobedient. They go to church regularly. They do good deeds. They declare their faith boldly. But could they be like the stay-at-home son? He is the one who does what the father expects. He tends the fields. He cares for the sheep. He is ready to do the father's will, but he keeps count of his deeds and he knows to a penny what he has received. He has it all marked down in the daily journal of debits and credits. He's sure his father is keeping a record. He doesn't have a father, but a bookkeeper for a parent. So when the father throws this wild party for the irresponsible son he is quick to remind the father, "Look! All these years I've been slaving for you and never disobeyed your orders. Yet you never gave me even a young goat so I could celebrate with my friends." Is it possible to live in the same house and never know one is loved? Is it possible to be related as family, but to live only as servant, a slave, and not a child? Is it possible to see the father as an accountant, a bookkeeper who knows our deeds and rewards us according to our works? The obedient son lives in the presence of his father and never knows how much he is loved. His father addresses him not as a slave, not as a servant, but "My son." The father is not an accountant!

The foolishness of the gospel is that at the heart of creation and history is one who loves us so much that he never lets us go. "While we were yet sinners, Christ died for us." We are not slaves, but friends of God. We are not economic functions, but children of "God the Father almighty." The Apostolic Faith declared that God the Father creates in love, redeems in suffering, and loves to throw wild parties.

Is it possible in our time that we see our heavenly Father as a meal ticket and we pray to get something, rather than "love, the source of all life and love"? Do we worship to give us peace of mind or make us healthy? The gospel does not say that we win God's approval, but that while we are sinners, God in Christ dies for us. There is hope for us, because God loves us not because we do it our way or because we never break a rule.

We all leave home at one time or another. I can remember when I first left home. I was off to college, a little state teacher's college in East Stroudsburg, Pennsylvania, about seventy miles from my home north of Scranton. I really didn't want my folks to take me to college, so my friend Billy Rosemorgy, who had a 1948 Hudson, agreed to drive me to school. The 1948 Hudson was a great car. We had that up to 100 miles an hour on the new Route 6. This car was impressive and our girl friends were going to go with us. We had visions of grandeur that all eighteen-year-old boys dream. So, I was on my best behavior for weeks, and I finally broke the news to my mother so she would soften up my father. "Mom, you and Dad won't have to take me to college. Bill has offered to drive me down." "Oh," she said, "Your Dad wants to take you to college."

Now I knew they wanted to take me, but my Dad and Mother embarrassed me. So I had developed a number of reasons why their presence wasn't necessary. I said, "Mom, you know how Dad hates these long trips. You know the old car is not trustworthy." She said, "Your Dad had the car into the garage three times and it is ready to go. He got maps from the AAA and we know the way. It will be a wonderful day." So I said, "You know how Dad hates to miss work. I wouldn't want him to miss work over me." She said, "Your Dad and I are so proud of you, we love you so much, we just want to be with you as you start college."

I was sure my parents just loved to embarrass me. They were an obstacle to my success. My father had a sixth-grade education, and here I was off to be with scholars with Ph.D.'s. My father was fat and wore suspenders, and his pants looked like they were about to fall off. He never wore a tie, and here I was with college professors who wore tweed sport

209

coats and flannels. My father was a small-town politician. He had views on everything, and talked to everyone and freely gave them his views. He was a Republican and most college professors, I thought, were liberal Democrats. Boy, he could embarrass me. My mother was a churchwoman — her dresses were always too long and the heels on her shoes always too short, and she had a tendency to testify about Jesus Christ to people who never asked. My only hope was to keep them out of contact with the college as much as possible, so my parents would not humiliate me.

We got to the registration center, and I convinced my parents to stay in the car while I got my assignment. Freshmen were housed off campus, because of the huge influx of Veterans from WWII. I was housed a few blocks away. When we arrived at the house, my father insisted on helping carry in my bags. My mother had to talk to the landlady. And my father sat down and began talking to my roommate (an older veteran). I could hear him tell him what a good student I was, and that I played on the basketball and baseball teams. He said I was a wonderful boy. I overheard my mother saying to the landlady, "You don't have to worry about Herbert — he's a born-again Christian." I was planning on being a born-again pagan.

Well, the damage was done, but I got my parents on their way. Dad wanted to take us out to dinner and Mom wanted to be sure I had a good meal, but I convinced them they needed to get home before dark. I went back up to my room, grabbed a pack of Lucky Strikes from my bag and stuck one in my mouth. Then I wrapped the pack in my T-shirt sleeve like Frank Sinatra and said to my roommate, "Do you have a light?" Boy, I was liberated.

My roommate pulled his legs over the side of the bed, reached under the bed and pulled out his cane and then struggled to his feet. He said to me, "This is going to be one awful year for me. I have a big fat jerk for a roommate. The only hope is that a jerk who is loved so much by two wonderful parents must be of some worth." (How many of us have lived in the presence of human love and never knew it?)

That's the gospel, folks. Not very uplifting, but I think it's true. Yes, it's true that we can live in the presence of loving parents and never know we are loved. Yes, it's true that we can live in the presence of the loving heavenly Father and never know we are loved. We're all big fat jerks, but God loves us so much that we have an eternal, everlasting possibility. We can come home.

But don't come home if you see God as a meal ticket. Don't come home as a servant. Don't come home and try to do better. Come home as a child of God, to wear the marks of royalty, to enjoy the banquet of grace, and to be loved.

What if you have never left home? If you have always obeyed the law and recorded all your good deeds? Throw the record books away; the Father is not an accountant. Come join the party, "My son, My daughter, for all that I have is yours." The only way with God is to know that God is love and love never ends. I pray that your relation with God is rooted in knowing that "God proves his love for us in that while we were still sinners, Christ died for us." You are a beloved child.

Enjoy the party and give thanks for that amazing grace!

Amen.

The Story Is Not a Secret

Roberta Heath

On the first Sunday evening of the month, a small group in our congregation meets for prayer. It's an informal gathering. We begin by sharing with one another the happy and the sad news in our lives, our concerns for the world, our families, and others. Then we pray, most times silently. Occasionally, someone will speak out in prayer, inviting the others to join in spirit as "two or three" agreeing together.

This past month, it seemed more than the usual burdens were raised. You could hear the sucking sound of despair as, one by one, those gathered told stories of struggles with children, of marriages in danger of failing, of sickness and loss. We heard a particularly heart-wrenching story of a young person who was systematically sexually used by her stepfather. Now, thankfully, the act was exposed. The young person, however, was moved to a foster home, separated from an important network of friends. Added on top of these concerns were the stories lifted off the front page of the newspaper. . . .

We went to prayer with heavy hearts. The silence was broken only by the occasional sound of sobbing, as the tragic stories we had heard seemed to overwhelm each soul. A long time of silence passed when Audrey, a young woman in the group, spoke. She was suffering from laryngitis. Her voice cracked and was barely audible. In a raspy whisper she prayed, "God, I can't speak long or loud tonight, but there's something I

This message was preached at Berkshire Community Church, Richmond, Massachusetts on May 6, 2001.

want you and the others here to know. I am so thankful for who I am today."

Through building tears, she continued, "Sometimes I'm shocked by how I've changed — the way I think, the way I live, the person I have become. I just thank you for Jesus. Knowing him has changed my life. I want the others to know that if you could change my life, then you can change anybody and anything. Just let them know Jesus. *Let them hear about Him. Amen.*"

Audrey's prayer was not theologically sophisticated, nor framed in the flowery words of a poet. She didn't quote passages of Scripture to affirm or defend the truth she spoke, and yet that simple, heartfelt prayer released our souls and called us from despair to faith, from hopelessness to courage. Audrey reminded us that there is another story, a Story of the Good News, which can overcome the darkness of all of the stories that we heard that night. Audrey reminded us of the Story of God — the story that someone once told her, the story that someone once told us, and the story that we must tell others.

Theological constructs or religious ideas can and do grow cumbersome and stale. Poetic words inspire, but may not empower. Biblical proof texts often prove little when brought to bear on the real world of evil and suffering. But the story, the Story of God, is never changing yet ever evolving. The Story of God brings new light, life, hope, and power to all who hear it. We must not keep it a secret.

Stories are powerful tools. They can cause us to joy or sorrow. They can lift us to new visions or drown us in an ocean of despair. They can help us to find clarity and hope for our life, or they can lead us into confusion and disillusionment. Stories can be vehicles of healing or burdens that make us sick. It all depends on the story we tell — on what story we invite to inform our life and frame our world. That night we heard tragic stories that evoked sorrow, despair, confusion — that made us soul-sick, so to speak. Had these been the only stories we heard; if suffering, sorrow, sin, and darkness was all that we had to frame our world, we would have left burdened, without a vision of hope for those for whom we prayed, for our world, or even for ourselves. Thankfully, Audrey lifted up another Story, a story that someone once told her, that someone once told us, and that we must tell to others. And, she reminded us that the One who stands at the center of that Story, arms outstretched, is never changing, but *the same yesterday, today, and forever.* We need to stop keeping that a secret.

The Bible is more than a collection of religious ideas, rules, or precepts designed to serve as a litmus test for the faithful. It is more than a compendium of ethical studies or a history of religious development. It is more than a platform for theological exercise and exchange. All of these good and useful disciplines can be derived from its study, but the Bible is, as Dr. Fackre's works have so eloquently proclaimed, *The Christian Story*.

A story is for telling. A story is for sharing. A story is a meeting place with others, and the Christian Story is also a meeting place with God. We must never keep this Story a secret. We must guard against the temptation to cloud it with complexity or dissect it to obscurity. We don't need to explain all of its subtleties or defend it against unbelief. We just need to tell it as simply and as clearly as we are able. If we believe that this Story is the very foundation of our hope today, just as it has been hope in ages past, we must tell it. We must tell it with our words, demonstrate it through our actions, speak it into each new day, each new situation, and hold it up to every new challenge. It is, as the hymn writer put it, an *old, old, story*. But it is not a dead story. It speaks anew into every age.

The Christian Story is as relevant in this so-called postmodern, global world as it was when it took formation in the hearts of those who shared it together in antiquity. When we engage the Story, just like those of old, we discover who God is, who we are, and what God's vision is for the world. We find answers to the many questions that plague humankind: Why are we here? Where do we fit in? Why does life seem so upside down at times? How should we get along with others? What does God expect of us? These questions lead us to the very center, the crisis of the Story so to speak, where we find Christ — God the Way, the Truth, and the Life for all, who is the same *yesterday, today, and forever*. These basics never change. They are the sum and substance of faith and life for me, for millions of others, and, I hope, for you.

The Story of God is never changing, but it is ever evolving. Like the evolutionary process of adaptation where a species survives change by asserting its greatest strength into the new circumstances, new challenges, the new context, if you will, of its existence, so it is with God's Story. Each new age throws challenges against it, but the Story survives. Accepted wisdom of past ages, theological understandings, and even ethical applications might pass to the tests of a new day or a new discovery, but the Story lives on. It speaks out afresh, informing and instructing, compelling those who engage it towards deeper reflection, challenging old notions in new ways. It is fresh every morning. And with each new challenge, with each new burst of light, with each new circumstance, the Story is our anchor. It holds us firmly to the center — to the core — the Christ of God, so we need not fear the challenges or retreat from the changing world. We have a safe harbor from which to put out onto the sea of life. We have a Word to keep us afloat and a Guide to navigate us through each age.

It's an amazing thing really. A Story as old as *in the beginning,* reaches into the future mystery of the *end of the age;* and yet, this same Story sends out the brilliant light of hope, life, and power for today, so that a young woman can know that if someone speaks the Story into a troubled world, it will bring healing peace. It is an amazing thing, isn't it? It is a precious gift this Story that God has called us to hear, ponder, and speak. We must never keep it a secret. We must never fail to tell it to others with love, tenderness, and the hopeful conviction that the God of the Story still reaches out to redeem, to guide, and to heal in *this* world, in *this* age.

The Bible is a Story for telling, for sharing with others. When we tell the Story, lives are changed. Too often, we treat the Bible like it's a manual for insiders. We lift up some principle that we feel particularly strongly about, quote a verse and turn some select words from the Story into a battering ram for our cause. Or we clothe it in liturgy, using insider church words. . . . *A reading from the Epistle.* . . . (I went to church for sixteen years and each week I listened to snippets read with a falsetto voice from the high pulpit. I never could figure out where the reading came from or put it all together with God.) We build our doctrines, take our positions, and believe that these alone contain the whole of all truth about God. We tell others about our church, our pastor, our choir, when all we really need to do is tell the Story. It is the Story, not our doctrines, not our church, not our opinions. It is the Story that is the meeting place with God. Where the Story is told, lives are changed and vision overcomes the paralyzing despair that is all too common in our world.

I was twenty-one years old. I had been in and out of church for most of my life. I understood the doctrine and the dogma. I could participate in the liturgy. I knew what the church believed. But none of it made much sense to me. None of it spoke to where I lived, or offered much *light for the paths* that I walked on. I had decided that religion really wasn't for me.

Then one day someone began a conversation with me about the Bible. I met the approach with ridicule. However, my ridicule and cynicism didn't stop this woman from telling me the Story, and better yet, challenging me to read it and refute it. I took up the challenge, certain of a victory. She had promised me that if I could prove that what was contained in the Bible was false, she would come over to my way of thinking. However, if it were discovered to be true, then I would have to come over to her way of thinking. She wasn't afraid of the challenge. She knew that the never-changing, ever-evolving Story could hold up to whatever I could bring to it. The Story didn't need her defense; it just needed to be told. She handed me the Book and I began to read.

I began to read of a God who created all that is. I read of God's joy and pride in the human creation and how those creatures failed. I read of the ongoing struggle of God to put it right again. I understood, I *felt* in my own soul, the arrogance and apathy of sin. Then I read of a Savior, and my life was changed. I could look into the future and see love, hope, and a vision for a life with meaning — with God. *I love to tell the Story, it did so much for me!* And to this day, each time I engage God's Story anew, I see more — more hope, more light, more life, more love.

What a remarkable Story, don't you think? What an astonishing Story God has entrusted into our care. Let's not keep it a secret. The Bible is not our own private diary, and Christ is not our own private deity. We *have* a *story to tell to the nations* and to our neighbors. We have a story to speak into darkness and suffering. We have a story to challenge the powers and principalities of this world. And speak it we must, if there is any love at all in us.

There is a rise in spirituality in this nation, and yet participation is declining in the mainline churches. Could this be because even we who express faith in Jesus Christ, who profess to know and love the Story of God, have failed to tell it to others? Are we hiding our light under a bushel, as the Sunday school song goes, or letting the darkness and evil of the world blow it out? Have we been too lopsided in our story telling — substituting our doctrines, our liturgy, or our opinions for the simple Story? Or are we really afraid of the test? Are we afraid to test the staying power of God's Story in this age? Thus, we keep it a secret, drawing the wagons of the faithful few around it and refusing to hold it up to new challenges of each new day. Do we really believe that the Story is as relevant today as it was in the past?

God doesn't need our protection. God's Story doesn't require our defense. Will it seem foolishness to some? Of course it will. Might it be a stumbling block to others? Without a doubt. It always has been. But to those who are being saved by the Christ that they meet with there, it is the power of God. We must tell the Story. It will hold up to the challenges of each new day, and those who hear will be blessed, transformed in vision and hope and power — yea, saved.

We all have a bag of tools that we use to meet the challenges of life. We have and often use the good tools of the modern world — psychology, education, political action, social agencies. These were the tools that so many of us wanted to bring to bear on the wrenching needs that were raised that night at prayer. However, they failed us in the darkness of the hour. We found ourselves lost in despair until one voice, weak and raspy, reminded us that we also have a tool which is much more powerful than all of the others. We have a Story of promise, hope, healing, and life. We have *the Christian Story*. She reminded us that it was this Story that changed her life and that has changed many, many lives down through the ages, and still changes lives today. We have this holy Story, this precious gift of God. We need not dissect it or defend it, but simply tell it, over and over again, with tenderness and love, into a world that needs to hear it so very desperately.

My friends, I give to you today, the never-changing, ever-evolving Story of our God. Go forth and tell it to all who will hear and *the kingdom of love and light* will come.

ADDENDUM

Aside from the person who first shared with me the Good News of God that literally changed my entire life (from mother on welfare to preacher is quite a change), the most influential person in my walk of faith and understanding has been Dr. Gabriel Fackre, in whose honor I was asked to write this sermon. I had the grandest blessing of studying with him both in my graduate and postgraduate work at Andover Newton.

Dr. Fackre possesses all of the credentials that one would expect to find on the faculty of a quality theological school. He is well-studied, well-known and respected as a modern theologian, broadly published, and always open to new thought. However, Dr. Fackre brought much more than his credentials to the classroom. He came to his students with an awareness of what he was teaching — the whole Story of God; with why he was teaching it — because the vision and power of God will bring peace and healing to a broken world; and whom he was teaching it to — foot soldiers of Christ destined to carry this precious Story out to the world. The richness of his narrative approach to theology provided me and countless others with an engaging process for reflection. It opened up the possibilities of preaching and teaching God's Word in new and creative ways. It empowered us for ministry. I am forever a grateful recipient of the Christian Story.

Divine Repose

Llewellyn Parsons Smith

Gabriel Fackre has made a significant contribution to theological conversation in the United Church of Christ through colloquy events held at Craigville on Cape Cod each summer, down the road from the Fackre home. Gabe Fackre took initiative in convening the first colloquy in 1984, commemorating the 1934 Barmen Declaration. Springing from several discussion groups active in the early 1980s, including Theological Tabletalk at Andover Newton Theological School, The Mercersburg Society, and the Biblical-Theological-Liturgical Group, the Craigville Theological Colloquies have been designed to deepen theological conversations in scholarly circles and church communities.

According to the format, plenary meetings and small group discussions have offered participants the opportunity to reflect on the year's selected topic, each small group giving a written report after five days of challenging conversation. An Ecumenical Observer is invited to comment on proceedings. An open invitation is given for anyone to submit a paper, usually yielding three chosen for presentation early in the colloquy period. These, along with keynote speakers, prompt us to discern and clarify theologically responsible positions on such subjects as Justification by Faith, Christian Formation, and the Resurrection. Worship and Bible study are always part of the colloquy program. Gabe Fackre has always been there, an important presence for his many students, friends, and colleagues in the faith.

On July 12, 1999, the sixteenth Craigville Theological Colloquy convened to explore the question: "How Shall We Understand Jesus as Savior Now?" At this event, the keynote speakers were Frederick R. Trost and

Bennie E. Whiten, Jr., U.C.C. conference ministers from Wisconsin and Massachusetts. For five days we reflected, explained, debated, and interpreted the meaning of salvation through Jesus Christ. Drafts of our conclusions were published to share with the wider church. I preached the following sermon at the opening worship service.

Scripture Lessons: Deuteronomy 18:15-20
John 1:29-34

The great Christian poet Gerard Manley Hopkins has a poem called "Peace" about the coming of the Holy Spirit. It begins: "When will you ever, Peace, wild wood dove, shy wings shut, You round me roaming end, and under be my boughs?" And it ends: "And when Peace here does house, He comes with work to do, He does not come to coo, He comes to brood and sit." As we gather for Holy Communion, we invoke the Holy Spirit, and we are grateful that the Spirit remains in the church through the centuries.

Yesterday, in my church in West Gloucester, we baptized a child of God named Benjamin. We heard the text in Romans about the power of the Holy Spirit and Benjamin listened to the sermon, as he has done every Sunday for many weeks though he is only eight months old. And I told him that we would be praying for the Holy Spirit, and he heard me say: "We will pray that the Holy Spirit will remain with you and bless you all the days of your life." But Benjamin, he knew nothing of this, gently resting in his father's arms.

I told him that Jesus was baptized in the Jordan River and the Holy Spirit came upon him there and, according to John's Gospel, it remained with him. It found a heavenly rest with him. It settled there, in divine repose, in holy fullness, in peace. But that little child knew nothing of this.

We sang "Breathe on Me, Breath of God," and I explained to Benjamin that the Spirit was the breath of God and had been given to the first earth creature, the Adam, when God breathed into his nostrils the breath of life. And the Spirit has to do with the breath of those who are part of the Body of Christ breathing the same air you do. So this congregation is breathing on you and passing on its Spirit. We pray for the Holy Spirit to be with us at a Baptism, and at Holy Communion, and Ordinations.

An early ordination rite took very seriously the supernatural power of the breath of a holy man. Do you remember the practice of insufflation? In Egypt, they had the custom of filling a skin bag with the holy breath of the Coptic Patriarch of Alexandria, tying it up, and transporting it upriver to Ethiopia where it was let loose on the one designated to be the Abuna or head of the Ethiopian church. In describing this practice, a confident comment comes down to us, through Raymond Brown: "Who can doubt apostolic succession when it comes in this form?"[1]

In my church yesterday, a real congregation with real breath was surrounding the child Benjamin at his baptism and sharing and, in a sense, passing on the Spirit of the church through the centuries. But that little child knew nothing of this, although he must have caught the feel of it.

I told Benjamin that people wondered for a long time what it meant that the Holy Spirit came to Jesus at his baptism. What was the relationship between Jesus and the Holy Spirit? Was the Spirit poured out by God on this human who then became empowered, as if he were at that moment adopted by God? Or did this story of the dove descending mean that Jesus already had the Spirit and the coming of the dove simply showed the world what the reality was? Little Benjamin seemed to shake his head.

Then I recalled for the congregation the role of Cyril of Alexandria who lived in Egypt; a Patriarch, he was. Cyril had a way of thinking about it that people found helpful. In fact, it was so helpful that his idea called the day and established the way faith was expressed in the fifth century.

In Christ, Cyril saw the full making divine of the human being: Christ, the Word of God, clothing Itself with humanity, albeit a rather impersonal humanity. Because Christ made humanity divine, we, too, shall be made partakers of the divine nature, sanctified. Our salvation is granted by God as we become partakers of divinity, sharing in the Holy Spirit. "Divinization" or "Theosis" as the process is called. For Cyril, the salvation of humankind is the sanctifying of our humble flesh. The Spirit that settled in Jesus, the incarnate Logos, remained with him and remains with the church.[2]

Cyril did not live long enough to attend what is known as the Fourth Ecumenical Council when 630 bishops met under the authority of Pope Leo I, in 451 at Chalcedon, up near Constantinople. They invoked the Holy Spirit, and then the Council of Chalcedon established that

---

1. Raymond Brown, *The Gospel According to John XIII-XXI*, Anchor Bible (Garden City, NY: Doubleday), p. 1023.

2. Daniel Keating, "The Baptism of Jesus in Cyril of Alexandria: The Re-creation of the Human Race," *Pro Ecclesia* 8 (Spring 1999): 201-222.

Christ is perfect in Godhead and also perfect in manhood, truly God and truly human, two natures, unconfusedly, unchangeably, indivisibly, inseparably, one in Christ. This established a norm of doctrine upheld by all but a handful of church communions (five Oriental, Monophysite church bodies), who refuse to admit two separate natures, in the language of Chalcedon.

Cyril, the subtle theologian and powerful Patriarch of Alexandria, had declared what became a watchword: "One physis (nature) of the logos (Word) and it made flesh." "Nature" here refers to a concrete existence, the Word made flesh — a living person. Nature for him was not the abstract totality of particular properties, human or divine. But now this word nature as used (after Cyril's death) at Chalcedon could be, as we can see, quite an ambiguous word, confusing (although it turned out to be useful at the time). However, its interpretation caused some sad ruptures in the church, between the Monophysites, or one-nature supporters, and those who strictly affirmed Chalcedon's "Two natures."

These distinctions may offer us ideas about how we may frame our thoughts about the meaning of salvation. Baby Benjamin isn't ready for it yet; but we are here to think about it. Perhaps we can say a special prayer on Friday, remembering that July 16th was the traditional day to celebrate the Feast of the Council of Chalcedon. In the liturgy for that day it says: "Let us with loud jubilation praise the mystical trumpets of the Spirit, the God-bearing [ones], those who took up the harmonious song of theology in the midst of the church."[3]

The language of Chalcedon has been regarded as the orthodox solution to the christological problem in Greek, Latin, and most Protestant churches. In our time, the question has been opened again with vigor, where once declarations of heresy and anathema damned the other side, through bilateral ecumenical dialogues fostered by the World Council of Churches. During the 1990s, the various official dialogues have looked closely at the Chalcedonian vocabulary and the substance it deals with, finding, frequently, that only terminology, not meaning, divides. The meaning of salvation in Christ is a vital concern in the 90s among Roman Catholic, Reformed, Orthodox, and Oriental churches. Dorothea Wendebourg compares the work being done and its possible accords to the breakthrough in the Leuenberg Intercommunion between Lutheran and Reformed churches.

3. Dorothea Wendebourg, "Chalcedon in Ecumenical Discourse," *Pro Ecclesia* 7 (Summer 1998): 307-332.

What of interfaith conversations? Are these christological distinctions of Chalcedon a help or a hindrance? In Egypt today, the World Council and the YMCA are encouraging dialogues at various levels. At a recent seminar sponsored by the YMCA, the report on dialogue groups said that many conversations "have discovered the need to begin with topics relating to economic, educational, political, or social issues. Once the participants have come to know and trust one another, they move on to religious and theological issues. Many Christians and Muslims are not yet ready to discuss theological questions with one another in an open, unprejudiced way. At the same time, it should be remembered that, particularly in Africa, theological issues and questions are an integral part of life. Not to discuss these would be unnatural. As men and women of faith, Christians and Muslims are longing to share at this deeper level."[4] If the Muslim says there is no God but Allah, and the Christian says Christ is fully God as well as fully human, the deeper conversation will be difficult, but all the more fascinating.

Looking at Egypt, we see how much has changed since the days of Cyril. Patriarch Cyril lived in Alexandria in an age of cultural grandeur, political eminence, and intellectual prominence. Alexandria was a center of learning and the arts in the fifth century. Cyril's theological ruminations drew on the resources of the Alexandrian library, numbering 700,000 rolls, the splendid university, the flourishing church, and his forbears, including Origen and Athanasius. When the wave of Islam flowed through Egypt in the seventh century, things changed. Many books, pagan, Jewish, and Christian, were deliberately destroyed. Muslim Arabs took Alexandria in 642 and later moved the capital of Egypt to Cairo. Now the Coptic Church represents only nine percent of the sixty million people in Egypt. Much of ancient Alexandria is underwater. Yet the tenacity of the faithful holds in the face of abuse and even persecution. The Holy Spirit remains with the church. Patriarch Parthenios of Alexandria said not long ago: "Let us not forget that the Spirit is Holy and the Church is holy, because the Spirit dwells in it. . . . We forget about its holiness. We forget that we have to become holy, as far as we can, since we enjoy the comfort of the Holy Spirit and the help of Christ's church. . . . Without holiness nothing comes to fruition."[5]

4. S. V. Sicard, "Ecumenical Task Force of the YMCA in Islamic Societies," Seminar in Nairobi, Kenya, May 1987, p. 47.

5. Patriarch Parthenios, presentation for the Seventh Assembly of the World Council of Churches, Canberra, February 1991.

I like to think of his predecessor, Patriarch Cyril, who wrote about the baptism of Jesus in John's Gospel, and pointed out emphatically that the Spirit *remains*. It remains with Jesus who is a representative human being, who represents the whole human race in its salvation. Or, in his words, "as human, he had the whole of human nature in himself, in order to renew all of humanity and restore it to its original state. . . . It was as though the only-begotten Word of God extended the stability which is proper to his own nature to us."[6] Here is how he is acclaimed on his feast day: "Rejoice most blessed Cyril, spring of theology and river of the knowledge of God. Never cease to intercede with Christ on our behalf."[7]

Last month, the Cape Ann Interfaith Commission called a meeting in Gloucester of Jewish, Christian, and Muslims to discuss and describe our personal experiences of our faith traditions. We had a most cordial and engaging time of "sharing" with friendly respect accorded all around. This was good. But if Cyril is right, we cannot just talk about salvation in our own time and place, but need to do so in the context of all church history and the worldwide church. When I wrote to the contemporary Patriarch of Alexandria a few years ago, he wrote back: "Your letter touched my heart. . . . Your love is a gift, which helps me, and your words are a gift from our Lord. May God bless you." It is a hand-written letter in ballpoint pen, which I brought with me today. When it arrived at my church the deacon who picks up the mail greeted me with the news: "Boy, a humdinger came in today." In discussing the World Council's work, Patriarch Parthenios said: "So dialogue begins, which is the only way to know one another in the Holy Spirit."

May each child of God washed and reborn at baptism receive a measure of the Holy Spirit, and may our little Benjamin come to enjoy theology. May the Spirit find rest and repose in each of us who come to the table today. We know the dove has not come here to coo in tranquility, but to work among us, to stir in us the witness to holiness, and to prompt what will happen here this week, as the days unfold. But we, as yet, know nothing of this. We simply pray that we may be blessed by the Holy Spirit that lit upon Jesus and remained. Amen.

6. J. Patout Burns and G. M. Fagin, *The Holy Spirit* (Wilmington, DE: M. Glazier, 1984), p. 162.

7. John A. McGuckin, *St. Cyril of Alexandria: The Christological Controversy* (Leiden: E. J. Brill, 1994), p. 32.

A View from the Congregational Platform

Joseph Bassett

Scripture Lessons: Psalm 84
John 3

The way the Psalmist holds up specific details is really quite lovely. In Psalm 84, we are told that the birds make their nests in the eaves of the Temple. Would that we were as faithful to detail when it comes to the Cambridge Platform ("Platform"). But, alas, we much prefer to reduce this critical document to sweeping generalities after Williston Walker gave us the critical edition of the text.[1] Subsequent scholars preferred the distractions of liberal religion to the words of the document itself. Thus, they lecture us about "congregational polity," an abstract construct that ignores the line in chapter two: "The term Independent, wee approve not" (II:5). Abstract Congregational Polity can be as provincial as it is independent. It leads scholars to dismiss the second stated purpose of the Platform, namely "[t]he holding forth of Unity and Harmony both amongst and with other churches" (Preface), as of absolutely no interest. So, on this day, let the Massachusetts Convention of Congregational Ministers listen to the Platform and remember those who wrote it. Let us hear what our tradition has to say to the ecumenical church. Let us pay attention to a few of the bird's nests in our eaves.

---

1. Williston Walker, *The Creeds and Platforms of Congregationalism* (Philadelphia: Pilgrim Press, 1960).

This sermon was delivered for the Massachusetts Convention of Congregational Ministers, at the First Congregational Church in Essex, Massachusetts, May 21, 1998.

The Synod that produced the Cambridge Platform came in three sessions: September 1646; June 1647; and August 1648. Of the three, the second — although the shortest — was the most interesting. John Eliot, the apostle to the Algonquins, preached a sermon to the Algonquins in their own language. Ezekiel Rogers of Rowley, ten miles up the road, then preached to the English in their language.

The second session of the Synod didn't last long. An epidemic was spreading throughout the land. The symptoms were "a cold and light fever with it." Governor Winthrop's wife had been carried off. This must have pained Ezekiel Rogers, because he had sailed to the Massachusetts Bay Colony on the *Lyon* with the governor's wife sixteen years earlier and had been her teacher. The Synod decided to adjourn and reconvene in August of 1648. Thomas Hooker returned to Connecticut and died, perhaps having caught the bug. John Eliot preached to the Algonquins and made a lasting impression. He is still remembered.

At the Chestnut Hill post office, there is a WPA mural showing Eliot preaching to Waban — an edifying sight as you stand in line for stamps. It is that figure of John Eliot preaching that stays with us. We know that Eliot not only preached in Algonquin, but he also translated the Scriptures into that language. The Roxbury minister presented a copy of his words to Jesus College in Cambridge, England. Every now and again you see a copy of Eliot's Bible — in places like the Boston Public Library. Eliot shared this preaching and translating with Jesuit missionaries in Canada. When Father Druillete came to the Massachusetts Bay Colony on a diplomatic mission in the winter of 1650, he visited with Eliot in Roxbury. The priest and the minister conversed in Latin, and compared notes in their work among the culture of Native Americans.

It has been repeatedly pointed out that by the time Eliot had translated the Bible into the Algonquin language, the Algonquins had all been pretty much obliterated by King Philip's war. Eliot's praying Indians had been shipped out to Deer Island, where they were rounded up and tied together with rope. There they were exposed to the weather and they suffered terribly in a harsh winter when the snowdrifts were shoulder high. Eliot then wrote: "the profane Indians p've [prove] a very sharp rod to the praying Indians."[2] Eliot himself was threatened while attempting to bring more food and medicine to the Algonquins on Deer Island.

The way the history is told, Eliot's preaching and translating were

2. Ola Winslow, *John Eliot: Apostle to the Indians* (Boston: Houghton Mifflin, 1968), p. 175.

peripheral. The story of European power — the military campaign, the political structures, the building of Natick — is considered more significant. Places like Bloody Brook and the Sudbury Fight are marked. The story of Mrs. Rowlandson of Lancaster has been recently republished. To all of this, John Eliot seems but a footnote.

For us, however, that cannot be. Eliot's preaching and translating receive our full attention. Some of the members of this Convocation occupy pulpits in towns where Eliot himself preached and prayed. Some UUA/UCC pulpits have preached the Word for two hundred, even three hundred, years. Moreover, like John Eliot, we live in a world where military and economic powers seem to dominate. Issues are decided by those with power to force their way on others.

Eliot wasn't in power. "Inculturation" was his ministry. He preached and translated the Word in order to "inculturate" the gospel in Native American communities. To inculturate is now something of a modern church buzz word. Today, the descendants of Father Druillete and Rev. Eliot study the dynamics of inculturation, as did their forebears.

This year, the Massachusetts Commission on Christian Unity discussed inculturation as it appears in a Faith and Order document, "Becoming a Christian." Father Edward O'Flaherty pointed out that adaptation is not the same as inculturation. There was a time when people thought the two were the same, but they are not.

John Eliot adapted the gospel to Algonquin culture when he organized praying Indian towns along the lines of Mosaic codes and legislation. Thus, for example, Eliot adapted the plan of Moses' father-in-law, Jethro, to govern Natick. These praying Algonquin chose their leaders in numbers of ten, fifty, and one hundred.[3] That is adaptation, not inculturation.

Inculturation is when the Gospel is incarnated into a particular culture. It is now recognized that translation is the first step in that process. So when John Eliot preached to the Algonquins in Algonquin and Ezekiel Rogers preached to the English in English, we have before us the inculturation of the gospel.

We are still involved in that process. We are still trying to find the right word to attest to the Word of God, which "living and active will pierce to the joints and marrow, discerning the thoughts and intentions of the heart" (Hebrews 4:12). Just think of the energy and controversy that have gone into the question of language in our hymns. In 1984, this con-

---

3. Winslow, *John Eliot,* p. 28.

vention took up inclusive language at Hancock church in Brookline. How to find the right word has been a continuing effort of the saints in New England. We can't just assume that words work. We are to pay attention to our translations. It is one of those details that count.

Thus, the first verse of Psalm 84 is found on the title page of the Cambridge Platform. We are most familiar with this verse as: "How lovely is thy dwelling place, O Lord of Hosts." The very mention of that verse and we think of Brahms' romantic anthem in the *Deutsche Requiem*. Therefore, it may come as a surprise to note that the Cambridge Platform doesn't translate that verse that way — and neither does the Authorized Version of the Bible sponsored by King James. That verse in the Bay Psalm Book is translated: "How amiable Lord of hosts they tabernacles bee."

The meetinghouses of New England were beautiful not in the sense of being "lovely," but in the sense of being "amiable"; amiable in the sense that they manifested the loving kindness and the grace of God for humanity. That was the purpose of these meetinghouses with their high pulpits — to preach the cordial consent of God's being to men and women, so that we could enjoy and glorify God forever.

That means preaching and teaching the person of Christ. That in itself involves inculturation. For what does "person" mean in English? We are called to affirm what Chalcedon called Christ's two natures without confusing them, on the one hand, or separating them, on the other. We are called to do this without making the mistake of William Ellery Channing, who said the word "person" destroyed the unity of God. We are called to do this without making the mistake of Moses Stuart, who replied that he didn't know what the word "person" meant, but because it was in the tradition he would use it just the same.

In unity and harmony, amongst and with other churches, we are called to preach the Word of God's loving kindness for creation and all who dwell therein. We do so in a modern world where, after they have set off atomic bombs, nuclear scientists think in terms of Vishnu from the *Bhagavad Gita*. In 1945, Robert Oppenheimer is reported to have quoted this line: "Now I am become Death, the destroyer of worlds."[4] But we preach in response that our gospel is not that of Vishnu, but the good news of Christ: "I came that people may have life and have it abundantly." Amen.

4. Richard Rhodes, *The Making of the Atomic Bomb* (New York: Simon and Schuster, 1989), p. 676.

The Ministry and The Center

Leander S. Harding

What is the central task of the church? What is the central task of the church's ordained ministers?

The official answers to these questions have varied little over centuries: To preach the gospel, to administer the sacraments, to pronounce blessing and pardon. In practice, in the time I have been an ordained servant of the church there have been at least three competitors for the answer to the question: "What should the clergy do and what should be its central occupation?" One model I would call the pastoral model. The church is seen as a community of healing, a place where people can come to find psychological and spiritual wholeness. In this model, the chief work of the clergy is to provide pastoral care. This pastoral care is often thought of in terms of one-to-one counseling, and the preparation and training are heavily therapeutic in orientation. The ideal pastor is sensitive, sympathetic, a skilled listener, non-judgmental, accepting — a good counselor. Another model is the prophetic model. Some of the seminaries of my denomination pride themselves on raising up and training a prophetic ministry. The central task of the church is seen as galvanizing Christian people to work together for a more just social order. The clergy are to empower people to overturn oppressive social and political structures and foster in their people "a liberative consciousness and praxis."

This sermon was preached at the Evensong of the joint SEAD and Confessing Christ Conference, November 4, 2000, in St. John's Episcopal Church, Stamford, Connecticut.

228

The ideal prophet is courageous and forthright, able to speak truth to power, no people-pleaser, well-trained in social and political analysis, adept in the skills of community organizing.

Lately, a third kind of rhetoric about the church and its ordained servants has been heard, the rhetoric of leadership. Commissions on ministry and seminaries now signal that they are weary of the introverted and the non-judgmental and the prophetic bull in the parochial china shop, and are now looking for natural leaders who can be given advanced training in aligning the resources of the organization toward a visionary future. The church is seen as an effective provider in the marketplace of religious needs, and the pastor is seen as an effective leader, who can build a robust and dynamic institution with a shrewd combination of responsiveness to constituencies and the capacity to articulate compelling dreams of future success.

Most of us have been both the beneficiaries and the victims of these models of the church and the work of its ordained ministers. The church as a whole and many individual clergy have been generously blessed by the insights and challenges of each of these models. We have also paid a price. Many churches and many pastors have become exhausted trying to live out these models. There is an unreality behind these models, a problem greater than their tendency to overemphasize one dimension of the church's mission at the expense of other dimensions. Each one of these models causes the clergy to act as though something were true when it really is not, when something very like its opposite is actually the case. The best of people in such circumstances become very tired and dispirited, and some simply break down. The breakdown can be mental, moral, or spiritual. (We hear a great deal about such breakdowns in the clergy today. The reports are exaggerated, but it is true enough.)

What is the lie — the unreality? All of these models assume that the central problem is to figure out what the church should do. They all assume that the church exists and will continue to exist. The problem is how to take care of a settled Christian people, or to challenge a settled Christian people to action or to organizational effectiveness.

In the current circumstances, in which most of the Protestant congregations consist of fewer than 100 souls at worship on Sunday morning, in which most congregations are plateaued or declining in membership, in which the mainline churches stand at the end of two decades of membership free fall (the Episcopal Church has gone from about 8 million members to fewer than 2 million members in this time), and when the median age of our congregations and clergy is 50+, it is unreal to take the existence of the church for granted and to take the continuing existence of the church for granted (at least in its present institutional form).

The truth is that we cannot take the continuing existence of the church for granted. Certainly we cannot take for granted the continuing existence of our denominations nor, in many, many cases, the continuing existence of the very congregation we are serving. The question has changed from, "What should the church do and what activities should occupy its ministers?" to "How can there be a church here and now, and how can this church reconstitute itself with a new people in a new generation?"

What has always been the official agenda, the setting forth of Christ — proclamation of the Gospel, administration of the sacraments (in Cranmer's words, "to set forth thy true and lively Word and rightly and duly administer thy holy sacraments") — becomes the practical agenda in a new way and with a new urgency.

The context has shifted. To a very great degree we do not serve a settled Christian people, but a profoundly unsettled Christian people within the churches and an increasingly secularized, yet neo-pagan world, that for all its technological prowess, is more superstitious and idolatrous than the age of the Caesars. We are confronted both without the churches and within, with people who have either never heard the Gospel or barely heard the Gospel or misheard the Gospel. To act, though with great skill and sincerity, in such a circumstance as though the existence of the church was secure and then to proceed to develop a pattern of ministry based on that assumption, is to be on a collision course with reality and to run the risk of spiritual shipwreck.

The central task of the church practically in our context, at this moment, is to tell the story of God's saving love made known to us in Jesus Christ, as though for the first time — to those who have never heard it, or barely heard it, or misheard it. (It is more difficult and complex a task, and one that requires greater persistence in the face of failure, to proclaim the Gospel to those who have barely heard it or misheard it.) There is a word for this — evangelism, even first evangelization. This is the central task of the church and its ordained ministers. Embracing this task allows us to acknowledge the reality of the mission upon which we have been sent, and the reality of the mission field to which we have been called.

In this present time, that which was assumed must be made explicit. To tell a story for the first time calls for a kind of clarity and simplicity that unmasks any ignorance or lack of conviction hiding behind equivocation or finesse.

The central task now is to tell the story of salvation over and over, as though for the first time. I want to say what I believe are the central chapters in that story, but first I want to say something about the heart of the pastor and the end to which the story is told. There is a word, an Italian word, which helps me a great deal. It comes from the work of a famous teacher of children. This makes sense because work with children is one of the places where the problem of first evangelization, the first telling of the story, has been pursued with great discipline in those churches in which otherwise the missionary impulse is fading. Sofia Cavalletti, an Italian religious educator, says that the purpose of sharing religious materials with the child is to make possible by God's grace, *innamoramento*, the moment of falling in love with God. The central task of the church and its ordained ministers in this moment is to tell the story as though for the first time — the story of God's love made known to us in Jesus Christ — to those who have never heard it or barely heard it or misheard it, in such a way that this moment of *innamoramento* becomes possible, either for the first time, or becomes possible again. What is required of the one called to do this is not so much this or that particular set of skills or virtues, but this fundamental posture of adoration and worship, the posture of one who has personally known the moment of falling in love with God.

There is a great need now for the clergy of the church to re-center their sense of vocation and to refocus their efforts on Christian Basics, on a very fundamental presentation of the Gospel, on telling the story in many cases actually for the first time and always as though for the first time, and in such a way as by God's grace to make possible this moment of falling in love with God. There is a need to re-center the ordained ministry of churches on what we have always said was the central task, even if our practice has belied it. There is also a need to recognize that the making of secondary things primary and primary things secondary has resulted in a loss of nerve, a loss of heart. There is a need for a new focus on things central, and a need for a new heart to tell the Story in a simple way, humbly and clearly, so that people may behold the fair beauty of the Lord and become lost in wonder, awe, and praise. This requires a heart that has itself been pierced by the beauty of the persevering, sacrificial love of God that has been made known to us in Jesus Christ.

If our central role is to tell a story — the true story of God's persevering love for us and all creation in such a way as to evoke love, gratitude and praise — a study of the Scriptures and the great teachers of the faith, which leads us to a greater apprehension of God's revelation of himself to us in Jesus Christ, must be at the heart of our work. Our study must be serious, rigorous, and disciplined, but it must also be different from other intellectual and scholarly pursuits as it turns toward contemplation, and from contemplation toward adoration and devotion.

What is this story that we have to tell? It is the story of God's love. Of how God made us and all that is, and that God's plan for us was that we should have hearts which reach up to Him in praise, thanksgiving, and worship, and hearts which reach out to each other in love and service. Of how we were made to know God and to serve Him by loving and serving each other and cherishing God's good creation. Of how we listened to the tempter and fell into sin and evil. Of how our hearts became hard toward God, and hard toward each other. Of how since then, each one has gone astray and done what is right in his or her own eyes.

I must say something about sin before I move on in this story. There is a great dispute about this chapter of the story now, and there are even attempts to tell the story without this chapter. In the Bible, sin is hardness of heart. *Sklerocardia* is one word the Bible has for sin. Sins are actions that are outer and visible consequences of the primary problem, which is a heart condition. There is a dispute in our churches about which sins are the most important sins and about whether some things are really sins at all. This debate is a symptom of the seriousness of the problem of sin, our hardness of heart toward God and toward each other. One of the symptoms of sin is that it is hard to hear and to obey God's Word. There will always be things which we say we do, but which we are unwilling to say are sin, and things which we are willing to say are sin, but which we are unwilling to say we do. The reality of the sin which is absolutely beyond dispute is a crushing weight which every human heart knows, "that memory which is grievous unto us and that burden which is intolerable to us," as our prayer book says, and from which every human heart looks for deliverance.

Sin is an important part of the story, but in spite of some ways in which the story has been told, it is not the beginning of the story or the end of the story. We do not begin in sin and evil, and God does not leave us there. He sends His Son who comes in the fullness of time, after great preparation and at great cost, to make it possible that the word of the prophets might come true and that we might have new hearts; hearts of flesh, not *sklerocardia,* hearts of stone. He spreads out His arms of love on the hard wood of the cross so that the whole world might come within the reach of His saving embrace. By the price of the cross and the power of the resurrection and the gift of the Spirit, He makes it possible that we might have in us the heart that was in Him, the heart we were meant to have in the beginning, the heart that goes up to God and out to others. He has come to give His life for us that He may give His life to us; a life of worship, praise, sacrifice, and service, a life which begins now and which the grave cannot hold.

There is an icon that has great meaning for me, and which helps me to focus on what is central to the vocation of the ordained. It is an image that is outside the ethos and aesthetic of the Protestant world. It is the icon of the sacred heart of Jesus. It is an image that has fascinated and horrified me most of my life. I remember seeing as a child the image of a heart, sometimes pierced, sometimes encircled with a crown of thorns, sometimes with a flame over it. It was mysterious and confusing. It is a common image in Roman churches. I was startled when I came to this church and noticed this same heart in the mosaic here, literally under our feet. It is part of a design representing the theological virtues of faith, hope, and love. Love, of course, abides forever. This heart doesn't have the thorns or the sword. It does have the flame, but as a radiating circle. It is an inflamed heart. Though the design is a little different it is, nonetheless, the same heart I have been seeing all these years, the sacred heart of Jesus. If you look carefully in our churches and are alert to all the different variations the design can take, you will be surprised at how common it actually is.

The meaning of this icon was brought home to me when one of the saints of our parish died. Arthur Cassell was a distinguished Liberian diplomat. He was the ambassador of Liberia to the United Nations. His life was tragically turned upside down by a coup in his country, and he lived out his exile in this parish. He was a person of deep faith. His father had been the Dean of the Cathedral in Monrovia. Arthur was one of those people who befriend and encourage the clergy. When he died his wife told me that Arthur had left something for me, something he got on a diplomatic trip to Iran. I could see it was a rug. I thought it was perhaps a Muslim prayer rug. It was, instead, a tapestry in very vivid colors and a very dramatic, even melodramatic style of Jesus. It was something that was about as far from the restrained and dignified aesthetic of Anglicanism as you can get. Jesus is pointing his finger at me, at you, and looking out with large searching eyes, and with his other hand he is pulling aside his robes, revealing and pointing to his heart, inflamed, circled with the hard thorns of our resistance, but radiating love, this heart, the one heart God has ever meant for you and for me to have, the sacred heart of Jesus, this heart which goes up to the Father and out to us. And Jesus is saying, "I have come that you may have this heart. I send you to give this heart to others." Make it so. Amen.

Publications

1949   "Creative Social Trends in British Christianity." *Baptist Divinity House News* (January 31, 1949): 1-3 (coauthor with Dorothy Fackre).

1957   *Under the Steeple.* Nashville: Abingdon Press, 1957 (coauthor with Dorothy Fackre).

1959   *The Purpose and Work of the Ministry.* Philadelphia: Christian Education Press, 1959.
"Ministering to Young Adults in the Industrial Area." *Chicago Seminary Register* 49:8 (November 1959): 42-46.

1960   "Heritage and Horizon — The Industrial Communities." *United Church Herald* 3:23 (December 15, 1960): 20-21.

1961   "What Is Dehumanization?" *Theology and Life* 4:4 (November 1961): 292-294.

Book Reviews:
Helmut Thielicke, *Nihilism.* In *Theology and Life* 4:3 (August 1961): 252-253.
Kendig Brubaker Cully, *Basic Writings in Christian Education.* In *The Christian Century* 78:17 (April 26, 1961): 537-538.

1962   "The Baptismal Encounter." Lancaster Seminary Occasional Papers, 1962. Reprinted in *Theology and Life* 5:3 (August 1962): 215-226.

Book Reviews:

Daniel Callahan, et al., *Christianity Divided.* In *Theology and Life* 5:2 (May 1962): 180-182.

Luigi Civardi, *Christianity and Social Justice.* In *The Christian Century* 79:37 (Sept. 12, 1962): 1099.

June Bingham, *Courage to Change: An Introduction to the Life and Thought of Reinhold Niebuhr.* In *Theology and Life* 5:4 (November 1962): 328-329.

1963   "Urban Mission: Parochial or Extra-Parochial?" *Theology and Life* 6:4 (Winter 1963): 342-344 (review essay of Gibson Winter, *The New Creation as Metropolis*).

"The Terror and Grandeur of Christmas." *Church School Worker* 14:4 (December 1963): 7-8.

"Lancaster Churches Sponsor Lay Center." *Christian Community* 16:4 (December 1963): 1.

Book Reviews:

Walter Wagoner, *Bachelor of Divinity.* In *The Christian Century* 80:42 (October 16, 1963): 1272.

Nels Ferré, *Reason in Religion.* In *United Church Herald* 6:23 (December 15, 1963): 15.

1964   *The Pastor and the World.* Philadelphia: United Church Press, 1964.

"Encounter and Pip's Place." *United Church Herald* 7:4 (February 15, 1964): 17-19, 34 (co-author with Herbert Davis). Reprinted in *Church of the Brethren Leader* 8:7 (July-August, 1965): 7-12.

"The Violet Band" (Feb. 16, 1964), "Holiness and Health" (Feb. 23, 1964), "The Imperative and the Indicative" (March 1, 1964), "One Great Hour of Sharing" (March 8, 1964), "God's Flesh and Blood" (March 15, 1964), "Lord of the Streets" (March 22, 1964), "The Path to Resurrection Faith" (March 29, 1964). *United Church of Christ Sunday Bulletins.*

"Storefront Meeting House." *The Home Missionary* (May 1964): 12-13.

"The Office of Pastor." *Theology and Life* 7:3 (Fall 1964): 197-204.

"Encounter — Mission in the World." *International Journal of Religious Education* 41:2 (October 1964): 6-7, 38.

Book Reviews:

William Stringfellow, *My People Is the Enemy.* In *Alumni Bulletin* (Bangor Theological Seminary) 39:4 (October 1964): 24-25.

Paul Tillich, *The Eternal Now.* In *United Church Herald* 7:18 (October 15, 1964): 32-33.

Julian Hartt, *The Lost Image of Man;* and Clara Mayer, *The Manmade Wilderness.* In *The Christian Century* 81:45 (November 4, 1964): 1370-1372.

1965   "Why an Ordained Ministry in a Modern Age?" *Youth* 16:3 (January 1965): 24-29.

"It Is Finished" (March, 1965). *United Church of Christ Sunday Bulletin.*

"The Death and Life of God." *Theology and Life* 8:3 (Fall 1965): 185-202.

"The New Morality." *Theology and Life* 8:4 (Winter 1965): 251-266.

"Secular Theology in the Church." *Ministers Quarterly* 21:4 (Winter 1965-66): 25-30.

Book Reviews:

Roger Mehl, *Society and Love.* In *Church School Worker* 15:10 (January-February 1965): 48 (co-author with Dorothy Fackre).

Robert Spike, *The Freedom Revolution and the Churches.* In *The Christian Century* 82:33 (August 18, 1965): 1013-1014.

Jean Rilliet, *Zwingli: Third Man of the Reformation.* In *The Christian Century* 82:40 (October 6, 1965): 1236-1238.

1966   "The Crisis of the Congregation: A Debate." In *Voluntary Associations: A Study of Groups in Free Societies:* Essays in Honor of James Luther Adams. Ed. D. B. Robertson. Richmond: John Knox, 1966.

"The Issue of Transcendence in the New Theology, the New Morality and the New Forms." *Theology and Life* 9:1 (Spring 1966): 35-50. Reprinted in *New Theology No. 4.* Ed. Martin E. Marty and Dean G. Peerman. New York: Macmillan, 1967; and in the *London Quarterly & Holborn Review* (January 1967): 1-11.

"Perspectives on Sex Morality." *Youth* 17:6 (June 1966): 17-25.

"Christian Secularity: Theological and Educational Implications." *Theology and Life* 9:2 (Summer 1966): 25-30.

"Witness Is a Two-Way Street." *United Church Herald* 9:15 (September 1, 1966): 17-19.

"Princeton Meeting on Renewal." *The Christian Century* 83:36 (September 7, 1966): 1095-1098.

"The Silence of God and the Noise of Men." *Preachers' Quarterly* (Great Britain) 12:4 (December 1966): 273-280.

Book Reviews:

Michael Novak, *Belief and Unbelief.* In *Theology and Life* 9:2 (Summer 1966): 181-183.

James Sellers, *Theological Ethics.* In *Religion and Life* 35:5 (Autumn 1966): 796-797.

Joseph Fletcher, *Situation Ethics*. In *United Church Herald* 9:17 (November 1966): 52-54.

1967 *What Happens in Baptism*. Living Faith Series. Philadelphia: Geneva Press, 1967.

"The New Morality." *Storm over Ethics*. Philadelphia: United Church Press, 1967.

"Voices for a World Come of Age." *Search for Identity*. The Methodist Church, 1967. Reprinted in *Protestant Women of the Chapel: Program Resource Guide*, 69-70. Washington, DC: Armed Forces Chaplains Board, 1970.

"Meddling." *Pulpit Digest* 47 (January 1967): 9-14. Reprinted in *The Schwenkenfelder* 64:2 (March 1967): 3-6.

"Love in Three Dimensions." *Children's Religion* 28:4 (April 1967): 18-20.

"The Church and Its Living Memory." *Church School Worker* 17:11 (July 1967): 7-10.

"The Church in Suburbia." *Reformed Journal* 17:7 (September 1967): 15-18.

"The Church and the Science-Man Questions." *Lancaster Seminary Bulletin* 2:1 (September 1967): 1-12.

"Is That Your Doing, Lord?" *Youth* 18 (October 1967): back cover.

"Emphasis: The Local Church in God's Mission." *United Church Herald* 10:11 (November 1967): 11M-13M.

"Secularization: Meaning, Value, Style." *Foundations* 10:4 (October-December 1967): 354-369.

"Celebrating in a Tangled World." *Religion in Life* 36:3 (Fall 1967): 334-342.

Book Reviews:

John Fish, et al., *The Edge of the Ghetto;* Stephen Rose, *The Grassroots Church;* Karl Rahner, *The Church in the Marketplace;* W. M. Bekkers, *God's People on the March;* Robert Adolfs, *The Church Is Different;* Earl Brill, *The Creative Edge of American Protestantism*. In *The Christian Century* 84:2 (January 11, 1967): 50-52.

Stephen Rose, *The Grassroots Church;* Richard E. Moore and Duane L. Day, *Urban Church Breakthrough*. In *Central Atlantic News* (Winter 1967).

Daisuke Kitagawa, *The Pastor and the Race Issue*. In *Review of Religious Research* 8:2 (Winter 1967): 119-120.

1968 *Conversation in Faith*. Philadelphia: United Church Press, 1968.
Secular Impact. Philadelphia: Pilgrim Press, 1968.

Second Fronts in Metropolitan Mission. Grand Rapids: Eerdmans, 1968.

"Witness Is a Two-Way Street." In _Creative Ministries._ Ed. David Marshall. Philadelphia: Pilgrim Press, 1968.

"Is This Your Doing, Lord?" In _Tune In._ Ed. Herman Ahrens. Philadelphia: Pilgrim Press, 1968.

"Faith and the Science-Man Questions." _Christianity and Crisis_ 27:23 (January 8, 1968): 315-318.

"Hope." _United Church Herald_ 4:1 (January 1968): 6M-12M (Ministry Edition).

"Public Education: A Missionary Model." _The Reformed Journal_ 18:4 (April 1968): 12-16.

"American Theology and the Cockney Milkman." _The Christian Century_ 85:32 (August 7, 1968): 987-989.

"The New Eschatology and the Old Realism." _Christianity and Crisis_ 28:16 (September 30, 1968): 225 (letter).

"Some Reflections on _The Church for Others._" _Concept_ (Blue). World Council of Churches. November, 1968.

Book Review:
Nelvin Vos, _For God's Sake, Laugh!_ In _Encounter_ 29:4 (Autumn 1968): 382.

1969   _Humiliation and Celebration: Post-Radical Themes in Doctrine, Morals and Mission._ New York: Sheed and Ward, 1969.

The Rainbow Sign: Christian Futurity. Grand Rapids: Eerdmans, 1969 and London: Epworth Press, 1969.

Christian Faith and Action in the Seventies. Council for Christian Social Action, 1969.

"Ethical Guidelines for the Control of Life." _Christianity and Crisis_ 29:5 (March 31, 1969): 68-72.

"The Blue Collar White and the Far Right." _The Christian Century_ 86:19 (May 7, 1969): 645-648. Reprinted in _Class and Group Behavior: A Book of Readings on Protest and Pressure in American Society,_ Vol. 1. Ed. John Florer, et al. Dubuque, IA: Kendall Hunt, 1971.

"Aiglatson." _United Church Herald_ 12:7 (July 1969): 10-12.

"A Voice for the Voiceless." _Journal_ 7:11 (September 1969): 3-7.

"Doing Theology in the Seminary of the 70s." _The Seminarian_ (Lancaster Theological Seminary) 20:4 (September 1969): 1-2.

"Some Observations on Nov. 15 in Washington." _The Seminarian_ (Lancaster Theological Seminary) 21:1 (December 4, 1969): 3-4.

Book Reviews:

Franklin H. Littell, *The Church and the Body Politic*. In *The Alumni Bulletin* (Bangor Theological Seminary) 44 (1969): 28.

Herman Kahn and Anthony Wiener, *The Year 2000*. In *The Voice* (Colgate Rochester Divinity School) 61:2 (April 1969): 19-20.

1970 *The Promise of Reinhold Niebuhr*. Philadelphia: Lippincott, 1970.

"Going into All the Future: The Congregation of the 1970s." *United Church Herald* 13:1 (January 1970): 14.

"Social Action in the Church of the 70s." *Worldview* (February 1970): 16-17.

"Realism and Vision." *Christianity and Crisis* 29:5 (April 1970): 72-77.

"Meditation on a Trip by Car and Foot in a City." *Youth* 21:13 (June 21, 1970): 26.

"Button, Button, Who's Got the Button?" *The Christian Ministry* 50:5 (July-August, 1970): 44-45 (with Dorothy Fackre).

"Banners Tell of a Festive Faith." *United Church Herald* 13:8 (August 1970): 22-27.

"Visionaries and Futurists: Hope's Partners." *The Christian Century* 87:36 (September 9, 1970): 1060-1063.

Book Reviews

George Lindbeck, *The Future of Roman Catholic Theology*. In *Religion in Life* 39:4 (Winter 1970): 620-621.

Frederick Sontag, *The Crisis of Faith*. In *Religion in Life* 49:4 (Winter 1970): 629-630.

1971 *Liberation in Middle America*. Philadelphia: Pilgrim Press, 1971.

"Redesigning Life: Scenarios and Guidelines." In *Should Doctors Play God?* Ed. Claude Frazier. Nashville: Broadman, 1971.

"Ethical Guidelines for the Control of Life." *Moral Issues and Christian Response*. Ed. Paul Jerisild and Dale Johnson. New York: Holt, Rinehart and Winston, 1971.

"Biomedical Reproduction." *Theology Today* 27:4 (January 1971): 409-421.

"Going East: Neomysticism and Christian Faith." *The Christian Century* 87:15 (April 24, 1971): 457-461. Reprinted in *Evangelische Kommentare*, 1971 and *Focus on Adults*, 1974.

"Ecology and Theology." *Religion in Life* 40:2 (Summer 1971): 210-224. Reprinted in *Western Man and Environmental Ethics*. Ed. Ian G. Barbour. Reading, MA: Addison-Wesley, 1973; and in *Moral Dilemmas*. Ed. Richard L. Purtill. Belmont, CA: Wadsworth, 1985.

"Reinhold Niebuhr: His Hope Was Real." *United Church Herald* 14:8 (August 1971): 42-43.

"COCU From the Ground Up." *Andover Newton Quarterly* 12:1 (September 1971): 34-41. Reprinted in *Church Union at Mid-Point.* Ed. Paul Crow, Jr. and William Boney. New York: Association Press, 1972.

"The Liberated Middle." *Christianity and Crisis* 31:18 (November 1, 1971): 226-228.

"*Times* Takes a Fresh View in '72." *The Newton Times* (December 29, 1971): 1.

1972   *Memory and Hope in a Time of Nostalgia.* Council for Lay Life and Work, 1972.

"The New Leisure: Planner and Citizen in Partnership." In *Leisure and the Quality of Life.* Ed. Edwin J. Staley and Norman P. Miller. Washington, DC: The American Association for Health, Physical Education and Recreation, 1972.

"A Catechism for Today's Storytellers: Prepared for Skye by Her Family." *Youth* 23:7 (July 1972): 24-41.

"Archie Bunker: Visions and Realities." *The Christian Century* 89:27 (August 7, 1972): 772-774.

"Rethinking Mission." *Action-Reaction* 4:3 (Winter 1972): 1-5.

Book Reviews:

Alan Geyer and Dean Peerman, eds., *Theological Crossings.* In *The Christian Century* 89:6 (February 9, 1972): 174-175.

Michael Novak, *All the Catholic People;* and Peter Schrag, *The Decline of the Wasp.* In *The Christian Century* 89:20 (May 17, 1972): 582-585.

Ruel Howe, *Survival Plus.* In *Religious Education* 67:3 (May-June 1972): 224-225.

James T. Baker, *Thomas Merton: Social Critic.* In *Religion in Life* 12:2 (Summer 1972): 287-288.

Carnegie Samuel Calian, *God, Grace and Guts.* In *Religion and Life* 41:2 (Autumn 1972): 427-428.

Martin Marty, *Protestantism.* In *The Christian Century* 89:41 (November 15, 1972): 1167-1168.

Lowell Strieker and Gerald Struber, *Religion and the New Majority.* In *Religious Education* 67:6 (November-December 1972): 478-480.

1973   *Do and Tell: Engagement Evangelism in the 70s.* Grand Rapids: Eerdmans, 1973.

"The Ethics of Abortion in Theological Perspective." *Andover Newton Quarterly* 13:3 (January 1973): 222-226.

"Evangelism: Meaning, Context, Mandate." *The Christian Ministry* 4:2 (March 1973): 7-13.

"Populism Revisited." *Bangor Seminary Review* 68:1 (Spring 1973): 3-14.

"The Education of Archie Bunker." *Colloquy* 6:5 (May 1973): 22-25.

"Dawn People." *Evangelism for a New Day* 1:4 (July 1973): 2. Reprinted in *Messenger* (Church of the Brethren) 124:10 (October 1975); and as "Das Volk der Morgenrote." *Jesus Christus Befreit und Eint.* Sektion 1, Bekenntnis zu Christus heute, 5. Vollversammlung Ökumenischer Rat der Kirchen, Jakarta 75. BRD: Verlag Otto Lembeck, 1975.

"Outside-In, Inside-Out." *Action: Planning for Evangelism* (1973): 27-29.

Book Review:

Carl Braaten, *Christ and Counter-Christ.* In *Andover Newton Quarterly* 13:4 (March 1973): 295-298.

1974   "Guide to *Do and Tell.*" *New Life Mission Handbook.* Nashville: Tidings, 1974.

"Conversion." *Andover Newton Quarterly* 14:5 (January 1974): 171-189.

"What Is Evangelism?" *United Church of Christ Sunday Bulletin.*

"Bicentennial: A Time for Word in Deed." *Evangelism for a New Day* 2:3 (May 1974): 2-3.

"Evangelism for Our Day." *A.D.* 3:11 (November 1974): 28-31.

"Evangelism and Social Action." *Engage/Social Action* 2:11 (November 1974): 6-14.

Book Reviews:

John Killinger, *The Salvation Tree* and *All You Lonely People, All You Lovely People.* In *The Christian Century* 91:2 (January 16, 1974): 50-51.

Harvey Cox, *Seduction of the Spirit.* In *Andover Newton Quarterly* 14:4 (March 1974): 276-281.

Charles E. Curran, *Politics, Medicine and Christian Ethics: A Dialogue with Paul Ramsey.* In *Review of Books on Religion* 3:5 (mid-February 1974): 1, 3.

Charles Davis, *Temptations of Religion.* In *The Christian Century* 91:38 (Nov. 6, 1974): 1045.

1975   *Word in Deed: Theological Themes in Evangelism.* Grand Rapids: Eerdmans, 1975.

Conversion. Disciples of Christ, 1975.

"Of Hope and Judgment." *Bicentennial Broadside* (January 1975): 5-6.

"Turning." *The Disciple* (Disciples of Christ) 2:1 (January 1975): 6-8.

"Quoted Summarily." *Catalyst Tape Talk* 7:1 (November 1975): 2.

"Dawn People." *Youth* 26:11 (November 1975): 55-63. With interpretation by Rick Casey of film produced by the Board for Homeland Ministries, United Church of Christ.

"A Theology of the Cross." *Andover Newton Quarterly* 16:2 (November 1975): 142-162.

Book Reviews:

Langdon Gilkey, *Catholicism Confronts Modernity.* In *The Christian Century* 92:4 (December 10, 1975): 1138-1139.

1976   "The Boston Affirmations: A Response." *Andover Newton Quarterly* 16:4 (March 1976): 250-252.

"Christ in Chiaroscuro." *Theology Today* 33:1 (April 1976): 40-49.

Book Reviews:

Fritz Staal, *Exploring Mysticism;* and Raymond Bailey, *Thomas Merton on Mysticism.* In *The Review of Books in Religion* 5:7 (Mid-April 1976): 12-13.

1977   *Book Reviews:*

"Cobb's *Christ in a Pluralistic Age.*" *Andover Newton Quarterly* 17:4 (March 1977): 308-315.

Stanley N. Gundry and Alan F. Johnson, *Conflicts in Contemporary Theology.* In *The New Review of Books and Religion* 1:6 (March 1977): 10.

John Hick, *Death and Eternal Life.* In *The Christian Century* 94:18 (May 18, 1977): 477.

Russell W. Aldwinckle, *More than Man: A Study in Christology.* In *The Christian Century* 94:40 (Nov. 16, 1977): 1073, 1076.

1978   *The Christian Story: A Narrative Interpretation of Christian Doctrine.* Grand Rapids: Eerdmans, 1978; Second Edition, Revised 1984; Third Edition, Revised 1996.

"The Struggle for Church Unity." *Festival of the Church.* New York: Office of Church Life and Leadership, 1978.

"Centering in Contemporary Theology." *The New Review of Books and Religion* 2:8 (April 1978): 4.

"Evangelism and Eschatology." *Evangelism for a New Day* 6:1 (April 1978): 1-2.

Book Reviews:

Frederick Buechner, *Telling the Truth.* In *The New Review of Books and Religion* 2:7 (March 1978): 6.

Frederick Sontag and John Roth, *God and America's Future.* In *St. Luke's Journal* (1978).

Publications

1979   *Youth Ministry: The Gospel and the People.* Philadelphia: Judson Press,
        1979; second edition, 1980 (co-author with Jan Chartier).
        "Theology and Forms of Confession in the United Church of Christ."
        Consultation on Church Union. Chicago: Disciples Divinity House,
        1979. Reprinted in *Andover Newton Quarterly* 10:3 (January 1979): 176-
        189; *Chicago Seminary Register* (Spring 1979): 12-24; and *Encounter* 4:1
        (Winter 1980): 37-52.
        "The New Morality." *Issues in Sexual Ethics.* Souderton, PA: UCPBW,
        1979.
        "Preface." *The Wisdom of the Heart,* by Wallace Robbins, Worcester, MA:
        First Unitarian Church, 1979.
        The Supper and Our Identity. Biblical Theological Liturgical Group, 1979.
        "Plural Shock and the Finality of Christ." *Update* (Thesis Theological
        Cassettes) 10:4 (May 1979): 2-5.
        "Ministries of Identity and Vitality." *Theology Today* 36:3 (October 1979):
        375-382. Reprinted in *Laity Exchange* (1981).

        Book Reviews:
        David Read, *Go Make Disciples;* George Sweazy, *The Church as Evangelist;*
        and Leroy Eims, *The Lost Art of Discipleship.* In *Occasional Bulletin* 3:3
        (July 1979): 113.
        Paul Jerisild, *Invitation to Faith.* In *TSF News and Reviews* 3:1 (October
        1979): 7-10.

1980   "Preface." *Who Dares to Preach?* by Wallace Fisher. Minneapolis:
        Augsburg Press, 1980.
        "An Agenda for the 80s." *The Christian Ministry* 2:1 (January 1980): 7-12.
        "Pastoral Witness to the Person and Work of Christ." *Catalyst* 12:7
        (April 1980): 2-3 (Part 1), and 12:8 (May 1980): 5-7 (Part 2).
        "Epistle to the Churches." *Living Faith* 1:1 (1980). (GF draft of consulta-
        tion text.)

1981   "Politics and Piety." *The Lantern* (Andover Newton) 1:2 (March 1981).
        "Corridor Light." *The American Baptist* 179:4 (April 1981): 3. Reprinted in
        The Maine Baptist, 1981.
        "Almighty God and the Problem of Evil." *Pacific Theological Review* (San
        Francisco Theological Seminary) 15:1 (Fall 1981): 11-16.

1982   *The Religious Right and Christian Faith.* Grand Rapids: Eerdmans, 1982,
        1983.
        Christ's Ministry and Ours. Laity Project, Andover Newton Theological
        School, 1982.

"The Nature of the Church." *The Leader's Box.* New York: Office of Church Life and Leadership, UCC, 1982, A26-A28.

"Personal Reflections on the Laity Project." *The Lantern* (Andover Newton) 2:3 (February 1982): 11.

"A Full-Orbed Gospel." *TSF Bulletin* 5:3 (March-April 1982): 17.

Book Reviews:

Lonnie Kliever, *The Shattered Spectrum.* In *The New Review of Books and Religion* 6:10 (Mid-March 1982): 1-3.

Herman Haring and Karl-Josef Kuschel, *Hans Küng: His Work and His Way.* In *TSF Bulletin* 5:8 (September-October 1982).

1983   "Antinomianism," "Blasphemy," "Evangelical, Evangelicalism," "Imputation," "Merit." In *The Westminster Dictionary of Christian Theology* (USA) and *The New Dictionary of Theology* (GB). Ed. Alan Richardson and John Bowden. Revised Edition. Philadelphia: Westminster Press, 1983; and London: SCM Press, 1983.

"Advent: Vision of Shalom and Hope of Glory." In *Social Themes of the Christian Year.* Ed. Dieter Hessel. Philadelphia: Geneva Press, 1983.

Consulting Editor, *Handbook of Christian Belief.* London: Lions Publishing Co. and Grand Rapids: Eerdmans, 1983.

"The Scandals of Particularity and Universality." *Mid-Stream* 22:1 (January 1983): 32-52.

"Narrative Theology: An Overview." *Interpretation* 37:4 (October 1983): 340-352.

"Bibliography: Jesus Christ." New York: Office of Church Life and Leadership, UCC, 1983 (co-author with Joan Nuth).

Book Reviews:

Robert Bellah and Phillip Hammond, *Varieties of Civil Religion.* In *St. Luke's Journal* (April 1983): 156-58.

Thomas Torrance, *Reality and Evangelical Theology.* In *Theology Today* 39:22 (July 1983): 449-453.

Bernard Ramm, *After Fundamentalism.* In *The Christian Century* 100:22 (July 22-27, 1983): 686-687.

Russell Aldwinckle, *Jesus: A Savior or the Savior?* In *TSF Bulletin* (November-December 1983): 22-23.

1984   "Carl Henry." In *A Handbook of Christian Theologians.* Enlarged Edition. Ed. Martin E. Marty and Dean G. Peerman. Nashville: Abingdon Press, 1984.

"Christ's Ministry and Ours." In *The Laity in Ministry*. Ed. George Peck and John Hoffman. Valley Forge: Judson Press, 1984.

"The Confessional Nature of the United Church of Christ." *EKU/UCC Newsletter* 5:1 (February 1984): 2-14.

"Bones Strong and Weak in the Skeletal Structure of Schillebeeckx's Christology." *Journal of Ecumenical Studies* 21:2 (Spring 1984): 248-277.

"Suffering and Hope." *No Other Foundation* 5:1 (Spring 1984): 14-18.

"Carl Henry's Reasoned Apologetic." *Theology Today* 41:2 (Summer 1984): 196-200.

"Pastoral Ministry in an Era of Prime-Time Preachers." *Theological Markings* (United Theological Seminary, MN) (Summer 1984): 1-6.

"Almighty God and the Problem of Evil." *MPL Journal* 4:3 (1984): 11-14.

Book Reviews:

John Cobb, *Beyond Dialogue*. In *International Bulletin of Missionary Research* 8:1 (January 1984): 42.

Otto Weber, *Foundations of Dogmatics*. In *The Christian Century* 101:1 (January 1984): 26-27.

1985   "Reinhold Niebuhr as Reformed Theologian." In *Reformed Theology: Essays in Its Modern Interpretation in America*. Ed. David Wells. Grand Rapids: Eerdmans, 1985.

"The Use of Scripture in My Work in Systematics." In *The Use of the Bible in Theology*. Ed. Robert Johnston. Richmond: John Knox Press, 1985.

"Defending the Faith Today." *Handbook of World Christianity*. London: Lion Publishing Co., 1985 (GB); and Grand Rapids: Eerdmans, 1985 (USA).

"Setting Up Signposts." *His* 45:4 (January 1985): 31.

"An Interpretation of the Craigville Colloquy," "Response," "A Telephone Conversation." *New Conversations* 9:1 (Spring 1985): 11-12, 33-35.

"Theological Soul-Searching in the United Church of Christ." *TSF Journal* 8:2 (November-December 1985): 5-9.

"Ministry in the Emerging Religious Context: The Neofundamentalist Phenomenon." *Word and World* 5:1 (Winter 1985): 12-23.

"Christian Theology and the Religious Right." *Bulletin of the Moravian Theological Seminary* (1985): 49-56.

Book Reviews:

James Barr, *Beyond Fundamentalism*. In *The Christian Century* 102:17 (May 15, 1985): 506, 508.

Clark Pinnock, *The Scripture Principle*. In *The Christian Century* 102:23 (July 17-24, 1985): 685-686.

1986   "Suffering and Hope." *Preaching* (January-February 1986): 16-19. Republication.

"BEM on the Eucharist: A United Church of Christ Perspective." *Prism* 1:2 (Fall 1986): 47-58.

Book Reviews:

Robert Roth, *Theater of God*. In *Word and World* 6:4 (Fall 1986): 478-479.

Frank Senn, ed., *Protestant Spiritual Traditions*. In *The Christian Century* 103:36 (November 19, 1986): 1037-1038.

1987   *The Christian Story*, Vol. 2. *Authority: Scripture in the Church for the World*. Grand Rapids: Eerdmans, 1987.

"Theology and Culture." *The Judson Bulletin* 6:2 (1987): 25-27.

"Sober Hope: Some Themes in Protestant Theology Today." *The Christian Century* 104:26 (September 13, 1987): 790-792.

"The Giftie Gie Us." *Voices* 2:3 (Winter 1987): 8-11.

"The Conversation Continued." *Unitarian Universalist Christian* 42:4 (Winter 1987): 16-17.

1988   "God the Discloser." In *Christian Faith and Practice in the Modern World*. Ed. Mark Noll and David Wells. Grand Rapids: Eerdmans, 1988.

"The Confessional Nature of the United Church of Christ." *New Conversations* 10:3 (Winter/Spring 1988): 12-21.

"The Kansas City Statement as a Confession of Faith." *Bulletin of the Congregational Library* 34:3 (Spring/Summer 1988): 3-12.

"Positive Witness and Honorable Intentions." *New Theology Review* 1:2 (May 1988): 58-73.

"The UCC in Reformed-Lutheran Dialogue." *Ecumenical News* (UCC) 1 (Fall 1988): 3.

"Evangelical Catholicity at Corinth." *The New Mercersburg Review* 4 (Autumn 1988): 14-17.

Book Review:

John Driver, *Understanding the Atonement*. In *International Bulletin of Missionary Research* 12:1 (January 1988): 32-33.

1989   "Theology: Ephemeral, Conjunctural and Perennial." In *Altered Landscapes* (festschrift for Robert Handy). Ed. David Lotz. Grand Rapids: Eerdmans, 1989.

"Political Fundamentalism." In *Theology, Politics and Piety*. Ed. T. Runyon. Maryknoll, NY: Orbis, 1989.

"Introduction." *Liberating News*, by Orlando Costas. Grand Rapids: Eerdmans, 1989.

"Summary Observations." *The Leuenberg Agreement and Lutheran-Reformed Relationships*. Ed. W. Rusch and D. Martensen. Philadelphia: Fortress Press, 1989.

"Evangelical Hermeneutics." *Interpretation* 43:2 (April 1989): 117-129.

"Welcome the Lutheran Connection." *United Church News* (Massachusetts edition) 5:3 (April 1989): 2.

"My Ecumenical Journey in Peace-Making." *The Cornerstonian* 4:3 (Summer 1989): 22-25.

Book Review:

Horst Reller, Herman Mueller, Martin Voight, *Evangelical Catechism*, American edition. In *The Lutheran Quarterly* 3 (Spring 1989): 112-114.

1990   "Ministry as Presence." In *Dictionary of Pastoral Care and Counseling*. Ed. R. Hunter. Nashville: Abingdon Press, 1990.

"God" and "Evangelism." In *Encyclopedia of Religious Education*. Ed. Kendig Brubaker Cully and Iris Cully. San Francisco: Harper & Row, 1990.

"Eschatology and Systematics." *Ex Auditu* 6 (1990): 101-118.

"Mutual Conversation, Consolation and Correction." *Dialog* 19:2 (Winter 1990): 88-91.

"Israel's Continuing Covenant and God's Deed in Christ," and "Perspectives on the Covenant with Israel and Christ." *New Conversations* 12:3 (Summer 1990).

"Evangelical Catholicity Today." *The New Mercersburg Review* 8 (Autumn 1990): 41-51.

"Life Together in Ministry." *Touchstone* (United Church of Canada) 8:3 (September 1990): 24-28.

"Perspectives on the Place of Israel in Christian Faith." *Andover Newton Review* 1:2 (Winter 1990): 7-17. Japanese trans., Yoichi Kabayaski, *Seinen Theological Review* (Winter 1995).

"The Reformed-Lutheran Conversation." *Craigville VII Theological Colloquy* (1990): 52-57.

Book Review:

James A. Carpenter, *Nature and Grace*. In *Interpretation* 44:2 (April 1990): 212-214.

1991   *Christian Basics: A Primer for Pilgrims.* Grand Rapids: Eerdmans, 1991,
        1992, 1993, 1995, revised edition, 1998, 2000 (co-author with Dorothy
        Fackre).

        "The Place of Israel in Christian Faith," In *Gott lieben und seine Gebote
        halten* (festschrift for Klaus Bockmuehl). Ed. Markus Bockmuehl
        and Helmut Borkhardt. Giessen: Brunnen Verlag, 1991.

        "Christian Doctrine in the United Church of Christ." In *Theology and
        Identity: Ministry, Tradition and Polity in the United Church of Christ.* Ed.
        Daniel Johnson and Charles Hambrick-Stowe. New York: Pilgrim
        Press, 1991.

        "Sin." *Words of Faith.* Cleveland: Office of Church Life and Leadership,
        UCC, 1991 (co-author with Dorothy Fackre).

        "Foreword." *Worthy to Raise Issues: Preaching and Public Responsibility,* by
        James Crawford. Cleveland: Pilgrim Press, 1991.

        "Reorientation and Retrieval in Seminary Theology." *The Christian Cen-
        tury* 108:20 (June 26-July 3, 1991): 653-656.

        Book Reviews:

        Hugh T. Kerr, ed., *Readings in Christian Thought,* rev. ed. In *Princeton Sem-
        inary Bulletin* 12:1 (New Series 1991): 82-83.

        Thomas Oden, *The Word of Life,* Vol. 2. In *Interpretation* 45:3 (July 1991):
        300-302.

1992   "Atonement." In *Encyclopedia of the Reformed Faith.* Ed. Donald McKim.
        Louisville: Westminster/John Knox Press, 1992.

        "Hope." In *Life as Liberty, Life as Trust.* Ed. Robert Nelson. Grand
        Rapids: Eerdmans, 1992.

        "Abortion." In *Handbook for Preaching.* Ed. James Cox. Louisville: West-
        minster/John Knox, 1992.

        "Evangelical Hermeneutics: Commonality and Diversity." In *Christian-
        ity for Tomorrow.* Ed. Charles Holland. Fort Worth: Biblical Studies,
        1992.

        "I Believe in the Resurrection of the Body." *Interpretation* 46:1 (January
        1992): 42-52.

        "Call and Catholicity." *Pro Ecclesia* 1:1 (Fall 1992): 20-26.

        "The State of Systematics." *Dialog* 31:1 (Winter 1992): 54-61.

        Book Reviews:

        James Leo Garrett, Jr., *Systematic Theology,* Vol. 1. In *Interpretation* 46:1
        (January 1992): 96-97.

        James Wall and David Heim, eds., *How My Mind Has Changed.* In *Per-
        spectives* 7:1 (January 1992): 19-21.

Wolfhart Pannenberg, *Systematic Theology,* Vol. 3. In *Perspectives* 7:4 (April 1992): 19-21.

Benjamin Reist, *A Reading of Calvin's Institutes.* In *Theology Today* 49:1 (April 1992): 136-137.

David Mueller, *Foundations of Karl Barth's Doctrine of Reconciliation.* In *Theological Studies* 53:4 (December 1992): 762-763.

Lesslie Newbigin, *The Gospel in a Pluralist Society.* In *Journal of the Academy for Evangelism in Theological Education* 7 (April 1992): 100-102.

1993   *Ecumenical Faith in Evangelical Perspective.* Grand Rapids: Eerdmans, 1993.

Sound Doctrine in the Church. 1992 Theodore Trost, Jr. Lecture, United Theological Seminary and St. Paul's United Church of Christ, St. Paul, MN, 1993.

"Reformed Heritage and Lutheran Connections in the Life of the UCC." In *A Common Calling: The Witness of Our Reformation Churches in North America Today.* Ed. Keith F. Nickle and Timothy F. Lull. Minneapolis: Augsburg Press, 1993.

"The Surge in Systematics: A Commentary on Current Works." In *Journal of Religion* 73:2 (April 1993): 223-227.

"Who Is This Jesus? The Christology of Henry Ware." *The Unitarian-Universalist Christian* 48 (Spring-Summer 1993): 9-18.

"Response to Chapman: A Common Calling." *Lutheran Forum* 27:3 (August 1993): 18-19.

"The Continuing Relevance of Reinhold Niebuhr." *Theology and Public Policy* 5:2 (Fall 1993): 4-14.

"Theological Reflections: Phil. 3:12-21, 4:1-13; 1 Thess. 1:1-10, 2:1-8, 9-13, 17-20." *Lectionary Homiletics* 4:11 (October 1993).

"An Altar Call for Evangelicals." *The Christian Century* 110:33 (Nov. 17-24, 1993): 1167-1169 (review essay of David Wells, *No Place for Truth*).

"Zur Lage der Systemischen Theologie in den USA." *Verkündigung und Forschung* 38 (1993), 5-20.

"Theological Standards in the UCC." *Craigville Colloquy X: Preparatory Booklet.* 1993. Pp. 223-237.

"Guide." *United Church of Christ: An Ecclesiology.* Cleveland: Board for Homeland Ministries, 1993.

Book Reviews:

Richard Neuhaus and George Weigel, eds., *Being a Christian Today: An American Conversation.* In *Pro Ecclesia* 2:3 (Summer 1993): 374-378.

Robert McAfee Brown, *Liberation Theology: An Introductory Guide.* In *Theology Today* 50:2 (July 1993): 332.

Wolfhart Pannenberg, *Systematic Theology*, Vol. I. In *Interpretation* 47:3 (July 1993): 304-306.

Avery Dulles, *The Craft of Theology: From Symbol to System*. In *Modern Theology* 9:3 (July 1993): 315-316.

Colin B. O'Connell, *A Study of Heinrich Ott's Theological Development: His Hermeneutical and Ontological Program*. In *Theological Studies* 54:3 (September 1993): 601.

T. H. L. Parker, *Calvin's Preaching*. In *Theological Studies* 54:4 (December 1993): 773-774.

1994   *The Promise of Reinhold Niebuhr*. Revised Edition. Lanham, MD: University Press of America, 1994.

"Confessing Christ: Theological Reflections" and "'Hermeneutics' as the Interpretation of Scripture." *Papers from the Initial Meeting of Confessing Christ*. De Forest, WI: Confessing Christ, 1994.

"In Quest of the Comprehensive: The Systematics Revival." *Religious Studies Review* 20:1 (January 1994): 7-12.

"The Ministry of OCC." *Newsletter: Order of Corpus Christi* 7:1 (January-March 1994).

"Ways of Inclusivity." *Prism* 9:1 (Spring 1994): 52-65.

"Carl Henry and Systematic Theology." *Religious and Theological Studies Bulletin* (April 1994): 5.

"Relating but Not Capitulating." *Touchstone* 9:1 (May 1994): 20-24.

"Listening for the Word." *New Conversations* 16:2 (Summer 1994): 5-15.

"Angels Heard and Demons Seen." *Theology Today* 41:3 (October 1994): 345-358.

"Culture-Protestantism and Confessing Christ." *Theology News and Notes* (Fuller Theological Seminary) 41:3 (October 1994): 19-23.

Book Reviews:

David Wells, *No Place for Truth*. In *Religious Studies Review* 20:1 (January 1994): 41.

Thomas C. Oden, *Life in the Spirit: Systematic Theology*, Vol. 3. In *Interpretation* 48:2 (April 1994): 183-185.

1995   *What About Those Who Have Never Heard?* Downers Grove: InterVarsity Press, 1995 (with John Sanders and Ronald Nash); Portuguese Edition, 2000.

"Last Things." In *The Christian Theology Reader*. Ed. Alister McGrath. Oxford: Blackwell, 1995.

"The Theological Commonplaces of Christian Education." *Christian Education Journal* 15:3 (Spring 1995): 25-36.

"Reclaiming the Center." *Perspectives* 10:3 (March 1995): 4-6.

"Confessing Christ: Thoughtful, Joyous, Imaginative Work." *Renewalife* 1:3 (Spring 1995): 3.

"Ecumenical View Offered." *United Church News: Massachusetts Conference Edition* (March 1995).

"An Evangelical Megashift? The Promise and Peril of an 'Open' View of God." *The Christian Century* 112:15 (May 3, 1995): 484-487 (review essay of Clark Pinnock, Richard Rice, et al., *The Openness of God* and Robert Brow, *Unbounded Love*).

"The Revival of Systematic Theology." *Interpretation* 49:3 (July 1995): 229-241.

"Angels." *Preaching* 11:3 (November-December 1995): 2-6.

1996   "Narrative: Evangelical, Postliberal, Ecumenical." In *The Nature of Confession*. Ed. Timothy Phillips and Dennis Okholm. Downers Grove: InterVarsity Press, 1996.

"The Future of Evangelical Theological Education." In *Theological Education in the Evangelical Tradition*. Ed. D. G. Hart and R. Albert Mohler. Grand Rapids: Baker, 1996.

"Communal Graces." *The Christian Century* 113:10 (March 20-27, 1996): 343-346 (review essay of James W. Wind and James W. Lewis, *American Congregations* and *New Perspectives in the Study of Congregations*, 1996).

"The United Church of Christ and the ELCA." *Forum Letter* 25:9 (September 1996): 6-8.

"Center Breaks Its Silence." *Renewalife* 2:2 (Winter 1996): 3.

Book Review:

Henry B. Clark, *Serenity, Courage, Wisdom: The Enduring Legacy of Reinhold Niebuhr.* In *Pro Ecclesia* 5:3 (Summer 1996): 377-378.

1997   *The Doctrine of Revelation: A Narrative Interpretation.* Edinburgh: Edinburgh University Press, 1997; and Grand Rapids: Eerdmans, 1997.

"Angels." In *The Library of Distinctive Sermons.* Ed. Stephen Gibson. Sisters, Oregon: Multnomah, 1997.

"United Church of Christ Basics: An Interpretation," and "Hymn Texts and Theology." In *How Shall We Sing the Lord's Song?* Ed. Richard Christensen. Pittsburgh: Pickwick Press, 1997.

"Confessing Christ: Year 4." *Renewalife* 3:1 (Spring 1997): 1-3.

"The Church of the Center." *Interpretation* 51:2 (April 1997): 130-142.

"The UCC and the ELCA." *Dialog* 36:2 (Spring 1997): 147-149.

"Gifts Given: Solidarity and Simultaneity," "Gifts Received: Sovereignty and Sanctification," "The Congregation and the Unity of the Church." *Currents in Theology and Mission* 24:2 (April 1997): 86-123.

"What the Lutherans and Reformed Have to Learn from One Another," and "Gabriel Fackre Replies to Allan E. Johnson." *The Christian Century* 114:18 (June 4-11, 1997): 558-561, 563-564. Reprinted in *On the Way* 14:1 (Summer 1997): 5-14.

"Commentary," and "Confessing Christ and 'the Church of the Center.'" *Joy in the Word!* 1:1 (Summer 1997): 3, 10.

"Perspectives from a Participant: A Conversation with Gabe Fackre." *Joy in the Word!* 1:2 (Winter 1997-1998): 6-9.

Book Review:

Colin Gunton, *A Brief Theology of Revelation*. In *Pro Ecclesia* 6:1 (Winter 1997): 119-120.

1998   *Affirmations and Admonitions.* Grand Rapids: Eerdmans, 1998 (co-author with Michael Root).

Restoring the Center. Downers Grove, IL: InterVarsity Press, 1998.

"Andover Theological Seminary." *Die Religion in Geschichte und Gegenwart,* Vol. 1. Mohr Siebeck Verlag, 1998.

"Mercersburg and the Mutualities of Affirmation and Admonition." *The New Mercersburg Review* 23 (Spring 1998): 25-34.

"Christ and Religious Pluralism: The Current Debate." *Pro Ecclesia* 7:4 (Fall 1998): 389-395.

"Snorkeling at the Seminaries." *Books and Culture* 4:6 (November-December 1998): 39-40 (review essay of Jackson Carroll, Barbara G. Wheeler, Daniel Aleshire and Penn Long Marler, *Being There: Culture and Formation in Two Theological Schools*).

"Confessing Christ — 1998." *Renewalife* 6:1 (Winter 1998-1999): 10, 13.

Book Reviews:

Joel Carpenter, *Revive Us Again*. In *Theological Studies* 59:2 (June 1998): 339-341.

Jürgen Moltmann, *The Coming of God: Christian Eschatology*. In *The Princeton Seminary Bulletin* 19:1, n. s. (1998): 56-58.

Donald Bloesch, *Jesus Christ: Savior and Lord*. In *The Princeton Seminary Bulletin* 19:2, n. s. (1998): 222-223.

Wolfhart Pannenberg, *Systematic Theology*, Vol. 3. In *Interpretation* 52:4 (Fall 1998): 440, 442.

1999   Editor, *Judgment Day at the White House* and author of chapter, "Christian Doctrine and Presidential Decisions." Grand Rapids: Eerdmans, 1999.

"Christology." In *Evangelical Theology in Transition: Theologians in Dialogue with Donald Bloesch.* Ed. Elmer Colyer. Downers Grove: InterVarsity Press, 1999.

"Suffering and Hope." In *The Library of Distinctive Sermons,* Vol. 8. Ed. Stephen Gibson. Sisters, Oregon: Multnomah Press, 1999.

"Tradition and Traditionalism." *A Confessing Christ Occasional Paper* 2:1 (Winter 1999-2000).

"Ecumenical Winter . . . or Summer?" *Boston Theological Institute Newsletter* 28:16 (January 1999): 1-2 (Reprinted in *The Pilot* [April 1999]).

"Christian Teaching and Inclusive Language Hymnody." *The Hymn* 50:2 (April 1999): 26-32.

"Bible, Community and Spirit." *Horizons in Biblical Theology* 21 (1999): 66-81.

"Ecumenical Admonitions." *The Christian Century* 116:23 (August 25–September 1, 1999): 817-819.

2000　*The Day After: A Retrospective on Religious Dissent in the Presidential Crisis.* Grand Rapids: Eerdmans, 2000.

"Kosovo: The Ethics of Heaven, Earth and Hell." In *Kosovo: Contending Voices in Balkan Interventions.* Ed. William J. Buckley. Grand Rapids: Eerdmans, 2000.

"The Lutheran *Capax* Lives." In *Trinity, Time and Church.* Ed. Colin Gunton (festschrift for Robert Jenson). Grand Rapids: Eerdmans, 2000.

"Foreword." *When I Survey the Wondrous Cross,* by Richard L. Floyd. Pittsburgh: Pickwick Press, 2000.

"Reformed Ecumenics." *The Bulletin of the Institute of Reformed Theology* 2:1 (Fall 2000): 1-2.

Book Review:

Kosuke Nishitani, *Niebuhr, Hromadka, Troeltsch and Barth: The Significance of Theology of History for Christian Social Ethics.* In *Ecumenical Review* 52:4 (October 2000): 550-551.

2001　"Confessing Christ Today." In *In Essentials Unity: Essays on the Nature and Purpose of the Church.* Ed. Douglas Meeks and Robert Mutton (festschrift for Frederick Trost). Minneapolis: Kirk House Publishers, 2001.

"Biblical Inerrancy" and "Inspiration, Biblical." In *Encyclopedia of Fun-*

damentalism. Ed. Brenda Brasher. Great Barrington, MA: Berkshire Reference Works/Routledge, 2001.

"Acts 2:42-57." In *The Lectionary Commentary: Theological Exegesis for Sunday's Texts*. Ed. Roger Van Harn. Vol. 1. Grand Rapids: Eerdmans, 2001.

"Acts 3:12-19." In *The Lectionary Commentary: Theological Exegesis for Sunday's Texts*. Ed. Roger Van Harn. Vol. 1. Grand Rapids: Eerdmans, 2001.

"Acts 4:5-12." In *The Lectionary Commentary: Theological Exegesis for Sunday's Texts*. Ed. Roger Van Harn. Vol. 1. Grand Rapids: Eerdmans, 2001.

"1 Peter 3:18-22." In *The Lectionary Commentary: Theological Exegesis for Sunday's Texts*. Ed. Roger Van Harn. Vol. 2. Grand Rapids: Eerdmans, 2001.

"John 14:1-14." In *The Lectionary Commentary: Theological Exegesis for Sunday's Texts*. Ed. Roger Van Harn. Vol. 3. Grand Rapids: Eerdmans, 2001.

"Narrative Theology from an Evangelical Perspective." In *Faith and Narrative*. Ed. Keith E. Yandell. New York: Oxford University Press, 2001.

"Theological Thoughts on the Present Crisis." In *He Comes, the Broken Heart to Bind: Reflections on September 11, 2001*. Ed. Theodore Trost. Confessing Christ, 2001.

"Five Things Clinton Taught Us." *Christianity Today* 45:1 (January 8, 2001): 56-58. Reprinted in *Ministry and Theology* [Korea] (Fall 2001).

"*Dominus Iesus:* A Reformed Response." *Pro Ecclesia* 10:1 (Winter 2001): 13-15.

"The Church of the Centre." *The Gospel and Our Culture* (Great Britain) 30 (Spring 2001): 7-8.

"The Confessional Heritage of the UCC." *The New Mercersburg Review* 28 (Spring 2001): 4-19.

"Three Types of Theology Today." *The Clergy Journal* (November-December 2001): 8-11.

"Let's Bind Up Wounds and Resist the Powers of Evil." *United Church News,* Focus on Faith, 17:8 (November 2001): A-7.

"On Being Gracious to Other Religions." *Cape Cod Times,* December 27, 2001, A-10.

2002   "A Reformed Perspective on the Joint Declaration on the Doctrine of Justification." In *Ecumenical Perspectives on the Joint Declaration*. Ed. William Rusch. Collegeville, MN: Liturgical Press, 2002.

"No Peace Is Worth Having without Justice." *Cape Cod Times,* January 13, 2002, G-1, G-6.

"The Teaching Life: Defining a Calling." *The Christian Century* 119:4 (February 13-20, 2002): 32-34.

"The Ecumenical Import of the Joint Declaration." *Reformed World* 52:1 (March 2002): 46-55 forthcoming.

"What Does the UCC Believe?" *Prism* 16:2 (Fall 2001): 78-91.

"Binding Up Wounds and Resisting the Powers." In *O God, Tender and Just: Reflections and Responses after September 11, 2001.* Cleveland: United Church Press, 2002.

" Was Reinhold Niebuhr a Christian?" *First Things,* forthcoming.

Book Reviews

Stanley Grenz, *Renewing the Center: Evangelical Theology in a Post-Theological Era.* In *The Princeton Seminary Bulletin* 23:1, n.s. (2002): 123-124.

Clark H. Pinnock, *Most Moved Mover: A Theology of God's Openness.* In *Theology Today* 59:2 (July 2002): 319-323.

Kevin J. Vanhoozer, ed., *Nothing Greater, Nothing Better: Theological Essays on the Love of God.* In *Theology Today* 59:2 (July 2002): 319-323.

Robert A. Gagnon, *The Bible and Homosexual Practice: Texts and Hermeneutics.* In *Pro Ecclesia,* forthcoming.

John Williamson Nevin, *The Mystical Presence: A Vindication of the Reformed or Calvinistic Doctrine of the Holy Eucharist,* ed. Augustine Thompson, O.P. In *Pro Ecclesia,* forthcoming.

2003 "Carl F. H. Henry." In *New Dictionary of Apologetics.* Leicester: Inter-Varsity Press, forthcoming 2003.

Book Reviews

The Living Theological Heritage of the United Church of Christ, vols. 1-6. In *Pro Ecclesia,* forthcoming.

Contributors

Elizabeth Achtemeier is a minister of the Presbyterian Church (USA), and formerly a professor at Union Theological Seminary in Virginia, having retired after teaching Bible and homiletics for forty years in five different seminaries.

Paul J. Achtemeier is a minister in the Presbyterian Church (USA), the Herbert Worth and Anne H. Jackson Professor Emeritus at Union Theological Seminary in Virginia, and former president of both the Catholic Biblical Association and the Society of Biblical Literature.

Joseph A. Bassett is the minister of the First Church in Chestnut Hill, Massachusetts.

Donald G. Bloesch is the Professor of Theology Emeritus at the University of Dubuque Theological Seminary in Dubuque, Iowa.

Carl Braaten is the Executive Director of the Center for Catholic and Evangelical Theology, and coeditor of *Pro Ecclesia*.

Elmer M. Colyer is an ordained elder in the United Methodist Church, professor of historical theology, and Stanley Professor of Wesley Studies at the University of Dubuque Theological Seminary.

Paul A. Crow, Jr., is the former President of the Council on Christian Unity (Chief Ecumenical Officer) of the Christian Church (Disciples of

Christ), and has been the co-Moderator of the Disciples of Christ–Roman Catholic International Dialogue since its beginning in 1977.

Herbert Davis is the minister emeritus of the Eliot Church, UCC, of Newton, Massachusetts, and a founder of the Craigville Theological Colloquies.

Avery Cardinal Dulles, S.J. is Laurence J. McGinley Professor of Religion and Society, Fordham University, and Professor Emeritus, The Catholic University of America, and is presently an advisor to the Committee on Doctrine of the National Conference of Catholic Bishops.

Richard L. Floyd is pastor of the First Church of Christ, Congregational, in Pittsfield, Massachusetts, and is a founding member of the Confessing Christ movement.

Kathryn Greene-McCreight teaches at Smith College and is a Research Fellow at Yale Divinity School. She was ordained in the United Church of Christ in 1988 and to the diaconate in the Episcopal Church in 2002.

Brother Jeffrey Gros, FSC, is the Associate Director, Secretariat for Ecumenical and Interreligious Affairs–NCCB/USCC in Washington, D.C.

Leander S. Harding is the pastor of St. John's Episcopal Church in Stamford, Connecticut, and a leader of the Scholars Engaged in Anglican Doctrine movement.

Roberta G. Heath is the pastor of Berkshire Community Church in Richmond, Massachusetts.

S. Mark Heim is the Samuel Abbot Professor of Christian Theology at Andover Newton Theological School and an ordained American Baptist minister.

Carl F. H. Henry is founding editor of *Christianity Today,* and professor and visiting lecturer at evangelical seminaries around the world.

George Hunsinger is McCord Professor of Systematic Theology, Princeton Theological Seminary.

Contributors

Robert W. Jenson is Senior Scholar for Research at the Center of Theological Inquiry in Princeton, New Jersey, and co-editor of *Pro Ecclesia*.

Leander E. Keck is the Winkley Professor of Biblical Theology, emeritus, Yale Divinity School, and former Dean. He is the Convener of the Editorial Board and Senior New Testament Editor of the *New Interpreter's Bible*.

Diane C. Kessler is Executive Director of the Massachusetts Council of Churches and an ordained minister in the United Church of Christ.

George Lindbeck is the Pitkin Professor Emeritus of Historical Theology at Yale University.

Martin E. Marty is the Fairfax M. Cone Distinguished Service Professor Emeritus at the University of Chicago.

Jürgen Moltmann is Professor Emeritus of the Faculty of Theology at the University of Tübingen, Germany.

Kenneth B. Mulholland is Dean of Columbia Biblical Seminary and School of Missions at Columbia International University, Columbia, South Carolina.

Richard H. Olmsted is the senior minister at Acton Congregational Church, Acton, Massachusetts, and former teacher of philosophy and religion at Colgate University in Hamilton, New York and at The College of St. Catherine in St. Paul, Minnesota.

Alan P. F. Sell holds the chair of Christian Doctrine and Philosophy of Religion, and is director of the Centre for the Study of British Christian Thought at the United Theological College, Aberystwyth, within the Aberystwyth and Lampeter School of Theology of the University of Wales.

Roger L. Shinn is Reinhold Niebuhr Professor Emeritus of Social Ethics, Union Theological Seminary, New York, and for twenty-five years Adjunct Professor of Religion and Society at Columbia University, New York.

Llewellyn Parsons Smith is the pastor of West Gloucester Trinitarian Congregational Church, in Massachusetts.

Contributors

Max L. Stackhouse is the Stephen Colwell Professor of Christian Ethics, Princeton Theological Seminary.

Frederick R. Trost has been president of the Wisconsin Conference of the United Church of Christ since 1981, and leader of the Confessing Christ movement.

Paul Westermeyer is Professor of Church Music at Luther Seminary, where he serves as Cantor for the Seminary, and is Director of the Master of Sacred Music degree, which is offered with St. Olaf College.

Index

For too many typos!

It would seem, Gentle Reader, that this author has taken her plot (intentionally or not) from "Nine Coaches Waiting" by Mary Stewart, an excellent book.

Wow! It up reaches only p. 55 and it seems almost as if she has copied Stewart's book, plot, characters, the whole shebang!

Ah well, as Kipling said;

"When Homer smote his bloomin'
lyre
He'd heard men sing on
land and sea
And what he thought he might
require
He went and took the same
as we"

(Drop the h's, please)

---

p. 140 is right out of the Stewart book. Ditto p. 345

Mary Stewart is, of course, a far better writer. At least until she took up with Merlin,

"A writer of rare intelligence and sensitivity."
Mary Jo Putney

She had no recourse but to accept the position...

Impoverished and untitled, with no marital prospects or so much as a single suitor, Beatrice Sinclair is forced to accept employment as governess to a frightened, lonely child from a noble family—ignoring rumors of dark intrigues to do so. Surely, no future could be as dark as the past she wishes to leave behind. And she admits a fascination with the young duke's adult cousin, Devlen Gordon, a seductive rogue who excites her from the first charged moment they meet. But she dares not trust him—even after he spirits them to isolation and safety when the life of her young charge is threatened.

...and no choice but to fall in love.

Devlen is charming, mysterious, powerful—and Beatrice cannot refuse him. He is opening new worlds for her, filling her life with passion...and peril. But what are Devlen's secrets? Is he her lover or her enemy? Will following her heart be foolishness or a path to lasting happiness?

By Karen Ranney

KAREN RANNEY

An Unlikely Governess

An Avon Romantic Treasure

AVON BOOKS

An Imprint of HarperCollinsPublishers

AVON BOOKS
An Imprint of HarperCollins*Publishers*
10 East 53rd Street
New York, New York 10022-5299

Copyright © 2006 by Karen Ranney
ISBN 0-7394-6025-0

Chapter 1

Kilbridden Village, Scotland
November 1832

"I'll work very hard, I promise."

"Gimme your hands."

Beatrice Sinclair stretched out her hands. Because she was trembling, she placed them palm up on the bar.

"You've got calluses all right. But you look like you'd fall over after a few hours of good work. I need a healthy lass, one who can be on her feet twelve hours."

"I'll be your best worker. I'll even work for free the first week to prove it."

"Can you wipe a table down in the wink of an eye? Or give a little saucy wiggle to the patrons?"

She nodded.

"Laugh at my customers' jokes, even if they be sorry ones?"

"I can."

"You don't look the type my customers like. You're too pale, and you've got an air about you." He frowned. "Are you sick?"

"I'm very healthy."

"Then why are you shaking?"

"I'm just cold."

He didn't look as if he believed her.

"Who told you I was looking for another tavern wench?"

"The owner of the Sword and Dragon."

"Went there, did you? Bet he wanted someone younger."

"He said he didn't have need for another helper."

"That's not true. His business has been near as good as mine. For the last half year, at least. Before that, no one came to drink or talk." He began to wipe down the bar with a spotted rag, looking as if he were thinking about the matter. "Did you have the sickness?"

She shook her head again, afraid to tell him the truth. But all the assurances in the world wouldn't matter. The minute the tavern maid entered the room Beatrice knew she'd lost the post. She couldn't wear a blouse that revealed all her assets or a skirt that bared her ankles. Nor was she given to simpering smiles or coy looks. While she didn't object to dispensing spirits, she wasn't about to sell herself along with them.

The innkeeper grinned. Several teeth were missing, and the effect was more of a leer.

"Go up to Castle Crannoch. They'll have a job for you."

She'd heard of Castle Crannoch ever since coming to Kilbridden Village, but she'd never considered it a source of employment.

"Castle Crannoch?"

He jerked his chin toward the ceiling.

"Aye, where the duke lives. Go ask the duke for a job. He'll give you one, but I won't."

Beatrice tightened her hands on her reticule and thanked the tavern owner with as much grace as she could muster. She'd come all this way for nothing.

She left the inn and stood outside. The cold rain seeped through her thin dress, a reminder that she'd traded her cloak for a sack of flour and a few eggs a week ago. Beatrice tightened her shawl around her hair, held it closed with one hand at her neck, and looked up at the mountain in front of her.

Castle Crannoch stood at the very top, overlooking the village. The fortress dominated the countryside, visible to anyone approaching, a sentinel of the past that looked capable of protecting its inhabitants well into the future.

Occasionally, word would seep down from the top of the mountain as to the lives of the occupants of Castle Crannoch. There had been tragedy there not long ago, she recalled. But her own life had been so difficult that she'd paid the gossip little attention.

The castle was oddly shaped, constructed as if it were a large box with a smaller box pulled from inside it. The two square buildings sat adjacent to each other atop the mountain, the smaller structure in stages of disrepair, the larger box topped by four turrets. The only way to the place was up a long and winding road. Not only did her legs ache but the climb looked to be a frightening one.

A voice, sounding too much like her father's, spoke against the fierce wind. *Do not go, Beatrice. No single woman of good character would seek employment there.* There were rumors about Castle Crannoch.

She no longer had a choice.

Slowly, she began to walk up the winding road, praying for endurance. She wouldn't allow herself to look up at the castle again. Doing so would only make the task seem interminable. She concentrated, instead, on putting one foot in front of the other, leaning into the rain.

Her shawl was sodden, but she tightened it around her head, holding it close at the neck. How long had she been walking? Hours? Surely not that long.

She heard the sound of the carriage and eased closer to the parapet. In the darkness she couldn't see the drop, but her imagination furnished the distance in her mind, adding jagged peaks and huge boulders at the bottom of the ravine.

The approaching carriage was a blur of motion, a dark shadow against the wall. Four horses pulled the ebony shape, the lead pair adorned with gleaming silver appointments. Twin lanterns, also silver, sat on either side of the door, but they were unlit, leaving her to wonder if the occupant of such a magnificent carriage wanted privacy. Or secrecy.

The coach took up the full width of the road, forcing her to the edge. Beatrice gripped the wall with her frayed gloves and felt them tear further. Was God punishing her for her daring, for her journey, for the thought of working in such a place as the duke's lair?

Only the curving half wall stood between her and the abyss. She held her breath as the carriage passed, the stallions from hell blending back into the shadows, their silver appointments winking out of sight.

Was it Black Donald, the devil himself? If so, it appeared he was not quite ready to abandon her. The carriage halted on the next curve. She gripped her reticule with both hands in front of her as if the small bag could offer some protection. She debated waiting until the carriage moved forward, but the rain was getting heavier. She had to make it to Castle Crannoch tonight.

Just as she would have walked by, the door abruptly opened. She stopped, halted not only by curiosity, but by fear. She was cold, wet, and exhausted, but cautious all the same.

"The road is dangerous." A human voice, low and deeply pitched. "You could easily have been run down by my horses."

The coachman didn't turn but remained huddled beneath his greatcoat.

Beatrice took one step forward. "Your horses were taking up the center of the road, sir."

"They are skittish of heights, and since they are so valuable, they are allowed to travel down the middle of the road if they wish."

"As opposed to people, sir, who must travel at the edge of it?"

"It's raining. The least I could do is offer you safe passage to Castle Crannoch."

She almost asked if he worked there before the ridiculousness of that question struck her. He was riding in a luxurious carriage, pulled by magnificent horses. He was probably the duke himself.

She would be foolish to accept a ride in a strange carriage. Almost as foolish as declining such an offer. The heavens growled overhead as if to convince her. The door opened wider, and she entered the carriage, stepping over the stranger's long legs to sit opposite him.

Two small pierced silver lanterns illuminated the interior. As the flames flickered, dots of light danced across the blue cushions and silk of the ceiling.

"Why are you going to the castle?"

Clearly, he wasn't the least reticent about prying into her concerns.

Beatrice debated whether or not to answer him, then realized his curiosity might well be the payment she owed for the ride up the mountain. She looked down at her clasped hands.

"I had hoped to obtain a position."

"Had you? They are notoriously parsimonious at Castle Crannoch. Did you know that?"

She shook her head.

Her rescuer was a man she would have noticed in any setting. His face was absolutely faultless, the nose, chin, and forehead perfectly crafted like the sculpture of an archangel she'd once seen. His hair was brown with touches of gold, and his eyes were so dark a brown as to appear black, and so arresting she felt as if he could pin her to the seat with his gaze.

One corner of his mouth curved up slightly, in amusement or a wry acknowledgment of her examination. Surprisingly, a dimple appeared in his cheek, and it was that particular feature she studied with great care.

Surely a man with a dimple could not be evil?

"Have you seen enough?" he asked finally.

"I have noted your appearance, sir. But appearance does not matter in this world."

"No doubt a homily told to you by an ugly woman. Ugly women are the only ones who think appearance does not matter."

"Have you ever heard of the story of the Ant and the Chrysalis?"

He looked intently at her for a moment, as if attempting to ascertain whether or not she'd lost her wits.

Without waiting for a response, she began to speak. "Once upon a time there was an ant and a chrysalis. It was very nearly at its time of change, and the only thing visible in the shell was a long tail that attracted the attention of an ant. He saw that this strange being was alive, and walked up to it and addressed the shell.

"'I'm very sorry for your fate. I'm an ant, you see, and able to walk and run and play if I wish. Poor you, for being trapped in such an ugly shell.'

"The chrysalis didn't bother to respond. All of its energy was spent in its transformation.

"A few days later, however, the ant was climbing a small hill, allowing himself to fall, then running up the hill again, laughing at his own silliness.

"He felt a breeze upon the back of his head and turned to find a large blue-and-purple butterfly hovering in the air. 'Dear ant,' the butterfly said. 'Do not pity me. I can fly whereas you can only walk.'

"The moral of this story is that appearances are deceptive."

"And you thought me a butterfly?"

"No. I thought you were Black Donald."

"I beg your pardon?"

"Satan might be a tempting master, but he demands eternal servitude."

He laughed, the carriage filling with the sound.

When she didn't respond to his amusement, a corner of his lip curved up in an almost smile.

"Does your virtue shelter you, then? Is that why you don't appear afraid? If I were Black Donald, I would think you'd be trembling in terror."

"Do you often do this? Insist upon demonstrating an act of kindness only to ridicule the person foolish enough to accept it?"

"Do you often chastise your hosts?"

"Stop the carriage and let me out. I shall trouble you no more."

"Don't be foolish. It's night and not safe for a lone female. Besides, we're there."

In the next moment, the carriage slowed, then stopped.

Beatrice slid her finger alongside the leather shade, peering into the darkness. A face leered at her, one so startling that she dropped the shade.

"Has something frightened you?"

"No," she said, not altogether certain the face she'd seen was real. Perhaps it was something she'd only seen in her mind.

The man opposite her reached over and opened the carriage door.

She hesitated, unwilling to face the monster outside the carriage. Her rescuer took her delay for the fear it was, but it was obvious he didn't fully understand it.

"I have not gnawed on a pretty virgin for many years. You're safe enough with me."

She doubted any virgin was safe with him, but she didn't stay to argue the point.

Instead, she pointed one toe out the door. The cold night air caressed her ankle, reminding her that time was passing too quickly. It was already dark, and she had yet to meet with the duke. She still had to make it down the mountain again, but she doubted she had the strength to walk the five miles back to her cottage. She'd probably have to find shelter on the side of the road in the rain. The thunder overhead punctuated that thought with a dull, ominous roar.

As she emerged from the carriage, the wind tugged at her dress, revealing her petticoat. A hand flew to her shawl to keep it anchored, while the other pressed against her skirt.

The creature materialized as she navigated the last step. He was tall and chunky, with thick bands of muscle where his shoulders would be. The uniform he wore was ill fitting, his wrists hanging beyond the cuffs. His face was misshapen, as if the bones of his face had been broken once and never properly healed. His eyes, however, were alert and kind, his gaze now fixed on her face.

"*Bienvenu à Château Crannoch,*" he said, in soft but perfect French.

Surprised, she only nodded back at him.

He translated his words, bowing slowly to her from his impressive height. "Welcome to Castle Crannoch."

"*Merci,*" she said. "*Il est mon plaisir.*" How much of a pleasure was doubtful, especially since the giant had made no effort to open the tall, arched, oak doors. Beatrice doubted if she could manage one of the iron-studded pair by herself.

"How may I assist you, mademoiselle?"

Must she get through this giant to reach the duke himself? Her stomach rumbled, vying in sound with the storm itself.

"I have come to speak with the duke about a position."

The giant looked at her curiously but said nothing. Instead, his attention was drawn to something behind her. Without turning, Beatrice knew the stranger had emerged from the carriage.

Her stomach clenched as he moved to stand too close behind her. She straightened her shoulders, avoiding the temptation to turn and ask him to move aside. He would be waiting for her to do something just that foolish. Or perhaps he was goading her to do so.

"The duke is not available, mademoiselle."

"It's all right, Gaston, I'll see to the lady."

"If you're sure, Mr. Devlen."

She turned to face him. He smiled down at her, nearly as tall as the giant, Gaston.

"Devlen?" His name was too close to devil. She *had* been transported here by Black Donald himself.

"Devlen Gordon. And you are?" He inclined his head, waiting.

"Beatrice Sinclair."

"I'll take Miss Sinclair to see my father, Gaston."

"Your father is the duke?"

"No, but be certain to address him as such, it would please him immeasurably."

He offered her his arm, leaving Beatrice with the choice of refusing his chivalry or touching him. After a moment, he dropped his arm, ending her indecision and her options. She had no alternative but to follow him as he strode up the steps.

Chapter 2

Castle Crannoch looked to be a vast place from the village, or even on the road leading up the mountain. Up close, however, it looked smaller, square and ugly, with turrets on all four corners and no windows to speak of facing civilization. On the other side of the castle there was the loch, and perhaps the defenders had allowed for some sunshine from that quarter. But they certainly hadn't planned for comfort when they constructed the castle of the Dukes of Brechin.

Beatrice followed Devlen into the shrouded darkness of the entranceway.

"Do you not have candles or lamps at Castle Crannoch?"

"My father is notoriously thrifty with a coin."

Beatrice had been without any source of funds for nearly a year, and in the past three months had been in dire straits indeed. She could stretch a meal to last three days, hoard provisions to last a month; but even she had lit a candle upon occasion, to keep her company during the long nights.

The only illumination was the pinpoint of light from a three-sided lantern set into an alcove far down the hall. Devlen headed toward it unerringly, as if he often traveled in the darkness and needed no marker or light.

The Devil could see in the dark.

Pray God to keep me safe and free from harm. See my sins, oh Lord, and forgive them with the alacrity I attempt to banish them from my soul. Keep me safe in this wicked place and with this wicked man.

She stumbled on the stone floor and made a sound, causing Devlen to turn. His expression was a mystery to her. She could no more see his face than she could the floor or her feet.

"Are you all right?"

No. She was tired and hungry, and more frightened than she'd been since the morning after she buried her parents.

She only nodded. He turned left and descended a set of stone steps carved into the earth. The musty, sour smell of the ground made her think this was a very old part of the castle.

There was nothing to fear with this man as her protector. He was so tall and broadly built, any ghost, goblin, or earthly presence would surely flee at the sight of him. There was nothing to fear unless it was the man himself.

Devlen abruptly stepped to the side of the corridor, as if he had some inkling of what would happen next. A keening sound echoed through the space, an unearthly noise that made her skin crawl. A small figure flew toward her, arms outstretched, a black void where his face should be. Beatrice pressed her back against the wall next to Devlen, praying the specter would pass. Instead, it halted only feet from her.

"Who are you?" he asked, pushing back the hood.

She expected to hear the voice of Hell itself, stentorian tones warning her this was no place for a gently reared woman. But the voice that emerged from the cloak was that of a young boy, high-pitched and curious.

Beatrice blinked at him.

The shadows were expansive, the single light from the end of the corridor barely enough to illuminate his narrow, pinched face. His nose was long for his face and his chin too prominent. His cheekbones were high, the skin stretched tight as if he'd lost weight recently or had always been a sickly child.

He was not an attractive boy, made even less so with his frown. His mouth was pinched and his eyes slitted into a narrow-eyed glare.

"Who are you?" he repeated.

At her silence, he glanced at Devlen.

"Cousin?"

Devlen turned to her, bowed slightly. "Miss Sinclair, may I present Robert Gordon, the twelfth Duke of Brechin."

She glanced at the boy, every faint and futile wish or hope for her future dissipating as they exchanged a long look.

"Your Grace," she said. The child acknowledged her light curtsy with a nod.

How was she possibly to obtain employment from this child?

She glanced at Devlen, wanting to slap the faint smile from his face. He'd known. All this time he'd known.

"Why did you not say something?" she asked.

"You insisted upon seeing the duke. I have provided you with a meeting."

There was nothing to do but straighten her shoulders and walk away from Castle Crannoch.

"Why did you want to see me?"

She was not used to obeying the summons of children, even one from an aristocratic child. But it was all too evident neither of them would move to allow her to pass until she gave him some sort of answer.

"I need employment. The innkeeper at the Hare and Hound said you might have need of me."

"In what capacity?" Devlen asked.

"Are you named for the Devil?" she asked, pushed to rudeness by the events of the past five minutes.

"The first duke, actually. He might well have been named for the Devil. I understand he deflowered his share of maidens."

Heat surged to her face at his words. Had he no sense of propriety?

She pushed away from the wall, clutching her reticule tightly. Hunger was making her dizzy, and the disorientation of the darkness made the situation worse. She stretched out one hand and gripped the edge of a protruding brick, hoping she would not shame herself as she retraced her steps.

Please, God, let me get through this. Endurance. One of the great assets of life. Patience, another. She doubted she had any more of the good emotions left. The last weeks had drained her.

"Let me pass," she said, reaching out and placing the fingers of her right hand on the wall.

She had to leave, to get out of here. There was nothing else to be done.

"I'll hire you," the diminutive Duke of Brechin said. "We're always needing wenches in the scullery."

Beatrice doubted she could manage the work in the scullery. In fact, she doubted she could continue to walk down this corridor without assistance. The walls were bending at the top to meet in the strangest sort of arch, and the floor was buckling beneath her feet.

She pushed past him, past Devlen, who didn't put up a hand to stop her, and down the corridor, following the beacon of that single light.

"I have not given you permission to leave me."

"I do not need it, Your Grace."

"You are at Castle Crannoch, and I am the Duke of Brechin."

"More like the Duke of Incivility," she murmured, but he heard her.

"I will set my guard on you. Or Devlen. Devlen, fetch her to me. Stop her!"

"Cousin, you have insulted Miss Sinclair," Devlen responded in a surprisingly somber voice. "I doubt the young lady would be suitable as a scullery wench."

"Then where shall I put her?"

"Perhaps somewhere where her education could be of benefit."

"How do you know she's educated?"

Beatrice slowed her steps, curious as to what they were saying about her. A part of her was loath to leave Castle Crannoch. There was nothing waiting for her outside its walls.

Her stomach no longer rumbled with hunger. There

was only pain, and a fierce sort of nausea that occasionally caught her off guard. It struck with a vengeance now, causing her to lean against the blackened brick. She climbed the steps with great deliberation.

They were still talking about her; she could hear them. Their words, however, were not as important as simply remaining upright. Dizziness threatened to level her, and it was with the greatest of wills she fought it back.

I will not faint. Not here, not in front of them.

"Are you all right, Miss Sinclair?"

"Yes, thank you."

But she wasn't. The world was tilting.

Devlen unexpectedly appeared beside her, putting his hand on her arm. She jerked away and lost her balance.

The stone floor seemed so very far away. She felt herself falling toward it, and reached out her hands to break her fall. The dizziness followed her down, became a voice etched with worry. A male voice called for assistance. How strange. How very odd.

She surrendered to the nothingness with a feeling of relief.

Devlen Gordon stared down at the figure of the young woman he'd escorted to Castle Crannoch.

"Damn." He sighed, then bent to rouse her, a feat more difficult than he'd expected. He gently tapped her cheeks with his fingertips. No sign of consciousness. She was breathing lightly, a fact he noted with some relief. The last thing he wanted was one more complication in his life.

"Do something, Devlen!"

"You would do better to cease commanding me,

cousin. In fact, I think it's about time someone advised you on your manners."

Robert didn't comment, a wise decision since Devlen was about ready to upend his young cousin and apply a few judicious paddles to his bottom.

He bent and scooped Miss Sinclair up in his arms, thinking she weighed less than he'd expected. In fact, she'd surprised him from the first moment she'd entered the carriage. She was a mouthy little thing, puffed up with prudery. But her mouth was made for kisses, and she had the blackest hair he'd ever seen. For a moment, when he'd caught sight of her in the carriage, he'd wanted to demand she remain still for as long as he wished so he might study the color of her eyes, such a light blue it looked as if she'd trapped a portion of a fair sky behind them. Where had she gotten that small mole beside one eye? It looked almost as if it were an affectation, one used often by the women of Paris.

Despite her threadbare dress, or perhaps because of it, he was most conscious of her long torso, the waist sloping gently from an overfull bodice down to long, beautifully shaped legs. She really should wear a heavier petticoat if she wanted to hide her figure.

But perhaps she didn't want to hide anything at all, and this story of applying for a position was just a ploy to wiggle her shapely little derriere past his father.

Still, she should weigh more. She wasn't a short woman. The top of her head came to his throat, and he was tall for a Gordon.

He was insatiably curious, a character trait that might be considered a flaw since he tended to use it to excess. Was she sick? The fever? Had he unwittingly brought disease to Castle Crannoch? He realized as he walked into the newer section of the castle the young woman in his arms prompted more questions than answers.

"Devlen!"

He didn't turn, didn't answer Robert.

The oldest part of the castle was comprised of a series of long, corridors sparsely lit by a candle here and there. No one could claim his father's stewardship of Robert's inheritance was rife with profligacy.

The walls widened as he climbed up the gently sloping corridor. There were no stairs in this section of the castle. When visitors came to Castle Crannoch, they did so through the north entrance, gaining a view of the sea and the surrounding undulating hills. He'd taken the family entrance, and had to pay for it now, carrying Miss Sinclair through the fortifications like a beast who'd captured a maiden and was taking her to his lair.

Chapter 3

Beatrice awoke to find herself in a strange bed. Her fingers trailed over the coverlet tucked beneath her neck. Silk. Ivory silk. Just like the heavily ruched canopy above her head. The four posters of the bed were intricately carved with trailing vines and leaves. The mattress felt as if it was stuffed with feathers. Was there lavender in the pillows?

She had never before slept in such a magnificent bed. Naked.

Not quite naked. One hand crept across her chest and lower to measure the extent of her coverage. This garment was not her shift. The yoke was heavily embroidered, and there was lace at the edge of her cuffs.

She flattened both hands against the smooth linen of the sheet and closed her eyes, trying to recall the events that led to her being in a strange bed in a strange place.

The last thing she could remember was walking up the long and winding road to Castle Crannoch and being stopped by the carriage. A black carriage with a daunting occupant.

Devlen.

Had he undressed her, then? Was this his chamber?

Her eyes slitted open to take in the rest of the room. A tall bureau with a pediment and many drawers, a washstand, an armoire, the bedside table, a man sitting in a chair.

A man?

Her eyes widened as she stared.

Her visitor was quite a handsome man, one with a decided resemblance to Devlen. For all his name, however, Devlen's face was that of an angel, and this man's face was marked by suffering. His mouth was thin, set inside deep grooves, parentheses in his flesh. A tracery of lines radiated from his brown eyes, and she had the impression humor hadn't caused them. His hair was brown, threaded with gray, and clubbed at the back with a blue ribbon matching the fabric of his jacket.

Emerald, lavender, and sky-blue embroidery depicting thistle and heather blossoms enlivened his waistcoat, granting a touch of abandon to his otherwise somber dark blue attire.

His mouth was faintly smiling, his expression one of self-directed mockery. Beatrice wished she had a clearer memory of the night before.

"Who are you?"

"Your host, Miss Sinclair."

Beatrice tried to sit up and promptly fell back against the pillow when the room whirled around her. She pulled the sheet up even tighter, rose cautiously on one elbow, and after ascertaining she was well and truly properly covered—as properly as one might be while lying in an unknown bed being addressed by an unknown personage—addressed him again.

"It would be less confusing, sir, if I knew your name. You are not the Duke of Brechin. I've met him."

"You do not sound impressed."

She was reasonably certain she was still at Castle Crannoch. It was hardly polite to criticize the Duke of Brechin, especially since she was partaking of his hospitality, however accidentally.

"My nephew has a great deal to learn, unfortunately," the man said at her silence. "One of those lessons is how to treat guests. I offer my apologies for his behavior."

"Nephew?"

The man floated toward her. The movement was so disorienting it took her a moment to realize her visitor was in a movable chair. Large wheels in the front and smaller ones in the back allowed him to glide across the floor while seated.

"You will have to forgive me if I don't get up, Miss Sinclair. My permanent posture is the result of a carriage accident."

"I am very sorry, sir."

"Pity is a common enough emotion, but it's not the reason I've sought you out, Miss Sinclair."

He reached the side of the bed. Slowly, he bowed from the waist, the same mocking smile still in place.

"Allow me to present myself," he said. "Cameron Gordon. I am the Duke of Brechin's guardian."

"And Devlen's father," she said, recalling snatches of last night's conversation.

"Have you known each other long?"

She could feel the warmth travel from her chest to

her face at his amusement. How improper of her to call
him by his first name.

"I met him only yesterday. Dear God, it was just yesterday, was it not?"

He nodded.

"How did I get here?"

"I understand from Gaston that you fainted. There
are several reasons a woman faints, Miss Sinclair. Are
you sickening? With child?"

She didn't comment on his rudeness, because just
then the faint scent of cooking wafted through the air.
For a moment, she was dizzy, then hunger like she'd
never known stripped any other thought from her.

"How long has it been since you've eaten?"

"Two days," she answered absently, wondering
where the smell originated.

A knock on the door preceded the arrival of a maid,
who entered struggling under the weight of a heavily
laden tray.

Beatrice sat up, uncaring that the sheet dropped to her
waist, or that she was trembling. Nothing mattered but
the sight of all that food heaped upon plates and coming
toward her.

She almost wept.

The maid approached the opposite side of the bed
and laid the tray on top of the silk coverlet beside her.

Her fingers touched the lace of the tray cloth, felt the
pattern of it. If it was real, then surely the toast was real
as well?

"Is there anything else you would like, miss?"

"It looks like George IV's breakfast."

Cameron looked startled at her statement. "What
would you know of the English king's eating habits?"

She glanced at him. "My father had a vast correspondence with men in England. They said his favorite breakfast was two roast pigeons, three beefsteaks, and a variety of spirits. Did you know he was purported to be England's fattest king?"

"If not its most inebriated."

His comment surprised her, but not as much as the sudden smile transforming his face. Humor lit his eyes and curved his lips, transforming him into a handsome man.

She turned back to the tray, telling herself she had not eaten in so long that she'd be sick if she consumed very much food at one sitting. But, oh, the choices. Oatmeal with cream, a rasher of bacon, nearly a loaf of toasted bread crusty brown and warm. A pot of butter, and a pitcher of chocolate. Her fingers trembled in the air, lit on one object after another as she tried to decide what to eat first.

"You say it's been two days since you've eaten, Miss Sinclair? And not steadily, I think, before that."

Beatrice nodded, picking up a piece of the thickly sliced toast and holding it in the palm of her hand. She was trembling, and wished, suddenly, he was gone, that no one could see the almost religious reverence she felt for this bread.

She bit into it, closed her eyes, and chewed slowly. Her stomach, as she expected, lurched in spasm, a final bit of pain in response to days of hunger. She swallowed, then bent her head, ashamed for not having thought to say Grace. But surely the Almighty understood her desperate eagerness.

Her prayer quickly done, she took another bite, and while she was chewing slathered a dark red jam on the remainder of the bread. If she took one piece of toast, and a few slices of bacon, surely she wouldn't become ill. One cup of chocolate, that was all she'd drink.

Her plans made, she dismissed her visitor with the single-mindedness of the starving. For long moments he seemed content to watch her eat, neither saying anything or moving so her entire concentration was on what she consumed.

Never had a meal tasted as good. Nor had she ever been as grateful for anything in her life.

"My son says you came to Castle Crannoch looking for employment."

She glanced at him.

"Yes."

"In what capacity, if I may ask?"

"Anything. I'm a hard worker. What I don't know, I can learn. I'm diligent, and focused."

He held up his hand as if to halt her recitation of virtues.

"You've met my nephew, have you not?"

"I have."

"From your expression, I can only imagine you found him ill-mannered and rude."

She remained silent.

"He is a singularly unlikable child, and it is my duty to rear him after the death of his parents." He glanced down at his covered legs. "The same accident, you see, managed to alter the lives of more than one person."

"I think he would benefit from a tutor," she said. There, a tactful way of stating the obvious. Perhaps if the tutor also had a small whip, that would even further benefit the Duke of Brechin.

"I have employed three tutors so far. None of them have stayed more than a month. He has tormented them in some fashion, left a frog in one's bed, told tales on another, and threatened the third with a bow and arrow, I believe, a present from my son. I can't decide if the world is becoming a softer place, or if I simply had the misfortune to employ three very frightened young men."

She stared at him, wondering why he was telling her this.

"I am in need of someone to instill some discipline into the brat. A governess, if you will. You, Miss Sinclair, are obviously in need of a livelihood."

"What makes you think I could do a better job than three tutors?"

He ignored her question. "In return, I will offer you a very handsome salary, to be paid in advance per quarter, a generous allowance for new books and the like for our young duke, and as much food as you choose to consume. I do warn you, however, there are numerous stairs at Castle Crannoch. If you begin to waddle, it will be difficult for you to master them."

Was he jesting? He must be, because he was smiling at her. But as far as becoming the Duke of Brechin's governess, that was a ludicrous idea. She stared down at the tray. Perhaps even more unbelievable was the idea of returning to the cottage with no money, no food, and no prospects, and expecting to survive the winter.

She sat back against the pillow. "You have not asked my qualifications, sir."

"Your speech indicates you have been educated, Miss Sinclair. You have the manners of a gentlewoman, even as hungry as you are. You know about the king, and speak of your father's correspondence. You have come down late in the world, I suspect."

She nodded, biting back the temptation to tell him of the past three months. Burdens shared do not necessarily become burdens lightened.

"You also speak French."

She looked at him, surprised.

"Gaston relayed as much to me. Robert has a penchant for speaking in nothing but French from time to time, as if to incessantly remind me his mother was French. Neither my wife nor I speak it. Gaston does, but it is problematic to have a servant attend dinner for the sole purpose of translation."

"Doesn't your son speak French?"

"My son does not live here."

Why was she disappointed? She'd been in Devlen Gordon's company for less than an hour, not enough time to acquire any feelings about the man at all.

"Well, Miss Sinclair?"

She looked at the tray, at the piece of toast remaining in her hand, and thought of the long trek down the winding road, then five miles more to her cottage.

"I have none of my belongings with me."

"Gaston will drive you where you need to go."

She took the last bite of toast and savored it as completely as she had the first.

"Yes, sir, I'll take the position."

Governess to a hellion. Still, it was a better life than the one she'd lived all these many months. That's what she told herself as Cameron Gordon smiled, then wheeled himself out the door.

Chapter 4

The family dining room faced east, and the view was of the sea in the distance now radiantly gold as the sun rose in the sky. As usual, his father sat at the head of the table, facing the view as if he commanded the land and all within it. As Robert's guardian, he did.

As always when he came to Castle Crannoch, Devlen marveled that generations of his family had coveted the place. This part of Scotland was a wild, open land harkening back to a time when they'd all painted themselves blue and fought the Romans. For some reason, there had always been strife among the Gordons for control of this castle, this acreage. Only during the last century had they become civilized, saving warfare for conflicts outside the family. Yet in the last generation, envy had risen again, to divide brother from brother.

As stark and arresting as Castle Crannoch was, Devlen preferred the civilization of Edinburgh, Paris, or London. He had homes and business interests in all three and could immerse himself in the activities of his businesses, or find some way of amusing himself. Not like his visits to the castle.

Devlen had rarely been to Castle Crannoch before his uncle's death. As a child he'd visited once when he was ten and due to be shipped off to school. His uncle hadn't married yet, and had given the impression of being a confirmed bachelor, a fact that had no doubt pleased his father. Little did Cameron know that ten years later, his brother would surprise everyone by marrying a young French countess who obviously adored her much older husband.

"There have always been men of adventure in the Gordon clan," his uncle had said on that day nearly twenty years ago. "What will you do with your life, Devlen?"

"I will be a wealthy man. I will own ships and buildings and shops. I'll be able to buy anything I want and never have to go away to school again if I don't wish."

His uncle had laughed. "I hope you do, my boy, I hope you do. The Gordon family could always use rich men."

Devlen had gone back to school, but he'd also acquired both wealth and power.

"Well, have you offered your proposition to Miss Sinclair?" he asked now. "More importantly, has she accepted?"

"I have done so, yes, my son. I'm pleased to say Miss Sinclair has accepted our little offer."

"Do not include me in your plan, Father. The less I have to do with your machinations, the happier I am." He moved toward the sideboard and selected his breakfast.

He returned to the table and sat at the opposite end of it, facing his father.

The Gordons weren't prolific breeders. He was an only child, while his father was one of two children. His uncle, in turn, had only one son. If they'd had more offspring, no doubt there would have been less rancor in the family.

"Does she know of the attempts on Robert's life?"

His father made a gesture in the air with his hand as if he brushed away the question. "The ramblings of an hysterical child. You know Robert is prone to imagining things. He has constant nightmares."

"I would have nightmares as well if I thought my uncle was trying to kill me."

All pretense of eating was forgotten. The two men stared at each other, Devlen's eyes the exact shade of his father's, his hair the same. His appearance was similar, but his nature was drastically different. While he couldn't give a flying farthing about being duke, his father lusted after the title.

Would he harm Robert in order to acquire it, however? That was a possibility, and one he'd not been able to discount. It was the reason he was here, after all, when it would have been more advantageous to be at the launch of his new ship. Or even accompanying Felicia to Paris. Anything but staring down the man he called sire, but who felt, even now, like a stranger.

"How can you think such a thing of me, son?"

"You only use that word when you're trying to charm me. Or confound others, Father."

Cameron's smile was part mockery, part amusement. "While you do the same. I've often thought we should just call each other by our given names and dispense with labels."

"Shall I tell you what I'd call you?"

Cameron laughed. "Do I look the fool? I can assure you, son," he said, accentuating the word, "that if I'd wanted the boy to come to harm, he wouldn't be alive now. And there would be no one to tell the tale."

"No witnesses? Just a frightened little boy who insists on sending me messages?"

"How did he ever manage to do that? Is that why you're here so soon after your last visit?"

"Does it matter? I'm here. How do you account for his most recent accident, Father?"

"Do not take such a tone with me, Devlen. You may command your businesses. You don't command me."

"Someone should. Why don't you spend your time in grateful appreciation for the life you have, Father, rather than in bitter contemplation of that which you cannot change?"

"My brother's death?"

"Your nephew's survival."

If his father could have stood, he would have. If he could have stormed from the room, he would have done that as well. Forced as he was to remain seated and in place, he fisted his hands on the edge of the table and stared at Devlen.

"I find it difficult to believe you would listen to the ramblings of an hysterical child," he said finally.

"Do you?"

Devlen studied his plate. In matters of food, his father never scrimped. None of the economies that showed throughout the rest of the estate were visible in the kitchen. But he had lost his appetite. His breakfast forgotten, Devlen sampled his coffee.

"I didn't harm the child."

Devlen didn't comment.

"Would it please you if I gave you my word?"

"It wouldn't matter one way or the other."

"You've grown into a cynic, Devlen."

He sat back and surveyed his father. Something was wrong at Castle Crannoch. It was unnatural for a child to be so afraid, an emotion Robert ably tucked beneath his less-than-pleasant behavior. Miss Sinclair would have her hands full.

"Is it cynical to know one's adversaries? You have a habit of twisting the truth to serve your purposes. You always have."

"Am I an adversary? Interesting."

"What else would you call our relationship?" From the moment he was old enough to understand, Devlen knew his father didn't care for him. He was an encumbrance, a nuisance, an irritant. All Cameron's interests were directed toward the shipbuilding empire his brother had given him to manage, and the ever-present need to demonstrate to his older brother that he was capable of doing so. Cameron was caught in a paradox— needing his brother's approval and despising the necessity for it at the same time.

"I'm surprised you offered the position to Miss Sinclair. She seems an unlikely choice."

"Why would you say that? I think Providence delivered her to our doorstep. The woman needs an occupation, and I have a position."

Devlen didn't answer, didn't comment what he truly

thought. Beatrice Sinclair looked too fragile for Castle Crannoch. In addition, there was sadness just beneath her bravado, something essentially courageous that made him feel oddly protective.

Now wasn't that an unusual thought for him to have?

Breakfast forsaken, Devlen stood and left the room, uncaring that his father wore a small and secretive smile. There were some things he didn't want to know.

Beatrice had been so afraid and so hungry in the last few weeks that the sudden absence of both sensations was almost heady. As she ate, she hummed a tune, an oddity witnessed by one curious bird settling on the edge of her window.

"Hello, little bird. Have you come to beg some scraps?"

He trilled a short song at her and flew away, no doubt annoyed because she wasn't sharing.

The knock on the door startled her. Beatrice stood, walked to the door, and opened it cautiously, holding the borrowed dressing gown closed tight at her throat.

"Mademoiselle? It is I, Gaston," the man said in the French of Paris.

She peeked through the opening to find the giant standing in front of the door, one beefy hand clutching her dress. "The maid, she ironed it for you."

Beatrice extended her hand and retrieved her dress. The maid had evidently mended the garment as well. The tear on the lace at the neck had been repaired, and a button had been replaced.

"Thank you, Gaston."

"Of a certainty, mademoiselle. Whenever you're ready to go fetch your belongings, I await you."

"Thank you."

"All you need to do is pull on the bell rope beside the bed, mademoiselle. Or, if you prefer, I can wait for you."

"I'm not quite finished with breakfast."

"Then I await your summons."

She closed the door, feeling a little bemused. No one had ever waited on her before.

After she finished eating, she dressed, smoothing her hands over the threadbare material of her dress. The maid had ironed it beautifully. The wool felt almost new, the smell emerging from the fabric something reminiscent of lavender. A simple thing really, but it brought tears to her eyes.

After she dressed, Beatrice found a brush sitting on a silver tray and used it to smooth her shortened hair. She, herself, had been ill with the same cholera that had taken her parents, and she'd been subjected to same treatments as the other survivors—their hair had been cut and they'd been purged, twin indignities she'd been too ill to protest.

The square mirror in front of her was trimmed in gold. The reflection revealed a woman too old for her years, perhaps. There was a look in her eyes that hadn't been there before, a bone-deep sadness, an enormous sorrow that didn't fade even when she practiced smiling.

The epidemic that had swept through Kilbridden Village had taken a member of every family. Some, like hers, had been doubly struck. Both her mother and father had died, three days after the first victim had succumbed. The swiftness of the disease had stunned her.

Not only her parents were gone, but also Beatrice's dreams, her hopes, and the simple, peaceful life she'd known.

There were those who might say she'd put herself in this predicament by being too choosy. She might have had her own home, own family. She'd received an offer of marriage but not, however, from the person she expected.

Jeremy MacLeod was a handsome young man who'd been her friend since she was twelve, their relationship changing to a form of awkwardness, and then interest as they'd both aged. He was kind, possessing a gentle temperament, and had a bright way of looking at the world. He was ambitious, filled with plans about the mill he'd inherited from his father. If he had one flaw, it was that he deferred too much to his mother. As the last surviving child of three, he was her baby. She was fiercely protective of him, and he allowed it.

After her parents died, Beatrice had expected Jeremy to come to her cottage and explain, in that earnest tone of his, why they should marry. Instead, he'd stayed away as if she were still contagious.

The only offer of marriage had come, surprisingly, from the young minister who had taken the place of the Reverend Matthew Hanson. She'd known him for all of three days when he'd proposed.

"The people here at Kilbridden Village speak highly of you, Beatrice."

"That is very kind of them."

"They also say that you're a very sensible woman."

"Thank you."

"You're no longer a girl, however."

She'd only glanced at him, wondering if he would correctly interpret her annoyance. He didn't.

"But you're not too old to be a helpmate."

"I suppose not."

"I have two children."

"Do you?"

"I'm a widower. Did you not know?"

She shook her head.

"My children will be joining me as soon as I'm settled. They need a mother, and I need a wife."

Hardly a flattering proposal, but he'd looked shocked when she refused.

She'd been too foolish, perhaps, in turning her back on his offer. Now she was alone in the world and forced to find her own way in it, a circumstance the minister had predicted.

"My offer will not stand open for long, Beatrice. In fact, I doubt you'll receive another like mine."

Bride—even the word sounded odd. She'd long since given up the thought of being a bride. She'd never felt desperate or even despondent about her single state. She'd been pleased to assist her father with his work.

It wasn't that she didn't wish to marry. She had, like other girls, her own chest of linens. Over the years, she and her mother had embroidered a dozen napkins with thistles and roses. There always seemed to be enough time to consider marriage, even if there were a paucity of candidates for husband.

She'd occupied herself with one task after another, and if she were occasionally lonely and longing to be a wife or mother, she assuaged her yearnings by minding her friend Sally's children. There were times when she'd confided in Sally that she might not ever be married, given the lack of men of her age in the village.

"Then he shall have to come from somewhere else,"

Sally had said, imminently practical. "You'll fall in love with him as he's riding through the village on his white horse."

"The only white horses in Kilbridden Village are used for plowing," Beatrice had said, and the two of them had laughed together.

Beatrice pulled on the bell rope and waited at the door, wondering if she should be at the entrance to Castle Crannoch instead. She was not, after all, a guest, but little more than a servant. A toady to the irritating young duke.

There was no choice. She had to take the position. Either that or return to the frigid cottage and starve silently to death. She wouldn't last the winter.

Chapter 5

Gaston arrived at her door less than five minutes later. He bowed slightly to her, a gesture she wished he wouldn't make. Beatrice followed him through the castle, but this journey was not in the darkness. Nor was she required to walk through a series of narrowing serpentine corridors. Castle Crannoch was not as wholly medieval as it had appeared the night before. Instead, this part of the structure was built less with protection in mind than beauty.

"Have you been with the duke long, Gaston?" she asked him in French.

"I have been with Mr. Cameron since before he was born, miss."

"I thought you were in the duke's employ."

He didn't comment.

"I understand his mother was French."

He nodded. "May I say your French is excellent?" he said.

That comment certainly put her in her place. Evidently, there were some questions she was not to ask.

"Thank you, my grandmother was French. I've spoken it since I was a child."

She halted at the top of the stairs, amazed. A pair of staircases began at the bottom, met at the second floor, then branched out again to sweep up to Castle Crannoch's third story. Both the banister and pilasters were heavily carved of a dark, well-polished wood, a stark contrast to the pale yellow silk of the adjoining walls.

In the center, suspended by a long chain from the third floor, was a massive chandelier. One of the footmen was balancing on a ladder, in the process of replacing the candles. He looked at her curiously, then evidently decided she was of no more interest than his chore.

Beatrice descended the steps slowly, glancing at the paintings on the walls. Each of the men featured in the life-size portraits resembled Cameron Gordon. Or his son.

"Are they the Dukes of Brechin?"

Gaston did not glance back at her. "No, mademoiselle, they are not all dukes. Some are men of importance to the family."

There was no time to ask any further questions, because Gaston had outdistanced her. She hurried to catch up.

The massive front doors looked to be old, banded with iron and studded with bolts. Gaston opened the left one and stepped aside, bowing lightly to her. "If you will, mademoiselle."

She stepped out onto the broad stone steps, transfixed by the view of the ocean to her left and the rolling hills before her. The sun was over the horizon, pink bands of clouds stretching like ruched ribbons across the sky.

In the night, winter had come. The grass was coated in a dull frost, and her breath clouded in front of her face. Soon, ice would hang from the trees, and snow would blanket the ground. The world would still, barely breathing, until spring.

She gripped her shawl tightly, feeling the cold seep past her skin into her bones.

A large shiny black carriage stood in the circular drive, four ebony horses being restrained by a liveried driver. The driver tipped the handle of his whip to the brim of his hat and bowed slightly. Beatrice nodded in return.

"Is that Devlen's carriage?"

"No," Devlen said from behind her. "It belongs to the Duke of Brechin, Miss Sinclair."

She turned and surveyed him. He was attired in a greatcoat that looked substantially more suited to the temperature than her shawl. She envied him the warmth of it.

"Aren't you cold?"

He studied her too intently, his gaze resting on her face, then her hands clutching the shawl around her shoulders. Finally, he looked at her shoes. Did he measure her appearance by her possessions? If so, he would judge her poorly indeed. She'd sold everything that might bring her a few coins. What was left was shabby and threadbare, hardly befitting the Duke of Brechin's servant.

"Have you nothing else to wear, Miss Sinclair?"

He unbuttoned his greatcoat and removed it, swinging it over her shoulders. Immediately, she felt warmer, and also dwarfed by the size of it. The coat puddled on the ground as he proceeded to button it.

"I can't take your coat."

He ignored her. Despite being attired only in a white shirt and black trousers, he didn't look affected by the cold.

"My father tells me you've accepted the position he offered you. Are you certain you've made the wisest decision?"

"Yes, quite sure."

"You might wish to consider the question for a moment before answering, Miss Sinclair."

"Why should I, Mr. Gordon? My decision has already been made."

She did wish he wouldn't smile at her in that annoying way.

When she stepped aside to descend the steps, he reached out and gripped her hand. She glanced down where his hand rested, then back up at his face. His smile had disappeared, replaced by a look so intent that she was startled by it.

"You need gloves as well."

"Please, let me go." She didn't tell him that her only gloves were shredded until they were nearly useless.

He released her but didn't step back.

"I don't think it's wise for you to remain at Castle Crannoch, Miss Sinclair."

"I thank you for your concern, sir, but I have made my decision and conveyed it to your father. He seems to think I would be acceptable in the role."

"You serve my father's purposes by being here, Miss Sinclair. Haven't you asked yourself why he would be willing to hire you for such a prestigious position? Candidates for the post are not normally interviewed in a bedroom."

Her face flamed. "If you will let me pass." She concentrated on his knee-high, shiny black boots. His clothing was plain but of an evident fine quality. He smelled of something pleasant, something she couldn't quite identify.

"You are a sheep in a den of wolves, Miss Sinclair."

Startled, she glanced up at him.

"Do you consider yourself one of the wolves, Mr. Gordon? The head of the pack, perhaps?"

She clapped her hand over her mouth, horrified at what she'd said.

"You're not prepared for the position you've assumed. Go home."

"And starve? This is the one position for which I have some training, and you would take it from me?"

She wanted to bite back the words the minute they were said. Who was he to know her circumstances? She wanted neither pity nor charity, simply a way to support herself.

"Is there no one to help you?"

Beatrice drew herself up, angered at having found comfort from the loan of his coat. She began to unbutton it, but he stopped her by placing his hands on top of hers.

"Keep it, Miss Sinclair. I refuse to watch you shiver for the sake of pride."

They looked at each other, the moments ticking by too swiftly.

"The cholera epidemic took everyone I loved," she said finally. "There is no one left. I'm alone."

"Not even a sweetheart?"

"No."

"Did the epidemic take him as well? Or was there more than one?"

The best course was simply to remain silent. He didn't need her participation in this conversation. He was doing quite well on his own.

"If you will forgive my impertinence, Miss Sinclair, you're an oddly striking woman. Once you've lost your thinness, you'll be beautiful, I think. Still, even now there's something about you that interests a man."

"No."

"No?" One of his eyebrows danced upward.

"No, I will not forgive your impertinence. Let me pass."

All this time, Gaston and the driver had been observing them with interest. Neither man made any pretense of ignoring their conversation. In fact, they looked as if they were taking mental notes, the better to describe it in detail for the rest of the staff.

The very last thing she needed was gossip to accompany her, especially when beginning a position that would keep her from poverty and ensure she was fed.

"Please," she said, deciding to soften her demand, "let me pass."

"Are you going home, Miss Sinclair?"

He really shouldn't say her name in that fashion. It had the effect of teasing her, as if the words traveled up from the back of her ankles to her spine. His voice was low, the syllables softly uttered, almost whispered.

"Yes, Mr. Gordon, I am going home. Now, will you let me pass?"

"Will you stay there?"

"No."

He nodded as if he weren't the least surprised by her answer.

"I hadn't intended to remain at Castle Crannoch long, Miss Sinclair, but I see I may have to delay my departure."

"Do not do so on my account, sir."

He placed his hand on hers again, but this touch was not to restrain. Instead, he trailed his fingers from her wrist to her forearm, inciting a shiver of sensation. She jerked away, a gesture that only deepened his smile.

"A few days, Miss Sinclair. Just to make certain you're settled in."

This time, he stepped back, allowing her to escape. She almost ran down the steps.

Gaston moved to open the carriage door. She gave him directions to her cottage before entering and sitting in the middle of the seat, away from the windows at either side, deliberately keeping her gaze on her feet. She didn't want to see Devlen Gordon. Not now, and certainly not when she returned.

She pulled the wool of his greatcoat up around her ears, smelling that strange and wonderful scent.

Gaston climbed up beside the driver. As they began to move, she glanced out the window. Why did she feel a surge of disappointment when she didn't see that most irritating man?

* * *

The last person they needed at Castle Crannoch was Beatrice Sinclair, with her soft blue eyes, restrained manner, and the hands that shook so very visibly.

Her hair was too black, and her complexion too white. Someone should tell her red lips were not in fashion. Did she color them?

She had a sharp tongue when she allowed herself to use it.

I was thinking you were Black Donald.

Someone really should do something about her wardrobe. Her clothes were too loose, but her bodice was entirely too snug. Her legs were too long as well, but he didn't suppose there was anything she could do about that.

She wasn't going to go away easily. For that matter, he couldn't blame her. His father had, no doubt, made being Robert's governess/nursemaid an enviable position while the truth was something else.

Still, it must have been better than what she'd experienced in the past year. Parts of Scotland had been decimated by the influx of cholera. In fact, he'd taken Robert to Edinburgh for the period, feeling a little more secure being away from Kilbridden Village. The stories he'd heard from Gaston had not been pleasant ones.

The last thing he wanted was to feel a surge of compassion for her. She wasn't safe at the castle. But even that revelation, subtly couched as it was, had been rejected. What would she have said if he'd told her the entire truth?

"Thank you, but I don't believe you." Or, "I'll take the position, regardless." Or, "Don't be absurd, Mr. Gordon. You've exaggerated." He could easily hear her make any of those responses.

He should be back in Edinburgh, where there were a

hundred details to see to. If nothing else, he could travel to Inverness and be about some of his business there.

Perhaps he should have accompanied Miss Sinclair to her home. There, he could have taken the measure of the woman more completely. But no one can measure where a man wants to go, or a woman for that matter, from their past. Futures were buried deep in the mind and soul, and rarely voiced.

He folded his arms, ignoring the cold as he watched the carriage begin the descent to the village.

She was going to be a problem.

Chapter 6

From a distance, Castle Crannoch appeared a somber gray, but the bricks were actually nearly black, and the mortar a much lighter shade. Only part of the older section of the castle was visible from the bowl of the valley, but the villagers could not see the four turrets with their crenellated tops so perfectly constructed they appeared like teeth, or the curving drive leading to the massive arched front doors.

But the stout lone tower, behind which sat the crumbling original castle, was easily visible. A facade, perhaps like the inhabitants of Castle Crannoch?

The descent to Kilbridden Village was done with great haste, as if the driver was a seasoned traveler of the curving road. Twice, Beatrice was nearly thrown to the door, and both times had to grab hold of the strap mounted above the window.

The lower half of the road, filled with serpentine twists and turns, was even more hastily navigated, which made her wonder if this particular driver had also been responsible for the carriage accident that had killed Robert's parents and put Cameron Gordon in a wheeled chair.

At the bottom, they hit ruts in the road that jarred the carriage and once made it sway so much Beatrice thought they would surely overturn. Instead of reducing his speed, the driver only cursed the horses so loudly Beatrice could hear his shouts inside the carriage.

With frenetic speed they drove on through the countryside, as if wolves were on their heels, the driver making no effort to slow or to even take the pitted roads into consideration.

Beatrice closed her eyes, both hands clutching the strap, and prayed all through Kilbridden Village.

A scant ten minutes later, she heard a high-pitched whine and a wheel went flying by the window, followed by the carriage lurching to one side and coming to an abrupt halt.

They'd snapped an axle.

Beatrice held on to the strap until the carriage stopped moving.

"Miss Sinclair?"

Gaston's voice was close to her left ear. She raised her head to find he had poked his head into the now open door. He extended his hand to her.

"Are you all right, Miss Sinclair?"

She nodded, even though her stomach still felt a bit unsteady.

"I'll help you out, Miss Sinclair. It would be more comfortable for you to wait outside the carriage while the wheel is being mended."

Since the carriage was perched at an angle, getting

out of the vehicle meant climbing up to the door on the left side, then allowing Gaston to lift her down. The feat was done as delicately as possible, given she didn't want her petticoats to show. On the descent, her skirt ballooned, and she revealed entirely too much of her legs. She hoped Gaston didn't notice, or if he did, he'd simply forget.

She bunched up her skirts demurely and maneuvered her way around the mud puddles to reach the side of the road. Only then did she realize exactly where she was. The mill. Jeremy MacLeod's property.

Beatrice must have made a sound because Gaston glanced in her direction. She waved her hand at him to signify everything was fine.

"It might be some time, Miss Sinclair. Thomas will have to return to Castle Crannoch for the parts. Or another carriage."

She was tempted to mention that if Thomas had had some degree of caution about the state of the roads, they wouldn't have been in this situation at all. But she only nodded.

The day kept getting worse and worse. The one person she had not wanted to see was striding toward her, his sandy hair uncovered, his face a little more bronzed by the sun.

Jeremy MacLeod.

"Beatrice, do you need assistance?"

"Good day, Jeremy. No, thank you."

"As you can see," Gaston said, gesturing toward the carriage, "we have had something of an accident."

Beatrice wondered if he deliberately pointed out the ducal crest, or if Jeremy had noticed it on his own.

"What is this you're about then, Beatrice?"

Beatrice clasped her hands together. "I've accepted a position at Castle Crannoch, and I've come to get my things."

"Castle Crannoch? I've done business with the castle before." That, it seemed, was all he was going to say.

She wanted to ask him questions about the inhabitants, but to do so would indicate she had lingering doubts about her decision. Therefore, she remained silent, and so did he.

Gaston interrupted, easing the awkwardness. "If you would give me instructions to your cottage, Miss Sinclair, I could go ahead on one of the horses and fetch what you need."

"That won't be necessary," Jeremy said. "I have a wagon you can borrow. The cottage is not far from here. Easy walking distance."

He should know. He had walked it often enough as a young man.

"Very well," she said, with as much grace as she could muster. "I would be grateful of the loan of your wagon."

Beatrice sincerely hoped the day would get better.

At that thought, it began to rain.

"Tell me about the nightmares," Devlen said.

Robert sat on the floor, busy arranging his troops. The oriental carpet in the Duke's Chamber served as a military battlefield, the various patterns being hills and valleys, rivers and streams. The toy soldiers had been Devlen's gift to his cousin last Christmas, a battalion of Hessians and English soldiers adding to Robert's already considerable army.

"Have they gotten worse?" Devlen sat beside his

cousin, took a handful of toy soldiers, and began to arrange them in a line.

"Not like that," Robert said, brushing away his hand. "I'll do it. They have to win, you know."

His cousin had an unholy love of war games, an interest that had been regrettably fueled by his father. Where other boys would have been content with tales of heroism, Robert wanted to know details of the battle. How many men had been killed, how many skirmishes until the war was done, topics Devlen was certain did not interest most seven-year-olds. But then again, he could be entirely wrong. Perhaps Miss Sinclair would know better. Or perhaps she was as inexperienced with children as he.

"So, you haven't been having any nightmares?"

Robert glanced at him but didn't say a word, evidently content in arranging his soldiers. Which battle were they fighting today? Robert knew an amazing wealth of detail about the placement of regiments and such. Since he'd never been militarily inclined, even as a child, Devlen fell back to watching Robert line up the troops. From Robert's scowl, his lack of activity wasn't approved of either, so Devlen scooped up the remaining men and put them on his side of the carpet like chess pieces he'd acquired.

"It's Hannibal," Robert said, leaning over and taking back the soldiers while giving Devlen an admonishing look. "The general who marched his elephants across the Alps."

Devlen leaned back on his hand and wondered if his cousin knew there were not many occasions when he crawled around on the floor. For that effort alone, he should be applauded. His memory furnished him with one unique episode with a former mistress, but it wouldn't do to dwell on that particular escapade. His knees had been chafed for a week.

Robert was intent upon reenacting some battle far back in history. Devlen decided not to ask more about Hannibal, in case it was a subject on which Robert was voluble. A sentence or two and he would be out of his element.

Devlen was quite able to converse on a variety of subjects, having spent many years in London as well as on the Continent. He'd traveled to America for one blissful summer, but he remembered more about the woman who'd accompanied him on that trip than he did the scenery of Washington and New York. His journeys through the Orient had been the most fascinating of all his travels, and he vowed he'd return one day. He'd become somewhat familiar with the Russians, although he doubted he'd ever return to that country. Too damn cold for his taste.

Yet, none of his experiences provided him with fodder for a conversation with his cousin. Still, he'd always liked the child, and Robert must have sensed his genuine affection, because he'd gravitated to Devlen ever since his parents had died.

The responsibility of being the only adult in the child's family who could tolerate him was heavy indeed. But there was something about Robert, as irritating as he could sometimes be, that summoned forth Devlen's compassion. Perhaps it was because Robert had suddenly been made an orphan. One moment he was the cherished son of a man older than his father and the next he was told his mummy and daddy had been killed in a carriage accident.

The intervening months had not been easy ones.

First, his home had suddenly been overtaken by an entourage. His uncle, now guardian, had arrived with his wife, her maid, and countless other servants, their sole purpose on earth to look after one very lonely child.

He'd been given a series of tutors, each selected by his uncle and each more disagreeable than the last. Robert, however, had defeated them to a man with the sheer brilliant tactic of being such a monstrous child they'd quit out of desperation.

Did his young cousin realize he was the greatest pawn in this invisible war? The enemy was not the French, or the English of a century earlier, but his own uncle.

Things were not well at Castle Crannoch or with Robert. Robert, however, was not talking. For the first time, his cousin wasn't sharing his misery, and his reticence was disturbing.

Yet, it wasn't Robert's fault he was suddenly and not unexpectedly irritated. Any more than it was his fault Cameron Gordon intensely disliked him.

"How's your ankle?" he asked, glancing at the wrapping visible below Robert's trousers. "You took a nasty fall down the stairs."

A fall that might well have killed an adult.

Robert nodded.

"You must be more careful."

Once again Robert glanced over at him. Those young eyes suddenly looked too old. In that moment Devlen wondered what, exactly, the child knew. Or suspected.

"You're going to get a governess tomorrow."

"I don't need a governess."

"To that I would probably agree. Nevertheless, Miss Sinclair is to begin tomorrow. Try to treat her nicely. No itchweed in her bed."

Robert looked intrigued by the thought, so much so Devlen wished he hadn't given the boy the idea. But Robert had managed to get rid of three tutors on his own; he didn't need Devlen's suggestions.

"Perhaps you can see your way clear to being polite to her. At least talk to her from time to time. I understand Miss Sinclair is an orphan as well."

Robert's face suddenly closed; there was no other word for it. The light in his eyes went out as if there were no intelligence behind them, as if nothing lived behind the face of Robert Gordon, twelfth Duke of Brechin. Devlen had never seen anyone vanish so quickly, and the effect was so complete it stirred the hairs on the back of his neck.

They could not travel fast in the farm wagon, but it was just as well. Beatrice had time enough to savor the view of the cottage she'd always known as home.

Although most of her memories were of Kilbridden Village, she'd come from somewhere else, a place near the border of Scotland and England. Her parents laughed about it sometimes, about her father acting as a reiver and her mother being the prize he'd stolen. But those were comments not for her ears. Even as a child Beatrice had known that.

Her parents had both come from large families, she'd been told. Yet in all these years, she'd never met any relatives. No aunts or uncles had come to Scotland to visit them, nor had she ever witnessed any correspondence.

There was an air of mystery about her parents. Once, when Beatrice had asked her mother why she never talked about the past, the older woman looked as if she might cry.

"There are some memories that shouldn't be recalled," she said, and wouldn't comment further.

When her parents had died, Beatrice had carefully searched through their belongings. She'd found nothing. No links with the past, no letters or documents that might lead to missing relatives.

Her father was an educated man, always talking about books and his lessons. He was a poor farmer, inept in those necessary tasks as if such menial work was unknown to him. The crops were often scraggly, and the chickens sickened and died more often than not. He was happiest when he was deep in his study of his few books, or when he called out to her mother and the two of them discussed a topic of interest.

Even with their poverty, life was pleasant for the three of them. The only time she could remember sorrow in the small cottage was when her mother gave birth to a baby boy who lived only an hour. She'd seen her father weep then as he sat beside her mother's bed. That was the first and only time she'd ever seen him cry; but as the years passed, she realized that of the two of them, her mother was the stronger person.

When she was fourteen, the village elders came to her father and offered him the newly created position as schoolmaster. All pretense of farming was forgotten, and from that day forward the family fortunes were different. There were never times in which money was plentiful, but they were less likely to starve. Her mother kept the chickens, and maintained a small garden, and her father left for the school each morning bearing a smile that was half anticipation, and half excitement.

Now the cottage looked forlorn and empty. Should she board up the windows, close the shutters? It would be some time before she returned here, if she could bear to return at all.

The cottage was far enough from the village that she had no neighbors. She'd often felt isolated during the past year. Perhaps that had been a good thing after all. No one had known of her precarious state, that she'd completely run out of money or objects to sell a month ago.

"Is it a difficult thing, miss?"

She glanced at Gaston, realizing the wagon had stopped, and Gaston was standing in the road.

"Is what difficult?"

"Leaving your home?"

She nodded.

How strange she'd given no thought to the care of the cottage while she'd be living at Castle Crannoch. Who would check the thatch to make sure it was repaired in the spring? Who would chip away the ice from the door and oil the latch and hinges? Who would guard her father's books and her parents' possessions, those she could not bear to sell in the last month?

She should tell Gaston she could not leave. A moment later, she chastised herself. Why would she stay? There was nothing here but the past, and she needed to put it aside, both memories of the happiness and laughter and the darker recollections of loss and grief.

"Miss?"

She came back to the present and left the wagon, walking down the path and deliberately blocking out memories. But they came flooding back despite her will. Her father had laid the path, and the task had taken him a full two months—six weeks for the planning of it and only two weeks to do the work. She and her mother had helped, hauling in the stones from the back of the property, laying them down exactly where he'd planned. She remembered he'd been so pleased at the finished result while she and her mother had merely been grateful the chore was done.

Her parents were so complete, so happy to be together, that she wasn't unduly surprised Fate had taken them within days of each other. Now they lay buried together, in the churchyard facing east. "In sure and certain hope of the Resurrection," the minister had said. "With a smile in their hearts and their souls enlivened with peace."

That was all very well and good for her parents, but what about her?

An entirely selfish thought, and she recognized it as such. However, she didn't chastise herself as much as she had in the beginning when grief was such a raw wound she would sit alone in the cottage staring out at the day and wondering how she was ever to live through the pain.

She had learned, in the last year, that she could live through anything, including the loss of her parents and her friends. She could endure loneliness and heartache, grief, pain, and even despair. But her body required food, water, and warmth.

For that, she'd agreed to Cameron Gordon's offer.

She entered the cottage, gathering up her belongings: a small brush, her mother's silver-backed mirror, her father's book of *Aesop's Fables,* her remaining two dresses, a spare set of stays, and two shifts. She was wearing everything else she owned. Within five minutes, she was done.

Beatrice left the cottage and closed the door behind her, taking care the latch caught and the wind couldn't blow it open as it had a habit of doing.

She turned and smiled resolutely. "I'm ready, Gaston."

He reached out to take the valise from her. "Are you certain, mademoiselle?" She half expected him to heft the bag in his hand as if measuring its contents.

"I'm certain," she said. The belongings were hardly worth the effort of the journey.

Should she contact her parents' friends, let them know where she would be? Just in case something happened, and any of them needed to reach her.

Who should she contact? Mrs. Fernleigh? A widow of indeterminate age, Mrs. Fernleigh had been old when Beatrice was a child. In the last few years, Mrs. Fernleigh had been increasingly forgetful, referring to people who were no longer alive as if she'd just spoken with them. The cholera epidemic had been difficult on her. She was often confused. Perhaps not Mrs. Fernleigh.

Mr. Brown? He'd lost his wife and son in the epidemic and often spent his days more intent on a tankard than the world around him.

Other than Jeremy, all her friends had perished in the epidemic. There was no one to tell, in the end.

With one last, lingering glance, she left the home she'd always known, walking down the path toward the carriage to, if not a better life, then one filled with less sorrow.

Chapter 7

Rowena Gordon surveyed herself in the mirror with a critical eye, not only to her appearance but her demeanor. She must show exactly the right appearance to the world. Her family was quick to judge, and she didn't want an errant tongue commenting she looked tired, or her lace was frayed, or there was a glint of disappointment in her eyes.

There must be nothing about her comportment to give anyone a reason to comment. If someone must say something, let him say the weather in Scotland agreed with her, her complexion had never looked clearer, the years had not seemed to touch her. Above all, dear God, do not let one of them whisper a word of pity or compassion about her husband.

Dear Cameron, what a shame for such a vital man to be trapped in a chair. How do you cope, my dearest Rowena?

Please, not that.

She was wearing red today, a daring color, a shocking one. Her jacket was cropped above the waist and trimmed in fur, as was the hem of her ankle-length skirt. There were little pompoms on her boots as well as on her hat. Another new outfit. Her relatives had not hesitated to comment on her spending habits, as if they envied her wealth. As if money could ever make up for the constant sorrow of her life.

She picked up the reticule and turned to address her maid.

"Well, Mary, will I do?" she asked.

Of all the people in the world, Mary was privy to her secrets more than anyone else.

Mary had sat beside her during those terrible hours when she hadn't known if Cameron would live or die. Mary had brought her countless cups of chocolate when she couldn't sleep. Mary had surreptitiously handed her a new handkerchief when she left her husband's room every morning. And Mary was the one who hung about like a wraith, an almost invisible creature simply waiting for the opportunity to be of service.

Mary nodded and smiled in response. "You look beautiful, madam."

"Thank you, Mary. If I do, it's no small thanks to your ministrations."

Mary's cheeks turned a becoming rose as she hurried to get the door.

"Will you be ready to leave by lunchtime?" Rowena asked as she left the room.

"Oh yes, madam. My bags are packed." She looked as if she'd like to say something, but kept silent.

"Will you not be anxious to see your brother again?" Thomas was one of Cameron's drivers, a most trusted employee.

"Indeed I will, madam. It's just that London is so very exciting a place."

"It is all that and more, Mary. But we must return to Castle Crannoch."

Mary nodded. "Yes, madam."

Did Mary know how desperately Rowena had wanted to leave Scotland? The despair of her life had become too much to bear. Mary had no choice but to accompany her. But these past two months in London had not eased her life one whit. Instead, she'd missed Cameron with every passing day.

Perhaps coming to London had been a good thing after all, because it had borne home to her the truth. She couldn't escape no matter where she was. She adored her husband, without his legs or not.

These past months, he'd withdrawn from her completely. He no longer even touched her in passing or friendship. She used to sit beside his chair and press the back of his hand against her cheek, remembering so many other times when such a gesture would lead to passion between them.

Now, however, there was not even that.

He would slowly withdraw his hand and look at her impassively, almost as if he didn't quite know her. Or didn't wish to.

Sometimes, she wondered what he would do if she told him just how lonely she was. Would he look right through her? Or would he allow her back into his bed? There were things they couldn't say to each other, even though they should and needed to be said.

She left her room, descending the steps holding her head high and feeling for the treads with her feet below her full skirts. Her mouth was arranged in a fixed smile and her face in a pleasant expression. She was on a stage of sorts, and the final curtain was about to rise.

Her family had changed, or perhaps she'd just now realized how sharp and aggressive they were in their curiosity. They didn't care that each one of their questions were like darts thrown at her exposed skin. Everywhere they landed they caused a wound.

As she entered the drawing room and faced her five cousins, two aunts, and her mother, Rowena realized she'd been an absolute fool. She'd come to London for comfort and been greeted by a hungry pack of she-wolves.

Not one of these females had once embraced her, or expressed their sorrow for her life's predicament. Instead, they had been jealous of Cameron's wealth and her stepson's notoriety.

She took a deep breath and greeted them.

The journey back to Castle Crannoch was delayed due to the repairs to the coach. Beatrice sat back against the cushions and folded her hands on her lap and made a pretense of looking out the window. She had planned to be back at the castle before the afternoon was well advanced. When they finally got on their way, it was gloaming. The saddest time of day, as if nature itself wept to see the coming of night.

She hated the darkness, the total blackness of it, the absence of light. Night reminded her too closely of death. She was a person who craved mornings, who sought the dawn. The first tentative touch of sunlight against a blackened sky brought a feeling of peace, of incipient joy.

Yet here she was, approaching Castle Crannoch once more with night looming on the horizon.

Was this the hand of God demonstrating that perhaps she should not feel such relief upon leaving her village? Had she been foolish to accept the post of governess?

They began the long arduous journey up the winding mountain to Castle Crannoch. Once again the trip was done in full darkness, the moon coming out from behind a bank of clouds to witness the ascent.

Beatrice tried to concentrate on anything but the knowledge of how steep the drop was to her right. Were the horses as afraid as she? Or were they simply immune to the danger?

"Tell me about Robert," she said, directing her attention back to Gaston, who'd remained silent and watchful for the last quarter hour. Instead of sitting with the driver, he rode with her inside the carriage.

"What would you like to know about him?" For the first time, she sensed his approval and felt ashamed she'd not asked about the child earlier.

"What are his favorite subjects to study? His favorite foods? That sort of thing."

"I think it best if you learn about His Grace on your own, Miss Sinclair. I will say this about the child, however. He loved his parents dearly and suffers for their loss even now."

"That is one thing we have in common, Gaston."

"Which is why I think you will do well for each other, Miss Sinclair. You're both orphans, and you will find there are other things you share as well."

"Tell me this, then, Gaston. Has no one seen to him

since his parents died? Is there no one to give him direction and to correct his manners?"

"He is the Duke of Brechin," he said, and shrugged. "He outranks anyone who would correct him."

"I don't care about his rank, Gaston. But I do care about his manners. If I am to be his governess, that must be understood."

Gaston sat back against the cushions and surveyed her. In the moonlight she could see the edge of the smile, as if he were genuinely amused.

"Before you can discipline a child, you must have affection for him."

"That might be a French sentiment, but it's not exactly what we Scots would say."

"What would the Scots say, Miss Sinclair?"

"That if a child is to be lovable, he must be disciplined first."

"Then these next weeks will prove interesting." His smile abruptly disappeared. "But you must promise me that if you need anything, anything at all, please seek me out. I will never be far from Robert."

"Are you his protector?"

"I have never known anyone—child or adult alike—who needed me more, but no. I tend to his uncle's needs."

She didn't respond, only subsided back against the cushions.

The carriage returned to the circular drive in front of the castle. Gaston left the vehicle first, then extended a hand to help her descend. She did, holding the greatcoat up so it didn't drag on the ground. She'd gotten mud on the hem earlier today, and regretted having to give it back in such bad condition.

Two lanterns on either side of the front door were

blazing brightly, and even the steps were adorned with candles, as if for a party.

"Are they entertaining?" Beatrice asked, surprised they would be doing so less than a year after the deaths of Robert's parents.

Gaston smiled again. "No, Mr. Devlen is profligate with candles. Whenever he is in residence, he orders them lit. Sometimes I think he would like to push back the night itself."

Perhaps she should have asked about Devlen as well as Robert.

It was too late, because he was suddenly there, dressed in a black formal suit of clothes and a white cravat. She'd thought him arresting in his day clothes but had to admit that now he was sartorially elegant. Perfectly handsome. As perfect as a prince.

"Gaston," he said. "My father is asking for you."

Gaston bowed once to her, then looked toward the castle.

"I should see to Robert," Beatrice said.

"Nonsense," Devlen said. "You can begin your duties tomorrow." He and Gaston shared a look. "I will see Miss Sinclair to her chamber."

Gaston bowed again and was gone, melting into the dark as if he were a creature of night itself.

Chapter 8

"**Y**ou needn't escort me," Beatrice said. "I believe I can find my way back to my chamber."

"Are you entirely certain? Castle Crannoch is a large and confusing structure."

"You saw me off, and here you are to welcome me on my return. Why?"

"Perhaps I have set myself up as the majordomo of Crannoch. Perhaps I simply missed you."

Did she take him seriously? Was he flirting with her? For some reason, she felt uncomfortable in his presence, as if he were larger than life and therefore made her feel so much smaller in comparison.

What a silly way to feel.

Devlen Gordon was simply a man. No more, no less than that. In that he was like a baker or a butcher or a silversmith or any of the men she'd met in the course of her lifetime. Some were braver than others, some more daring in their speech or dress. Some were courteous, and others used the courtesies they'd been taught in an offhanded way that made her think they truly didn't mean to be polite but only did so because it was less effort than rudeness.

None had been so handsome, though. Nor had any of them been graced with such a low voice, its tone having a strange effect on her. She wanted to hear him say mundane things, simply to hear his voice.

She was no doubt tired, and still suffering from near starvation.

"I can assure you, Mr. Gordon, I'm quite aware of how large a castle this is. At the same time, it is no great feat to find the room I slept in last night."

"How will you find the dining room from there, Miss Sinclair?"

He stopped in front of her and held out his arm, leaving her with the choice of being insufferably rude or putting her hand upon it.

She had not been reared to be impolite, and it would have caused her as much embarrassment as it would have caused him if she slighted him right at this moment. She reached out tentatively and rested her fingers as lightly as possible upon the fine material of his jacket. But her hand had a will of its own and her fingers moved over the cloth, her thumb stroking over and over as if to test the resiliency of the muscles she felt.

He glanced at her as she lifted her head. The look they exchanged made her breath tight. She felt as if someone had relaced her corset so she couldn't breathe. The bone and the leather pressed into her flesh, making her acutely conscious of her entire body. She could almost feel the outline of her hips, her waist, and the breasts that didn't feel like hers at all, but creations too full and pillowy to belong to her.

She almost said something to him then, some word to make him look toward the sea or the sky or even toward her feet. Anywhere but keep staring at her. She couldn't look away, and the lanternlight flickered over his face, alternately painting it as the face of an angel or a devil. He was too handsome and too arresting a personage to be standing here in the dark with her. The horses moved; one stamped and the others blew through their noses. No doubt a reminder to the humans that the night was growing colder, and they wanted their stalls and feed.

"I must go inside," she said, drawing his coat closer to her shoulders. She really should return it to him, but she didn't unbutton it, didn't surrender the garment.

He is dangerous. She didn't know why she thought those words, but she understood their meaning well enough. He was the type of man mothers warned their daughters about, the type of man who was mentioned in whispers and shocked expressions. Gossip would follow him all of the days of his life. Women, even virtuous women, would forever notice him. And the other kind of woman would wonder, deep in her heart, if the look in his eyes was really a promise.

"You're a guest. It would be the height of crudeness to allow you to find your chamber on your own."

"I am not a guest, or have you forgotten? I'm the governess."

"Still, the same courtesies apply."

"Then fetch the chambermaid," she dared him. "Or one of the footmen. Or even one of the stable lads with some knowledge of the castle. Any of them can assist me."

"We have a very small staff at Castle Crannoch. My father believes in being penurious to a fault. We employ only a fraction of the individuals needed to maintain my cousin's birthright. It would be a hardship to take one of them from their duties."

"Do you resent him?"

"I beg your pardon?"

The moment the question was out of her mouth, she wished it back. How could she have dared? She wanted to blame him for bringing out the worst in her, but Devlen Gordon was not at fault here. The flaw was unfortunately in her own nature.

"Do you always say exactly what you think?"

"I apologize. It was not well-done of me, and I do know better."

"I find you remarkably refreshing, Miss Sinclair. Perhaps you're what my cousin needs after all."

"Why do you object to my taking the position?"

"I have a whole host of objections, I'm afraid, Miss Sinclair. You're too young. Too attractive. You are, no doubt, naïve. You're no match for my father, and I doubt you can control my cousin."

She stared at him, nonplussed. What did she say to such a litany? She decided to address the insults alone. The compliment she would mull over later in the privacy of her chamber.

"I'm not naïve. I'm very well read."

"Reading, while virtuous in and of itself, cannot grant any true experience in life."

"Nor am I a child, sir."

"If I had seen you on an Edinburgh street, Miss Sinclair, my first thought would not have been your resemblance to a child."

She could feel her fingers and toes tingle, not to mention the tip of her nose. She was certain she was in full blush right up to her hairline. Beatrice desperately wanted to ask him what he would have thought, but restraint, absent until now, finally made itself known. She didn't dare walk into his net of words.

"Very well," she said in her most matronly tone, "I will just have to prove you wrong. I will show you I can do a very good job as Robert's governess."

For the longest moment he didn't say a word, simply looked at her as if she had issued him a challenge of some sort, and he was debating whether or not to accept.

"Did I insult you, Miss Sinclair? I can assure you I didn't mean to do so."

"I can assure you, Mr. Gordon, I am not in the least insulted."

He looked beyond her to where the driver stood patiently at the head of the restless horses. He nodded, only that, and the driver began leading them away, toward the road branching off from the entrance. Beatrice assumed the stables were in that direction, as well as the other outbuildings necessary to support the castle.

"Gaston tells me you're responsible for all the candles," she said, staring at Castle Crannoch lit up to greet the night. The building was an impressive sight indeed, tinged golden by the hundreds of flickering beeswax candles.

"I find it foolish not to use my wealth where it might bring me the most comfort. I dislike night."

She glanced at him, surprised by his admission. "Are you afraid of the dark?"

"Not at all. But darkness limits my movements, robs me of time, and I dislike wasting time intensely."

"So you change night into day."

"If I can."

"Are you very rich? Does it make you happy?"

Why on earth had she said that? To mitigate her words, she asked him another question, "Do you travel with trunks of candles?"

"As a matter of fact, I do, Miss Sinclair. I also travel with pistols in my carriage, and other objects that provide me with some protection. My dislike of the darkness is not simply limited to Castle Crannoch."

"What happens when you travel by ship? I understand fire is a very real concern. Do they allow you your candles?"

"I travel aboard my own ships, and therefore do not have the difficulty of trying to convince a captain to overlook my peculiarities. However, I restrain myself to lanterns and only in fair weather. I had a very interesting, if pitch-dark journey, around Cape Horn during a storm. It was not an experience I wish to duplicate. It was like going to hell by way of the ocean."

She had never met anyone like him, so aware of his own idiosyncrasies and yet so uncaring of them. He simply accepted that his dislike of darkness was part of his character, but he didn't offer excuses for himself.

"I am not fond of the darkness as well," she said, as he opened the door for her. She entered the castle and immediately looked up at the chandelier above their heads, now filled with hundreds of lit candles, which cast a honeyed glow over the entranceway. "Unlike you, I've never been wealthy enough to change night into day."

"So how do you manage, Miss Sinclair?"

"I simply endure, Mr. Gordon."

"Ah, there is the difference between us. I don't have the patience for endurance. I think it a specious virtue."

As they mounted the steps, he glanced down at her. "What do you do when you wake in the middle of the night? Or do you always sleep the sleep of the just?"

She smiled at his curiosity and her own pleasure in it. "I shut my eyes very tightly and pray for sleep. As a child I used to spend most of my nighttime hours below the covers. I would create a little cave for myself with my doll, my imagination, and my dreams."

"What did you dream about?" he asked, holding his arm out for her again.

She gripped the banister instead. The journey upward was done slowly and leisurely, almost as if they were taking a walk in the garden. She thought about his question.

"I dreamed of singing, even though I have no voice. Or of being a storyteller. In my imagination, people were always sitting and listening to me as if my words were important."

"So you were a teacher in your imagination."

"I've never thought about it that way, but perhaps. Or perhaps I simply wanted someone to pay me attention. I was an only child and, as such, I was lonely a great deal of the time."

"We have that in common, it seems. My mother died shortly after my birth."

"What did you dream about as a little boy? Were you a knight or Robert the Bruce?"

"If anything, I probably fought on the English side," he said, smiling. "My family has not been nationalistic for a good hundred years. I think the events at Culloden had a tendency to expunge those sentiments from most Scots' hearts."

"Another thing we have in common. My grandmother was French, and she believed France was the greatest country on earth. She ridiculed anything Scottish or English, for that matter. I was left thinking, even as a child, it was best not to be any one thing, but to be an amalgam of all countries. So, I have a great deal of English practicality, and the fervor of the Scots."

"And the passion of the French?"

There was that warmth again, sliding up her body and down, and pooling in places where she'd never felt warm before.

"The French aren't the only people who have passion, Mr. Gordon. The Scots have their share of it as well."

At the head of the stairs he turned left. She didn't tell him that perhaps it was a good thing he'd accompanied her. She would have turned right.

Here the candles were not as abundant, but they were in evidence in the embrasures and wall sconces.

Despite the fact that the staff of Castle Crannoch was not abundant, the wooden floors were highly waxed and polished. There was not a speck of dust to be seen on the occasional tables and chests lining the hallway. Even the mirrors at both ends of the corridor were brightly polished.

They turned left again and up a short flight of stairs to another wide corridor. At the third door, he stopped.

They stood facing the door for a moment, neither speaking.

He turned and faced her, retrieving her hand and holding it between his. Her skin felt cool against his warmth. She tried to pull away, but he increased his grip so she gave up the effort, telling herself it would be a rudeness to continue.

"Why are you pulling away?"

"Because you won't let go. You shouldn't hold my hand like this."

"I like holding your hand."

"I like it, too. That's what makes it disturbing."

He smiled at her, and she had a silly notion to reach out and push that errant lock of his hair back into place so he'd look less approachable.

"You make me feel protected, Mr. Gordon, as if someone actually cares about me. But that's a foolish and naïve thought."

"Dinner will be in an hour," he said, staring down at her palm. "You have a fascinating palm, Miss Sinclair. You reveal all sorts of traits."

"Do I?"

Once more, she gently tried to extricate herself from his grasp but he wouldn't allow it. His hold on her wrist tightened lightly but firmly enough that she knew he would release her only when he was ready.

"It seems you have a passionate nature. Do you?"

The warmth had never truly receded and it was returning in full measure.

"I also believe you have a very long life ahead of you. An enjoyable one, if one believes in such things."

"In a long, enjoyable life? Or in reading palms?"

This time she did succeed in pulling her hand away.

"Thank you very much for your kindness in seeing

me to my chamber, Mr. Gordon. I appreciate your courtesies."

His smile deepened as she entered her room, and as she was trying to close the door, he sniffed her hair.

For a moment all she could do was stare at him in disbelief. She pressed her hand against her temple, and patted her hair into place, discomfited by his gesture.

"You smell of roses," he said, drawing back. "Or violets. I can't tell which. Do you perfume your hair, or do you simply use scent when you wash it?"

No man had ever asked her such an intimate question. Not even her father, who sometimes looked taken aback at living with two women.

"Did you ask me such a thing to see if it would fluster me? To see if I would fall apart in girlish giggles or tears? I can assure you I will do nothing of the sort. You're a very annoying man, Mr. Gordon."

"Ah, but just a moment ago, I was your protector."

"How would you know such things about women, being a bachelor yourself? Unless, of course, you have a score of mistresses?" A second later, she pressed her hand over her mouth as if to call back the words.

He laughed then, as if he were pleased with her response, as if her irritation had been his aim all along.

She closed the door so quickly she caught her skirt and petticoat. He was the one who opened it again, bent down, and pushed the offending garments to safety.

"I'll send a maid to show you to the dining room, Miss Sinclair. You must believe me when I say I am looking forward to dinner."

Chapter 9

Beatrice told herself she was a fool, but that didn't stop her from brushing her hair at least a hundred times as she did every night, in the vain hope it would grow faster. She studied herself in the mirror and made a face.

A maid had left a fresh pitcher of water and a few clean cloths at the washstand. She unbuttoned the dress to her waist and washed herself, taking care especially at her throat and chest where the heat still gathered.

He'd said her hair smelled of perfume. She put a tiny drop of scent, the last of the bottle she'd been given for her birthday two years ago, behind her ear and on both temples. Would he think she smelled like attar of roses?

She really should show a little more care in his presence. Oh, but he was so handsome, and there was something about him that excited her. Even when he did nothing but stand close to her, she could feel her pulse leap. She was silly to be so affected by his charm, especially since it was quite evident he was practiced at it. She was awkward at social events, and especially with men.

The only person who'd ever shown her so much attention was Jeremy and only for a few short weeks, that was all. After that, his mother had probably sat him down and explained to him Beatrice was a poor teacher's daughter and no match for him, up and coming in the world as he was.

What would Jeremy say to know she was being charmed by the cousin of a duke?

Did she look too gaunt? A little. A few weeks of eating three meals a day, and she would not look so lean and hungry. Her eyes did not look as haunted as they had a few days ago. It was remarkable what employment could do for one's hope.

She didn't fool herself that the position was permanent. She didn't know if she'd last the week, especially if Robert was as difficult as he appeared to be upon their first meeting. But she would try her very best, and perhaps when this experience, however short-lived, was over she could obtain another position. Surely it would be a good thing to have worked for a duke?

Finally, she sat on the bed and tightened her stockings, then took a cloth and wiped off her shoes until the scuffed leather was clean. She stood again and smoothed her hands down her bodice and skirt before readjusting the fabric at her waist. Should she relace her stays? No, they were tight enough. Perhaps too tight, because they thrust her bosom forward like the prow of a ship.

At least the dress had been ironed that morning by one

of the maids and was in better shape, in all honesty, than her other two garments, since it had been her mother's and rarely worn. The hem still showed where she'd let it out, but there was nothing to be done with that.

She buttoned the bodice, smoothing her hands over her skirt one last time. Her palms were damp, so she washed her hands, and dried them, facing herself in the mirror when she was finished.

The knock on the door was expected, but it wasn't a maid come to show her to the dining room. Instead, it was Cameron Gordon on the other side of the door, seated in his wheeled chair. A large package sat on his lap, and as she watched, he handed it to her.

She took it from him, and opened the door wide, uncertain whether to curtsy or to invite him into her chamber. He was such a personage, even seated as he was. He gave her the impression of a king on his throne.

He ended her awkward dilemma by putting his hands on the wheels and wheeling himself into the room. With a hand gesture, he indicated she should close the door behind him.

"It's not a gift," he said, pointing to the package she'd yet to open. "But a necessity."

He waited, and she realized he wanted her to open the package right away.

Inside was a beautiful dark blue wool cloak, the fabric so thickly woven she could feel the warmth against her stroking palm.

"It's lovely."

"It belonged to my first wife. You're of the same size, Miss Sinclair. It's more appropriate than wearing my son's greatcoat."

She felt the blush creep to her cheeks. Did he know everything that happened at Castle Crannoch?

"I regret to say I am here in the guise of your employer, Miss Sinclair."

He wheeled himself to the window and indicated she should sit beside him at the table.

Part of her awkwardness around Cameron Gordon was due to the fact she was so much taller than he. Also, she'd never before known anyone who was confined to a chair.

She wanted to express how very sorry she was that he couldn't walk. How did she do that, especially when the object of her pity so obviously didn't want it? Instead, she remained silent, sat and folded her hands on top of the table, waiting for him to continue.

"As your employer, I feel it only fair to warn you about certain things here at Castle Crannoch."

"Have I done something wrong, Mr. Cameron?"

"Nothing except be a young woman without family, Miss Sinclair." He paused for a moment. "My son is a very handsome man."

The warmth was there again, the blush no doubt in full force. Had she blushed so much while living at Kilbridden Village?

"I would hate for you to become one more of his conquests."

Now she was doubly embarrassed. Being foolish was one thing; to be called on it was quite another.

"You and my son have held several intimate conversations, have you not?"

"I have spoken to him upon occasion, yes."

"That's how it begins, Miss Sinclair. Impressionable

young ladies such as yourself are caught first by conversation, then charm. Before they know it, they are
engaged in behavior that would shock their parents.
Since you are alone in the world, I find it necessary to
warn you."

She pressed her hands flat against the table, linking
her fingers together. She focused on her nails, clasped
her hands together again, then placed them on her lap.

"Simply because I am alone in the world does not
make me foolish, sir."

"I'm heartened to hear it. Therefore, I'm sure you'll
understand why I think it best you not join us for dinner.
At least, not until my wife returns from London. We
have a bachelor household until then. I think it would
be advisable for you to have a tray in your room."

"Of course." She kept her gaze focused on her hands,
unwilling to show her disappointment.

Cameron Gordon left her, and as she closed the door
behind him, she had the oddest thought it wouldn't be
wise to reveal her emotions to any of the Gordons.

A few minutes later, a maid brought her a tray, and
like the morning, there was a huge selection. Once laid
out, the plates and bowls covered the entire top of the
table.

She was still too close to hunger not to savor a meal.
After a taste of the onion soup, it simply didn't matter
she was eating alone in her room.

There were potatoes and carrots and beans in a sauce
tasting like vinegar and sugar at the same time. There
was roast beef so succulent she didn't need a knife to
cut it, and crusty rolls and pots of butter and one of
honey. The maid had brought her a carafe of wine,

enough for one large glass. She sipped it as she ate, taking an hour for her dinner and enjoying every single morsel.

She didn't close the drapes while she ate but sat and looked out at the view of the hills and the village below. The lights twinkling on and off looked like faraway stars, but she knew they were candles being lit in rooms where people met and sat and talked and argued, perhaps.

The rest of the world was coming together. The day was being discussed, problems being aired, questions about life and love and the sheer drudgery of living being asked and answered.

Sometimes she missed the touch of another person so much she could cry. Sometimes she simply missed the conversation, the laughter. There was no one in the world who cared whether she lived or died.

For a moment, the temptation to give in to the despair of that thought was too tempting, but she pushed it aside. If she had no one left to love her, then she would simply have to find someone who would, a friend, an acquaintance, perhaps even a child like Robert. Someone who would find some comfort in being with her.

People were not designed to live alone, to live without affection or caring. Nor was it normal to go through days and days without one person saying: How are you? Are you well? Why are you smiling? Are those tears I see?

She'd sipped the wine slowly, but she looked at the empty glass with annoyance. Perhaps the wine had brought about this maudlin mood.

She stood and opened the window, breathing the

night air. The wind was mild, but the temperature had lowered. Instead of closing the window, however, she gathered her new cloak and covered her shoulders, staring out at the flickering lights below in the village. She was both ferociously lonely and angry about it.

Her friend, Sally, would laugh at her. "Silly girl, you never know what's going to happen tomorrow. Something wonderful could happen, and here you are, moping about now." But she had never been as optimistic as Sally or as much of a dreamer. In the end Sally's dreams had not saved her from the cholera.

The knock on the door roused her from her mood. She opened it, thinking it was the maid come to gather up the dishes. Instead, it was Devlen Gordon.

While she'd felt no reluctance in allowing his father into her room, the voice of caution urged her not to be as welcoming with him. He was not confined to a wheelchair. He was young, handsome, and, according to his father, a rake.

She was not going to be his conquest.

"Miss Sinclair," he said bowing slightly, "I came to ensure myself of your health. My father said you're not feeling well."

"Did he?"

"I wanted to make sure such was not the case. You appeared in good health when I left you earlier."

"I am well, thank you."

How very polite they were. His eyes, however, were entirely too invasive. His face suddenly changed. His smile disappeared and his expression became somber.

"Have I done anything to offend you?"

The question so surprised her that she stood looking up at him, her hand on the door. "No, you have not."

"Then why didn't you come down to dinner?"

She'd been employed for less than a day and already she was being caught up in family drama. What did she tell him? That his father had warned her against him? Devlen Gordon was not a resident of Castle Crannoch. He was only a visitor, and his father was her employer.

Still, she felt guilty about lying to him, so she didn't answer him directly. "I thoroughly enjoyed my dinner here," she said, hoping he would cease questioning her.

He looked dubious, but didn't say anything else.

She felt too vulnerable at the moment, too desirous of another human being's company. But he was one man she should not wish to be near. What had his father said? First it begins with conversation, then charm. Oh, and he had charm in abundance, didn't he?

He reached up and touched her cheek.

"How fascinating you are, Miss Sinclair. Why do you look so sad?"

It was the very worst time to ask a question of that sort. She wanted to tell him she had no armor against kindness. Instead, she began to close the door. When he pressed one hand against it, she looked up at him again.

"Please." The only word she could manage.

"Miss Sinclair." He really shouldn't say her name in such a fashion, in such a low tone it sounded almost like an endearment.

"Please," she said again, and slid her hand up until it covered his. Slowly, she pulled his fingers away from the wood and then held his hand in midair. He reached out with his other hand and cupped hers.

Shouldn't she be closing the door?

Then he leaned over and did something entirely shocking. He pressed his lips against her cheek. A kiss. She'd never been kissed.

She expected more of it, and conversely less.

His lips were warm, soft and comforting; his breath against her skin surprisingly and strangely exciting.

He drew back and bowed slightly once more. In apology? Or mere politeness?

She shut the door and leaned against it, her forehead pressing against the wood. She placed her fingers against her cheek. He was gone and yet the memory of this kiss was there still, confusing and unsettling her.

"Leave the sparrow alone."

Devlen turned to see his father sitting in the shadows at the end of the hall.

"Miss Sinclair? Why do you call her sparrow? Do you see yourself as a hawk? If so, your wings have been clipped, Father."

"If you were close enough, I would backhand you because of that comment."

His father rolled himself out into the light. Not for the first time, he gave Devlen the impression of a malevolent spider, creeping around on leather-bound wheels. Cameron had had a series of ramps built at Castle Crannoch so he could navigate almost anywhere, except atop the towers.

"I think it's time for you to go back to Edinburgh, Devlen. You wear out your welcome very quickly."

"I think you're right."

He walked away, then stopped midway down the hall.

He turned and addressed his father again. "Leave her alone. Do not make her another one of your victims."

Cameron laughed. "Strange, Devlen, but I told her the very same thing about you."

Chapter 10

Beatrice readied herself for bed, pulling out the nightgown from her valise.

In the morning she would tell Devlen Gordon she wasn't to be kissed whenever he felt like it. Such expressions of affection were only between couples who were engaged, and only surreptitiously.

As the governess, she was to be considered above such dalliances. She was not the upstairs maid to be grabbed in a shadowy corner, her skirts upturned while she was groped.

How odd the vision came so quickly to her mind of Devlen Gordon doing exactly that. And how very strange that it made her angry to think of him engaged in such an immoral act. Exactly how many conquests had he made at Castle Crannoch? No doubt every single maid employed here had experienced the full extent of his charm.

How dare he kiss her?

As children she and Sally had often talked about such things, wondering exactly what loving was like between a man and woman. Each had ventured several theories as to how it must feel and what exactly a man does. What would Sally have said about Devlen Gordon?

Her friend would no doubt have teased her about that kiss. A kiss on the cheek, that was all it was.

She went to the bed, plumped up the pillows, and pulled down the coverlet.

A snake was in the middle of her bed.

In the middle of the lovely bed, on top of the ivory-colored sheets was a very dead snake with its head bashed in, and its poor twisted body stretched down the middle of the mattress. On the whole, it was an innocuous-looking creature. She'd found one in the garden often enough.

She went to the bell rope and tugged on it. When the maid appeared, looking tired and more than a little groggy, Beatrice asked for directions to Robert's room.

"You need to know where His Grace's room is?"

Surely, it couldn't be a good thing for a seven-year-old to be constantly referred to as His Grace.

"Yes, please."

"The Duke's Chamber is at the end of the hallway, miss. The big double doors."

Beatrice stuck her head out the door and looked down the hall. Just as the maid had said, at the end of the hall was a set of double doors.

"When his parents died, His Grace insisted upon moving to their suite. It's customary for the Dukes of Brechin to live there."

"Even if he's seven?"

The maid looked a little confused at this question, and Beatrice took pity on her and bid her good night.

Before the girl left, Beatrice called out to her. "What is your name?"

"Abigail, miss," she said, bobbing another curtsy.

"Thank you, Abigail. I'm sorry to have troubled you."

The girl smiled, her plump cheeks reddening as she did so. "It's quite all right, miss."

Beatrice donned her wrapper, buttoned it closed, then gathered the poor snake and left her room. At the end of the hallway, she knocked firmly on one of the doors. When her knock wasn't answered, she turned the handle and entered.

A small lamp was burning in the foyer. A set of drapes separated the area from the rest of the suite. She pushed them aside and stood marveling at the sheer size of the room. From its dimensions, she gauged it took up the whole eastern portion of Castle Crannoch.

On a dais at the other side of the room sat a massive canopied bed draped in crimson and gold. The bed itself was easily twice as wide as hers and at least that deep. As she approached it, a small figure sat up in the middle of the bed and stared at her.

"What are you doing here?" Robert asked.

"I came to deliver your snake," she said, "and to ask you one question."

She still held the poor dead creature in her hand. Carefully, she laid it on the end of the bed. "Did you kill it? Or did you simply leave it in my bed to frighten me?"

"What difference does it make?"

"If you killed it, I would think you a monster. The snake did nothing to deserve its death."

He sat back on his haunches, his fists on his thighs.

"It might have bitten me."

"If it did, it was to protect itself. You're much larger than it."

"I didn't kill it. It was already dead. I think a carriage ran over it."

"Good," she said, and turned to leave.

"Weren't you afraid?"

"I've lived through a cholera epidemic. Nothing could frighten me after that. Besides, some snakes are our friends. They eat rodents and bugs."

"How do you know that?"

"It was in a book I read, I think."

"Would you show me that book?"

"Perhaps," she said. "If you don't put any more snakes in my bed."

"I command you to show me that book."

"You can command me until hell comes to earth," she said calmly. "I'm your governess, not your servant. Nor do I ever want to hear you talking to the servants in such a fashion. If you're a duke, then behave like one."

He looked as surprised as if she'd told him he had two heads.

"Now go to sleep. Tomorrow we'll bury that poor creature."

"I command you to stay."

She studied him for a moment. "I think you're a very spoiled boy who's had a great deal of sorrow in his life. But that's no excuse for you to be rude to others, especially to me."

He looked surprised again. "Why not to you?"

"Because I've experienced the same kind of sorrow, and I know what it's like to lose my parents."

"Do you sleep?"

"What a strange question. Yes, I sleep."

"I don't. When I do, I have nightmares."

Beatrice walked back to the end of the bed and put the dead snake on the floor before sitting on the end of the mattress. She leaned against one of the massive posts supporting the bed, drew up her legs and wrapped her arms around her knees.

"Tell me about the nightmares," she said.

He stared at her for a moment as if he would like to tell her to get off his bed or go away. But evidently, the lure of companionship was too great. In him, she recognized the same weakness she herself felt. They were separated by two decades, by sex, and by role, but she couldn't help but feel akin to this young duke, spoiled though he was.

"Tell me about the nightmares," she said again.

He folded his legs in front of him, placing a hand on each knee like a pasha sitting on a throne of cushions. She smothered her smile at his unconscious arrogance. Cameron Gordon had done his nephew no favor by catering to his every whim.

"I dream someone is watching me while I sleep. They're standing in the shadows and just watching."

She felt a shiver race across her skin.

"What a horrible dream. No wonder you're in no hurry to sleep. Do you ever dream about your parents?"

He nodded. "When I dream of them, it feels just like it happened. I was waiting for them to come home. But they never did. In my dream, they never do, either, and I stand there at the window waiting and waiting."

He was too young to feel the weight of such sorrow. But she could not eliminate it from his life any more than she could wave a wand and make her own situation different. The secret was in finding a way to live until the loss became bearable.

How did she help a seven-year-old child endure such grief?

"So you keep a lamp lit."

"Devlen says it helps. You can hear noises in the darkness you can never hear during the day. As if there are things there, whispering to each other. As if they know you're asleep and defenseless and can't fight them off."

She felt another chill race down her spine. The child had wanted to frighten her with the snake and had ended up doing so with his own words.

"Shall I tell you a story? It might help you sleep."

"I'm too old for fairy tales."

"I will tell you one of Aesop's fables," she said. "They are simply stories, but each one has a lesson. Anyone, even someone of your great age, might enjoy them."

She arranged herself so she was more comfortable and began: "Once upon a time, the queen bee of a very large hive traveled all the way to Mount Olympus. Everyone knows Mount Olympus is the home of the Greek gods. Once there, she told the gatekeeper she wished to visit with Jupiter. She waited some time until he could meet with her and once in front of him, she bowed low, spreading her wings upon the golden floor.

'I give you a gift,' she said. 'A gift of my honey. My workers have labored diligently these past weeks and months to produce only the finest honey for you, Jupiter.'

"Jupiter, very pleased, thanked her, and took a bite of the honey. So impressed was he at its quality, he asked what he could give her in return for her gift.

" 'I ask only one thing, Jupiter, and that is to be able to protect my people. Mankind comes and invades my hives. They steal my honey, and they frighten and kill my workers. Give me the power that I might wound,' she added, pointing to her stinger.

"Now Jupiter was a friend of man, and he was very much troubled by the queen's request. But he granted her the ability to wound any with her stinger.

"Excited her wish had been granted, the queen returned to her hive. That very next day, a man approached the hive and she flew out of it and stung him over and over until he collapsed on the ground.

"But something strange happened to the queen. Once she stung the man, she lost her stinger, and with the loss of it, she fell to the ground and died.

"The moral of this story is evil wishes, like chickens, come home to roost."

"That's a stupid story," Robert said.

"Would you like to hear another?"

"Another fable?"

Beatrice nodded.

"No. They're stupid stories."

"Then I won't tell you another one," Beatrice said.

"Why didn't you scream when you saw the snake?" Robert asked.

"Are you disappointed? I could scream now if you wish."

Robert surprised her by smiling. "You almost screamed last night."

"You're right, I did."

"But you fainted instead. Did I scare you that much?" The little boy sounded proud of himself.

"I fainted because I was hungry."

"People don't faint because they're hungry."

"Have you ever been hungry? I doubt you have."

"Why were you hungry?"

"Because there was no food to eat, and I had no way of earning a living."

"We give food to the poor." Robert moved up in the bed.

"Some people would much rather work than take charity."

He had no comment to this, for which she was eternally grateful. Despite the fact he was only seven years old, he was an arrogant seven-year-old, and exceedingly irritating.

He slid down in bed beneath the covers. "Are you going to stay here until I fall asleep?"

"Do you want me to?"

"Is it something governesses are supposed to do?"

"I don't believe so, no. But since I have never been a governess before, I don't quite know."

"I am the duke," he said sleepily. "I should have a governess with experience."

"If you had an experienced governess, no doubt she would have left you after the experience with the snake."

"Do you truly think so?"

"I do."

"Perhaps that's why my tutors left. They were all very experienced."

"Did you put snakes in their beds?"

"No."

"Then it's to your advantage I have no more experience than I do. I shall practice on you."

"I am the duke. I should not be practiced on."

"We can learn together. Whenever I do something you dislike, I give you leave to tell me. Not to put snakes in my bed, but to tell me. Together, we'll discuss the matter."

He murmured something, an incoherent response that summoned her smile.

She sat there in the darkness at the end of the ducal bed and listened to his breathing.

When she was certain she would not disturb him, Beatrice slid off the end of the bed and stepped down from the dais, walking to the windows. Not surprisingly, Robert had not drawn the drapes against the night.

The stars blanketed the sky, twinkling back at her as if to say she was not alone. But stars were so far away and they neither conversed nor held hands nor smiled. The glass was cold against her fingers, and there was a draft as if one of the panes was not properly sealed. The gentle breeze ruffled the curtains as if someone were standing there. But she knew she was alone except for the sleeping boy.

There was a certain emptiness to the cavernous chamber, as if life needed to be inserted into it. A life that was exuberant and noisy and filled with laughter. Not one that dealt in whispers and fear.

The chamber, for all its riches, and for all it belonged to Robert, somehow did not suit him. He needed a brightly painted room, one that wasn't adorned with portraits of ancestors on the walls, and ornate and heavy furnishings.

He needed to be a boy before he became a duke.

From her vantage point at the window she could see the ocean surface brightly illuminated by the moon until it looked silvery white, and the curving road winding around to the entrance and then behind the castle to the stables. As she watched, a carriage led by four striking ebony horses slowly made its way to the front of the castle.

She had seen that carriage before, more richly crafted than the duke's, but without a crest on its door. Was Devlen Gordon leaving so soon?

How silly to feel suddenly abandoned. He was a stranger who'd dared take liberties. He'd kissed her when she'd not given him leave to do so. He'd smelled her hair, and treated her as if she were a loose woman, and oh, perhaps she was, because she couldn't forget either gesture. Foolish Beatrice. She was a governess, late of Kilbridden Village, a schoolteacher's daughter with hardly any accomplishments to her name. Yet she had a yearning for more, more excitement in her life, more sin perhaps.

At the moment, she only had the energy to be safe, well fed and secure. Perhaps one day she would venture out into the world and have some excitement. For now she was content.

Then why did she feel so suddenly bereft? Devlen Gordon was about to embark upon an adventure, she knew it. Anyone else would have departed Castle Crannoch in the brightness of day, but not Devlen Gordon. As much as he disliked the night, it suited him. Who else traveled in darkness?

She put her finger to the window again and blocked out the sight of his carriage, and the feeling of abandonment eased somewhat. If she could not see him leave, then she need not feel disappointed. Some errant idiotic notion, some girlish sensibility, some silliness that hadn't been leached out of her by the travails of the past three months no doubt was responsible for the feeling. Or curiosity. That's what it was. He was simply the most interesting, most compelling man she had ever met. The most dark and dangerous.

Movement below caught her attention. Devlen strode from the castle door to his coach and stood in conversation for some time with the driver. He wore a long coat notched at the collar, his black hair uncovered. The horses stamped their feet, their breaths white billows in the night. A moment later, Devlen glanced up toward the window where she stood. She didn't move, didn't step backward, didn't hide herself from his gaze. To do so would mark her as a coward, and she had no reason to be afraid. He was leaving.

For a long moment they exchanged a look, her with her fingers on the glass and him with a question in his eyes she couldn't decipher.

She wanted to ask him where he was going and why it was so important he leave for his destination tonight.

And what question did he wish to ask of her?

She would never know.

One by one, Beatrice drew the drapes, moving along the wall of windows until she was done. She stood at the last of the windows, looking down at the drive. From here, she could barely see the coach. She didn't want to see him leave. Everyone in her life had left her, and she had come to dislike departures of any sort, transitory or permanent.

Chapter 11

S he was half-hidden by the drapes when she heard a sound. Beatrice stepped back, allowing the billowing fabric to conceal her.

Soft footsteps crossed the room, hesitated.

She pulled back the fabric of the curtains to see Devlen standing at the end of the bed, staring at Robert.

Her heart beat so fiercely in her chest she thought he must surely hear it. At that moment he turned and looked directly at her.

He walked to where she stood, and pulled back the curtains.

"Are you hiding, Miss Sinclair?"

"Of course not."

"Then may I inquire why you've made no effort to announce your presence?"

She was not dressed. She was attired in only her nightgown and wrapper, but rather than call attention to her clothing, she said, "To do so might have awakened Robert."

"Is he all right?" There was a tone of concern in his voice she'd not heard before.

"Why do you ask?"

"I should think that was obvious. You are here. Why are you in his room, Miss Sinclair?"

She didn't want Robert to be punished for what was a childish prank. "I told him a story."

"And sat with him until he fell asleep."

"Yes."

"You have a tender heart, Miss Sinclair."

"He has nightmares."

"Did he tell you?"

She nodded. "Has he always had them? Or only since the death of his parents?"

"I regret to say I don't know. I hadn't much to do with my cousin before his parents died. I had other interests I deemed more pressing."

"Like the ones that are causing you to leave now?"

"I've been told I'm unwelcome. Besides, you of all people should be glad I'm going back to Edinburgh."

"What do you mean?" Her heartbeat escalated, her breath grew short. Devlen Gordon had an odd effect on her, one that was not altogether unpleasant. She felt as if excitement was flowing through her veins, as if she'd just sipped the finest chocolate, or just finished a potent glass of wine.

"Will you watch after him?" He turned back to watch the sleeping boy.

"Of course," she said. "I'm his governess."

"He needs a friend more than he needs a governess.

If anything untoward happens, tell one of the drivers, and he'll come to Edinburgh."

"What do you mean, untoward? What do you expect to happen?"

"It's not what I expect, Miss Sinclair. I expect the sun to rise every morning and those I care about to continue living happily. However, I have learned what I expect and what happens are not necessarily the same."

"If you have such dire thoughts about the future, how can you leave?"

"I would think you'd be relieved."

"I'm afraid I don't understand."

"I think you do, Miss Sinclair. But I also think you choose to remain cloaked in ignorance or virtue, either one. One of us has to be wise in this instance. I applaud your wisdom."

"Are you normally so cryptic?"

"Are you normally so obtuse?"

She smiled, startled into amusement by his rudeness.

"I'm not obtuse at all, Mr. Gordon. I have attempted to be a lady at every one of our encounters."

"Cloaked in virtue."

In the light, he was devastatingly handsome, but in the darkness, he was even more alluring.

"Tell me, Miss Sinclair, do you ever wish to be simply a woman? Simply a female? Unencumbered by rules or expectations?"

"What you are speaking of, sir, is anarchy."

"Anarchy of the self. An apt description. Do you not ever wish to rebel, Beatrice? Before you answer no, let me warn you. I see flickers of rebellion in your eyes."

How on earth was she to answer such a challenge?

"Is there not one single part of you that wants to put aside your strict upbringing, that wants to loosen your stays and laugh at convention?"

He stepped closer, reached out one finger, and traced the edge of her bottom lip, a tingling touch reaching all the way down to her toes.

"Is that how you talk women into your bed? By daring them?"

He smiled at her. "Would it work with you?"

"No."

"Do you really want to know why I'm leaving, Beatrice?"

"You'll say it's because of me, but it isn't. You can find your share of willing partners at the next inn. No doubt you have a mistress in readiness, eagerly waiting for your return."

"Is there nothing here that would tempt me?"

"Not me. I'm cloaked in virtue. I'm not an antidote to your boredom, Mr. Gordon."

"Is that what you think it is?"

She nodded.

"I could agree except for one thing. I have an eagerness to share your mind as much as your body. What do you call that?"

"Foolish."

His fingers trailed across her cheek, behind her ear, and down to her throat. Did he know how difficult it was to swallow suddenly? Did he feel how frantically her pulse was beating?

Let me go. But the words didn't come. She opened her mouth to speak, but the only sound to emerge was a sigh.

"You are the most unlikely governess, Beatrice."

He really shouldn't call her by her first name. It wasn't

proper, but at the same time she dared herself to answer in kind.

"Why, Devlen?"

"Because, my dear Miss Sinclair, you really are tempting. If I stay, I will bed you. I'll take you to my bed or to yours or to any surface we find amenable and comfortable, be it the floor or a washstand or a table. And I will plant myself in you so deeply that when you swallow you'll be certain that it's me. I'll have you again and again and again until you are as wanton and tempestuous as I think you could be. And we would both enjoy it."

She slapped him. Her hand reached up so quickly he couldn't anticipate the blow. When she did it again, he didn't flinch, didn't move away or otherwise shield himself. He merely stood there quietly, a towering presence, a shadow, a force.

Beatrice could feel the smoothness of his cheek against her palm even through the tingling. He'd recently shaved, and he smelled of spices and something delicious. A scent she'd forever associate with darkness and Devlen.

She stepped back and crossed her arms around her waist not because she was cold. Not because she was suddenly frightened at the somber look on his face, but because she needed to restrain herself from placing her hand gently against the cheek she had just slapped. Or raising up on tiptoe and kissing his skin tenderly in apology.

"Are you done?"

She nodded.

"You are quite correct to be outraged," he said softly. "I am a rake and a lecher and a despoiler of innocents. And you, Miss Sinclair, are very much in danger from me. But I suspect you're innocent only in your experience, and not in your wishes or your deepest heart."

He took one step closer to her, and she pressed herself against the window. The glass was cold against her wrapper.

"But if it makes you feel safer to deny your nature, then so be it. As I said, the reason I'm leaving is for your benefit and not mine."

"Have you no control?" The words were out of her mouth before she could call them back.

"As I said, Miss Sinclair, I've been in your company for one day. An extremely painful day, but I don't suppose you know what I mean."

She shook her head.

"At the risk of being slapped again, let me show you."

He reached out and grabbed her hand and pressed it against his waist. No, not against his waist. Against something hard and unmistakably masculine.

She jerked back her hand, horrified.

"I haven't the slightest idea why it should be so. You are not, after all, the kind of woman who attracts me. I hunger for blondes and statuesque beauties. Although your bodice is certainly plentiful and your legs long, you lack a certain flair, a certain blowsy charm I find attractive."

She could still feel him against her hand.

"Then do not let me stop you from going out and finding the type of woman who attracts you, Mr. Gordon. I wish you well. May all your conquests be easy ones."

"Will you be thinking about me, then?"

"Your coach is waiting, and the night is cold."

"You sound so very angry, Miss Sinclair. Would you like to slap me again?"

"I would very much like to, Mr. Gordon, but it would no doubt be a waste of effort."

"Then you think I'm not capable of being educated?"

"I think you're capable of being educated. I just don't think you're capable of being trained."

His bark of laughter surprised her.

Robert made a sound in his sleep, and Devlen looked back at the bed.

"Care for him, Miss Sinclair, regardless of what you think of me."

"You have some affection for him, don't you?"

"You sound surprised."

She was, but she didn't answer him.

"Have you a kiss to send me on my way?" He bent down and breathed against her hair. Was he smelling her again? "Some token of your regard for me?"

His hand came up and smoothed against her waist. Her uncorseted waist. His hand splayed until his fingertips almost reached the underside of her breast.

She jerked away from him, and to the other side of the drape, making her escape as quickly as she could. She raced across the Duke's Chamber, her bare feet making no sound on the polished wooden floor and to her own room, where she locked the door with trembling fingers, her heart beating so fast she felt faint with it.

For a long moment she stood there, palms pressed against the door until she heard a light tap. Just that. A tap of his hand as if to acknowledge she was safe, and he was leaving.

The winding drive from Castle Crannoch was illuminated at night by a series of twenty lanterns. One man—

or boy, as he sometimes was—kept watch over all the lanterns to ensure they lasted until morning. Devlen had given the orders himself when he first began visiting.

He doubted the lanterns were used in his absence, but he liked having the freedom to arrive and to leave whenever he wished.

Now he didn't want to go back to Edinburgh as much as he wanted to remain at Castle Crannoch, but the voice of his conscience, not often loud enough to be heard, warned him he would be wiser to get away as quickly as his horses could carry him.

He wanted to touch Beatrice. He wanted to touch her so badly he hurt with it.

She smelled of roses. Warm roses and woman, as the heat of her had traveled upward to tease him with her scent. He wanted to reach out, and with not quite steady fingers, unbutton that one button keeping her modest wrapper fastened.

He'd push back the full sleeves with their lace cuffs and kiss her elbow. A teasing kiss while he parted the top of her nightgown. Another, while he slid his hand inside.

One finger would smooth in between the creamy mounds of her breasts, stroking the soft, plump skin there.

His erection swelled at the thought. A button, that's all. The thought of loosening a button, and he was hard as an iron staff.

Very well, he would imagine the button gone, and Miss Sinclair standing bare to the waist, nothing covering her. The warmth would nearly scorch his palm as it rested against a hard nipple.

She would look surprised by the reaction of her own

body to his touch and then slowly, he would use two fingers to hold a nipple so sweetly she'd gasp in awareness.

He would feel the outline of that sweet protuberant nipple and measure the length of it as it grew. His mouth would suckle it, his lips provide a gentle resting place, his tongue tasting her.

He would pull up the rest of her nightgown where it bunched around her waist until it was in folds, then toss it to the floor.

He'd pull her close so he could warm her in his embrace and she would moan at the sensation of being so heated in the chilled air.

He needed to be closer to her, so he could touch his erection to some part of her body. He needed to feel her against him, move her up and down to mimic the action of love.

Do not move, sweet Beatrice, I am imagining myself inside you.

What would she say to that?

No doubt banish him for his torment, or send him away with a teasing smile.

What would it be like to bed the surprising Miss Sinclair?

Just thinking about doing so had him close to erupting in his trousers, and he had yet to press his lips against hers or against her neck or his mouth against those bounteous breasts.

Damn it.

Sleep came with great difficulty that night. Beatrice lay awake staring at the tester above her head and when that sight dulled, she turned and stared out the window at the night sky. When she was tired, she closed her eyes and thought about what Devlen Gordon had said to her.

Any virtuous woman would have been shocked and appalled at the things he had said. Any virtuous woman would have demanded an apology. Most certainly, she would have made her displeasure known to Cameron Gordon. Or she should have marched downhill with her valise beneath her arm, intent on her lonely cottage and some measure of propriety.

A virtuous woman would not be lying here, thinking of all the things he said and wondering at the heaviness of her own limbs and the heat of her body.

Finally, she threw aside the coverlet and the sheet before drawing up the nightgown until her knees were exposed. But it was not enough; she was still too hot to sleep. She sat up on the side of the bed and dangled her feet in a back-and-forth, back-and-forth movement that did nothing to assuage the restlessness inside her body.

She was lusting after Devlen Gordon. There, she'd confessed it.

She placed both hands beneath her breasts and hefted them, feeling their weight. They were entirely too large. No matter how much weight she lost, her breasts never seemed to change. The gesture made her nipples rub against the cotton of her nightgown, gently abrading them. The feeling was so strange and yet so pleasurable she continued it for a moment.

How shocking to be touching herself while thinking of a man.

As penance, she gave herself the task of reciting the books of the Bible. She got all the way to Job before she realized she was thinking of him again.

She sighed, stared up at the elaborate plasterwork of the crown molding. The guest room she'd been given was a lovely chamber, decorated in shades of deep rose. She'd never liked the color much, but it suited the heavy mahogany furniture, offsetting the darkness and adding a touch of femininity.

Had Cameron Gordon's wife chosen the fabric? Or had Robert's mother been responsible for the décor of Castle Crannoch?

How foolish to pretend she was interested in such things when all she truly wanted to know was why she felt so decidedly odd.

She unbuttoned the top button of her nightgown and spread the placket open. Reaching in one hand, she palmed her breast. Then, experimentally and feeling wicked, she pressed two fingers around her nipple and felt an answering sensation deep inside. Without much effort, she could imagine they were his fingers on her, his whispers in her ear to continue.

"Sweet Beatrice. You want so much to feel pleasure, don't you?"

In the next moment she stood and slid her nightgown off her head, tossing it to the end of the bed. With a quick glance to the door to make sure it was locked, she went to the chest of drawers and tilted the mirror on top of it until she could see her body.

She had never before done such a thing, never looked at herself with an eye to what a man might see. Her shoulders were straight and simply shoulders. Her arms were the same. Her hands were formed like hands, her fingers long. Her waist tapered nicely from her chest before flaring gently to her hips. She placed her hand on her stomach, her thumb resting at the indentation of her navel, her little finger stretched out and touching the very beginning of the triangle of hair between her legs.

Her abdomen was flat, her bones in sharp relief, but a few more meals like the one she'd eaten that night and she would not be so thin.

She placed a palm flat on each nipple, but the friction of her touch only made them ache even more.

She turned and looked over her shoulder at her bottom. She liked the shape of it. Turning, she faced herself again, placing a hand on either thigh, splaying her hands until her thumbs met, then slowly, daring herself, she touched herself where she was most swollen and aching.

A soft moan escaped her.

She remembered the feel of him against her hand, hard and erect. The shape of him felt imprinted on her palm. Instead of delighting in the memory, she should be ashamed. Or angry at the very least. He'd done something unspeakably wrong. Shocking. Lurid.

She got back into bed and covered herself with the sheet. A moment later, she left the bed again and opened the window. This time when she returned to the bed, the chill of the room cooled her and eased the unbearable heat she was feeling.

Beatrice closed her eyes, determined not to think of him. Devlen Gordon was on the way to Edinburgh. Yet, in her mind, she could see him leaning over her. She could hear his voice whispering to her, encouraging her to find release in her dreams of him.

Shame seeped through her, shame and a loneliness so desperately painful that if he were here, she might have gone to him. That's what he'd meant. He'd gone back to Edinburgh not to protect her from him, but to keep her sheltered from her own nature.

Chapter 12

The scream was so loud it awakened her. Beatrice bolted upright in bed, staring at the opposite wall, uncertain from where the noise had originated. The scream came again, and this time she knew.

She flew from the bed, threw her nightgown on, grabbed her wrapper, and raced out the door and down the hall. She was opening the door to the Duke's Chamber when Gaston appeared in the doorway of the adjoining room.

He swore, in perfectly accented French.

The lamp in the foyer was still burning, but because she had closed the curtains the night before, the room was nearly suffocating in darkness. Gaston moved in the direction of the bed while she went to the windows, opening up the drapes and letting in the light from a dawn sky.

She turned to find Robert kneeling in the middle of the bed, Gaston's arms around the trembling boy. She didn't have to ask to know Gaston had done this often.

"What is it? Is it one of your nightmares, Robert?"

"Someone was here," he said. "Someone was in my room."

"Devlen was here earlier, but he's gone now."

"I want him. I command you to get him."

She walked toward the bed. "I'm sorry, I can't. He's gone back to Edinburgh."

He shot her a look of such dislike she almost reeled from it. How foolish she'd been to think the hour or so they'd spent together the night before might soften his manners.

She reached out and touched his shoulder, but he jerked away, burying his face against Gaston's chest.

"I don't want you here," he said. "Go away."

"Perhaps it would be best, mademoiselle. Just until he recovers."

Since she was scantily dressed, and Gaston was in his nightshirt, she decided retreat was the best option for the moment. She nodded and left the room, closing the door behind her.

Once in her own chamber, she took care of her morning ablutions before dressing in the same clothing she'd worn the day before. She brushed her hair, uncaring if it grew or not.

She stared at herself in the mirror. She was too pale, but at least she no longer felt as she had last night, confused, uncertain, and heated from her own thoughts.

She tapped her cheeks with her fingers, but she still looked pale, and her lips appeared nearly bloodless. Perhaps she needed embarrassment to bring color to her face. Or shame.

She wrapped the shawl around her shoulders. Castle Crannoch was drafty and cold, despite the fact it was a ducal residence.

In the corridor she hesitated, uncertain where to go next. Should she go back to Robert's chamber? Or to the dining room? Surely Cameron Gordon wouldn't insist upon her eating breakfast alone?

As she was debating, the doors to the ducal suite swung open, and Robert stood there.

He looked as he was, a seven-year-old boy. A title could not change the fact his hair would not quite lie down in the back. He had dressed in an outfit the miniature of his cousin's, even down to the white stock, but Robert's was tied less than perfectly around at the throat. He bowed slightly to her, his chin at an arrogant angle.

"Did you sleep well?" she asked. "Before your nightmare, I mean?"

"It wasn't a nightmare. Someone was in my room. Was it you?"

"I can assure you it was not."

He nodded as if he believed her. But she decided to change topics and start the day off in a better frame of mind. Consequently, she forced a smile to her face, and asked him, "Would you mind escorting me to breakfast?"

For a moment he looked as if he would refuse, and as she was contemplating an impasse, he came and offered his arm to her.

"I will be happy to escort you to breakfast, Miss Sinclair. And perhaps over the meal we can discuss your duties."

She bit back her retort and kept her smile with some difficulty.

"Perhaps we can at that."

Breakfast was not in the main dining room, but in something called the Family Dining Room, a dark and somber-looking place dominated by heavy mahogany furniture.

Two large cabinets filled with china sat against adjoining walls, while the fireplace was built into the third. The fourth wall was covered in heavy burgundy drapes. She would have liked to open them, to view the day outside, but no one else looked as if they were oppressed by the closed-in nature of the room.

Cameron Gordon sat to her left, while Robert was to her right. If Devlen had still been here, he no doubt would have taken the place opposite, while the setting to Cameron's right was probably reserved for his wife.

"Are you expecting Mrs. Gordon home soon?" she asked.

"My wife decides to come and go as she wishes, Miss Sinclair. I am not privy to her plans."

She nodded, feeling awkward for having asked.

A moment later she excused herself and stood at the buffet, deciding what she would eat among the huge array of breakfast foods. Surely, the staff had prepared more food than for just the four of them? The food here could have kept her for a week.

She selected a few pieces of ham, a dish of oatmeal, and a cup of something with the delightful fragrance of strong coffee mixed with dark chocolate. Her stomach rumbled, but it was not so much in hunger as delight.

For the next quarter hour, she was more intent on her meal than she was her breakfast companions. Their conversation, or the lack of it, didn't occur to her until Cameron Gordon asked his nephew a question.

"What plans have you for today, Robert?"

"I want to see the new foal. Devlen said Molly finally delivered. And then I shall play with my toy soldiers. Devlen brought me some new ones from Edinburgh."

"How kind of Devlen," Cameron murmured.

Beatrice put down her fork and folded her hands. "We shall have lessons this morning, Robert. You may see the foal later, and if you do well in your reading, perhaps you can play with your soldiers as a reward."

He ignored her.

Cameron glanced at her, a small smile on his lips, as if he were amused by the exchange.

"Is there a nursery? Or someplace set aside as a schoolroom?" she asked him.

"There are over two hundred rooms at Castle Crannoch. Surely one of them can be modified for your use."

"Did you not grow up here?"

"I did."

"Did you never take your lessons here? Or have a tutor?"

"I was sent off to school at quite a young age, Miss Sinclair. Both my brother and I were. There was never a need for a schoolroom. But I believe you can take what books you need from the library, and as for space, pick one of the rooms. I'll give the order it should be cleaned and ready for your use."

"Very well," she said to Robert. "Perhaps we can meet in my chamber this morning so I can assess your reading ability. If you have a favorite book, please bring it."

"I shan't come," he said, giving her a thoroughly disagreeable look.

She would have been sent to her room had she dared to look at any adult in such a way.

"I shall expect you at nine," she said sternly.

"I shall be with the horses."

She glanced up at Cameron, who remained silent and unsupportive.

She had the distinct feeling this was a test of sorts. Neither Cameron nor Robert Gordon knew her. She never gave up. In fact, her father had always teased her that her epitaph should read: Beatrice Sinclair—I shall prevail.

She wasn't about to let a seven-year-old child, regardless of his rank, outmaneuver her.

"I shall give orders you are not to be shown the new foal until I approve."

Robert threw down his fork and stood beside the table. "You cannot give any orders at Castle Crannoch. *I* am the only person who can give orders. Do you hear me? *I* am the Duke of Brechin."

"You're the duke of rudeness. And unless you want to grow up to be an uncivilized, ignorant creature, you'll do as I say."

He glared at his uncle, and when Cameron didn't say a word, turned and sent the same expression in her direction. She wasn't impressed.

"Nine," she repeated. Instead of commenting further, Robert left the room.

She would have gone after him, would have demanded Cameron's support but for one small, almost unnoticeable thing that kept her silent. The small hand that had been clenched beside the table, the one nearly hidden in the drape of tablecloth, had been trembling.

Beatrice watched as he stormed from the room, slamming the dining room door shut behind him.

"You have to understand, Miss Sinclair, my nephew *is* the Duke of Brechin. He is not to be treated like a normal pupil. Some allowances must be given to the fact of his rank."

She pressed her hands against her waist below the table and decided she had two choices. She could accede to Cameron Gordon's wishes, or she could choose a harder path, one that would ultimately benefit Robert.

In the end, however, it wasn't a hard decision to make.

"I am afraid, sir, I can't agree with you," she said. "He should earn what allowances he's given and not be fawned upon simply because he's inherited the title. You, yourself, have complained about his manners. He needs discipline, I believe you said. If something isn't done now, he'll grow to be a despot, and no credit to his title or his family."

Cameron looked surprised at her vehemence.

He leaned back in his chair and studied her for a moment.

"I have rarely had my words tossed so charmingly back in my face, Miss Sinclair."

"Have you changed your expectations, Mr. Gordon?"

"I have not. You're right to remind me. I was given to understand you have little experience as a governess, Miss Sinclair. Was I wrong?"

"I have a great deal of experience in learning, sir. Also, I assisted my father for many years. In addition to being the schoolteacher for the village, he was a tutor as well."

"I wasn't asking about your qualifications, Miss Sinclair, but your experience. They are two different issues."

She felt cold inside. Is this what failure felt like?

"No, sir, I have no experience as a governess. That doesn't mean, however, that my opinion is without merit."

"You surprise me, Miss Sinclair," he said calmly. "I'd no idea the heart of a tiger beat beneath your rather scrawny abandoned-kitten facade."

Before she could counter his insult, he spoke again. "I only meant you seem to be quite able in the role. Gaston tells me you were with Robert last night and rushed to his side this morning."

She nodded.

"I commend you on your duties so far. Do as you see fit. Remember, however, even if rarely, that he is the Duke of Brechin."

"Will you send word he is not to visit the stables?"

"I will send word you are to be obeyed, Miss Sinclair. That will do you more good, I think."

He snapped his fingers, and Gaston emerged from the shadows, nodded to her, and placed his hands on the hidden handles behind the tall chair and pushed Cameron Gordon from the room.

Chapter 13

Robert had disappeared. There were a hundred places a boy of seven could hide.

"You might find him at the chapel, miss," one of the maids said. She glanced at her, stopped, and retraced her steps. The girl was emerging from a cunningly concealed door, a bucket and cloth in her hand.

"How did you know I was looking for Robert?"

The girl shrugged. "His Grace flew out of here like a bat from a cave. I thought it likely someone would be after him. Normally, it's Gaston."

"Where is the chapel?"

The girl gave her directions, a complicated process considering Castle Crannoch was so large.

"Does he often go there?" Robert didn't strike her as a particularly religious child.

"When His Grace is disturbed, he does." The girl turned to leave. "You know why, miss, don't you?" she asked over her shoulder.

Beatrice shook her head.

"His parents are buried there."

Before going in search of Robert, she returned to the second floor, opened the door to Robert's room, and gathered up his coat and the snake, still on the floor. She returned to her room for her cloak and followed the maid's directions to the chapel.

She didn't want to feel sorry for Robert Gordon. He was a thoroughly unlikable child. She didn't want to remember the sight of his trembling hands, or think about what it must be like for a boy of seven to endure the loss of his parents. She was two decades older, and she'd found the same loss almost intolerable.

The journey to the chapel took a good quarter hour, all the right and left turns through the old part of Castle Crannoch dizzying. An arched pair of double doors, heavily inscribed with a carved cross, marked the entrance.

For a moment she hesitated, wondering if she would find him inside. If she did, what on earth would she say to him? Perhaps now was not the time to be rigid in her requirements. But if not now, then when? Someone had to say no to the boy sooner or later, and it would be better for him if it were done earlier than not. He couldn't rear himself. Someone must be his adult.

She pushed open the door to find the chapel awash in light. Not from candles this time, but from the light pouring through the stained-glass windows in the chancellery. The altar, set across the entrance to an alcove, was covered in an ivory lace cloth and furnished with two goblets and a series of plates that looked as if they were made of solid gold. In front of the altar was a kneeling bench upholstered in a crimson fabric. At the end of the bench, his head bowed and his hands in a prayerful attitude, was Robert, the twelfth Duke of Brechin.

Beatrice did not want to disturb the child at his prayers, so she sat in a pew in the middle of the room and remained as quiet as she could.

Robert, however, began to pray aloud, his implorations to the Almighty stated rather loudly.

"Please, God, take her away. Take her back to where she come from. A big wind would do it, God. Or a lightning bolt."

"Dear God, please inject into your servant some humility," she prayed, in a voice as loud as Robert's. "Please let him see I intend to do my best by him, and that means insisting upon his diligence with his studies. His parents would not wish for him to be an uneducated boor."

There was only silence in response, and she glanced up to find Robert standing at the end of the pew.

"No one talks about my parents. It's not allowed."

"Whose rule? Yours?"

He shook his head. "My uncle's."

"Does he think it will harm you to hear of them? If so, that's silly. We need to remember those we mourn."

He sat down on the end of the pew. "I don't like you, you know."

"You don't know me. You just dislike the idea of a governess or anyone telling you what to do."

"No one else does."

"Which is why, I don't doubt, any of the boys from

Kilbridden Village could beat you in mathematics or geography."

He glanced at her out of the corner of his eye.

"Geography, Robert. It's the study of the world. If you're to be a duke, you must know as much about the world as you can."

"I am a duke."

"Then if you're to be a proper duke, you must know as much as you can."

"What do I have to know?"

"What your parents knew. What they would want you to know. How to calculate a field's production, the tally of your herds, reading the writings of the day, the authors of the past, the Bible. How to reason out a problem, protect your heritage, guard your fortune, and perhaps expand it."

"How to rid Castle Crannoch of my uncle?"

The question startled her into silence. "Yes, I suppose that, as well," she finally said.

He nodded, as if in agreement.

"Ignorant is not a good title for any man to wear, Robert. Being a duke does not equip you with knowledge. You have intelligence. You must use it to acquire knowledge, and knowledge will help you be the best Duke of Brechin."

"Did you know my parents?"

"I did not have that pleasure. Will you tell me about them?"

He shook his head.

"My parents died a year ago," she said. "Within three days of each other. I miss them every day."

"Do you ever talk about them?"

For the first time, his voice sounded like that of a

seven-year-old boy, slightly tremulous, wanting to know but too afraid to hear the answer.

"Sometimes. It took a while for me to do so. I always cried when I did."

"My parents have been dead six months."

"That's not very long, is it?"

He shook his head.

"You'll find time doesn't go by very fast when it comes to grief."

For a few moments they sat silently together. Beatrice didn't fool herself it was a harmonious interlude. Robert would either revert to being obnoxious, or he would rush off and leave her sitting there.

"My mother had a wonderful laugh," Robert said abruptly. "It made everybody smile when she was happy."

Her heart felt as if it would break. She almost wished the child was being difficult again.

"My father always said we should keep her happy because she was the queen of our castle."

Don't tell me any more. But she was as incapable of halting the child's words as she was of halting her compassion.

"She used to come and tuck me in every night."

"Did you ever have nightmares when they were alive?"

He didn't answer. Instead, he stood and walked away, and for a moment she thought he'd left her. But he called out to her. "Would you like to see them?"

She followed the sound of his voice to where he stood at the side of the chapel, in a nave she'd not seen earlier. The floor looked freshly laid, the mortar binding the stones looking too white and new.

Amee Alison Gordon lay side by side with Marcus Harold Gordon, their birth dates different, but the dates of death the same.

She carefully stepped back, but not Robert. He stood on the stones covering his parents' graves and looked down at their markers.

"Do you come here every day?"

He glanced over his shoulder at her. "Yes."

He would never heal if he kept plucking at the wound. Only time would help him understand, at least it had for her. But were seven-year-old boys different? Even in the midst of his tragedy, there must be something interesting him, that excited him.

"What is your favorite place at Castle Crannoch?"

He looked surprised at the question. "The woods. And then the towers."

"Take me there."

"Which place?"

"Your choice. But first, we have something we must do."

"What?"

She went to the pew where she'd placed their coats and handed him his before donning the cloak Cameron had given her.

Beatrice walked out of the chapel and away from Castle Crannoch, acting as if she were unconcerned if Robert followed her or not. In actuality, she was very attuned to the boy, listening intently to his footfalls behind her on the floor.

She went to a copse of trees on top of a knoll. While the child watched, she dropped to her knees, and with a stick began to dig a small hole.

"What are you doing?"

She didn't answer him. Robert demanded, and the staff of Castle Crannoch immediately gratified his every wish. She was not about to do so.

When the hole was complete, she withdrew the napkin from her cloak and uncovered it.

"The snake."

She nodded. She bent and very gently laid the dead snake inside his grave and covered it with soil. When she stood, she looked at Robert. "You must say something."

"What?"

"I don't know. A prayer."

"I don't know any prayers."

"You were praying in the chapel."

"That was a made-up prayer."

"Then make one up now."

"You first."

She decided since the departed was, in this case, a snake, she should amend the service. "Go forth, dear snake, from this world, in the name of the Almighty Father who created thee. May God receive you in His goodly habitation of light. May the angels lead thee into Abraham's bosom."

"Requiem aeternam dona eis, Domine, et lux perpetua luceat eis."

Startled, she glanced at Robert.

"Rest eternal grant to them, O Lord, and may light perpetual shine upon them," he translated, his gaze on the snake's grave.

"You learned that for your parents?"

He nodded. "For their funeral. My father liked to recite Latin."

"That's very nice, Your Grace."

She stared down at the mound of earth she'd made, a last resting place for a trampled snake.

Robert was continually surprising her.

"Shall I take you to the woods now?"

She nodded and allowed him to lead her down the path and around the castle.

Rowena Gordon folded her hands in her lap, stared out at the sky, and ignored her maid with as much determination as possible.

Mary, however, had made her presence known these last few minutes by making a series of unforgettable sounds: tiny little yelps as if she were being pinched, and deep heartfelt sighs. When those failed to garner her attention, Mary had resorted to moans and then high-pitched squeals. If ghosts truly existed, they must sound the same.

Finally, unable to take any more, Rowena slapped her reticule down on the seat beside her and stared at her maid. "We will soon be home, Mary. There is no need for such histrionics."

"But, madam, this is such a perilous journey. We could so easily fall down the mountain. Why, this road could be a way to heaven itself."

Rowena sighed. She'd heard the same thing every time their carriage approached Castle Crannoch.

"It is a very dangerous series of turns. If the horses become tired or frightened, they could easily go over the side." Mary peered out the window, then shivered before letting the shade fall back over the window.

"How many times have you made this journey?"

"In the last six months? Surely a dozen."

"The horses know the route only too well, Mary, and nothing has happened to us in all this time. Calm yourself. We'll be at Castle Crannoch in less than five minutes."

Mary subsided against the seat, a mulish expression on her face. "Very well, madam. I shall not trouble you any longer."

Rowena held back her sigh with some difficulty. Mary's feelings were often hurt. In fact, she had to be the most sensitive creature Rowena had ever known. But she'd had plenty of time to acquaint herself with Mary's idiosyncrasies since the woman had been in her employ for eleven years, ever since she'd been a young girl in London.

"Mary, there is truly nothing to worry about. If you must be concerned about anything, worry about whether or not all those items we purchased in London survived the trip."

Mary glanced over at her.

"Remember the shepherdess and the shepherd statues I purchased? And the porcelain fox for the mantel?"

"They were packed in straw, madam." But the line above Mary's nose creased in concern. "Unless they did not follow my instructions, madam; and then I'm very much afraid of what we'll find when we begin the unpacking."

Good, she'd already begun to worry about the trunks. At least she wouldn't be afraid of the sharp curves still to come.

Rowena wedged herself into the corner of the carriage and smiled determinedly. As long as Mary had something to occupy her, she was content, and bearable to be around.

The day promised to be a sunny one. Clouds had obscured the morning sky, turning it gray, but the closer they came to Castle Crannoch, the bluer the sky. An omen for her homecoming?

She hated Castle Crannoch as strongly as if it were a person and had a personality. She hated the place because it was the scene of defeat, of demoralization, of despair. She hated it because Cameron loved it and lusted after it with more affection and emotion than he'd shown her in the last six months.

The last six months had not been easy ones for Cameron or for her. There'd been times when she'd despaired of surviving from one day to the next. Not that she would ever do anything to harm herself, but there were times when her heart almost shriveled up and died.

Gradually she learned to accept that she and Cameron would never be the way they once were. Whereas previously they had never spent a night apart, now they had two separate chambers, two separate dressing rooms, two separate sets of servants, and gradually, two separate lives.

Regardless of how many times she went to London or to Paris or to Edinburgh, she always came back to Castle Crannoch again, drawn not like a moth to a flame, but like a lovesick woman for the man she adored. Because whether he walked or not, whether he acknowledged her presence or not, whether he cared if she lived or not, she loved him.

The carriage slowed, a sign they were coming close to the end of their journey. Rowena didn't bother opening the shade. She heard the driver call out to the horses and prepared herself to make an entrance. A few minutes later, the door was opened. Rowena put on her gloves and stepped down from the carriage.

Rowena fixed a smile upon her face and looked up at the edifice of Castle Crannoch with what she hoped could be interpreted as enthusiasm and not the dread she really felt.

"It seems a very long time since we've been gone," Mary said. "Two whole months. Nothing has changed one whit, has it, madam?"

"Castle Crannoch has endured for centuries. Two months will not change it."

"That's true." Mary stared up at the castle with awe on her face. Unlike her, Mary had admired the place ever since they'd moved here from Edinburgh. Romantic, Mary had said reverentially, upon first seeing Castle Crannoch.

"I imagine Mr. Cameron will be so very happy to see you, madam."

So happy he'd not yet put in an appearance. So happy no one stood at the broad front doors to greet them. Not a servant walked down the steps; the door didn't even open.

If she'd been so foolish as to confide in Mary, she'd tell her that not once in the months since she'd been gone had Cameron ever written her. She had no idea if the time without her had been a lonely one, or if he'd missed her, if his health was good. In short, her husband was a stranger.

The morning was fair, the sun greeted her brightly, but no human being of her acquaintance stood at the door and welcomed her home.

"Perhaps Mr. Gordon woke late, madam, and he's just now dressing," Mary said.

Not a good sign that her maid had noticed her discomfiture. In just a moment, Mary would be dabbing at the corners of her eyes with her ever-present handkerchief, a sign she empathized for Rowena's plight—being the unloved wife of an invalid.

"There was no way to let him know of our arrival, Mary. We shall simply let them know we are here now."

There was no need to instruct the driver, he was well aware of where to have the trunks taken. What a pity all the new clothing she'd purchased in London wouldn't mitigate this bitter disappointment.

In addition to her new wardrobe, she'd purchased presents for Cameron and Devlen, and added to Robert's collection of toy soldiers. She knew the child would be pleasantly surprised. They'd had little or nothing to do with each other, and she suspected he preferred their current arrangement as much as she.

She'd always been careful around children, cautious and reserved. She didn't go out of her way to view a child in its pram, and when a friend whispered to her she was with child, Rowena's first thought was to mentally bless the poor soul and hope she made it through the travail of childbirth.

After marrying Cameron five years ago, she'd given some thought to children, but since he was twelve years older, it hadn't been a subject concerning her overmuch. He had his heir in Devlen. After the accident, she'd had to accept the closest she would ever come to her own child would be acting as aunt to Robert, the twelfth Duke of Brechin.

She mounted the steps holding her skirts up to her ankles. Her dress was a gray merino trimmed in silk. The bodice was fitted in the waist, and the color accented her red hair. Perhaps after two months Cameron would notice she was not unattractive, at least not according to several men in London.

Would he comment upon her pale complexion? She'd been careful not to acquire any sun. Or lovers. More than once, she'd been approached by an attractive man, and more than once she'd wondered at her own virtue.

Would Cameron have been as restrained if the circumstances were reversed? That was not a question she was foolish enough to ask herself.

Mary opened the door for her, as properly as a footman. She smiled at her, a forced expression, not quite sincere. But the dear woman only smiled back at her and hurried to close the door behind her.

Dear Mary, always so accommodating.

Rowena took the stairs to the right. Her chamber was adjacent to Cameron's in the same wing, on the opposite side of the castle from the Duke's Chamber. As if Cameron did not wish to be reminded daily his nephew had ascended to the title.

How could he ever forget?

If she did nothing else, she needed to convince Cameron a few more servants would not be amiss. If for no other reason than to be able to smile at a friendly face from time to time and not make the journey from her chamber down to the drawing room without seeing a solitary soul.

At the second floor, she hesitated. A wiser woman

would have gone straight to her room to refresh herself and rest from the journey. But she had waited for this moment for the last two months, less one day.

During that first day after she'd left Castle Crannoch, she'd been happy about her decision. Then regret had crept in, and she'd been so desperately lonely she'd immediately wanted to turn around and return to the castle. During these past two months she'd imagined all sorts of homecomings, and none of them had been so dry and desolate as the real one.

How foolish she was to desperately want something that would never happen.

She stopped and turned, changing her mind and walking back to her chamber. She opened the door before Mary could do so and entered the room.

Rowena turned away from the door and went to her vanity. Mary followed, intent on helping her. For the moment, however, she only wanted to be alone.

"See to yourself, my dear," she said, with as much kindness as she could summon. "If you could come before dinner, perhaps."

Cameron insisted everyone dress for dinner, and since it was often the only time during the day when she saw her husband, Rowena took great pains with her attire.

Mary chattered at her side, and she nodded from time to time so as to appear attentive. In actuality, there were times when she simply ignored Mary. Her maid shared every thought traveling through her mind, however transiently. Given any encouragement at all, the poor dear would go on and on and on about the most trivial matter. The squeaking of the latches on the coach door, the slap of the shade against the window, all these things reminded her of when she was a child and embarked upon a journey with her father while her mother stayed behind caring for a sibling.

In addition, Mary liked to gossip, and these little snippets of conversation would shortly contain tidbits about every single individual who lived at Castle Crannoch. Rowena would be privy to the activities of every single servant, guest, or inhabitant of the castle. Except, of course, herself and Cameron. But she didn't hold out any hope Mary had any restraint whatsoever when it came to sensitive matters.

"Please, take this time for yourself."

"Very well, madam, if you're sure," Mary said. "I can stay, if you prefer. Your trunks will be delivered shortly, and we need to unpack your things. Otherwise, those lovely new gowns will be irreparably damaged."

Rowena could not see how sitting in a trunk a few more hours might ruin them when they had been sitting there for days already. But she only smiled.

"There's time enough later."

Mary finally left, closing the door softly behind her. Rowena stared at herself in the mirror, slowing removing her hat, an ethereal bit of fluff and veil that enhanced her green eyes.

She was too pale, but other than that, the last part of the journey from London had not altered her looks. She looked well, healthy, and vibrant, a woman of youth who still had the ability to turn a man's head. Her cheeks were pink, her mouth turned up in a smile, the freckles on her nose barely visible through the dusting of powder. Her eyes sparkled, but she knew it wasn't anticipation but tears making them look so deeply green.

One tear escaped and trailed from the corner of her eye down her cheek, then to her chin. She brushed it away slowly.

Cameron would know by now she'd arrived. Perhaps he was even supervising the arrival of her trunks and looking at all of the things she'd purchased with that smile of his, half-wry, half-cynical.

But he hadn't come to her room and he hadn't made the effort to greet her. Two months had evidently made no difference in Cameron's affections.

Very well, if this was how she was to live the rest of her life, she would do so with grace. He would never know how devastated she felt at this moment. Instead, let him look at her and wonder at her smile. Let him imagine what might have transpired in London. Let him think her beautiful and desirable. Let him decide she was wanton. Let him think anything at all about her other than she was a poor despicable creature yearning for the affections of the one man who wouldn't grant them. Who held his heart aloof because of what she'd done.

He had his pride. Very well, so did she, and he would learn just how very much pride she had from this moment on.

She repaired her hair, and blotted at her face so no trace of her earlier tears would show. She stood, straightened her attire, grateful for the gray wool she wore. The dress flattered both her coloring and her figure.

Once armored, she left the room, intent for the library on the first floor. Cameron had claimed the room as his, and if he wasn't in his chamber, he was holed up in the library, playing at being the Duke of Brechin. Even if he could not bear the title in actuality, he governed Castle Crannoch as if he were the true owner.

Cameron was a genius at management. He knew the exact number of cattle, sheep, goats, chickens, or horses and where they were at any one time. He knew the tally of each field and how many bushels it produced. The ships belonging to the child duke, the various possessions scattered all over Scotland, were all kept in perfect order by Cameron for the child's majority.

Once Robert no longer required a guardian, he could destroy his own birthright if he chose. When he reached twenty-one, Cameron would be forced to turn away and surrender all he'd stewarded for all these years. She'd asked him once if he would be able to simply walk away from Castle Crannoch. He'd only stared at her as if she weren't there. A ghost of who she'd been, perhaps. A wifely spirit.

She knew exactly when his love had turned to hate. Marcus and his wife had been visiting Edinburgh to celebrate his birthday. A carriage accident had killed the duke and duchess instantly, and injured Cameron to the extent she'd had to make a fateful decision.

She'd sat at the side of his bed every moment since the operation. Cameron's life force was so strong he couldn't help but survive. If anything, she would will it. For days she sat beside his bed and prayed.

When he finally awoke, it was her duty to tell him what had happened. Because his legs had been crushed beneath the carriage he would never walk again.

But he would survive, his life would go on.

"Not without my legs, Rowena." He'd turned away

from her then, and ever since, he'd treated her as if she weren't quite there, never looking at her directly and rarely addressing her personally. When he'd made the decision to move to Castle Crannoch, she acquiesced. There was nothing, after all, she could do.

How strange she could love someone so deeply and hate him at the same time.

Chapter 14

The air was chilled, but the sky was blue. The grass was lightly browned from the nightly freezing temperature. Yet there was something about the day that spoke not of winter, but of springtime. Beatrice halted on the lee of the hill and looked beyond her, to the vista of blue-shrouded hills in the distance.

There was something about the scenery, the sight of an eagle soaring high above, its wings black and gray against the blue of the sky, the feel of the air itself, holding a bite even in summer. She closed her eyes and thought she could even smell the faint odor of peat fires and smoke.

Her father was Scots, and he loved the country with the same fervency she felt. But he had no illusions as to its history, its future, or its people.

"The word no is an anthem for Scotland, my dear Beatrice. You'll never find a more recalcitrant lot than the Scots. Nor will you ever find a nobler race of people or a greater friend than a Scotsman."

Her mother, half-French, always smiled in tolerance. Perhaps she'd learned it wasn't important to worry about nationalities.

At the moment, Beatrice couldn't help but feel as though she were born to this land.

She glanced behind Robert at the looming castle. From here, the older part of the castle was clearly visible, including the lone tower, now crumbling in places.

"Why is it the past seems so much more romantic than the present? Your ancestors lived here a very long time ago, and no doubt suffered a great many privations. But one doesn't think of what they suffered, only of their pride and their determination."

"Do you know nothing of the Gordons, Miss Sinclair?" Robert stopped on the path and glanced back at her. "They were a bloodthirsty lot. My father used to tell me stories of all the raids they went on, and all the cattle they stole from places along the border."

"Really?"

"My father and I used to spend every Friday afternoon discussing a Gordon. There are thirteen generations of Gordon men, Miss Sinclair, and each of them should be studied. Some were foolish, while some were heroes."

His voice proudly echoed his father's words. She looked down at him and smiled.

"I think I would've liked your father."

She thought for a moment Robert was going to say something in return, but he didn't.

Perhaps if she could get him to talk more it would be a healing step for him. She knew loss was never truly eased, but it became a part of the fabric of one's character, like a hole through a once-loved garment. Even after mending, the tear was still there, and the garment altered because of it. She didn't discard a garment because it had one flaw, and she couldn't stop living her life simply because grief had visited her. If she imparted no other lesson to Robert, she'd try to teach him this one.

The young duke was, after all, only seven years old. He had a lifetime of living ahead of him. True, his early years would always be filled with the bittersweet memories of the parents he loved, but he must begin to create other memories.

The graveled path they followed was bordered by large rocks on either side and was too narrow for two people to walk abreast. Like the road leading down the mountain, it meandered from side to side through the glen. The distance to the woods was longer, but conversely, the journey was easier, given the height they descended on the zigzag trail.

Someone, a very long time ago, had cut steps into the stone where the hill abruptly dropped, and they'd become part of the path itself. As she followed him, Beatrice noticed Robert's step became less reluctant, his arms began to swing back and forth, and his head came up as if eager to see what was ahead of him.

How long had it been since he'd ventured outside the castle? Castle Crannoch might be his birthright, but there was no sunlight there, nothing but a dark warren of lavish rooms lit by hundreds of candles. A child needed sunlight and activity, chores to perform and responsibilities, even if he was duke.

To the right, following the curve of the hill, was a

dense strip of forest. The trees were thick, and the underbrush looked as if it hadn't been cleared away for years. At first glance, the wood appeared black and unfriendly. But as they grew closer, Beatrice realized it was just the kind of place a boy would like to explore.

He thrust both fists into his pants pockets. His stock had already come untied, and there was a spot on his jacket and one on the knee of his trousers. He was not the most sartorially perfect of aristocrats.

She wanted suddenly to hug him. Though he had moments in which he was rude and unbearable, she found herself softening toward him the longer she was in his company.

"What do you do in the woods?"

"I pretend I'm duke."

She glanced at him, surprised.

"I'm not really the Duke of Brechin at Castle Crannoch, Miss Sinclair."

"Why on earth would you say that? It's your home."

He looked at her as if he couldn't believe her stupidity. It was such a boyish thing to do she found herself smiling.

"It was my home when my parents were alive. Now it's filled with people who do not like me and wish I'd never been born."

He turned and marched toward the forest again, leaving her with a choice of either to follow him or stare after him incredulously.

Finally, Beatrice lengthened her strides until she was only a few feet behind him.

"Surely you don't feel that way about Gaston?"

"Gaston is my uncle's servant." He stopped again, turned and looked at her. "Did you know, Miss Sinclair, none of the servants who were employed at Castle Crannoch when my parents were alive are here now?"

She shook her head, surprised.

"Most of the servants below stairs are rotated every three months. They come from Edinburgh or Glasgow. My uncle imports them here with a bonus and promises them they will only have to serve for a quarter of the year. Even if they wish to stay, they are not allowed to."

Was her tenure to be as short-lived? The selfishness of that thought shamed her.

"Why would he do that?"

He shrugged. "You tell me, Miss Sinclair. My uncle tells me nothing. I think he'd rather pretend I wasn't around."

"And Devlen?" she found herself asking. "How do you feel about Devlen?"

He turned away, relentless in his approach toward the woods. She had to nearly sprint to catch up with him.

"Devlen is my one true friend. I would live in Edinburgh with him if I could, but my uncle wouldn't allow it."

"Why wouldn't he?"

"Because Devlen would be a bad influence upon me." He grinned, a thoroughly masculine, albeit seven-year-old version, grin. "He stays out late, you know, and he has a great many lady companions."

"Does he?"

He stopped one more time and looked at her. "I found a deer once," he said, looking as if he were dubious about confiding in her.

"I trust you treated him with more care than the snake."

He raised his eyebrows in an imitation of his cousin's gesture. "I'm the Duke of Brechin, Miss Sinclair. I'm the only one allowed to hunt in these woods. But the deer was already dead, I'm afraid."

"You have your morbid moments, Robert. Is that why we've come to the woods? To find some other poor dead creature?"

He gave her another pitying stare, and she decided to refrain from further comment.

They were beyond the first of the trees when Beatrice heard a loud cracking noise. She looked down, thinking she had stepped on a branch, but the noise came again, this time from behind her. She glanced back toward Castle Crannoch. Something stung her face and she recoiled, pressing her hand to her cheek. When she drew it away, there was blood on her palm.

Robert ran up to her, grabbed her arm, and before she could ask him what he was about, had pulled her into the woods and to the ground.

"Someone's shooting at us, Miss Sinclair!"

Another shot rang out and this time she didn't need Robert's urging to flatten herself behind a fallen tree. The earth was a pungent combination of pine and decay, the discarded needles from the mature trees above sticking to her hands.

Her face hurt, but a delicate exploration revealed she wasn't actually hurt. Instead, she must have been struck by splinters from one of the shots.

"I'm afraid someone else believes they have the right to use your woods, Robert," she said. Another shot rang out. This one was close enough she could hear the zing of the bullet before it struck a tree. "Thank the Lord he's not a very good shot."

There wasn't much left of the tree trunk they were hiding behind. Time and the insects had hollowed out a majority of it, but the tree was enough of a shield she felt somewhat protected. She peered through the trees, in the direction she thought the bullets had originated.

In front of her was the entire hill, with Castle Crannoch to the upper left. Below was a cottage, half in ruin, evidently the gamekeeper's cottage at one time. Her eyes followed the path they'd taken. Several large boulders might shield a man with a gun.

"It wasn't a hunter, Miss Sinclair. The shots came from the castle," Robert said with a terrifying certainty. His voice was low, and if her hand hadn't been resting on his shoulder, she wouldn't have known he was trembling.

She wrapped her arm around him as they stared out at the sun-dappled day.

"It was probably a hunter with very bad aim."

"No one is allowed to hunt on Gordon land."

"Rules don't stop a man trying to feed his hungry family."

"It wasn't a hunter," he said again. "Someone was trying to kill me."

The comment was uttered so matter of factly she wanted to ask him how he had learned such *sang-froid* at such a young age. How could he view an attempt on his life so calmly?

"What a very odd thing to say, Robert."

"It isn't the first time it's happened."

Shocked, she drew back, and turned him to face her. "What do you mean?"

"On the day my last tutor left, I'd gone to the gamekeeper's cottage instead of saying good-bye." He pointed to the ruined structure down the hill.

"You mean you'd hidden there when people were trying to find you."

He looked away rather than at her.

"I was nearly caught in a trap. It wasn't there before. I almost stepped in it."

"An accident."

"We don't use traps at Castle Crannoch. Ask my uncle. He'll tell you."

He pulled away from her and stood, drawing up the leg of his trousers to reveal a bandage she hadn't noticed.

"And someone pushed me down the stairs a few days ago."

They stared at each other, Beatrice left without a word to say. What kind of hornets' nest had she stumbled into?

She stood and went to the edge of the forest, keeping Robert behind her. Several moments had passed since the last shot, and she wondered if they were being stalked. Or, had it truly been a hunter, and he'd belatedly realized they weren't game?

Her cloak was a deep blue, but Robert's jacket was a fawn color.

"You were probably mistaken for a deer," she said, even though she was beginning to be doubtful of her own claim.

He only shook his head.

A moment later, she dared herself to step out onto the

path again. Right now, all she wanted to do was reach the relative safety of the castle. But how safe was Castle Crannoch, especially if what Robert said was true?

A quarter hour later, when no further shots had come, Beatrice decided it was safe to return. They climbed the hill, taking the path back to Castle Crannoch, in full view of anyone who might wish to harm them. The only concession to Robert's safety was that he remained behind her. If what he said was correct, whoever was shooting at them would have a clear view of her, but not of him.

The journey was a harrowing one, and when they finally made it back to the castle grounds, Beatrice almost wept with relief.

"Your uncle needs to know what happened," she said when they'd reached the safety of the outer courtyard.

He stopped and looked at her in a way no seven-year-old should ever look, with wisdom and a certain amount of sadness in his eyes.

"Go ahead and tell him, Miss Sinclair. He will say it was an accident. Or that it didn't happen, and it was all my imagination. That's what he said before."

"He's your uncle. He wouldn't want anything bad to happen to you."

The child's laughter was eerie, and almost adult. He turned and looked out at the land stretching in front of Castle Crannoch.

"Miss Sinclair, my father married late in life. Up until then, my uncle believed he was the heir to the title. I was a surprise, and not a welcome one. If something happens to me, my uncle becomes duke."

Shocked, she could only stare at him. "Robert,

surely you cannot believe your uncle responsible," she finally said.

The boy began to climb the steps up to the broad double doors. At the top, he turned to face her again.

"You can talk to my uncle if you wish, Miss Sinclair. But I can tell you now it will make the situation worse rather than better."

She watched him enter the castle and wondered what, exactly, she should do. If Devlen were here, she might have confided in him. Instead, she chose Gaston, and went in search of the manservant. She found him in the kitchen.

"Do you have a moment to speak with me?" she asked.

"You've been hurt, Miss Sinclair."

She touched her cheek. Up until that moment, she'd forgotten.

"A scratch, that's all."

"We've some ointment that will aid in preventing a scar."

She had no choice but to follow him, sitting at the table when he pointed to a chair, tilting her head just this way as he cleaned the scratch and then treated it with a foul-smelling salve. He handed her a small jar of it when he was done and gave her instructions to use it twice a day.

"Now, what did you wish to talk about?"

She glanced around her at the interested servants.

"Could we go somewhere more private?"

"Certainly, Miss Sinclair." He left the tray of salves and ointments on the table and led her through a series of tunnel-like corridors. She vaguely remembered the path she took that first night.

They exited the castle to a small courtyard, and she knew her memory had been right. Devlen's coach had stopped here.

"What is it, Miss Sinclair?"

"Can you keep a confidence, Gaston? Even if it is from your employer?"

"I do not know how to answer that question, not unless I know exactly what type of confidence."

She admired loyalty, but she also needed to show some loyalty to Robert. He hadn't asked for her word, but she felt as if he deserved it, for no other reason than his courage.

"Is Robert in any danger? Has anything happened to him since his parents died that might be construed as unusual?"

She'd expected Gaston to answer her quickly and in the negative. Instead, the manservant studied her for several long moments as if to gauge the meaning behind her question.

"There have been some incidents regarding the duke. Accidents any small boy would have."

"Such as being pushed down the stairs?"

"His Grace often neglects wearing his shoes, Miss Sinclair, and takes to sliding on the floors in his stocking feet. It was an accident, nothing more."

"And the trap?"

"We were not able to find the trap he spoke of."

She almost mentioned the shots, then knew Gaston would explain them away just as she had. A zealous hunter, with an overabundance of gunpowder and a paucity of skill.

"Does Mr. Gordon know of these incidents?"

"My master does know, Miss Sinclair. He knows

everything that goes on at Castle Crannoch. Simply because he does not comment about it or make it public knowledge is no reason to think he is not aware of the situation.

"If there are more such incidents in the near future, Miss Sinclair, it might be because of you."

She stepped back. "Me?"

"His Grace might see you have a kind heart. He may use these stories to encourage you to leave Castle Crannoch."

"You believe it's his imagination?"

"Perhaps the ramblings of a child still grieving for his family."

She looked down the mountain at the torturous corkscrew of a road. If she had any sense at all, she would leave this place with its hint of mystery and tragedy. But something had changed in the last two days. She'd found herself touched to the core by a little boy who was arrogant, obnoxious, yet startlingly brave.

No, she couldn't desert Robert. She might well be the only person who believed him. Because the hunter—if he was truly a hunter—had shot at her as well as the boy.

Beatrice turned on her heel and left Gaston before she was tempted to say something she shouldn't. She didn't even ask him to keep what she'd said in confidence, knowing he wouldn't. Instead, he would no doubt visit Cameron Gordon and within the next quarter hour relate to him everything she had said.

She took the back stairs to the second floor and knocked on Robert's door. There was no answer, but this time she didn't make the effort to find the boy. No doubt he had places to hide throughout the castle. A safe place, she fervently hoped.

Instead, she entered her chamber and slammed the door, feeling both childish and frightened.

Chapter 15

"When I used to slam doors," Robert said, "My parents reprimanded me."

She glanced at the other side of the room, where Robert sat on the edge of her bed, his feet dangling over the side.

"Should I ask what you're doing in my chamber?" Nevertheless, she was oddly relieved to see him. "Are you placing another snake in my bed? Or is it to be a toad this time?"

His smile was utterly charming and he laughed like a little boy might laugh, not a serious young duke.

"Did I tell you I shot one of my tutors in the rump? It was an accident, of course, but he didn't believe that. He told my uncle I was the spawn of Satan and should be sent away to prison, not to school. I shall have to think long and hard about what to do next with you, Miss Sinclair. I suspect you are not often frightened."

"I was today. That incident," she said, using Gaston's word for it, "frightened me enough."

"Yet you were very brave," he said. "You stood out in the path and dared someone to shoot you."

"I was not daring. I was hoping with all my heart the shooter was a hunter and by seeing me clearly he might realize I wasn't a deer."

"Did you tell my uncle?"

"Ah, the real reason you're here. No, I didn't."

She sat on the bed beside him. "But I'm very surprised someone didn't hear the shot."

"They might have thought it really was a hunter. Perhaps my uncle has a yen for rabbit and sent one of the servants out."

The inference being, of course, that Cameron Gordon was responsible, either directly or indirectly, for the events of this afternoon.

"I think you're very brave, Miss Sinclair."

The compliment was said in such a calm and pleasant tone, so unlike the autocratic whine Robert normally used, that she looked at the boy in surprise. Without his cloak of arrogance, Robert was a very pleasant individual indeed. In fact, she'd enjoyed being in his company this morning, something she hadn't expected.

"What shall we do now?" he asked.

She would dearly like to lie down and put a cold compress over her eyes and ignore the throbbing headache that had grown ever since she'd been shot at, but she had to keep going for Robert's sake.

"Can you show me where the library is?"

He shook his head.

She was surprised at his sudden recalcitrance, and

wondered if she'd been too kind to think him pleasant only a moment earlier.

"My uncle uses that room during the day."

Now she understood. She didn't want to be in the company of Cameron Gordon either.

"Well, then it's impossible for us to acquire some books to begin your education. Where did you and your tutors study?"

He looked away, brushed his hands across his trousers, studied a hole that had suddenly appeared in his stockings, anything but look at her.

"Robert?"

He glanced at her and then found the view from the window to be so intriguing it commanded his attention.

"Robert."

He sighed heavily and turned to look at her finally.

"I had three tutors, Miss Sinclair."

She waited.

"Two of them thought Castle Crannoch was too far from civilization and complained from the moment they arrived, so I wasn't sorry to see them go. One of them wasn't such a bad sort, but he kept telling me how handsome my uncle was and nearly swooning whenever he saw him. I had nothing to do with his leaving, truly. The arrow didn't hurt him that badly. My uncle dismissed him."

"So they weren't here long enough for you to learn anything from them?"

He nodded.

"But where did you study?"

"There's a small sitting room next to my bedroom."

"Then we shall meet there in the morning."

Instead of answering her, he slid off the bed, his eyes

lighting up. "Would you like to see the attics, Miss Sinclair? There are lots and lots of empty rooms up there. There's one I know that is perfect for a schoolroom."

"The attics?"

He held out his hand for her. "Come with me, Miss Sinclair. I know the castle very, very well."

"Who taught you when your parents were alive?"

"My father."

She nodded, not unduly surprised. No wonder Robert resented having a governess or tutor. Their presence was a living reminder his father was not here to teach him.

As to Robert's excitement over the attic, there was an answer for that as well. No doubt Cameron Gordon couldn't navigate the stairs because of his wheelchair. She had the impression Robert's uncle oversaw everything within his domain. For the time being, Robert, twelfth Duke of Brechin, was very much within his control. She wouldn't be surprised if the child was always thinking of schemes to avoid his uncle.

Beatrice couldn't say she blamed him much.

His rebellion, however, would be short-lived. Wherever they decided to study, Cameron Gordon would no doubt make an appearance. Nor would she be surprised if he commanded them to choose an accessible room. He was, after all, Robert's guardian.

Robert led her down the hall, turned left, then right, evidently following a path he knew well. At the end of the hall, he reached out and pressed one of the decorations below the top frame of a painting. The wall instantly moved, revealing a small corridor. She'd seen one of the maids disappear into a similar one downstairs just that morning.

"A secret passage?"

"Just a way for the maids and the footmen to travel between floors. I think once they were used to hide treasure. My father said that some of our ancestors were thieves and rogues." He grinned at her. "I think they're haunted. I once saw the very first Gordon and his horse."

She raised one eyebrow at him, and he shrugged.

"My uncle doesn't like to see servants, so whenever they hear him coming, they sort of melt into the walls." He giggled, sounding like a seven-year-old boy.

"Are there places like this throughout the castle?"

"No, only the newer part. This section of Castle Crannoch is only about a hundred years old. If there are any secret passages in the old part, I haven't been able to find them."

"Do you do a lot of exploring?"

"What else is there to do?"

"Well, from this moment on, your lessons."

He made a face but didn't comment.

She followed him into the small anteroom leading to a circular iron staircase. Evidently, the space had originally been a tower. Sunlight spilled in through the archer slits, but so did the chill. In the depths of winter, it must be unbearably cold to serve the Gordon family.

He dropped his voice and whispered, "You can go down to the kitchen from here, as well as climbing up to the attics."

"Why are you whispering?"

"You have to be careful because anyone can hear you. Sound carries very well."

She held on to the railing and climbed, feeling as if

they would never make it to the top. Heights made her uncomfortable.

Finally, they were at the top, the staircase ending in a wooden landing. There was a gap of some space between the top step and the first board, and Beatrice made it across without looking down.

"It's all right, Miss Sinclair," he whispered. "We're almost there."

He pushed open the door, and she found herself in a well-lit corridor, but narrower than the second floor. There was no effort to hide the entrance to the servant's staircase.

"We're at the top of the castle," he said, and for the first time, the pride of ownership was in his voice. "There's one room on this floor that has nothing but windows for a ceiling. It's filled with trunks right now, but you can see the ocean from it."

She was intrigued by his description, enough to silence her doubts for the moment.

"When we used to have a lot of servants, they slept up here. But they use the third floor now."

"How many servants are there at Castle Crannoch?"

"Only about seven. We need at least five times as many to care for the castle."

"Why don't you employ them?"

"My uncle says he's saving my fortune. I think it's because he doesn't like to have people around him."

"You don't like your uncle, do you?"

He gave her a look that made her want to retract the question.

A moment later, he spoke again. "My father used to say people have to choose between being good or evil."

"Your father sounds like a very wise man."

"My father was the best man in the whole wide world. Nothing my uncle could ever say would ever change my mind."

She glanced down at him, wondering if Cameron Gordon was guilty of maligning the dead.

He didn't say anything further about Cameron, and Beatrice felt strangely relieved. She had held her position for only two days. Yet those two days had been very peculiar ones.

Robert walked to the end of the hall and pushed open the door. Instantly, he was bathed in sunlight. Curious, she followed him and peered into the room.

The windows started midway along the outside wall and stretched up to the ceiling and angled upward. Sunlight flooded into the room, warming the space and tinting it golden. Beatrice felt as if she were inside a bright yellow jewel.

"Isn't it nice, Miss Sinclair?"

"I think it's absolutely perfect," she said, awed.

To the right was the line of mountains, to the left the ocean sparkling in the early-afternoon sun. Ahead were the hills and valleys of the land belonging to Castle Crannoch.

"If nothing else," she said, smiling, "the vista will be an inspiration for your learning, Your Grace. You'll want to become the most learned duke of all, especially viewing your birthright each and every day."

"Do you know you only say 'Your Grace' when you're pleased with me?"

"Do I?" She glanced him and smiled. "Then you should try to make me say it often."

She studied the room. Someone had made this beautiful room a storehouse for empty crates and trunks.

"It will take some time to clear out all this mess. We'll have to remove the trunks and put them somewhere else."

Robert began to drag one out the door. "No, we can't go about this all willy-nilly. We have to have a little organization."

She began to count the trunks. "What we really need is help. It's called division of labor."

"Call one of the footmen."

She glanced at him.

"I'm the Duke of Brechin, Miss Sinclair. I can still command my own servants."

Just when she thought he was uncomplicated and childlike, Robert surprised her.

"Very well, is there a bellpull up here? Or do we need to go down to the second floor?"

He grinned at her, evidently pleased about something. He walked to the end of the corridor and waved his hands at her to get her attention.

She folded her arms over her chest and tapped her foot impatiently.

"Yes?"

Mounted on the wall above his head was a metal triangle. He jumped up to grab it, succeeding on the first try. Wrapping his arms around it, he allowed his weight to carry him nearly to the floor. When he released the triangle, the tension made it bounce back almost to the ceiling.

"What is that?" Beatrice said, coming to investigate the curious instrument.

"It's a fire alarm," Roberts said. "It only rings in the kitchen. In moments we'll have all sorts of servants here."

"Robert Gordon! Have you no sense? You will scare everyone to death."

She frowned at him, but he blithely ignored her.

Within five minutes at least four of the seven servants employed at Castle Crannoch appeared at the entrance to the servants' stair, red-faced and carrying buckets. Just as she'd feared, every single one of them looked terrified.

Beatrice dismissed them all except one footman, who looked less breathless than the others. He and Robert exchanged a glance and a conspiratorial smile, and she wanted to ask him if he'd been Robert's partner in illicit activities before.

Perhaps ignorance was the better course, at least for the moment.

The two of them set about moving the crates from the room while she investigated the trunks. Most of them were empty except for a few wedged into the corner. Two of them were badly damaged, the tops nearly crushed.

She didn't know where to put them. When she'd tried to move them, both felt as if they were full.

"They belonged to my parents," Robert said from beside her. "I wondered where they'd gone." He pointed to another trunk against the wall. "That's my mother's."

"Where should they go?"

"Could they stay here?"

Thankfully he didn't ask they be opened, only that they remain in the room, almost as if both parents would be present during their lessons. She understood, since she had done similar foolish things, such as lighting her father's pipe so the scent of his tobacco would permeate the empty cottage and putting her mother's apron on the cabinet so it looked as if she'd just stepped away.

"Of course they can," she said, smiling.

Robert made an attempt at a smile in return.

Their efforts were rewarded, two hours later, by an almost empty room. They could move a table into the center, leaving space for some bookshelves against the wall. Another discovery they'd made was the fireplace against one wall. A blaze in the hearth would warm the room on even the coldest of days.

The three of them worked together in perfect harmony, the physical labor helping to push aside the frightening events of the morning. When the room was empty, she went in search of something to clean the floor, leaving Robert behind with the footman as company. When she returned from the scullery armed with a bucket and a mop, she found the footman had disappeared, but Robert was still there. This time, however, his companion was a woman.

"You must be the amazing Miss Sinclair."

Staring at her was one of the most beautiful women she'd ever seen. A tall crown of bright red hair was piled on the top of her head and framed a face as smooth and flawless as porcelain. Her green eyes, however, were hard as chips of stone.

"Robert," she said, glancing down at the boy. "Go and ready yourself for dinner."

"I'm not hungry."

Beatrice sighed. Evidently, the child's arrogance had not dissipated completely.

"Your Grace," she said, "remember your manners."

He glared at her, but Beatrice frowned right back at him.

"Very well," he said. He made a perfect little bow from the waist. "Miss Sinclair."

She nodded, pleased with him. He turned and bowed to the redheaded woman. "Aunt Rowena."

"Forgive me," Beatrice said. "I didn't know you'd returned. I'm Robert's governess."

"So I understand. Did you know my husband prior to being employed by him, Miss Sinclair?" the other woman asked in an icy tone.

"No, I didn't."

"Extraordinary, especially since my husband likes to surround himself with attractive women."

Beatrice had never been faced with another woman's instant dislike. Nor had she ever been so certain that another person's antipathy was based on false information and misplaced jealousy.

"You won't like Castle Crannoch, Miss Sinclair. There is nothing here to keep you occupied. Nothing to interest a young woman such as you."

At the risk of sounding insolent, Beatrice remained silent.

Rowena Gordon swept by her and left the room, giving Beatrice the distinct impression life at Castle Crannoch had just gotten more difficult. Coming as it was after this morning's unsettling events, the knowledge wasn't comforting in the least.

Chapter 16

Beatrice finished dressing, tilted the mirror above the bureau and surveyed herself one last time. This was to be her first family dinner, now that Rowena had returned to the castle. Frankly, she would have preferred another tray in her room.

She closed the door quietly behind her and walked down the hall to the Duke's Chamber. As Robert's governess, it was incumbent upon her to ensure that his manners were perfect for this evening. Perhaps a little conversation before they descended to the dining room wouldn't be amiss.

Her knock wasn't answered. Slowly, she turned the handle and pushed the door ajar. The room was empty. Hopefully, Robert had gone down to dinner early and was not hiding somewhere. She really didn't have the energy to find him.

Halfway down the staircase, she gestured to a maid just as the girl was sliding behind a hidden panel.

"Where is the dining room?"

"On the first floor, the third room in the east wing."

She bobbed a curtsy and disappeared from sight, much as Beatrice would like to do. The directions were sparse, but she finally found the room.

Unlike the area where they'd eaten breakfast, the formal dining room at Castle Crannoch was a monument to the family's history. There were claymores, shields, tartans, and banners hanging from the ceiling and the wall, interspersed with hunting pictures and portraits of dogs and horses. It was the most fantastic juxtaposition of really bad art she'd ever seen in her entire life.

To her relief, Robert was already seated at the table. Not at the head of it, but to his uncle's left. Rowena was on Cameron's right. Another place was set far down on the left side of the table, far enough to be considered an insult. She took her place without comment, nodding to the family. The only response she received was Robert's smile.

Dinner was a strange affair. Robert was in rare form, finding the silliest things about which to giggle. Otherwise, however, the young duke minded his manners without being prompted to do so.

Rowena Gordon ignored her for the entire meal. Whenever Cameron addressed a remark in her direction, Rowena affected to study the sconce on the far wall, no doubt measuring the length and width of the candle since the last time she had done so.

Was Rowena Gordon jealous of every female at Castle Crannoch? Was it simply because Beatrice was new or that she'd been hired without Rowena's consent?

"Were you in London long, Mrs. Gordon?" she asked.

Once again, Rowena studied the sconce. Was she going to answer her? Or simply ignore her again? Equal parts of embarrassment and irritation made Beatrice wish she hadn't asked.

"Not long, no. But long enough, perhaps."

"Two months, Miss Sinclair," Cameron said.

"Did you find London to your liking?"

"I enjoyed it as well as I was able, being separated from my husband."

"They say that sooner or later the entire world goes to London."

"Do they?" Rowena smiled absently, in that exasperating way beautiful women do, as if they could not be bothered to curve their lips. Perhaps the effort was too exhausting, and they needed to save their energy for flirtatious glances and fanning themselves.

She should not be so intent upon initiating a conversation with the other woman. Yet, politeness dictated she at least attempt to do so. Rowena, however, was making it exceedingly difficult to be polite.

Finally, the woman looked directly at her, the first time she'd done so during the whole of dinner.

"What are your qualifications to be the Duke of Brechin's governess, Miss Sinclair? Have you impeccable references?"

She had no references.

Beatrice glanced at Cameron Gordon, who was watching her with an inscrutable expression on his face, almost like a cat watching a mouse. There was going to be no assistance from him. Why? Because she'd dared to challenge him this morning?

Once again, she had the thought she'd be better off simply marching down the mountain. She'd find some type of employment. Better yet, perhaps she'd even return to Edinburgh with Devlen when he next visited. Surely in Edinburgh she could find a position with a normal family.

As it was, however, she needed to answer the woman.

"While it is true my stitchery is not very competent," she said calmly, "I can read three languages. I speak French as well as Italian and German, and can converse on a variety of subjects secular or religious. I've helped tutor young men in Latin, and I've had sufficient training in mathematics, geography, and economics."

"It seems you're talented in a variety of tasks, Miss Sinclair. However, you need not narrow your employment to that of a governess. You could be suitable for a diversity of employment, such as a milliner's assistant or a barmaid, for example."

"I've no interest in hats, and while I don't object to spirits because of any moral stance, I simply cannot abide the smell of ale. Oddly enough, the owner of the tavern at which I applied thought I was too old and ugly to be employed by him." She looked directly at Rowena. "I'm gratified you don't feel the same."

She didn't mention she'd no longer had a choice as to what she would do. She had to become employed or sell her body for a meal. "Virtue" was a word having meaning only for the well fed, the warm, and the secure.

Had she simply exchanged one set of problems for another? Perhaps, but the present set of problems came equipped with a well-stocked larder and a salary that had been mentioned in passing but still had the power to make her jaw drop in shock.

She forced a smile to her face, and returned to her dinner, wishing Rowena Gordon had remained in London.

Dinner was excellent, roast beef and duckling, each in a creamy sauce, vegetables, and a wonderful sweet torte that was so light it almost floated off the plate. But Beatrice couldn't help but wonder if being fed, however fulsomely, was enough to offset living a furtive life among people who suspected each other of unspeakable acts and hidden desires.

For the first time, she could understand why Robert didn't want Cameron to know about the incident in the woods. The two of them, boy and governess, exchanged a glance. She smiled, a look of collusion, and vowed to keep his secret.

"I didn't expect to see you home so soon, sir." Saunders stepped back, placed his fingers deftly around the collar of Devlen's snug jacket and helped him skin it off.

"To tell you the truth," Devlen told the other man, "I didn't expect to return home this early."

He walked into his library, satisfied when he noticed his staff had lit all the candles in the sconces and the oil lamps on the mantel and the desk.

"Was the gathering not to your taste, sir? I understand some members of the royal family were to be in attendance."

"They were, Saunders. Edinburgh society was graced tonight with a few inbred cousins and more than enough titles to throw around. They would have, I believe, gladly dispensed with the titles in exchange for another fortune or two. Why is it, Saunders, that the higher up in society one goes, the more one affects not to need money and yet the more one must have it?"

"I'm sure I don't know, sir."

"You may go," he said, dismissing the other man

with a flick of his hand. Saunders disappeared from a room with a relieved sigh.

Devlen was used to being alone, but this last week, he'd begun to crave company. He disliked mysteries, especially those of his own nature. Why was he so restless?

The knock on the door was unexpected, and he turned, waiting.

Saunders peered inside the room, his usual affable appearance marred by a disconcerted expression.

"Sir, you have a visitor."

"At this hour?" He glanced at the mantel clock. Nine o'clock. Not late enough to retire, but certainly too late for a business appointment.

"A Mr. Martin, sir. He says it's vital he speak with you."

Martin was the owner of a company he was thinking of buying. The man had developed a type of percussion powder that interested him. His company, however, was lamentably run, without organization, and in financial chaos. Martin was facing ruin, unless Devlen purchased the sagging company as well as the man's new invention.

Devlen sat behind his desk and nodded to Saunders.

When Martin was ushered into his library, he gestured to the chair opposite his desk.

Martin sat, hat held tightly between his hands.

"Have you thought about my proposal?" Devlen asked.

"I have. I don't want to sell. But I've no choice, have I?"

"You always have a choice. I don't want it said I browbeat you into a decision."

He stood, offered the man a glass of whiskey. Martin took it, drank it too quickly, and set the tumbler down on the edge of the desk. Devlen took his own glass and returned to his chair.

"I want to be partners instead of giving you everything. I'll sell you half."

He raised one eyebrow. "What good is half a company to me?"

Martin didn't answer.

Devlen leaned back in the chair, waiting.

Because I have the knowledge and you don't. Because I'll make you money. Because I'll keep my new invention unless you agree to my terms. All comments Devlen expected to hear from the man sitting opposite him.

Martin, however, simply stared down at his hat and remained mute.

Devlen had no patience with people who couldn't define exactly what they wanted and how they wanted it. A man should always be able to articulate his wishes and goals.

"Well?"

Still, the man didn't look at him.

"Why would it be to my advantage to buy half your company? I'm not used to being a partner. I prefer to own things outright."

Martin looked up. Devlen was horrified to note tears in the other man's eyes.

"It's all I have."

Devlen stood and walked to the window.

A more compassionate man might have given in at that point. But he'd never been judged as exceptionally compassionate. Shrewd, yes. Sensible, certainly. Dogmatic, intense, ambitious, all labels he accepted because society insisted upon tagging its members.

"Are you married, Mr. Martin?" He didn't turn to look at the other man.

"Yes, I am. Twenty years now."

"Do you love your wife?"

"Sir?"

Devlen turned to face the other man. "A curious question, but humor me. Do you love your wife?"

Martin nodded.

"How did you decide you loved her?"

The other man looked confused, and Devlen couldn't blame him.

"Well, it was an arranged marriage, sir. Her father knew my father."

"So, you decided you loved her after a few years?"

Martin smiled. "More like a few weeks. She was a pretty little thing, with blond hair and the prettiest eyes. Hazel-like, but if she wore a blue dress, they were blue. She has this green thing she likes to wear for special occasions, and I could stare at her eyes for hours when she does. It's like they're pools or ponds." He shook his head and stared down at his shoes.

"Do you love her for her appearance, Mr. Martin?"

He rapidly shook his head, his attention still on his shoes. "She's the kindest soul I've ever known. She'll rescue a person as soon as she will a stray dog, Mr. Gordon. You might even say she's rescued me."

"Then your company isn't the only thing you have, Mr. Martin. It's not even the most important thing in your life."

Martin looked up at him curiously. "You believe a man's marriage is more important than his business, sir? Then why have you never married?"

Devlen returned to his desk.

"You haven't given me a good enough answer, Martin. Why should I settle for half?"

Martin had run his company into the ground. He'd taken a brilliant idea and let it fester. Yet, if the man had been able to verbalize an idea, a solution, or even a proposition, he might have, for the sake of experimentation, given the man the money and written it off as a bad debt.

"What I'll pay you is more than your company's worth, Mr. Martin."

"But it's mine."

"Then keep it." He leaned back in his chair. "You came to me initially, as I recall. You asked me to buy your company. Have you changed your mind?"

"I'm ruined if you don't. I've lost everything if you do."

"Then it seems you have some decisions to make."

He stood and picked up a bell on the corner of his desk. When the door opened and Saunders peered inside, Devlen glanced at his visitor again. "See Mr. Martin to the door."

Before the man left the room, he glanced back at Devlen. "Why did you ask me all those questions about my wife?"

"Curiosity, and nothing more."

Martin didn't look convinced. As he turned to leave, Devlen spoke. "I'll give you five days, Mr. Martin. At the end of that time, I'll either buy your company or I'll walk away from my offer."

After the other man left, he returned to the chair behind his desk.

Martin wasn't the only one who needed to make a decision.

He didn't want to sit and work, didn't want to retire, read, or occupy himself in mental pursuits. He was restless, annoyed, on edge. He was never this uncertain of himself. He could always find something meaningful to do. Meaningful, in this instance, translated to expanding his empire. He liked money, liked what he could do with it, enjoyed the power of it, as well as the fact his worth—as far as society gauged it—was built on his bank balance and not his character.

Some would rate him among the most eligible bachelors in Scotland.

There was never a time when his conscience bothered him. Before he made a decision, he analyzed it thoroughly, considering every angle, every permutation of its effect. He was sometimes brutal in his assessment, but he never lied, either to his business associates or those others would classify as his enemies. Perhaps his emotions were involved, but they were so tempered by reason he didn't experience any highs or lows in success or failure. He didn't gloat.

Are you very rich? Does it make you happy?

Beatrice Sinclair. Why was she so often in his mind?

He'd never before met a woman so like him in the directness of her speech. The look of horror on her face when she'd said something particularly pointed was something he'd come to look for more than the comment itself.

Most of the time she acted as if she didn't care what he thought of her.

What *did* he think of her?

She was a woman of Kilbridden Village, a governess to his cousin, an employee, a servant of the family. A woman of mystery.

He returned to his desk and began writing his list for the next day. Every night he did the same, concentrating on the responsibilities he set for himself in the morning. He'd always had the ability to focus intently on a task until it was accomplished. Until it was done, he allowed nothing or no one to interfere.

His life was marked by goals, never further from his mind than a thought.

Ever since he had left school, he'd known exactly what he wanted: to be richer than anyone he knew, to own more property than any other Scotsman of his acquaintance, to create an empire. He'd spent every single day in the accomplishment of these goals.

That was not to say he didn't enjoy pleasure. In seeking enjoyment, he knew a respite would only make him stronger, better, and sharper for the next event, acquisition, or business meeting. He deliberately planned some time in each day for enjoyment, either through a good horse, a relaxing game of cards, or even the attention of a favorite mistress.

He hadn't ridden in days, he wasn't in the mood for games, and the fact he didn't call upon Felicia was a warning so dire it signaled the reason he was annoyed and irritated.

Beatrice Sinclair.

Why her, of all people? Why was she sticking in his mind like a particularly attentive burr?

She was a bit pale, and too slender for his taste. He wondered what a month at Castle Crannoch would do for her. Fatten her up, no doubt, and add luster to her hair. But would being Robert's governess dismiss that stricken look in her eyes?

Strange, he didn't have many protective impulses.

He was known as a demanding lover but a generous one. When he ended a relationship with a woman, he always bestowed something lovely and expensive on her, a gift by which to remember him.

Whenever he saw a recently dismissed mistress in the company of another man at one of the society soirees which nowadays bored him to extremes, she'd be flashing a bracelet, or brooch, or a particularly fine diamond necklace he'd purchased in Amsterdam. He'd nod and she'd incline her head, the two of them utterly polite to each other, conveniently forgetting the last time they saw each other she was flushed from weeping as he'd abruptly ended their affair.

He walked to the window and stared out at the night. Perhaps what he needed to do was dismiss his current mistress and install someone else in her place.

Miss Sinclair?

Hardly the type he'd pick for a mistress. She was too argumentative. Too . . . intelligent? She hadn't discussed hats once in their conversations. Nor had she asked him if he liked her dress in a thinly veiled solicitation of a compliment. He hadn't, of course—her clothing was nearly threadbare. Her hands were too red, her fingers callused. She'd done more than her share of physical work before coming to Castle Crannoch.

She was a prideful thing, with her habit of forcing a smile to her face, one that never quite made it to her eyes. He'd like to hear her laugh, long and loudly, as if genuinely amused. He'd like to buy her chocolate and watch her savor it with delight. He'd like to see her in a red dress, something to flatter her unusual coloring and bring a sparkle to those fascinating light eyes of hers.

He wanted to talk to her again, that's all. A little curiosity had never made him irritable before.

He forced himself to return to his desk and concentrate on his list. He'd just purchased part of a shipyard in Leith along with two new ships, the new clippers that would add to the China trade.

A woman didn't cause this mild irritation; it was simply inactivity.

He wasn't a man like Martin, incapable of deciding what he wanted.

Yet, it was all too clear he wanted Beatrice Sinclair.

Damn it.

Chapter 17

According to Robert, Cameron Gordon had made the library his. Beatrice had no wish to be near him, and with the arrival of Rowena Gordon, it was even less wise.

For a week she and Robert had met in the attic schoolroom. His lessons were done from Beatrice's memory. He wanted to learn geography the most, and they began with the British Empire. She had a love of antiquity, and all too soon they were talking about Egypt and the recent discoveries of an entirely unknown civilization.

The time had come, however, to invade Cameron's library. Consequently, she chose dawn one morning to survey the library shelves for books she needed to continue Robert's education. From what she'd been able to ascertain, his father had grounded him well in the basics. She needed to include Latin, a study of history, and some literature to provide him a well-rounded body of knowledge.

She felt guilty for not having told anybody about the incident in the woods. She felt even worse when she realized there wasn't anyone at Castle Crannoch who genuinely cared about the child. Rowena's attitude had been cold. Cameron's had been critical. Devlen was the only one who'd shown Robert any warmth. Perhaps, if he returned soon, she'd confide in him.

The library door looked like it dated from the castle's origins, the oak studded with many tiny wormholes, and the iron banding pitted and scarred. She pushed down on the latch and opened the door cautiously, half-expecting Cameron to be seated inside. Blessedly, however, he was nowhere in sight.

Beatrice stepped across the threshold and held her breath in delight. She'd expected, perhaps, a few volumes in a room as old and worn as the door. But it was evident someone cared for the library. Of all the chambers, this was the true heart of Castle Crannoch.

The predominant color of the room was burgundy, and it was present on the upholstered chairs sitting before the desk and those in front of the fireplace. The drapes flanking the two large windows on either side of the fireplace were of a burgundy velvet as were the valances embroidered with the crest of the Duke of Brechin in gold.

There was a space behind the desk, and she realized the chair was missing. No doubt to make it easier for Cameron to wheel himself into position. Tall bookcases covered the other walls, and each of them was filled with volumes encased in leather and gilt bindings.

Sconces hung discreetly between the bookcases, and two ornate brass lanterns sat on each end of the desk, on either side of the burgundy leather blotter. She went to the desk and lit one of the lanterns from the candle in her hand. The soft glow was enough to read the spines.

A narrow ladder was propped up against one of the bookshelves. She made her way around the desk and grabbed the bottom of the ladder, pulling it out a little bit more so it would be safer to mount. She climbed the steps, daring herself as she did so. Even though she was not comfortable with heights, and could feel herself trembling, she made herself remain in place.

Her life could not be constrained by her fears.

One by one, she selected a volume, opened it, thumbed through it, and either chose it or rejected it based on a set of criteria only Robert would understand.

She wanted to combine the child's two great needs—talking about his parents and his education. Therefore, she selected volumes that might bring his father to mind, or might have once been selected by the older duke. She chose *Ivanhoe*, because Robert was a seven-year-old boy and such a tale might spark his imagination. The French poets were next, and she thought he might enjoy them because of his mother. By the time she was finished, she'd picked out six books, more than enough to continue their studies.

She took her time descending the two steps, and once her feet hit the floor, she shook her head at her own foolishness. She hadn't been but a foot or two off the floor, and yet it had felt as if it were five times that distance.

Reaching up, she grabbed the books from another step, and with her arms around them, turned in preparation to leave the library.

Devlen Gordon was standing there watching her.

Perhaps another woman would have made a sound of surprise. Or even giggled, and said something silly. "I didn't see you standing there." Or "When did you come in?"

Surprisingly, it felt as if she'd been waiting for him, as if he'd told her somehow in words she couldn't hear, in a language she didn't realize she spoke, that he'd be back, and soon. She'd kept a vigil waiting for him, clicking off the hours and the minutes and the seconds until he suddenly appeared again like a conjurer's trick.

Her arms tightened around the books and she deliberately curved her mouth into a smile. How foolish she should be expecting him and yet didn't want him to know.

He didn't answer her smile with one of his own. His face was solemn, his gaze piercing. He studied her as if he had never seen her before, or perhaps knew her too well, measuring her against some fixed notion of her in his mind.

Beatrice slowly withdrew one book and placed it on the desk beside her.

She was safer with the books in her arms, because without them she'd be tempted to go to him, place her arms around his waist, and lean her head against his chest, waiting for his hands to press against her back to hold her there, immobile and safe.

She removed one more book and placed it beside the first one.

Still, he didn't speak, only stood there with his arms folded, one leg crossed in front of the other. A nonchalant pose, if one could ignore the flex of the muscle in his cheek and the fact that his bearing, while appearing relaxed, was rigid. His shoulders were level, his hands tight on his upper arms, his face unsmiling.

She removed yet another book. Now there were three on the desk and three in her arms.

"I nearly killed my horses because of you."

She put another book on the table.

"I've spent entirely too much time on the road between Castle Crannoch and Edinburgh lately. The distance gives me considerable time for reflection. I've come to believe you're a woman to be avoided."

He moved away from the door and rounded the desk, making a show of studying the volumes in one of the bookcases. He withdrew a slim volume, replaced it, and removed a larger book and studied one of the drawings.

How did she answer him? The air was heavy was silence, and there was a beat to it as if a celestial drummer was measuring off the cadence of their discord.

He turned abruptly and stared at her, the book in his hands no more than a prop, something to justify his being in the library.

It was dawn, and the world outside was waking to yet another day. In some places it would bring delight and grandeur. In others, trauma and perhaps heartache. The circumstances varied with the locale. Some people would forever mark this day upon their internal calendars and say oh yes, this was the day when I lost my loved one. Or this was the day when my beloved was born. Outside this place, in a world regulated by the ordinary, people would go about their lives in decency and squalor, luxury and chaos.

Here, however, the world slowed, and time itself didn't matter.

She put another book on the desk. Now they were

equally matched. He held one book as did she. He walked behind the desk, coming toward her with an implacable and fierce look on his face. She turned and took a step toward him, unafraid and resolute.

"You've been gone nine days," she said.

"And you thought of me nearly every moment, didn't you?"

She extended her hand, the one still holding the book. He took it from her and tossed it on the top of the desk before doing the same with the volume he still held. Their hands met, their fingers entwined.

"Are you Satan himself, Devlen Gordon?" she asked, surprised he knew how often she'd thought of him.

"Some would no doubt say I am," he said, smiling for the first time. "But I don't think such a creature truly exists. We create Hell for ourselves here on earth. Why invent Satan?"

He pulled her to him with the most gentle touch, but she suspected he might be more forceful if she didn't acquiesce. She took two more steps toward him. Just their linked fingers joined them. Or perhaps it was their willingness to dare convention.

She wondered if her gaze was as smoldering as his, or if he could read a flicker of uncertainty there. Had she imagined it in his gaze?

Devlen Gordon had no vulnerabilities. No weaknesses. She almost smiled at that thought. There was not a man or woman alive who did not have his own share of fears. The wise person knew his and compensated for the lack. The fool pretended he was never afraid.

Which one was Devlen?

He was intelligent, charming, direct, and forceful. She doubted if he was also a fool. He would be wise to be afraid, wise to be cautious of what flowed between them. The emotion was too strong to be usual or normal.

Outside, she could hear the wind battering the castle. Overhead, the clouds raced to hide the dawn sun. It would be a stormy day, almost as tumultuous as this particular moment.

Slowly, he lowered her hand and took a step backward. One single step. A test, then. She knew it without his saying a word, just as she knew she was going to close the distance between them.

Beatrice took one step forward and raised her right hand to place it on the wall of his coat. The fabric was so thick she couldn't feel him beneath it, had no measure of his warmth or his heartbeat. She wanted to tunnel through all the layers of material until she felt him, his skin, his flesh.

She was no doubt doomed to perdition. Or the hell he said they created in their minds. If so, that was a demise she gladly accepted. What a shocking thing, to contemplate dying of pleasure.

He didn't move, didn't say a word when she took one more step, one foot sliding to rest between his. She raised her left hand and placed it on his chest, her fingers brushing back and forth over the fabric.

In the next moment, he reached out both hands and placed them on her arms and drew her gently forward.

He bent his head, and kissed her temple, his lips warm, the touch amazingly soft and amazingly wrong.

"I want you in my bed. I want you naked and impatient."

She shivered, and a feeling like ice traveled up the back of her spine to settle in the pit of her stomach.

Now was the time for her to tremble. Now was the time to feel fear. Instead, the ice heated and bubbled, and the shiver turned to a sigh of anticipation, as if a demon long living inside of her, deeper where she was ignorant and unaware, had suddenly come to life, making its presence known. She was Persephone and he was Hades. Yet there was no good reason for her surrender other than the sheer joy of it.

She hurt in places she shouldn't hurt.

He breathed against her ear. She turned her head and brushed her lips against his bristly cheek. He'd traveled all night to be with her. He traveled in the darkness like a demon, and in the dawn light, he offered her a hint of depravity.

Dear God, she wanted it so.

Her lips stretched across his cheek and rested at the lobe of his ear. Her tongue licked at the very tip of it, and she felt him jerk in surprise. He pulled back and looked at her, a small smile curving his lips.

"Are you a virgin, Miss Sinclair?"

His fingers trailed from her waist, ignoring the press of her breasts against the fabric. His finger traced a T against her bodice just below her neck, as if to demarcate where he would next touch.

As a taunt, it was deliberate. As a tease, it was goading.

What did he want her to say? Touch me? She reached out and, in another daring move, adjusted his hand so it rested over her left breast.

His smile grew wider.

"I am a virgin, Mr. Gordon."

"But an impatient one, I'm thinking. Would you care to alter your state?"

"And become like the girl in the rhyme?"

"What rhyme is that?" He slowly moved his hand so he was cupping her breast, his thumb moving back and forth over her nipple. It drew up tight until it was no bigger than a pebble, aching and sensitive.

"There once was a woman named Charlotte. She began as a virgin and died a harlot."

"Ah, virtue. Another creation of people who invent Hell, I think."

"Such as ministers and clergy? Such as the righteous among us?"

"Good God," he said in a low voice, "do you count yourself among them?"

A shuddering sigh escaped her. "I doubt anyone could think that, with your hand on my breast."

"And you enjoying it."

"I was raised to be good."

"I know."

"I was raised to be good. I was."

"I know. Poor Beatrice."

He held her nipple with his two fingers, the touch keeping her restrained, and shivering with awareness.

"Come to my bed."

"No."

"Come to my bed now, and I'll lure you to do things you've never thought of doing."

"You probably would."

"You would enjoy it, Miss Sinclair. You might even scream in pleasure."

She closed her eyes and forced herself to take one step back from him.

"I want you naked, Miss Sinclair. We'll tease each other until dinner, then feast on one another for dessert."

She took another step away, her breath shallow, her blood too hot.

Then, before he could defeat the better angels of her nature, she grabbed the books and left the room, as if he were indeed the devil.

Chapter 18

Beatrice retreated to the schoolroom, grateful to notice her hands had stopped shaking by the time she reached the third-floor landing. However, the feeling hadn't gone away. Instead, she felt as if a fire was burning inside her body, the flames licking out to touch every exposed inch of skin.

She wanted to be kissed. She wanted Devlen to whisper decadent, immoral things against her cheek. She wanted him to breathe against her ear and touch his fingertips to the nape of her neck. Perhaps trace a path with his thumbs down her throat.

Why was it so difficult to swallow suddenly?

She placed the books she'd taken from the library on the table, straightened her skirt, readjusted her bodice, and pressed her hands against her hair, hoping she looked more presentable than she felt.

Robert would be here soon, and they would have a full day of learning. Perhaps, if the weather cleared, they would go outside and take a walk after lunch. Or perhaps it would be safer simply to remain in the schoolroom, a proper governess. A woman who had a strict code of behavior ingrained in her from birth and acted in a proper fashion except in Devlen Gordon's presence.

What was he doing now? Was he going to leave again soon, and why had he come back? Was it simply to seduce her?

She walked to the window and pressed her fingers against her lips. Her lips felt swollen, as if she'd spent hours kissing him.

Beatrice smiled, recalling a memory. As a girl, she'd practiced kissing the corner of her pillow late at night, a confession she'd never made to another living soul, not even Sally.

She pressed her hands against the window, feeling the cold against her palms and feeling heated inside in contrast. The ice melted on the other side of the glass and slid slowly down to the sill.

He'd touched her breasts and fingered her nipple. She pressed her palm hard against herself, feeling a tingling between her legs. He'd have touched her there if she hadn't fled.

They'd forgotten where they were. He'd not been concerned that the library was his father's lair, or that Cameron Gordon might interrupt them any moment. Then again, neither had she.

Dear God, what kind of creature was she becoming? One of a lascivious nature, that was certain. One who craved the touch of one man. In her very thoughts, she was becoming carnal.

She returned to the table and sat, organizing her

thoughts and forcing her mind from the scene in the library. Dwelling on it would only keep the yearning alive.

Better to wish him gone than to crave her own ruin.

She arranged and rearranged the books, trying to decide where she would begin—with the French poetry or the geography, or with the essays on religion? Or would it be better to concentrate on Robert's reading?

Thumbing through the French poetry intrigued her. She began to read aloud, not having spoken French for a while before coming to Castle Crannoch. The poem she'd happened on had a special significance, as if Providence itself was demanding she aspire to better pursuits than thinking of Devlen Gordon.

> *'Twas thus those pleasures I lamented,*
> *Which I so oft in youth repented;*
> *My soul replete with soft desire,*
> *Vainly regretted youthful fire.*

How could she regret that which she'd never experienced?

Besides, she didn't want to be good, pure, or virtuous anymore. She simply wanted an ease to her life, to wake in the morning and know the day to come wouldn't be frightening, that there was enough food to feed her and warmth to keep her from being cold. She had clothing and an occupation, and some few moments of entertainment, however she devised it. There would be, in this life she created in her mind, a purpose, even if that purpose was simply to exist without pain and without lack. She wanted nothing more than these simple pleasures, and yet it had been more than she'd had for the last three months.

If Devlen was right and we created Hell in our minds, was it done to keep mankind rigorously constrained and proper? If Hell was not real, then was Heaven? If it didn't exist, then were the virtues necessary to achieve an angelic state also false? Decency, kindness, purity, were these all spurious virtues?

Or was she, perhaps, simply seeking an excuse for her depravity?

Who was she to reorder the universe? To question all she'd been reared to believe?

She stood and walked around the table, creating a restless circle from window to door and back again. The first time she circled she clasped her hands tightly together in front of her. The second time, her hands were at her back. The third time, she folded her arms in front of her, and on the fourth occasion, she met Robert coming into the door.

"Good morning, Miss Sinclair," he said, taking his seat at the table as polite and well-mannered as any young boy of her acquaintance.

Beatrice inclined her head and looked at him and mulled over the startling thought that her pupil was becoming better mannered while the teacher was descending into madness.

She sat as well, suddenly deciding which book she'd use to begin their lessons. She handed him a small volume with an intricate sketch of Castle Crannoch on the front cover.

"Did you know your father had written a book?"

He nodded and took it from her. With his arms

rigid on the table, he held the book between both hands, studying it as if it were the most wonderful treasure he'd ever imagined. For the longest moment, he didn't speak, and when he did his voice trembled just a little.

"It's the history of Castle Crannoch," he said. "He worked on it for years and years, he told me."

"Would you like to begin reading?"

He nodded and turned to the first page.

"Aloud please."

At first, his voice was halting, and she wondered if she should spend some time with him on his reading. But then, he became more involved with the words, and his voice lost its hesitancy.

" 'Castle Crannoch,' " he read, " 'was built four hundred years ago by the third Duke of Brechin. What had once been a mound of earth was transformed in two decades to a large and sprawling castle. Although no more than the south tower currently exists of the original structure, it is enough to demonstrate the building techniques, advanced for their era.' "

He continued reading, his voice impossibly young yet filled with pride, not only for his heritage, but for the man whose words he read. She sat back and studied him, wondering what there was about Robert that was so engaging. Upon her first meeting, she could have cheerfully throttled the boy.

When he was done with the passage she congratulated him on his reading.

"My father taught me," he said. "I've been reading ever since I was little."

She wanted to point out that he was still little, then

realized doing so would be foolish. His grief alone had aged him.

But even though he appeared older, he was still only seven. There was a great gulf between the responsibilities he would one day assume and the boy he was now. He was a child, despite having inherited the title and being addressed as Your Grace.

Beatrice realized her duties might well be not those of a governess, but more Robert's protector, especially in view of the shooting incident. How remarkably ill equipped she felt for the task.

They spent the rest of the morning doing math problems. Here, the young duke was as adept as he had been at reading. They'd begun memorizing the multiplication tables when a knock at the door interrupted them.

Her initial reaction was a surge of excitement followed by a frisson of fear. She both wanted to see Devlen and didn't, needed to see him, and knew it would be foolish to do so.

When the door opened, however, it wasn't Devlen but a maid. She placed a tray carefully on the table between the two of them.

"I was sent with your noon meal, miss."

"Is it that late?"

"The rest of the family has already eaten. Mr. Cameron said you must be busy with your lessons to have forgotten and all."

The girl made a quick and perfect curtsy to Robert and backed out of the room, closing the door behind her.

Robert jumped up from his chair, leaned over the table, and peered under one of the covers.

"Soup. I don't like soup."

"Then you've never truly been hungry," Beatrice said, annoyed with him. "If you were, you'd eat anything on your plate and be glad of it."

"I'm the Duke of Brechin. I'll never go hungry."

Evidently, her charge needed some education in something other than books.

"You might go hungry if there is a drought and your lush farmland withers and dies. You might if your cattle grow sick and your sheep as well. You might, if cholera kills all your workers, if the castle itself begins to crumble. You are a fortunate young man now, and I pray your luck always holds. But it's foolishness itself to think your title will protect you from hardship. You've had a lesson in loss already, Robert. Learn from it. You need to become as smart as you can in order to grow into your inheritance, to shield it and protect it for those who come after."

He didn't say anything for a moment, and when he did, his comment surprised her. "My father said the same thing."

"Did he? Then he would be proud of your showing here today. You're a good student."

"I must be, Miss Sinclair. I am the Duke of Brechin. 'To whom much is given, much is expected.' "

"Your father's words?"

He laughed, the first time he'd done so. "No, Miss Sinclair. Thomas of Aquinas."

He peered under the second cover, allowing her time to steep in her own embarrassment for not knowing the quote. "Cook has sent us cinnamon biscuits. I *love* Cook's cinnamon biscuits."

Besides two bowls of steaming soup and the beloved biscuits, Cook had also provided a loaf of crusty bread, and a pot of tea serving both as a beverage and a restorative.

Beatrice cleared off an area at the other end of the table and moved her chair around, bidding Robert to do the same. For a few moments they were occupied with their meal. She only had to correct Robert's table manners twice. Both times he looked annoyed she'd done so, and she responded to his irritation with a bright smile.

Perhaps after lunch she might address the concept of arrogance with the young duke.

She sat back and eyed their bread. She would rather have a biscuit, she decided, and picked one up and nibbled at the edge of it. Cook had outdone herself. She closed her eyes to better savor the taste. When she opened them it was to find the remainder of the biscuits had disappeared from the plate.

Robert smiled at her innocently.

She wasn't fooled. "Are you hoarding those for this evening?" she asked. "So you might have a snack before bedtime?"

His smile didn't dim one whit.

"Or are you planning on eating them all now?"

He nodded.

"I should confiscate them, you know. Or only give one to you after you've completed your geography. But you've done so well this morning I'm going to ignore the fact five biscuits have disappeared."

His smile became a little less feigned angelic and more genuine.

"I do like you, Miss Sinclair," he said.

"Because I let you have sweets?"

"Partly. I also like you because you let me talk about

my mother and father, and because you can keep a secret."

Before she could comment on that startling announcement, he stood, grabbed the loaf of bread, and went to the window. Placing the bread on the sill, he pushed open the window.

"Robert! It's cold outside!"

He stood on tiptoe and peered outside, as if looking for something. He nodded once, as if he'd found it and then grabbed the bread, tearing it into little pieces.

"But the birds are cold, too, Miss Sinclair. My father used to feed them every day. He always said God looks after the sparrows and so must we."

Was he old enough to have learned manipulation? Or could a seven-year-old boy know, instinctively, just how to tug at her heartstrings? Every single time she became annoyed at him, Robert Gordon did something that made her wish to weep.

He stood on tiptoe and continued to toss the bread out the window, feeding the birds in memory of his father.

If she had the power of God, if she were somehow blessed with the ability to raise the dead, she would summon Robert's parents back to Castle Crannoch. Their lives had been taken too quickly and their child had nearly been destroyed because of it. But she was not the Almighty and had no such power. All she could do, in her limited way, was offer what education she'd been given, and protect the child as much as she could.

"Let's keep at your lessons," she said, reaching out and closing the window, then cleaning up the bread crumbs. "You've given the birds the entire loaf. They'll be lucky if they can fly."

"Perhaps they'll waddle," he said, tucking his hands

into his armpits and making silly little flapping motions with his elbows. When she laughed, he pushed out his stomach and walked with his toes turned in.

"An amazing demonstration, Miss Sinclair. Dare I hope other lessons will be more appropriate?"

Robert froze. Beatrice turned toward the door to find Cameron Gordon sitting there. He'd appeared silently, gliding on his leather-bound wheels.

"Mr. Gordon." There was no way to explain to Cameron Gordon they had been indulging in a simple bit of nonsense. Today was the first time she'd ever seen Robert acting like a normal boy.

Robert's uncle raised one eyebrow and stared at her.

He and his son were remarkably alike in appearance. By looking at Cameron, she could almost predict what Devlen would look like in twenty or thirty years. But would Devlen ever be as embittered? Possibly, if his life had been altered by a carriage accident. She couldn't help but think, however, that Devlen would've found a way to turn the entire situation to his advantage.

"We were just finishing our lunch, Mr. Gordon. Thank you for thinking of us."

He didn't respond.

"Robert, if you'll be seated, we'll begin our lessons again."

She glanced at Cameron. "Would you care to observe, sir?" she asked, pulling the door wider.

Instead of entering the room, however, Cameron rolled back into the hallway.

How had he ever made it to the third floor? By the look on Robert's face, he wondered as well. The sanctuary they'd found for themselves was no longer inviolate.

"I think not, Miss Sinclair. But I do expect weekly

progress reports. I would like to know what Robert is learning besides levity."

"His Grace is seven, sir. A bit of levity is not going to alter his character. Indeed, it may add to it."

"You're a very surprising woman, Miss Sinclair."

And one who was going to find herself dismissed if the fact he was clenching his hands on the arms of the chair was any indication. He was obviously annoyed by her comment.

"My only concern is Robert's well-being."

"I commend your loyalty, Miss Sinclair. And your diligence. Time alone will prove whether or not I've made a very great mistake in hiring you."

With that, he slid back into the hall and snapped his fingers. Gaston appeared, placed his hands on the handles and wheeled him away.

A sigh escaped her as she closed the door.

"Are we in trouble, Miss Sinclair?"

"I'm very much afraid we are," she said, and pushed away a feeling of doom.

Chapter 19

Devlen realized that he was a fool to return to Castle Crannoch so soon after leaving.

There were a dozen women he could have called upon in Edinburgh if he'd grown tired of Felicia. Any one of them would have been pleased to see him. Some of them would have urged him to extend his stay until morning. Instead, he'd traveled through the night to have an assignation in the library with a young miss who intrigued him every time he saw her.

How did she do it?

With a directness he found curiously erotic. He was not a satyr by any means, but neither was he inexperienced. Beatrice Sinclair made him feel as if he were a hybrid of the two.

She was a distraction he didn't need at the moment. She could complicate his life. She *had* complicated his life already.

Why, then, was he anticipating dinner like a schoolboy? Why was he taking special care in his appearance? For that matter, why had he made a special trip to his tailors to ensure his newest suit of clothing was completed? Not for his father's sake, his stepmother's, or even his own.

He wanted to dazzle Miss Beatrice Sinclair. He wanted her to be cognizant of the fact other women saw him and admired him. If nothing else, she should be aware it was a great privilege and honor for him to single her out for his attention.

He had no business seducing a governess, or even dreaming about her. She was better left alone with her books and her quill and that studious little frown between her eyes. He didn't want to recall the dawning confusion her smile awoke in him.

He looked down at his hands and thought it was a test of his will that he could still feel her. The scent she wore was either fashioned from lilies or roses or something curiously and simply Miss Beatrice Sinclair.

His tailor had told him the blue wool of his coat was flattering. He'd only glanced at the man, momentarily discomfited by the look of admiration on the tailor's face.

Instantly, he'd thought about Beatrice and wondered if she would think the same.

He didn't know the chit. His only encounters with her had been odd ones. Yet during each and every occasion in her company, he'd felt enlivened, and strangely excited. Even when she attempted to defuse his lust and spear him with her intellect.

No, she certainly wasn't a bit of fluff, but neither was she someone who should bedevil him in quite this manner. Bed her and be done with it. Go to her room and make love to her all night long. Give her what she invited with those long fluttery lashes and that wise little smile. Wear her out. Wear himself out. That should ease the enchantment, or the momentary loss of his reason.

The image of doing exactly that gave him a few uncomfortable moments as he adjusted his trousers. Dinner would prove to be an interesting affair, especially if she gave him those sidelong glances of hers. He would be hard-pressed to make it through the meal.

She was a virgin. He made it a point not to bed virgins. They were too much trouble. The first time was rarely successfully executed, and he didn't want to be the source of pain to any woman.

Virgins were for marriage, not for fun. Marriage could wait. He wasn't overly eager to form an alliance with another family and have it consummated with a show of bloodletting. No, virgins were for later, when one was unavoidable.

He should have stayed in Edinburgh. He should have devoted himself to matters of work such as the contract to purchase Martin's company if the man came to some decision.

If the need for a woman grew too strident to ignore, he'd simply call upon his mistress. Felicia was pouting lately that he hadn't visited her often enough. Perhaps she'd do better with another protector.

He'd managed to come full circle in the matter of Beatrice Sinclair. Now, he was reluctant to go down to dinner. Perhaps it would be wiser for him to turn around and go back to Edinburgh with the alacrity he had made the journey from the city.

Devlen shook his head at his reflection, patted the silk stock in place, adjusted his sleeves once more, and inspected his immaculately polished shoes. He looked the perfect picture of a wealthy man. Thank God the image he portrayed didn't reveal his confusion and his sudden annoyance.

He needed to get her out of his system—assuage his curiosity, that's all. Once he learned a little more about her, she'd just be one more woman. Just one of many.

An hour before dinner, Beatrice finished dressing and made a decision. She strode down the corridor, knocked on the duke's door, and waited until she heard Robert's voice before entering his room.

Every lantern in the room had a fresh candle now flickering against the darkness. Robert was sitting on the floor in front of the bed on a large circular carpet. Arrayed in front of him were at least a hundred toy soldiers. A sheet from the bed was bunched up on one side and formed a mountain range.

He studiously ignored her, while she overlooked the fact he was being rude.

"It's very unusual for a child of your age to be with adults every night. If you weren't the duke, you'd be having your dinner with me in the schoolroom. Would you like to do that tonight? A tray, either in the schoolroom or your sitting room?"

Without looking up, Robert said, "You just don't want to be around my uncle."

"You will not stay seven years old, will you?" She shook her head. "Whenever I think you're just a boy, you say something very old and very wise."

Robert glanced up. "I feel the same way about him. My insides always get knotted up when I go down to dinner. Sometimes, I'd rather say I was sick."

"Since you've been so honest with me, I've no choice but to reciprocate. I doubt he will allow us to avoid the dinner table completely. But you look very tired today. You've spent an entire day on your lessons. I don't want to insist that you come down to dinner when you could fall asleep in your chair."

He nodded, a slow smile coming to his face. "I am very, very tired, Miss Sinclair. But very, very hungry."

"Very well, Your Grace, if you insist," she said, sighing dramatically. "I'll ring for a tray."

"Could we, perhaps, have more of Cook's cinnamon biscuits?"

"I concur," she said. She turned and left the room, grateful she wouldn't have to suffer Rowena's glowers and Cameron's intensity for one meal. Not to mention that she was pointedly avoiding Devlen Gordon—or attempting to do so.

Less than an hour later, they were seated in the sitting room attached to the Duke's Chamber, at a large circular table that had been placed in the center of the room in front of the fire. The drapes were still open, revealing the night sky, cloudless and deep, the stars flickering like the windows in Kilbridden Village. The evening was the most pleasant time she'd ever spent at Castle Crannoch.

Their dinner done, she and Robert were attempting to fairly divide up the cinnamon biscuits Cook had sent them.

"If you eat too much," Beatrice said, "you won't be able to sleep."

"I can't sleep very much anyway," Robert said with some degree of equanimity. He reached for two of the biscuits and slid them onto his plate with no apology. "But if you eat too many, Miss Sinclair, you won't be able to fit into your dresses."

Beatrice folded her arms and rested them on the table, staring at her charge. He grinned and took a bite of the purloined pastry.

"You aren't supposed to notice a woman's attire," she said, curiously embarrassed by his comment. "At least not at seven years of age."

"You'll find Gordon men are prodigies in the realm of women, Miss Sinclair. We tend to notice females early in my family."

She removed her arms from the table and sat back in the chair, not looking in the direction of the doorway. His voice was similar to his father's, but Devlen's was lower, almost a purr.

"Devlen!"

Robert abandoned his dessert, leaving the table and throwing himself at Devlen with an exuberance only demonstrated by young boys. She turned her head to witness the reunion, smiling at his excitement. Devlen bent down and effortlessly elevated the boy until they were eye to eye.

"I've been gone less than a fortnight. Has Miss Sinclair been mistreating you that much? If I'd known, I'd have returned much sooner." He glanced at her, but his look wasn't teasing. Instead, something flickered in his eyes, a look recalling this morning and their almost kiss.

"We found a schoolroom, Devlen. We cleaned and cleaned, and it's where I take my lessons now."

"Have you? No more sitting room for you, then?"

Robert shook his head from side to side.

"I missed you at dinner," he said, not looking in her

direction. The comment was for Robert, and not for her, but she couldn't help but feel a frisson of pleasure nevertheless.

"If I'd known you were here, Devlen," Robert said, "we would have come down to dinner." He glanced over at her. "Did you know Devlen had returned, Miss Sinclair?"

"Yes," she said. "I did."

Robert frowned at her. "You should have told me."

"And I will do so in the future," she said, carefully smoothing the napkin on her lap.

She wished she had the power to read thoughts. The look Robert was giving her right at this particular moment was so inscrutable she'd no clue to what he was thinking.

"Are you annoyed with me, Robert?"

He remained silent.

"Very well, Robert, whenever your cousin returns to Castle Crannoch," she promised, "I will make sure you know immediately."

Robert nodded, evidently satisfied.

Devlen turned and addressed his remarks to Robert. "Let this be a lesson to you about women, Robert. They twist the truth from time to time. The sin of omission is as great a sin as a lie."

"Are you lecturing Robert on virtue, Mr. Gordon?"

"No, Miss Sinclair, simply on women. As a species, they're not the most forthcoming of creatures."

She stood and faced him. "Have you been wounded by a woman in your past?"

His eyebrow arched and tugged a corner of his mouth with it. "Not to my knowledge."

"No unrequited loves?"

"Indeed not."

"Were you left at the altar?"

"Since I've never proposed to a woman, that would be an impossibility."

"Has a woman ever stolen anything from you?"

"Just my time."

"And your good name? Has it ever been besmirched because of a woman?"

"Isn't that normally what happens to women, Miss Sinclair?"

"Then why your antipathy? Before you continue lecturing Robert, perhaps it would be wiser for you to remember that it was not a woman who betrayed Jesus with a kiss."

"Let that be another lesson to you, Robert," he said, his gaze never veering from her face. "Do not trade barbs with an intelligent and beautiful woman. You will lose most of the time. When your mind should be on the next rejoinder, you'll be thinking how fetching she looks in candlelight. Or in dawn light, for that matter."

"And if you would like to know anything about your own species, Robert, then please be advised there are times when men are ruled by their baser instincts and not their higher ones. The mind is to be obeyed, but too often it is the loins that rule a man."

"Spoken as a woman not unaware of her capacity to stir the loins," Devlen said, smiling an altogether wolfish smile.

Theirs was hardly an appropriate topic of conversation, especially since Robert was looking from one to the other as if he were thoroughly enjoying the sparring.

She smoothed her hands down her skirt, thinking it would be better to make a hasty retreat from this room as soon as possible. Certainly before Devlen Gordon moved closer to her.

He looked splendid. He was dressed in blue, so dark it looked almost black. His eyes were crinkled at the corners as if he had spent a great deal of time outdoors or in the act of smiling. His teeth were white and even. His neck. Her thoughts stopped. Why would she suddenly notice a man's neck? Because even his neck, the part that appeared above his stock, was splendidly made. Everything about him was glorious, from his broad shoulders tapering to a narrow waist and long legs that were so muscled she could see the hint of their shape below the fabric of his trousers. And it wasn't entirely fair a man had such an attractive backside.

That was one subject she and Sally had never discussed, the fact a man could look as attractive from the rear as he did from the front.

The longer she was in the same room with him, the worse her agitation became. All day long, she had not been able to stop thinking about him. Seeing him here so finely attired, so handsome and utterly charming, was a guarantee she wouldn't be able to sleep well either.

Perhaps she and Robert should keep themselves company tonight. She'd play games with the boy through the long hours, anything to avoid experiencing this fevered longing for Devlen Gordon.

Touch me. The need was so strong she almost said the words. The yearning was there in the clasp of her hands tightly at her waist, in the fact she couldn't look up at him but stared at the pattern of the carpet under her feet.

She would have to pass him to leave the room, but coming too close to him was as dangerous as teasing the flames in the fireplace with her petticoat.

He was tall, large, and commanding. In addition, he smelled as he had before, the scent reminding her of spices and hinting at exotic locales. Never before had she noticed how a man smelled. Not once had she ever wanted to touch someone as desperately as she did now, or have him touch her. Just a fingertip, please, on the edge of her jaw, or tracing the curve of her lips.

Or, and this could be too much to ask for, then give her a kiss. Just one kiss, and she would be satisfied until the next dream, or the next time she saw him, or the next time she felt lonely.

A dangerous man, Devlen Gordon.

"Are you leaving us?"

"Yes, I must concentrate upon my lesson plan for tomorrow. I must admit," she added, smiling down at Robert, "that I didn't expect my pupil to be so advanced in so many ways. It will mean I will have to reassess what I plan to teach him."

"Indeed. Will this lesson plan take so much of your time you must leave now?"

"Are you implying something else, Mr. Gordon?"

"Every time we meet, you seem anxious to depart. Have I offended you somehow?"

He knew it wasn't that.

"May I join you in the schoolroom tomorrow?"

"Please don't," she said, too quickly for it to be anything but rude. "I prefer you don't," she said, amending her statement. "It disrupts the learning process," she said, and smiled, genuinely relieved to have come up with some plausible explanation.

"When will I see you again?"

"Why is it necessary to do so?"

"Perhaps I'm concerned as to my cousin's education."

"No."

"No?"

"It wouldn't be wise."

"I don't like being told what's wise or not, Miss Sinclair. When you know me better, you'll realize it's a challenge. I'm not a man to back down from challenges."

"Nor am I a woman to avoid them, Mr. Gordon. But don't take it as a challenge. Rather a plea."

"I can't."

She faced him finally, tilting back her head.

"I've come all this way. What a pity if the journey is wasted."

Robert was being too quiet, his interest in this conversation too apparent. If nothing else, she must think of him. She moved past Devlen and out into the hall. Unfortunately, Devlen followed her.

"When are you returning to Edinburgh?"

"I have no plans at the moment. The length of my stay depends on nothing more than my whim."

"There are no doubt matters awaiting you in Edinburgh."

"But none here? I think you're wrong, Miss Sinclair. I think there are pressing concerns at Castle Crannoch."

"Do you have a mistress?"

He smiled as if charmed by her rudeness.

"I do. Felicia is her name. A lovely woman, quite talented in a variety of ways."

"Go back to Felicia. She no doubt yearns for your presence."

"While you don't?"

"I do not, Mr. Gordon."

"I think you're lying, Miss Sinclair. A governess ought to be a paragon of the virtues she thinks to instill in her pupils, don't you agree? How can you possibly teach Robert to be an honest man if you lie?"

"I must leave," she said, hearing the quaver in her own voice and hating it. Not because it revealed her trembling uncertainty, but because every time she was around him her fascination about him grew. He knew it, surely he must.

"I must leave," she repeated, and this time he stretched out his hand to touch her as she moved past him. His fingertips grazed her hand at her waist.

She halted for a moment, and they exchanged another look. Slowly, his fingers dropped from her hand.

"I'll not keep you, Miss Sinclair. Sleep well and deeply."

The look on his face didn't quite match the amiability of his words. In fact, he looked as if he wished her a sleepless night, and tormented dreams. She didn't tell him it was altogether possible he would get his unspoken wish.

"You look disappointed that your little governess wasn't at dinner," Rowena said, standing at the threshold of Cameron's room.

She was surprised he'd answered the door or that Gaston was nowhere in sight. Was this a sign of his softening toward her? Cameron wheeled himself to the other side of the room, and Rowena closed the door behind her.

Could it be he was lonely?

"On the contrary, my dear wife, it was my son who looked bereft. Didn't you notice? Any interest I express about Miss Sinclair is simply because I'm concerned about Robert's well-being."

"To the exclusion of anyone else."

He didn't say anything, only sat and studied her. He hadn't lost his looks in the last six months. Her longing for him would have been easier to bear, perhaps, if he had.

"I admit, she is lovely, but not your type. I've always thought you liked a certain dramatic sort of woman."

"Like you, Rowena?"

She smiled.

"Like me, dearest Cameron. Except, of course, you haven't given any indication of liking my looks of late. Strange, I thought your legs didn't work. Not your manhood."

He looked startled at her bluntness. She had never before assaulted him with words. She'd attempted to seduce him. She'd hinted at her loneliness, and when nothing else worked, she'd taken herself off to London, only to realize the only way to storm the citadel was by a direct and frontal attack.

She'd no intention of allowing someone like Beatrice Sinclair to take one iota of her husband's attention away from her.

"She's frightened of you, you know. I don't know if it's because you're in that chair or simply because she doesn't like you."

"How did you come to that conclusion?"

"She avoids you at all costs, does she not?"

"What Miss Sinclair does or does not feel for me is none of my concern, Rowena."

"I could have told her, of course, that you were kinder when you were walking. You've changed, Cameron, become more angry, more embittered, more annoyed with life."

"Is there a reason for this litany of my sins, Rowena?"

"You have always enjoyed my humor, Cameron. You once said you enjoyed my intelligence. Perhaps you'll come to admire my bluntness."

She advanced on him, then changed her mind and walked toward the door and locked it.

A small smile was playing around his lips, and it angered her. She wanted to punish him for all of his avoidance, for the nights in which she'd lain awake desperate for his touch. Now, however, was not the time.

She pulled up a chair and sat beside him, loosening her wrapper. She was naked beneath the thin garment and the cold had tightened her nipples, making them as hard and erect as if she were aroused.

He didn't need to know she was almost desperately afraid at this moment, afraid he would reject her. She reached out and grabbed his hand and pulled it to her, placing his palm over her nipple.

"How you used to love my breasts, Cameron. You used to love to touch them, to pull on my nipples. To taste me."

Despite the fact he was attempting to pull his hand away, she was stronger in her need than he was in his annoyance. She took two of his fingers and deliberately stroked herself with them.

"Do you remember being inside me, Cameron? Do you remember when we would exhaust ourselves with each other?"

Before he could respond, before he could pull away and renounce her with words that would no doubt hurt and wound, she reached out her left hand and gripped him between the legs.

"You're hard for me. What do you do every night?

Do you will it away? Or you think of your Miss Sinclair and bring yourself to satisfaction?"

"I am but an animal in several ways," he said, allowing his hand to drop. "The sight of a lovely woman, any lovely woman, is enough to get me hard."

She pulled back. "Why do you hate me?"

"You know the answer to that, madam, more clearly than I could ever articulate."

"We've only been married five years, Cameron. Five years. Am I to live like this for the rest of my life?"

"Go back to London, Rowena. Find yourself a lover."

He wheeled himself to the door, turned the lock, and swung it open.

"Or coax one of the footmen to your bed, I don't care. Just don't come here again."

She stood and pulled her wrapper around her, affecting a nonchalant pose she didn't feel.

He didn't say another word to her as she left his room.

Chapter 20

Surprisingly, Beatrice slept well, waking at dawn as she normally did. This morning, like her entire stay at Castle Crannoch, was different from the mornings of the past three months, however. She was not awakened with a raging headache, an empty stomach, and an obsession for food.

She'd have liked some of the biscuits from last night, but she doubted if Robert had left any. Never mind, she'd find something to eat.

Dressing took no more than fifteen minutes, talking to herself sternly took a half an hour.

You will not flirt with Devlen Gordon.

You will not even look in his direction.

You should not wish for excitement. Or adventure. You have had enough of those since coming to Castle Crannoch.

There was something to be said for a placid life, for a sameness of routine. Ah, but that life didn't include people like Devlen Gordon, handsome and dangerous. She sighed.

Ensuring every hair was in place, and her attire was suitable for a governess took a little longer, as did washing her face and staring at herself in the mirror until the color on her face subsided. Her eyes sparkled too much, but she doubted if there was anything she could do about that. She tried to think sober thoughts, but her mind was not cooperating either.

An hour after she rose, she walked down the hall in search of her charge.

There was time before breakfast for a brisk walk. Doing so would no doubt enliven the constitution, and make it easier to sit for hours in the schoolroom during lessons.

When she mentioned as much to Robert, he looked startled at the suggestion.

"Miss Sinclair, do you think it's safe?"

Until that moment, she'd forgotten about the shooting incident. What kind of governess was she, that she could forget such a horrid thing?

"We'll stay close to the castle," she said. "But we need some fresh air. And despite the fact it's cold, it looks to be a fair day."

In fact, it was nothing of the sort. The sky was cloudy, and it looked like snow, but her mood was such it could have been a bright summer day.

She bundled Robert up in his greatcoat while she wore her dark blue cloak. Once they were out of the castle, she turned to Robert.

"Are you going to tell your cousin about what happened?"

He looked straight ahead, and she wondered if he

was going answer her. After several silent moments, he sighed.

"Do you think I should?"

They walked for a few minutes, rounding the front part of the castle.

She hadn't expected him to ask her opinion. She turned the question on its ear and back to him. "Do you think you shouldn't?"

He stopped abruptly, and stood there thinking. After a moment, she noticed he was trembling.

"Robert? What is it?"

He raised his arm and pointed, his finger shaking.

"Look, Miss Sinclair. The birds."

She followed his glance, then walked past him, staring down at the dozen or more birds lying dead on the ground, their plump gray bodies surrounded by a few chunks of frozen bread.

"Go and get Devlen," Beatrice said, as calmly as she could.

Robert didn't ask any questions, only set off in a run to obey her.

She thrust her hands into the cloak and tried to assume an aura of nonchalance, of outward calm. Inside, however, she was panic-stricken. She clasped her hands together, and stood looking down at the dead birds. Above them was the schoolroom. She tilted her head back and viewed the window where yesterday Robert had been so excited to be feeding the birds. If she thought about what she saw, she might well scream. Or run as far from Castle Crannoch as she could.

Neither action would be helpful or productive.

Despite her resolve, however, she couldn't help but

feel the first cold icicles of fear. Someone was trying to harm Robert. First, the shots, which she had tried to pretend were an accident, and now the birds. This, however, was even more horrible. Someone had actually poisoned his food. Someone inside Castle Crannoch. Someone who wanted a child dead.

Who?

Was Cameron Gordon so bitter about being disinherited by a seven-year-old child that he'd want Robert dead?

Another icicle of fear slid down her back. She could have easily eaten the bread, too.

If it hadn't been for the child, she might have given her notice on the spot. Though poverty, the loss of her pride, possibly even starvation was all that awaited her back in her village, at least she would be alive, and it's doubtful anyone would care enough to wish her dead.

Beatrice heard the running footsteps and felt an easing of that curious, immobilizing fear. She turned her head and watched as both Devlen and Robert entered the clearing.

Devlen didn't say a word either in greeting or reassurance. He glanced down at the dead birds, looked up to the window high above, then bent to retrieve a piece of the bread.

"Did I poison them, Devlen?" Robert asked, his small voice out of keeping with his usual bravado.

He was an intelligent child. Too intelligent, perhaps. Surely she should say something to assuage his worry, to ease his mind. But she had never been a good liar. There was no hope of sheltering him or shielding him from the truth. But she reached out anyway and enfolded him in her arms, pressing his cheek against her waist.

She spoke to him the way a mother might, saying, "It's all right. It's all right." Nonsensical words, in actuality, because she wasn't at all sure things were going to be all right. But he didn't challenge her, only held on to her waist with both arms, as if she had suddenly become his anchor.

Even through the heavy wool of his coat, she could feel him tremble, and suddenly the child's fear made her angry.

Devlen stood, and she looked up at him, her eyes dry and furious.

"This is not right," she said. "For whatever reason someone is doing this, it's not right." She glanced down at the child. "Tell him, Robert," she urged.

He looked up at her, then over at Devlen.

"He'll get mad."

"I doubt he will."

"Why am I being talked about as if I'm not standing here?" Devlen said. "What will I get mad about, Robert?"

"He won't get mad, Robert. I promise," she added, glancing at Devlen.

He nodded.

Robert told him about the shooting. As the story progressed, she watched Devlen become more and more rigid until his spine could have been made of iron.

"Go and pack your things," he said.

Her grip tightened on Robert. "You do not have the power to dismiss me. Nor will I leave."

"Your loyalty is admirable," he said in an unconscious repetition of his father's words earlier. "However, I have no intention of dismissing you. Pack Robert's things as well. You're coming to Edinburgh with me."

Robert was in danger, but then again so was she. Not, this time, from someone who wanted her dead. As they exchanged a look, she knew full well if she went to Edinburgh with him she might well be putting herself in peril.

"Will you come?" he asked, his voice soft, low, and dangerous.

She had no choice, and yet she had a world of choices.

"Yes," she said, in agreement with her own ruin.

Devlen turned to his cousin.

"Would you like to come to Edinburgh, Robert?"

Robert pulled back, releasing his grip on Beatrice's waist.

He nodded. His eyes were red, traces of tears still on his cheeks. Beatrice smoothed his hair back and placed her palm on his hot cheek, feeling an incredible tenderness for the young duke.

"Then we should go and pack," she said. "Shall we make a game of it? Who'll be the first to finish?"

"You, Miss Sinclair. I have so much more than you. I must take my soldiers, you see."

"Do not pack too much, Robert," Devlen said with a smile. "Think of my horses."

She forced an answering smile to her face and took Robert's hand. There were times as an adult when she had to feign an emotion until it was real. But now she found herself in the curious position of having to hide what she felt.

"I'm half-tempted to put you in a carriage now, without giving you time to pack. How soon can you be ready?"

"A quarter hour," Beatrice said, shortening the time she needed by half. But she was nearly desperate to leave Castle Crannoch, and if doing so quickly meant her valise was packed in haste and her clothing was wrinkled, she truly didn't care.

"Then do so," he said. "I'll have my coach brought around."

She walked with Robert to the front of the castle, realizing she could easily have abandoned anything in her room. She didn't feel comfortable staying at Castle Crannoch anymore. Something was desperately wrong here, something so evil and pervasive it seeped through the very bricks.

Suddenly, she wanted her old life back. Not the way it had been a month ago, but as it was a year ago, with her parents alive and her content, if a little restless.

She had wanted something to happen, and dear God it had, but not quite in the way she'd expected. Was God a literal deity? Should she be careful about the wording of her prayers?

Then let her amend them. She wanted peace in the morning and a feeling of contentment during the day. She wanted laughter and lightness in her heart, and a dozen other pleasant emotions.

"Is it going to be all right, Miss Sinclair?"

"Of course it is," she said crisply, her voice conveying no uncertainty, no hesitation. Robert mustn't know of her own fears.

Less than half an hour later, they left Castle Crannoch. Together, she and Robert walked slowly to the coach, all the while Beatrice expecting to hear her name being called. But Cameron Gordon didn't shout for her to return with her charge. No one knew they were leaving.

She opened the coach door herself and unfolded the steps, urging Robert into the carriage. She followed him and sat next to him, taking his hand and holding it between her ungloved ones. The day was cold, the hint of snow still in the air, but someone had thought to furnish a brazier and it sat on the floor of the carriage, the glowing coals inside the pierced brass vessel radiating heat.

"I think someone's trying to kill me, Miss Sinclair."

"Don't be silly," she said, her voice pure governess. "The incident in the woods was a hunter, and the poor birds outside the schoolroom window had just frozen to death. The temperature is cold enough for it."

Robert didn't look convinced.

Finally, she relented. He was too intelligent, and she'd been too dismissive. "I don't know what's happening, Robert. But I don't like it."

He nodded, as if he approved of her honesty.

She opened up the shade.

"I think it's going to snow soon, Robert, perhaps during our journey to Edinburgh."

He nodded and stared out the window. She would much rather have him be acting like the aristocratic little snob she'd first met than this silent waif.

"Do you like the snow, Robert?"

He shrugged, but otherwise didn't answer her.

"I like the snow very much," she said, well aware she was sounding a little like a woman she knew in her village. The poor dear had a comment about anything and everything, and couldn't manage a quiet moment in the entire day. "I think it's beautiful to see, especially when it clings to the branches of the trees. At night, when it snows, it's like a full moon. The night is not quite so dark, is it? Snow seems to glow."

A thought struck her, one tinged with horror. Had someone tried to kill Robert in his sleep? Was that why the child was plagued with wakefulness?

I think someone comes into my room at night.

Dear God.

"I don't think I've ever seen the snow at night, Miss Sinclair," he said, looking interested.

"Then we'll just have to arrange it, won't we?"

"My father used to say you can't arrange nature. If we could get rain when we needed it, all farmers would be wealthy men."

"I think I would've liked your father." The eleventh Duke of Brechin sounded like a very pragmatic man with a generous spirit, a father who honestly loved his child.

The door opened, and Devlen stepped into the coach. Instantly, it felt warmer inside, and much smaller.

His fingers brushed against her skin in passing, alerting the fine golden hairs on her arms.

Gently, she pulled away, disliking the touch. No, liking the touch, but disliking the feeling of vulnerability being so close to him gave her.

He made her feel weak and feminine, as if she needed his strength and the very fact he was male. She wanted him to put his arm around her and hold her close, shelter her, protect her. She'd never before had such thoughts.

Devlen gave the signal to his driver, and the carriage began to move. Blessedly, he concentrated on the passing scenery and the faint flutter of snow.

"Do you still have your guns in here?" Robert suddenly asked.

Devlen smiled. "I do. I carry them with me at all times."

"In case of robbers," Robert said to Beatrice. "Devlen sometimes carries a lot of gold with him."

"Really?"

"I only carry the pistols to protect myself." He reached over and pushed against the wall of the carriage. Instantly, a small rectangular section popped open, revealing two gleaming guns mounted inside. "I dislike being unprepared."

"Have you ever used them?"

"Once."

"I trust you will not have to do so on this journey."

"I will protect that which I believe to be valuable."

What did he consider valuable? Or whom? His cousin, surely. Her? A woman who'd exchanged barbs with him, a village inhabitant with an expansive education taught by books but little experience in life. Would he consider her as valuable?

He said something to Robert, who smiled in return, the exchange one of longtime friends, confidants, almost brothers.

The descent down the mountain was done with some caution, she was happy to note. There was little need for haste even though she wanted to be as far from Castle Crannoch as she could be, as quickly as possible.

She glanced at Robert to find him yawning. "You didn't sleep well last night," she said.

He only nodded.

Robert shifted in the seat, leaning his head back against the cushion. She spread the blanket over his legs.

"You can put your feet up here," she offered, "if you'd like to stretch out a little more."

"It isn't polite," he said, once more the proper young duke.

Beatrice smiled, amused that Robert vacillated between an old-fashioned courtliness and an autocratic arrogance.

She patted her lap, and he was finally convinced to prop his feet up on the lap robe. He arranged one of the blankets behind him as a makeshift pillow and burrowed beneath another until only his nose showed.

Within moments, he was asleep.

In the snug carriage, with the brazier heating her feet and her legs kept warm from the blanket she and Robert shared, it was difficult to remember they might be in danger.

She pretended an interest in the increasing snowfall, but in actuality she was studying Devlen.

All in all, it was an arresting face, one drawing her gaze time and again. Was she the only woman to feel so attracted, or did Devlen Gordon simply have that effect on all females in his environment? When he walked into a crowded ballroom, did every woman there turn to regard him? Were they coy in their glances? Or did they make no secret of their fascination for him?

He glanced at her then, as if he had the power to understand her confusion and her curiosity. A corner of his lip curled upward, a mocking acceptance of her studious assessment.

"What can you be thinking, Miss Sinclair?"

"I was thinking you must charm women," she said, giving him the truth with no reluctance whatsoever.

He looked momentarily disconcerted, and she vowed from that moment always to be direct with him. Doing so equalized them. He was evidently unfamiliar with those who spoke the truth, and she was equally so with those who spoke falsehoods.

"I have no lack of companions, if that's what you're asking."

"I wasn't, actually. You've already spoken of Felicia. Are you bragging? Or simply letting me know how many women you have?"

"You're very constrained, Miss Sinclair."

"Am I?"

"I've never seen a woman as constrained as you."

"Is that as great a sin in your eyes as the ability to stretch the truth?"

"It's a characteristic that concerns me, oddly enough."

She fisted her hands in her lap and glanced at him. "Why is that?"

"You're too calm. I've never seen you angry, although I've given you ample reason to be. You might be afraid, but you don't appear to be."

"Why should I indulge in drama?"

"Who hurt you, Miss Sinclair?"

For a moment she could only stare at him, flummoxed.

"Was it life itself? Too much unexpected grief? Too many disappointments?"

"Are you this rude to every woman of your acquaintance?"

"Most women don't incite my curiosity. They bore me, instead. But you, Miss Sinclair, are a different situation entirely."

"Should I pray to be boring, Mr. Gordon?"

"It's too late for that. I'm already intrigued."

She looked out the window at the falling snow. The winter scene was starkly beautiful. There was no reason to be touched to tears, but she suddenly wanted to cry. Or worse, confide in him about the previous year, living in the cottage after burying her parents. Systematically burying her friends, too, while she waited for cholera to sicken her.

Over the years, she'd developed her mind, and whenever emotions persisted, she allowed them some freedom before restraining them and tucking them back into their proper place. Even her grief had been similarly controlled. She needed to concentrate on living in the present.

After all, she was pragmatic and practical, a survivor.

She turned to face him again. "Shouldn't you be more concerned about what's been happening to Robert?"

The incident in the woods and the dead birds were enough to be concerned about.

"I'll protect Robert. You needn't worry. For that matter, Miss Sinclair, I'll protect you."

"Physically, Mr. Gordon? Or morally?"

There, the challenge was out in the open.

He only smiled.

An image of his black-on-black coach thundering through the countryside, faintly illuminated by the lanterns on the outside, came to her. He'd terrified her the first time she'd seen it.

She'd be a fool not to be afraid. How odd she wasn't. The emotion coursing through her wasn't remotely like fear.

"For someone who dislikes the dark, you certainly use it to your advantage."

"I don't sleep very much. Three hours at the most. Why waste the time?"

She had no answer for that.

The snow fell in a cloud of flakes, as if they were feathers wafting on the chilled breeze. They clung to every surface, trees, bushes, and grass, transforming the world into a white fairyland, a place so delicate and ethereal it stopped her breath.

Her eyes tickled with unshed tears. An odd moment to cry. Or perhaps the best moment, after all. There was so much loveliness in the world, the same world in which there dwelt so much horror. A paradox, one in which they were forced to live.

She wanted something at this moment, something she couldn't quite define or explain. Something that would answer the restlessness deep inside her. She was either hungry or lonely or distraught and more than a little curious as to why she couldn't identify the feelings completely. Perhaps it was because all this time, she'd cocooned herself, protecting herself from the grief and fear that were too painful to experience on a daily basis. Perhaps she was separated from her own discomfort, like stubbing her toe and not feeling the pain until hours later.

Was she just now recognizing the full extent of her own loneliness?

Devlen Gordon made it difficult not to feel. Every time she was in his presence, she was different . . . alive, somehow. As if he had the capacity to stir her— or awaken her—in some way.

He was too strong a personality, too forceful to ignore. Nor could she avoid the fact that he was so quintessentially male. There were times, like now, when she wanted to reach out and touch him, to see if the muscles hinted at below his shirtsleeves were truly real.

Her gaze was entirely too intent on his trousers. She was even curious about his feet, encased in knee-high boots. His chest looked too broad to be completely real, and she had the absurd and horrified thought that perhaps he wore padding beneath his clothes.

Not Devlen Gordon. He wasn't the type to engage in artifice. He was more the kind of man who would dare society to judge him for what he truly was—handsome or ugly, short or tall, rich or poor.

But of course he was handsome, tall and rich, and the relative of a duke. No doubt he was extremely popular in Edinburgh.

"Why haven't you ever married?"

"Is it any of your concern, Miss Sinclair?"

"None at all."

"You're very curious. In that, we're alike. If I answer your question, will you forfeit one to me?"

She didn't answer for a moment.

"Afraid?"

"Not afraid," she said. "Wise, perhaps."

"Perhaps I'll ask you something improper."

"I expect you to."

"Then why the hesitation?" Devlen asked.

"I'm trying to decide if I'll answer."

He smiled at her again.

"Shall I start then? The answer to your question, Miss Sinclair, is that I've never made the time for marriage."

"The time?"

"Courtship takes a measure of time I've never been willing to spare."

"Not to mention emotion," Beatrice said.

"There is that."

"Have you ever been in love?"

"Ah, but it was only one question. I think it's my turn now. Have you ever been in love, Miss Sinclair? Not an improper question after all."

"No. Never."

"A pity. The emotion is said to be very heady."

"Really?"

"Love makes fools of us all, I've heard."

"Have you?" Beatrice asked.

"Can't you envision me playing the fool, Miss Sinclair?"

"Not unless it was to your advantage, Mr. Gordon."

His smile broadened. "You think me a cynic?"

"Aren't you?"

"Cynicism is just another word for wisdom."

"So, you're too wise to fall in love?" she asked.

"I don't think love has anything to do with wisdom. I think it simply occurs when it will."

"Like a bolt of lightning?"

"Do you believe in love at first sight, Miss Sinclair?"

"No."

He laughed softly. "Now who's the cynic?"

"Why fall in love with someone's appearance? People get sick, or grow old. The character matters more than looks, Mr. Gordon. Wit, intelligence, kindness, all matter more than appearance."

"So, you would have love come after a conversation?"

"Perhaps."

"How long would it take?"

"The conversation?"

His smile chided her. "Falling in love."

"How should I know if it's never happened to me?"

"Perhaps we should talk longer, Miss Sinclair, have a few more conversations."

He looked away, and it was just as well, because she didn't know how to answer him.

Chapter 21

The weather was growing worse. The snow formed a curtain between them and the rest of the world. She couldn't see the trees or the bushes lining the road anymore, and it was evident the driver was having difficulty with the horses as well because their speed had slowed considerably. Twice, the driver had rapped on the small window separating him from the passengers, and twice Devlen had reassured him there was no need for haste.

"Take your time, Peter," he'd said on the last occasion. "We'll make an inn soon enough."

"So, we are going to stay the night?" Beatrice asked.

He sat back against the seat and surveyed her indolently. "The weather has made further travel an impossibility."

"Is it entirely proper?"

"You and I staying at an inn together, chaperoned only by my seven-year-old cousin? You alone can decide the answer, Miss Sinclair."

"I'm not entirely certain I like the way you say my name. It always has a touch of sarcasm about it."

"My apologies, Miss Sinclair. I meant no affront."

She frowned at him.

"Unless we sleep in the same chamber, I'm certain your reputation will remain as pure tomorrow as it is today. Or perhaps I am assuming too much. Is your reputation unsullied?"

She looked over at him, more than a little offended. "Of course."

"Then I should worry about other things, Miss Sinclair. Reputation does not seem to be an important one."

"Possibly because you have none to lose," she said.

But he only looked amused at her comment. "If that is your opinion of me, then you have joined a great many other people. I wonder what it is about me that makes people immediately label me a sinner?"

He glanced at her. "Do you have a great deal of experience in recognizing sinners, Miss Sinclair?"

"My father was schoolteacher, not a minister. But it seems to me with your penchant for dark coaches and traveling at night, you encourage people to think the worst of you."

"Simply because I hate to waste time, I'm now to be punished as an evildoer. How very quaint."

"Perhaps people are afraid of you. They often label as evil what they don't understand."

"Therefore, in order to counter their bad opinion, I should endeavor to make myself understandable?"

"Perhaps."

"The fact is, Miss Sinclair, that I don't care what a great many people think of me. Does my attitude surprise you?"

"Not in the least."

"There are, however, several people whose opinion I do value. Would it further surprise you to know you are among that small and select cadre?"

"Very much," she said, finding it difficult to hold his gaze.

"I find I do care what you think about me. I am not the lecher my father would make me out to be."

"I have not often discussed you with your father."

"But you have discussed me. How novel, an honest woman."

"That's not the first time you've alluded to dishonesty being a female trait. I would venture as many men are dishonest as women."

"On the contrary, it's been my experience that women as a whole do not tell the truth unless it suits their purpose."

"I think perhaps, as a representative of my species, I should be insulted."

"But you aren't, and I wonder why that is? In fact, you're rarely upset, Miss Sinclair. Do you ever cry?"

"A rather personal question, isn't it? I demand a forfeit."

"Very well. But answer first."

"No, I don't cry often."

"Why not? And before you protest, Miss Sinclair, it's only part of the original question. A clarification, if you will."

"Because I've never found tears were worth shedding. Why cry? It will not make the situation easier to bear."

"Do you ever feel any strong emotion? Anger, joy?"

"It's my turn to ask a question."

He sat back and folded his arms, waiting.

"Why do you have such a bad opinion of women? Who hurt you?"

He smiled. "I'm sorry to disappoint you, Miss Sinclair, but no one. If I have a somewhat jaundiced view of women, it's because I only view them as companions for the evening. I have no women friends, and I've rarely spent time with them unless it was in amatory pursuits."

"You should. You'd discover that women do not, as you think, use honesty or the lack of it to manipulate others."

"Then you are very sheltered, Miss Sinclair, because I could show you five or six women in Edinburgh alone who have a singular ability to do exactly that."

Despite his words, she still had the feeling he'd been hurt in the past. But Devlen Gordon was not a person for whom she should have any compassion or pity. First of all, he would be amused at it. Secondly, she doubted those poor women were ever able to harm him. More like he'd broken their hearts.

The carriage slowed even further. She flicked a finger beneath the shade and surveyed the white world outside the carriage.

"It's gotten so much colder," she said, looking up at the gray-white sky.

"I'm afraid we're in for a blizzard, sir," the driver said, peering down into the window again.

"A blizzard?" She glanced at Devlen. "Does that mean we won't be able to travel through to Edinburgh?"

"What that means, Miss Sinclair, is we need to take shelter and wait out the storm." He glanced up at Peter. "The horses will be freezing. Make for the nearest inn."

"Yes, sir."

She glanced at Devlen, surprised he should feel such compassion for four-legged creatures and none at all for women.

He smiled at her then, as if gauging the tenor of her thoughts. If so, she should mind her features with greater skill.

Less than a quarter hour later, a tall gray building appeared out of the white blur of snow. The windows were lit like welcoming beacons.

Beatrice sat back among the cushions, grateful they'd finally found shelter.

She glanced down at the sleeping boy and reached out one hand to gently cup his cheek.

"Robert," she said softly. "You need to wake."

"Leave him," Devlen said. "I'll carry him inside." There was an expression on his face she had never before seen, a tenderness oddly suiting him.

She didn't say anything in return, merely pulled the lap robe up around Robert's shoulders and tented it so his face was shielded.

The carriage stopped, and the door opened, the driver standing there coated in snow, his cheeks red as he moved from one foot to the other to warm himself.

"After you've done with the team, Peter," Devlen told the driver, "get yourself inside. You needn't stay with the horses tonight."

The man looked surprised, and Beatrice wondered if it was his habit to sleep in the stables. That impression was strengthened when Devlen held out his hand and gave Peter a small drawstring bag to his obvious surprise.

"Buy yourself something warm to drink," he said. "You've earned it, getting us here safely."

"Thank you, sir." The driver's seat face split into a smile. "Thank you, Mr. Gordon. I'll do just that."

Devlen left the coach first and helped her out. Once she was standing on the frozen ground, he reached into the carriage and emerged with Robert in his arms, the blanket half over the boy's face to protect him from the falling snow.

"Will we be able to travel in the morning?"

Devlen's smile was remarkably warm considering she could barely see him through the snow flurries.

"Shall we let the snow take care of itself? We won't know until the morning."

Until then, she had to get through the whole long night.

Despite the fact the inn was large, it wasn't especially prosperous. The greeting they received from the effusive innkeeper was so fawning Beatrice wondered if he thought them royalty. The weather had evidently driven most of his regular clientele away, and the taproom was empty except for one man sitting huddled before the fire.

"Your best rooms," Devlen said, shifting Robert's weight in his arms. He acted as if he was familiar with being obeyed and quickly.

The innkeeper bowed, still smiling. "Of course, sir. How many would that be?" He glanced at Beatrice and back at Devlen.

"Two," Devlen said. "If you do not object to staying with Robert," he said in an aside to her. "I'd prefer someone be with him, especially in view of what happened with the birds."

"Surely you don't think . . ." The rest of her question was silenced when he shook his head slightly. Now was not the time to question him as to Robert's safety, not with the innkeeper listening. "No, I don't mind," she said. The child would serve as her chaperone.

The innkeeper gestured to the stairs, and she followed, ascending the steps and hearing the two men's conversation behind her.

She hesitated at the landing and the innkeeper pushed by her, leading her to a room at the end of the hall. The second room was next door. Entirely too close.

The innkeeper opened the door and bowed to Devlen, but he made a gesture that she should precede him. The room was cold, but the fire was hurriedly lit by the innkeeper himself as he kept up a running commentary on the weather.

"This room is larger," Devlen said. "You and Robert can stay in here."

Beatrice stepped close to the window for a view of the snow-encrusted countryside. Icicles hung like frozen tears from the branches of the trees. Bushes were laden with layers of snow until they appeared like dozens of hulking shapes huddled against the wind. The road was a mirrored path, the lanternlight reflected in its icy surface.

The snow had stopped falling, and the sky had cleared, revealing a full moon hanging like a snowball in the sky. The snow sparkled, and the ice glistened. Her breath fogged up the window, and she stepped back from the draft.

On this cold night there would be no comfort to be

found outside the inn, but inside there was the warmth
from the fire, a thick mattress, and plenty of blankets.

Devlen laid Robert in the high bed and removed the
boy's shoes before tucking him beneath the covers.

The room she and Robert had been given was undoubtedly the inn's very best. A massive four-poster
took up much of the space. What was left was occupied
by a washstand, a small folding screen, and a chair sagging so much in the seat that it looked to be a castoff
from the taproom downstairs.

The innkeeper melted away after showing Devlen
his room, spurred on his departure by Devlen's coin. A
moment later, the tavern maid left as well, and Beatrice
was oddly reminded of the time when she'd been so
disappointed not to get the job at the Sword and
Dragon. What would her life have been like in the last
two weeks?

She would not be standing here beside the window,
wouldn't be surreptitiously glancing at Devlen occasionally, would not be worrying about what he was doing when he came around the end of the bed and headed
in her direction. There were so many things that would
not have happened, let alone the sheer excitement of his
taking her hand.

"You look frightened. Are you?"

"Should I be?"

He smiled. "You never seem to answer any of my
questions directly."

"Then, yes, you frighten me sometimes. Sometimes,
my own reaction to you frightens me."

There, an honest answer, one without prevarication.

"Why are you afraid of me?"

She turned and looked out the window. "Because you lure me to do what I should not. Because you entice, Devlen Gordon, and your enticements are not for maidens like me."

"I normally eschew maidens, Miss Sinclair. I avoid them with all haste and vow never to bother with them. They're too much trouble, you see, and I'm a man who knows my own worth and the value of my time."

"So maidens are a waste of time?"

"I've found so, yes."

"Then I should feel safer, shouldn't I?"

"Do you?"

"Not appreciably, no."

"I've promised to protect you, don't you remember? I never break a promise."

"What if I don't wish to be protected?"

He smiled in response. "I'll go and see if the innkeeper can find us something to eat," he said, closing the door behind him. The room was suddenly much smaller.

"You like my cousin, don't you, Miss Sinclair?"

She smiled in Robert's direction, not completely surprised he'd feigned sleep.

"Yes, I do. Is that acceptable to you, Your Grace?"

He smiled sleepily. "He's a very nice man when he wants to be. But he can be ruthless."

Not a word a seven-year-old should be using to describe an adult.

"Where did you hear that?"

He sat up and rubbed his eyes. "My uncle. But I don't think he likes Devlen very much. Devlen's very rich."

"One man's ruthless is another man's determined."

He sat up, looking around. "It's not a very big place, is it?"

"But we're lucky to be out of the storm."

"Devlen would never let anything happen to his horses. He spent a lot of money for them."

"Then we should consider ourselves fortunate he has such great concern for his horses. We are therefore protected by default."

"Oh, I'm certain he would never let anything happen to me, either, Miss Sinclair."

"Yes, you're the Duke of Brechin."

He nodded. "But he loves me, too."

She found herself silenced by the wisdom of a child.

"Remember our conversation about snow at nighttime?"

He nodded.

"Come and look."

He slid off the bed and came to the window. After a moment, he smiled up at her. "It looks like you could eat it, Miss Sinclair. As if Cook had spread her frosting all over the world."

Beatrice smiled. "You're right, it does."

A few minutes later, Devlen arrived at the door followed by a chambermaid. The girl bobbed an awkward curtsy, a rather remarkable feat considering she was balancing a tray filled with food.

She laid it on the table doubling as a washstand and curtsied once again. Not to Beatrice, who was rather unused to the sight, but to Devlen, who further confounded the young girl by smiling at her.

"You really shouldn't do that," she said after the maid left the room.

"Do what?"

"Smile at young things. It confuses them entirely. I noticed at Castle Crannoch you made the maids lose the ability to talk. As if their wits had flown out of their heads."

"You exaggerate."

"I speak only the truth," she said, amused at the flush coloring his cheekbones.

Could it be that Devlen Gordon was embarrassed? Or only flummoxed because she'd called him on his ability to charm the female sex?

"My cousin has always had that effect on women."

"Do you ever sound like a seven-year-old?" Beatrice asked him. "Sometimes I think you're really twenty, and you're only masquerading as a child."

"That's because I'm very intelligent."

She and Devlen exchanged looks, and she couldn't help but wonder if he felt as bemused around Robert as she often did.

But she was grateful to notice in the next few minutes he reverted to being his age as he bounced in the middle of the bed and insisted upon having a picnic there, with the cloth spread out in the middle.

"You sit there," he said to Beatrice, pointing at the opposite corner of the bed. "You, there," he said to Devlen, indicating the pillows at the head of the bed. "We'll pretend we're sitting beneath a tree at Castle Crannoch."

She'd prefer a safer place.

"I think we should envision a different scene," Beatrice said. "Somewhere we've never seen before."

"The moors outside of Edinburgh," Devlen contributed. "Beneath a large oak tree."

"Pine," Beatrice countered. "Pines smell so much better."

"I wasn't aware oaks smelled."

"Which proves my point."

She reached for one of the crusty rolls as Devlen did. Their fingers met, touched, and she reluctantly withdrew her hand.

Robert reached down into the basket and grabbed a roll and handed it to her. "Here, Miss Sinclair."

"My troubadour. Thank you, Robert." She spent some time slicing it in half and piling some of the ham on top of it, anything but look in Devlen's direction. She was as foolish as one of the maids. His very presence had an effect on her. He needn't smile. Even one of his frowns was captivating.

"Don't you think so, Miss Sinclair?" Robert was saying.

She glanced over at the boy. "I'm sorry, but I was engrossed in my own thoughts. What was it you asked me?"

"I was saying we might be trapped here for days and days."

"Well, at least we have food to eat," she said, gesturing toward the lavish dinner Devlen had procured for them. "And we're warm." Only just, however. There was still a chill in the air since the fire was just lit.

"And Devlen's horses are in the barn," Robert added. "But I want to see Edinburgh again. I want to see Devlen's house. It's the most wondrous place, Miss Sinclair. You have never seen anything like it. It's three stories, and it's filled with furniture and marvelous rooms, and it has a hidden staircase just like Castle Crannoch and a secret passage from the library to the stables."

She glanced at Devlen to find him smiling fondly at the boy.

"Some of what I've told you is a secret just between you and me," he said, smiling.

Robert looked shamefaced, then brightened. "But she doesn't know exactly where the secret passages are, Devlen."

"Why would you build a secret passage in your house?"

"I didn't build it," he said. "I bought the house that way. Edinburgh has long been known for its intrigues, and evidently the previous owner had some connection with the court. He no doubt thought it wise to provide some type of escape for himself and his family."

"Did he ever use it?"

"I'm not entirely certain. I decided not to delve too deeply into the family history when I bought the property."

The rest of their meal was pleasant, their conversation innocuous bordering on bland, as if both of them were conscious of the innocent boy sitting between them.

They also carefully avoided discussing the attempts on Robert's life.

Their meal done, Devlen took the tray and stacked the dishes on it.

"You surprise me," she said.

He glanced at her and resumed his chore.

"Why, because I don't need a servant to do my every bidding or because I'm not afraid to do for myself?"

"Perhaps both."

He put the tray down, opened the door, and picked up the tray again.

"Things are not always as they seem, Miss Sinclair. Nor are people."

He glanced at Robert. "We'll make our travel decisions in the morning."

She nodded, and a moment later he was gone.

"You need to wash, Robert," she said, handing him a small ceramic jar she'd taken from her valise.

He didn't fuss but did as she instructed, lathering his face and hands with the soap, then making a point of shivering as he rinsed. She handed him a small towel embroidered with the Brechin crest. He dried himself off and changed into his nightshirt, making a point of stepping behind the folding screen and making her promise not to look.

Beatrice smiled and promised, and lit one of the lanterns, but because of the size of the room, didn't bother to light the other.

"It's very cold in here, Miss Sinclair," Robert said, emerging from behind the screen.

"Bundle up in bed, and you'll soon be warm enough."

"Tell me a story," he said with all the arrogance of a fully grown duke.

"Not if you command me."

"You're my employee."

"You're my charge."

"I'm Brechin."

"You're seven is what you are."

She sat down on the edge of the bed. "Do you think your father would be proud of you to hear you talk like this? From what you've said of him, he was very conscious of the feelings of others."

Robert's eyes widened, but he didn't answer her.

"Would he be glad you announce your title so often?

He strikes me as a most modest man, someone who wanted to do good in his life more than he wanted to impose fear."

To her absolute horror, the child began to cry, the huge tears rolling down his cheeks all the more powerful for the fact they were soundless. Stricken, she reached out and enfolded him in a hug.

She'd never thought herself maternal. In fact, when a baby was born in the village, she was not inclined to gather around the child and ooh and aah about its face, toes, or its likeness to either parent. But at the moment, when she began rocking back and forth in an effort to comfort the child, she felt absurdly protective.

Who would dare to hurt a child?

The thought was so sudden and invasive she was taken aback. This was not a holiday. This was not an adventure. There was only reason they were going to Edinburgh and that was to keep Robert safe.

Someone wanted him dead.

"I will tell you a story, my young duke," she said, kissing the top of his warm head. He smelled of the soap he'd used before getting into bed.

"Once upon a time, a peacock with a glorious tail noticed a tall and ugly crane passing by. The peacock made fun of the crane's gray plumage. 'I am robed like a king,' he said, 'in gold and purple, and all the colors of the rainbow, while you have not a bit of color on your wings.'

"He proceeded to parade around the crane, making a great presentation of his tail feathers, spreading them wide beneath the bright sun. Indeed, they were magnificent feathers in shades of red, blue, and green.

"The crane said not a word. When he walked, he did so awkwardly, and it's true there wasn't a bit of color on his feathers. He was nearly ugly, just like the peacock said.

"But while the peacock was laughing at the crane with the other peacocks, the crane suddenly picked up his feet, flapped his wings, and began to run. A moment later, while the peacocks watched in amazement and awe, he soared into the heavens.

"Up and up and around the clouds he flew, into the face of the sun itself.

"The peacocks could barely hear the crane's voice as he climbed higher into the sky, but hear it they did. 'It is true you are beautiful, much more beautiful than I. But I wing my way to the heights of heaven and lift up my voice to the stars. You can only walk below among the birds of the dunghill.'

"The moral of this story? Fine feathers don't make fine birds."

"Do all Aesop's fables have a moral, Miss Sinclair?"

"Every single one of them."

"Are any of them interesting?"

She only shook her head and tucked him in, taking care to ensure he was warm.

Once Robert was tucked in, he fell asleep without much difficulty. She sat and watched him, convinced he would rest tonight without nightmares. The room might be small, but there was a pleasantness to the inn somehow lacking at Castle Crannoch.

A half hour later, she stood and undressed, replacing her clothing with her nightgown and wrapper.

She was about to do something very foolish, something even Sally would caution her against. But if nothing else, the last year had taught her something. Life was fleeting and could be stripped from her without warning, without a hint.

She didn't want to waste one second of the time she had. She didn't want to pretend that there would be years and years to be wise and sensible, to find love.

Love. The word described all the incredible acts of passion mankind was capable of, all the acts of sacrifice, all the illogical and nonsensical acts. Love. She wasn't under any illusions that what she was about to do was based on love. She was intrigued by Devlen Gordon, and fascinated by him. His smile caused desire to curl up at the base of her spine, then extend its silky tail through her body, but she didn't love him.

Nor was time a certainty. All she knew was that she had this moment.

Still, she hesitated at the door, her hand on the handle. She felt greedy for life in the same way she'd been hungry for food, as if she'd been starving for experiences all these years. The hunger she felt easily overcame the soft whisper from her conscience.

She left the room, closing the door softly behind her.

Chapter 22

Beatrice stood before Devlen's room a full minute before summoning the courage to knock.

The sound was too loud in the silence, the echo of it carrying down the hall and back. She heard his footsteps nearing the door, then he hesitated, as if questioning whether or not he should open it.

She didn't knock again, but neither did she turn and go back to her room. Instead, she stood there with hands clasped in front of her, waiting.

Finally, the door opened, and he stood there, half-undressed. His stock was askew, his shift unbuttoned. But he didn't apologize for the state of his appearance.

Nor did he question her presence.

"Who do you think might have tried to harm Robert?"

It was a valid question, and one that needed to be asked and answered. But that wasn't why she was here, and they both knew it.

He reached out and pulled her into the room, then closed the door behind her.

"You wouldn't enjoy it, Miss Sinclair. In the morning, you'll wonder why you gave up your virtue so easily."

"Will I?"

"You'll wonder why you gave up so much for so little."

"You sound as if you have some experience in the regrets of virgins."

"No, I don't. Nor do I wish to. Go back to your room."

His voice was so well modulated, his smile so firmly fixed in place she would have thought him unaffected by her presence. Except, he kept his hands thrust in his pockets and there was a little pulsebeat at his neck where his skin moved up and down furiously, a cadence that was remarkably similar to her own frantically beating heart.

"Devlen?" She reached out with her hand, placed her fingers against his cheek. He jerked away at her touch.

"You tempt fate, Miss Sinclair."

"Beatrice," she said softly. "Have we not progressed to that, at least? I shall call you Devlen, since I do so in my mind already, and you may call me Beatrice."

"I would be better to call you ill-advised or foolish, Beatrice Sinclair. Without a smidgen of sense."

"You have teased me for days, if not weeks. And tempted me to your bed. Now you warn me away from it."

"Someone should warn you."

"I didn't expect you to warn me. I expected you to be my lover."

His smile abruptly disappeared.

"Have you no sense of self-preservation, Beatrice Sinclair? Nothing that warns you it isn't wise to tease the wolf?"

"Is that what I'm doing?" How utterly strange. Her pulse beat so hard she could feel it in her lips, her eyelids trembled, the whole of her body was vibrating.

She forced her hands to open. Her palms were wet.

"Is it such a terrible thing being here, Devlen?"

"You're leaving Robert alone."

"Yes, I am."

She turned to go, angry at him. He'd seized upon the one thing that could force her away. When she would have left the room, his hand on her arm held her back.

"He'll be fine."

"No, you were right to remind me of my duty. After all, I'm an employee. A governess."

"A woman."

His voice was low, his hand on her wrist warm. She didn't turn to look at him, but she wanted to. When he moved to stand close to her, her breath hitched and held, then slowly, slowly, released.

"I have never met anyone like you, Beatrice Sinclair. What kind of woman are you?"

"One derelict in my duty, Mr. Gordon, as you reminded me. Please release me."

"Tomorrow, perhaps, at dawn."

He turned her slowly.

A fingertip rested on her bottom lip, tapped it lightly. "You frighten me a little, you know."

"Do I?"

"My conscience wants to send you in all haste from this room. After all, I promised to protect you. My curiosity and my need begs you to remain."

"Then protect me tonight. Protect me from loneliness and despair. From questioning myself, from being cold."

"Beatrice."

"I can't explain what I feel, because I've never felt it before. I have no descriptions for the sensations rushing through my body, no way to convey the emotions I'm feeling. Maybe I need a poem to do so. Or a symphony. Music, as a way to express words I can't find."

"Damn it, Beatrice."

"Tell me what to do to rid myself of these feelings, and I'll do it. I won't trouble you any longer. Is there something I can drink? Something I can eat? Would sleep do it?"

"Touch yourself."

"What?" Shocked, she stared at him.

"Touch yourself and think of me. Hold your breast and tell yourself Devlen would touch me just this way. Stroke your nipple, and pretend it's my tongue. Let your hands wander over your body until you manage to convince yourself they're my hands."

"If I still crave your touch after that?"

He reached behind her, opened the door, and abruptly left the room, leaving Beatrice to stare after him.

Did she wait? Or return to her chamber?

After deciding to come to him, she wasn't going to leave. She walked to the bed, removing her wrapper, then mounted the steps and slid beneath the covers, feeling the shivery chill of the sheets.

Devlen would warm her.

Why was she here? Because she was lonely? Because he offered her something that had sparked her curiosity? Possibly both reasons, or neither of them.

Her body was capable of so many wondrous feelings, from first waking in the morning and stretching to feeling the warmth of the sun on her arms to walking barefoot through the spring grass. She could close her eyes at that moment and recollect the summer breeze across her cheek or the feel of the linen as she donned her shift.

What would she recall tomorrow morning?

The room was cold and silent, the only sounds the tearing wind outside and the hiss and pop of the fire. Her feet warmed, and she burrowed deeper beneath the covers, staring up at the ceiling and wondering if she should have some sort of trepidation for what was soon to follow.

The door opened then, and she was done with introspection. He closed the door softly and stood with his back to it, surveying her with a somber look.

"You have time to get out of my bed, Beatrice Sinclair," he said. "But I warn you, if you're not gone by the time I get there, you won't be able to escape."

"Do I look as if I'm attempting to escape?" She rose on her elbow.

"You should. You should be frightened for your life. I'm offering you nothing, you know."

"I know."

Silence stretched between them.

"Where did you go?"

"I hired the maid to sit outside Robert's room for the night. She'll fetch me if he awakes."

"You're a better protector than I, Devlen Gordon."

He didn't answer her. Instead, he came to the bed, pulled the covers down, and held out his hand. Curious, she sat up, then rose to her knees.

Her nightgown was gone in a few swift movements.

"Perhaps you have some experience in this, after

all," she said, amazed at the speed with which he'd divested her of her clothing.

"Now's not the time to discuss my experience."

"Then pray, remember that, when you would mention my lack of experience."

"Ah, but you are a virgin. Virgins are special creatures."

"You make me sound like a unicorn. Surely I'm not all that rarefied a creature?"

"In my bed you are."

She shouldn't have felt a shiver of pleasure at those words. He hadn't complimented her, after all.

"So, I'm your first virgin."

"You needn't look so pleased," he said, sitting on the bed.

"Why ever not? A woman likes to think she is special to a man in some degree or another. If for no other reason, you'll remember me because I was a virgin."

He shook his head, and she couldn't help but smile. It amused her to confound Devlen Gordon.

"Have you given no thought to your future?"

"You mean a child?"

The atmosphere in the room suddenly changed. It was no longer a secluded bower, a warm oasis from the cold. The chill of the winter night seeped in through the windows. Beatrice wouldn't have been surprised to look outside the bed to find snow piled high around it.

Devlen moved from the bed, walking to where the innkeeper had placed his trunk.

"I hadn't thought that far ahead," he said. "But luckily I do not travel unprepared."

He returned to the bed holding something in his hand. Instead of showing it to her, he slid it beneath the pillow.

"They're *les redingotes anglaises.*"

"English riding coats?"

"Precisely. They're to prevent you from becoming with child."

"I've chosen well," she said. "If I had to be deflowered by anyone, it was wise to choose a rake, someone versed in the skill. Do you make a point of keeping them next to your candles and your pistols?"

"You sound annoyed."

"I am not. Truly, I'm not. Very well, I am. I want both to be protected and to be protected from the knowledge of being protected."

"You want to be loved by a rake who's a virgin."

"It does sound nonsensical, doesn't it?"

"It would be better if you went back to your room. Then we wouldn't have to discuss English riding coats or preventing children."

"Yes," she said, "it would be better if I went back to my room." It was suddenly cold, and she was chilled. She hadn't felt so acutely naked before, but she did now, with her nipples drawing up tight against the chill.

He looked at her intently, and she wished he wouldn't. She felt vulnerable now while she hadn't been earlier. Instead, she'd been caught up in the daring of her deed. Now she just felt foolish.

She raised an arm to cover herself and just as she did, he reached out and prevented her from doing so.

"If you deny me your company for this evening, then at least let me look my fill. The sight of you will fuel my dreams."

How could he do that? With just a few words, he'd made her warm again.

She reached out her hand, and he took it. She rose to her knees, put her hands on his shoulders, and placed a soft kiss on his cheek.

"Being here is foolish, I know," she murmured next to his ear. "But I'm rarely foolish, Devlen."

"You want a taste of sin."

She nodded.

"And if you're ruined for marriage?"

"I'm not titled. Nor am I wealthy, and I doubt such considerations will matter if I ever marry. My husband will have to take me as I am or not take me at all."

"You'd bend the rules, Beatrice? Challenge society itself?"

"I suspect you've done your share of bending and challenging, Devlen Gordon."

"It's different for men, I think."

"Because we are vessels. What an odd way to think about women, don't you agree?"

"I don't believe I've ever considered a woman a vessel before, Beatrice."

"You must have," she said, drawing back. "If you hadn't, you wouldn't be carrying English riding coats in your trunk."

"Why are you so content to get nothing in return?"

"In return?"

"For the gift of your virginity?"

"Is it a gift? Or a burden?"

"You won't enjoy it, you know."

She looked at him for a long moment. "Are you a bad lover, Devlen? How odd I'd never considered it."

His smile was barely there, anchored by a wisp of

emotion. A wish, perhaps, that she would cease questioning him. Or meekly acquiesce to what she'd already chosen as her fate.

She sat back on her haunches and regarded him.

He didn't look away or appear the least uncomfortable.

Instead, he pulled his stock away from his throat slowly, so she could almost feel the slow slide of fabric against skin. Then his waistcoat, unbuttoned by large, long fingers, was falling to the floor with casual disregard.

"Your valet isn't here, Devlen," she said, amused.

"Perhaps I can convince you to straighten up after me."

"I have one charge. I am in no hurry to gain another."

How silly she should want to smile at this moment. The time was not ripe for humor, or the buoyant feeling in her chest. But she was absurdly happy as she watched him slowly undress, his gaze still fixed on her face and her dawning smile.

"You are enjoying this, aren't you?"

"The sight of you undressing? Very much. I must admit, however, I've never actually seen a naked man." An instant later, she corrected herself. "Not alive at any rate."

He halted in the act of unfastening his trousers. "Not alive?"

"During the epidemic, anyone was pressed into service to help bury the dead, Devlen. I was very good at sewing shrouds."

"You have a disconcerting habit of flummoxing me with your conversation, Beatrice Sinclair."

"You don't have to call me by my first and last name, you know. You could call me Beatrice. Or my middle name."

"Angelica?"

"No, nothing so ironic. Angel and devil." She smiled. "Anne. Much more prosaic."

"At first glance, however, Beatrice, it would not seem you're the angel in this mix. I suggest you're the devilish one."

"Really?" She was absurdly delighted by his comment.

He sat at the end of the bed, removed his boots and stockings, then slipped his trousers off his long, long legs.

"My," she said, and then fell into a long silence, interrupted only by the wind pushing against the windowpane. "Have you always been so large?"

A bark of laughter had her lifting her gaze to his face.

"Not a question I've ever been asked before," he admitted. "I don't think I was this large as a boy, no."

"Is it practice that makes it large? Does it get larger the more you use it?"

"Where do you get these questions?"

"Curiosity. I've always been curious."

"I find it oddly disconcerting to be questioned about my sexual exploits."

"Have you had none?"

He startled her by jumping onto the end of the bed. "Enough, Beatrice Sinclair. You have the devil's own tongue."

"Thank you," she said, and was further surprised by his dawning smile.

"Whatever for?"

"For not regaling me with stories of your conquests."

"That wouldn't be well-done of me, would it, Beatrice?" He leaned over and kissed her on the nose, a thoroughly confusing kiss.

He knelt before her, allowing her to look her fill.

She should have turned away, perhaps. But then, she shouldn't have been here at all. Instead, she looked, starting at his shoulders, rounded with muscle, to his chest, crafted like a Roman soldier's hammered breastplate, to his lean hips, to other places far more interesting.

"You look, dare I say it, enthralled."

"I've not had the opportunity to witness a naked man so close."

"One who's alive."

She nodded.

"I trust you approve of the sight."

"You're very beautiful. Do many women tell you that?"

"Considering the circumstances, perhaps it would be better if we didn't discuss other women."

"That means they have, of course," she said, stretching out her hand. Before she could touch him, she halted, her fingers resting on his thigh. As she watched, his manhood grew, stretching like a sleeping snake.

Oh my.

He picked up her hand and placed it on him.

"You're very warm," she said, when she'd regained the use of her voice. The comment came out as a croak. "Almost hot," she added.

His skin could burn her. She brushed the back of her hand against his thigh, and watched as his eyes half closed. He was like a cat she could pet. A warm cat who'd been sunning in the window. The fine black hair on his skin was not unlike a pelt. But there all resemblance to a domesticated animal fled from her mind. He was not a tame kitty, even though he was sitting patiently beneath her touch. His muscles were taut, his expression one of barely restrained civility.

His hand clenched, then moved to rest against her breast, to cup it as if to measure it against his palm. Her breast looked small and white and defenseless against his hand and she wanted to urge him to take some care with her. With all of her, naked and trembling yet too wild for maidenhood.

His thumb strummed against the tip of her breast, and she closed her eyes at the feeling. A sound trapped inside of her escaped through her tightened lips. A soft moan, or a sigh, no more than that.

Suddenly, she was on her back, and he was above her.

"Last time, Beatrice Sinclair, unicorn, if you will."

"I wish you'd urge me to stay with as much eagerness as you urge me to flee."

"I only wish to give you fair warning."

"It cannot be such a dour thing, Devlen, or the world would not hold it in such esteem. Nor would preachers sermonize about the doom and gloom of hell. Do only men enjoy it?"

"The first time, I'm afraid so."

"Then shall we dispense with the first time as quickly as possible? I shall hold you blameless if I feel the least bit ill from it."

"It's not a purgative, Beatrice."

"At least that, Devlen, or you wouldn't be warning me so."

He bent and kissed her and there were no more warnings. Or if he ventured any, she was not in the mood to hear them. His kisses were hot and drugging, leading her into a state of nothingness she'd never before known, a place where only sensation ruled. The touch of the tip of his tongue against her mouth, the soft sigh he made when deepening the kiss, the taste of him were all things she noted with the small part of her mind not adrift in wonder. The rest of her was aflame, curling beneath his fingers, his palms, her skin ablaze with feeling. Not even her toes were exempt from sensation, because they brushed against the long, wiry hair on his legs, and teased the soles of his feet.

She undulated like a wild thing, arching and retreating, enjoying each touch. He palmed her breasts, and she marveled they'd never been so sensitive. His thumb reached out and with his forefinger, teased her nipples, and she knew she'd never again be unaware of herself and her capacity for sheer enjoyment.

When his fingers explored her intimately, spreading swollen folds and entering her, it was as if he was demonstrating to her the body she'd inhabited all these years. His thumb bore down on one spot, his fingers curled into her, and she arched her back in an effort to get closer to him. Her arms wrapped around his shoulders and her lips pressed against his ear and it still wasn't close enough. Not nearly enough.

His fingers flicked against her. She felt caught up in a whirlwind, a vortex that was sucking her higher and higher. He whispered something to her, some words that had no meaning because she'd lost the ability to filter sound, so entranced was she in the magic he'd created with his touch.

She reached out with one hand and pressed against his fingers, urgent in a way she couldn't articulate. He said something else, and the only thing she noted was the amusement in his tone.

There was nothing remotely funny about what she was feeling.

He inserted another finger into her, his murmur less amused than coaxing. His thumb was insistent, probing, magic. Suddenly, her mind numbed, the sensation silvery, an explosion that crested, halting her breath. She hung, suspended, in midair, then exhaled a sigh, floating back to earth slowly on a current of bliss.

Devlen slid his hand beneath the pillow. He pulled away from her, and when he returned, he entered her with a smooth and practiced movement.

Just as swiftly, the bliss she'd felt turned to discomfort. "No."

He halted, staring down at her, gripping the pillow on either side of her head.

"No?"

She nodded.

"For the love of God, Beatrice, you can't say no now!"

"You won't fit, Devlen. I know you think you can, but it's all too obvious you won't."

He sighed, and lowered himself until he rested his forehead against hers. "Let me show you, Beatrice. Remember how I said it wouldn't be very comfortable?"

She nodded again.

"This is the not-comfortable part. But I promise, I shall be very kind."

"Am I still a virgin?"

"Only half."

"Then, please, finish."

"If you're sure?"

She nodded for the third time and was rewarded by his very determined expression.

He withdrew, and surged forward, and she immediately wanted to scream at him that he hadn't been kind at all. She felt stretched and invaded, and where he rested it burned. But then he withdrew once more, and this time she did scream, but only a little as he buried himself to the hilt in her.

She closed her eyes and tried to distance herself from what she was feeling.

"Beatrice?"

"Yes?"

"Are you crying?"

"A little."

"I'm very sorry, but I did tell you."

"Do you feel better being right, Devlen?"

"Not appreciably."

"Is it very enjoyable for you?"

"Not at the moment, no."

"I don't think I'm a virgin anymore, am I?"

"Definitely not."

"Well, that's done."

A moment passed, and she realized he was still hard inside her, a state of affairs that surely wasn't right. Short of asking him to hurry up and finish, however, what did a virgin do?

"Devlen?"

"Yes, Beatrice."

"Are you waiting for something?"

"For you to grow accustomed to me."

"I doubt that will ever happen, Devlen. You mustn't wait any longer."

"I've never been asked to depart with such grace, Beatrice."

She didn't have anything to say to that, so she remained silent.

"You're quite large."

"That's a compliment, you know. Thank you."

"I feel very small in return."

"You're supposed to be. You're a virgin."

She flexed her internal muscles, trying to ease the ache. He glanced down at her and smiled.

"That feels interesting, Beatrice."

"Can you feel that?"

"Too much more, and so will you."

She did it again, and he closed his eyes.

"Beatrice."

Once more and he moved, raising himself on his forearms and looking down at her as he did so. The discomfort wasn't quite as bad this time.

Once, twice, three times he surged into her, and when he did, she flexed her muscles. Several more minutes went by, with him moving above and in her. Her discomfort had almost completely eased now, but his, evidently, had not.

Devlen's expression was almost pained, his eyes closed, his movements more and more forceful and less restrained. She was being moved with each forward thrust, until she placed her hands on the headboard, palms upside down, bracing herself as he surged into her.

Suddenly, he made a sound and collapsed against her, his breathing ragged, his heart beating so frantically she feared for him.

A moment later he raised his head, his face flushed, his eyes sparkling wildly.

"You're wondering what the hell you've done."

"You were right. It wasn't very enjoyable. Oh, there was a moment there, but . . ."

"On the whole, you'd rather not have done it."

She nodded.

"I very much regret that fact, Beatrice. I shall have to change your mind."

She shook her head. She didn't want to do this again. Ever.

He lay beside her and held her close, but the comfort of his embrace didn't make up for her soreness or the lingering discomfort.

However, she couldn't berate herself until dawn came. She gave up, sighed deeply, and surrendered to sleep.

Chapter 23

The first thing Beatrice was aware of the next morning was Devlen leaving the bed. He went to the window and opened the sash, scooping the snow off the sill and forming it into a ball. He closed the window with his elbow and returned to the bed and did something utterly shocking: he placed the ball of snow between her legs and pressed it against her.

She nearly flew off the bed.

"Devlen! What are you doing?"

"Be still," he said. "Try to bear it as long as you can. The snow will help the swelling."

She subsided against the pillows.

"You'll be sore, but there's nothing I can do about that."

"I think I'm numb," she said. "Hasn't it been long enough?"

He removed the snow for a moment, but then when

she thought he might cease his ministrations, pressed the snow to her again.

"For someone who has never had a virgin in his bed, you seem to know a great deal about the care and feeding of them."

"Unicorns," he said, smiling.

There was nothing else for her to do but lie back and enjoy being cared for, albeit in such an intimate manner. His attitude, his entire demeanor, made it so casual that she couldn't help but be grateful.

When he was done, and most of the snow melted, he dumped the rest of it in the basin and pressed the towel against her. True to his word, she felt better already.

"I should be leaving," she said, glancing out the window. Dawn was already lightening the sky.

He nodded and stood, returning to the window.

"It hasn't snowed for quite a few hours. We'll be able to travel today."

She sat up in the bed, folding the towel he'd placed beneath her. The silence stretching between them wasn't so much awkward as it was filled with unspoken thoughts.

She wanted to thank him for his care of her, and his honesty. She wanted to explain why she'd come to his room, what she'd wanted from him. He'd eased her loneliness and satisfied her curiosity, but in doing so had only incited so many other questions.

If she asked him, would he give her the truth?

Why were men the only ones allowed pleasure? Was it because women were given the greater blessing of carrying a child? Was she odd in wanting to experience the same type of bliss Devlen had felt?

She slid off the edge of the bed and donned first her

nightgown, then her wrapper. Still, he didn't turn from the window, obviously impervious to the cold or to the fact he was naked in full view of anyone who might look up.

What a sight they would see.

"I'm going now," she said, and only then did he turn. His gaze, when he looked at her, was somber. There was not a remnant of the sparkle in his eyes. His mouth looked like he had never smiled, and his face might have been etched in marble, so stern and unapproachable was he at that moment. If she'd never before known him, he would have given her pause. She might have been afraid of him, or at the very least wary. But they'd shared their bodies the night before, and he'd cared for her only minutes earlier.

"Let me go and dismiss the maid. If you have no care for your reputation, at least I do."

When he returned, he didn't glance at her. "Go and wake Robert. Tell him I want to get an early start." She nodded.

"We'll break our fast on the road. I'll have the innkeeper pack us a basket."

Once again, she nodded, his perfect servant.

She opened the door, glanced at him once more, but he'd turned back to stare out the window again. In the reflection, however, he was looking at her. She drew the wrapper closer at her throat as if to hide all the places on her body where his hands had made a mark, where his whiskers had abraded her, where his lips had sucked and his tongue touched.

But she didn't say a word as she closed the door behind her, regret thick in the air.

* * *

The sun was so bright against the drifts of snow that Beatrice had to shield her eyes from the glare.

Robert grumbled as they left the inn and entered the carriage. She ignored his complaints about the early hour, that he was hungry, cold, and tired.

"It doesn't do any good to complain endlessly. It doesn't make a situation easier to endure."

To her surprise, he subsided against the seat, folded his arms across his chest, and remained silent until Devlen joined them.

"How long until we get to Edinburgh, Devlen?"

Devlen closed the door behind him, choosing to sit beside Beatrice. He had never done that before and she rearranged her skirts twice before realizing what she was doing.

"In fair weather, it would be a matter of hours, Robert. But with the snowdrifts, I've no idea. If the roads are impassable, we'll simply have to turn around and come back."

"But I want to get to Edinburgh."

Beatrice leveled a look at him, almost daring him to have a tantrum at this particular moment. She was in no mood for petulant dukes, or ill-mannered children.

To his credit, Robert was very good at reading her expression, because once again he sank back against the seat without another word.

Devlen tapped on the top of the roof twice, a signal to the driver. The carriage began to move, the horses evidently restive and willing to show their mettle.

Twice they were forced to stop because of the ice. The driver and Devlen laid down a bed of straw, a large bundle of which had been purchased from the innkeeper and now sat atop the carriage for just such a use. Other than those two occasions, the journey was uneventful. As the day lengthened and grew warmer, the snow began to melt, and the danger was getting trapped by the muddy roads.

Beatrice had heard about Edinburgh all her life. Her father was enamored of the city and once they'd actually had the funds to take a coach there. He'd conferred with an academic friend, and they'd stayed in the man's narrow little house in a tiny airless room. The discomfort of their visit had never mattered to her father, who'd regaled Beatrice with every single sight of historical interest and the history of each.

As they drove into the city, she experienced an incredible sense of sadness. Her father would have been so happy to have been able to return here. As she looked around, she could almost hear him exclaim at all the changes that had taken place since she was fifteen and a wide-eyed girl.

She knew the city was divided into two sections, called Old Town and New Town, and she wasn't appreciably surprised when the carriage continued toward the newer section of the city. They stopped in front of a set of iron gates and waited as two men appeared and swung them inward.

Beneath the folds of her skirts, Devlen's hand found hers. He gave her a reassuring squeeze, as if she were a child frightened of the dark.

She turned and looked at him, but he was staring out the window. She did the same, pretending an interest in the scenery rather than the feel of his warm fingers intertwined with hers.

Here, in the city, the snow had not been so plentiful,

but what still lay on the road and on the trees was a sparkling mantle. The carriage turned, traveling down a wide road of crushed shells. A few moments later, she glimpsed his house for the first time, an enormous mansion easily the equal in size to Castle Crannoch, set in the middle of a parkland.

She'd heard Devlen described as wealthy, had known he had some business affairs, but until this moment, she'd not considered exactly who Devlen Gordon might be. As she stared at the house, she realized she'd misjudged him again.

"What kind of businesses do you have?"

He turned and looked at her. "Do you want the types of industries, or a listing of the companies I own?"

"What's shorter?"

He smiled. "The industries. The companies take up two pages in my ledger. There's shipping, textiles, import and export. I build things, and I make soap."

"Soap?"

"The soap making is a new venture, I confess. But we've been experimenting with putting all different types of scents into soap."

"Is that why you always smell so wonderful?"

His smile dimmed, and he glanced at Robert. What would he have done if Robert hadn't been in the carriage? She didn't have a chance to wonder, because he continued with his litany.

"I make a great many things as well. Nails, for example. And cotton. There's a new loom I'm trying out. Do not, I pray you, forget about my ships or my glassworks. Plus, I'm negotiating for a company that makes gunpowder."

"I had no idea."

"Did you think me a hedonist?"

She shook her head. She hadn't thought of him as an industrialist, a man interested in glassworks and ammunition. When she thought of him, it was as he'd first appeared to her, sitting in his carriage, or teasing her in Robert's sitting room.

Devlen's house was built of red brick, three stories tall with two wings outstretched like arms around the curved drive. A dozen white-framed windows stretched along each floor. The entrance was a double white door level with the drive, a sedate brass knocker the only ornamentation.

The house was as far from Castle Crannoch as she could imagine.

As she exited the coach, and stood smoothing down her skirts, Beatrice had the oddest notion her cottage could have fit inside his home at least thirty times over. Devlen extended his arm to her and she took it as if she were accustomed to always visiting such a magnificent place on the arm of its owner.

Robert, not content to walk sedately, gamboled in front of them. She didn't bother to correct him. The last several hours in the coach had only bottled up his energies. Better he should expend them now than when he needed to be on his best manners.

She and Devlen were silent as the door opened. They still had not spoken of the night before. It might not have ever happened except in her memory or except for the small aches and pains reminding her it was all too real. At the moment, Devlen felt like a stranger, proper and hospitable. They might never have talked or shared a meal or been intimate.

She had no inkling of his life, and how could he possibly understand what she'd gone through in the last year? Every single conversation came back to her and replayed itself as she made her way across the gravel drive, still holding on to the arm of the man who'd taken her virginity. The stranger who'd been almost a friend until this moment, until her awareness of the vast gulf separating them.

A man stepped out in front of the door and nodded to two footmen. Like marionettes, they bowed to Devlen before opening the door. Robert preceded them, silent for once.

Once inside the foyer, she stopped and looked around her, her breath leaving her in a gasp. She couldn't swallow, and she was certain she couldn't speak. Neither Robert nor Devlen acted as if anything was amiss.

The foyer was three stories tall with sunlight pouring down onto the tile floor. In the ceiling was a rotunda fitted with at least a dozen panes of glittering glass. Surrounding the carved dome were a dozen birds in all shapes and sizes, carved from plaster and incredibly lifelike.

The tile floor beneath her feet was black and white in alternating squares. In a smaller space the pattern would have been overwhelming, but the entranceway of Devlen's home stretched on forever.

Ahead of them was a massive round mahogany table resting on a single pedestal. In the middle of it was a silver epergne filled with flowers.

"You have flowers," she said, grateful to note she'd been able to form a coherent sentence. "There's snow on the ground, but you have flowers."

"There are greenhouses behind the house. We have flowers year 'round."

"Of course you do," she said, sounding a great deal more cosmopolitan than she felt. "You have a great many parties here, don't you? Balls, and the like."

"I've entertained some, yes." He looked amused.

She felt like a country girl who'd never been far from Kilbridden Village. But she'd come to Edinburgh before, had seen the sights. But she'd never thought to stay in one of the wonders of the city, to reside in one of its stately mansions. Devlen's house was far more grand than anything she could have imagined.

"You could fit an orchestra into one corner of the foyer and it would barely be noticed."

"Actually, they play on the second floor. There's a ballroom there."

She didn't have a chance to ask any more questions. A woman was walking down the hall, her look smoothing from surprise to one of welcome.

"Sir, I didn't expect to see you back so soon."

"Castle Crannoch proved to be inhospitable, Mrs. Anderson. I trust you will not be discommoded by our unexpected guests?"

"Of course not, sir. You know our guest chambers are always ready for any of your friends."

Exactly how many friends did Devlen have? And how often did they stay at his home? That she would even entertain such thoughts was an indication of how disoriented she was. His life was none of her concern.

Mrs. Anderson glanced in her direction, then immediately dismissed her to smile at Robert.

"Your Grace," she said, performing a very credible curtsy considering the woman was not young. "What a pleasure to have you with us again."

"Thank you, Mrs. Anderson," Robert said without being prompted. But his next words were not so polite. "Do you have any of those chocolate biscuits?"

"I believe we can find some for you, Your Grace. Shall I send them up to your room?"

To his credit, Robert glanced in Beatrice's direction. "Is it all right, Miss Sinclair?"

"Since breakfast was a long time ago, it's very all right."

"Perhaps you would like some biscuits as well," Devlen said with a smile. "Mrs. Anderson?"

Once again the woman glanced at her, then away.

"I can have lunch in the family dining room in a matter of moments, sir."

"I think we're more tired than hungry, Mrs. Anderson. It's been an eventful journey. We can subsist on biscuits for now, but let's plan on an early dinner."

"Of course, sir."

"Miss Sinclair is Robert's governess and will be staying with us as well."

"Miss Sinclair." Mrs. Anderson executed a stiff inclination of the head while her lips curved in an infinitesimal smile barely warmer than the frosty weather outside. What concessions she made to politeness were for Devlen's benefit entirely, and they both knew it.

"I'll show you to your room."

"That is not necessary, Mrs. Anderson," Devlen said, all cordial hospitality. "I'll show Miss Sinclair her chamber. The blue room, I think."

"It's quite some distance from the Duke's apartments, sir."

For a moment, the two of them, servant and employer, just stared at each other.

"Quite right, Mrs. Anderson," Devlen said finally. "Miss Sinclair is His Grace's governess, not his nurse. I think the blue room will do fine."

This time the smile he received was at least as wintry as the one bestowed upon Beatrice. Mrs. Anderson obviously didn't approve.

Beatrice's cheeks felt warm, but she didn't say a word as she followed Devlen and Robert up the sweeping staircase. She'd thought the architecture at Castle Crannoch impressive, but it was no match for this magnificent home in the middle of Edinburgh.

"How many people do you employ?" she asked, not merely to make conversation. She was genuinely interested.

"Seventeen. A damn sight more than at Castle Crannoch."

"Don't forget the stables, Devlen. He has four groomsmen and a stable master, too, Miss Sinclair."

"Truly?"

"My horses are at least as important as any dust that might appear in my home," he said, but blunted the edge of his comment with a smile. "I will have to show you my horses, Miss Sinclair."

"I'm lamentably ignorant when it comes to horses," she confessed. "We've never kept any, and they always seemed so very large."

"We shall have to see if we can add to your education. And Robert's. We'll consider it a lesson, perhaps."

They were on the second floor now, looking down at the foyer and up to the sunlit dome at the top of the house. She could see the birds more clearly, each so ornately carved and true to life they looked as if they could all fly away in a flutter of wings.

"What kind of bird is that?" she asked, extending her arm and pointing to one particularly odd looking specimen.

"A white pelican. Indigenous to North America."

He was looking at her oddly, and she supposed she was acting irrational. But she couldn't get over the impression she'd totally misjudged Devlen Gordon. It wasn't because of his wealth, but because of his industry. He was genuinely excited when he was talking about making soap, of all things.

She'd always admired people who had a fire inside, who knew exactly what they wanted to do or to be in life and who pursued it with single-minded ambition.

Because she was female, she was supposed to want, first, to be a wife, then a mother. Any other interests she pursued would be supplanted by those roles. Except, of course, she was lacking sufficient suitors, and she had only one true talent: she was very, very good at survival. In the last year she'd managed to stay alive, and that was still her primary goal and focus.

Devlen led the way down the corridor, and she followed, wondering how close her room would be to his. Had he shocked his housekeeper? Should she protest?

She wished he wouldn't look at her in quite that way, out of the corner of his eye, as if measuring the distance between them. Then he would always follow up that glance with another one toward Robert.

There were too many emotions, too many feelings to sort out, too much had happened in the last day, and she'd yet to reason it all through. First, the birds dying, then this hasty retreat to Edinburgh, and finally, most importantly, last night.

What a fool she'd been. What a silly, idiotic fool.

And yet, if the circumstances were the same again, she would no doubt do exactly what she'd done last night. Lovemaking was overrated and painful, but at least she had experienced it.

She was no longer simply Beatrice Sinclair, of Kilbridden Village. She was Beatrice Sinclair, the governess of the Duke of Brechin. A woman whose virginity had been taken by Devlen Gordon, industrialist extraordinaire.

When the time came for her to return to her village, she would never again be the same gray, nondescript person she had been. People would notice her, if for no other reason than the look of nostalgia in her eyes.

When the time came. She couldn't predict how many weeks or months or days it might be until he sent her from Edinburgh, until Robert went off to school, until Cameron Gordon was so incensed by the fact they'd left Castle Crannoch that he dismissed her.

Time was not one of those commodities she could predict with any certainty. Nor could she gauge another human being's behavior or actions. Therefore, she'd have to be content with simply living each day to its full measure, to savoring all she could when it was placed before her. If she were at a banquet, she'd be foolish to deny her hunger.

At least for the next few days, she'd be living in a beautiful home in the middle of an exciting city, with a man as handsome and distracting as Devlen Gordon.

Devlen halted before a chamber door. Robert had lost no time opening the door and inspecting the premises.

"You haven't changed it," he said.

"Why should I?" Devlen asked. "It's your room. I promised you that, the last time you were here."

Robert nodded, but still went from wardrobe to chest, opening doors and drawers as if to acquaint himself with the contents and ensure himself nothing was missing.

"Your room is in the next wing," Devlen said. "Come and see, Robert. In case you need your governess."

"We shan't be having lessons, shall we, Miss Sinclair?" he asked, as they walked down the hall. "This is a holiday, isn't it? Because of the birds?"

She glanced at Devlen, then away, startled to find he'd been watching her. "We should find a schoolroom here. Your lessons shouldn't be neglected."

His mouth was set in a mulish pout, but after looking at Devlen, he evidently thought better of protesting right at that moment.

Devlen halted before another door, turned the handle, and threw the door open wide for her.

The chamber she'd been given was unlike anything she'd ever seen. The predominant color was blue, from the draperies in front of the long windows to those that hung at the corners of the four-poster atop the dais. The mattress was easily double the size of the one she'd slept on at Castle Crannoch and covered with a thickly embroidered coverlet, again in blue, with a medallion of gold in the center. In the middle of the ceiling was a second medallion, this one in ivory, directly over a blue-and-gold-flowered carpet.

The furnishings were perfectly proportioned for the room's dimensions. A vanity with delicately turned legs sat against one wall, swags of blue damask matching the bed hangings draped from the mirror perched halfway up the wall down to the floor, where they puddled in large folds. A washstand in the corner was partially concealed by a folding screen, and a small secretary sat next to the window. The writing surface sat open, a quill, inkstand, and a supply of paper lay in readiness as if to welcome a correspondent.

"If you need anything, Miss Sinclair, all you need do is summon a maid." Devlen walked to the bell rope near the fireplace and fingered the tassel.

"Thank you," she said. "This is all rather grand."

"So are you."

For a moment she only stared at him, startled by his words. What could she possibly say to that?

There was something about him that would have attracted her even if they'd met on a street in a crowded city. She would have looked back at him if their carriages had passed, if she'd walked near him, if she'd been introduced to him by a mutual friend.

She might have caused a scandal anywhere, at any time.

"Devlen," she said in warning.

He only smiled, turned, and glanced at Robert, who was investigating the balcony beyond the French doors.

"My chamber is across the hall."

An arrangement similar to that at the inn. Did he think she was going to come and visit him?

"No wonder Mrs. Anderson was scandalized."

"Mrs. Anderson is an employee."

"So am I."

"Ah, but I don't pay your salary. My father does. So technically, you aren't."

"You look at the finer point of things, Devlen."

"I'm trained to do so."

She was as well, and yet she didn't think like him. Her education had been in using her mind to analyze a point, to converse in one of three languages, to consider the past. She had no experience in shading the truth or cutting the corners from it.

The moment the door closed behind him, Robert in tow, she let out a breath she hadn't been aware she'd been holding.

What on earth had she done?

It was one thing, her father had always said, to make a mistake. Quite another to refuse to admit it.

We are, Beatrice, my dear, a strange and wondrous species. We go willy-nilly through life making mistake after mistake, only at the end of it to look back and see where our course should have been corrected, made less difficult by a simple turn.

She needed to make a turn now, that was evident, needed a room in the servants' quarters, and not be treated as if she were a beloved guest. Nor should she be across the hall from Devlen's own suite of rooms.

Her cheeks warmed even further at the thought of Mrs. Anderson's pursed lips and disapproving glance. No doubt the woman knew, almost as if she had been standing outside the room last night, exactly what had transpired between them.

Anyone who happened to interpret the glances between them would know. Even Robert had looked from one to the other, curiously, as if he'd sensed an undercurrent.

Very well, she'd been foolish, but if they still took precautions, there was nothing to be concerned about other than her slightly dented reputation. That was something that needn't carry further than Devlen and her. No one in her tiny village would know. No one at Castle Crannoch would have any inkling. Therefore, if she wished, she could return there almost as if she were unsullied and pure and as maidenly as she had been two nights ago.

In actuality, she couldn't see what all the fuss was about. Lovemaking might prove to be very pleasurable to men, but women must simply grit their teeth and pray during the entire experience.

Besides, she had more to be concerned about than her reputation. There was Robert's safety and the mystery of who wanted him harmed, or dead. There was the uncertainty of his future—and hers. At this point, she couldn't even imagine returning to Castle Crannoch.

Although it was only early afternoon, she was tired. The night before had been filled with a fitful sleep. She was unused to sleeping beside another person and found herself awake more often than not, looking at Devlen as he slept.

Would it be acceptable to take a nap? Or would it be considered unpardonably rude?

The question was answered a few minutes later when she responded to a knock at the door. For one moment, she hoped it wasn't Devlen, coming to speak with her. He would kiss her, she knew, and the meaning of his longing glances were clear enough. He wanted to replicate what had transpired between them the night before.

How did she tell him no?

But it wasn't Devlen after all, for which she was grateful, but a footman bringing her valise. Behind him was Mrs. Anderson, bearing a tray.

"Mr. Gordon asked me to bring you something to eat,

miss. He thought you might be tired and would like to rest."

She nodded, feeling tongue-tied and shy in the presence of the older woman.

"Thank you," she said, after the woman had placed the tray down on the table. "It looks delicious."

"It's just some greens and some soup. Along with one of Cook's tarts. Mr. Gordon is very partial to Cook's apple tarts."

"I appreciate your efforts on my behalf."

"It's what I would do for any of Mr. Gordon's guests."

"Does he have many?"

"It's not for me to say."

After the woman left, she sat at the table and ate the meal, finding it tastier than anything she'd eaten at Castle Crannoch.

Once done, she removed her dress and her stays, and placed the garments in the armoire before retrieving her wrapper from the valise. She crawled into the big, wide bed and slid beneath the covers, thinking heaven itself could not feel more sumptuous.

Wealth could not bring a man happiness, she'd always been told, a saying she questioned as she burrowed into the feather pillow. Perhaps it couldn't buy happiness, but it certainly could provide comfort.

Devlen had a hundred things he could do, a dozen things that must be done. There were, no doubt, people waiting for him in his office to make decisions. He needed to go by the shipyards, and the new machinery was due to be delivered to the warehouse he was converting to a textile factory.

Instead, he sat in Beatrice's room, watching her while she slept.

If nothing else, he could be interviewing Robert, coaxing details from the boy about the poisoning of the birds, and the shot in the forest.

His mind shied away from doing that, and it didn't require any great thought to understand why. His father had always wanted to be duke. Enough to kill a child?

He would have to protect Robert, at least until he determined who was at the bottom of the incidents surrounding him. Who had shot at him, and who had poisoned his food? Why would anyone want to kill the boy? His thoughts came full circle, back to his father.

Tomorrow, he would visit with his solicitor, have him send something to his father. Anything to keep Cameron away from Robert, at least until Devlen could assure Robert's safety. Castle Crannoch wasn't the place for the boy. For the time being, Robert would remain with him. At least in Edinburgh he was safe.

His bachelor life could be expanded somewhat to include a child. He was growing tired of the endless round of parties and entertainments. The idea of staying in was growing in appeal.

How much did Beatrice Sinclair have to do with that idea? Probably too much to warrant investigation. He hadn't lied to her—he thought virgins too much trouble. She, especially, with her air of directness and her way of puncturing his conscience.

He'd eschewed the substances in life proving to be addictive. He didn't indulge in opium, or too much drink. While he engaged in selective breeding of his horses, and treated them well, he didn't think that hobby a vice. He'd been attracted to gambling, only to find himself feeling certain that he'd been singled out to be different. When he won, he felt as if his luck was special, his destiny unique. He'd felt blessed, as if a light from heaven shone down on him to illuminate to the rest of the world that he, alone, was anointed.

He had to almost lose his fortune before he realized what a fool he'd been.

Was Beatrice as dangerous as gambling?

She was proving to be a distraction of major proportions. He anticipated her smile, and he wanted to hear her laugh. Deflowering her had been one of the single most unforgettable experiences of his life. He hadn't wanted to cause her pain, and had felt acute regret when he'd done so, enough that his own pleasure had been muted. When she'd carefully avoided him this morning, he'd wanted to enfold her in his arms, kiss her tenderly, and tell her the experience would be a better one the next time. But it was all too obvious she wanted nothing to do with any further forays into passion.

Was that why he was here?

Perhaps he was more concerned about his reputation as a lover. He couldn't let her continue with the thought that lovemaking was a painful event, especially with him. That's what it was—he was simply concerned she not have a bad opinion of his skills.

He smiled in the darkness, amused by his attempts at delusion.

There was none so blind as he who will not see. Who said that? And did he ever sit in a darkened bedroom and gaze at the object who was causing him so much mental discomfort, feeling helpless and wanting?

She had the power to charm him, keep him awake.

From the moment he'd met her, only weeks ago, he'd been fascinated.

He had a hundred acquaintances, but few friends. He wasn't given to confidences, and he was so single-minded and focused in his work that he was impatient with the necessities of friendship. He didn't want to spend any time cultivating an acquaintance into a friend, didn't want to spend the time to listen to their travails, their thoughts, or the experiences of their days. There were only so many hours in each day, and he spent most of them productively.

For the first time he felt the lack of friendship, acutely lonely in a way that surprised him at his core. Was that another aspect to his life brought about by Beatrice Sinclair?

She was proving to be quite an irritant.

It occurred to him then, as he sat in the darkness, that she occupied the role of friend more closely than anyone ever had. He actually wanted to hear her thoughts, and had solicited her opinions quite often. The way her mind worked was vastly fascinating to him to a degree that startled him.

That was it. She was simply a friend, and he was acting in a capacity of friendship. That was all.

This time, he didn't smile at his delusion.

Chapter 24

When Beatrice awoke, the drapes had been closed against the night. She lay there in the dark, disoriented at first before she pieced everything together. She was in Edinburgh, the city she'd always wanted to revisit. Her parents and her friends were dead, her life had changed drastically. The man she'd taken as her lover was, for all intents and purposes, her employer, and he'd given her this lovely room.

In exchange for her virginity?

How foolish a thought if it were true. Devlen owed her nothing. Although the experiment itself had a disappointing outcome, she would not have traded the experience.

Knowledge was never to be shunned.

She sat up and wished whoever had closed the drapes had thought to light a candle or a lamp. But just as she was wondering where there might be a box of matches, she heard a sound. A rustle of fabric, a movement of a shoe against the flowered carpet, no more than that, but it had the power to freeze her.

She gripped the sheet and pulled it up to her chin.

"Who's there?"

"Forgive me," Devlen said. He struck a match and instantly, an oil lamp flared to life. His shadow grew to encompass the corner where he sat, looming to a point on the ceiling.

He stood, and his shadow danced down to a normal size even as the man himself grew taller.

"How long have you been there? Have you been watching me sleep?"

"Not long. I had plans to take you on a carriage ride at sundown, but time got away from us."

"I'm sorry, I didn't mean to sleep so late."

"You were tired. Neither of us got much sleep last night."

"No." She was proud of the fact she could sound so calm when speaking of last night. How utterly civilized both of them were being. Usually, such circumstance might lead to high drama, but she couldn't imagine Devlen Gordon being histrionic about anything, let alone the seduction of a woman of some naïveté.

"Could we go tomorrow night?"

"We can do anything you wish." He'd reached the side of the bed now and leaned over to smooth her hair back from her cheek. She'd not thought to braid it, and it would take some time to rid it of its tangles.

She wished he'd not seen her in such disarray.

The oil lamp barely illuminated the room; they were two shadows approaching each other.

"I really should see about Robert."

"He's fine. He's pestering the cook for more biscuits and grateful you're nowhere in sight."

"I've been an errant governess."

"Every boy needs a chance to escape from authority, even as delightful an authority as you."

"Stop doing that."

"Doing what?"

"You're very effusive in your compliments, Devlen."

"And you don't know quite how to handle them. Or me."

"Is that your intent?"

"To keep you off-balance? Perhaps. I like you discomfited, Miss Sinclair. You're charming when you're confused."

"You're just too charming."

"Ah, you're learning too quickly, I think. I must warn you, however, I'm not nearly as overcome by compliments as you seem to be. I've grown accustomed to praise."

There was silence while she wondered what next to say. She was often fighting for her verbal survival around him.

"Which brings up the subject we need to discuss."

She had a good idea what subject he wanted to discuss and she preferred to avoid it.

"I told you it wouldn't be an enjoyable experience."

"Yes, you did. I'm grateful you aren't a liar, Devlen."

His bark of laughter startled her. "Only a despoiler of innocents."

"Absolutely not. You did nothing I didn't want done."

"Tell me this, since we're so intent on the truth, you and I. Would you have done it if you'd known what it was to be like?"

She considered the question for a few moments. "Probably not," she said finally. When he remained silent, she continued, "I'd much rather not do it again, please."

"So much for honesty. I'm beginning to believe it isn't as much of a virtue as I've always thought."

She slid from the other side of the bed. "You sound annoyed."

"Not annoyed, Beatrice." He came around the end to meet her. "Very well, annoyed. I'd expected you to say differently. I wanted you to have some pleasure in our closeness, perhaps. Enough to want to replicate the experience. Only then could I show you it was a great deal more pleasurable than the first occasion."

"For you, perhaps, Devlen. I'll grant you that."

"I've never been considered a selfish lover, Beatrice. Pardon me if I'm slightly irritated by that comment."

"Shouldn't we be arguing over something that makes a bit more sense?"

He didn't say anything for a moment.

"I didn't mean to insult you, Devlen." She touched him on the arm, and the muscle jerked at her touch. "Forgive me."

When he still didn't say anything, she moved closer. "You said yourself virgins are too much trouble."

"I've come to show you something," he said. "A little renovation of mine."

"I really should see about Robert."

Suddenly he reached out his hand and touched her cheek with his fingers, trailing a path across her face to the corner of her lips, then back to her ear.

She half turned her face away, uncomfortable with his gentleness. That feeling was beginning again, where her breath was tight and her heart beat too loudly. Her mind knew what was to come, but her body had not yet learned that lesson, evidently.

"He's fine, Beatrice. When he finishes badgering Cook, he'll see the new soldiers I bought for him."

She pressed her hand against his chest, feeling the fine linen weave of his shirt. A wealthy man's garment, the stitches so fine as to be invisible, the fabric so closely woven as to feel like silk.

Leave me alone. I beg you.

But how strange she didn't speak the words. One hand splayed on his chest, and she placed the second one there, thumb to thumb. And still she didn't measure the full breadth of his chest.

"Beatrice."

Just her name, softly said. She let her eyes flutter shut and bowed her head until her forehead rested against his chest, unsurprised to feel his arms extending around her. Her traitorous body was so foolish, she took two tiny steps closer.

She wanted to be kissed, and when she tilted her head back, he obliged her. The consummate host, giving what a guest desired.

She opened her mouth below his, inviting the invasion of his tongue, feeling a spear of excitement deep inside when he touched his tongue to hers and deepened the kiss. Her hands spread wide, reached up to grip his shoulders. She stood on tiptoe and wound her arms around his neck, pressing her nearly unclad body so close a sigh could not have separated them.

His hands reached down and cupped her buttocks and pulled her closer and higher so his erection rested at the V of her thighs. He lifted her slightly, then let her slide down again, to mimic the act of love in a standing position.

The excitement she felt deepened as her body heated, and their kiss became more carnal.

Too quickly done. Within a moment, she was aflame. Her thoughts, wishes, decisions might have been thrown out the window. If he'd suggested they go back to her bed, she would have thrown herself atop the mattress. Thankfully, he did no such thing.

He slowly pulled back, gave her one last kiss, then bent his head again and pressed his lips against her cheek. His breathing was ragged, the words barely audible.

"Not yet, Beatrice. I've a surprise to show you."

She didn't want a surprise. Or dinner. Or to be proper. She wanted her breath to come back in full measure and her heart to quit its erratic beat. Most of all, she wanted that feeling inside her to ease. Her body waited for something, anticipated something, and yet her mind knew full well exactly what she wanted. His hands on her. His fingers on her pressing against her, bringing her release. But if that happened, there would be pain, and she wasn't eager for that part of the experience to be repeated.

"Come with me." His hand trailed down her arm until their fingers linked. He headed toward the door with her following.

"I'm not dressed," she protested.

"You don't have to be. In fact," he added enigmatically, "you shouldn't be."

He opened the door and looked both ways, and she fervently hoped none of the maids or footmen were in the hall.

He led her out of the room, closed the door behind

her, and walked across the hall to his own chamber. She tugged at his hand, but she was no match for Devlen's insistence.

Seduction was evidently not on his mind. Inside his suite he turned away from the bed mounted on a dais, and led the way across the room to a door set in the wall. He turned the latch and pushed in the door and let her into another chamber.

She'd never seen anything like it.

There was no carpet on the floor, nothing adorning the stone walls. The chamber would have been as cold as a mausoleum had it not been for the floor-to-ceiling fireplace in one wall. A large copper pot sat bubbling over a well-tended fire. The only furnishing in the entire room was a large copper vessel sitting in the middle of the room, a series of pipes leading from it to the fireplace, then down into a drain in the floor.

"It's a bath," Devlen said with obvious pride. "If you want hot water, all you do is turn that spigot," he said, pointing to a handle mounted at the edge of the tub. "The other leads to the cistern on the roof and provides cold water."

"Good heavens."

But the wonders weren't over.

"When you're done, merely unplug the tub and the water disappears into a drainage area in the garden."

She had never seen anything quite like it, and when she said as much, his smile was that of a young boy.

He reached into his pocket and handed something to her. She looked down at the key on her palm.

"To the room," he said. "I thought you might enjoy the experience. Alone. With no interruptions."

She'd revel in it.

They'd had a tub at the cottage, but the effort of heating all that water was a chore. It was easier to simply bathe in bits from a basin.

She nodded, grateful for his consideration, and absurdly glad he was wealthy.

Before she could thank him, he'd slipped from the room.

She turned the key in the lock, removed her wrapper, and hung it on a hook near the door. Before removing her shift, however, she went to the tub and peered inside. Devlen could have fit inside. In fact, it was commodious enough for two people.

The stopper was easy to fit into the hole at the bottom. She was leery about the hot water lever but after turning it just halfway, a steady stream of steaming water filled the tub. After adding cold water, she removed her shift and climbed the small wooden step next to the tub. She put one foot and then the other inside, sinking down into the hot water with a blissful sigh. A few minutes later, she leaned back in the water, submerged up to her neck, happier and more relaxed than she could remember being in months.

"I thought you'd like it."

Her eyes opened and she jerked to a sitting position, using her arms to hide her breasts.

"I neglected to mention I have a second key," he said, entering the room and closing the door behind him.

"Yes," she said, "you did."

"Are you angry?"

"I should be. You're very presumptuous."

"But you aren't. Good. I came to bring you this." *This*

turned out to be a tray on which a dozen or so ceramic jars were arranged, each bearing a label in a distinctive script.

"My newest venture," he said, setting the tray down beside the tub.

She read a few of the labels: SANDALWOOD, BERGAMOT, LAVENDER. "Soap?"

He nodded. "Would you like to try one?"

Before she could say yes, she would, but only in private, or ask him to leave, or a few other rejoinders that would no doubt be more proper and less suggestive, he moved the stool to the back of the tub and sat down, grabbing one of the containers from the tray.

"Sandalwood," he said, and reached out with one hand to grip her shoulder. He gently pulled her until she was resting her head against the back of the tub again, staring up at the ceiling.

A word from her would send him away, she was certain. She didn't speak.

Using both hands, he massaged the creamy soap into her shoulders and neck. The scent mixed with the steaming water and strengthened.

"It's very exotic," she said, surprised her voice sounded so level. His hands were very gentle, never dipping below the level of her shoulders, never going above her neck. Every once in a while, however, he would brush his thumbs up her throat to rest behind her ears, a gesture that had the power to incite shivers.

"I think of Far Eastern bazaars and women in veils."

"You use it, don't you?"

"Occasionally."

"I've smelled it on you."

He reached for another jar, and she let out a sigh. It was to be seduction, then. He would use his hands and bring her delight. In return, she would endure the discomfort and the pain for a few moments.

She would concentrate on the delight, and the other would take care of itself.

He lathered his hands with a scent reminiscent of flowers. He began at her shoulders, but this time trailed his hands down her arms, leaning forward until his cheek rested against hers. His breathing was steady and even, the antithesis of hers.

He had that power over her. At another time she'd feel irritated. Now, she was too occupied anticipating his touch.

His fingers entwined with hers, and she dropped her head back and closed her eyes, pretending not to know her breasts rested half-in, half-out of the water, her nipples pointed and hard and wanting to be touched.

He withdrew his hands to reach for another container. This scent was definitely lavender, and his hands, thick with soap, went immediately to her breasts.

A soft gasp escaped her at the sensuous slide of the soap, coupled with the hardness of his palms against her sensitive nipples.

He placed a gentle kiss against her ear. A tender, almost soothing kiss as if to calm her while his palms were making circles around her breasts.

She shifted restlessly, causing the water to lap near the edge of the tub.

Still, he cleaned her breasts with minute detail, careful to ensure the nipples were given their share of attention. Another scoop of soap and his fingers devoted another minute, two, to the task.

Beatrice licked her lips and turned her head. His beard was beginning to show, and she found that impossibly arousing. She licked at his skin and kissed the spot her tongue touched.

He made a sound low in his throat and gently squeezed both breasts.

The sensation flew like an arrow through her.

He removed his hands, but she didn't complain. She knew he'd pick another container and return soon enough. This scent was something herbal and green, smelling of a garden after the rain. He leaned against her back, his arms almost completely surrounding her, his cheek once more next to hers.

"Kiss me," she said, her eyes still closed.

"Turn your head."

She did so cautiously, opening her eyes slowly. His lips were so close. She wanted them on her, wanted to feel them.

He drew back, and she raised one hand, placed it on his cheek.

"Now," she said, demanding. He'd teased her into becoming this creature, and she felt no shame.

He kissed her, and she clung to his lips, parting them with her tongue, teasing him just as he'd done her.

In a few moments, he'd want to be inside her, but there was a price he had to pay first. He must pleasure her, softly and with great skill.

She pulled back and looked at him.

His hands dipped into the water, found her, and he slid one finger across her swollen folds. It wasn't nearly enough, but just when she would have begged for more, he stood, dragging her upward so forcefully she had no choice but to cling to him.

"Damn it to hell, Beatrice."

He was angry, his cheeks flushed, his eyes dancing with something that wasn't quite rage.

She didn't have a towel, but she didn't need one as long as he was holding her so close. His shirt and trousers were sodden.

He marched across the bathing chamber with her in his arms, opened the door, and stalked through his bedroom. Suddenly, she was airborne, then landing on his mattress with a bounce.

This wasn't supposed to happen at all.

"Damn it," he said, stripping off his clothes.

He was naked and atop her, but before she could say a word, he was inside, surging so deeply into her she expected the pain to be unbearable.

Her eyes widened, but the only sound she made was a gasp of surprise.

"I told you, damn it. I told you it wouldn't hurt."

"Why are you so angry?"

"Because this time was supposed to be slow and deliberate. But you've made me lose all control."

He hadn't been slow, but this felt very, very deliberate.

"Are you all right?"

She nodded.

"Are you certain?"

He moved then, and abruptly she wasn't certain at all. The sensations she was experiencing weren't at all what she'd felt the night before, and although he was still large, she was accommodating him quite easily.

She placed her hands flat on the bed and pushed upward a little. The resultant feeling was interesting. More than interesting—she felt positively exultant with it.

"I think you're enjoying this." Devlen smiled.

"Wasn't that what you wanted?"

"We should be gentle. Restrained. You're too close to a virgin."

"Unicorn," she said, smiling.

"Damn it, Beatrice."

Her smile broadened, and she felt, absurdly, like laughing.

"Does it always feel this way? Once you're not a unicorn, that is."

"How does it feel?"

"A heaviness," she said, considering. "No, nicer. Like something soothing and not at the same time. Does that make any sense?"

"Shall I tell you what it feels like for me?"

She nodded, curious.

"It's a damnable itch, and it makes me want to slide in and out of you until it's satisfied. I'm so hard it's painful, and yet every time you move, or sigh, I get harder. I want to bury myself in you so deeply you'll never be able to forget how I felt."

"Oh."

"Indeed. Oh."

He moved, sliding just a fraction of an inch out of her, and she gasped. Instinctively, her hips arched up to entice him back, and he returned, bending his head to kiss her.

She reached up and kissed him, sighing with relief when he returned to her. He pulled back a few moments later, his breathing labored, and braced himself on his elbows.

"You have beautiful breasts."

She wasn't particularly in the mood for conversation right at the moment. Again, she pulled his head down for a kiss, but he hesitated just before reaching her lips.

"Impatient?"

"Kiss me."

"Dearest Beatrice, so autocratic."

She didn't care what he called her as long as he kissed her. She flexed her internal muscles and heard him groan. He bent to kiss her then, and her lips curved against his smile.

His fingers measured her swollen folds, danced where they joined, and she almost came off the bed when his thumb circled her and coaxed her to pleasure.

Loving would cease to be simply a word. The very mention of the word *love* would summon images to her mind: his smile, the way he looked down at her with each surging thrust, the flex of the muscles in his arms, the tightening of his neck. Their bodies pushed against each other for that last bit of feeling. Again and again he arched his hips, his buttocks flexing beneath her spread fingers.

He bent his head, his lips near her ear, praising her response. "You're so tight, Beatrice. So very hot inside."

Each word, each soft stroke of his fingers on her body, was an incitement. When she lifted her hips, urging his invasion once more, he whispered to her, "Soar for me, Beatrice. Fly."

She did, feeling as if she touched the sun.

When he followed her a moment later, she held him

tight, her arms wrapped around his shoulders, and wept against his neck.

"What do you mean, he's gone?"

"I heard," Mary said, "they left yesterday. Both of them. Mr. Devlen and the governess. And the boy, of course."

"That odious child. He causes more problems than he's worth."

"Mr. Gordon is having a fit, madam. He's throwing things around in the library and threatening to go after them."

"Is he?"

Mary handed her the cup of tea, bustling around her to adjust the pillows on the settee, straighten the blanket on her lap.

Sometimes, the woman could be busy as a bee and about as annoying.

"Settle yourself, Mary," Rowena said.

The older woman did so, choosing a footstool near a chair.

"Cameron is going after them?" She hadn't spoken to Cameron since that disastrous night she'd gone to his room. Nor did she want to. Her pride was all she had left.

"He hasn't told me, madam."

"Gaston might know."

"Gaston would never tell, madam."

"That's true. It amazes me the loyalty Cameron is able to inspire."

Mary looked away.

"Not that you're not loyal, Mary. But you are not fanatical about it."

"I don't know what you mean, madam."

Rowena sighed. "Never mind." She held her hands out. "There's a draft near the window."

Mary hurried to close the drapes, throwing the room into a clouded sort of darkness. She lit a candle, and the blaze from the fire provided some illumination as well.

"The entire castle is cold, madam."

Rowena didn't bother to answer.

She wanted to go back to London. At least there she could pretend her life was ordinary. If Cameron didn't wish to speak to her, she could attend a play or an entertainment. If he barred her from his bedroom, perhaps she could engage in a flirtation with someone else.

How foolish she was being. As if anyone else could ever measure up to Cameron.

"I hate that child."

Mary looked stricken.

"Madam, you're crying."

Rowena wiped at her face with one hand. "Am I? How very odd."

She stood, returned to the dressing table, and allowed Mary to flutter around her as she usually did.

"I would like to wear the green today, I think, Mary," she said. The dress was a new one, purchased in London with the thought it might interest Cameron. The garment required a special set of stays because it was so closely fitted. At least she looked the part of Chatelaine of Castle Crannoch, at least until Robert grew and took a wife.

Damnable child.

She didn't want to hear about Robert, didn't want to worry about Robert, didn't want to even think about Robert until it was absolutely necessary. Every time she saw the child she was reminded of that horrible day of the accident.

She dropped her head in her hands and said a prayer, hoping God would forgive her because she knew Cameron wouldn't.

Chapter 25

"**D**evlen!" Two knocks on the door, followed by another of Robert's shouts. "Devlen!" They looked at each other.

"Good heavens!" She sat up, forgetting her nakedness. Devlen's eyes traveled down her torso, and she slapped him on the chest before pulling up the sheet.

"Go into the bathing chamber, and I'll get rid of him."

"I know Robert, he won't be rid of easily."

"I'll take him down to the dining room. You can go to your room. When you're dressed, summon one of the maids to show you where it is."

She couldn't just sit across the table from him. Not now.

"Shouldn't I just have a tray in my room?"

"No."

She raised her eyebrows at him. "No?"

"I want you at the table with us."

He stood, and walked to the washstand, supremely unconcerned about his nakedness.

"I enjoy your company, Beatrice." He glanced at her, then halted. "Stop looking at me like that."

"You're very attractive. I like looking at you."

"Devlen! Answer the door!"

Beatrice pulled the sheet off the bed and wrapped it around her, entering the bathing chamber and closing the door behind her.

Devlen said something in response to Robert's summons. The child was evidently mollified because she didn't hear him shouting again.

She flattened herself against the door and looked at the disarray all around her. The towels had tumbled to the floor, the box of soaps was askew. Water puddled near the drain and in a path to the door, and the tub was still filled.

What a strange time to want to laugh.

A half hour later Beatrice was dressed, descending the staircase with her thoughts still full of Devlen. A maid greeted her at the base of the stairs, her face, if not sullen, then strangely without expression. Did Mrs. Anderson force such a conformity of expression on her staff?

She was led to the drawing room, a room of such beauty that at any other time she would have stopped in the doorway and admired the pale yellow walls and the art mounted on them.

The sight of Cameron Gordon, however, sent every thought flying from her mind.

He'd lost no time in following them.

"You're looking well, Miss Sinclair," he said.

Robert sat on a couch not far away, looking small, pale, and cowed.

How dare he frighten a child.

Devlen stood behind him, but at her entrance, he moved beside her.

"You didn't tell me you had plans for a holiday in the city, Devlen. I might have allowed it had I known."

"There was no reason to inform you since you were the reason we left."

Cameron raised one eyebrow and studied his son. "Are you going to explain that statement, or shall I use my powers of divination?"

Devlen put his arm around her back, his hand on her waist, a physical gesture of support she'd not expected.

"There were too many attempts on Robert's life for me to be comfortable with him remaining at Castle Crannoch."

"Indeed."

"And you, Father, seemed disinterested in his welfare."

"I'm his guardian. Of course I'm interested in his welfare."

"Did you know someone shot at him? And poisoned his food?" A movement caught her eye, and she glanced to where Gaston stood, silent and until now unobtrusive.

"Robert is a very excitable, very imaginative little boy. He sees goblins where there are none, Miss Sinclair."

Robert simply looked at his shoes, a miserable expression on his face.

"He didn't imagine those incidents," she said. "I was with him when they occurred."

"Then perhaps if you are no longer with him, they will not occur. I think I will dispense with your services, Miss Sinclair. Your propensity for attracting danger cannot be a good thing for Robert."

"You're dismissing me? Is that your answer to protecting Robert?"

"No, Miss Sinclair. My answer to protecting Robert is to remove him from your care. He belongs at Castle Crannoch. Robert," he said, turning to the boy, "we'll be leaving in the morning. Edinburgh is not the place for you."

"I'm not going." He stood and faced his uncle, his fists balled up at his sides. Beatrice wondered if he was trembling as he was the last time he confronted Cameron.

"Indeed you are, child."

"I wouldn't be so certain, Father." Devlen stepped closer to Robert, standing behind the boy and placing his hands on Robert's shoulders. "Robert isn't going anywhere. I've already contacted my solicitor. I'm contesting your guardianship."

Cameron's face changed. In that moment he was no longer the charming, almost courtly invalid. Instead, he was obviously angry, his hands gripping the arms of his chair so tightly his knuckles were white.

"Robert is going to stay here with me, Father, until the courts decide," Devlen said. "I suggest, however, that you return to Castle Crannoch."

"You can pretend to be duke without me there," Robert said.

The look in Cameron's eyes did not bode well for the child. He signaled to Gaston, who stepped to the rear of Cameron's chair and deftly wheeled him to the door. When he was gone, Beatrice turned and looked at Devlen.

Robert stared at the empty doorway. "He wants me dead."

She had no answer to such a statement. The horror was that Robert uttered it in such a calm voice, as if accusing his uncle of murderous impulses was an everyday occurrence.

"I don't have to go, do I, Devlen?"

"No, you don't, Robert," he said somberly. "I promise."

She almost wept at the look in the child's eyes, and was certain she'd worn the very same expression after her own parents' deaths: grief, loss, and pain so deep it was almost tangible.

"Go and ask Cook if she has some treats," Devlen said.

Robert nodded, leaving the room without a backward glance.

"My father has always been dissatisfied with his life," Devlen said. "My earliest memories are of his anger toward his brother for being duke. He always told me that his brother would much rather prefer to be a scholar than head of the family."

"While he would much rather be the head of the family."

He nodded. "He was destined to be duke, at least in his mind."

"Could he harm Robert?"

He didn't answer her. Instead, he walked to the fire, stirred the coals with the poker. Several minutes elapsed before he turned back to her. "I've been asking myself the same question for weeks, ever since I learned of Robert's penchant for accidents."

"If not your father, then who else could be behind it?"

"Gaston?"

She must have looked surprised, because he smiled. "Gaston is my father's loyal servant. He would be the most likely candidate, being my father's legs, so to speak."

"I went to him," she said. "When Robert was shot at in the woods, I went to Gaston." He had been in the kitchen, she remembered. Not far from the courtyard. He could have seen them descending the hill.

Devlen came to her side. "It's too easy to blame yourself in hindsight. I do the same. Why didn't I take Robert from Castle Crannoch in the beginning?"

"If you had, we never would have met."

"A circumstance that would have occurred in some fashion, I'm sure."

"Fate?"

"You sound as if you don't believe in it," he said, with a smile.

She shook her head. "You can't say you do."

"Actually, I don't."

"But for Fate you might be a duke yourself one day."

"I am content to be a mister, nothing more."

She tilted his head and surveyed him. A corner of his mouth turned up as she continued to study him. The moments ticked by as their gaze held.

"Are you disappointed that I'm not a duke?"

She laughed, genuinely amused. "Heavens, why should I be? You've created your own wealth, and you look the part of a prince. The title would just be redundant."

"I created my own wealth because I didn't want to depend on anyone for my livelihood, and my looks are beyond my control."

"You've just proven my point. You have the arrogance of a duke."

He smiled at her. "Why, I wonder, does your opinion matter so much to me?"

"It shouldn't. I'm just a governess. And not even that, now."

"You're my angel of goodness."

Amused, she reached out and let her fingers stray over his coat, palm flattening over his heart. "You're my devil of delight."

"You frighten me," he said.

A confession that disturbed him, she could tell. His eyes were suddenly somber, and the expression on his face was that of a man forced to speak the truth.

She placed her palm against his cheek. He frightened her as well—or more correctly—what she felt for him frightened her.

"Devlen."

He bent and kissed her, a soft and charming kiss, but not a passionate one.

"I have duties to perform," he said. "Work I could do."

"Yes."

"We haven't eaten dinner yet."

"No." She shook her head.

"Every time I kiss you, it always leads to more."

"I'm sorry." She smiled.

"I believe you plan it that way," he said.

"Not truly."

"I thought, once, you would change my life."

"Have I?"

"More than you know."

"Perhaps it would be better if I left," she said.

"Perhaps it would. But I haven't always done the wisest thing in regard to you, Beatrice."

"Nor I you."

"We are a pair, aren't we?" he asked.

She stepped away, allowing her hand to drop. "For the meantime."

His face darkened, as if he didn't like the truth she'd offered him. They didn't belong to the same life, and they'd only borrowed this time.

"I'll go and see about dinner. Robert is probably coaxing Cook into giving him all sorts of forbidden treats."

"He'd be happier that way."

"Yes, but life isn't all cake, Devlen."

"Beatrice."

She glanced at him, but he only shook his head, as if his thoughts must forever remain unspoken.

Beatrice left before she, too, could say more.

Chapter 26

Two weeks later, Devlen stood in a ballroom staring out at the newest crop of virgins, all too aware that he was being watched by the matrons of society to ensure he didn't violate any unwritten rule, therefore proving himself good enough for their daughters. The daughters, on the other hand, were less judgmental.

One brave young miss reminded him of Beatrice, not because of her appearance—she was short, blond, petite, and graced with a bodice that must be half handkerchiefs for all the overflowing lace—but because of her daring. She was batting her eyelashes and her fan at him.

"That one has her eye on you, Gordon."

He turned to see a business acquaintance staring at the same young lady. She looked pleased rather than daunted by the increased attention.

"I think I'll pass. Be my guest."

"Haven't the money. Rumor is her mother is trolling

for a title. Barring that, a fortune. Too bad, the girl really is a looker."

Devlen didn't comment, an omission that had the other man glancing at him curiously.

"Surprised to see you tonight. These types of things aren't usually your style."

"I felt the need to show myself."

"In the marriage mart are you?"

"God, no."

"Wouldn't think so with that gorgeous creature of yours."

"How the devil do you know about her?"

"Hell, Gordon, everybody knows about Felicia."

"Oh, her."

"Whom did you think I meant?"

He shook his head, but the other man wasn't satisfied. What the devil was the man's name? Richards? Something like that.

Devlen wished his hostess approved of something more potent than a sugary sweet pink punch as a refreshment. Whiskey, for example.

"Is the fair Felicia about to get the boot, then?" He leaned closer. "Want to share who your newest mistress is?"

"No."

"But you do have a new one?"

"I don't know why the hell I'm here," Devlen said. He turned to the man beside him. "Why are you here?"

"I'm being harassed at all sides to marry," his acquaintance said. "I just need to find an heiress, myself. Someone with a penchant for poor men who will worship at their feet forever."

"Is that what women want?"

"Damned if I know," the other man said, smiling ruefully. "I have five sisters, and they all seem different. Sometimes different from themselves, depending on the mood."

Beatrice had been herself, consistently. She had a variety of moods, however, each of them more fascinating than the last. He even enjoyed her annoyance, and found himself going out of his way to argue a point of view he didn't even agree with simply to see her impassioned anger.

How idiotic was that?

They discussed literature, languages, history. He'd even found himself expounding on his plans for a new racing stable. They argued politics, religion, women's rights, and various other subjects he'd never once discussed with a male acquaintance.

"Never seen you look so down, Gordon. Deal fall through? Heard Martin is being stubborn."

"He can keep his munitions works if he wants. I've offered him a fair price."

"Then you don't really want it. The word is out, you know."

"I didn't know I was that easily deciphered."

"If you don't want something, it's not worth buying. Surely you've seen that most of the market follows your lead like carp? They're bottom feeders, Gordon."

At another time he might be amused by the analogy.

The orchestra was beginning again, and the girl with the fan was fluttering a little madly.

"You really should give her a go."

"I don't dance."

His companion glanced at him. "There's nothing to

it, Gordon. You simply go out there and resign yourself to playing the fool. It's done all the time."

"Not by me."

"Then it's a good thing you're not in search of a wife. It's a requirement, you know."

He fingered the box in his pocket. It was time to leave. He'd come to this idiotic evening to prove, at least to himself, that his life hadn't changed in the past few weeks. He could go and come as he liked, unfettered by conscience or guilt. He'd enjoy himself, and when it was time, he'd return home.

The problem with his plan was that it didn't work. He wasn't enjoying himself, and he wanted to be home more than he wanted to be in company. Every woman of his acquaintance was either insipid or too obvious, and none of them was graced with wit or intelligence or the ability to tell him what she really thought.

None of them was Beatrice.

He bid farewell to the man at his side and spent the next quarter hour locating and saying good night to his host and hostess. That done, he made his way to the entrance and spent an enjoyable few minutes chatting with another man of his acquaintance while waiting for his carriage to be brought around.

When it arrived, he gave Peter a destination the driver knew well.

The interior lantern was lit and illuminated the necklace as he drew it out of its box. A magnificent collection of yellow diamonds. "A necklace fit for a queen," the jeweler had said.

He hoped Felicia thought so as well.

* * *

Beatrice sat in the middle of Robert's bed in the room Devlen had set aside as his. Unlike the Duke's Chamber at Castle Crannoch, this room obviously belonged to a child. The walls were painted a soft blue, and there were blue silk draperies on the windows. There were three armoires aligned against one wall, and two of them held an abundance of toys, anything a duke—or any child—might want.

Beatrice was an observer as Robert arranged his toy soldiers around the pillows and featherbed coverlet. He had already described several battles to her, and since her knowledge of anything military was somewhat lacking, she could only nod sagely and pretend an interest she didn't have.

From time to time she glanced at the mantel clock, then away, pretending the lateness of the hour didn't matter. In actuality, she was conscious of the passing of every minute. Robert, however, having readied for bed, was professing to not being able to sleep.

"I feel like I might have a nightmare tonight, Miss Sinclair."

Of course she hadn't believed him. Was it even possible to predict when one might have bad dreams? Nor had Robert had any nightmares since leaving Castle Crannoch.

It wasn't concern for him that held her there or allowed him to remain awake and playing. She was lonely and angry and sad, and all three emotions were keeping her unsettled. Perhaps a little guilt kept her here as well. She hadn't been the best or most attentive governess since leaving the castle.

The last weeks had been part of an idyll, weeks of hedonistic pleasure, and if she made up for it by playing toy soldiers until midnight, then it was a small price to pay.

Still, he was yawning every few minutes.

Earlier, she and Robert had had their dinner on a tray. Devlen had a social engagement he'd had to attend, and the house was oddly empty without him.

As the minutes advanced, she was all too certain that, for the first time since coming to Edinburgh, she was going to spend the night alone.

Where was he? What was he doing?

The clock struck midnight, and despite Robert's protests, she began to gather up his toy soldiers.

"If you don't sleep now, or at least try, you will be worthless for your lessons tomorrow."

He gave her a rude look, and she returned it with a strict expression.

"You'll be too sleepy to go on an adventure."

"An adventure? Are you bribing me, Miss Sinclair?"

"I believe I am, Robert. But we should explore Edinburgh a little, don't you think? Perhaps we can go and find a sweet shop."

"Really?"

She nodded.

He allowed her to tuck him in and light one lantern. It was hardly necessary. Devlen's home was lit up as bright as a harvest moon.

He was the most unusual man she'd ever known, and the most fascinating.

"You haven't had nightmares since we left Castle Crannoch, have you?"

He shook his head. "Castle Crannoch doesn't feel like home," he said, scooting up in the bed and gathering the sheet around him. "Not since my parents died."

Since she felt the same way about her own little cottage, she only smiled.

There were some things a child, even one of seven, was certain to understand. Death was regrettably one of them. Loss of parents changed everything, made the world a dark and unfriendly place.

Beatrice stretched out her hand and smoothed back his hair. He yawned in response.

"Tell me a story. But not a fable."

"They're the only stories I know."

"Tell me about when you were a little girl."

"When I was little? How little?"

"My age."

"You don't seem very little at all. One moment you're seven and the next you're twenty-seven."

"You're avoiding the subject, Miss Sinclair."

She smiled. "I am, actually. I haven't had a very exciting life. My grandmother lived with us until her death, and it was from her that I learned French. When she died we came to live at Kilbridden Village. I was almost twelve. I remember because two days after we arrived was my birthday."

"Did you have a celebration? Get a present?"

She shook her head. "There was so much chaos no one remembered. It wasn't until nearly a month later my mother realized it."

"I should have had a fit, Miss Sinclair. No one should forget my birthday. It's June 26," he added for good measure.

"I shall make a note of it."

"But where did you live before?"

"In a small house on the border of Scotland and England. A very small farm but a lovely place. I don't re-

member very much about it, but I know I was happy."
She tucked the sheet around his shoulders. "That is the
extent of my adventures. See, I told you I didn't have a
very exciting life."

"Didn't you have any friends?"

"My very best friend lived at Kilbridden Village. I
met her on my birthday, as a matter of fact. Her name
was Sally."

"Is she still your friend?"

Sally had been among those who'd died in the cholera
epidemic. On the day Sally had died, a storm had suddenly appeared, turbulent and wild, stripping the
branches bare until it appeared to be raining leaves. The
birds had ceased their song, and even the raindrops, drip-
ping ponderously from the heavens, were more like tears.

But for Robert's benefit, she only nodded.

"But what's all these questions about friends?"

"I haven't any. I'm the Duke of Brechin. Shouldn't I
have friends?"

She bent and before he could draw away, kissed him
on the forehead. "Indeed you will. When you go away
to school, perhaps."

"Why not here in Edinburgh?"

"I shall have to send out notices to all my business
acquaintances, I see. Announce to all of them the Duke
of Brechin is accepting visitors, but only those around
the age of seven." Devlen strode into the room.

Robert grinned. "Could you do that?"

Beatrice turned and smiled at Devlen. He was so utterly handsome, her heart stilled at the sight of him.

She stood and walked around the end of the bed.

Devlen joined her there and grabbed her hand, bringing it up to his lips to kiss her knuckles.

"How have you been?"

"In the four hours since you've been gone? Fine."

He bent his head, but just before his lips met hers, he glanced to the side.

"Turn your head, Robert. I'm about to kiss your governess senseless."

"I'm a duke," Robert said. "I should learn about such things."

"Not at this particular moment. And not from me."

He turned her so his back was to Robert's bed, and proceeded to kiss her until her lips were numb.

"May I escort you to your room?" he asked when he released her.

"I would like that."

She stood at the doorway and watched Robert for a moment. "Sleep well."

He feigned sleep for a moment before opening his eyes. "I'm hungry."

"Tomorrow."

"I'm thirsty."

"Tomorrow."

He sighed dramatically. "Good night, Miss Sinclair."

"Good night, Robert."

"Good night, Devlen."

"Go to sleep," Devlen said. He still held her hand, and she felt as if they were children themselves, walking swiftly down the corridor to the next wing. For the first time, she was grateful for his advance planning in having installed her in a room far from Robert's.

Instead of saying farewell to her at her door, he opened it and stepped aside. When she entered the room, he followed her and closed the door behind him.

They were immersed in shadows. The darkness gave

her a freedom she'd never before felt. She linked her hands to the back of his neck and stood on tiptoe to press a kiss against his lips.

"Thank you," she softly said.

"Why am I being thanked?"

"For your kindness to Robert."

"Anyone would be kind to the child," he said.

"Someone isn't."

"Must we talk about that at this moment?"

"Must we talk?"

"Beatrice, I'm shocked."

"Are you?" She reached up to kiss his smiling mouth.

"The dress looks very complicated."

"On the contrary, it is supremely easy."

He placed both hands at her waist, his thumbs meeting in the front. Slowly, he drew them upward until he cupped both of her breasts.

"Have you many dresses? I would just as soon tear this one from you."

"I only have three, and before you suggest it, no, I shall not accept any clothing from you."

"How did you know I was going to offer?"

"It sounds like something you'd do. You're very generous."

He bent and placed his cheek against hers. "I'm not especially generous with other people, Beatrice, but I find myself wanting to give you things."

"Then restrain yourself with the knowledge I will not accept them."

"Do you dance?"

"Dance?" She pulled back to look at him, but the room was too dark to see his expression. "I do. Country dances mostly. Why?"

"I'd dance with you. I just realized that tonight."

"You would? How very sweet of you to say that."

"I'm not sweet. I despise the word."

"Very well. You're kind and well-mannered."

"If I am, it's because you summon forth my better nature."

Slowly and with great dexterity, he unfastened her bodice, and spread it wide, unlacing her stays with such skill it was as if his fingers could see in the darkness.

In a matter of moments she was down to her shift, her dress thrown on the nearest chair, along with her stays.

Her fingers found his coat, eased it off his shoulders, uncaring it fell to the floor. His waistcoat was next, and she unbuttoned it with the same skill he'd shown earlier. Over the past weeks, they'd learned each other's clothing. His shirt came next. She unbuttoned one button and bent forward to kiss his bare chest. Another button, another kiss.

While she was intent upon removing his clothing, he was equally intent upon learning her curves beneath her shift. His hands roamed from her shoulders to her elbows to her hips to her buttocks and up her back, soothing strokes that made her shiver.

They were matched in sensuality, the only part of their lives where they were equals. His wealth was enormous, his position enviable, his possessions covetable. Her status was not so high-flown, and she had nothing to her name but a cottage and the contents of a well-worn valise. No one would ever clamor for her presence at dinner, and there would not be hordes of invitations awaiting her perusal as there were for him daily.

Suddenly, she was in his arms, and he was taking her to bed. This loving would be slower, less fevered, and perhaps more devastating. There was a component of tenderness now that made her want to simply hold him to her. She framed his face with her hands and kissed him sweetly.

Don't ever forget me.

They didn't speak, didn't tease each other with words.

When he entered her, a lifetime later, she arched off the bed, a small gasp of wonder escaping her.

"Please," she said, knowing he was the only one who could end this eternal wanting.

When it ended, and she was sated, she turned in his arms, exhausted. She heard him whisper her name, just before she slid into sleep, feeling safe and protected for the first time in a very long time.

Devlen left the bed and donned enough clothes so that he wouldn't shock a footman if he were seen. He left her room, soundlessly closing the door behind him.

The lovemaking was one thing, but it had a remarkable ability to put him in a reflective mood, and he was damn tired of feeling guilty about Beatrice Sinclair.

She was driving him mad.

He wanted her constantly, and it was obvious she felt the same. But her conscience was evidently not bothering her as much as his; witness the fact she'd rolled over and gone to sleep, and he was prowling through his home like some nocturnal creature.

He should leave her alone. Why couldn't he?

He should send her back to her village with enough money to live for the rest of her life. A dowry, if you

Chapter 27

When Beatrice awoke Devlen was gone. Her first thought was that she missed him, and her second was that she was being foolish. He hadn't been in her life long enough for her to miss him. He wasn't firmly fixed in place, wasn't someone to whom she could point with pride and announce he belonged to her.

Devlen Gordon was so much himself that the idea of him belonging to anyone was amusing.

The snow was full on the ground, and they were months away from spring. The squirrels were hiding away in their burrows, and there was a wild and fierce wind blowing against the building, but nevertheless the day looked to be one of promise. She felt like the happiest person alive. Was that tempting Providence?

The garment she chose was a dark blue dress with red piping along the cuffs and collar. It was cinched at the waist and fastened up the front. Very proper attire by any standards. Perhaps not grand enough for a guest will. She'd marry a farmer, maybe a brewer or a shop-keeper, and bring to that union assets of her own.

Why should he banish her?

Because hiding in the shadows was no life for a woman like her. Because he was not used to skulking around like a passion-crazed weakling who couldn't get enough of a woman.

Because he didn't want to keep her as his mistress.

She was probably better educated than he was, and no doubt had a more traditional upbringing. Her manners were impeccable, her speech upper-class, and she had an annoying tendency to be right during most of their arguments.

Then why treat her like a doxy on the London wharves?

Damn it.

at Devlen's Edinburgh home, nevertheless, it was the best of her three dresses and must do.

In the last three weeks, Devlen had tried to convince her to accept the services of a dressmaker, and she'd repeatedly declined. It was one thing to engage in an idyll, sharing weeks of hedonism for the sake of it. Quite another to be kept openly like a mistress.

Devlen's mistress. The label should have shocked her, and the fact it didn't was an indication of how utterly depraved she'd become.

She left her chamber and went to Robert's room, not unduly surprised to find it empty. The child was no doubt down in the kitchen again. He was often to be found there, chatting away with the cook and her helpers, and stuffing himself full of purloined treats.

The staff had still not warmed to her, and she wasn't surprised. During the day, she and Devlen practiced a careful avoidance of each other in front of the servants. Were they fooling any of them? Or was the staff at this enormous home busy speculating behind closed doors about the master and the governess?

She found her way to the kitchens, and there was Robert, perched on a chair, one hand braced on the top of the table, the other in a large ceramic bowl.

At the sight of her, he grinned.

Evidently, the Duke of Brechin was in the process of picking another biscuit. One or a dozen, she couldn't be certain. A selection was already arrayed on the table in front of him.

She reached him and brushed off the crumbs from the front of his shirt.

"Biscuits for breakfast?"

"Annie's biscuits," he corrected. "The best."

"Do not talk with your mouth full."

He nodded and smiled.

"Good morning, miss," Cook said, turning from the stove. She performed an awkward curtsy, especially as she had a spoon in one hand and a pot in the other. The odor of chocolate filled the room, and she suddenly understood why Robert couldn't stop grinning.

When his biscuit was finished, he said, "We're going to have chocolate to drink, Miss Sinclair. In honor of the day."

"In honor of the day?"

"It's Wednesday. Don't you think every day should be special?"

She smiled at him and reached to take a biscuit herself. Tomorrow, she'd fuss at him about eating a proper meal.

"I'm sure Annie wouldn't mind if you had some chocolate, too."

"Thank you, Your Grace, you're more than kind."

He grinned at her and took another bite of his newest biscuit acquisition. She was tempted to ask if he intended to hoard the others, but didn't.

Beatrice smiled her good-bye and made her way into the family dining room, where the table was set for breakfast. In a sense, the chamber was indicative of her life. From the kitchen, she could hear the sound of laughter and conversation. Somewhere, Devlen was no doubt occupied in a myriad of duties. Here, in this room, she was alone, strangely segregated from others. Proper, alone, and suddenly lonely.

In the year since her parents had died, she'd learned to accept the silence of her life, learned to live with the aloneness of loss and grief. It had been a habit she'd suddenly lost the ability to endure. She suddenly knew she'd never be able to go back to that life.

She moved to the line of serving dishes and inspected the contents one by one before replacing the lids.

At the cottage, she had been occupied with a daily tedium. Washing, weeding her tiny garden, carrying water to the struggling plants, cleaning, mending her garments and those she could still use that had once belonged to her mother. Her life hadn't been interesting, but it had been busy. Her new life was fascinating and yet was steeped in tedium.

She sat at the table and folded her hands, intent upon studying her nails. They'd lost their bluish tinge since she'd been eating well. Her hands no longer looked so frail or skeletal. Her body had filled out, her clothing was almost too snug. There were no lasting ill effects of her near starvation during that last hideous month before coming to Castle Crannoch.

After a few moments, she stood again and walked around the table and took another chair. The view was different, and she could look out the lone window at least. The day was a gray one and looked to be cold. Too cold for a walk, perhaps? She needed to stretch her legs, to do something other than simply wait until breakfast was done to begin her teaching chores.

Even that was not onerous. Robert was a good student when he wished to be, and when he didn't, one look from Devlen changed his mind about misbehaving.

The morning that had begun with such promise was now proving to be interminable.

She stood once again and left the dining room.

The fact they were lovers did not give her the authority to invade Devlen's privacy. Otherwise, she'd have used some of her free time to explore, to investigate some of this grand house Devlen had created for himself. She should retreat to the library and pick out a book. But she would be there soon enough to begin Robert's lessons. She needed something to do other than think of Devlen, some occupation that would take her mind from her enthrallment.

What was she but a slave to Devlen Gordon? A slave to pleasure, one who had begged him to bind her with chains.

Finally, with nowhere else to go, she retreated to her room, but before she entered, she turned and stared at the double doors leading to Devlen's chamber.

She strode across the hall and knocked gently on his door. There was no answer. Had he already left for the day? With such an empire to run, he must be occupied every moment of the day. If so, she was envious. She wanted something to do other than to think of him.

She heard a sound, and pushed on the latch, surprised to find the door unlocked.

He'd opened the drapes, and the weak sunlight spilled into the room, illuminating the midnight blue of the carpet and the draperies surrounding the bed.

The sound came again and she suddenly knew where he was.

Slowly, she pushed open the door of the bathing chamber and leaned against the jamb, watching him.

He was reclining in the copper tub, his arms on the sides, his head back with his eyes closed. Steam rose around him as he hummed a tune, some little ditty that had bawdy lyrics, no doubt.

After a moment, she stepped into the room, closing

the door behind her, but taking the precaution of locking it before turning to face him.

He glanced behind him and now sat looking at her, his features impassive, but a twinkle sparkling in his eyes.

"Are you going to tell me what's sauce for the goose is sauce for the gander?"

"I should, shouldn't I? But I must confess any thought I had has simply flown from my mind."

"At the sight of me?"

"Of course."

Beatrice retrieved the three-legged stool and set it beside the tub. She sat and dipped her hand into the hot water, playfully flicking water onto his chest.

"Dare I hope you're going to bathe me?"

"Do you want me to?"

"I'd be a fool to say no, wouldn't I?"

"We're both fools, of one kind or another."

He was dangerous, addictive, fascinating, and bad for her. She was virtuous, educated, and—to the world outside this house—imbued with sense and decorum. There was some type of future ahead of her now that she'd been the Duke of Brechin's governess.

She resented him at the same time she was fascinated by him. Nothing good could come of her relationship with Devlen Gordon.

He smiled at her, as if he understood her sudden irritation.

"You didn't use the English riding coats last night."

"I know. I remembered later."

"Does that mean I'm going to have a child?"

"Not necessarily. But it does mean I can't be trusted around you. I've never forgotten before."

What a silly time to feel a surge of pure, feminine pleasure.

His erection broke the surface of the water like a creature emerging from the deep.

"Does it always grow like that? Is it the hot water?"

His laughter echoed against the stone walls. "Not the hot water, Beatrice. It's you, I'm afraid. Frankly, even the idea of your hand being so close."

"Oh."

"Indeed. Oh. You see, I have been sitting here thinking of you touching me, and in you come, locking the door behind you."

"Really."

"You have the most fascinating look on your face. Why?"

"If you must know, I'm trying to envision what it must look like right at the moment."

He abruptly stood, water cascading from his body in sheets. "There, does that help?"

He was most gloriously made, a man in his prime, muscled and splendid. His buttocks were round and formed like two perfect buns. She trailed her fingers over one and watched as it flexed beneath her hand. But it was his impressive array of male attributes that caught her attention and held it.

His erection was long and thick, growing as she watched. It pointed to his stomach, and he pushed it down with a hand as if preparing to use it as a lance. If she'd still been a virgin, she would have been terrified.

She knew, however, what absolute wonder he could perform with such a weapon, and was only fascinated at its girth and length. Slowly, she extended one finger and trailed a path from its bulbous head to the nest of surprisingly soft hair at its base.

"It's very hard," she said. "And hot. Does it hurt?"

"Yes."

She glanced up at him to see him watching her intently. Her finger strolled from base to tip, and then softly circled the head.

"Indeed?"

"I'm in great pain at the moment."

"You should take advantage of a long, soaking bath I think. Something that would take the swelling down."

"Is that what you would recommend?"

"A snow pack, perhaps, would be better."

"It would certainly cool any ardor."

She stroked his erection again, and it trembled beneath her ministrations.

"You must certainly seek some treatment for it."

"Kiss it."

She glanced up at him, shocked. His eyes were glittering, his face ruddy with color. "Kiss it, Beatrice."

Slowly, she rose and, with one hand on the edge of the tub for balance, reached over and pressed her lips against him. His erection bobbed in response, hot and eager, and so soft she was tempted to kiss him again. She held him with one hand, her fingers gently resting against his length as if to coax him still. Her other hand curved around one buttock as her lips found him, and opened just a little.

The bulbous head was soft against her lips. She opened her mouth just a little wider, enough for her tongue to dart out. A teasing touch, one eliciting a groan from Devlen.

She smiled, her lips curving against the shaft.

The steam from the water dampened her face, plastered the fabric of her bodice against her chest. She wished she was naked with him. She ran her palms up his thighs, combing the hair on his legs with playful fingers. His buttocks were smooth, so beautifully shaped she couldn't help but caress them with her hand.

All the while, he stood motionless, his hand on the back of her head, fingers spread through her hair. She didn't move her lips, but from time to time she would blow a warm breath on the head of his erection to see it jerk and throb in response.

She loved having him under her power.

He smelled of the soap he'd used, something scented with sandalwood. Reaching out with her right hand, she scooped some up from the tin and placed it on his knee, rubbing it into his skin in a circular pattern.

"Beatrice."

She sat back and looked up at him. "I want to wash you, Devlen."

He grabbed her hair, and tugged gently. "There. Wash me there."

She only smiled.

One leg was washed slowly, from the knee down to his foot, submerged in the steaming water. Then the other, using the same slow, rhythmic touch.

His erection grew as if to attract her attention. She was not likely to forget about it.

When she was done with his legs, she lathered the base of hair between his legs, taking care to soap the testicles with a gentle circular motion. Finally, it was time to wash his erection. She covered both palms with the sandalwood soap before placing them on the shaft.

He made a noise halfway between a groan and a laugh.

Beatrice smiled.

Using both hands, she stroked him from the base to the tip, her grip firm and unrelenting. He said something to her, some caution she blithely ignored. She wanted him to explode in her hands, wanted him to lose control as she did every time he touched her.

She grew breathless and heated—she wanted the same from him. Her heart pounded so loudly her chest quivered with it. Her mind opened and her soul poured out to him. She wanted him as desperate and longing as she felt.

Both hands were on him, holding him still, and she bent forward and opened her mouth, encircling the head with her lips. He arched his hips forward, and she felt an answering response deep inside, where her body readied for him.

A few drops of water splashed from the faucet into the tub, a log dropped in the fire, but they only accompanied the kissing sounds she made when teasing the head in and out of her mouth. Devlen whispered something, a warning perhaps, and she only moved slightly so she could grip one of his buttocks with each hand.

She moved, releasing his erection, compelled to do something shocking. She bit him tenderly on that beautiful backside, kissed the spot, and then rubbed her cheek against his buttock. He made a sound in his throat, a cross between a laugh and an oath.

The moment was so decadent, completely sensual, and probably wrong, but her breasts tightened, and her body heated.

She trailed a path of kisses back to his erection.

He was arching his hips back and forth as if to urge her to mouth more of him. But despite pressing her head forward with his hand, she wouldn't do what he wished. This moment was for his satisfaction, but she would be the architect of it.

She pulled back and gripped the shaft again, looking up at him.

He'd always used words to such advantage with her. Could she do the same?

"I want you to explode in my hands, Devlen." She gripped him tightly, using the remainder of the soap as a lubricant to slide her hands tightly down his shaft to ring the head with her fingers.

"A waste, Beatrice."

He looked fierce and proud and almost angry with passion. At that moment, she wanted him in her, rising over her and into her. But her satisfaction would have to wait.

One more stroke and he closed his eyes.

"Open your eyes, Devlen. Look at me."

She licked the head of his erection, never breaking eye contact.

His gaze grew even more fierce as the color on his cheekbones deepened.

"You taste sweet. Is that your soap? Or you?"

One more lick.

"Did you make the formula of your soap for just this purpose? How inventive of you."

She licked him again, tightening her grip around his shaft and sliding her hands up and down once more. He felt hotter and harder than before.

"What a marvelous instrument this is," she said,

speaking to his erection. She licked the head again. "You taste of salt."

He tightened the grip on her hair.

Another stroke, and a rhythm began between them, not unlike when he was inside her. He arched, she stroked, her gestures accompanied by words of encouragement.

"It will be soon, won't it, Devlen?"

"Is that what you want?"

"Oh yes."

"If you don't stop teasing me, I'll be more than happy to deliver."

"Please do. I want to taste you."

"Damn it, Beatrice."

That's when she knew he was hers. She had him between her hands, at the end of her licking, teasing tongue. She smiled and bent to taste him again and he swore once more, his hips jerking forward before his erection shivered and arched and throbbed. His testicles drew up and she held him as he exploded between her hands.

He dragged her up against his body. His eyes were glittering, the flush on his face had darkened. His kiss was punishing and exhilarating. She held on to his shoulders for balance as he pulled her closer, her dress sodden.

For once he was powerless, and her mood was exhilarated and wild.

A strange and wonderful time to realize she was in love.

Chapter 28

Beatrice sat on the leather sofa in Devlen's library, Robert on the floor in front of the circular table. The room was palatial in comparison to the library at Castle Crannoch, both in terms of numbers of volumes on the shelves as well as the furnishings. Two leather couches, tufted and designed for comfort, sat sideways in front of a roaring fire. Between them was a low round table adorned with a crystal bowl filled with flowers.

When they studied, Beatrice took the precaution of moving the crystal bowl to the floor.

The mahogany shelves surrounding the room were crafted with intricate dentil molding and filled with leather-bound books with gilt titles. She'd examined most of them, fascinated with the depth and breadth of Devlen's curiosity.

The room was shaped like an L; at the other end was Devlen's desk where he sat working on a stack of papers. He glanced over at her from time to time, and smiled, then returned to his task.

"We're going to discuss Pliny the Younger this morning," she said, forcing herself to pay attention to Robert's lessons. She would have liked to sit and study Devlen, instead, since he was such a commanding personage, especially dressed casually as he was this morning. But that wouldn't be proper, not to mention a colossal waste of time.

She wouldn't be any closer to understanding him than she was now. Nor would she have an inkling of what plans she should make.

Time. Time had never before raced by as quickly as it had these last weeks. Some permanent provisions would have to be made for Robert, and she was very much afraid the plans wouldn't include her.

Beatrice didn't want the child returning to Castle Crannoch, however. If she could do nothing else, she'd convince Devlen not to allow him to return to that dark and brooding place.

As for her, she needed to find another position. Cameron Gordon had dismissed her, and she was without prospects. She wasn't going to starve again.

She could always remain as Devlen's mistress. If he wished her in that role, that is. What kind of life would she have if she remained? One of pleasure and luxury, no doubt. But little regard from others, and she doubted she'd have friends. And security? As much money as Devlen would promise her, perhaps. She'd be a rich man's mistress.

She'd be Devlen's mistress.

She'd be Devlen's lover.

Life was quickly done and easily over. She'd

learned that lesson in the past year. Even Robert in his youth had learned how temporary life could be. Should she return to her cottage to spend the rest of her life as a virtuous woman, repentant of her time of lust? Or should she live her life as best she could, as fully as she could?

She bent to her lessons, blocking out the sight of Devlen with some difficulty.

Instead of looking for another room in the house to do their lessons, Devlen had urged her to use his library, which was all well and good, but he had occupied it as well.

At first, she'd been a little self-conscious to instruct Robert in front of his cousin, but Devlen rarely appeared to be listening. A few times she caught him smiling, however, like now.

"Do you think my methods amusing?"

"You're so very earnest, Miss Sinclair. You seem to care very much whether or not Robert learns from you."

"Of course I care. What sort of governess would I be if I did not?"

"My tutors didn't seem to care," Robert offered.

"That's because you put frogs in their beds."

"I put a snake in yours."

"Did you?" Devlen asked.

"He did."

"What did Miss Sinclair do?"

"She gave the snake a funeral," Robert said.

"Miss Sinclair has a very soft heart."

She glanced at him and then away.

"You're a very good teacher," Devlen said.

She really shouldn't have been so pleased, but she was, of course.

"I have an errand to do this afternoon," Devlen said. "Would you like to accompany me?"

Her initial response was the same excitement Robert immediately showed. Instead, caution reared its head, and she shook her head. During the day she was Robert's governess. At night she was Devlen's lover. The two roles never overlapped. In the library she was Miss Sinclair. In the bedroom she was dear Beatrice.

"I think it would be better if Robert and I take a walk. The snow has kept us inside for days. I need to stretch my legs."

"There are several shops you might enjoy not too far away." He glanced at Robert. "You must make a point of stopping by Mr. McElwee's Confectionary Shop. They make excellent sweets."

Robert looked hopeful again. Beatrice smiled at him and nodded. "You've been working very hard lately. I think that deserves a treat."

They finished their morning lessons. Devlen left the room before they did, calling her attention to a pouch he left on his desk.

"A little money for your outing."

She didn't bother arguing with him, only thanked him and watched as he left the room. Instantly, she missed him.

The day was cold, but the sun was shining. Beatrice bundled up in her cloak and ensured that Robert was similarly attired. He needed new gloves but for this outing was using a pair of Devlen's. They were much too large, of course, but he insisted upon wearing them, waving the fingers comically at her.

She wrapped a scarf around his throat and wished the

snow was not so deep, but they would look for a well-traveled route so they could avoid the worse of it.

"Shall we take the carriage, Miss Sinclair?"

"I am heartily tired of riding in a carriage, Robert. Aren't you?"

He nodded a moment later, but she could tell his heart wasn't in it.

"You'll see. The walking will do us good. We'll be hungry for lunch when we return."

"I'm hungry now."

"You," she said, ruffling his hair, "are hungry any-time."

He didn't fuss any more about the walk, and twenty minutes later she was grateful she'd decided to go on foot.

Edinburgh's streets were narrow in places, and mostly cobbled. London had the reputation of being the city the world came to visit, but it felt as if Edinburgh also shared that distinction this morning. She heard French being spoken as well as three other languages, one of which was German. The other two she couldn't identify, but she stood there unabashedly listening to the speakers in an attempt to do so.

The city was perched on several hills, so walking was a vigorous exercise. Devlen's home was in the newer section of Edinburgh, its neatly arranged streets and parks a marked contrast to Old Town.

"The residents of Edinburgh are certainly well-read," she said, when they passed yet another bookstore.

"Yes, but do they eat any sweeties?" Robert frowned up at her, a not-too-gentle reminder they were on a quest for a confectioner's shop.

She consulted her directions and led him to the shop

Devlen recommended. There, she spent some of the money Devlen had given her on fudge in various flavors, including chocolate with raisins, hazelnut, and something delicious called Highland Cream. At Robert's insistence, she tried a sweet that made her feel as if the top of her head was coming off.

"It's hot, isn't it, Miss Sinclair?"

She waved her hand in front of her mouth. She'd tasted cloves and cinnamon, but there was something else in the chewy toffee as well—pepper and ginger?

"You put another snake in my bed, didn't you?"

The boy laughed, the first time he'd done so in so long that her discomfort was worth it.

She saw the carriage as they left the confectioners, but other than to remark upon its similarity to Devlen's vehicle, didn't pay it much attention. But when it was still there, lingering on the crowded street when they emerged from a bookshop, she studied it with more care.

The horses looked the same. She wasn't an expert on the animals, but their coloring was similar, and they were perfectly matched.

Had Devlen sent a carriage to wait for them?

She walked a few feet before realizing that Robert wasn't with her. She turned to see him standing at the edge of the street, his attention caught by a dead rodent.

"Come away, Robert."

"It's dead."

"Robert."

He glanced at her and for a moment she thought he might disobey, but he kicked at the animal, then stepped back when a score of flies swarmed upward.

The coach was looming directly in front of them.

There was something oddly reminiscent of the first time she'd seen Devlen's carriage on the winding road to Castle Crannoch.

Before Robert reached her, however, the carriage swerved, heading directly for the boy. For a horrified second, Beatrice froze. In the next breath, she ran for Robert, grabbing him by both arms and pulling him with her. They both slammed into a retaining wall beside the road.

Beatrice reached down and grabbed the boy under the arms, pushing Robert up to the top of the wall. His shoes scraped her forehead as he scrambled to reach the top.

Please, please, please. There was no way she could escape the carriage. She buried her head below her arms, and pressed herself as close to the wall as she could.

She couldn't think, could only feel time measured in tiny blips of seconds. She wanted to run, as quickly as she could, but was trapped against the wall. Her arms stretched wide to minimize her breadth. The horses were so close she could feel their heated breath on her face.

Screams of equine terror echoed in her ear.

Help me.

"That's all," Devlen said to his secretary.

"Sir?"

"I can't work."

"Are you feeling all right, sir?"

"Fine, damn it."

"Could I bring you something to drink, sir? Or ring for Mrs. Anderson? She could bring you some tea. Or chocolate."

"I'm not hungry, Lawrence. I simply can't work."

"You must make a decision, sir, on the new cotton mill."

"Later."

"What about the new hull design?"

Devlen leaned back in his chair. "Tomorrow."

"But the negotiations for the mine, sir, in Wales. That can't wait. Sir?"

"Have you ever been in love, Lawrence?"

"Sir?"

The young man's face flamed. Deven had employed Lawrence because he'd been impressed with the young man's business acumen. His youth, however, was always an issue.

"Never mind." He thumbed through the stack of papers on his desk. "Do you think my empire is going to be in shambles if I don't work today?"

"With all due respect, sir, you haven't worked very much for the last three weeks. Not since . . ." His face deepened in color.

Devlen didn't bother to answer his accusation. Lawrence was right.

Even if his own business affairs were done, there was the matter of the solicitor's report. He wanted to amend Robert's guardianship, and there was a slight chance the courts would grant him custody of the child, only because of his father's infirmity. He didn't want to fight Cameron, especially in the courts, and he didn't want to bring to light—and to the public—what had happened to him. But Robert's welfare was greater than Cameron's reputation, and if the latter needed to be sullied in order to protect the child, then Devlen would do so.

If, however, he could get his mind off Beatrice. He'd come to the wharf office to do some work, approve the off-loaded inventory, and meet with two of his captains. Not sit here like some weak-minded lad, remembering Beatrice as if he hadn't just left her.

One particular memory was his favorite. They were studying Plutarch's Lives, and when he'd inquired as to whether doing so was a little advanced for Robert, she'd smiled.

"He dislikes *Aesop's Fables*, and Plutarch offers stories about mortal men who really lived. But the study of their lives also offers a moral."

"Did you always learn that way? Every lesson having a moral?"

She considered the question for a moment. "My father once said animals can teach their young without seeming to do so. A kitten will obey its mother, or perhaps its nature, while a baby has no inkling of the lessons the parent has learned. Education must fill the gap. We must learn from the mistakes and triumphs of others. It's not enough simply to know the sum of a column of figures, or to be familiar with a poet's work. Learning must be about a man's life. How to make it better."

"Has learning made your life better?"

She glanced at him and then smiled. "Some would say learning is wasted on women. I've heard that thought espoused on more than one occasion. Plutarch taught me to be resigned rather than angry about my life."

"I think a little anger wouldn't have been amiss. Less logic and more feeling, perhaps."

"Do you think I don't have any feelings?"

"I think you push them down so deep inside so they'll not trouble you. Even Plutarch acknowledged

the weaknesses of men. He believed men could be promoted to angels but for their passions."

"He also believed men are subjected to death and rebirth. Do you believe that?"

"A clever way of deflecting the subject, Miss Sinclair."

He'd stood, then, and left the room. Otherwise, he
would have kissed her, in front of Robert and the
young maid who'd entered with a tray of biscuits and
chocolate.

She had the most alluring voice. Low, but imbued
with a rounded tone to it, as if laughter hid just behind
the words. She looked as if she hid a smile as well, her
lips curving as if teasing him to leave his desk and
come across the room to kiss her.

Beatrice. The name truly didn't suit her, and yet at
the same time it did. It was much too modest a name for
such a wanton creature. Only he knew how wanton. He
leaned back in the chair and contemplated a series of
memories, plucking one at random. Until the day he
died, he'd remember how she looked this morning as
he'd opened the curtains and watched her sleep. The
sun had filtered into the room, stealing across the carpet
to rest at her feet, and then, catlike, creeping to bathe a
hand, and then a cheek. She'd blinked open her eyes,
shielding them with that same sun-warmed hand, and
smiled at him, a look of such beauty and delight he'd
been charmed to his toes. And something else. He'd
been struck by a fear so pervasive and sudden he'd lost
his breath because of it.

What would he do if she left him?

She couldn't.

Where were they now? Had they already visited the
confectioner's shop? Was she tired of walking Edin-

burgh's endless hills? Should he send a carriage to bring her home?

How could he keep her with him?

Too many questions, and regrettably, he didn't have the answers.

The carriage missed her by an inch, no more. Beatrice could feel the heat of the horses, then the slap of their leads against her back. The axle of the wheel grazed the back of her legs, tearing her skirt.

The wheels ground against the cobbles, combined with the whinny of the frightened horses, and Robert's shouts.

When it was gone, she sagged against the wall, feeling herself slip to the ground, her palms abraded against the brick.

"Miss! Are you all right?" She was suddenly surrounded by strangers, people she didn't know, whose faces were as white as hers must be.

"Criminal, the way some people drive!"

"You're bleeding, miss." A woman pressed her lavender-scented handkerchief into her palm, and Beatrice dabbed at the cut on her lip.

"Miss Sinclair! Miss Sinclair!" She folded herself against the wall, her cheek pressing against it. The carriage was careening down the crowded street, pedestrians turning to witness its departure, more than a few people surrounding her, inquiring as to her well-being. She had to get up. She was causing a scene, sitting there.

She stood with some difficulty, her legs shaking beneath her.

"Miss Sinclair?"

She turned to see Robert standing there. How had he descended from the wall?

"Miss Sinclair, are you all right?"

She wasn't, but she forced a smile to her face. "How are you, Robert?"

"It happened again, didn't it?"

There was no point in mistaking his meaning. Someone had tried to run him over, in a carriage looking too much like Devlen's for comfort.

"It was Thomas, Miss Sinclair."

"Thomas?"

"The driver. He works for my uncle."

She pressed her hands against her waist, and prayed for composure.

Beatrice grabbed Robert's hand and started retracing their steps to Devlen's house. The return trip was mostly uphill and too long. She was trying not to think as she walked, but she couldn't do anything about the fear. It was there like a third person.

Robert was silent at her side and she wanted to reassure the child they were safe, but she couldn't lie to him. Edinburgh was proving to be as dangerous as Castle Crannoch.

As they walked past the wrought-iron gate and entered Devlen's property, Beatrice felt some of the tension leave her. Devlen would know what to do. The thought brought her up short. When had she begun to place all her trust in Devlen?

"Miss Sinclair."

She glanced down at Robert. The boy had stopped in the drive and was staring at the carriage parked in front of the house.

"It isn't your uncle's."

She tugged at his hand, walked behind the carriage, and opened the front door. There, in animated conversation with Mrs. Anderson, was one of the most beautiful women Beatrice had ever seen.

The black cloak she wore was made of a soft wool, Beatrice could tell that much by the way the garment draped. Pearl buttons held it closed at the neck, while a white fur collar emphasized the blue of the wearer's eyes, the delicate pale complexion, and the shine of her auburn hair, arranged in a style designed to be taken down with the artful removal of only a few pins.

She was shorter than Beatrice by some measure, enough that she felt like a giant in comparison. Everything about her was petite, from the pointed shoe peeping out from beneath her cloak, to the hand holding the white fur muff.

"Who are you?"

Even her voice was small. Small, and breathy, as if she was too delicate to take a full breath. No doubt doing so would test the stamina of her chest, and it looked like she was doing all she could to stand upright with such a massive bosom.

"Mrs. Anderson, who is this woman?" she asked, her voice accented with the barest hint of a Scottish burr. No doubt the men of her acquaintance thought it charming.

Mrs. Anderson didn't even look in Beatrice's direction. "His Grace, the Duke of Brechin and his governess, Miss Sinclair."

"Devlen's cousin," she said, dismissing Robert as unimportant. Why not? He was only seven and therefore too young a male to attract.

"I'll wait for Devlen in his library."

Beatrice glanced at Mrs. Anderson. "Is that wise?

Devlen doesn't like people in his library when he isn't there."

The other woman turned and surveyed Beatrice again. "You're a bit forward to be the governess, aren't you?" She hesitated for a moment, then began to smile. "You think to coax him to your bed, don't you?" An instant later, her eyes narrowed. "Or have you already? How very convenient for Devlen to have installed you as the governess." She smiled. "You're available both day and night, and he gets two positions in paying for only one. Devlen does have a head for business."

She calmly unbuttoned her cloak, revealing a green silk dress clinging to her overripe curves before falling to her ankles in a long, shimmering cascade of fabric.

"Does he give you presents as well?" She fingered a diamond necklace at her throat. "It's his latest gift."

Devlen's mistress.

"It's too showy for my taste," Beatrice said calmly. "I prefer pearls. So much more understated."

Felicia smiled, but the look in her eyes could have melted ice.

"You might want to thank him in the bathing chamber. He has a partiality for that room."

Before Felicia could say another word, or the estimable Mrs. Anderson could comment, Beatrice took Robert by the hand, turned, and walked out the door.

"Where are we going, Miss Sinclair?"

"Somewhere safe," she said.

"Will anyone be able to find us?"

"No."

"Miss Sinclair? You're shaking."

"I'm cold, that's all."

She was shaking, but it wasn't cold or even fear.

Anger raced through her, as spicy as the chocolate she'd eaten earlier. How dare he! How dare he keep her in his house and keep his mistress as well.

Was Devlen to blame? Or was she the more culpable? She'd wanted adventure and excitement to the exclusion of good sense. She'd pushed down every condemning thought, every weak whisper of her conscience because of pleasure.

She should have been wiser, smarter, less innocent, unwary. Instead, she'd given him everything: her affection, her body, her trust. Her love.

"Miss Sinclair?"

"It's all right, Robert. It will be all right."

She reached into her reticule and pulled out the money Devlen had insisted she take for their outing. He'd been incredibly generous, and they'd purchased enough sweets to give Robert a stomachache for a week. The remainder of the money would be enough to leave Edinburgh.

Beatrice halted at the corner and wondered where she could go to hire a carriage. A simple enough question as it turned out. She inquired of a passerby, who pointed her in the direction of an inn. The innkeeper in turn directed her to a stable. The owner was not happy to rent his carriage for a one-way journey, so she ended up paying twice as much as it was worth.

"I need to go to Kilbridden Village," she said, giving him directions.

"I know the place, but it's an out-of-the-way hamlet, miss. Inverness might be more to your liking."

Robert had been silent beside her, his eyes wide. But it was an indication of how desperate their straits that he didn't question her actions.

"Return in an hour, and we'll leave then."

"Now."

He stared at her and then spit on the ground. "I've not had my dinner."

"Your horses are rested, are they not? Have they been fed and watered? What else must you do?"

"Are you fleeing for some purpose, miss? I'm not carrying a felon, am I?"

"I've done nothing. But my son and I need to travel this afternoon."

"The roads might be bad, we might need to spend the night."

"I've the money to pay for lodging."

"Son is it? He doesn't look like you."

"Mommy," Robert said just at that moment, "I want a candy."

"Not now. Later." She brushed his hair back and wondered at the speed at which they had both become accomplished liars.

"Very well, get inside, and we'll be off." He added a few more moments of grumbling before he began to lead the horses to the front of the coach.

She and Robert climbed inside, and in the silence he asked her the one question she dreaded.

"Does Devlen want me dead?"

"I don't know."

She didn't want Devlen to be involved. He couldn't be. She couldn't be that wrong about someone. He loved Robert; that was plain to see by anyone who viewed them together.

And her? What did he feel about her?

"I'd give it up if I could," Robert said. She glanced down to find Robert crying. Large tears all the more touching for the fact they were silent. "I don't want to be duke."

She wrapped him in the folds of her cloak. At the moment, she wanted to cry, too. She was so frightened, and she didn't know what to do.

Robert slid his hand into hers, and she was grateful for the comfort of it. Together, they sat as the driver made the carriage ready. She was grateful for the silence. There was nothing she could say to the child.

She'd almost failed him.

Chapter 29

The journey home took them five hours, far longer than it would have taken if the driver had made an earnest attempt to hurry. Perhaps the roads were as bad as he complained. They were certainly icy, but neither snow-filled nor rutted. If he'd been paid by the distance instead of the hour, Beatrice was certain they could have reached Kilbridden Village in half the time.

The cottage looked more than empty; it looked deserted and oddly sad, its thatched roof drooping beneath the night sky. The stone of the walls was from a quarry outside of the village and was the color of mud when it rained. In the spring they were saved from dullness by climbing ivy. But now it looked forlorn and humble, hardly a fit place to bring the Duke of Brechin.

She left the carriage and paid the driver the rest of his money, before taking Robert's hand and following the path to the front door.

At the door she turned the latch and entered, feeling

as if she'd been gone for years instead of just a few weeks. She halted on the threshold, feeling the memories flooding back.

"Father, why did they build such funny-looking buildings?"

"They're called pyramids, Beatrice, and they're for worshiping their gods."

"Beatrice Anne Sinclair. What are you doing? Come down from there this instant!" But in the next moment, her mother had dissolved into laughter to see both her husband and her daughter sitting in the high branches of a tree.

"It's a nest, Mother. Father thinks it's an eagle."

"I shall not ever want to leave you. I promise and cross my heart, Father."

"Ah, but you will, Beatrice, and it will be a good thing. One's children are only on loan, you see. They are gifts to be surrendered when the time comes."

Robert entered the cottage after her, and she wondered what he saw. A plain structure, with three windows and a door, a wooden floor sagging in spots. There was one place near the hearth where the floor squeaked.

The kitchen table was square and old, two of the chairs matched, but the third did not. Her mother had made the curtains over the windows a few years ago, sitting by the fire and hemming the embroidered linen with careful stitches. A rug in front of the fireplace had been her resting place many evenings as she'd sat and listened to her parents talk or her father read aloud. Two overstuffed chairs sat in front of the fire with a small table between them. On it sat a lantern, and a store of candles. A door led to her parents' room, and a staircase to her loft bed.

All in all, a snug place to live. Nothing as grand as Castle Crannoch. But there was love here, the remnants of it clinging to the very air. At Castle Crannoch there were only dark shadows and suspicion.

And in Edinburgh? She could not think of Edinburgh right now.

After lighting the candles on the mantel, she knelt and prepared the fire. The room was chilled, and it would take several hours for the cottage to warm.

She opened the door beside the fireplace, revealing her parents' small but comfortable room, one she'd never occupied.

"You'll sleep here," she told Robert, who was still looking around him with wide-eyed wonder. Ever since they'd left Edinburgh he'd been strangely quiet.

There was nothing to eat in the larder or pantry, so she and Robert sat at the end of her parents' bed and ate the rest of the sweets for dinner. When she tucked him into bed, his voice was subdued and more childlike than she'd ever heard.

"Miss Sinclair? Could I have a candle lit, please?"

"Of course," she said, and bent down to brush his hair off his forehead. Before he could object, she kissed his cheek, feeling a curious and maternal protectiveness for the Duke of Brechin.

"Sleep well, Robert."

"You'll be close?"

"Just in the loft," she said, pointing to the ceiling. "A call will bring me running."

He nodded, evidently satisfied.

She sat in the main room of the cottage, staring at the fire. She was cold, but it wasn't the type of chill that could be warmed.

Had she made a mistake in leaving Edinburgh without meeting with Devlen? Robert's safety came first, and her wishes and wants far behind. Did she suspect him? That was the question, wasn't it?

She stood and walked around the room, touching the table where she and her parents had taken their meals, the mantel where her mother's most prized possessions, a pair of statues of a shepherd and shepherdess, had once rested. She'd sold them after the epidemic, in order to afford the gravestones for her parents.

She gripped the mantel and leaned forward, resting her head on her hands. The heat from the fire warmed her face.

What would her father have thought of Devlen? He would have warned her to be wary of men with such a charming smile and way with women. A despoiler of innocents. A hunter of unicorns. Her mother would have adored him.

She stood, and walked back to the chair her father had often occupied. The upholstery still bore the scent of his pipe.

Dear God, how was she to endure this, too?

The pain felt like a bandage being removed from a wound. Until now, until this exact moment, she'd thought everything was bearable. The discovery there was agony beneath the surface was shocking, stripping her breath from her.

She wrapped her arms around herself and bent over,

stifling the sharp, keening cry. She wanted to scream, but the sound traveled inward, careening through her mind and heart and forcing her to her knees. Beatrice slid to the floor, holding on to the arms of the chair to keep herself upright. She could barely breathe for the pain.

Devlen.

Her tears came grudgingly. She wept for her parents, for Robert's loss, for the girl she'd been and was no more. She cried for the lost innocence not of her body but of her heart. She cried because she was betrayed, and in love, and the enormity of those twin emotions was too great a burden after all.

Devlen couldn't remember ever being as angry as he was right at this particular moment.

He'd come home, only to find that Beatrice and Robert hadn't returned from their outing. He'd paced in the library for a few hours, calming himself with the thought that they were no doubt enjoying the day. But by dusk he was summoning the servants, intent on retracing their path through the shops.

He told himself it was annoyance that incited his search, but he couldn't maintain that pretense for long, especially after visiting a shopkeeper along the route.

"Aye, sir, it was a close call. I seen them both, the little boy and the woman. Why, the woman nearly got herself trampled trying to save the lad. Magnificent horses, though. Matched pairs, both of them. Rarely seen the like."

"But you haven't seen them again?"

"The horses? Oh, you mean the woman and the boy. After a close call like that? I'd go to the nearest tavern and down a whiskey." The shopkeeper shrugged. "No, I never saw them after that."

The carriage was too slow, and he pounded on the top of the roof as a signal to the driver to pick up speed.

The idea she'd almost been hurt had caused him no end of grief. His stomach still rolled thinking about it.

Where in blazes was she?

He'd sent Saunders to Castle Crannoch to ensure she wasn't there. He didn't believe she'd go back to the castle but he couldn't afford to overlook any possibility. At dawn he'd visited Felicia, which proved to be both interesting and profoundly disturbing. Up until Mrs. Anderson told him he'd no idea the two women had ever met, let alone that Beatrice had returned to the house earlier. At least one question had been answered: Why hadn't she come to him? She had, and found Felicia.

"What did you say to her?" he asked.

"Nothing of consequence. Has she gone away, Devlen?"

Felicia began to smile, reaching up to place her hands on his chest. He had the strangest thought she was not unlike a cat. He didn't particularly like cats.

"Why, Devlen darling. Are you lonely?"

"What did you say?"

She pulled back, and then stepped away.

"Are you this proprietary with your women, Devlen? If so, I should have been flattered during our time together."

She began to laugh, her wrapper falling open to reveal a plenteous bosom. He should know. She'd been his mistress for two years.

"You're in love with her. Oh, Devlen, that truly is a jest."

There was nothing he could say. To argue the point would be futile, especially since it occurred to him just at that moment, standing in his former mistress's parlor, that she might be right.

Beatrice couldn't have simply left. She wouldn't have, not after last night. Or this morning. She'd glanced at him before he'd left the room and he could swear there was something warm in her look, an affection, some type of fondness.

But there was nothing to tie her to him. No reason for her to stay. Perhaps he should settle an obscene amount of money on her and bribe her to remain with him. Or hire her in some capacity. Perhaps he could lock her up in his house for a year or two. Keep her sated and well loved in his bed, so exhausted she couldn't leave it. The idea of her needing to sleep to recuperate from their loving and then being seduced again was enough to deflect his anger for a few moments.

She'd come from Kilbridden Village. Is it possible she might have returned there? Where else would she go? Beatrice was alone in the world, with few options. She had no money, nothing but the care of an occasionally obnoxious seven-year-old duke.

The thought they were in danger was sudden, overwhelming, and nearly paralyzing.

Beatrice ended up sleeping in her father's chair, fully dressed. Her feet were swollen when she awoke and her shoes pinched, so she slipped them off and wished the fire hadn't burned down to cinders. She eased up from the chair, feeling stiff. A price to pay for sleeping sitting up, her head braced against the chair's side. She'd caught her father doing that only too often in the past.

Last night they'd survived on sweets, but today she must arrange to buy some food. She'd become accustomed to eating three times a day in Edinburgh, and her stomach rumbled as if to remind her a meal was due.

Later, she'd go to see Jeremy. He'd know the name of the magistrate, or some other official to whom she could tell her story. There must be someone impartial who could offer protection to Robert. If nothing else, his title should be able to garner some interest in his plight.

There was enough money to tide them over for a week or two, especially if she were careful. And after that?

That decision could wait until later.

She pulled at the wrinkles of her skirt, slipped on her shoes, and went to the well in the back garden. The rusted pulley wheel squeaked as she hauled the bucket up from the bottom. Once the bucket was full she returned to the cottage, intent on her morning's chores.

Mary stood in the middle of the cottage's main room. Rowena's maid was dressed for the weather in a full cloak trimmed in fur. Both hands held a basket.

"Miss Sinclair," she said, inclining her head. "How tired you look."

"What are you doing here? For that matter, how did you know I was here?"

"Devlen sent his man to Castle Crannoch looking for you. My brother and I wondered if you'd be here, instead. You do remember my brother, don't you? Thomas? The driver? Or perhaps you don't. People often ignore servants, as if they're not there. We're invisible."

She strode forward and put the basket down on the table. "I've brought you some pastries. I'm quite a skillful cook, you know."

"That was very kind of you."

"You look wary. I wonder why."

"I don't know you. Why should you bring me pastries?"

"Miss Sinclair?"

Robert came out of her parents' room, rubbing his eyes. He had clearly just awakened. Before she could go to his side, before she could urge him back into the room, Mary grabbed her.

The knife in her hand bit deep into her throat.

She gasped, half in shock, half in pain.

"Take a muffin from the basket, Robert." Mary moved the knife closer. Beatrice could feel the blade cut into her skin and the warmth of her blood trickle down her neck.

Beatrice didn't understand. Not until Mary moved closer and unfolded the napkin from the basket. There was an assortment of plump muffins resting there, each of them sprinkled with what looked like sugar.

The birds. The bread.

"Don't," she said, the only word she was able to get out before Mary tightened her grip.

"If you don't want your governess to die, Your Grace, you'll do as I say. It won't be bad. You'll just get sleepy, that's all. Then you'll go and meet your father and mother. You miss them, don't you, lad?"

Robert reached out and picked up a muffin, his eyes wide and frightened. He was only seven, young enough to trust the words of an adult, even a madwoman. But Beatrice knew the moment he ate the biscuit, Mary would kill her.

She made a noise in her throat, and the knife sliced deeper.

Her neighbors were too far away to be of any assistance. No one else knew she'd returned to Kilbridden Village.

"I'm the Duke of Brechin," Robert suddenly said, putting the muffin down. "No one commands me to do anything."

Mary made a sound in her throat. "Do you want Miss Sinclair to die, you foolish child?"

He picked up the muffin again and looked away, his attention momentarily distracted. Beatrice wanted to shout at him to move, to run away, anything but allow himself to be poisoned.

What a hideous time to discover Robert felt some affection for her.

A sound at the door made Mary turn, still holding the knife. Beatrice was bleeding freely now, and she didn't know if the sudden dizziness she felt was from loss of blood or terror.

A thousand cannons suddenly exploded. The small cottage absorbed the boom of thunder and a high tinny ringing Beatrice realized was only in her ears.

Mary dropped to the floor, her mouth forming a perfect O as she fell. Instantly, a crimson flower formed on the floor around her. No, not a flower. Blood.

Beatrice looked toward the door, eyes wide. Devlen stood there, holding one of his carriage pistols, a look of such ferocity on his face she almost flinched from it. As Robert ran to him, she sank down into her father's chair, holding a hand to her throat.

Chapter 30

"**W**hy?"
Devlen glanced at her, and Beatrice tightened her arms around Robert. "Why would Mary do such a thing?"

"Unfortunately, the person who really knows the answer to that question can no longer tell us."

The wheels of the carriage were loud on the gravel-covered road. The wind, sharp and fast, sounded a high-pitched keening as if to mourn Mary.

"But you suspect," Beatrice said.

"For the sake of love. It makes fools of all of us."

"But did it make her a murderer?"

"I suspect she wanted my father to be duke," Devlen said.

"Did she love him so much she was willing to kill a child?"

"Not for him. For Rowena."

She closed her eyes, placed her cheek against Robert's

head, and exhaled a breath. "To make her the Duchess of Brechin."

"There was that, but I don't think she thought of it like that. Rowena and my father have not seen eye to eye since the accident. My father wanted the dukedom. If he was happy, perhaps Rowena would be."

"But when Robert was shot at, they weren't even at Castle Crannoch."

"No, but I think if you look closer to Mary's family, you'll find her accomplice."

"Thomas."

She looked out the window. The day had been spent with the magistrate, a very somber gentleman who owned land to the north of Kilbridden Village. He hadn't been overly impressed with either the Duke of Brechin's title or Devlen's wealth.

"How did you come to find Miss Sinclair, sir?"

"I asked in the village. I woke up more than one person, I admit, until I got an answer."

Evidently, Thomas had driven his sister to her house, and waited outside while Mary carried out her plot. Devlen had easily overpowered him and given the other gun to his driver, with instructions to shoot if Thomas moved.

Now, the magistrate was taking Thomas somewhere to be held for trial.

"You'll be here to testify, sir?" he asked Devlen.

"I will."

The magistrate also arranged to have Mary's body taken back to Castle Crannoch.

The man had had some training as a physician, and insisted upon inspecting the temporary bandage Beatrice had placed on her own throat.

"If she'd cut you any deeper, miss, you wouldn't

have survived the wound." He'd wrapped her throat tightly and given her some precautions. She'd listened and nodded from time to time, trying to ignore the fact Devlen was glowering at her.

Robert was being so quiet every few moments she bent forward to look at his face. He was awake, but only barely. He looked tired, his face too pale. A few minutes later, he grew heavier in her arms, and she glanced at him to find him asleep. She couldn't blame him. The day had been a long one with the interviews with the magistrate, and the inquiry about the shooting.

"Was Thomas responsible for pushing Robert down the stairs as well?" she whispered, not wishing to wake the child.

Devlen looked down at his cousin. "I'm afraid the incident on the stairs was a genuine accident. Too much haste, combined with a young boy in his stocking feet. The floors are well waxed."

"Will there be any ramifications for you because of what you did? Will you be arrested?"

"For killing a woman who was going to kill you? No. Don't forget, she'd planned to kill Robert as well."

She nodded.

"I wouldn't want you to be punished."

"I shall not be."

"Thank you for what you did."

"I would have protected anyone in my care."

Her eyes flew to his, but then she looked away, anything but try to interpret that stony stare.

"What about Felicia?" she asked.

"What about Felicia?"

"She came to see you."

"And met you instead. Is that why you left Edinburgh?"

She glanced over at him. He didn't look the least ashamed.

"I thought you weren't seeing her anymore."

He didn't answer. "Is that why you left Edinburgh?"

She blew out a breath. "Perhaps." She'd been angry and afraid, emotions that didn't necessarily lead to logic. "I wanted to get away, to be safe."

"And you didn't think it would be safe with me."

"I couldn't stay there."

"Because you thought I was still with Felicia."

She looked away, and only then nodded. "Yes," she said in the silence.

"I haven't been with her since I met you. I've only seen her once, to give her a ruinously expensive diamond necklace."

"She mentioned it."

"You should have stayed in Edinburgh."

She turned her head and stared at him. "I'm no longer your employee, Devlen. Don't presume to tell me what I should or should not have done. I did what I thought was right at the time."

"Forgive my impertinence, Lady Beatrice."

"Is that your attempt at humor?"

"Believe me, I'm not feeling at all amused at the moment."

The moments stretched between them, silent and uncomfortable.

"You could have asked me," he said finally. "About Felicia. I thought we had that much trust between us."

She didn't speak.

Finally, several moments later, she spoke again. "Does it ever ice up so you're trapped at the castle?" There, a casual question, one not containing emotion of any sort.

"No. There's always a way down, even if it must be done on foot."

The weather was growing colder, and a fine mist was falling. The fog was rising as they mounted the hill, their journey slower than usual.

Devlen didn't speak again. She was forced to silence only because she didn't know what to say. It was only too clear he was angry. No, not angry. Not even furious. He appeared encaged by rage. The wrong word might set him free. She wasn't entirely certain she wanted to face an infuriated Devlen.

At the entrance to the castle, he exited the carriage first and reached in to take Robert from her, all without a word spoken. She was left to follow him, up the winding staircase and to the Duke's Chamber. Robert still slept, but she wasn't surprised.

Devlen left the room after placing Robert on the bed, leaving her to remove the boy's shoes and tuck the counterpane around him. Later she would worry about undressing him properly. For now, she wanted to let him sleep.

The room was the same. The maid had straightened the bed and replaced the toweling, but otherwise the room looked as if they'd just left it and not been gone a month.

The pillows smelled of fresh herbs, and it was evident someone had beaten the dust from the four-poster's drapes. The circular table near the window had been treated with lemon oil and the scent permeated the room. Everything was in readiness for the Duke of Brechin.

Home and safety. For the first time, Robert might feel a little of both.

"You wanted to see me?"

Rowena tried, and failed, to push hope away. But it was the first time since the accident Cameron had sent for her, and she stood on the threshold of his library dressed in one of her new purchases from London, a blue silk that flattered her complexion. She'd taken the precaution of coloring her lips a soft pink and adding drops to her eyes so they gleamed in the candlelight.

In the mirror she'd looked like a woman going to her lover.

"Mary is dead."

"Yes, I heard."

"You don't seem overly affected by the news."

She shrugged. "She was a good maid."

"Is that all you have to say? She's been with you for what, a decade?"

"Do you wish me to weep for her, Cameron? Doing so would hardly put me in a good light, would it?"

"I can't remember you being this calculating when we first met, Rowena. But perhaps I was blind to your true character, being as besotted as I was."

"Were you besotted, Cameron?"

She took a few steps toward his desk, wishing he wasn't sitting on the other side. He used the sheer size of it like a barrier, a bulwark behind which to position himself. That was very well when he was addressing the staff, but hardly necessary when he was talking with his wife.

"I've decided it's best if you return to London."

She stared at him, disappointment rapidly overcoming any other emotion. "Why?" she finally said.

"Because I cannot bear the sight of you, my dear Rowena. Even the scent of your perfume renders me nauseous."

She took another step toward him. "I don't understand."

"I'm much happier when you're nowhere to be seen. London is far enough away, I think."

"You can't be serious, Cameron."

"On the contrary, Rowena. I don't believe it's possible to measure the exact degree of my hatred for you."

She took a step backward, almost physically affected by his words. The contemptuous look in his eyes made her suddenly wary.

"I spoke to the doctor, you see. At length, as a matter of fact. While you were in London. We had an interesting conversation, he and I."

Her stomach lurched, and she placed a hand against her waist. She was going to be sick, she was certain of it.

"What I cannot comprehend was the reason for it. Did you hate me so much?"

"I love you."

Her skin was so cold she could feel the heat of her own blood racing beneath it.

"You will never get me to believe that, Rowena. Not now, not ever."

He emerged from behind the desk, wheeling himself toward her. She remained where she was, determined not to flee in the face of his hatred.

"What about Robert? Did you know about Mary, about what she and Thomas were doing? Let's have a little honesty between us."

"No, I didn't know. I don't like the child, but I wouldn't harm him. And you, Cameron? Don't tell me you're unhappy she almost succeeded."

"Unlike you, Rowena, there are certain things I won't do in order to get my way. Killing a child is one of them."

He studied her, such a disinterested glance she felt the coldness of it. It was over. Finally, it was over. She turned, intent upon leaving the room, the castle, and him.

Before she could leave, he spoke again. "Don't ever come back, Rowena."

She hesitated at the door, squared her shoulders, and forced a smile to her face. She glanced back at him once. "I won't, you can be assured of that. But you will miss me, Cameron. Perhaps you'll even long for me."

"No, madam, on that score, you're wrong. I would sooner wish for the devil himself."

Devlen was determined not to be an idiot about Beatrice. However, he was very certain he was going to do just that, which is why he was intent on his errand.

Gaston was driving him, but before he got into the carriage, he ventured a question to the other man.

"Have you ever been in love, Gaston?"

The other man looked surprised at such a question. Just when he thought it wouldn't be answered, Gaston nodded.

"I have, Mr. Devlen. It's not a gentle emotion, for all that the books would have you believe."

"On that I agree. It's a damnable feeling, isn't it? It gets a hook right into the middle of you and won't let go."

"Even when it does, sir, you remember the feeling."

Devlen nodded. "Like being a salmon, Gaston. A salmon with a smile on his face."

He entered the carriage and closed the door, staring back at the castle.

She needed to follow the magistrate's instructions about that cut on her throat. Would she? She'd always have a scar. He was damned if all she thought of when she looked in the mirror every day was the memory of nearly dying for Robert.

He'd been a fool—he wouldn't deny that. From the very first moment he'd ever seen her he'd been an idiot. A lustful idiot.

There was her window. If he threw a stone at the glass, would she look down?

He'd never been so confused, uncertain, and definite about a woman in all his life. She made him want to pull his hair out, wander around naked in his own home, and vow monastic celibacy all at the same time.

She couldn't stay here. While the danger to Robert had been eliminated, the atmosphere still wasn't suitable for Beatrice. She needed laughter and a touch of silliness. She needed to attend the opera and listen to music. He'd take her to his soap factory, and she'd sample the new scents. Or to the glassworks and let her see the new patterns.

Anywhere.

Instead, he nodded to his driver and got in the carriage.

Maybe he'd be better off simply riding down the mountain on a surefooted horse. The faster he was about his errand, the better.

"Devlen told me what happened. Please accept my apologies as well as my thanks, Miss Sinclair. I truly didn't know."

Beatrice turned, surprised she hadn't heard Cameron's

arrival. She glanced at the bed, grateful Robert was still asleep. For his benefit, she left the room and stepped out into the hallway.

She waited until Cameron followed her to answer him.

"I don't care about your apology or your thanks, Mr. Gordon. All I care about is that Robert is safe. Can you promise me that?"

"I can see why you fascinate my son so much, Miss Sinclair."

"I don't know how to respond to that comment. Do you expect me to be flattered?"

"You don't hesitate to speak your mind while at the same time insisting upon being very female. And yes, I promise to protect Robert to the best of my ability, Miss Sinclair. Not for your sake or mine, but for his."

She walked down the corridor, wondering if he would follow her. He did, his manipulation of the wheelchair done gracefully.

"My son may be enamored of you, Miss Sinclair, but he's ruthless, all the same."

When she didn't comment, he continued, "How do you think he created his own empire? With a please and a thank-you? He's accustomed to getting his own way, to doing exactly what he wants."

"Is there a reason you're telling me this?"

"I feel a curious responsibility for you, Miss Sinclair, especially in view of all you've suffered on our behalf."

"I would think you'd be proud of him."

"I am, but I'm not blind to his faults. My son is stubborn, opinionated, aggravating, talented, generous, loyal, and the most irritating human being I've ever loved."

"He's determined, Mr. Gordon," she said, turning and facing him. "As determined in his way as you are in yours."

One eyebrow rose, an expression so similar to Devlen's that she smiled.

"Just how am I determined?"

"You could have easily died in the carriage accident, I understand. Yet you survived."

"On the contrary, Miss Sinclair. I was barely injured."

He smiled, an expression so odd she felt a trickle of ice slide down her spine.

"Do you know what it's like to love, Miss Sinclair? To love so desperately you would surrender your very soul?" He glanced at her. "Ah, I see you do. People can twist the force of that love into something else, something distorted and possibly evil."

Slowly, he drew the lap robe off his legs. All this time she'd thought he was paralyzed, but there were only neatly hemmed trousers beneath his knees. Nothing else.

"My wife did that." He stared at himself, his smile mocking. "She instructed the surgeon to amputate both my legs, even though there was no need. I might have lost a few toes, or had to use a cane perhaps, but that was the extent of my injuries."

She stared at him, horrified. "Why?"

"Why does one cage a bird, Miss Sinclair, but to hear it sing? We don't think about the bird's freedom, only our own gratification."

She held on to the doorjamb.

"My wife believed I was interested in other women. Are you up to hearing a confession? I was not a faithful husband. But I hardly think I deserved this punishment for my sins."

She shook her head.

"All this time, I thought she was somehow behind the incidents involving Robert. She was capable of it." He rolled to the end of the hall, stared out the small window at the vista of mountains in the distance. "I thought she wanted Robert to die to absolve herself of her great crimes. She would present me with the dukedom as if it could make up for the loss of my legs."

Speech was beyond her. She'd never heard of anything more horrible. She'd been right all this time to think the atmosphere at Castle Crannoch malevolent.

Beatrice opened her door, suddenly wanting to be away from Cameron Gordon.

"He's left, you know." He glanced at her. "Devlen's left the castle."

"Has he?" She folded her hands together, determined not to betray any of her emotions.

"You can still catch him, if you try."

"I doubt he wants to see me again."

"Love should always be given a chance, Miss Sinclair. Real love." With that, he wheeled himself down the hall. In her mind, he'd always been an object of pity. Now she saw him as he was, a man altered by circumstances but not yet felled by them.

She walked to the window, staring down at the entrance to the castle. Devlen's carriage rounded the corner of Castle Crannoch and disappeared from sight. From here, she couldn't see the serpentine curves leading down to the valley.

How strange that anyone would begin a journey at the edge of nightfall. The sun was setting, the dying rays touching remnants of snow, and casting the world in a golden glow.

She might catch him. If she were brave enough.

The road curved back on itself in at least three places. The area closest to the castle was too high and too perilous to climb, but halfway down, embankments jutted out beside the road. By cutting across the retaining walls, she could shorten the distance. If she could make it past the first long curve not long after Devlen's coach, she had a chance of reaching him before he made it to the bottom.

She left the cloak behind since it would only weigh her down, and raced for the stairs. Sunset colored the steps of the castle orange and red, and she blessed the fact night had not yet fallen. Even so, she would have taken the chance.

Beatrice took a deep breath, and began to run. She fell once, when slipping on a patch of ice, but picked herself up and raced for the curve. In the distance, she could see Devlen's coach.

Dear God, please don't let him leave. Don't let him leave me.

She made it past the first curve, nearly falling again, but managing to find her balance as she skidded to the edge. Finally, she made it to the second curve, and without stopping to think, to reason, or to be afraid, she put one leg over the edge and said a quick prayer that the ground was stable and not covered with ice. A few scrub bushes aided her descent, and she held on to them as she made her way past the last curve. She was now almost even with the carriage. Either Devlen was traveling uncharacteristically slowly down the road, or she was blessed by Providence.

And faster than she thought she could be.

At the base of the mountain, she only had a few moments to spare. She stood in the middle of the road, stretched out her arms, and closed her eyes, wondering if she was destined to die by coach after all.

The driver shouted, standing and pulling on the reins in an effort to halt the horses. The road was slick beneath the carriage's oversized wheels, and it began to slide around the last curve.

In that second Beatrice wondered if all she'd succeeded in doing was sending the coach catapulting off the mountain. Instead, the horses lost their footing, and the carriage slid sideways into a snowdrift like a ship nestling into its berth.

The driver was still shouting at her in French, the comments not polite in the least. She recognized Gaston finally, but she didn't move, only lowered her arms.

The door opened, and Devlen emerged, looking like an emissary of the devil himself. In the faint light of a waning sun, she flinched from the look in his eyes. She tilted back her chin and took a deep breath as he reached her.

"You stupid fool! You could have been killed!"

"I couldn't let you go. I couldn't let you leave without knowing."

She was hiccupping softly while she cried, the tears falling freely.

"Knowing what?"

"I never thought you were responsible." Honesty compelled her to add, "Perhaps for a little while. After Edinburgh. But I knew that a man who'd taken a child to safety wouldn't have then tried to kill him."

"How very reasonable of you."

"You couldn't have done it." Her tears continued. She didn't know how she would be able to stop them. Right now she felt as if she could cry forever.

"I knew you would prove to be a problem."

"You hate me, don't you?" She looked up at him, uncaring that tears sheened her face.

"I don't hate you, Beatrice."

"Then why are you so angry?"

"Anger is one of those essentially worthless emotions."

"One of those? What would be the other ones?"

His smile grew more genuine.

"You're expecting me to say love, aren't you? Or a host of other gentle feelings. Dear Beatrice, you lay such sweet traps for me."

The snow began.

His look was intent, somber. She was reminded of the first time she'd seen him, on this same road, at almost this same spot. She'd been transfixed by the sight of him as she was now.

Finally, he spoke again. "It's better to be angry than afraid. It's foolish to feel fear when a little knowledge will normally overcome it. Fear is caused by uncertainty, by ignorance."

"I'm not afraid of you." Well, perhaps she had been, but only in the first five minutes of their meeting. Fascination had easily taken the place of fear.

"My dearest Beatrice, I wasn't referring to you. But of myself. I've been afraid ever since I met you."

"You have?"

"All this time, I was afraid you'd leave me."

"I never wanted to."

"But you would. One day you would."

Perhaps he was right.

"Stay with me."

"Are you asking me to be your mistress? I thought Felicia held that post. The beautiful, tiny Felicia."

"Thank God I didn't witness that meeting," he said, smiling. "As to being my current mistress, I think it would be amusing to have a wife who acted the part."

For a moment she couldn't speak.

"Where did you think I was going?" he asked.

"To Edinburgh."

He shook his head. "I was in search of a minister, my dearest Miss Sinclair. I have no intention of losing you again. The bonds of matrimony must surely be strong enough to keep you with me."

The snow was piling up on his shoulders, and she reached up to brush it away.

"You love me?"

He smiled, and the expression was a faint effort at best, not quite reaching the somber expression in his eyes.

"With all my heart, dear Beatrice. Or do you think I kidnap governesses without a care to their reputation or mine? It's not my way of doing things."

"You love me?" The thought was so alien she found repeating it the only possible solace.

"Even though you thought I was a murderer. We shall have to work on trust, I think."

"I never thought you were a murderer. I thought your father was. I didn't want to put you in a position where you'd have to choose."

"Between you and anyone else? I choose you. Between you and the world, Beatrice? Surely you know that answer."

"Your father says you're ruthless."

"Indeed."

"I suspect he's right, Devlen."

"You're correct, Beatrice. In certain matters, I am. With you? Of a certainty. I feel it only fair to warn you I'm about to kidnap you again."

"Are you?"

"And Robert as well. I think the boy would do better in Edinburgh for a while. Although, while we're on our honeymoon, he should attend school."

"You want to marry me, even though I'm a governess?"

His laughter echoed up the mountain and back. "You're the most unlikely governess I've ever known."

She took a deep breath. "You asked me once if life had affected me. Maybe it has, I don't know. I do know I don't want to dread every day. I want a roof over my head, and food to eat. I want to be warm and have pretty clothes. I want to be healthy, and I want to be happy. But most of all, I want you. I deserve you."

She wiped her tears away with her fingertips, but they kept coming.

He placed his hands on her waist and pulled her to him. "I think you deserve a great deal more than me, but I'm afraid I won't let you go. You'll have to say yes."

She looked up at his face, thinking a year ago she wouldn't have thought there was any reason to feel joy or wonder or such delight it spread through her body like a warm flood.

"Do you have such great experience with being in love, Devlen?" She'd asked him the question once, and he'd never answered her.

"None. It feels like an ache, Beatrice, a damnable irritation right here." He reached for her hand and placed it over his heart. "You're the only one who can heal me."

"It's a contagious disease, Devlen."

"I should hope so."

"I do love you."

"I know, dearest Beatrice."

"You love me, too."

"With all my heart and what's left of my mind." He smiled and enfolded her in his arms.

There, in the darkness, just below Castle Crannoch, they kissed. When they broke apart, it was with a smile toward the sky, at the large snowflakes wafting down on them like a celestial blessing.

"Yes, Beatrice?"

"Oh yes, Devlen."

With a laugh, they turned and walked hand in hand toward the carriage.